DON'T GET EATEN BY ANYTHING

A COLLECTION OF "THE DAILIES"
2011 ~ 2013

DAKOTA McFADZEAN

Conundrum Press
Greenwich, Nova Scotia

dakotamcfadzean.com

FIRST EDITION
PRINTED BY TWP IN SINGAPORE

LIBRARY AND ARCHIVES CANADA CATALOGUING IN PUBLICATION

McFADZEAN, DAKOTA, AUTHOR
DON'T GET EATEN BY ANYTHING: A COLLECTION OF THE DAILIES / DAKOTA McFADZEAN

ISBN 978-1-894994-90-3 (bound)

1. GRAPHIC NOVELS I. TITLE

PN6733.M325D65 2015 741.5'971 C2014-907918-4

THE STRIPS CONTAINED IN THIS VOLUME ARE WORKS OF FICTION. ANY SIMILARITIES TO REAL EVENTS OR PEOPLE, LIVING OR DEAD, IS PURELY COINCIDENTAL.

PUBLISHED BY ANDY BROWN AT CONUNDRUM PRESS, GREENWICH, NS, CANADA
conundrumpress.com

CONUNDRUM PRESS ACKNOWLEDGES THE FINANCIAL SUPPORT OF THE CANADA COUNCIL FOR THE ARTS AND THE GOVERNMENT OF CANADA THROUGH THE CANADA BOOK FUND TOWARD ITS PUBLISHING ACTIVITIES.

Canada Council for the Arts | Conseil des Arts du Canada

Canada

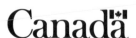

FOR MY PARENTS,

WHO KEPT ME
FROM BEING EATEN.

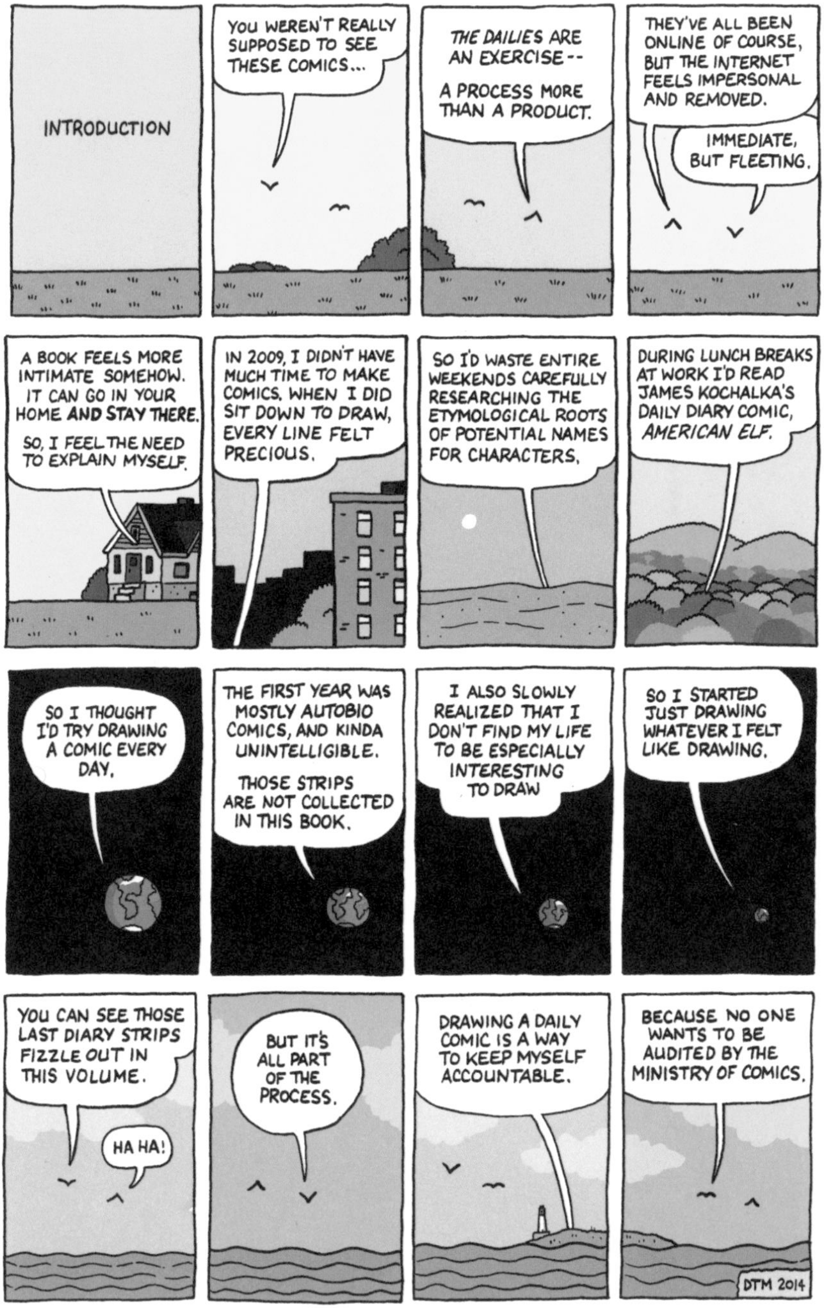
INTRODUCTION
YOU WEREN'T REALLY SUPPOSED TO SEE THESE COMICS...
THE DAILIES ARE AN EXERCISE --
A PROCESS MORE THAN A PRODUCT.
THEY'VE ALL BEEN ONLINE OF COURSE, BUT THE INTERNET FEELS IMPERSONAL AND REMOVED.
IMMEDIATE, BUT FLEETING.
A BOOK FEELS MORE INTIMATE SOMEHOW. IT CAN GO IN YOUR HOME **AND STAY THERE.**
SO, I FEEL THE NEED TO EXPLAIN MYSELF.
IN 2009, I DIDN'T HAVE MUCH TIME TO MAKE COMICS. WHEN I DID SIT DOWN TO DRAW, EVERY LINE FELT PRECIOUS.
SO I'D WASTE ENTIRE WEEKENDS CAREFULLY RESEARCHING THE ETYMOLOGICAL ROOTS OF POTENTIAL NAMES FOR CHARACTERS.
DURING LUNCH BREAKS AT WORK I'D READ JAMES KOCHALKA'S DAILY DIARY COMIC, *AMERICAN ELF.*
SO I THOUGHT I'D TRY DRAWING A COMIC EVERY DAY.
THE FIRST YEAR WAS MOSTLY AUTOBIO COMICS, AND KINDA UNINTELLIGIBLE.
THOSE STRIPS ARE NOT COLLECTED IN THIS BOOK.
I ALSO SLOWLY REALIZED THAT I DON'T FIND MY LIFE TO BE ESPECIALLY INTERESTING TO DRAW
SO I STARTED JUST DRAWING WHATEVER I FELT LIKE DRAWING.
YOU CAN SEE THOSE LAST DIARY STRIPS FIZZLE OUT IN THIS VOLUME.
HA HA!
BUT IT'S ALL PART OF THE PROCESS.
DRAWING A DAILY COMIC IS A WAY TO KEEP MYSELF ACCOUNTABLE.
BECAUSE NO ONE WANTS TO BE AUDITED BY THE MINISTRY OF COMICS.
DTM 2014

SAT JAN 1, 2011

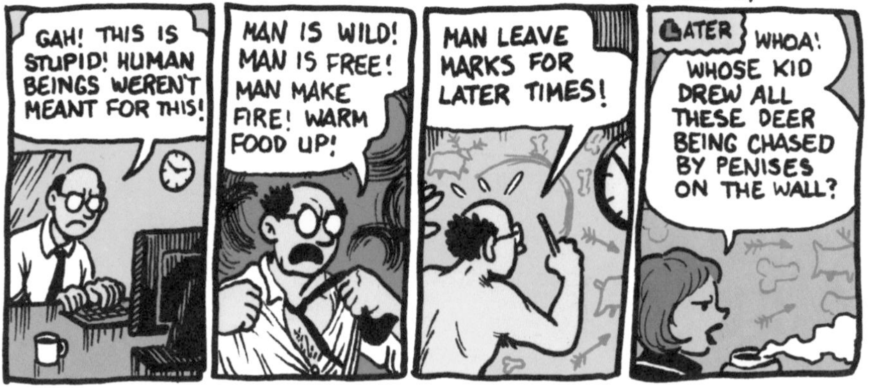
GAH! THIS IS STUPID! HUMAN BEINGS WEREN'T MEANT FOR THIS!
MAN IS WILD! MAN IS FREE! MAN MAKE FIRE! WARM FOOD UP!
MAN LEAVE MARKS FOR LATER TIMES!
LATER
WHOA! WHOSE KID DREW ALL THESE DEER BEING CHASED BY PENISES ON THE WALL?

SUN JAN 2, 2011

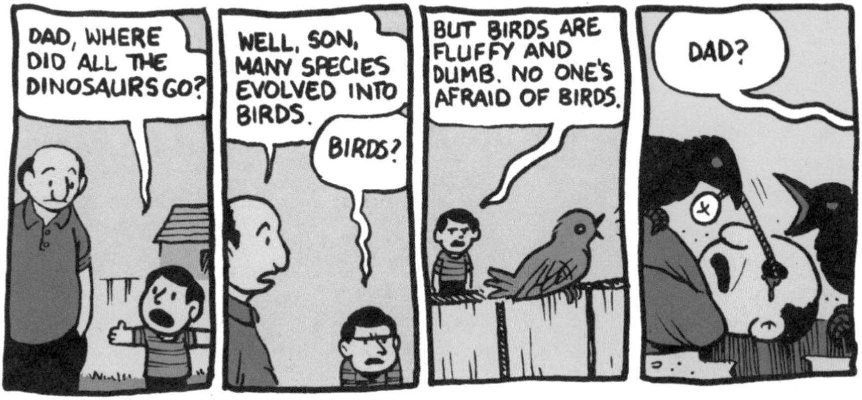
DAD, WHERE DID ALL THE DINOSAURS GO?
WELL, SON, MANY SPECIES EVOLVED INTO BIRDS.
BIRDS?
BUT BIRDS ARE FLUFFY AND DUMB. NO ONE'S AFRAID OF BIRDS.
DAD?

MON JAN 3, 2011

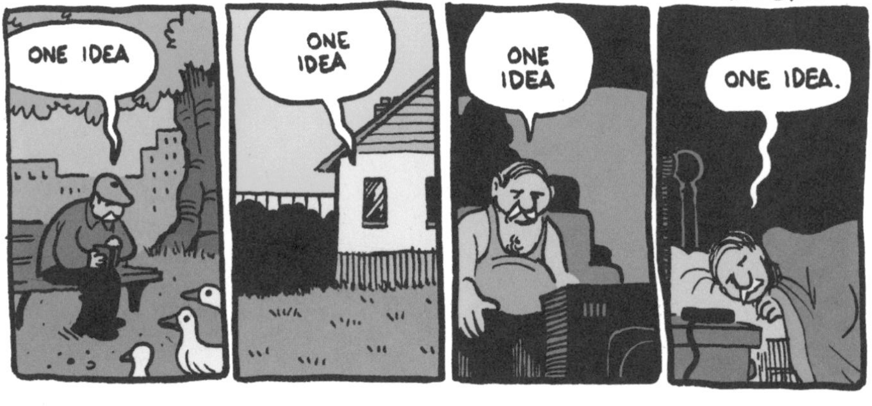
ONE IDEA
ONE IDEA
ONE IDEA
ONE IDEA.

TUE JAN 4, 2011

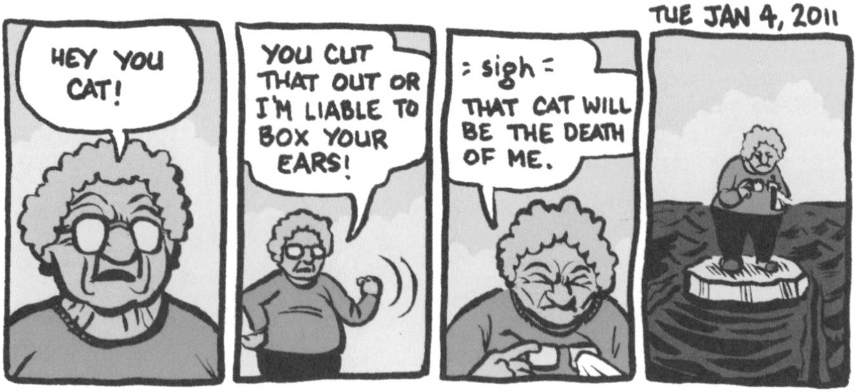
HEY YOU CAT!
YOU CUT THAT OUT OR I'M LIABLE TO BOX YOUR EARS!
= sigh =
THAT CAT WILL BE THE DEATH OF ME.

WED JAN 5, 2011

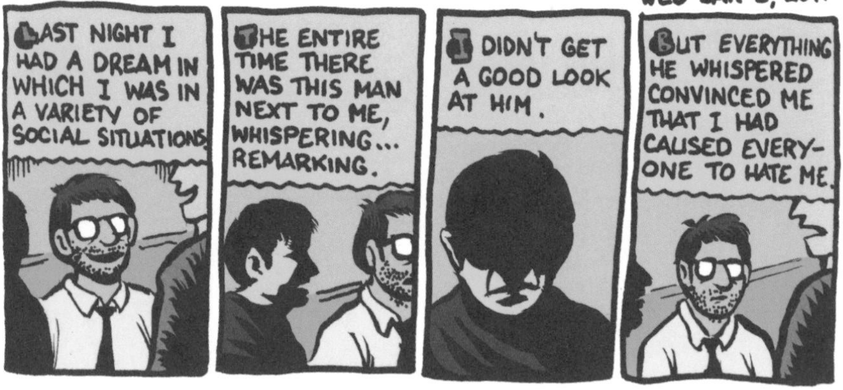
LAST NIGHT I HAD A DREAM IN WHICH I WAS IN A VARIETY OF SOCIAL SITUATIONS.
THE ENTIRE TIME THERE WAS THIS MAN NEXT TO ME, WHISPERING... REMARKING.
I DIDN'T GET A GOOD LOOK AT HIM.
BUT EVERYTHING HE WHISPERED CONVINCED ME THAT I HAD CAUSED EVERY-ONE TO HATE ME.

THU JAN 6, 2011

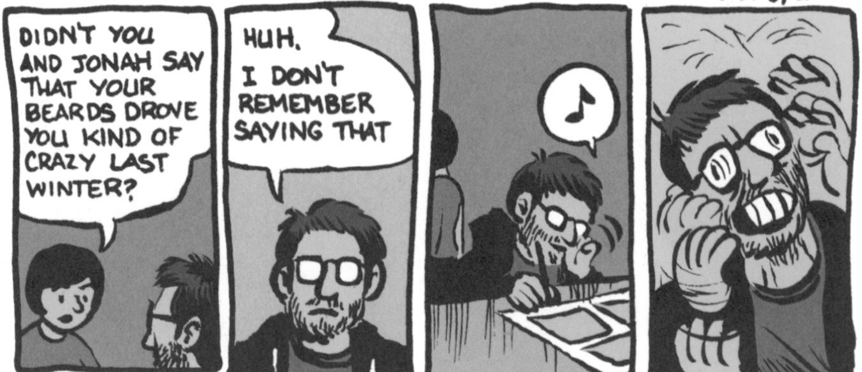
DIDN'T YOU AND JONAH SAY THAT YOUR BEARDS DROVE YOU KIND OF CRAZY LAST WINTER?
HUH.
I DON'T REMEMBER SAYING THAT

NICE COMICS

FRI JAN 7, 2011

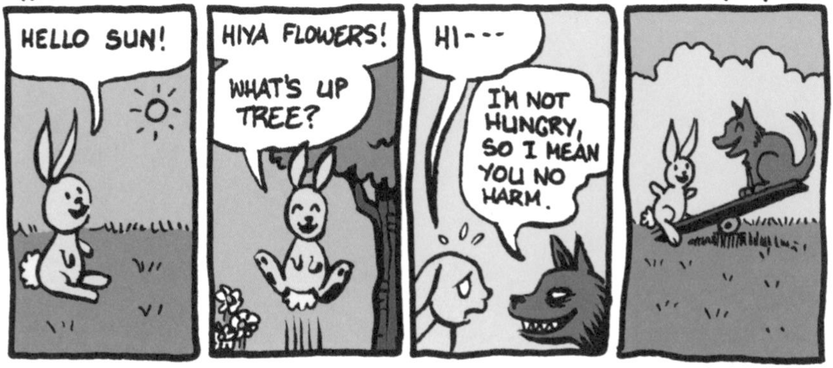
HELLO SUN!
HIYA FLOWERS!
WHAT'S UP TREE?
HI---
I'M NOT HUNGRY, SO I MEAN YOU NO HARM.

SAT JAN 8, 2011

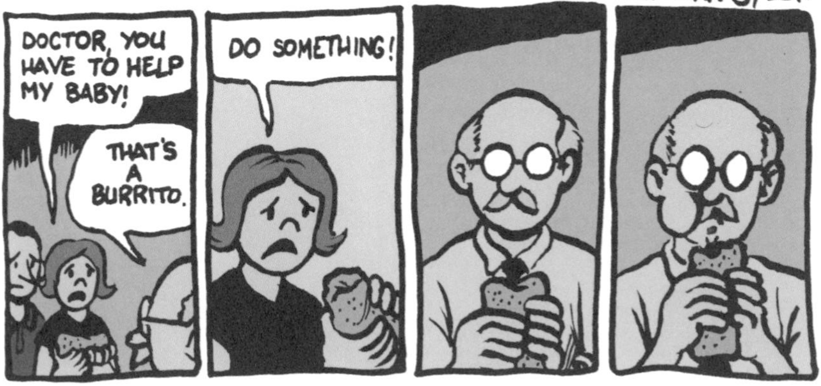
DOCTOR, YOU HAVE TO HELP MY BABY!
THAT'S A BURRITO.
DO SOMETHING!

SUN JAN 9, 2011

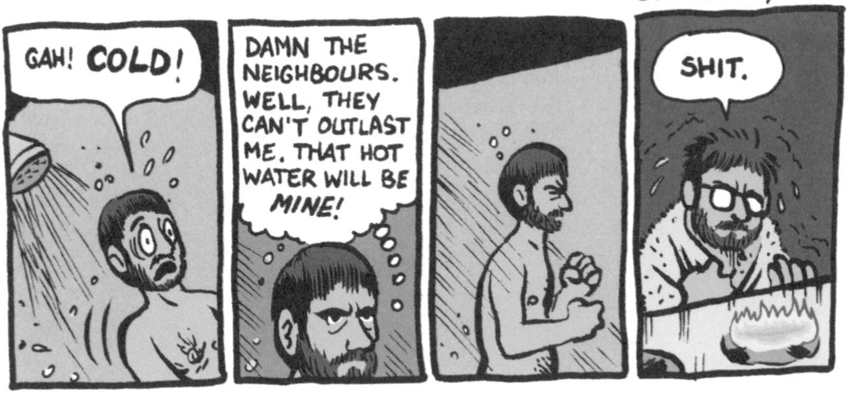
GAH! COLD!
DAMN THE NEIGHBOURS. WELL, THEY CAN'T OUTLAST ME. THAT HOT WATER WILL BE MINE!
SHIT.

A THING I SAW

MON JAN 10, 2011

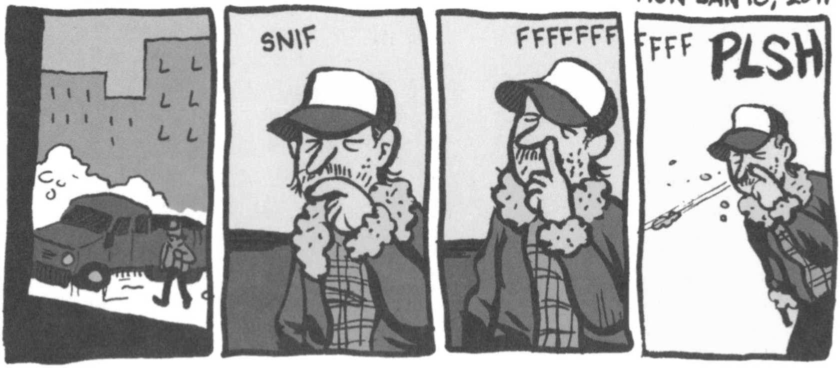

SNIF
FFFFFFF
FFFF
PLSH

TUE JAN 11, 2011

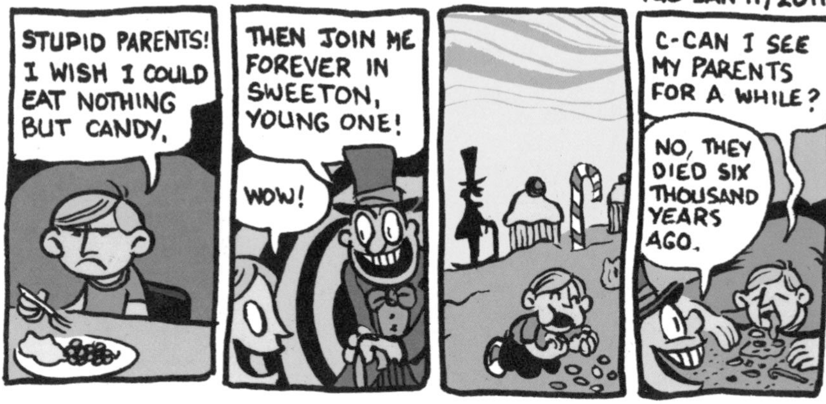

STUPID PARENTS! I WISH I COULD EAT NOTHING BUT CANDY.
THEN JOIN ME FOREVER IN SWEETON, YOUNG ONE!
WOW!
C-CAN I SEE MY PARENTS FOR A WHILE?
NO, THEY DIED SIX THOUSAND YEARS AGO.

WED JAN 12, 2011

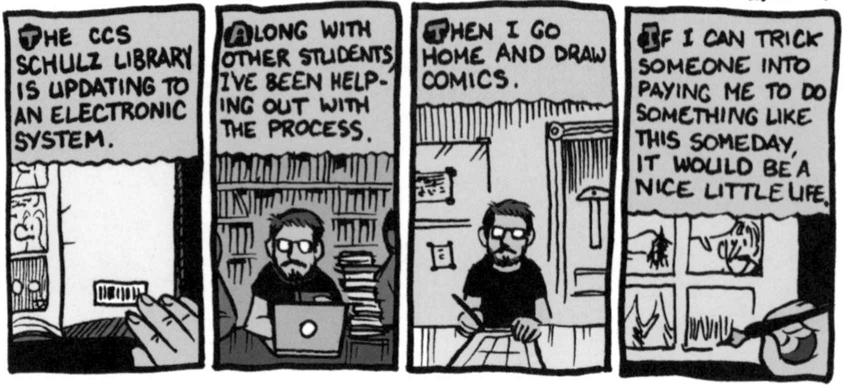

THE CCS SCHULZ LIBRARY IS UPDATING TO AN ELECTRONIC SYSTEM.
ALONG WITH OTHER STUDENTS, I'VE BEEN HELPING OUT WITH THE PROCESS.
THEN I GO HOME AND DRAW COMICS.
IF I CAN TRICK SOMEONE INTO PAYING ME TO DO SOMETHING LIKE THIS SOMEDAY, IT WOULD BE A NICE LITTLE LIFE.

THU JAN 13, 2011

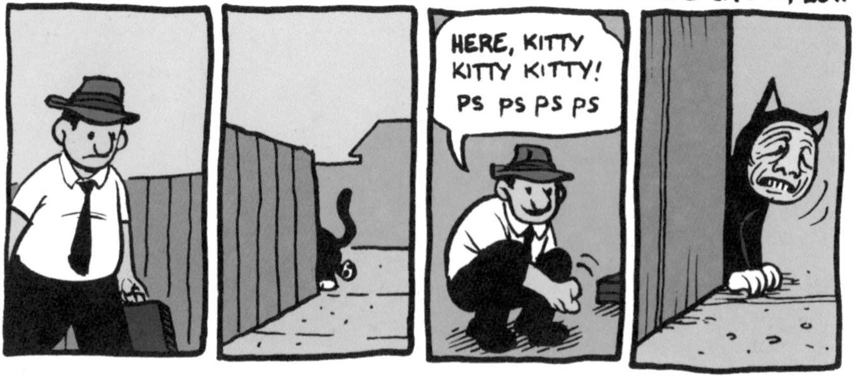
HERE, KITTY KITTY KITTY!
PS PS PS PS

FRI JAN 14, 2011

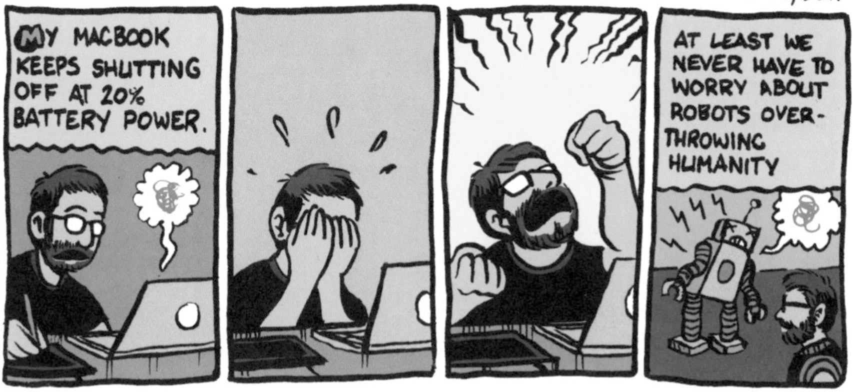
MY MACBOOK KEEPS SHUTTING OFF AT 20% BATTERY POWER.
AT LEAST WE NEVER HAVE TO WORRY ABOUT ROBOTS OVER-THROWING HUMANITY

SAT JAN 15, 2011

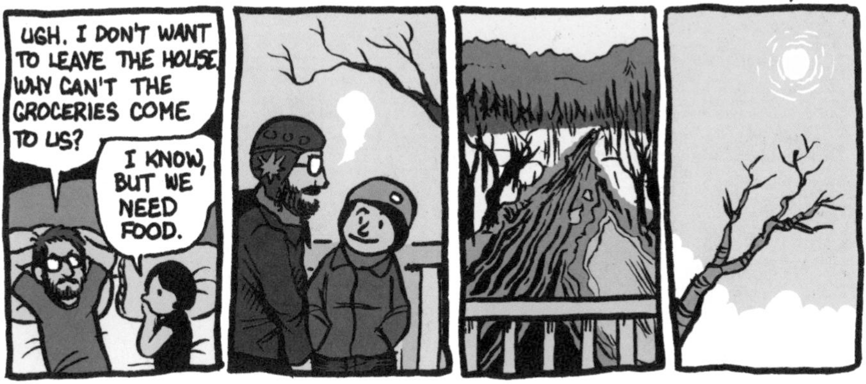
UGH. I DON'T WANT TO LEAVE THE HOUSE. WHY CAN'T THE GROCERIES COME TO US?
I KNOW, BUT WE NEED FOOD.

SUN JAN 16, 2011

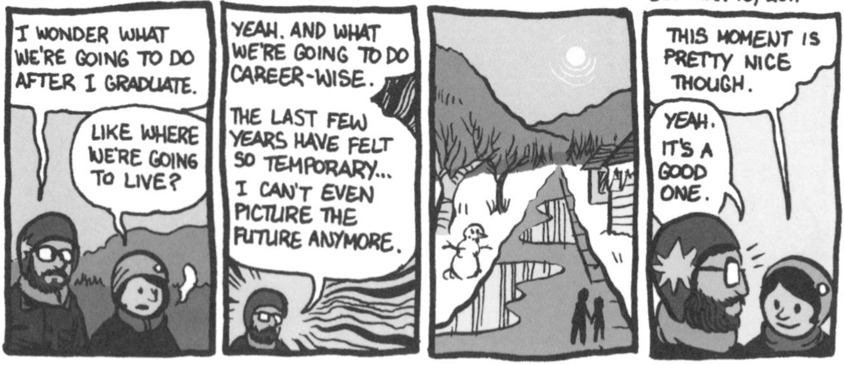
I WONDER WHAT WE'RE GOING TO DO AFTER I GRADUATE.
LIKE WHERE WE'RE GOING TO LIVE?
YEAH. AND WHAT WE'RE GOING TO DO CAREER-WISE.
THE LAST FEW YEARS HAVE FELT SO TEMPORARY... I CAN'T EVEN PICTURE THE FUTURE ANYMORE.
THIS MOMENT IS PRETTY NICE THOUGH.
YEAH. IT'S A GOOD ONE.

SLEDDING WITH FRIENDS

MON JAN 17, 2011

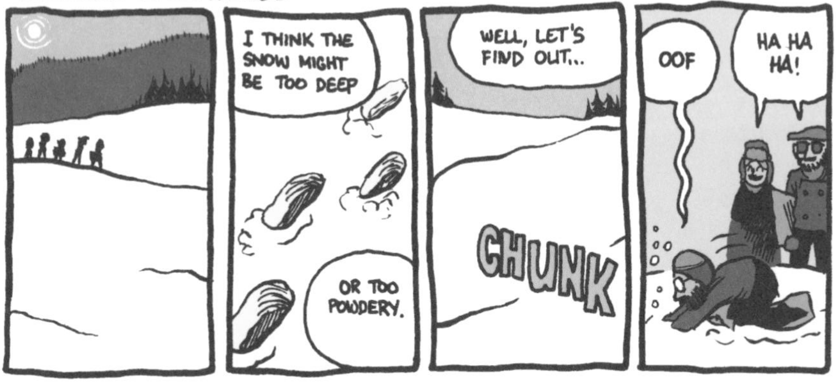
I THINK THE SNOW MIGHT BE TOO DEEP
OR TOO POWDERY.
WELL, LET'S FIND OUT...
CHUNK
OOF
HA HA HA!

TUE JAN 18, 2011

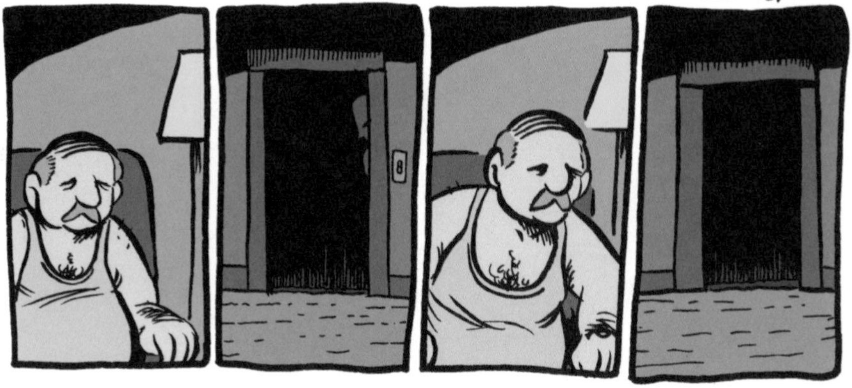

WED JAN 19, 2011

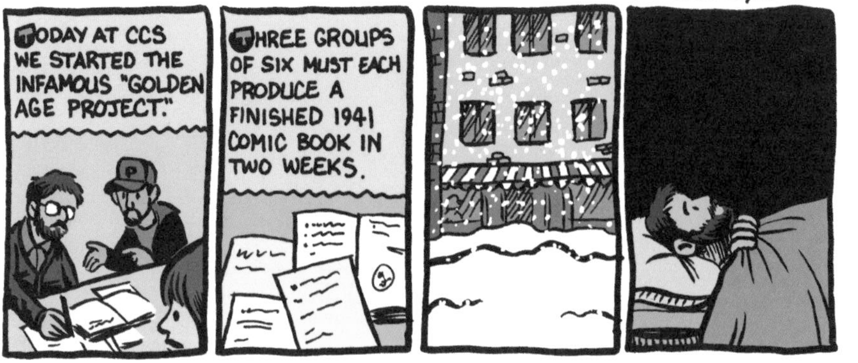
TODAY AT CCS WE STARTED THE INFAMOUS "GOLDEN AGE PROJECT."
THREE GROUPS OF SIX MUST EACH PRODUCE A FINISHED 1941 COMIC BOOK IN TWO WEEKS.

THU JAN 20, 2011

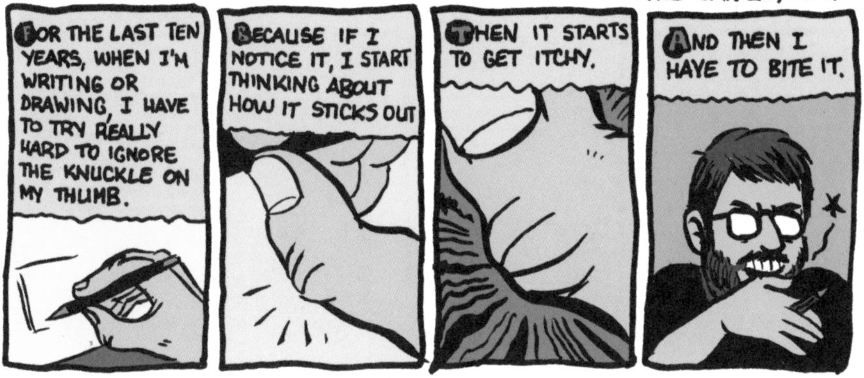
FOR THE LAST TEN YEARS, WHEN I'M WRITING OR DRAWING, I HAVE TO TRY REALLY HARD TO IGNORE THE KNUCKLE ON MY THUMB.
BECAUSE IF I NOTICE IT, I START THINKING ABOUT HOW IT STICKS OUT
THEN IT STARTS TO GET ITCHY.
AND THEN I HAVE TO BITE IT.

CLOSE-UP MAN

FRI JAN 21, 2011

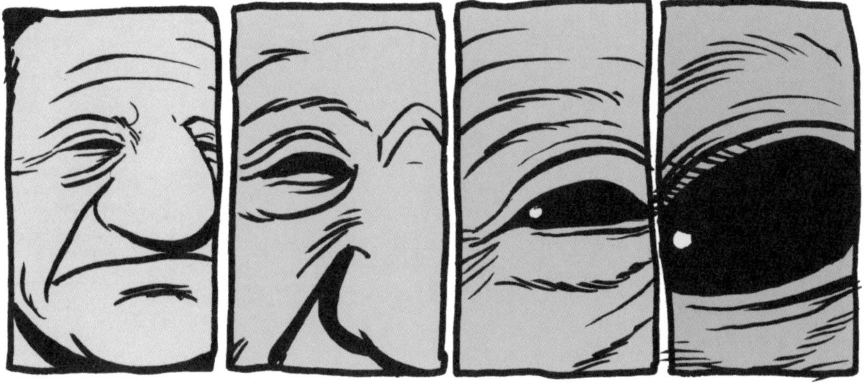

FLYING KITTY

SAT JAN 22, 2011

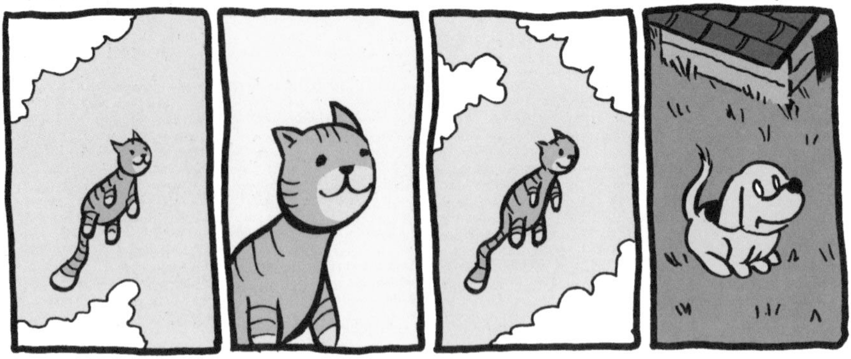

SUN JAN 23, 2011

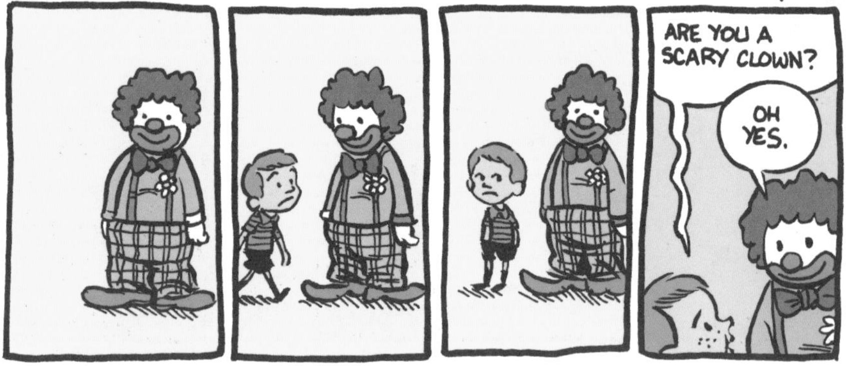
ARE YOU A SCARY CLOWN?
OH YES.

"MY LIFE"

MON JAN 24, 2011

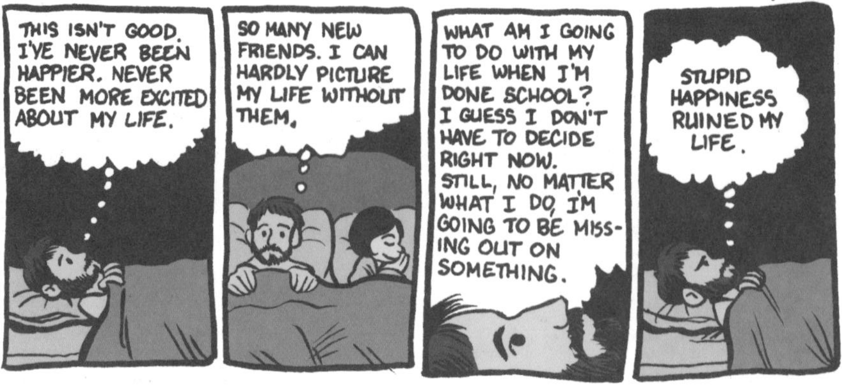
THIS ISN'T GOOD. I'VE NEVER BEEN HAPPIER. NEVER BEEN MORE EXCITED ABOUT MY LIFE.
SO MANY NEW FRIENDS. I CAN HARDLY PICTURE MY LIFE WITHOUT THEM.
WHAT AM I GOING TO DO WITH MY LIFE WHEN I'M DONE SCHOOL? I GUESS I DON'T HAVE TO DECIDE RIGHT NOW. STILL, NO MATTER WHAT I DO, I'M GOING TO BE MISS-ING OUT ON SOMETHING.
STUPID HAPPINESS RUINED MY LIFE.

GOD COMICS

TUE JAN 25, 2011

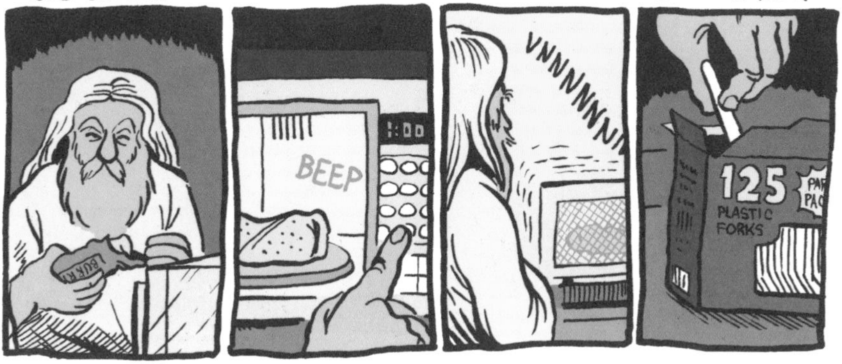
BEEP
VNNNNNN
125
PLASTIC FORKS

TIME TRAVELLING RABBIT

WED JAN 26, 2011

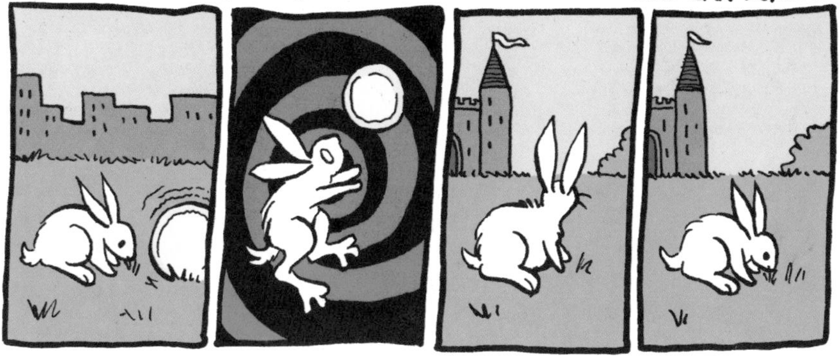

THU JAN 27, 2011

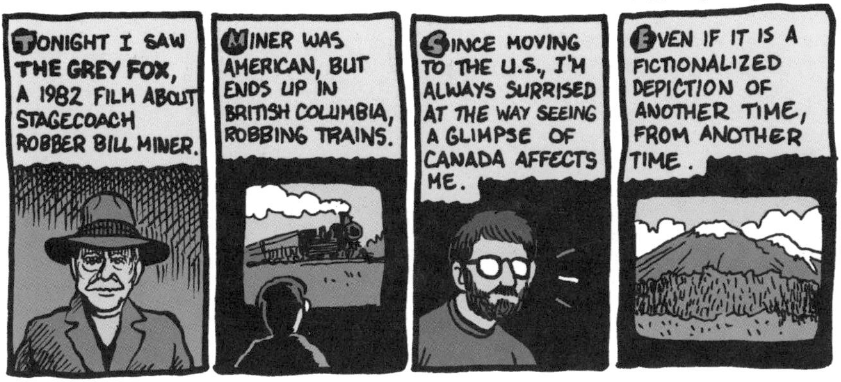
TONIGHT I SAW THE GREY FOX, A 1982 FILM ABOUT STAGECOACH ROBBER BILL MINER.
MINER WAS AMERICAN, BUT ENDS UP IN BRITISH COLUMBIA, ROBBING TRAINS.
SINCE MOVING TO THE U.S., I'M ALWAYS SURRISED AT THE WAY SEEING A GLIMPSE OF CANADA AFFECTS ME.
EVEN IF IT IS A FICTIONALIZED DEPICTION OF ANOTHER TIME, FROM ANOTHER TIME.

FRI JAN 28, 2011

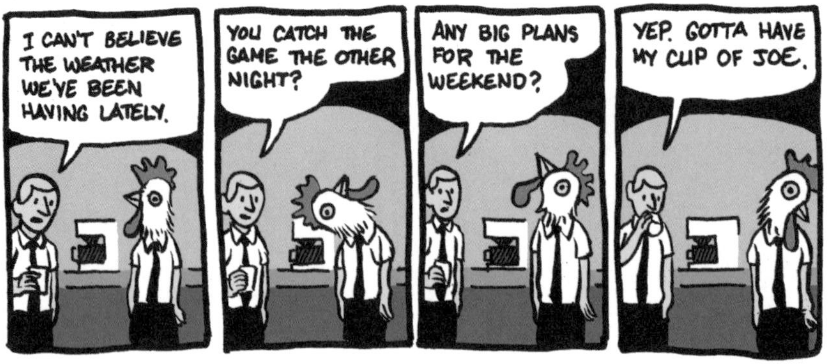
I CAN'T BELIEVE THE WEATHER WE'VE BEEN HAVING LATELY.
YOU CATCH THE GAME THE OTHER NIGHT?
ANY BIG PLANS FOR THE WEEKEND?
YEP. GOTTA HAVE MY CUP OF JOE.

GHOST COMICS

SAT JAN 29, 2011

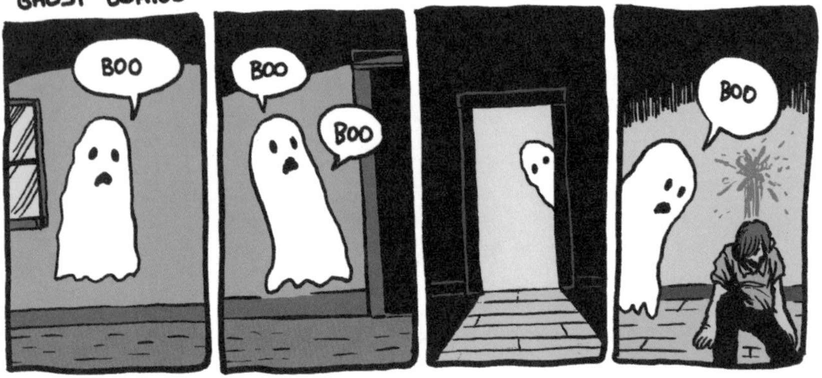
BOO
BOO
BOO
BOO

SUN JAN 30, 2011

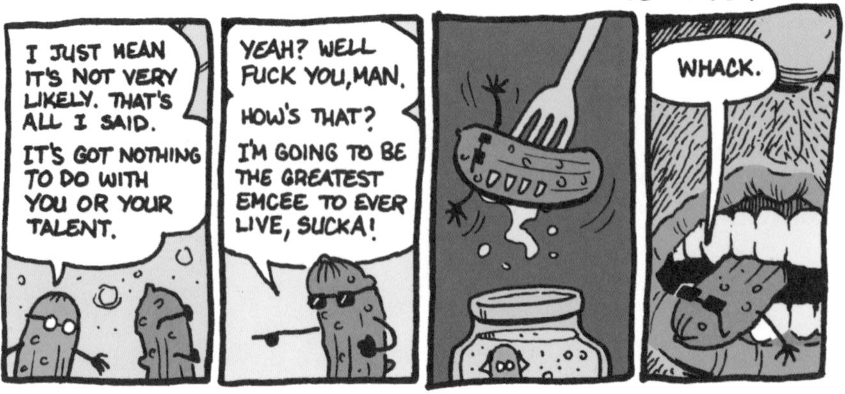
I JUST MEAN IT'S NOT VERY LIKELY. THAT'S ALL I SAID.
IT'S GOT NOTHING TO DO WITH YOU OR YOUR TALENT.
YEAH? WELL FUCK YOU, MAN.
HOW'S THAT?
I'M GOING TO BE THE GREATEST EMCEE TO EVER LIVE, SUCKA!
WHACK.

MON JAN 31, 2011

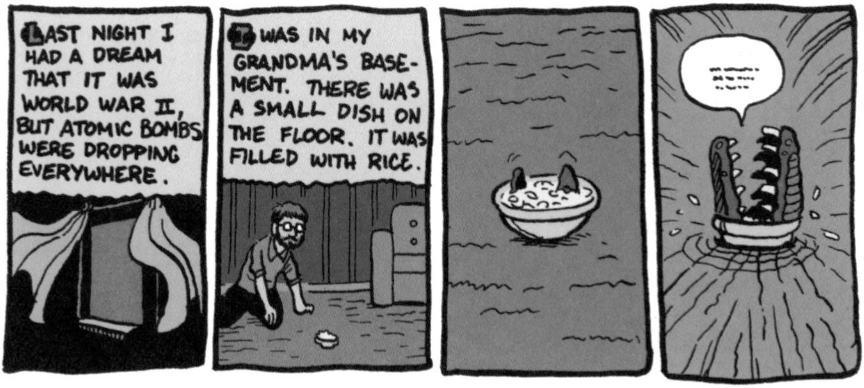
LAST NIGHT I HAD A DREAM THAT IT WAS WORLD WAR II, BUT ATOMIC BOMBS WERE DROPPING EVERYWHERE.
I WAS IN MY GRANDMA'S BASEMENT. THERE WAS A SMALL DISH ON THE FLOOR. IT WAS FILLED WITH RICE.

OFFENSIVE THOUGHTS

TUE FEB 1, 2011

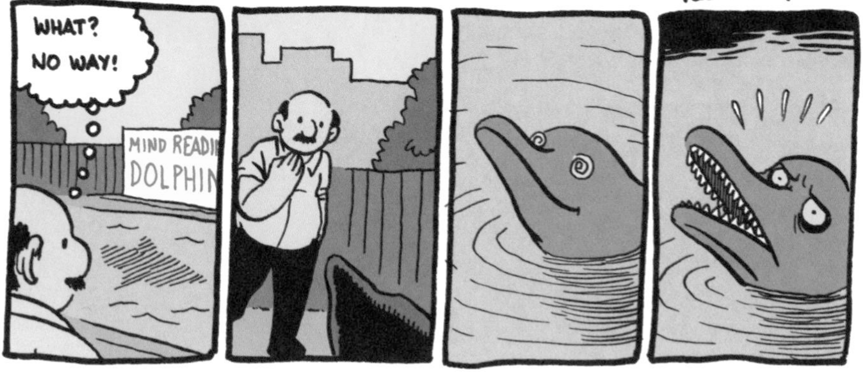
WHAT?
NO WAY!
MIND READI
DOLPHIN

CCS GOLDEN AGE

WED FEB 2, 2011

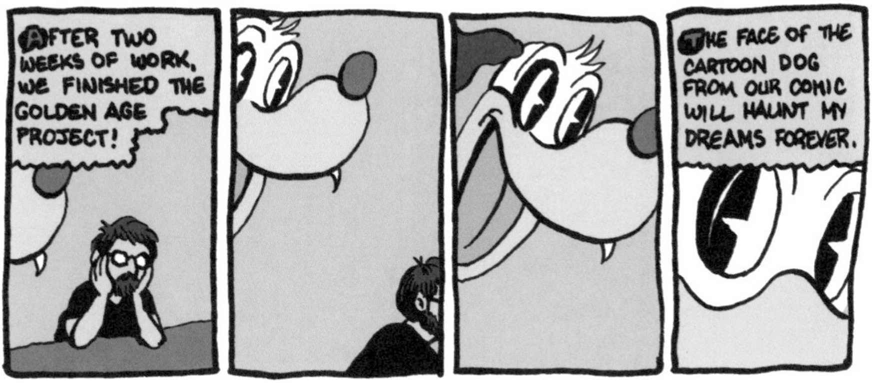
AFTER TWO WEEKS OF WORK, WE FINISHED THE GOLDEN AGE PROJECT!
THE FACE OF THE CARTOON DOG FROM OUR COMIC WILL HAUNT MY DREAMS FOREVER.

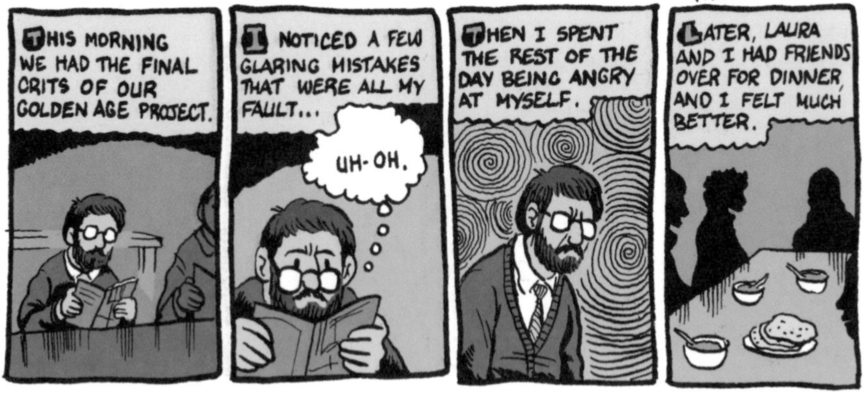
THIS MORNING WE HAD THE FINAL CRITS OF OUR GOLDEN AGE PROJECT.
I NOTICED A FEW GLARING MISTAKES THAT WERE ALL MY FAULT...
UH-OH.
THEN I SPENT THE REST OF THE DAY BEING ANGRY AT MYSELF.
LATER, LAURA AND I HAD FRIENDS OVER FOR DINNER, AND I FELT MUCH BETTER.

SNEAKY CAT

FRI FEB 4, 2011

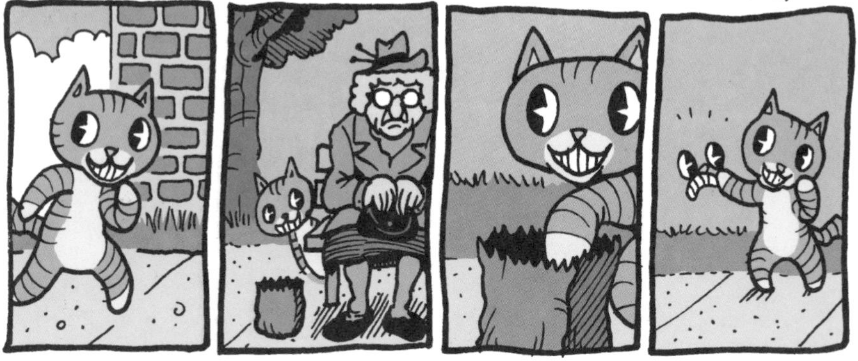

ELEPHANT COMICS

SAT FEB 5, 2011

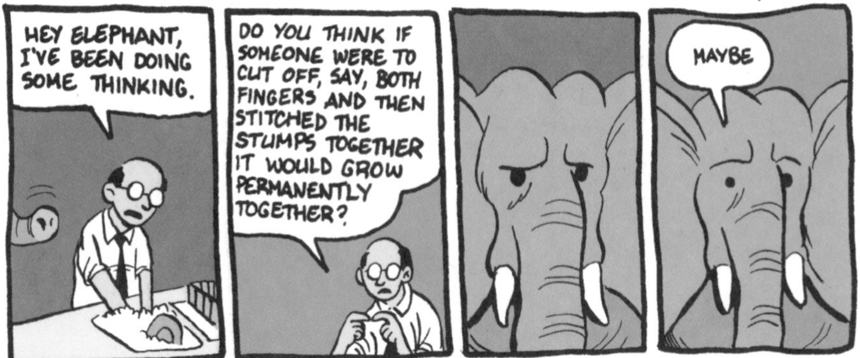
HEY ELEPHANT, I'VE BEEN DOING SOME THINKING.
DO YOU THINK IF SOMEONE WERE TO CUT OFF, SAY, BOTH FINGERS AND THEN STITCHED THE STUMPS TOGETHER IT WOULD GROW PERMANENTLY TOGETHER?
MAYBE

SUN FEB 6, 2011

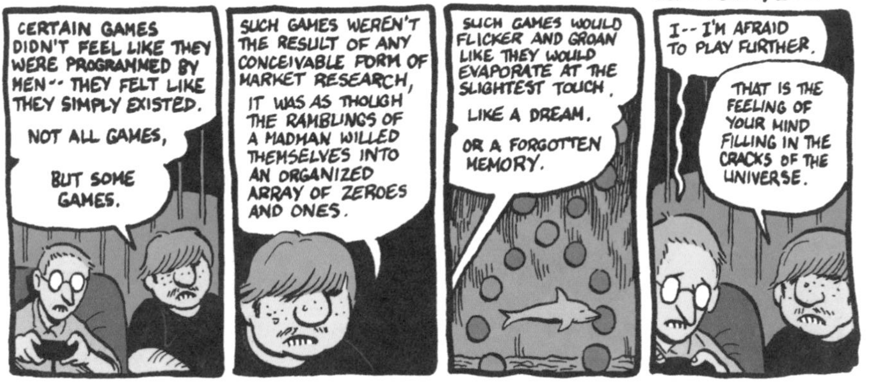
CERTAIN GAMES DIDN'T FEEL LIKE THEY WERE PROGRAMMED BY MEN-- THEY FELT LIKE THEY SIMPLY EXISTED.
NOT ALL GAMES,
BUT SOME GAMES.
SUCH GAMES WEREN'T THE RESULT OF ANY CONCEIVABLE FORM OF MARKET RESEARCH,
IT WAS AS THOUGH THE RAMBLINGS OF A MADMAN WILLED THEMSELVES INTO AN ORGANIZED ARRAY OF ZEROES AND ONES.
SUCH GAMES WOULD FLICKER AND GROAN LIKE THEY WOULD EVAPORATE AT THE SLIGHTEST TOUCH.
LIKE A DREAM.
OR A FORGOTTEN MEMORY.
I-- I'M AFRAID TO PLAY FURTHER.
THAT IS THE FEELING OF YOUR MIND FILLING IN THE CRACKS OF THE UNIVERSE.

GOD COMICS

MON FEB 7, 2011

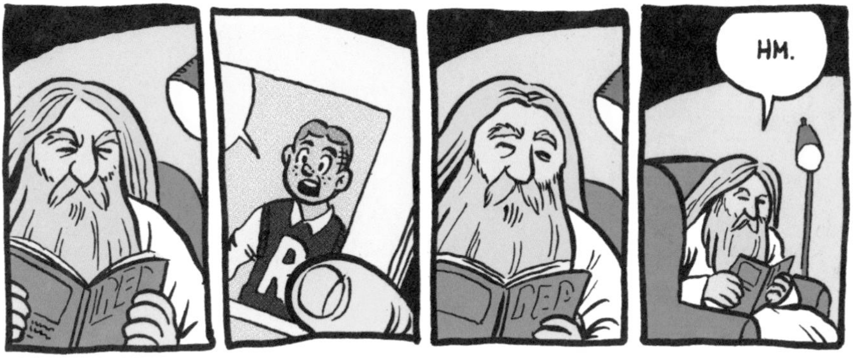
HM.

TUE FEB 8, 2011

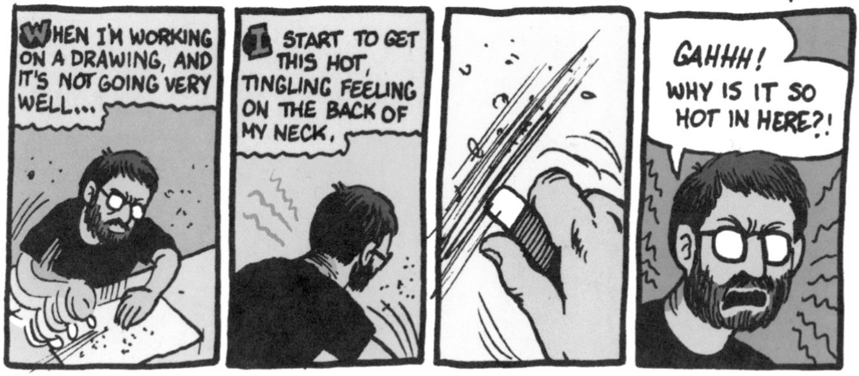
WHEN I'M WORKING ON A DRAWING, AND IT'S NOT GOING VERY WELL...
I START TO GET THIS HOT, TINGLING FEELING ON THE BACK OF MY NECK.
GAHHH!
WHY IS IT SO HOT IN HERE?!

WED FEB 9, 2011

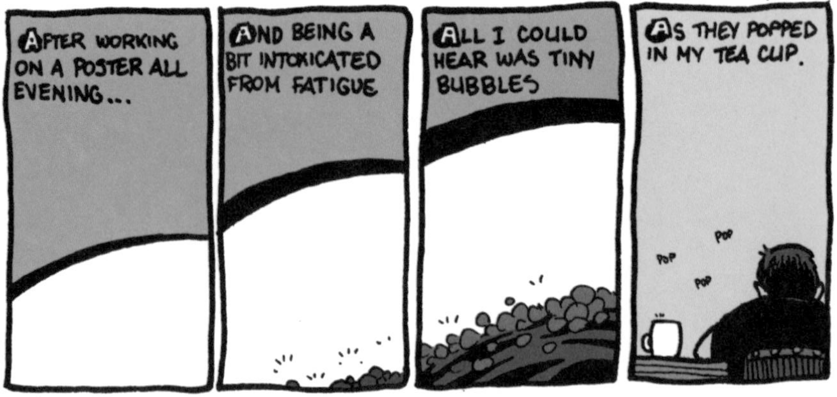
AFTER WORKING ON A POSTER ALL EVENING...
AND BEING A BIT INTOXICATED FROM FATIGUE
ALL I COULD HEAR WAS TINY BUBBLES
AS THEY POPPED IN MY TEA CUP.
POP
POP
POP

THU FEB 10, 2011

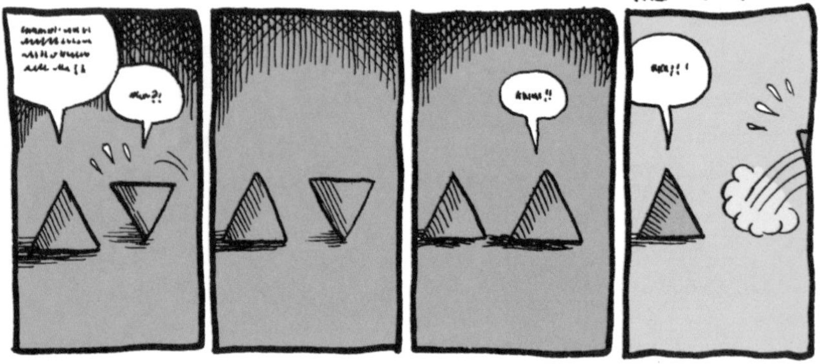

NEIGHBOURS - 12:16 am

FRI FEB 11, 2011

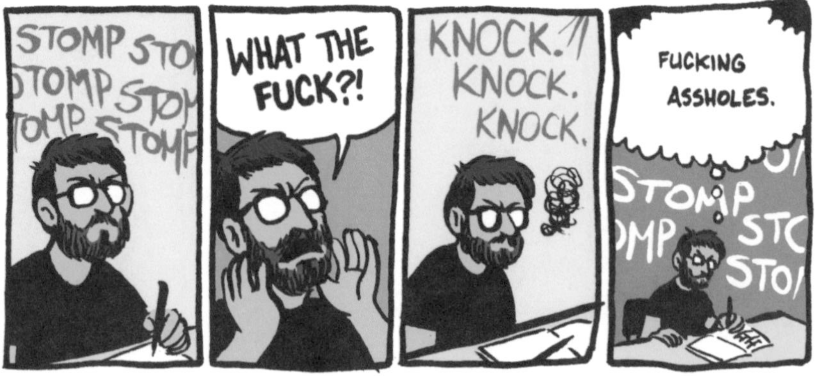
STOMP STOMP STOMP STOMP STOMP STOMP
WHAT THE FUCK?!
KNOCK. KNOCK. KNOCK.
FUCKING ASSHOLES.
STOMP STOMP

SAT FEB 12, 2011

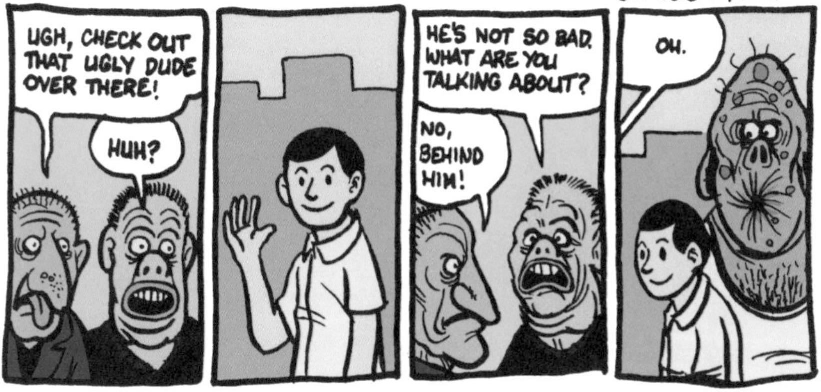
UGH, CHECK OUT THAT UGLY DUDE OVER THERE!
HUH?
HE'S NOT SO BAD. WHAT ARE YOU TALKING ABOUT?
NO, BEHIND HIM!
OH.

SUN FEB 13, 2011

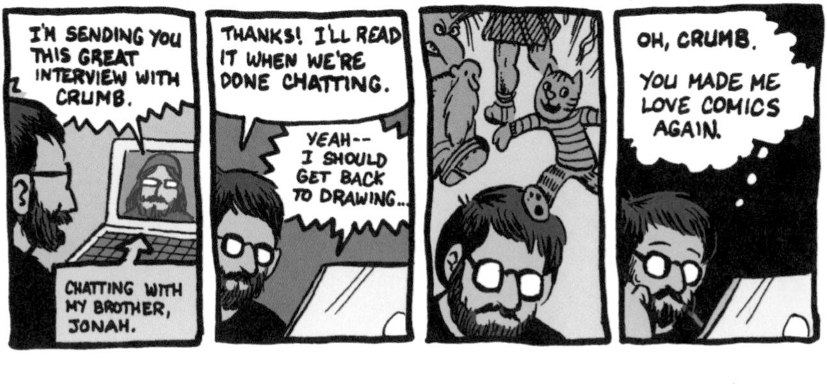
I'M SENDING YOU THIS GREAT INTERVIEW WITH CRUMB.
CHATTING WITH MY BROTHER, JONAH.
THANKS! I'LL READ IT WHEN WE'RE DONE CHATTING.
YEAH-- I SHOULD GET BACK TO DRAWING...
OH, CRUMB.
YOU MADE ME LOVE COMICS AGAIN.

MON FEB 14, 2011

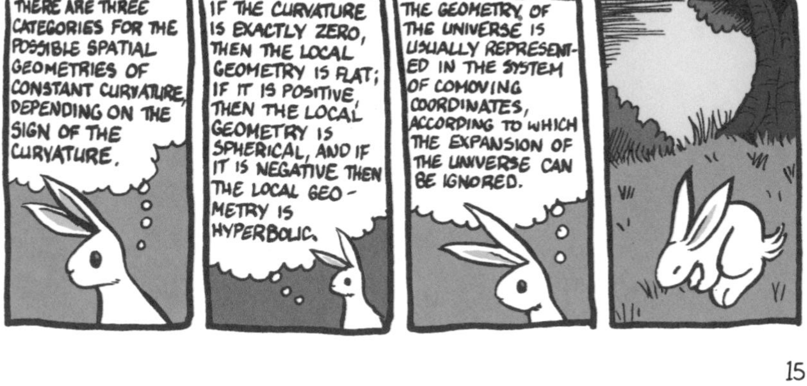
THERE ARE THREE CATEGORIES FOR THE POSSIBLE SPATIAL GEOMETRIES OF CONSTANT CURVATURE, DEPENDING ON THE SIGN OF THE CURVATURE.
IF THE CURVATURE IS EXACTLY ZERO, THEN THE LOCAL GEOMETRY IS FLAT; IF IT IS POSITIVE, THEN THE LOCAL GEOMETRY IS SPHERICAL, AND IF IT IS NEGATIVE THEN THE LOCAL GEO-METRY IS HYPERBOLIC.
THE GEOMETRY OF THE UNIVERSE IS USUALLY REPRESENT-ED IN THE SYSTEM OF COMOVING COORDINATES, ACCORDING TO WHICH THE EXPANSION OF THE UNIVERSE CAN BE IGNORED.

TUE FEB 15, 2011

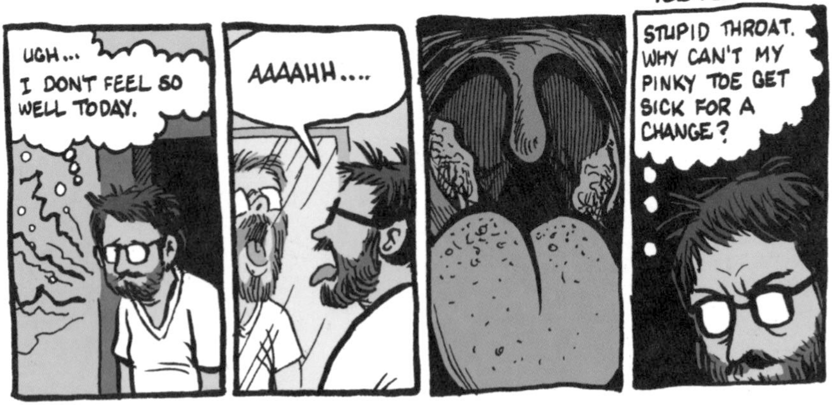
UGH...
I DON'T FEEL SO WELL TODAY.
AAAAHH....
STUPID THROAT. WHY CAN'T MY PINKY TOE GET SICK FOR A CHANGE?

WED FEB 16, 2011

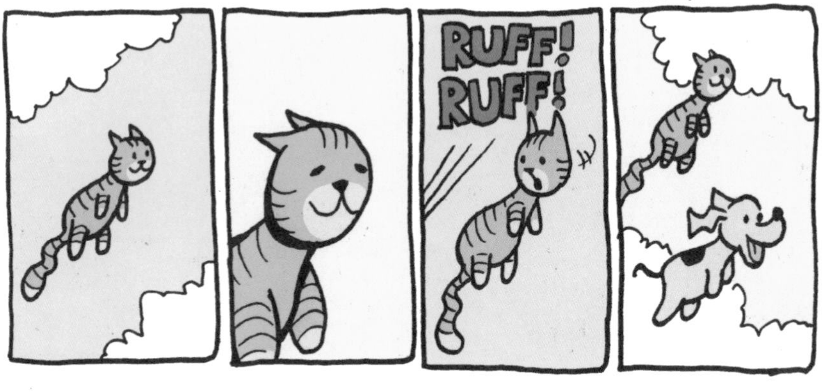
RUFF!
RUFF!

THU FEB 17, 2011

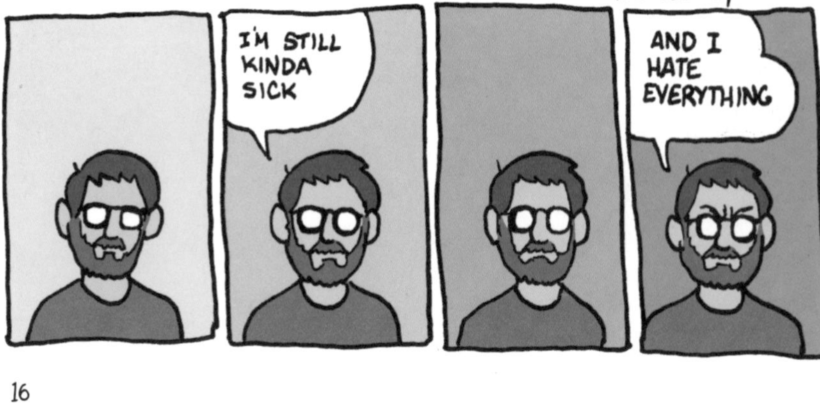
I'M STILL KINDA SICK
AND I HATE EVERYTHING

FRI FEB 18, 2011

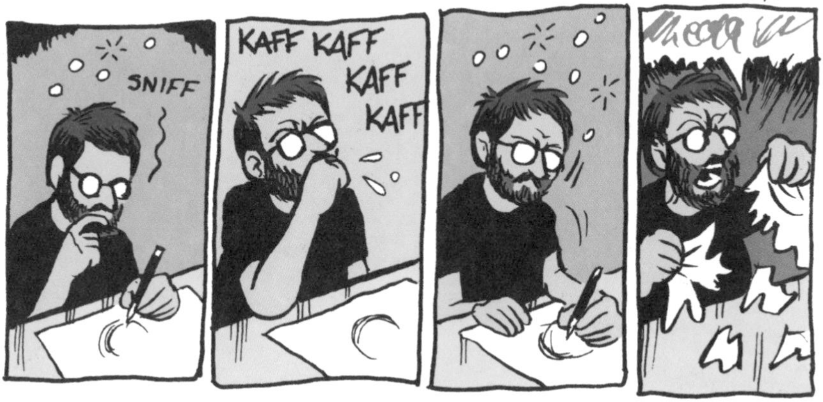
SNIFF
KAFF KAFF
KAFF
KAFF

SAT FEB 19, 2011

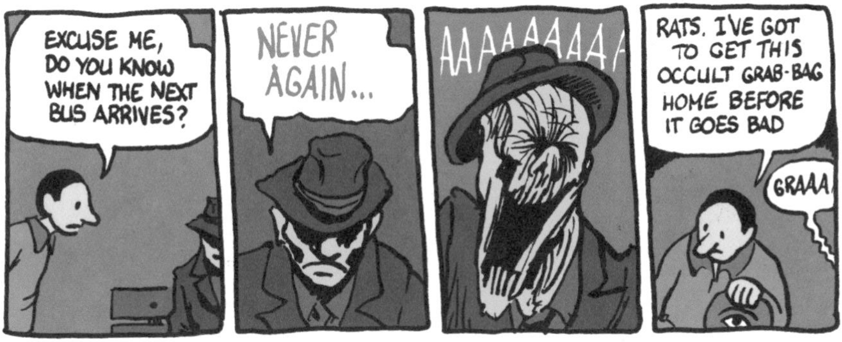
EXCUSE ME, DO YOU KNOW WHEN THE NEXT BUS ARRIVES?
NEVER AGAIN...
AAAAAAAA
RATS. I'VE GOT TO GET THIS OCCULT GRAB-BAG HOME BEFORE IT GOES BAD
GRAAA

SUN FEB 20, 2011

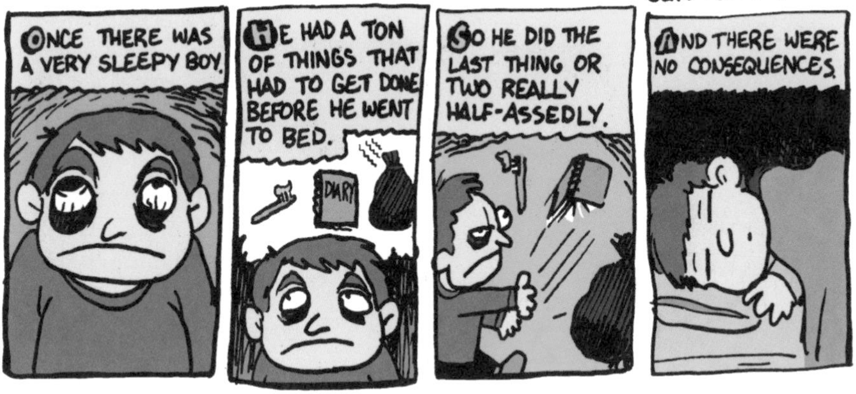
ONCE THERE WAS A VERY SLEEPY BOY.
HE HAD A TON OF THINGS THAT HAD TO GET DONE BEFORE HE WENT TO BED.
DIARY
SO HE DID THE LAST THING OR TWO REALLY HALF-ASSEDLY.
AND THERE WERE NO CONSEQUENCES.

MON FEB 21, 2011

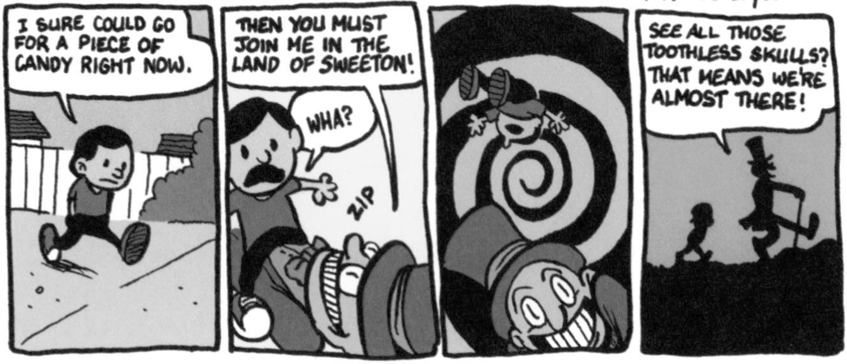
I SURE COULD GO FOR A PIECE OF CANDY RIGHT NOW.
THEN YOU MUST JOIN ME IN THE LAND OF SWEETON!
WHA?
ZIP
SEE ALL THOSE TOOTHLESS SKULLS? THAT MEANS WE'RE ALMOST THERE!

TUE FEB 22, 2011

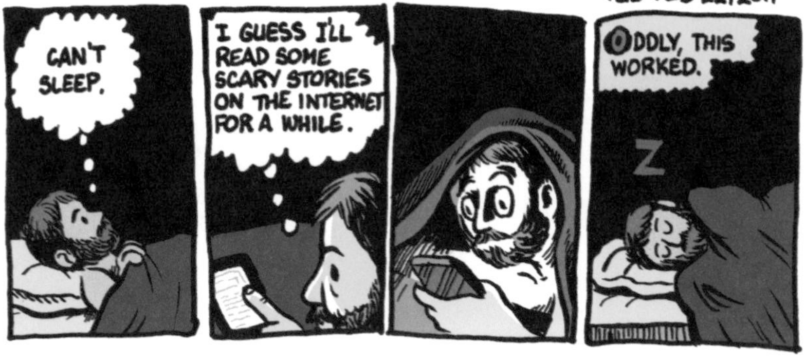
CAN'T SLEEP.
I GUESS I'LL READ SOME SCARY STORIES ON THE INTERNET FOR A WHILE.
ODDLY, THIS WORKED.
Z

WED FEB 23, 2011

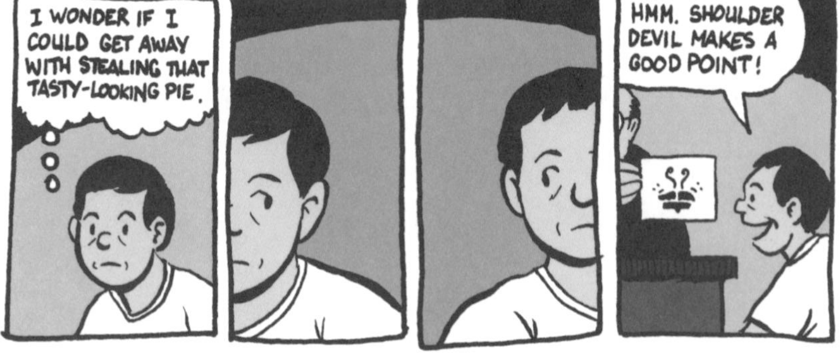
I WONDER IF I COULD GET AWAY WITH STEALING THAT TASTY-LOOKING PIE.
HMM. SHOULDER DEVIL MAKES A GOOD POINT!

THU FEB 24, 2011

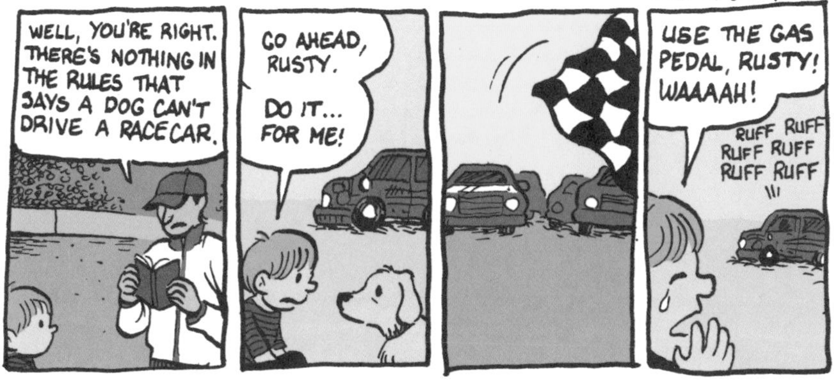
WELL, YOU'RE RIGHT. THERE'S NOTHING IN THE RULES THAT SAYS A DOG CAN'T DRIVE A RACECAR.
GO AHEAD, RUSTY.
DO IT... FOR ME!
USE THE GAS PEDAL, RUSTY! WAAAAH!
RUFF RUFF RUFF RUFF RUFF RUFF

HAPPY COMICS

FRI FEB 25, 2011

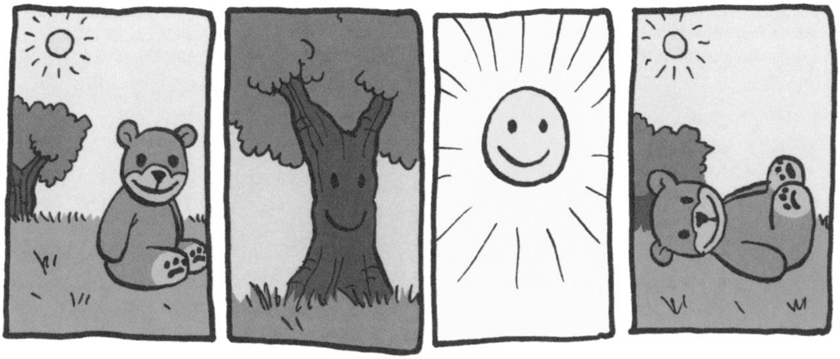

SAT FEB 26, 2011

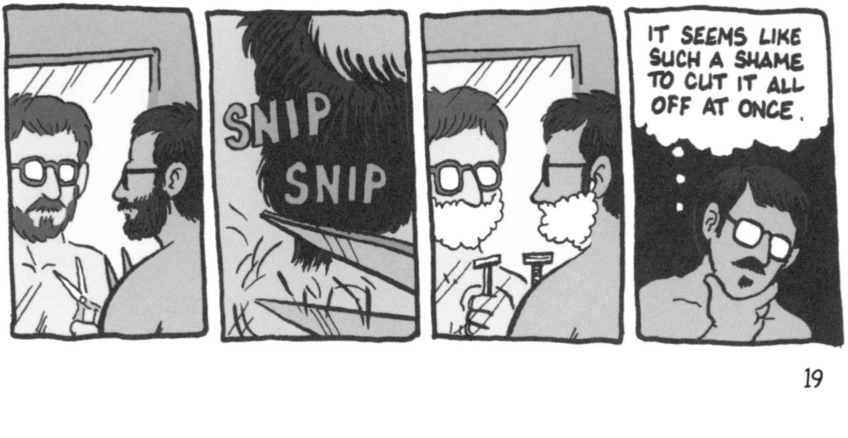
SNIP
SNIP
IT SEEMS LIKE SUCH A SHAME TO CUT IT ALL OFF AT ONCE.

SUN FEB 27, 2011

OH BOY, IS MY HUSBAND EVER A GOD DAMN MORON.

YEAH? WELL AT LEAST I'M NOT A FUCKING NAG.

THIS PURGATORIAL LIMBO IS WITHOUT CONTEXT OR CONSEQUENCE. I USED TO THINK WE WERE IN HELL, BUT EVEN THE DAMNED WRITHE IN PAIN.

After the 2003 death of beloved cartoonist Clarence Royale, an unpublished 'final year' of his long-running strip, Mr. & Mrs. Bliss, was discovered in his Florida Beach House.

MON FEB 28, 2011

I OFTEN FIND MYSELF WISHING I COULD GO BACK IN TIME TO POINTS IN MY LIFE WITH THE KNOWLEDGE I HAVE NOW

LIKE WHEN WE LIVED IN MONTREAL. I HAD MY SAVINGS AND NOTHING BUT TIME TO KILL.

WHY DIDN'T I DRAW MORE COMICS BACK THEN? I'LL PROBABLY NEVER HAVE THAT KIND OF FREEDOM EVER AGAIN.

ONCE I PAY OFF MY SCHOOL LOAN, WE'LL PROBABLY HAVE KIDS, THEY'LL GROW UP, AND THEN I'LL BE OLD.

OH COME ON NOW.

INFINITELY-FALLING BABY

TUE MAR 1 2011

WED MAR 2, 2011

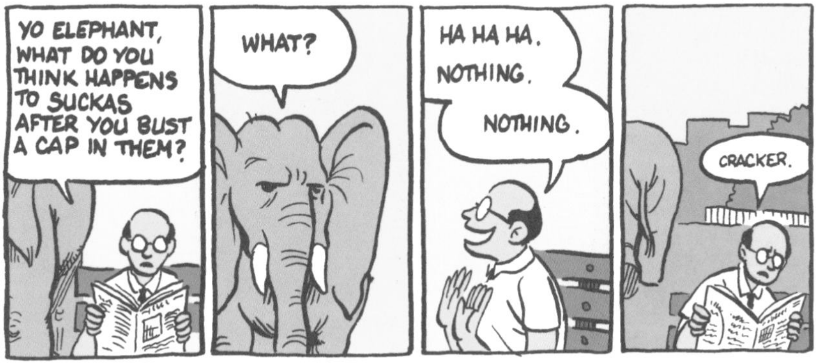
YO ELEPHANT, WHAT DO YOU THINK HAPPENS TO SUCKAS AFTER YOU BUST A CAP IN THEM?
WHAT?
HA HA HA.
NOTHING.
NOTHING.
CRACKER.

THU MAR 3, 2011

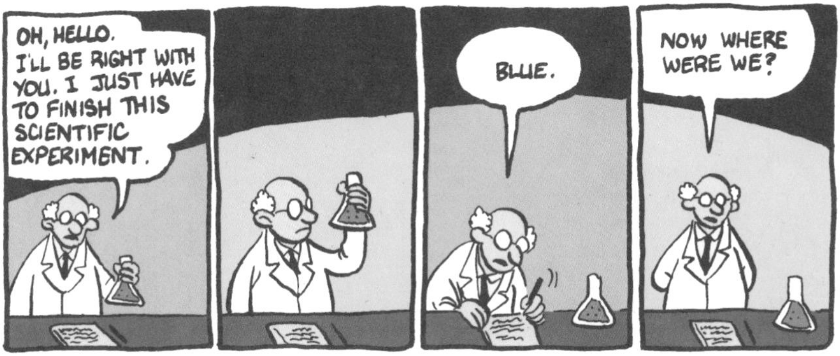
OH, HELLO. I'LL BE RIGHT WITH YOU. I JUST HAVE TO FINISH THIS SCIENTIFIC EXPERIMENT.
BLUE.
NOW WHERE WERE WE?

FRI MAR 4, 2011

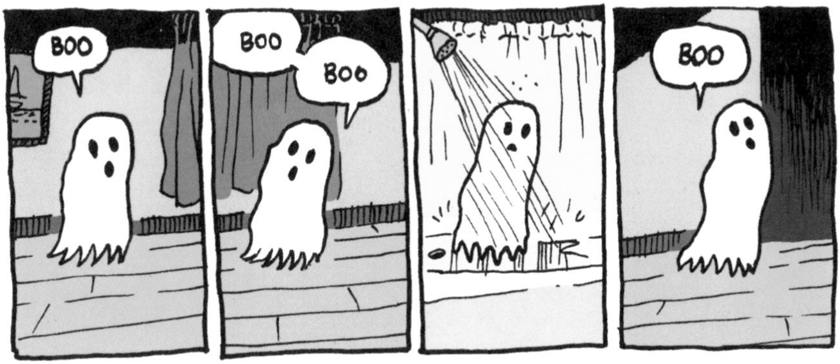
BOO
BOO
BOO
BOO

SAT MAR 5, 2011

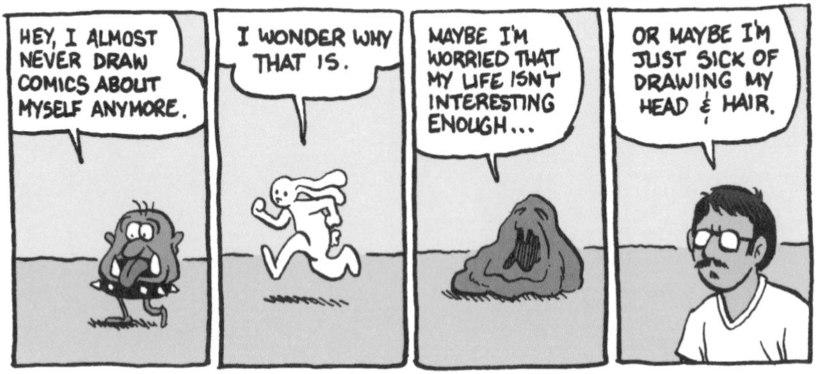
HEY, I ALMOST NEVER DRAW COMICS ABOUT MYSELF ANYMORE.
I WONDER WHY THAT IS.
MAYBE I'M WORRIED THAT MY LIFE ISN'T INTERESTING ENOUGH...
OR MAYBE I'M JUST SICK OF DRAWING MY HEAD & HAIR.

SUN MAR 6, 2011

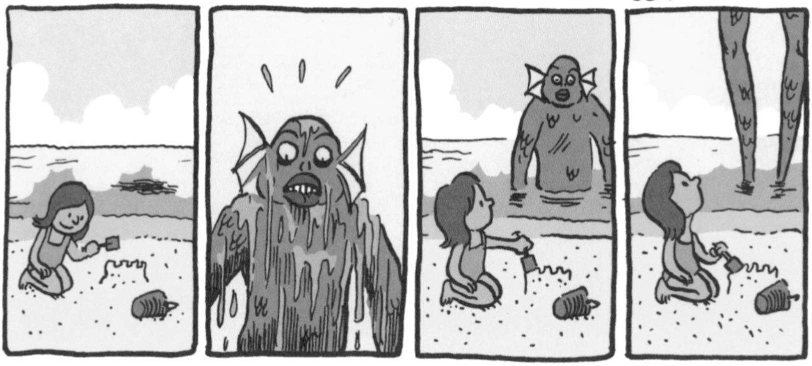

MON MAR 7, 2011

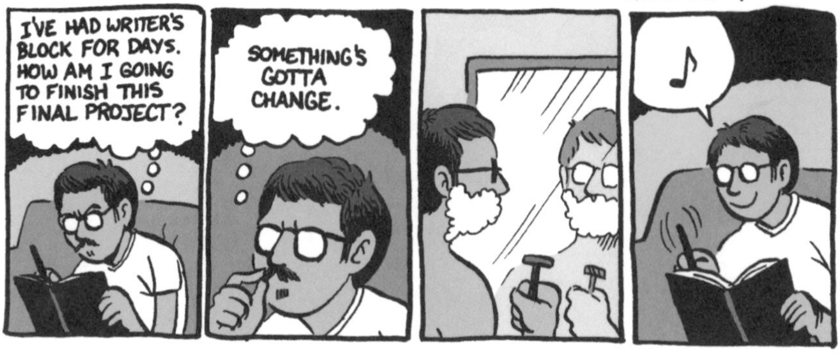
I'VE HAD WRITER'S BLOCK FOR DAYS. HOW AM I GOING TO FINISH THIS FINAL PROJECT?
SOMETHING'S GOTTA CHANGE.
♪

TUE MAR 8, 2011

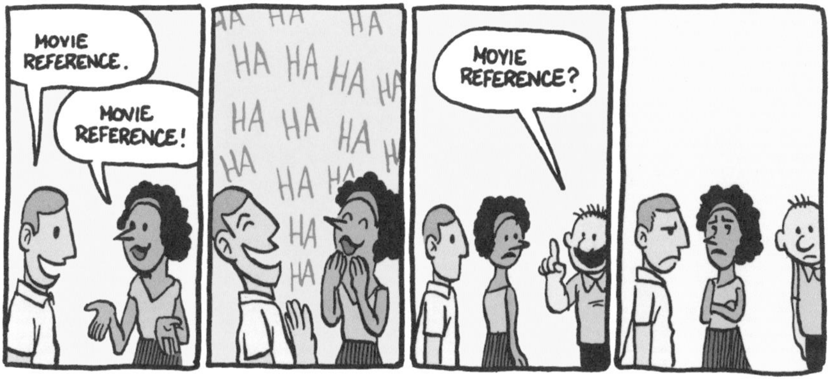
MOVIE REFERENCE.
MOVIE REFERENCE!
HA HA HA HA HA HA HA HA HA HA HA HA HA HA HA HA
MOVIE REFERENCE?

WED MAR 9, 2011

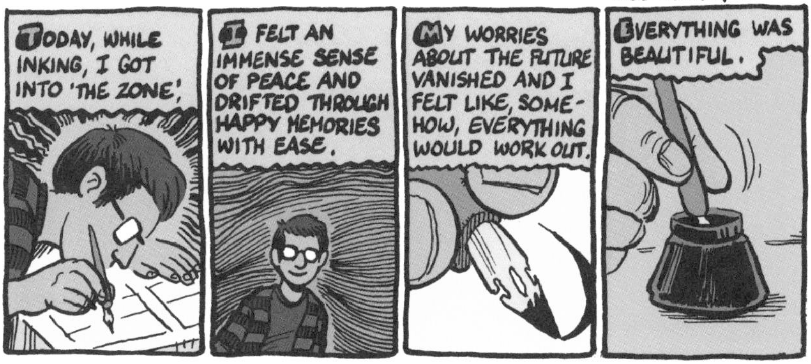
TODAY, WHILE INKING, I GOT INTO 'THE ZONE',
I FELT AN IMMENSE SENSE OF PEACE AND DRIFTED THROUGH HAPPY MEMORIES WITH EASE.
MY WORRIES ABOUT THE FUTURE VANISHED AND I FELT LIKE, SOMEHOW, EVERYTHING WOULD WORK OUT.
EVERYTHING WAS BEAUTIFUL.

THU MAR 10, 2011

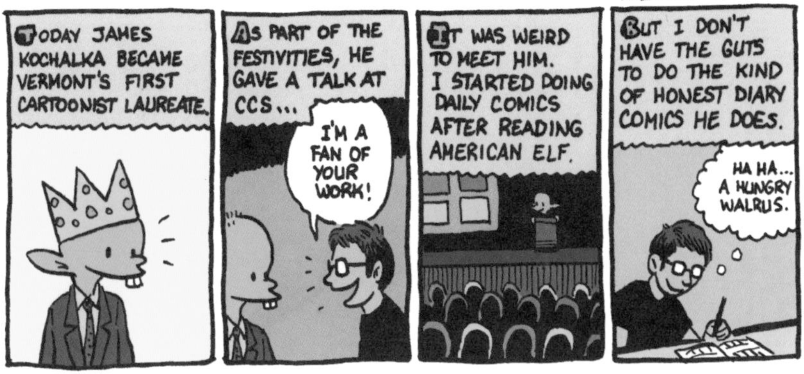
TODAY JAMES KOCHALKA BECAME VERMONT'S FIRST CARTOONIST LAUREATE.
AS PART OF THE FESTIVITIES, HE GAVE A TALK AT CCS...
I'M A FAN OF YOUR WORK!
IT WAS WEIRD TO MEET HIM. I STARTED DOING DAILY COMICS AFTER READING AMERICAN ELF.
BUT I DON'T HAVE THE GUTS TO DO THE KIND OF HONEST DIARY COMICS HE DOES.
HA HA... A HUNGRY WALRUS.

FRI MAR 11, 2011

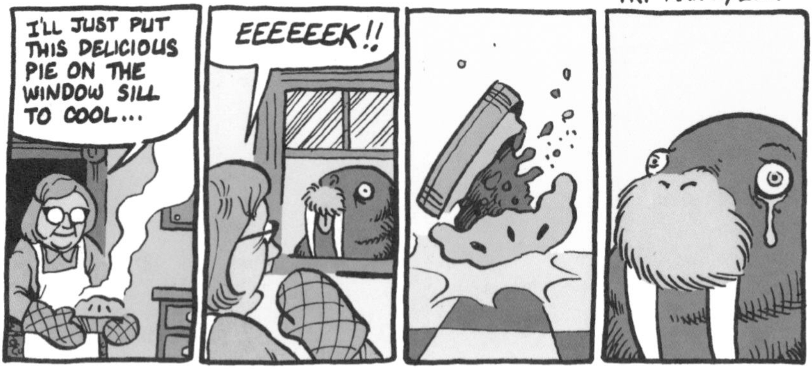
I'LL JUST PUT THIS DELICIOUS PIE ON THE WINDOW SILL TO COOL...
EEEEEEK!!

SAT MAR 12, 2011

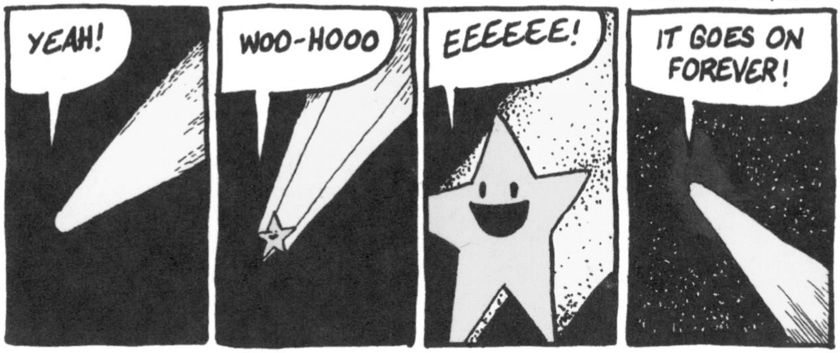
YEAH!
WOO-HOOO
EEEEEE!
IT GOES ON FOREVER!

CRYING MAN

SUN MAR 13, 2011

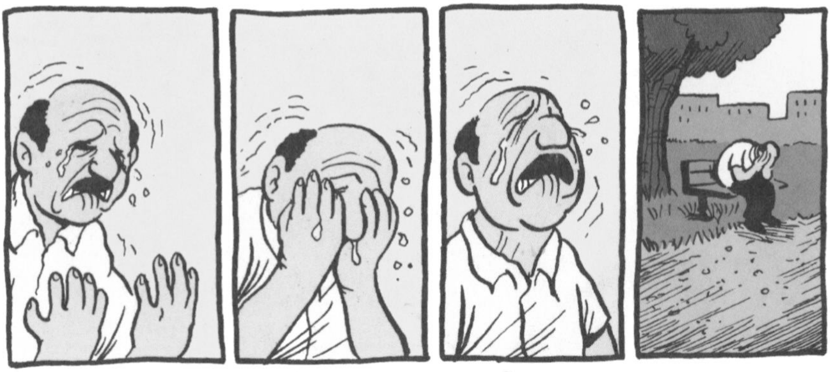

MON MAR 14, 2011

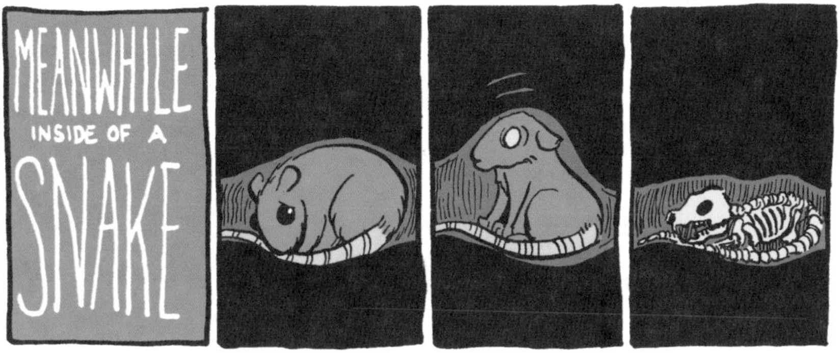
MEANWHILE
INSIDE OF A
SNAKE

HISTORY CLASS

TUE MAR 15, 2011

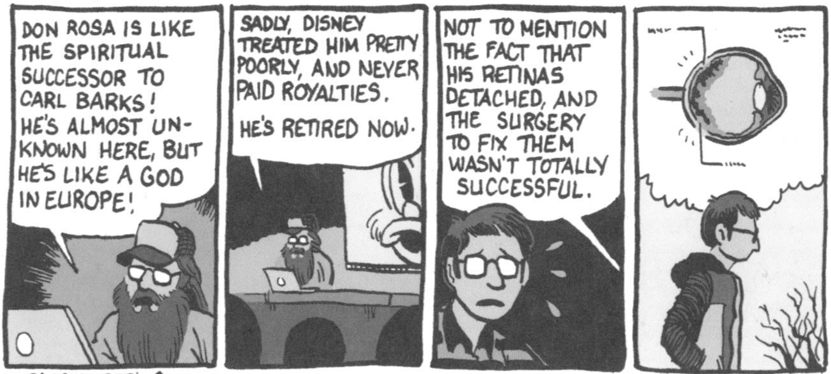
DON ROSA IS LIKE THE SPIRITUAL SUCCESSOR TO CARL BARKS! HE'S ALMOST UN-KNOWN HERE, BUT HE'S LIKE A GOD IN EUROPE!
SADLY, DISNEY TREATED HIM PRETTY POORLY, AND NEVER PAID ROYALTIES.
HE'S RETIRED NOW.
NOT TO MENTION THE FACT THAT HIS RETINAS DETACHED, AND THE SURGERY TO FIX THEM WASN'T TOTALLY SUCCESSFUL.

ALEC LONGSTRETH

TIME TRAVELLING TOROSAURUS

WED MAR 16, 2011

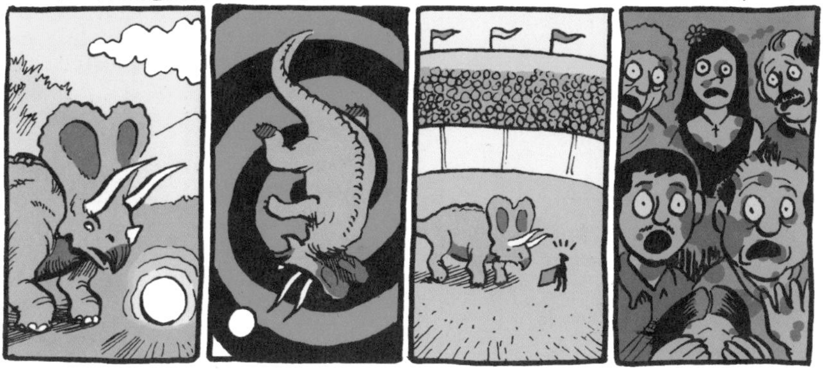

THU MAR 17, 2011

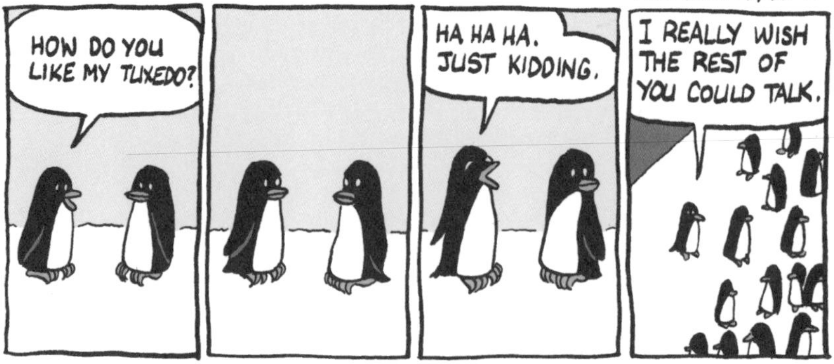
HOW DO YOU LIKE MY TUXEDO?
HA HA HA. JUST KIDDING.
I REALLY WISH THE REST OF YOU COULD TALK.

WE GO FOR LUNCH

FRI MAR 18, 2011

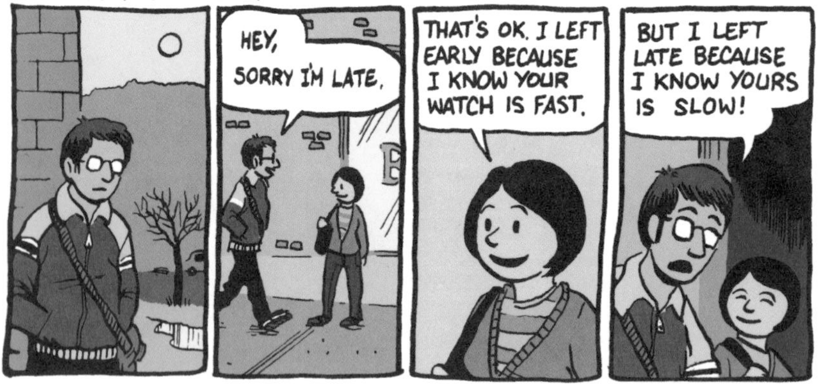
HEY,
SORRY I'M LATE.
THAT'S OK. I LEFT EARLY BECAUSE I KNOW YOUR WATCH IS FAST.
BUT I LEFT LATE BECAUSE I KNOW YOURS IS SLOW!

SAT MAR 19, 2011

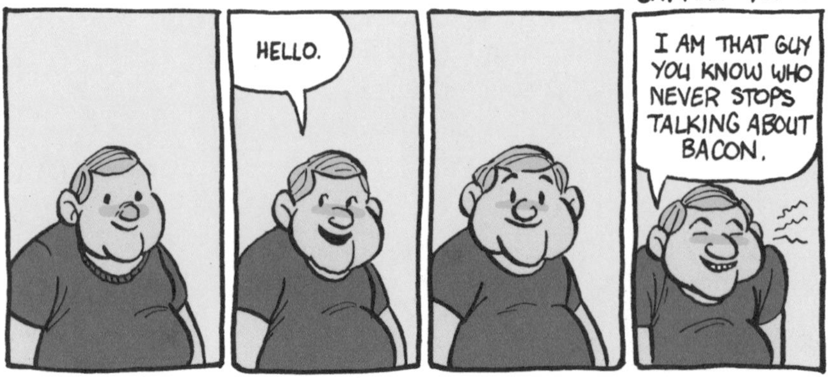
HELLO.
I AM THAT GUY YOU KNOW WHO NEVER STOPS TALKING ABOUT BACON.

SUN MAR 20, 2011

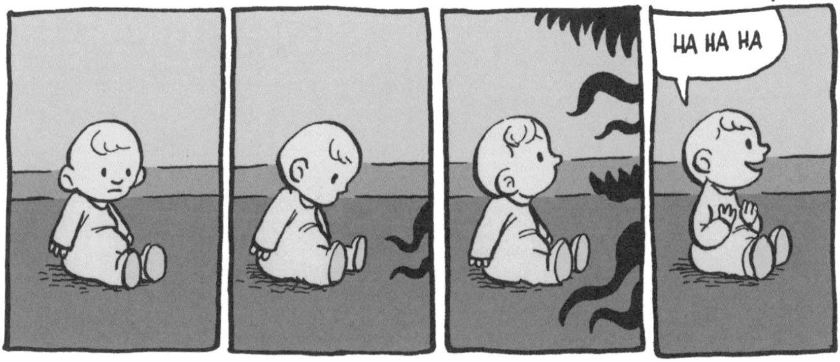
HA HA HA

A DREAM I HAD

MON MAR 21, 2011

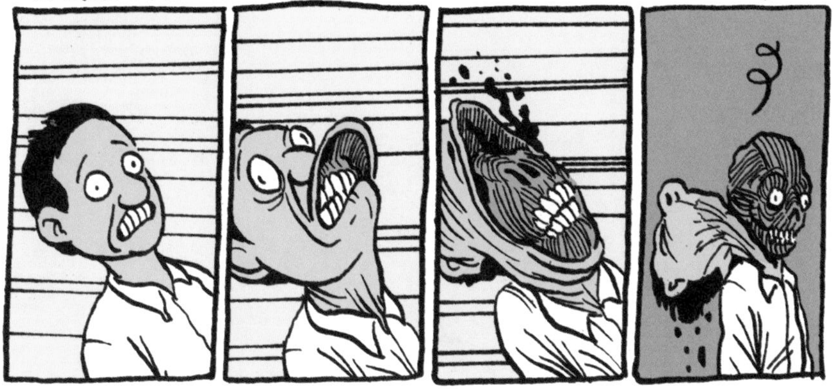

CAN'T THINK STRAIGHT...

TUE MAR 22, 2011

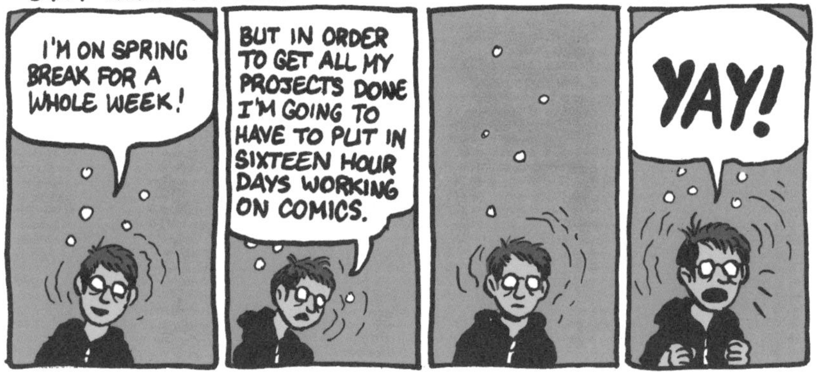
I'M ON SPRING BREAK FOR A WHOLE WEEK!
BUT IN ORDER TO GET ALL MY PROJECTS DONE I'M GOING TO HAVE TO PUT IN SIXTEEN HOUR DAYS WORKING ON COMICS.
YAY!

WED MAR 23, 2011

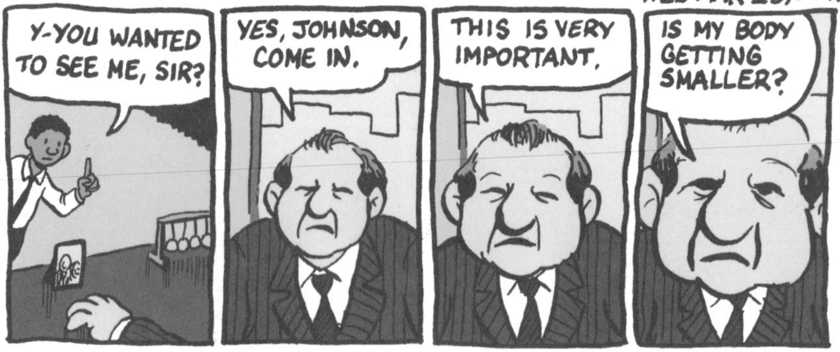
Y-YOU WANTED TO SEE ME, SIR?
YES, JOHNSON, COME IN.
THIS IS VERY IMPORTANT.
IS MY BODY GETTING SMALLER?

THU MAR 24, 2011

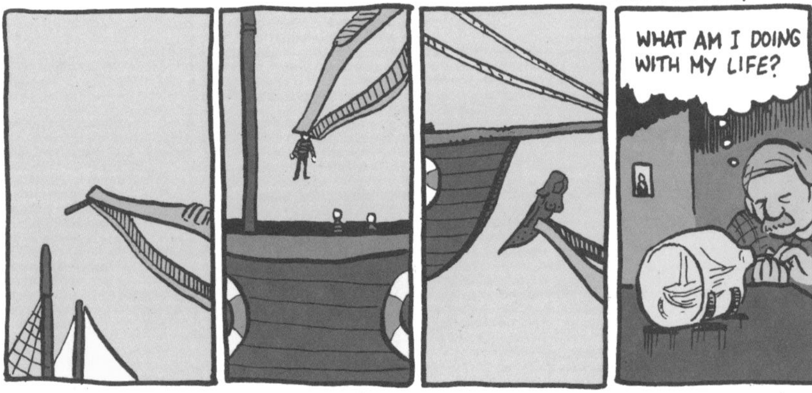
WHAT AM I DOING WITH MY LIFE?

FRI MAR 25, 2011

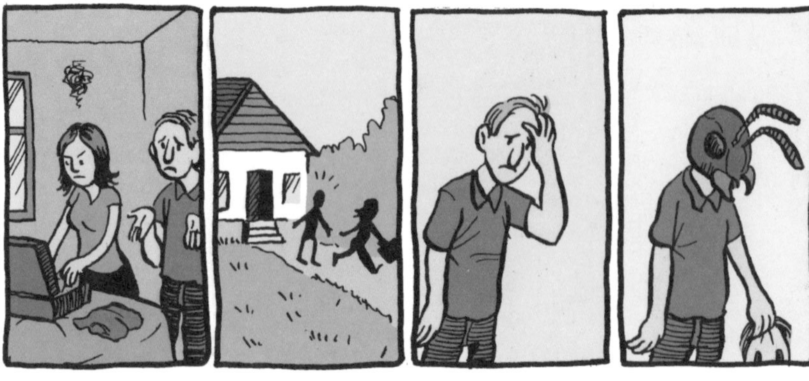

SAT MAR 26, 2011

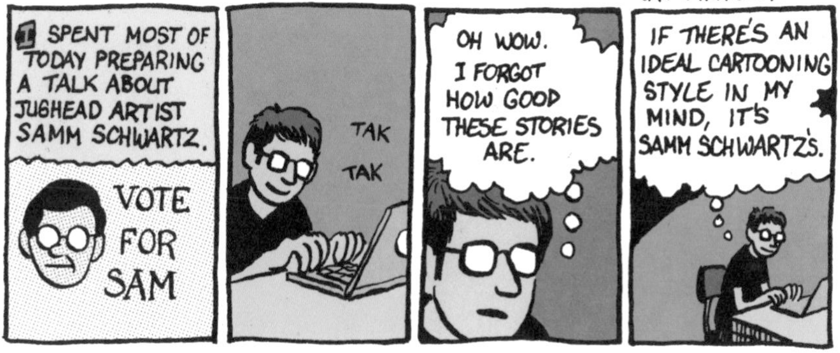
I SPENT MOST OF TODAY PREPARING A TALK ABOUT JUGHEAD ARTIST SAMM SCHWARTZ.
VOTE FOR SAM
TAK
TAK
OH WOW. I FORGOT HOW GOOD THESE STORIES ARE.
IF THERE'S AN IDEAL CARTOONING STYLE IN MY MIND, IT'S SAMM SCHWARTZ'S.

INVISIBLE DINOSAUR

SUN MAR 27, 2011

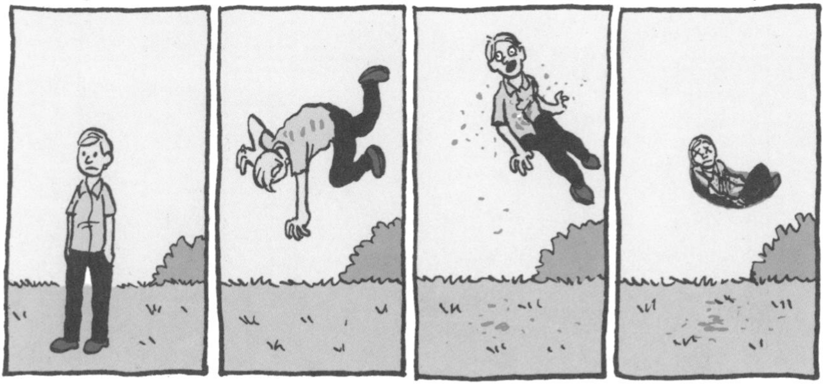

A DREAM I HAD

MON MAR 28, 2011

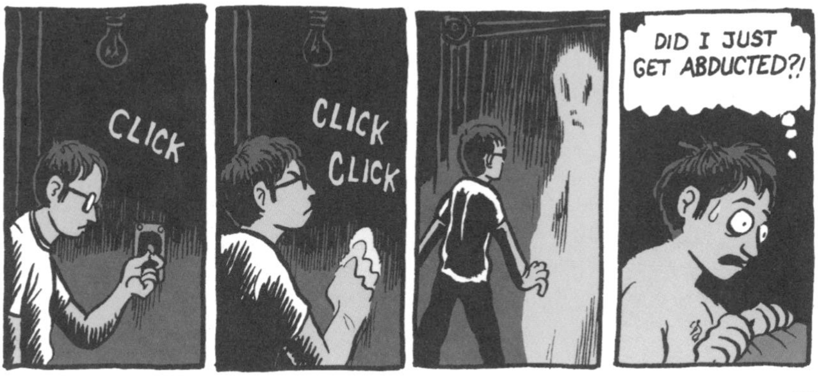
CLICK
CLICK
CLICK
DID I JUST GET ABDUCTED?!

ANOTHER DREAM I HAD

TUE MAR 29, 2011

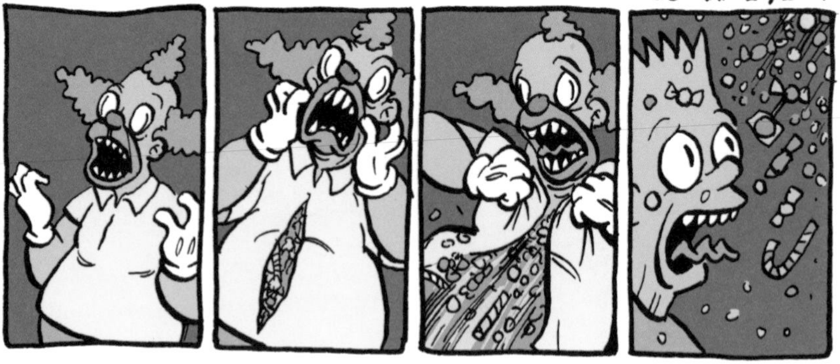

ELEPHANT COMICS

WED MAR 30, 2011

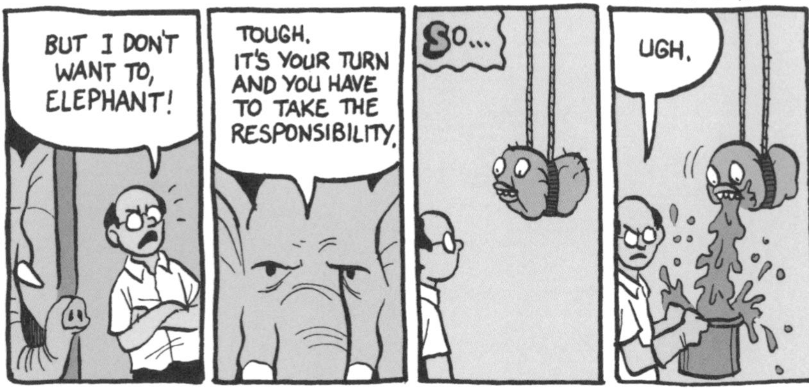
BUT I DON'T WANT TO, ELEPHANT!
TOUGH. IT'S YOUR TURN AND YOU HAVE TO TAKE THE RESPONSIBILITY.
SO...
UGH.

EXPLODING DOG

THU MAR 31, 2011

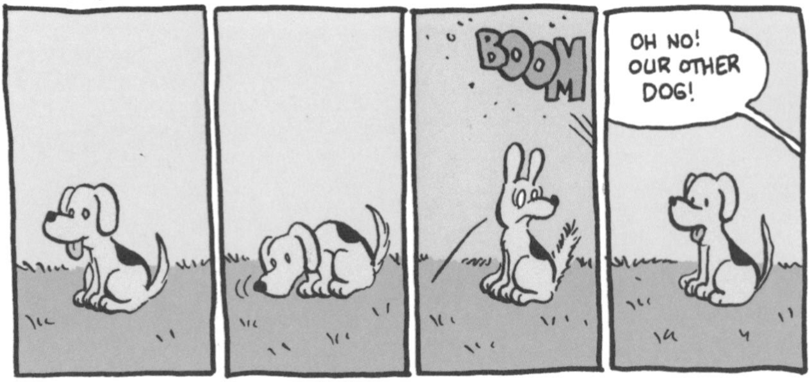
BOOM
OH NO! OUR OTHER DOG!

FRI APR 1, 2011

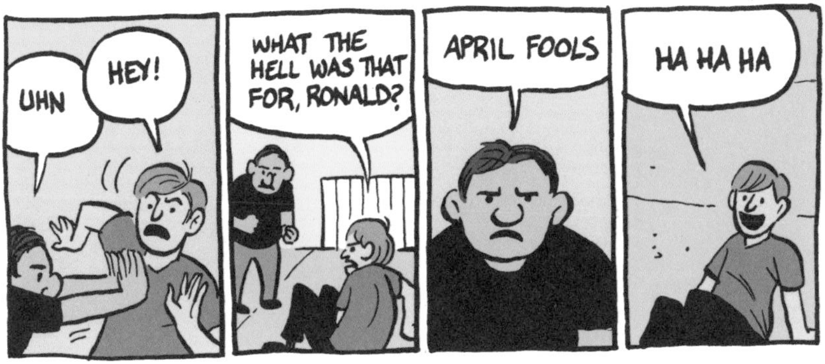
UHN
HEY!
WHAT THE HELL WAS THAT FOR, RONALD?
APRIL FOOLS
HA HA HA

SAT APR 2, 2011

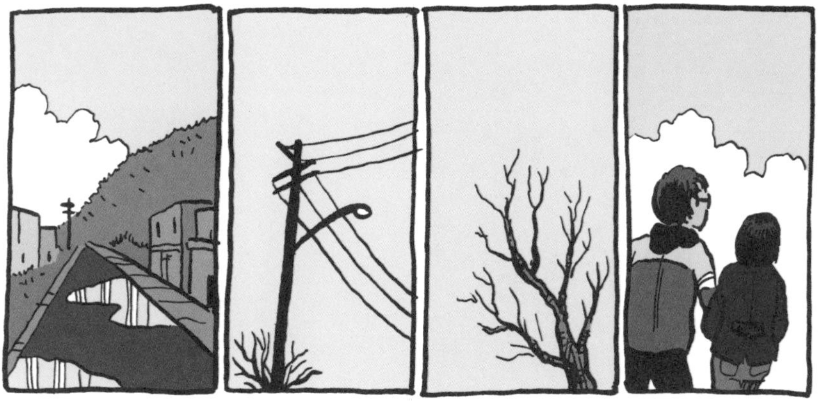

SUN APR 3, 2011

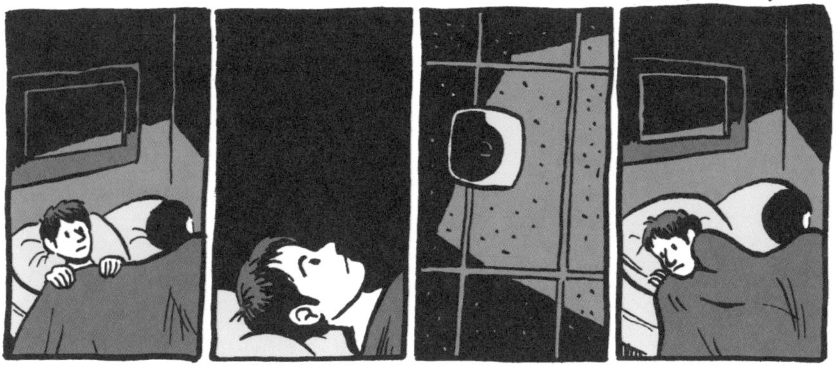

GOD COMICS

MON APRIL 4, 2011

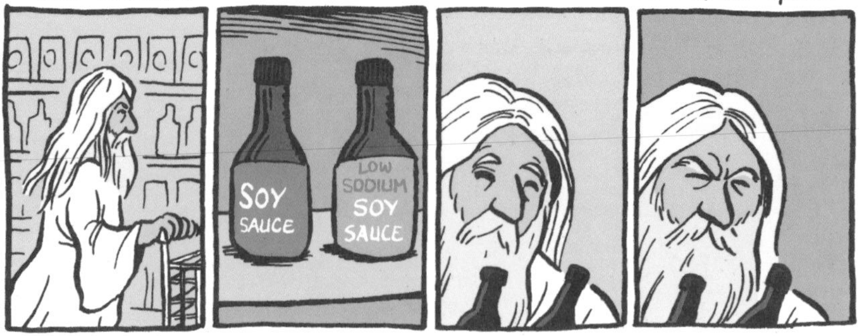
SOY SAUCE
LOW SODIUM SOY SAUCE

TUE APR 5, 2011

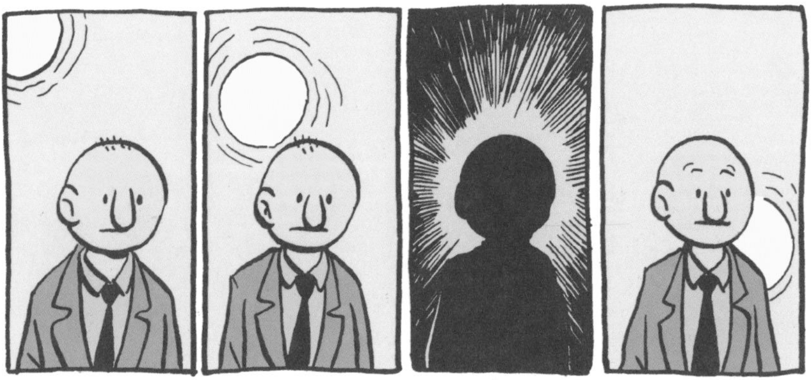

NAP

WED APR 6, 2011

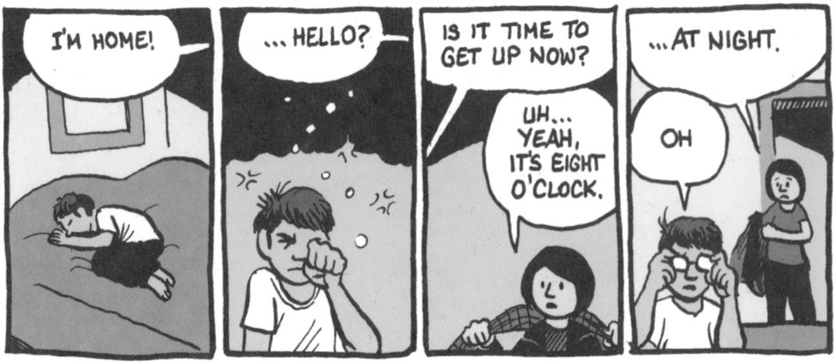
I'M HOME!
...HELLO?
IS IT TIME TO GET UP NOW?
UH... YEAH, IT'S EIGHT O'CLOCK.
...AT NIGHT.
OH

THU APR 7, 2011

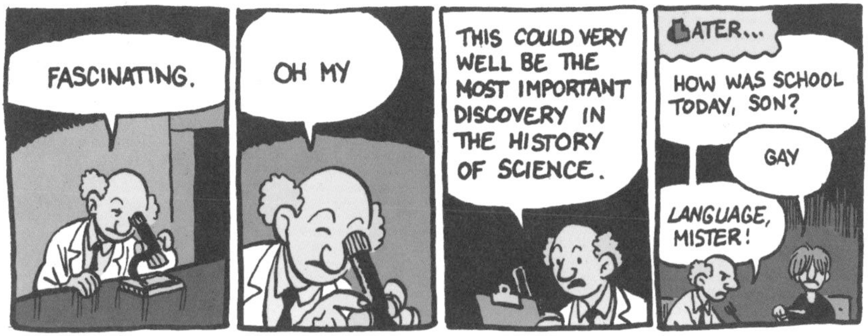
FASCINATING.
OH MY
THIS COULD VERY WELL BE THE MOST IMPORTANT DISCOVERY IN THE HISTORY OF SCIENCE.
LATER...
HOW WAS SCHOOL TODAY, SON?
GAY
LANGUAGE, MISTER!

IN NEW YORK

FRI APR 8, 2011

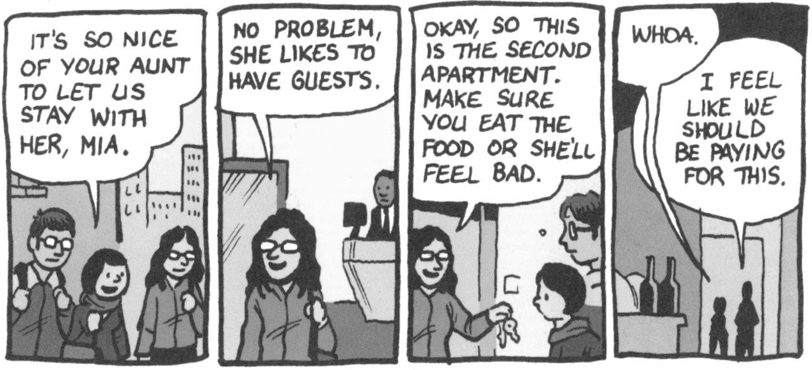
IT'S SO NICE OF YOUR AUNT TO LET US STAY WITH HER, MIA.
NO PROBLEM, SHE LIKES TO HAVE GUESTS.
OKAY, SO THIS IS THE SECOND APARTMENT. MAKE SURE YOU EAT THE FOOD OR SHE'LL FEEL BAD.
WHOA.
I FEEL LIKE WE SHOULD BE PAYING FOR THIS.

TABLING AT MoCCA...

SAT APR 9, 2011

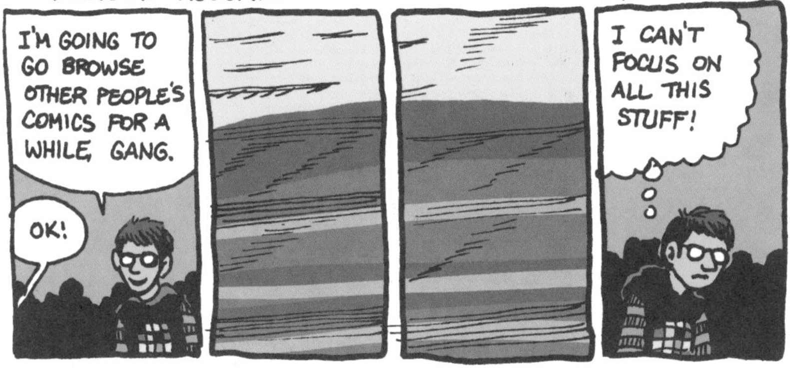
I'M GOING TO GO BROWSE OTHER PEOPLE'S COMICS FOR A WHILE, GANG.
OK!
I CAN'T FOCUS ON ALL THIS STUFF!

SUN APR 10, 2011

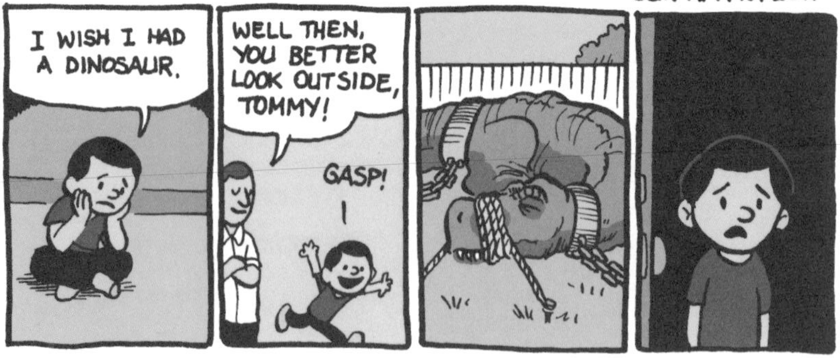
I WISH I HAD A DINOSAUR.
WELL THEN, YOU BETTER LOOK OUTSIDE, TOMMY!
GASP!

MON APR 11, 2011

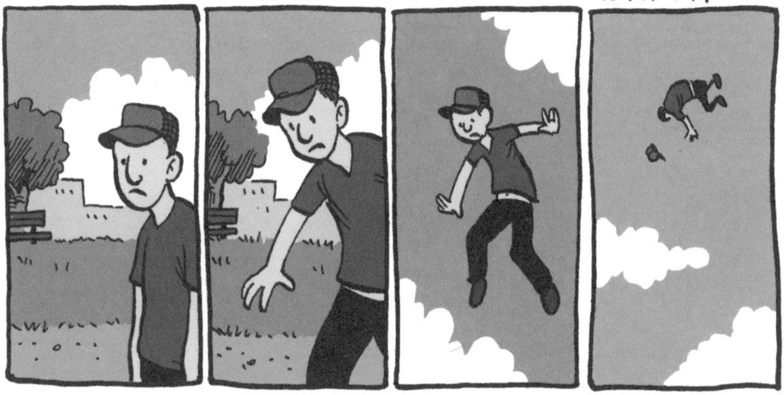

TUE APR 12, 2011

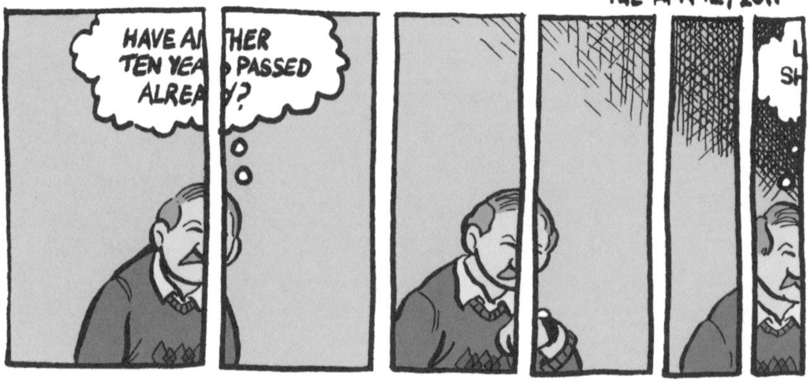
HAVE A THER TEN YEA PASSED ALREA ?

ANTI GRAVITY CAT

WED APR 13, 2011

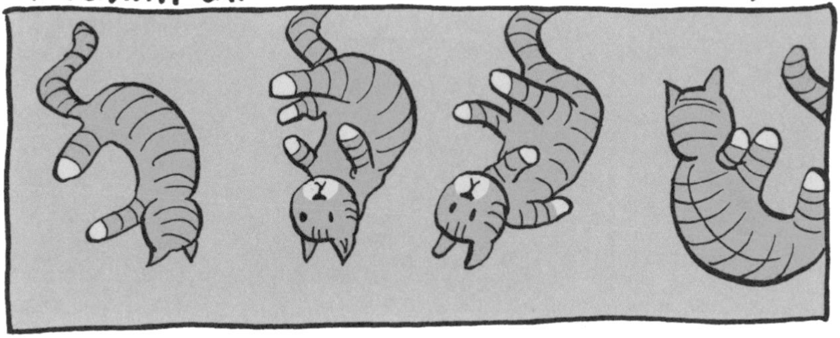

THU APR 14, 2011

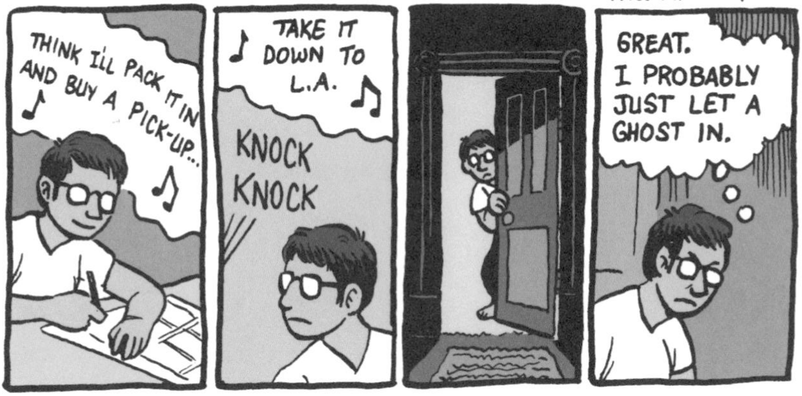
THINK I'LL PACK IT IN AND BUY A PICK-UP...
TAKE IT DOWN TO L.A.
KNOCK KNOCK
GREAT. I PROBABLY JUST LET A GHOST IN.

FRI APR 15, 2011

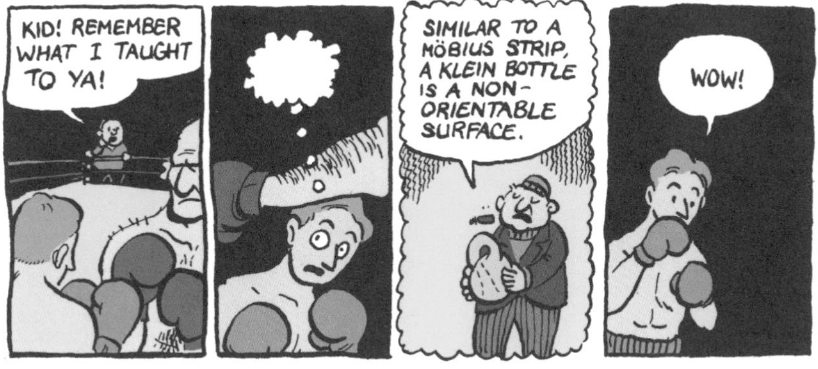
KID! REMEMBER WHAT I TAUGHT TO YA!
SIMILAR TO A MÖBIUS STRIP, A KLEIN BOTTLE IS A NON-ORIENTABLE SURFACE.
WOW!

SAT APR 16, 2011

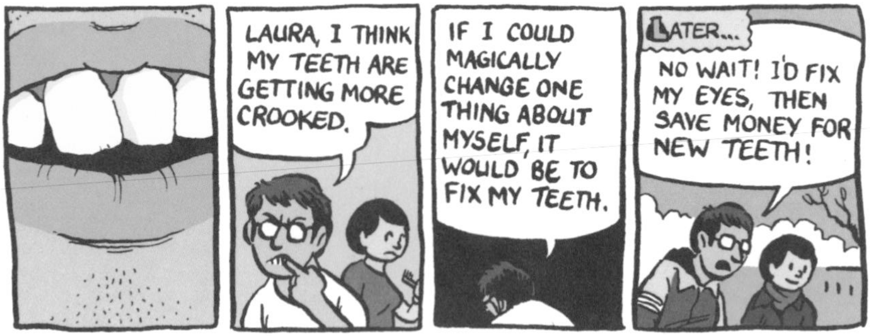
LAURA, I THINK MY TEETH ARE GETTING MORE CROOKED.
IF I COULD MAGICALLY CHANGE ONE THING ABOUT MYSELF, IT WOULD BE TO FIX MY TEETH.
LATER...
NO WAIT! I'D FIX MY EYES, THEN SAVE MONEY FOR NEW TEETH!

SUN APR 17, 2011

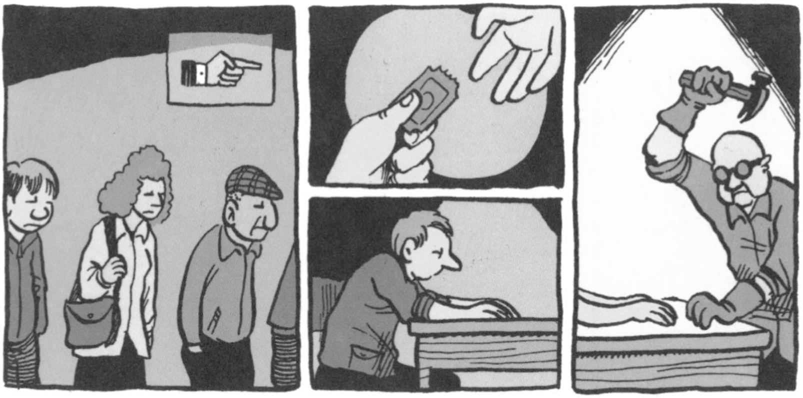

MON APR 18, 2011

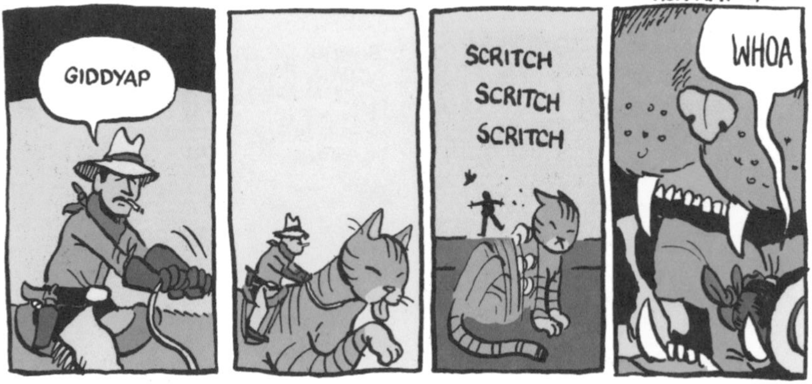
GIDDYAP
SCRITCH
SCRITCH
SCRITCH
WHOA

TUE APR 19, 2011

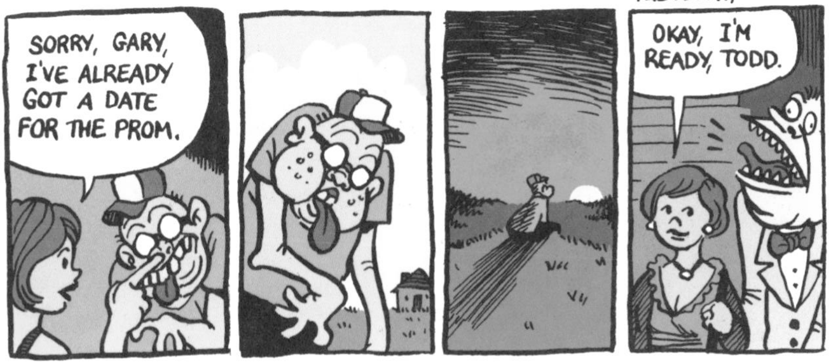

SORRY, GARY, I'VE ALREADY GOT A DATE FOR THE PROM.
OKAY, I'M READY, TODD.

ELEPHANT COMICS

WED APR 20, 2011

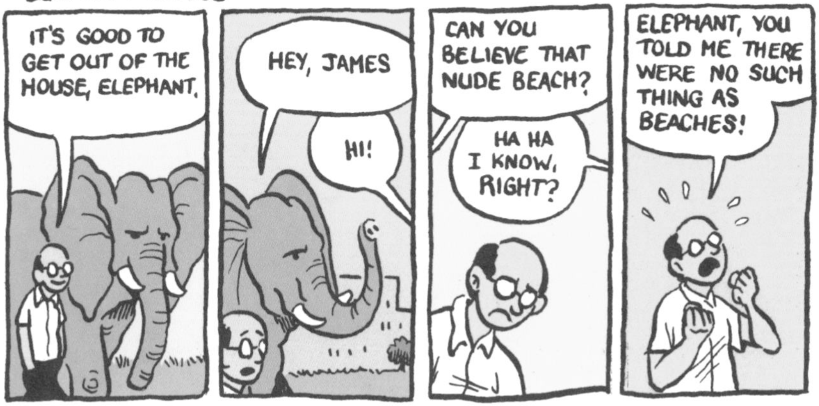

IT'S GOOD TO GET OUT OF THE HOUSE, ELEPHANT.
HEY, JAMES
HI!
CAN YOU BELIEVE THAT NUDE BEACH?
HA HA I KNOW, RIGHT?
ELEPHANT, YOU TOLD ME THERE WERE NO SUCH THING AS BEACHES!

DUMB COMICS

THU APR 21, 2011

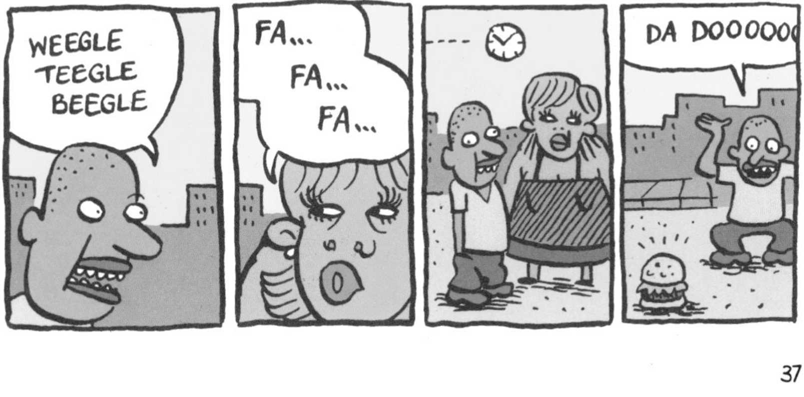

WEEGLE TEEGLE BEEGLE
FA... FA... FA...
DA DOOOOO

FRI APR 22, 2011

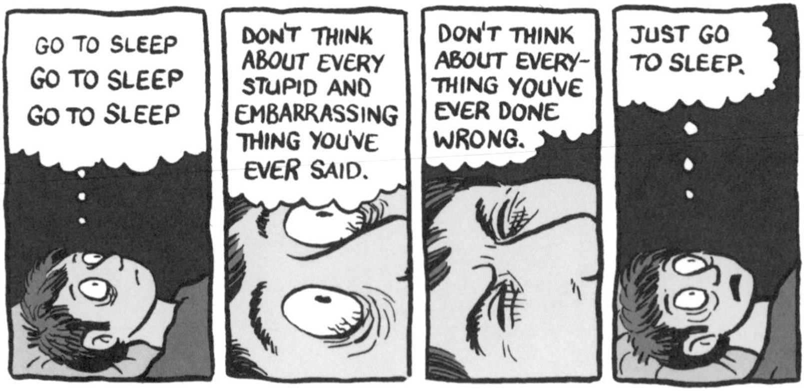
GO TO SLEEP GO TO SLEEP GO TO SLEEP
DON'T THINK ABOUT EVERY STUPID AND EMBARRASSING THING YOU'VE EVER SAID.
DON'T THINK ABOUT EVERYTHING YOU'VE EVER DONE WRONG.
JUST GO TO SLEEP.

SAT APR 23, 2011

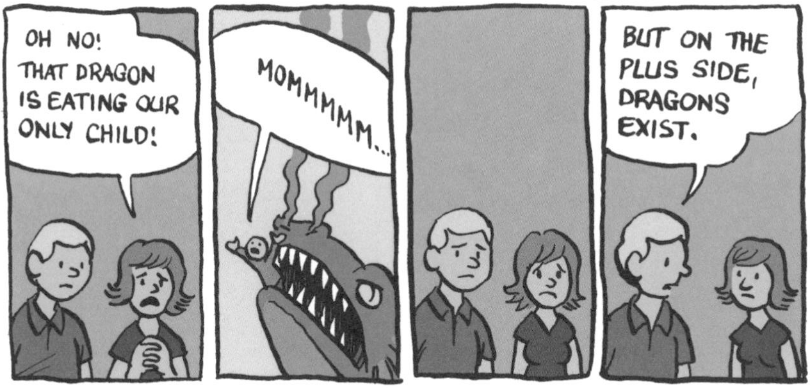
OH NO! THAT DRAGON IS EATING OUR ONLY CHILD!
MOMMMMMM...
BUT ON THE PLUS SIDE, DRAGONS EXIST.

SUN APR 24, 2011

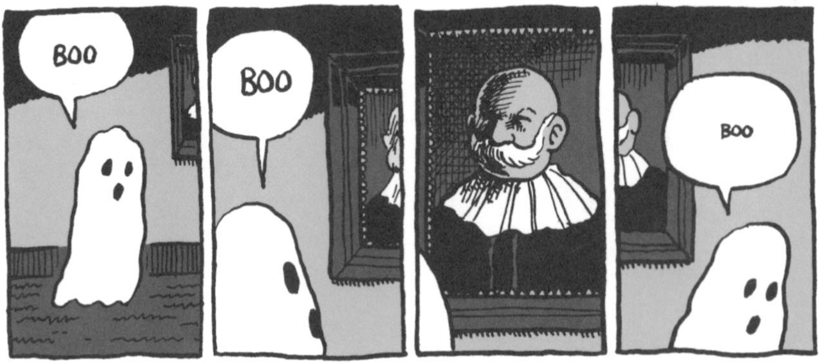
BOO
BOO
BOO

GHOST RABBIT

MON APRIL 25, 2011

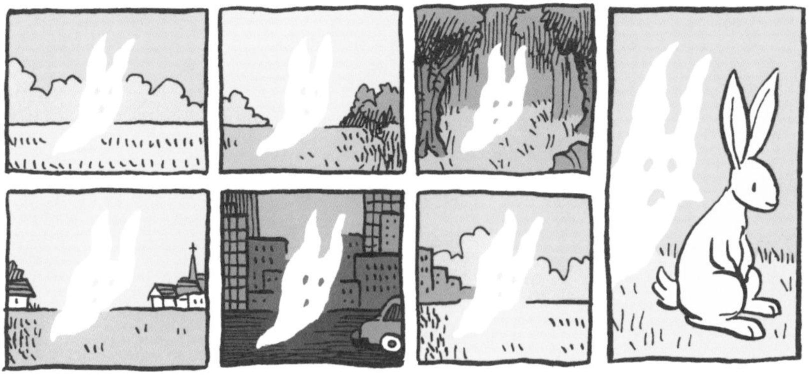

TUE APR 26, 2011

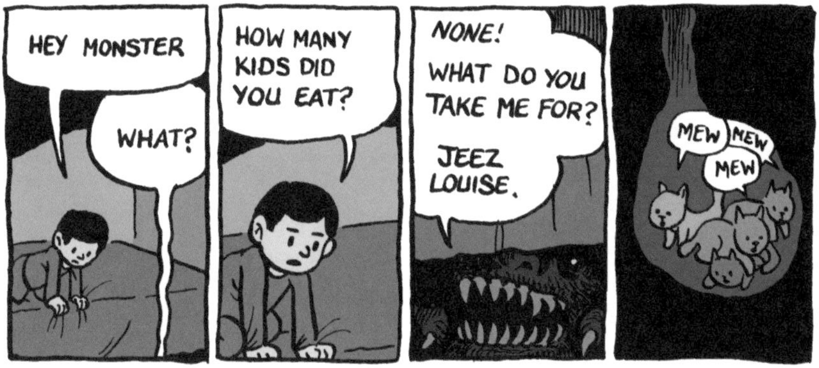
HEY MONSTER
WHAT?
HOW MANY KIDS DID YOU EAT?
NONE!
WHAT DO YOU TAKE ME FOR?
JEEZ LOUISE.
MEW
MEW
MEW

WED APR 27, 2011

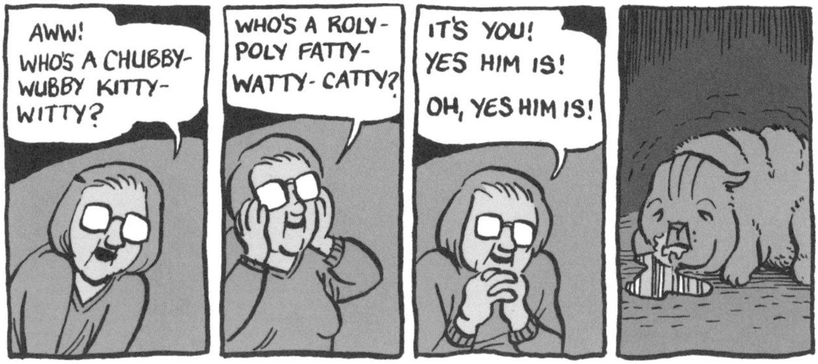
AWW!
WHO'S A CHUBBY-WUBBY KITTY-WITTY?
WHO'S A ROLY-POLY FATTY-WATTY-CATTY?
IT'S YOU!
YES HIM IS!
OH, YES HIM IS!

THU APR 28, 2011

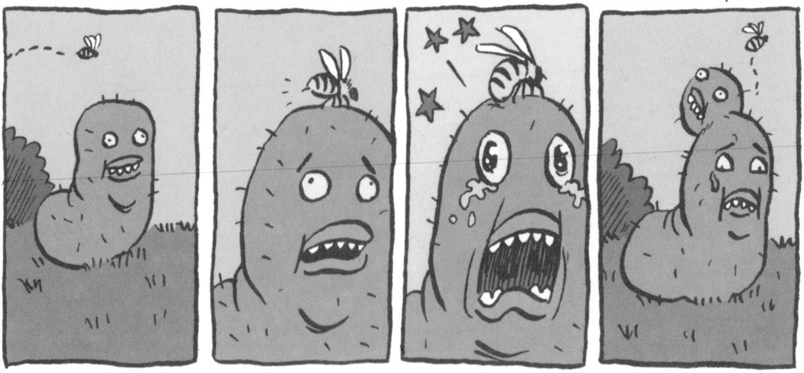

NO MORE HOMEWORK

FRI APR 29, 2011

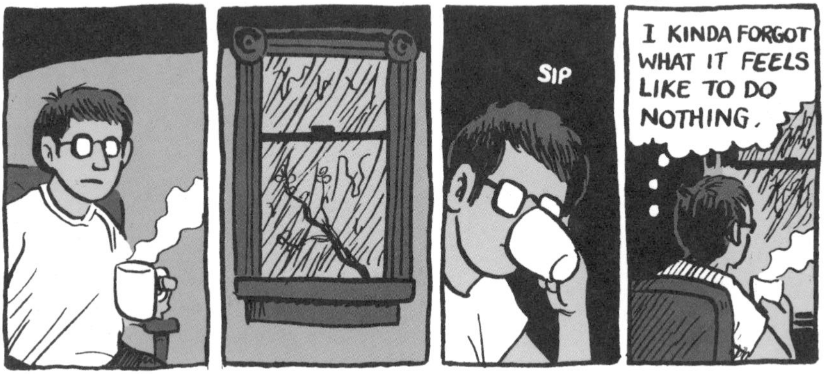
SIP
I KINDA FORGOT WHAT IT FEELS LIKE TO DO NOTHING.

SAT APR 30, 2011

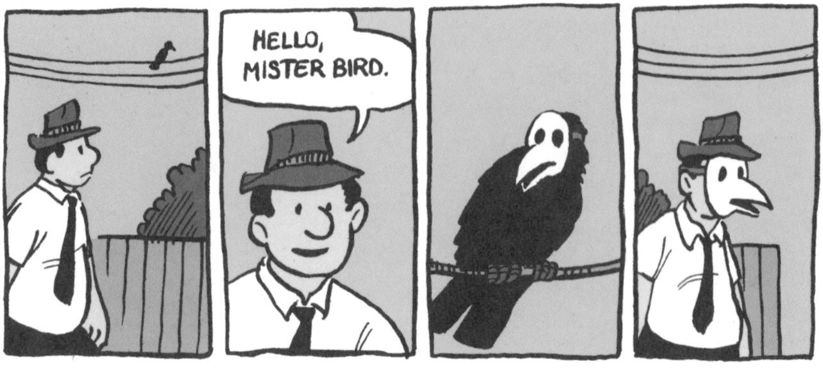
HELLO, MISTER BIRD.

SUN MAY 1, 2011

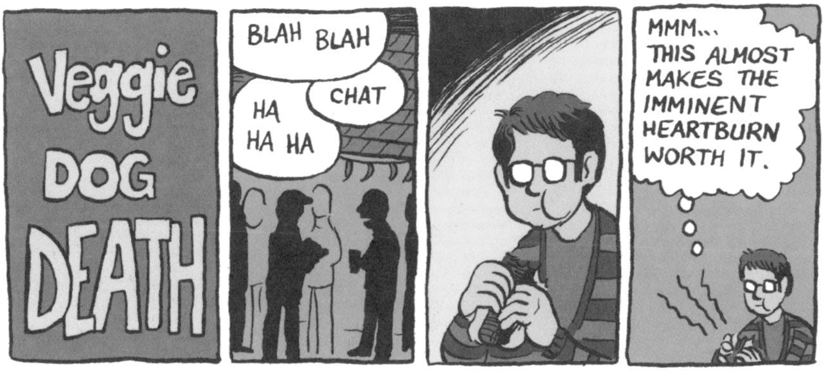
Veggie DOG DEATH
BLAH BLAH
CHAT
HA HA HA
MMM... THIS ALMOST MAKES THE IMMINENT HEARTBURN WORTH IT.

MON MAY 2, 2011

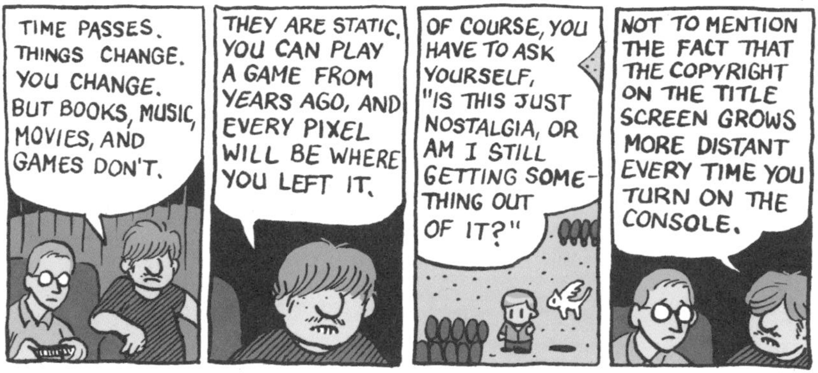
TIME PASSES. THINGS CHANGE. YOU CHANGE. BUT BOOKS, MUSIC, MOVIES, AND GAMES DON'T.
THEY ARE STATIC. YOU CAN PLAY A GAME FROM YEARS AGO, AND EVERY PIXEL WILL BE WHERE YOU LEFT IT.
OF COURSE, YOU HAVE TO ASK YOURSELF, "IS THIS JUST NOSTALGIA, OR AM I STILL GETTING SOME-THING OUT OF IT?"
NOT TO MENTION THE FACT THAT THE COPYRIGHT ON THE TITLE SCREEN GROWS MORE DISTANT EVERY TIME YOU TURN ON THE CONSOLE.

TUE MAY 3, 2011

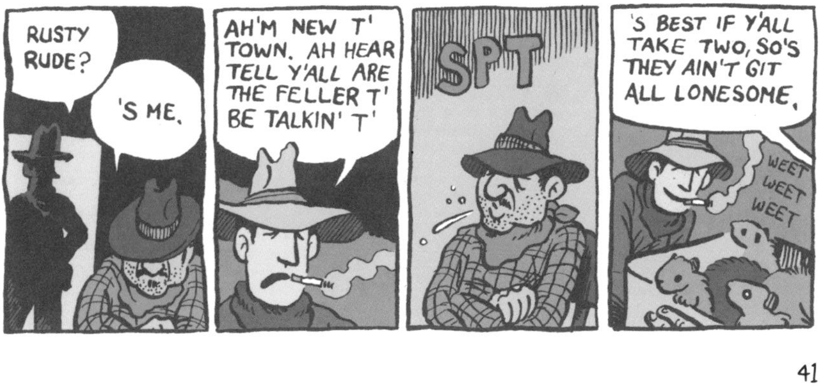
RUSTY RUDE?
'S ME.
AH'M NEW T' TOWN. AH HEAR TELL Y'ALL ARE THE FELLER T' BE TALKIN' T'
SPT
'S BEST IF Y'ALL TAKE TWO, SO'S THEY AIN'T GIT ALL LONESOME.
WEET WEET WEET

WED MAY 4, 2011

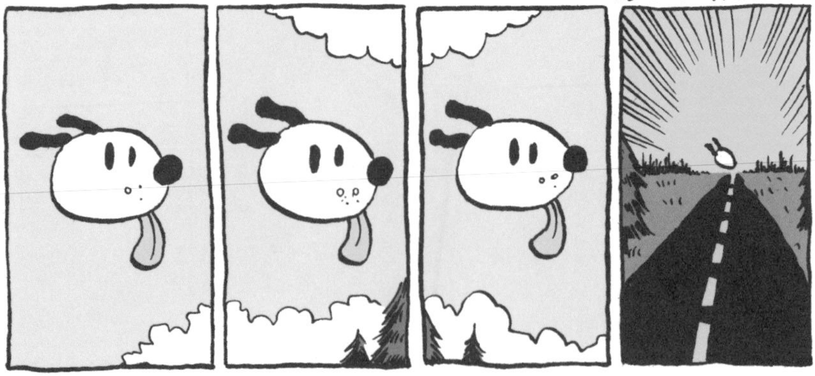

THU MAY 5, 2011

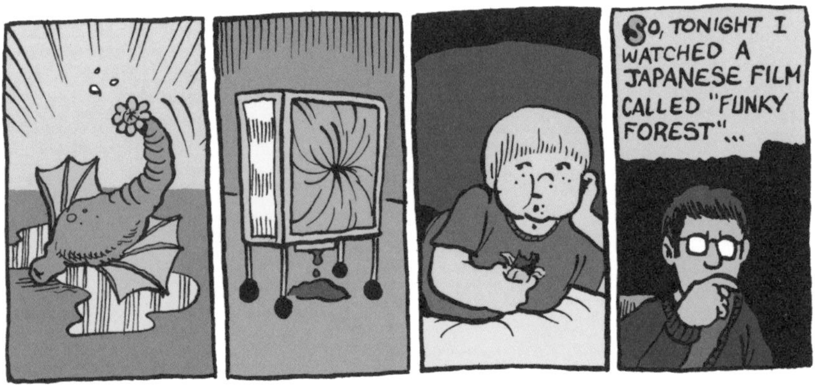
SO, TONIGHT I WATCHED A JAPANESE FILM CALLED "FUNKY FOREST"...

FRI MAY 6, 2011

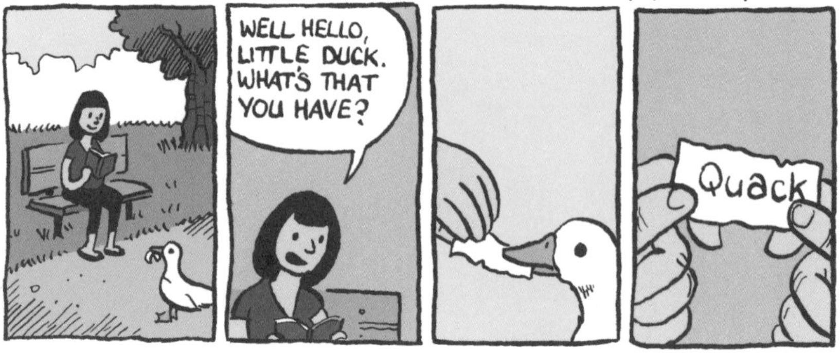
WELL HELLO, LITTLE DUCK. WHAT'S THAT YOU HAVE?
Quack

SAT MAY 7, 2011

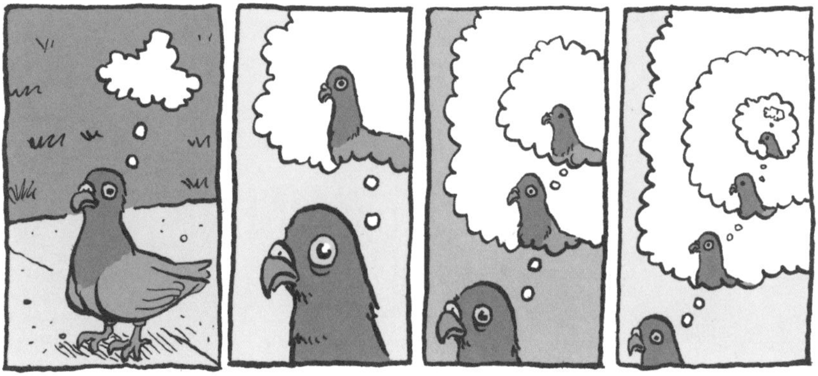

SUN MAY 8, 2011

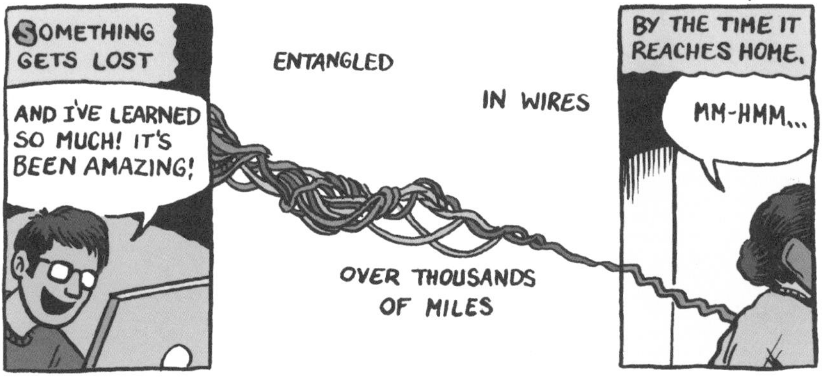
SOMETHING GETS LOST
AND I'VE LEARNED SO MUCH! IT'S BEEN AMAZING!
ENTANGLED
IN WIRES
OVER THOUSANDS OF MILES
BY THE TIME IT REACHES HOME.
MM-HMM...

MON MAY 9, 2011

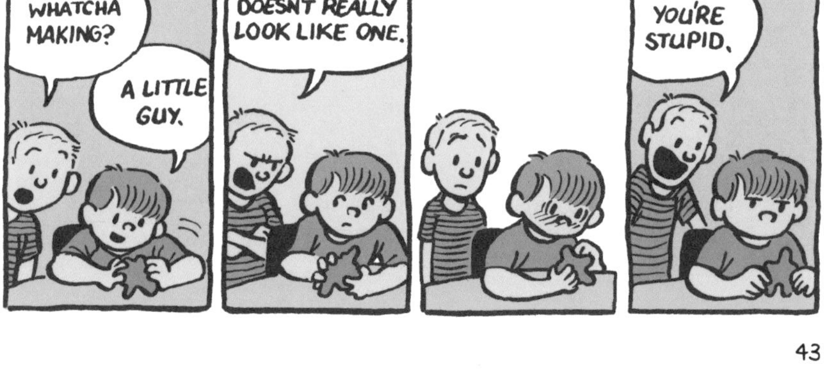
WHATCHA MAKING?
A LITTLE GUY.
DOESN'T REALLY LOOK LIKE ONE.
YOU'RE STUPID.

ELEPHANT COMICS

TUE MAY 10, 2011

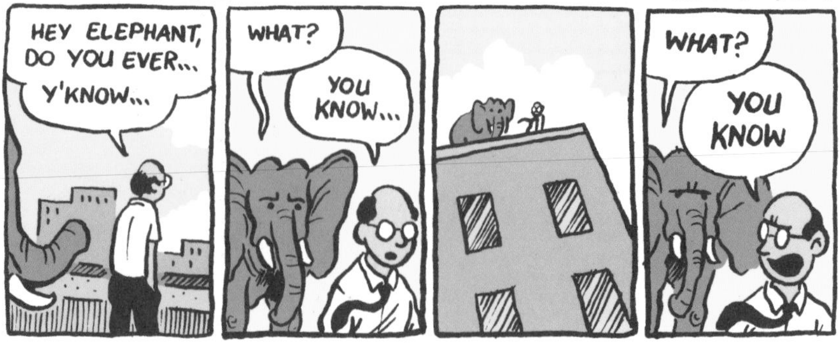
HEY ELEPHANT, DO YOU EVER... Y'KNOW...
WHAT?
YOU KNOW...
WHAT?
YOU KNOW

WED MAY 11, 2011

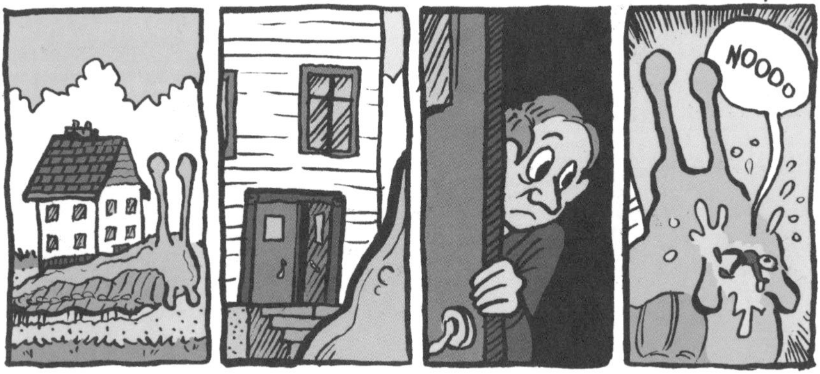
NOOOO

THU MAY 12, 2011

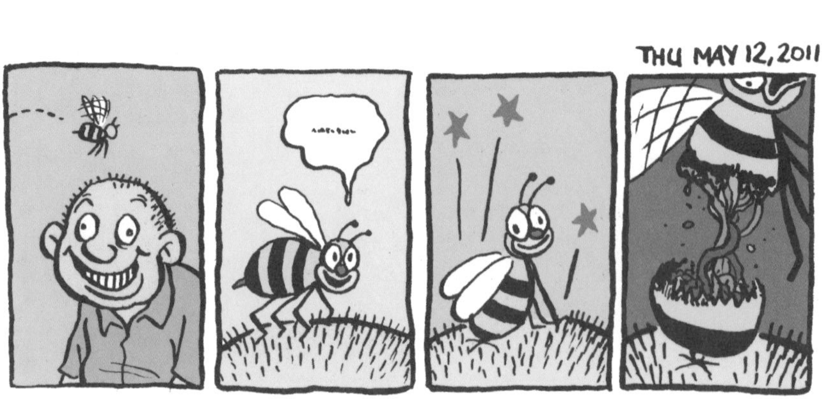

INVINCIBLE BABY

FRI MAY 13, 2011

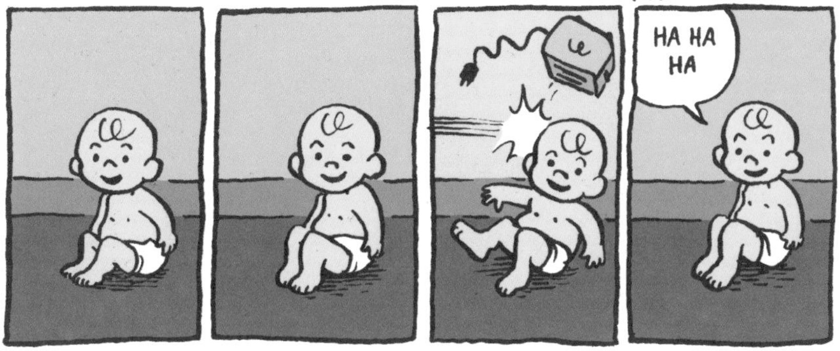
HA HA HA

SAT MAY 14, 2011

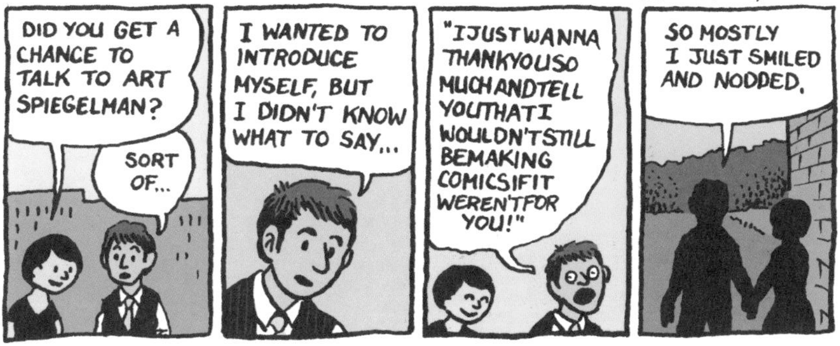
DID YOU GET A CHANCE TO TALK TO ART SPIEGELMAN?
SORT OF...
I WANTED TO INTRODUCE MYSELF, BUT I DIDN'T KNOW WHAT TO SAY...
"IJUSTWANNA THANKYOUSO MUCHANDTELL YOUTHATI WOULDN'TSTILL BEMAKING COMICSIFIT WEREN'TFOR YOU!"
SO MOSTLY I JUST SMILED AND NODDED.

TEENAGERS

SUN MAY 15, 2011

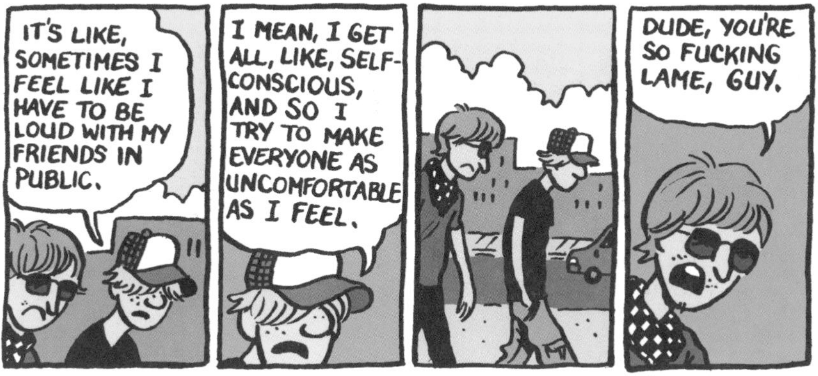
IT'S LIKE, SOMETIMES I FEEL LIKE I HAVE TO BE LOUD WITH MY FRIENDS IN PUBLIC.
I MEAN, I GET ALL, LIKE, SELF-CONSCIOUS, AND SO I TRY TO MAKE EVERYONE AS UNCOMFORTABLE AS I FEEL.
DUDE, YOU'RE SO FUCKING LAME, GUY.

FLYING CAT

MON MAY 16, 2011

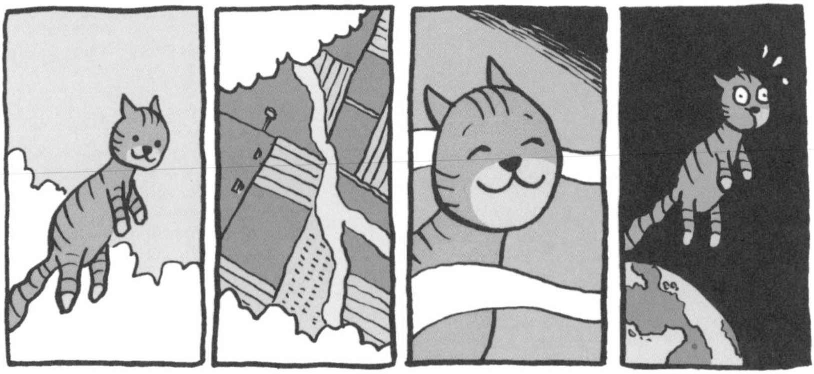

TUE MAY 17, 2011

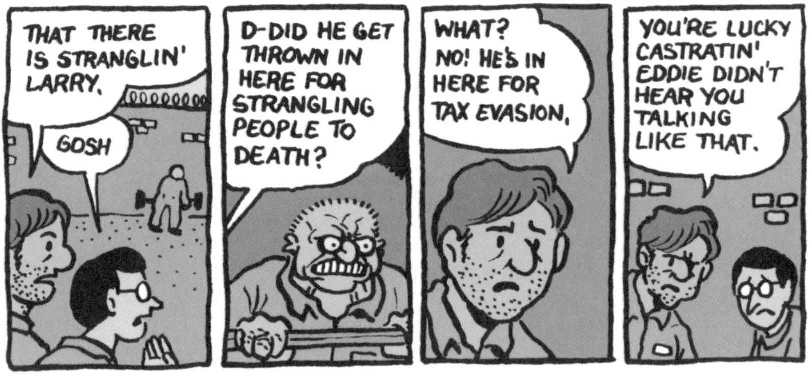
THAT THERE IS STRANGLIN' LARRY.
GOSH
D-DID HE GET THROWN IN HERE FOR STRANGLING PEOPLE TO DEATH?
WHAT? NO! HE'S IN HERE FOR TAX EVASION.
YOU'RE LUCKY CASTRATIN' EDDIE DIDN'T HEAR YOU TALKING LIKE THAT.

FAT HAMSTER

WED MAY 18, 2011

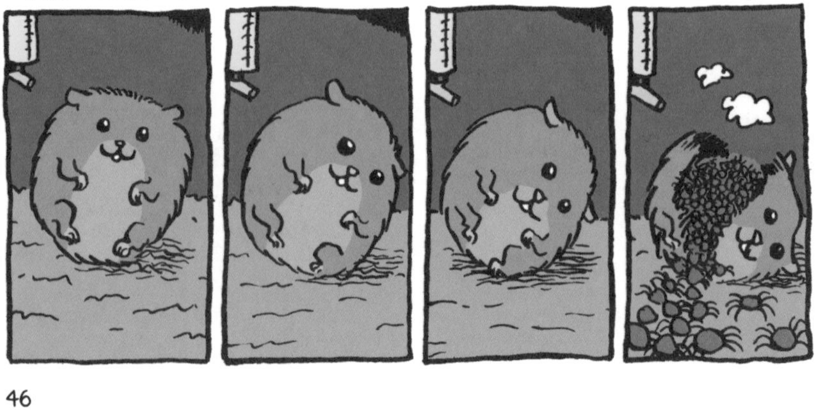

THU MAY 19, 2011

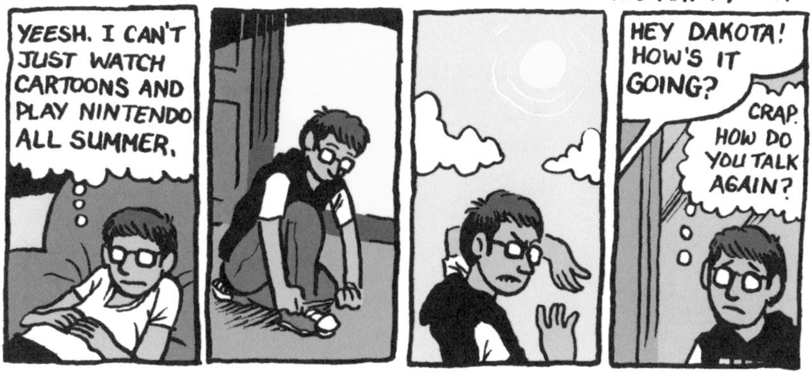
YEESH. I CAN'T JUST WATCH CARTOONS AND PLAY NINTENDO ALL SUMMER.
HEY DAKOTA! HOW'S IT GOING?
CRAP. HOW DO YOU TALK AGAIN?

CONSTANT HEART ATTACKS MAN

FRI MAY 20, 2011

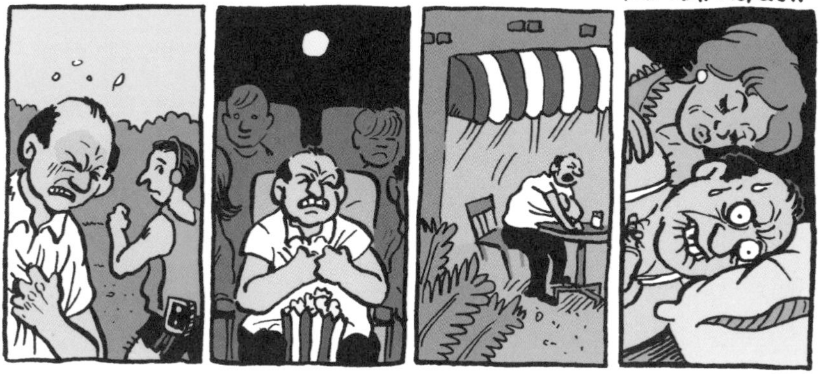

SAT MAY 21, 2011

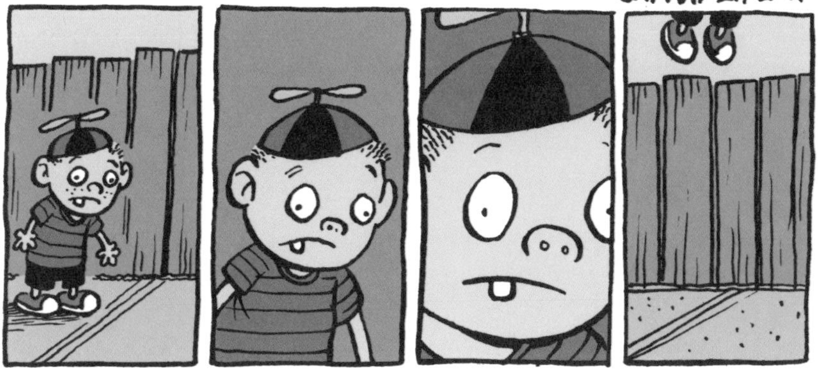

SUN MAY 22, 2011

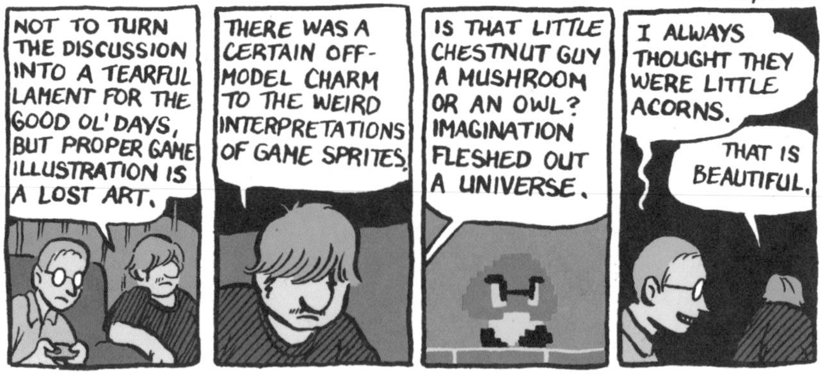
NOT TO TURN THE DISCUSSION INTO A TEARFUL LAMENT FOR THE GOOD OL' DAYS, BUT PROPER GAME ILLUSTRATION IS A LOST ART.
THERE WAS A CERTAIN OFF-MODEL CHARM TO THE WEIRD INTERPRETATIONS OF GAME SPRITES.
IS THAT LITTLE CHESTNUT GUY A MUSHROOM OR AN OWL? IMAGINATION FLESHED OUT A UNIVERSE.
I ALWAYS THOUGHT THEY WERE LITTLE ACORNS.
THAT IS BEAUTIFUL.

MON MAY 23, 2011

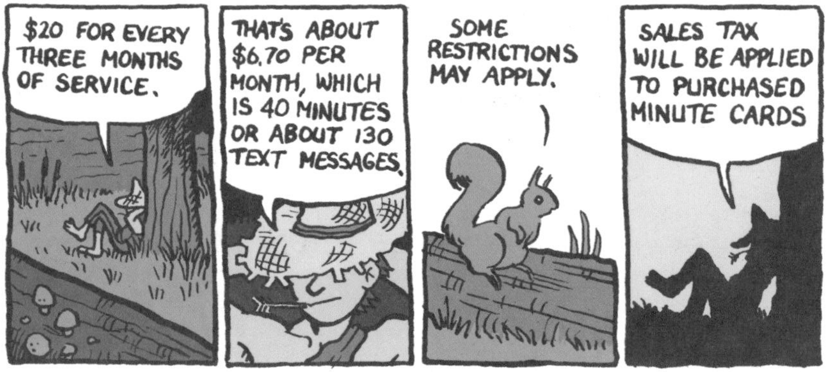
$20 FOR EVERY THREE MONTHS OF SERVICE.
THAT'S ABOUT $6.70 PER MONTH, WHICH IS 40 MINUTES OR ABOUT 130 TEXT MESSAGES.
SOME RESTRICTIONS MAY APPLY.
SALES TAX WILL BE APPLIED TO PURCHASED MINUTE CARDS

TUE MAY 24, 2011

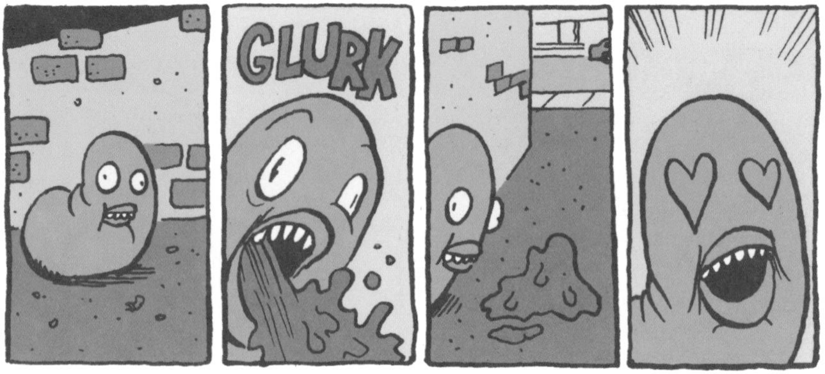
GLURK

WED MAY 25, 2011

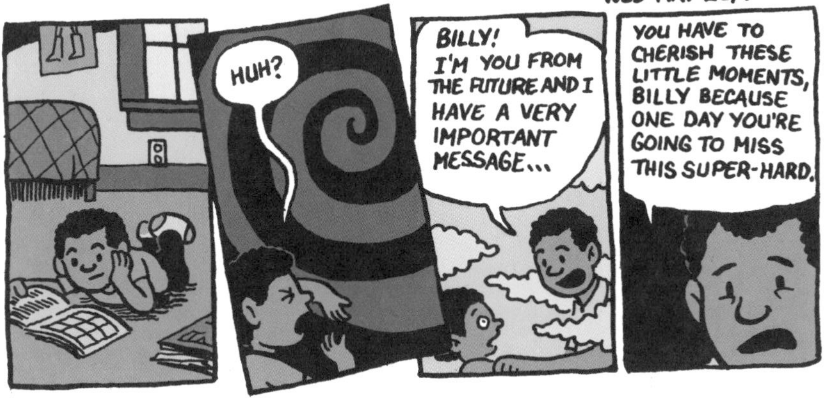
HUH?
BILLY! I'M YOU FROM THE FUTURE AND I HAVE A VERY IMPORTANT MESSAGE...
YOU HAVE TO CHERISH THESE LITTLE MOMENTS, BILLY BECAUSE ONE DAY YOU'RE GOING TO MISS THIS SUPER-HARD.

THU MAY 26, 2011

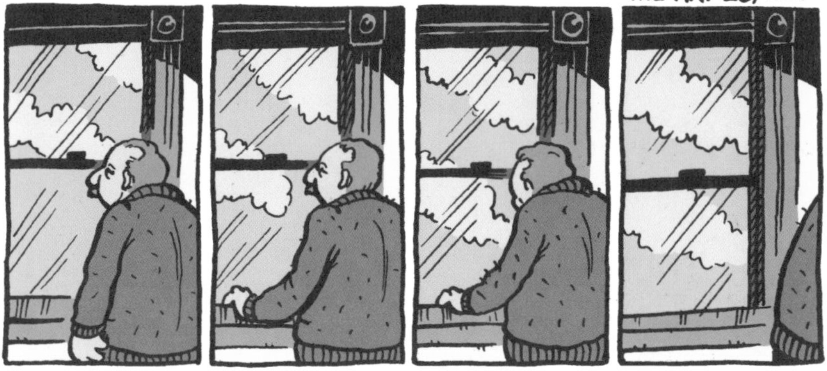

FRI MAY 27, 2011

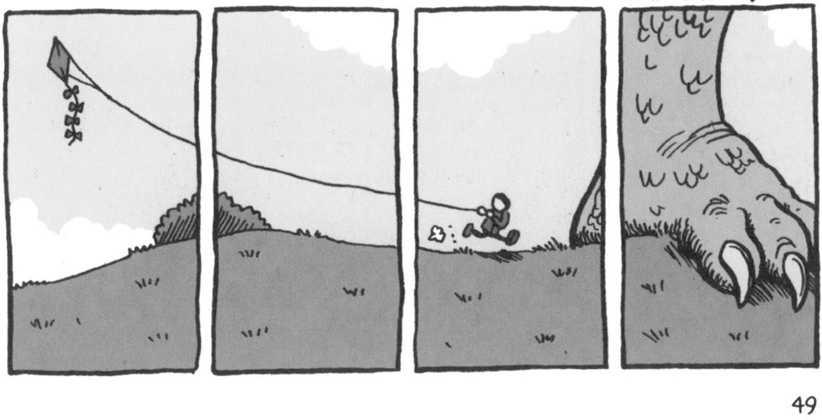

SAT MAY 28, 2011

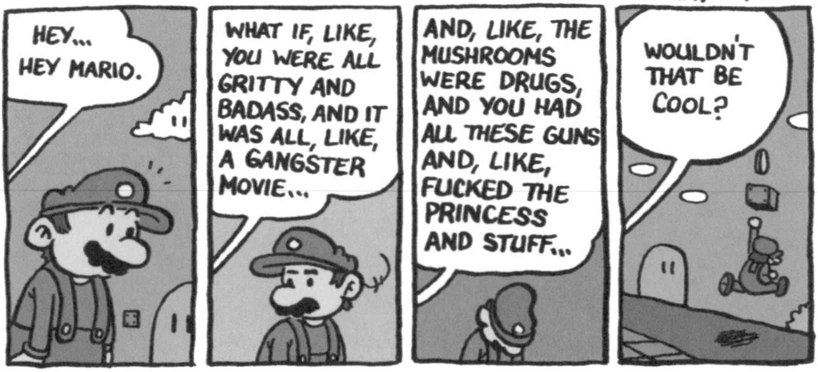
HEY... HEY MARIO.
WHAT IF, LIKE, YOU WERE ALL GRITTY AND BADASS, AND IT WAS ALL, LIKE, A GANGSTER MOVIE...
AND, LIKE, THE MUSHROOMS WERE DRUGS, AND YOU HAD ALL THESE GUNS AND, LIKE, FUCKED THE PRINCESS AND STUFF...
WOULDN'T THAT BE COOL?

SUN MAY 29, 2011

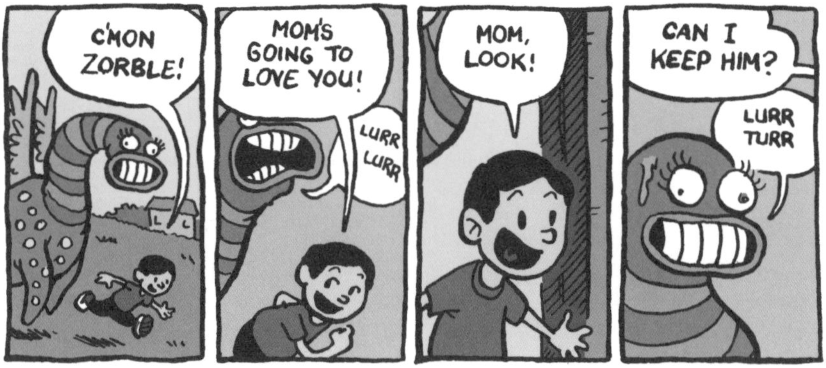
C'MON ZORBLE!
MOM'S GOING TO LOVE YOU!
LURR LURR
MOM, LOOK!
CAN I KEEP HIM?
LURR TURR

MON MAY 30, 2011

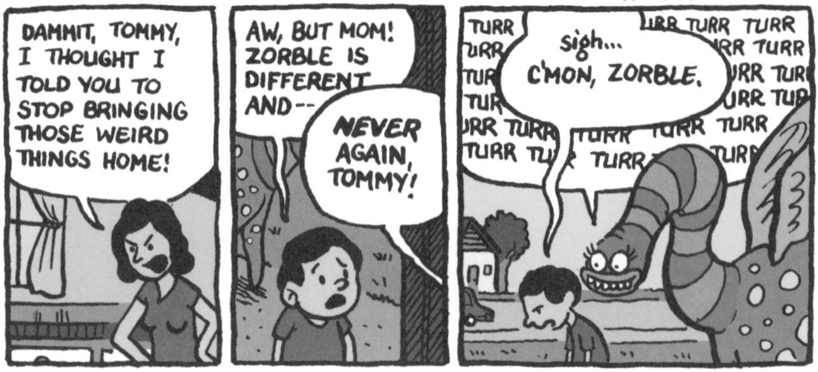
DAMMIT, TOMMY, I THOUGHT I TOLD YOU TO STOP BRINGING THOSE WEIRD THINGS HOME!
AW, BUT MOM! ZORBLE IS DIFFERENT AND--
NEVER AGAIN, TOMMY!
sigh... C'MON, ZORBLE.

TUE MAY 31, 2011

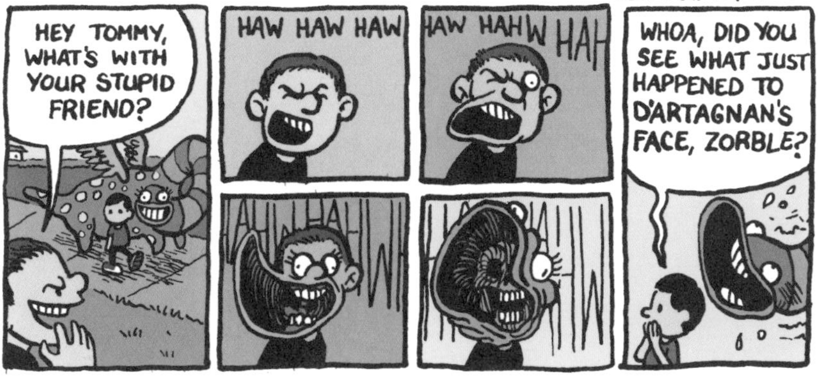
HEY TOMMY, WHAT'S WITH YOUR STUPID FRIEND?
HAW HAW HAW
HAW HAHW HAH
WHOA, DID YOU SEE WHAT JUST HAPPENED TO D'ARTAGNAN'S FACE, ZORBLE?

WED JUNE 1, 2011

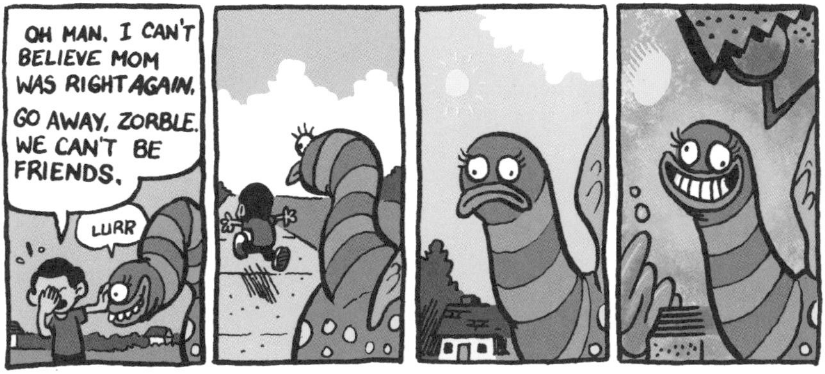
OH MAN. I CAN'T BELIEVE MOM WAS RIGHT AGAIN.
GO AWAY, ZORBLE. WE CAN'T BE FRIENDS.
LURR

THU JUNE 2, 2011

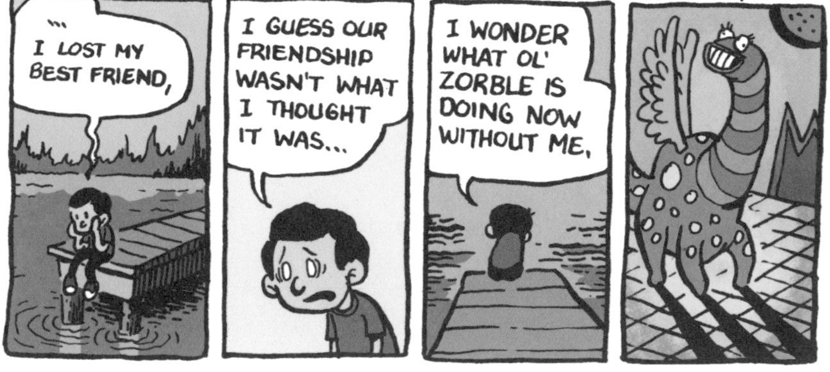
... I LOST MY BEST FRIEND.
I GUESS OUR FRIENDSHIP WASN'T WHAT I THOUGHT IT WAS...
I WONDER WHAT OL' ZORBLE IS DOING NOW WITHOUT ME.

FRI JUNE 3, 2011

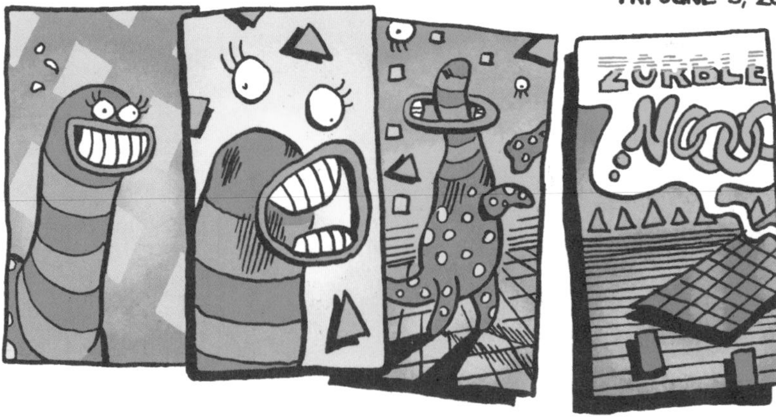
ZORBLE

SAT JUNE 4, 2011

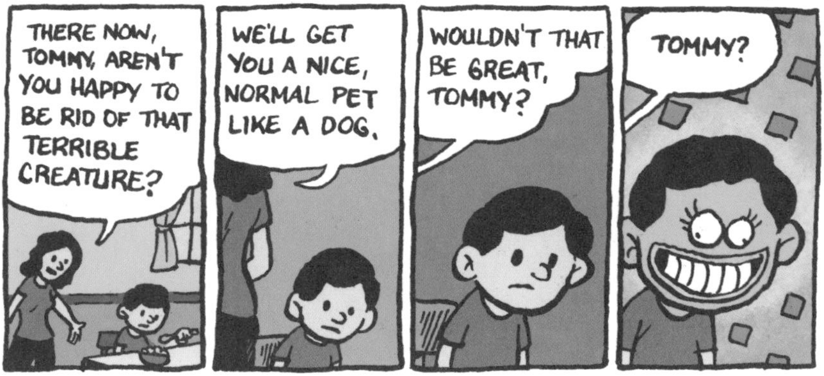
THERE NOW, TOMMY, AREN'T YOU HAPPY TO BE RID OF THAT TERRIBLE CREATURE?
WE'LL GET YOU A NICE, NORMAL PET LIKE A DOG.
WOULDN'T THAT BE GREAT, TOMMY?
TOMMY?

SUN JUNE 5, 2011

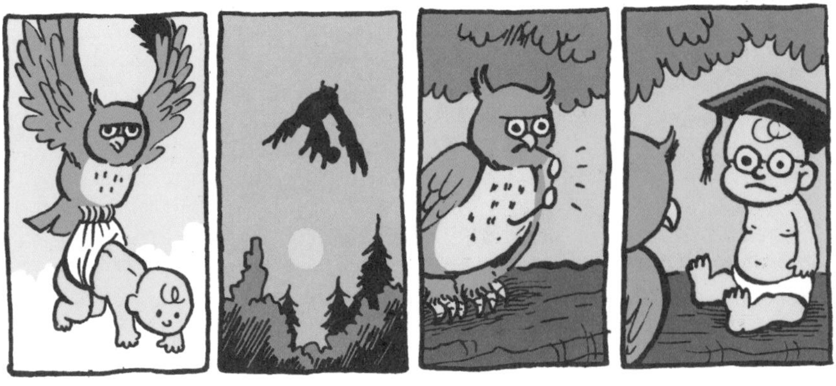

MON JUNE 6, 2011

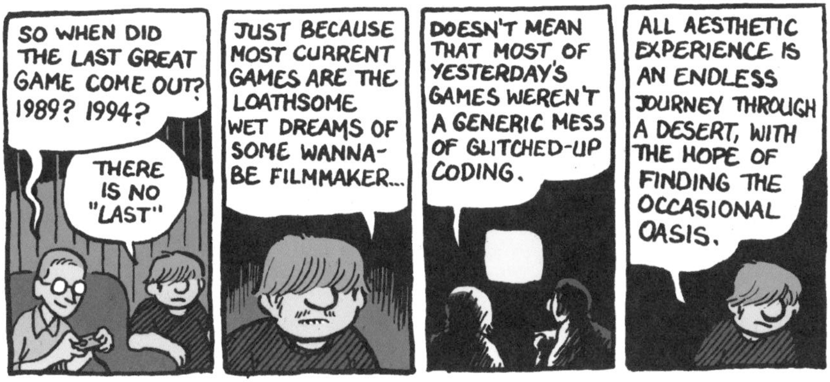

SO WHEN DID THE LAST GREAT GAME COME OUT? 1989? 1994?
THERE IS NO "LAST"
JUST BECAUSE MOST CURRENT GAMES ARE THE LOATHSOME WET DREAMS OF SOME WANNA-BE FILMMAKER...
DOESN'T MEAN THAT MOST OF YESTERDAY'S GAMES WEREN'T A GENERIC MESS OF GLITCHED-UP CODING.
ALL AESTHETIC EXPERIENCE IS AN ENDLESS JOURNEY THROUGH A DESERT, WITH THE HOPE OF FINDING THE OCCASIONAL OASIS.

TUE JUNE 7, 2011

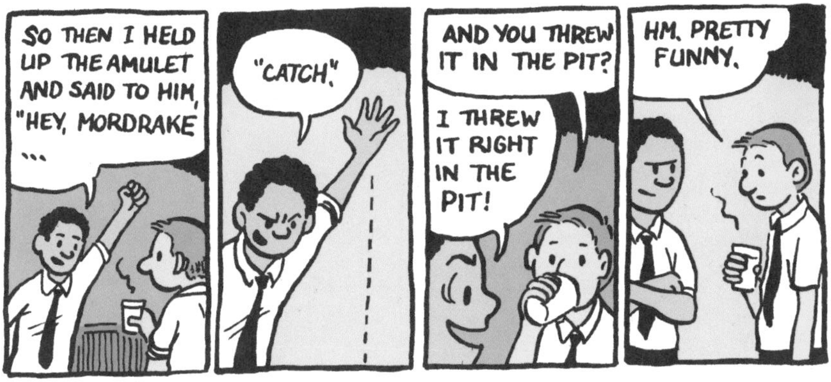

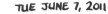

SO THEN I HELD UP THE AMULET AND SAID TO HIM, "HEY, MORDRAKE ...
"CATCH."
AND YOU THREW IT IN THE PIT?
I THREW IT RIGHT IN THE PIT!
HM. PRETTY FUNNY.

GOD COMICS

WED JUNE 8 2011

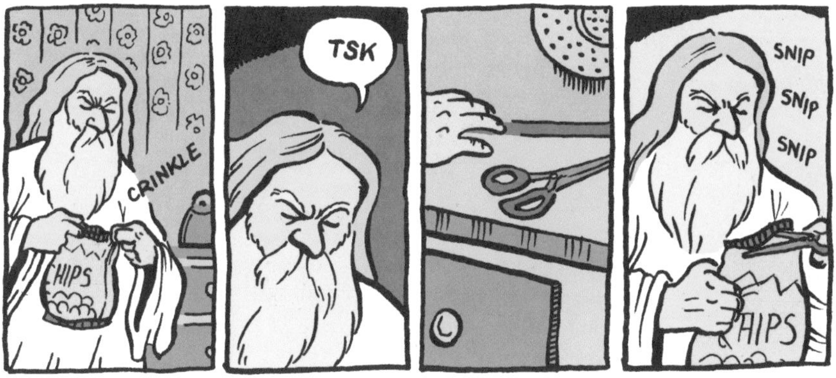

CRINKLE
CHIPS
TSK
SNIP
SNIP
SNIP
CHIPS

THU JUNE 9, 2011

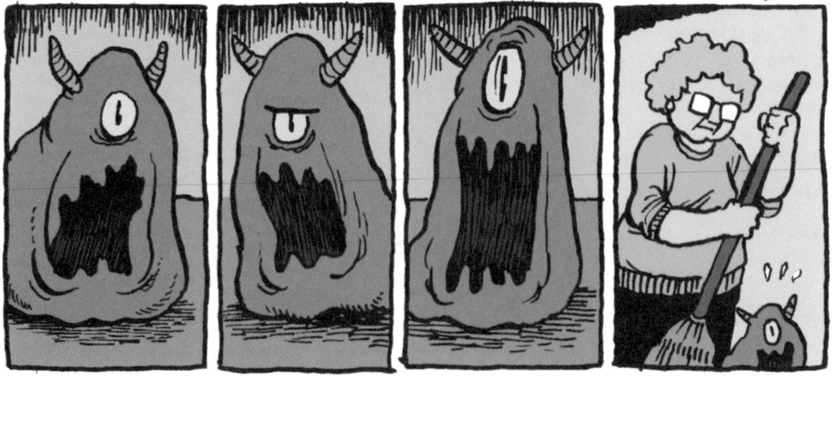

GODZILLA

FRI JUNE 10, 2011

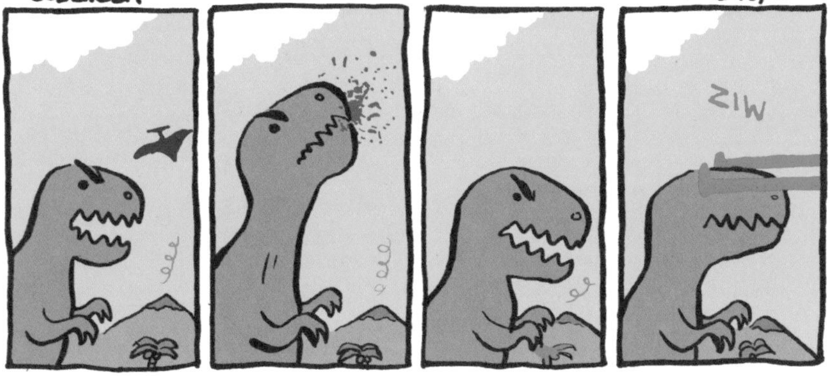

SAT JUNE 11, 2011

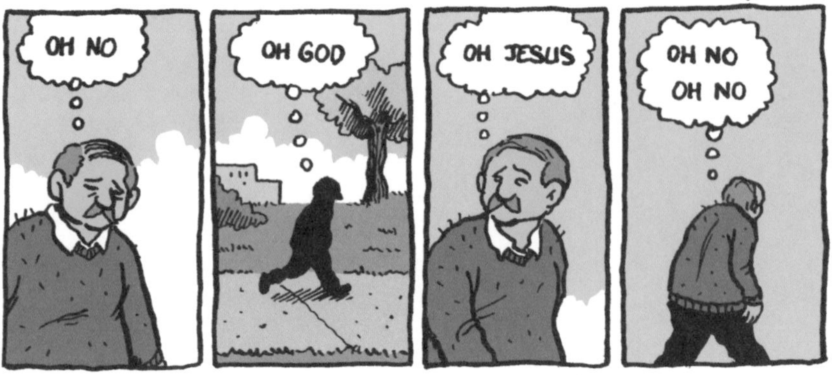
OH NO
OH GOD
OH JESUS
OH NO
OH NO

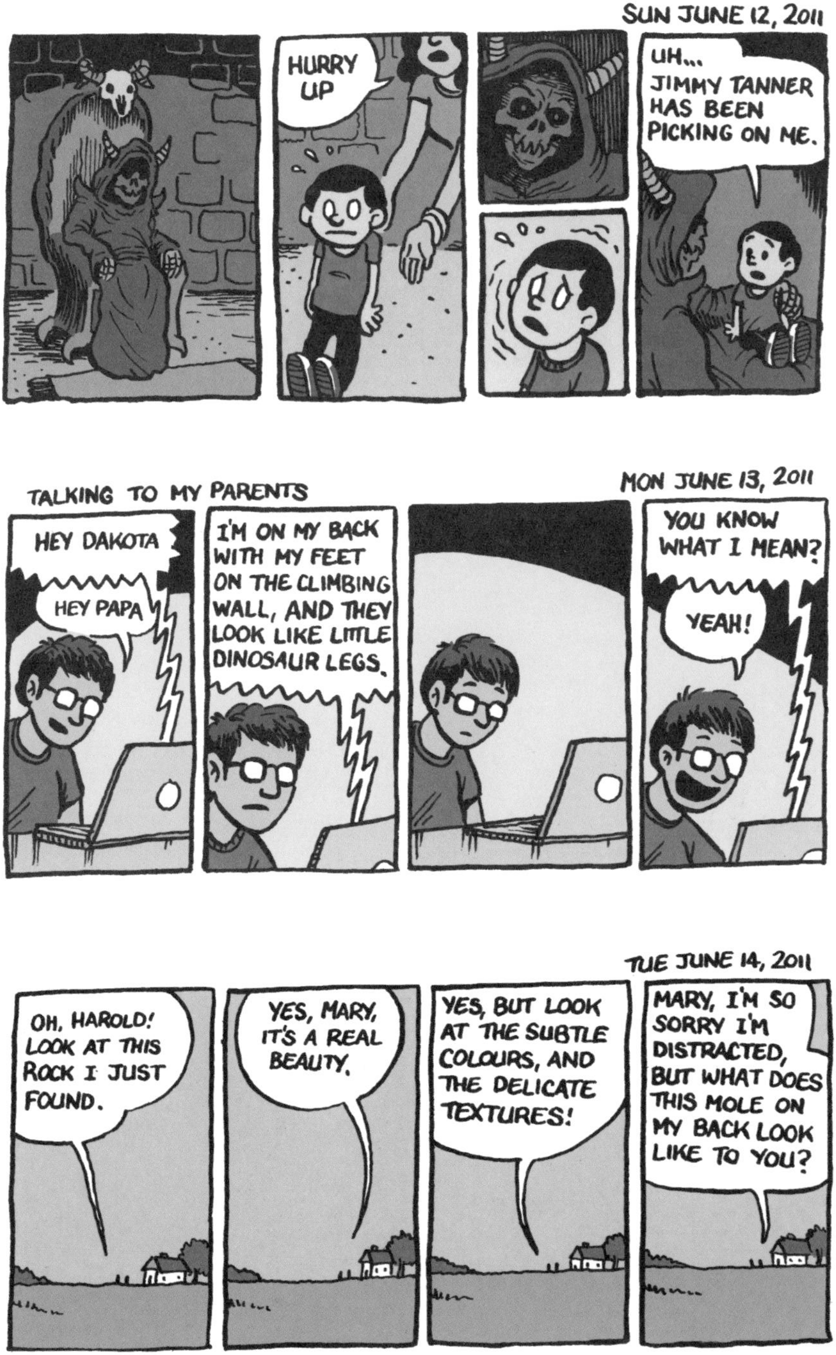
SUN JUNE 12, 2011
HURRY UP
UH... JIMMY TANNER HAS BEEN PICKING ON ME.
TALKING TO MY PARENTS
MON JUNE 13, 2011
HEY DAKOTA
HEY PAPA
I'M ON MY BACK WITH MY FEET ON THE CLIMBING WALL, AND THEY LOOK LIKE LITTLE DINOSAUR LEGS.
YOU KNOW WHAT I MEAN?
YEAH!
TUE JUNE 14, 2011
OH, HAROLD! LOOK AT THIS ROCK I JUST FOUND.
YES, MARY, IT'S A REAL BEAUTY.
YES, BUT LOOK AT THE SUBTLE COLOURS, AND THE DELICATE TEXTURES!
MARY, I'M SO SORRY I'M DISTRACTED, BUT WHAT DOES THIS MOLE ON MY BACK LOOK LIKE TO YOU?

WED JUNE 15, 2011

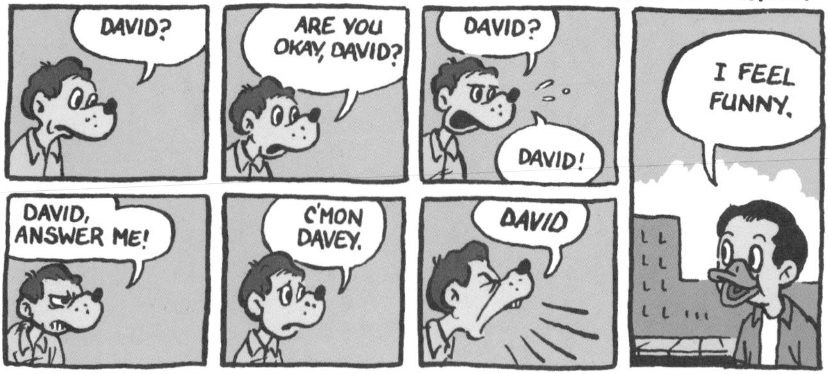
DAVID?
ARE YOU OKAY, DAVID?
DAVID?
DAVID!
DAVID, ANSWER ME!
C'MON DAVEY.
DAVID
I FEEL FUNNY.

THU JUNE 16, 2011

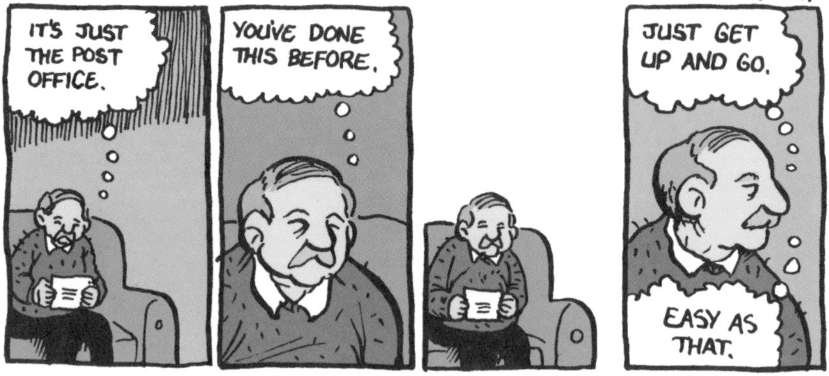
IT'S JUST THE POST OFFICE.
YOU'VE DONE THIS BEFORE.
JUST GET UP AND GO.
EASY AS THAT.

FRI JUNE 17, 2011

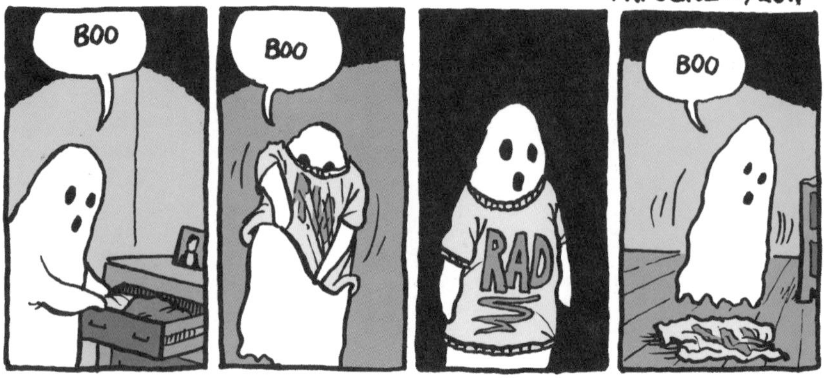
BOO
BOO
RAD
BOO

SAT JUNE 18, 2011

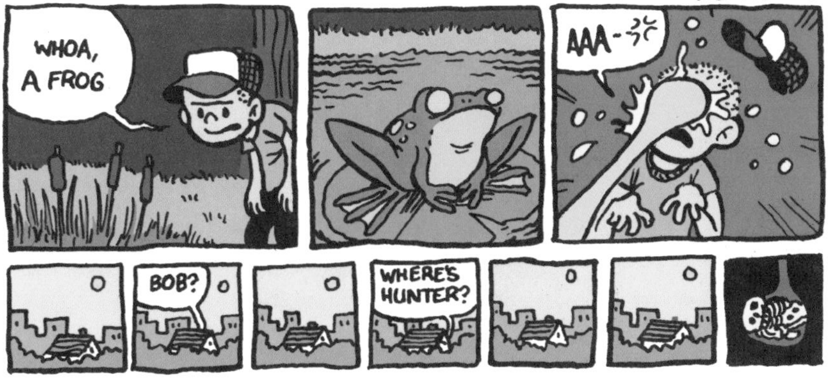
WHOA, A FROG
AAA-
BOB?
WHERE'S HUNTER?

SUN JUNE 19, 2011

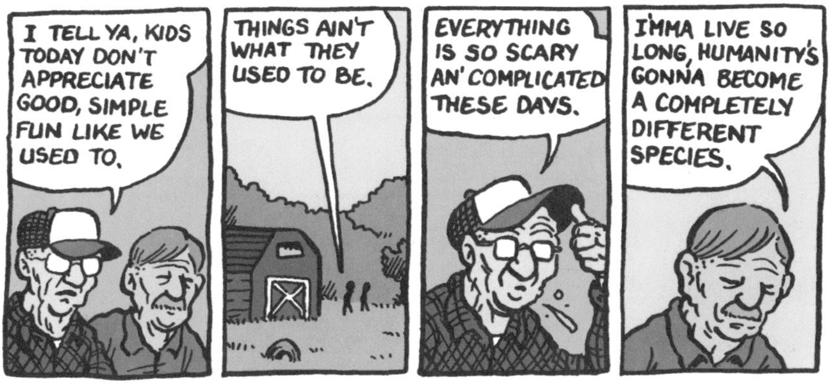
I TELL YA, KIDS TODAY DON'T APPRECIATE GOOD, SIMPLE FUN LIKE WE USED TO.
THINGS AIN'T WHAT THEY USED TO BE.
EVERYTHING IS SO SCARY AN' COMPLICATED THESE DAYS.
I'MMA LIVE SO LONG, HUMANITY'S GONNA BECOME A COMPLETELY DIFFERENT SPECIES.

MON JUNE 20, 2011

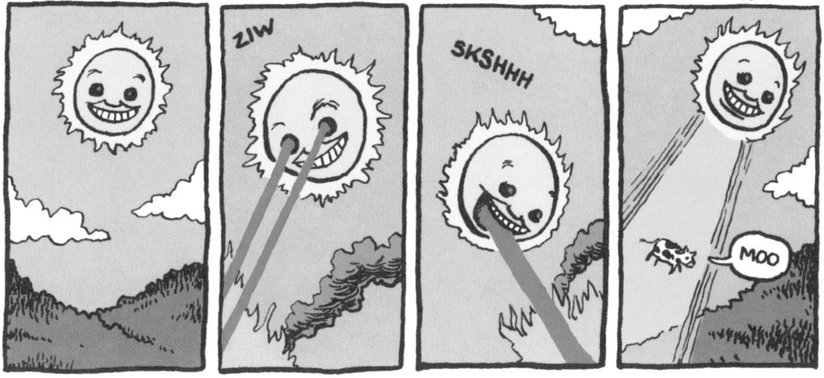
ZIW
SKSHHH
MOO

TUE JUNE 21, 2011

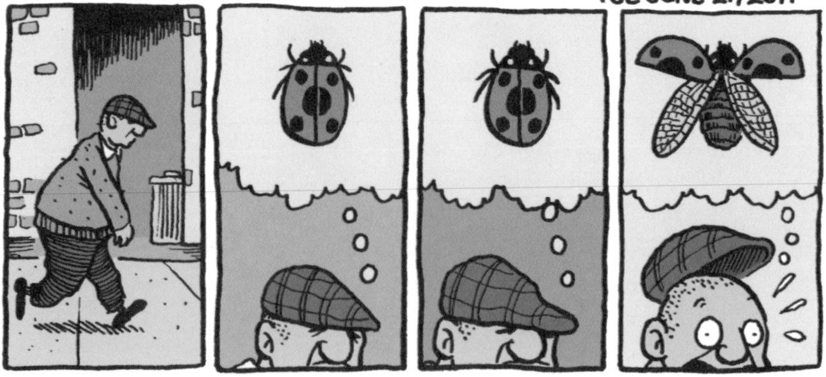

WED JUNE 22, 2011

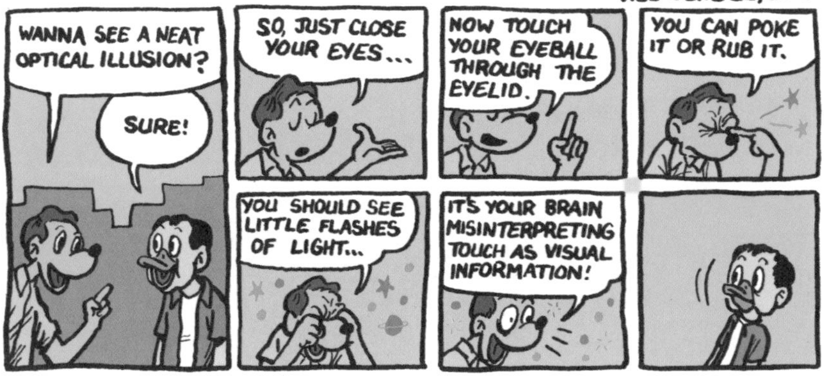
WANNA SEE A NEAT OPTICAL ILLUSION?
SURE!
SO, JUST CLOSE YOUR EYES...
NOW TOUCH YOUR EYEBALL THROUGH THE EYELID.
YOU CAN POKE IT OR RUB IT.
YOU SHOULD SEE LITTLE FLASHES OF LIGHT...
IT'S YOUR BRAIN MISINTERPRETING TOUCH AS VISUAL INFORMATION!

ELEPHANT COMICS

THU JUNE 23, 2011

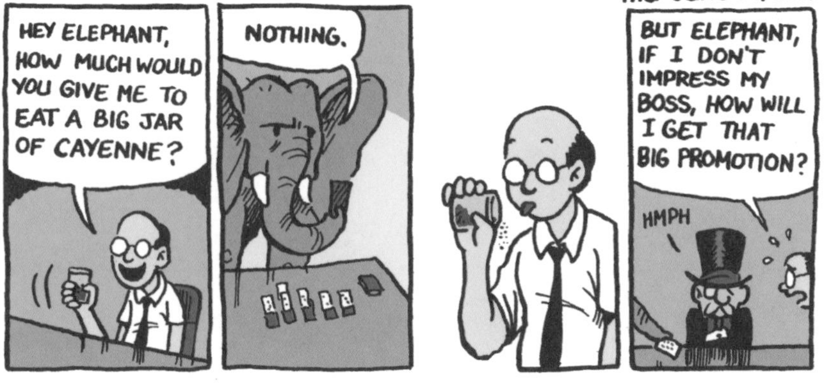
HEY ELEPHANT, HOW MUCH WOULD YOU GIVE ME TO EAT A BIG JAR OF CAYENNE?
NOTHING.
BUT ELEPHANT, IF I DON'T IMPRESS MY BOSS, HOW WILL I GET THAT BIG PROMOTION?
HMPH

CONSTANT VOMIT MAN

FRI JUNE 24, 2011

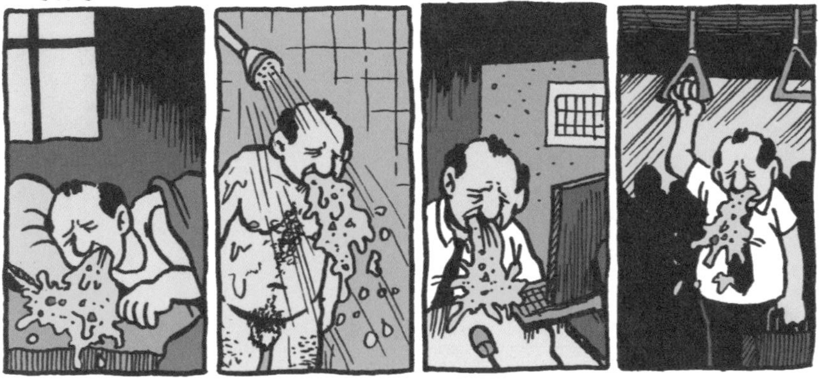

SAT JUNE 25, 2011

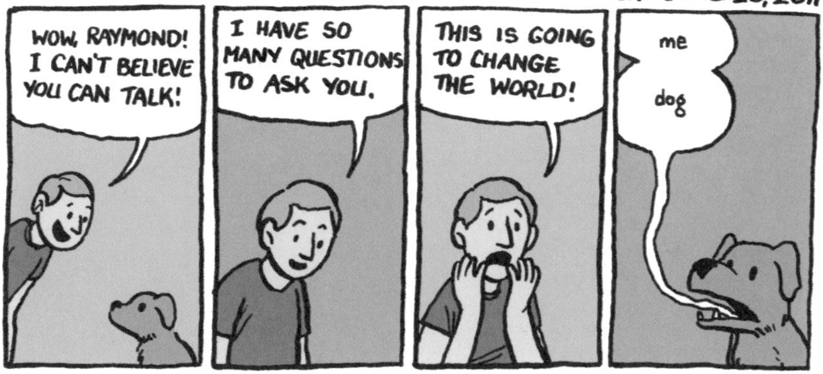
WOW, RAYMOND! I CAN'T BELIEVE YOU CAN TALK!
I HAVE SO MANY QUESTIONS TO ASK YOU.
THIS IS GOING TO CHANGE THE WORLD!
me dog

SUN JUNE 26, 2011

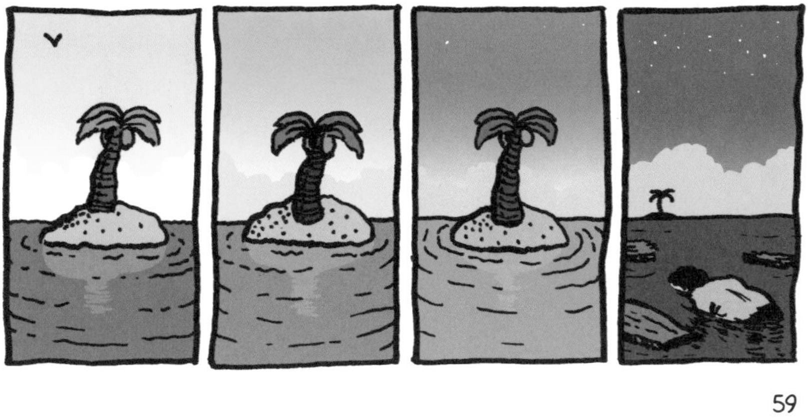

MON JUNE 27, 2011

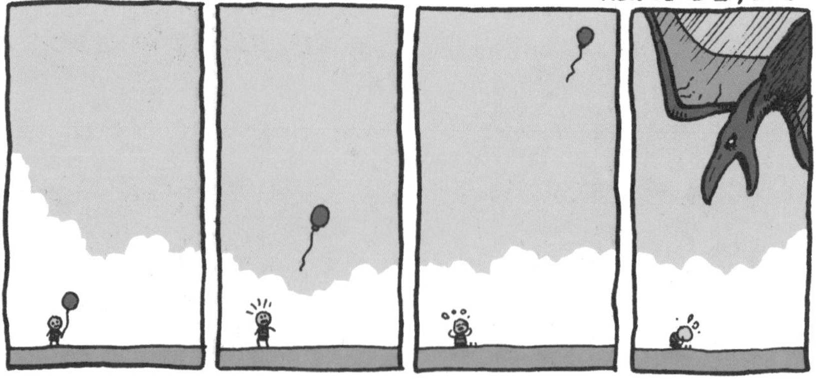

TUE JUNE 28, 2011

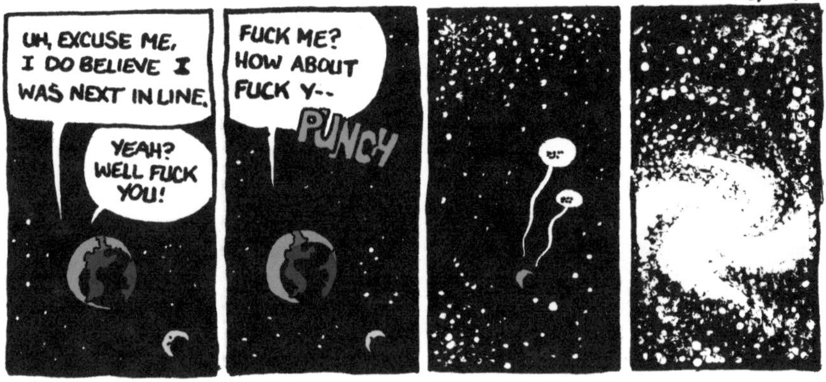
UH, EXCUSE ME, I DO BELIEVE I WAS NEXT IN LINE.
YEAH? WELL FUCK YOU!
FUCK ME? HOW ABOUT FUCK Y--
PUNCH

RHINOCEROS COMICS

WED JUNE 29, 2011

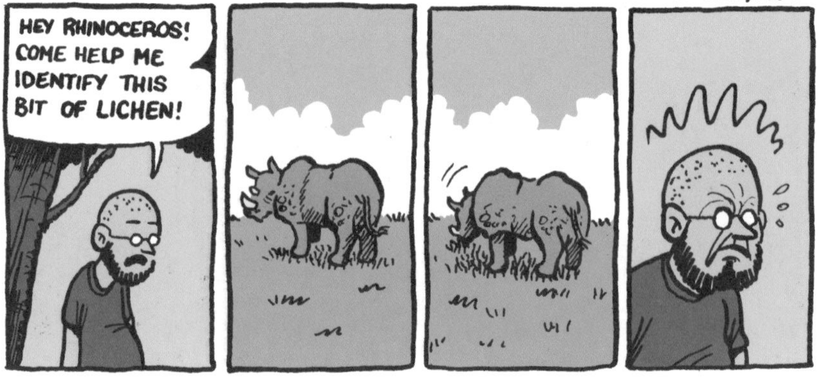
HEY RHINOCEROS! COME HELP ME IDENTIFY THIS BIT OF LICHEN!

GODZILLA

THU JUNE 30, 2011

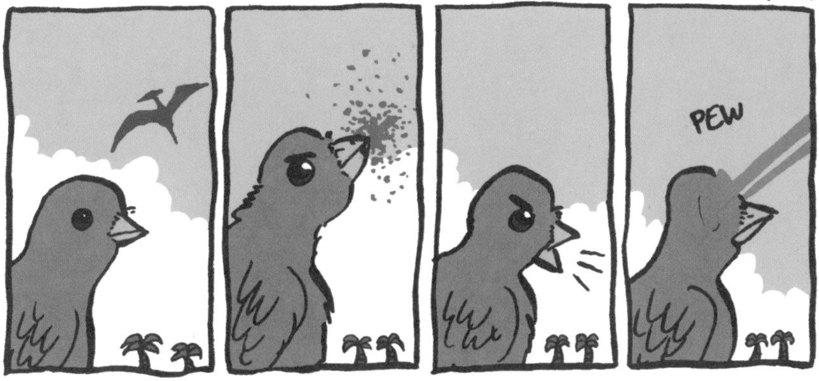
PEW

FRI JULY 1, 2011

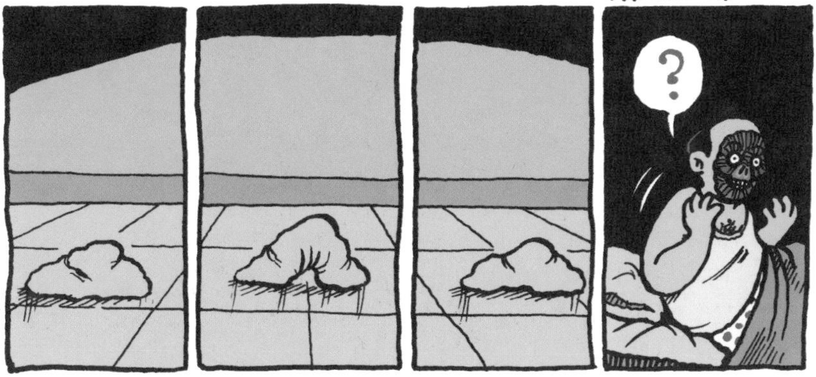
?

LYNCH IN LOVE

SAT JULY 2, 2011

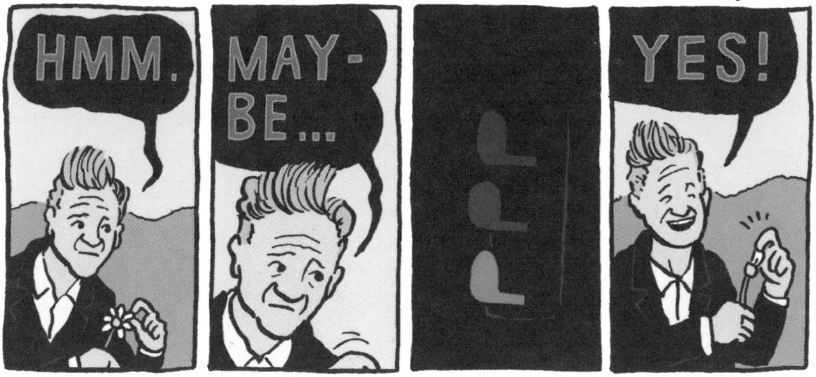
HMM.
MAY-
BE...
YES!

DUMB COMICS

SUN JULY 3, 2011

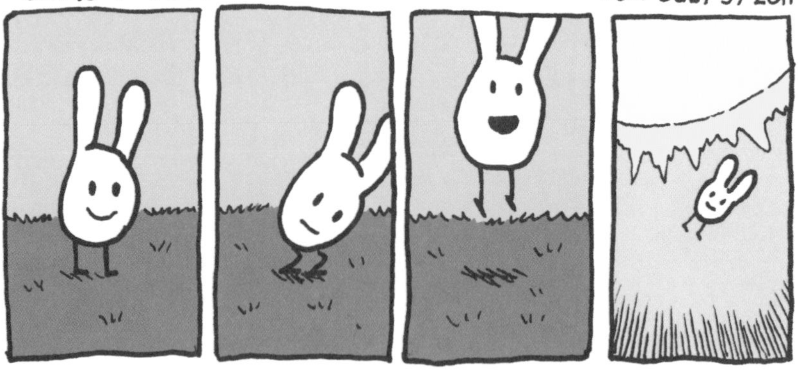

MON JULY 4, 2011

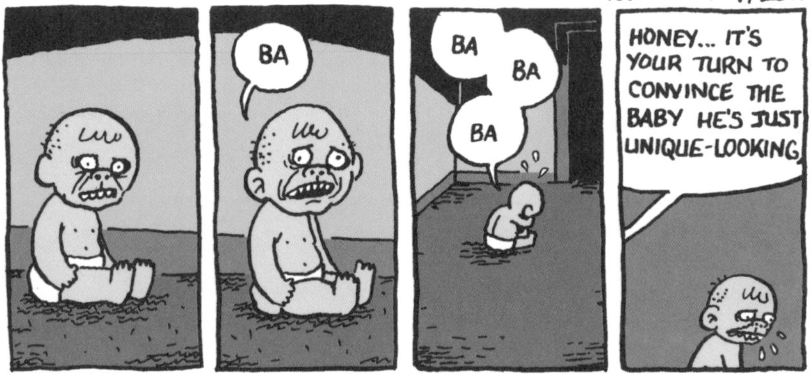
BA
BA
BA
BA
HONEY... IT'S YOUR TURN TO CONVINCE THE BABY HE'S JUST UNIQUE-LOOKING.

TUE JULY 5, 2011

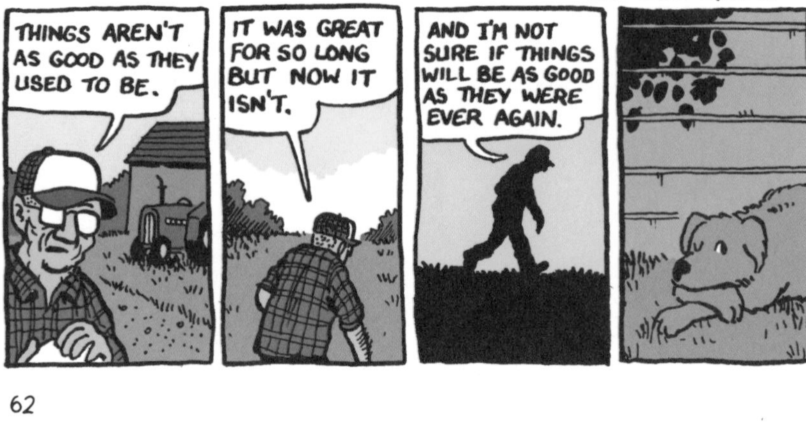
THINGS AREN'T AS GOOD AS THEY USED TO BE.
IT WAS GREAT FOR SO LONG BUT NOW IT ISN'T.
AND I'M NOT SURE IF THINGS WILL BE AS GOOD AS THEY WERE EVER AGAIN.

WED JULY 6, 2011

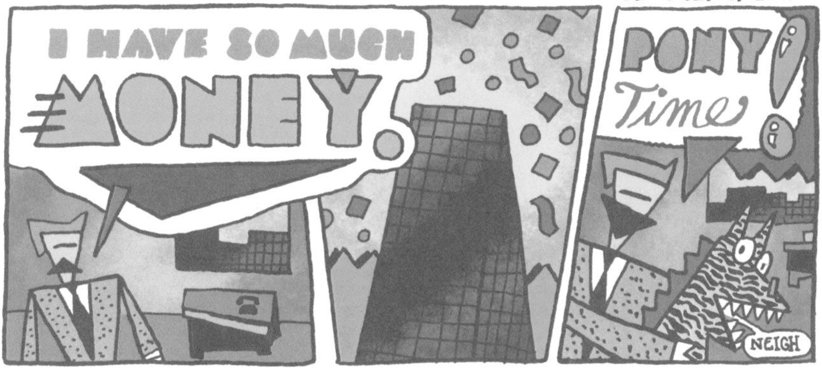
I HAVE SO MUCH
MONEY.
PONY Time!
NEIGH

THU JULY 7, 2011

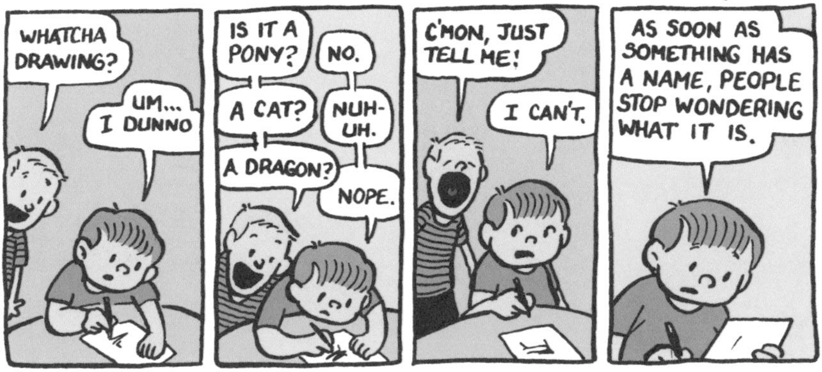
WHATCHA DRAWING?
UM... I DUNNO
IS IT A PONY?
NO.
A CAT?
NUH-UH.
A DRAGON?
NOPE.
C'MON, JUST TELL ME!
I CAN'T.
AS SOON AS SOMETHING HAS A NAME, PEOPLE STOP WONDERING WHAT IT IS.

GOD COMICS

FRI JULY 8, 2011

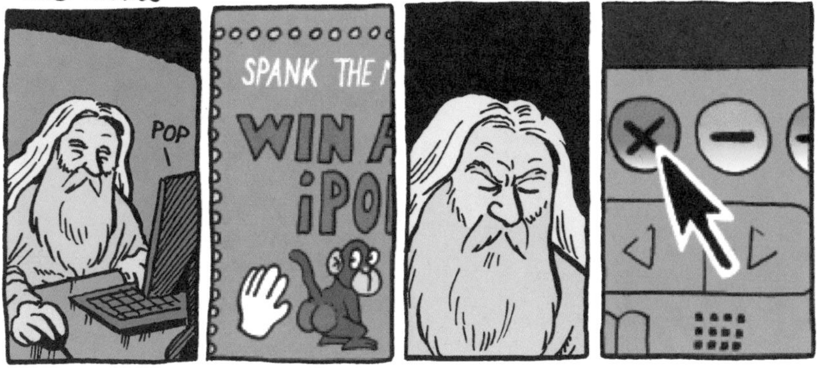
POP
SPANK THE
WIN A
iPO

THE ANGRIEST MAN SAT JULY 9, 2011

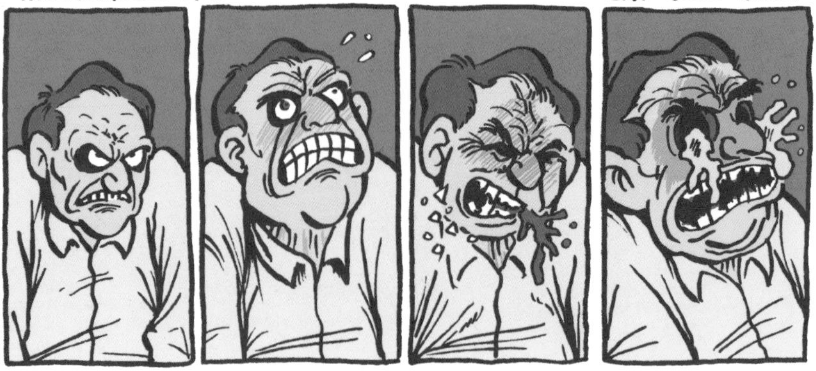

SUN JULY 10, 2011

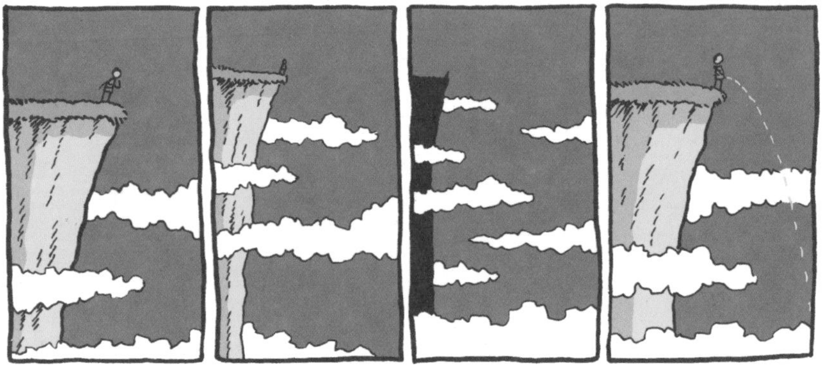

MON JULY 11, 2011

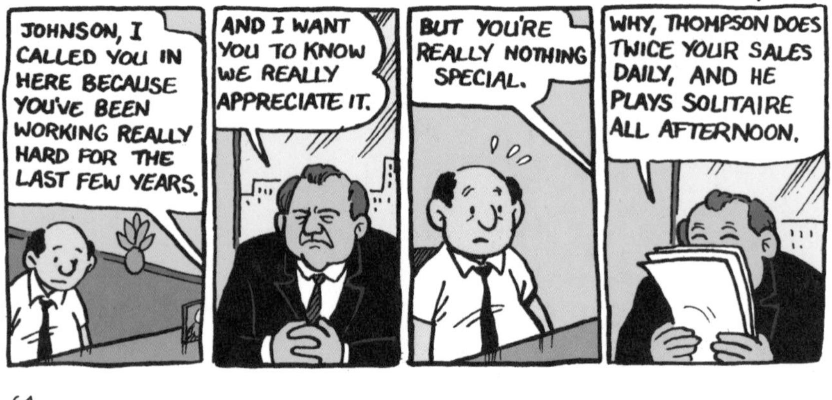
JOHNSON, I CALLED YOU IN HERE BECAUSE YOU'VE BEEN WORKING REALLY HARD FOR THE LAST FEW YEARS.
AND I WANT YOU TO KNOW WE REALLY APPRECIATE IT.
BUT YOU'RE REALLY NOTHING SPECIAL.
WHY, THOMPSON DOES TWICE YOUR SALES DAILY, AND HE PLAYS SOLITAIRE ALL AFTERNOON.

TUE JULY, 12, 2011

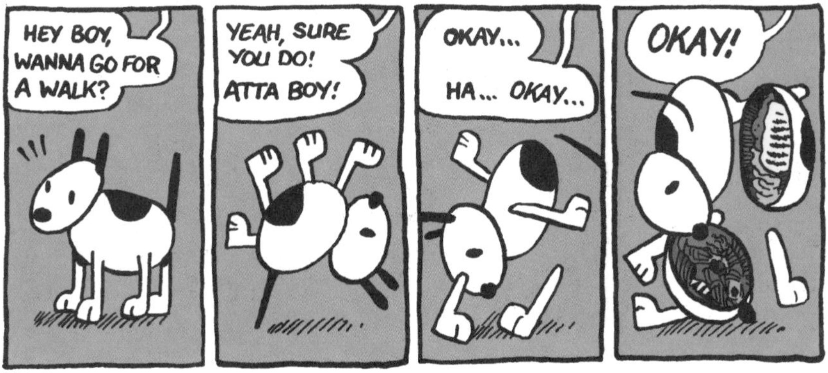
HEY BOY, WANNA GO FOR A WALK?
YEAH, SURE YOU DO! ATTA BOY!
OKAY...
HA... OKAY...
OKAY!

WED JULY 13, 2011

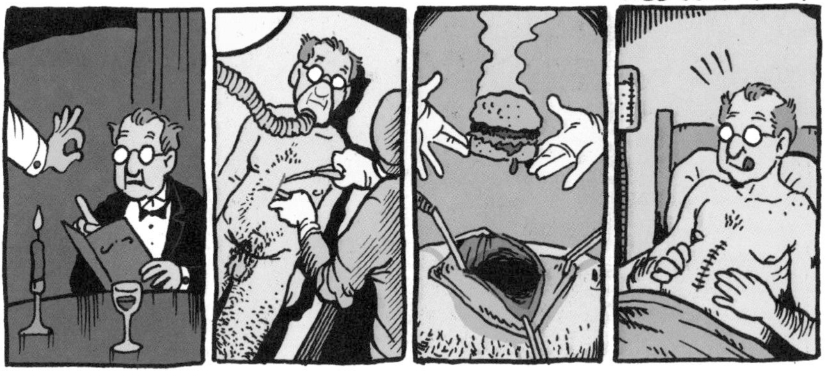

THU JULY 14, 2011

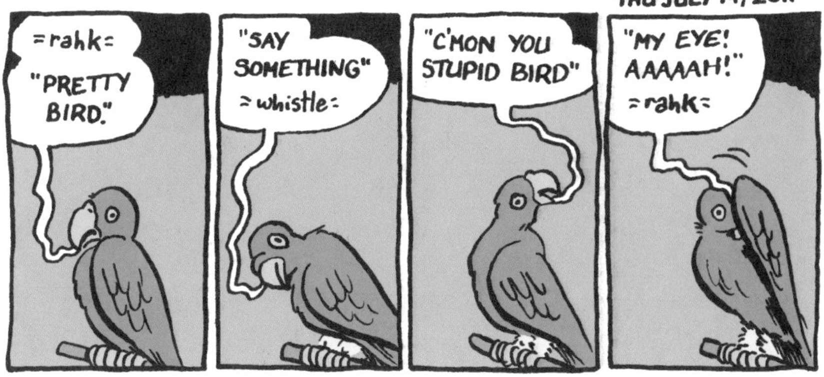
=rahk=
"PRETTY BIRD."
"SAY SOMETHING"
=whistle=
"C'MON YOU STUPID BIRD"
"MY EYE! AAAAAH!"
=rahk=

FRI JULY 15, 2011

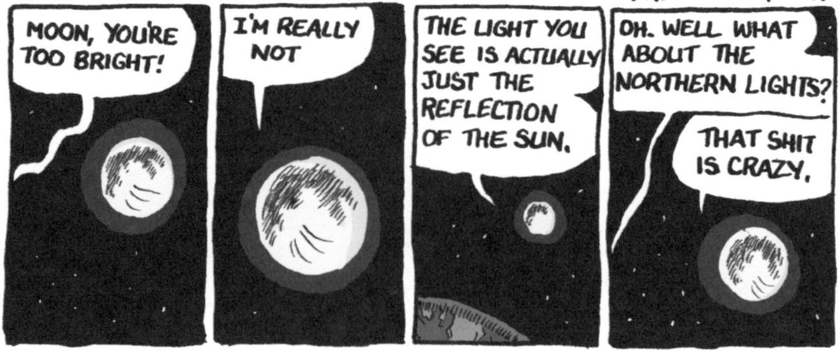
MOON, YOU'RE TOO BRIGHT!
I'M REALLY NOT
THE LIGHT YOU SEE IS ACTUALLY JUST THE REFLECTION OF THE SUN.
OH. WELL WHAT ABOUT THE NORTHERN LIGHTS?
THAT SHIT IS CRAZY.

SAT JULY 16, 2011

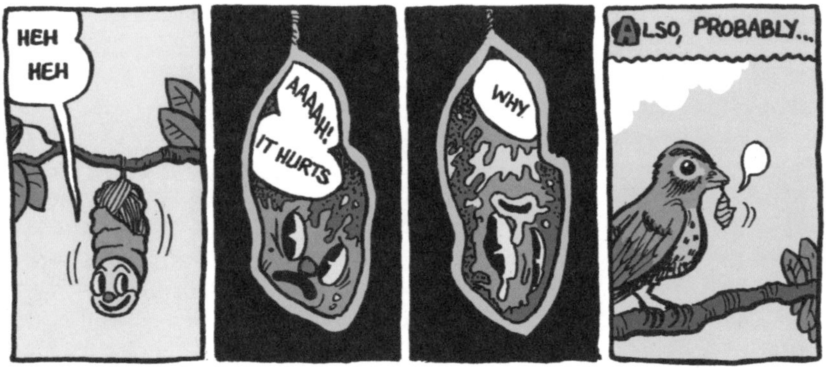
HEH HEH
AAAAH! IT HURTS
WHY
ALSO, PROBABLY...

SUN JULY 17, 2011

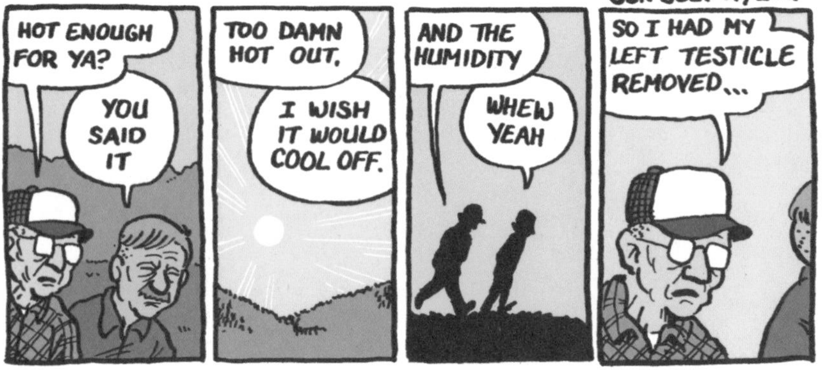
HOT ENOUGH FOR YA?
YOU SAID IT
TOO DAMN HOT OUT.
I WISH IT WOULD COOL OFF.
AND THE HUMIDITY
WHEW YEAH
SO I HAD MY LEFT TESTICLE REMOVED...

MON JULY 18, 2011

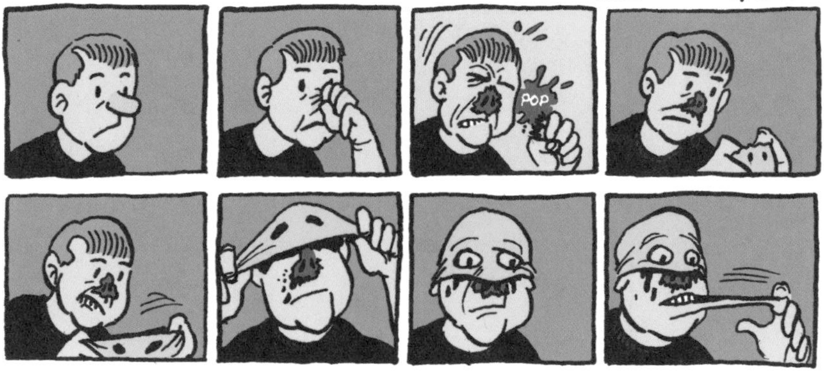
POP

TUE JULY 19, 2011

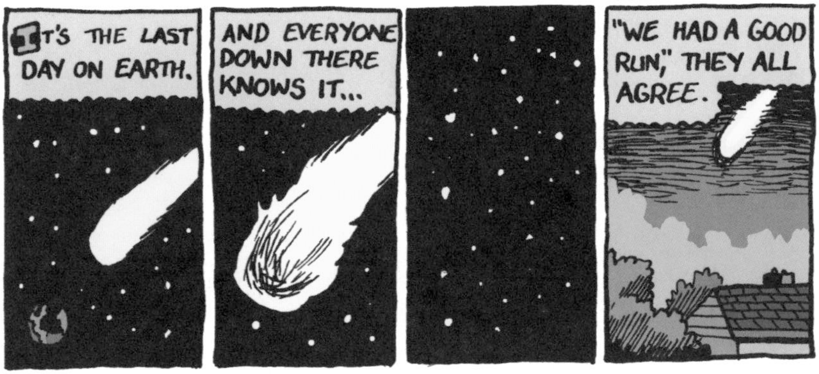
IT'S THE LAST DAY ON EARTH.
AND EVERYONE DOWN THERE KNOWS IT...
"WE HAD A GOOD RUN," THEY ALL AGREE.

WED JULY 20, 2011

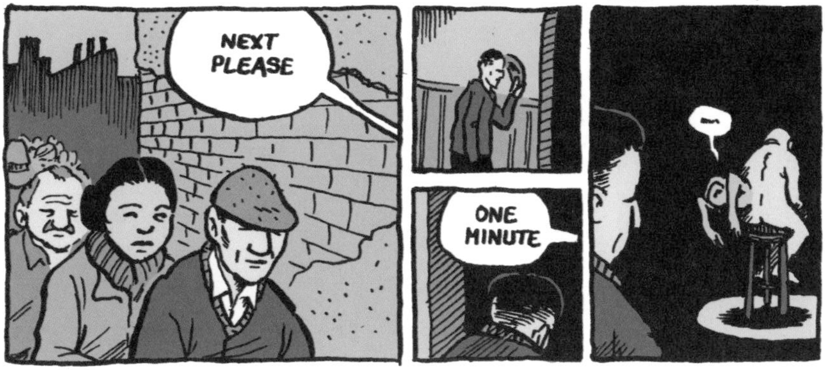
NEXT PLEASE
ONE MINUTE

THU JULY 21, 2011

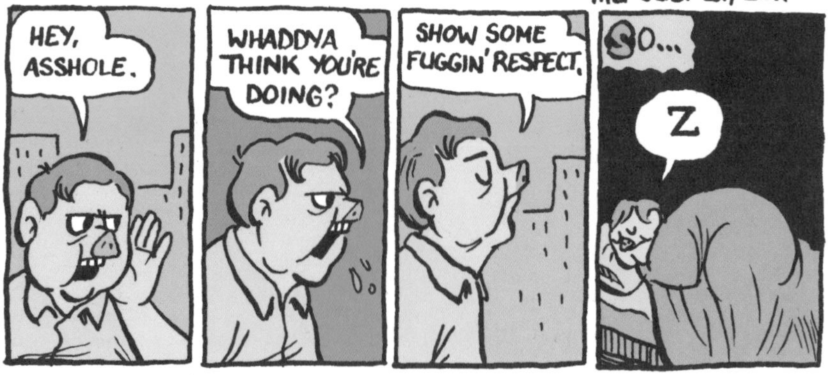
HEY, ASSHOLE.
WHADDYA THINK YOU'RE DOING?
SHOW SOME FUGGIN' RESPECT.
SO...
Z

FRI JULY 22, 2011

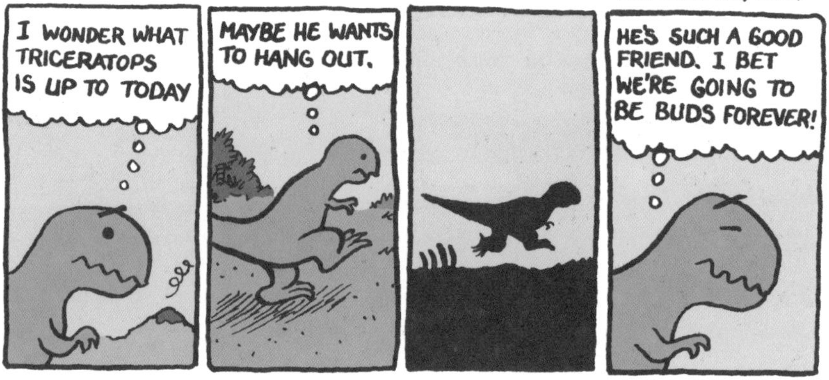
I WONDER WHAT TRICERATOPS IS UP TO TODAY
MAYBE HE WANTS TO HANG OUT.
HE'S SUCH A GOOD FRIEND. I BET WE'RE GOING TO BE BUDS FOREVER!

SAT JULY 23, 2011

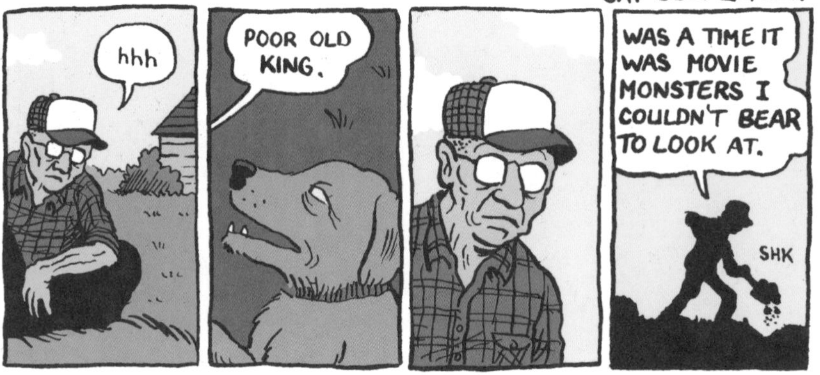
hhh
POOR OLD KING.
WAS A TIME IT WAS MOVIE MONSTERS I COULDN'T BEAR TO LOOK AT.
SHK

OH, UH EUNICE...

I -- HA HA ... UH GOSH.

SORRY, SAM I GOTTA GET TO BIOLOGY.

OH WELL. WE PROBABLY WOULDN'T HAVE MADE IT ANYWAY...

HA HA... WHOOPS HA...

HAH

YOU'RE UH... HA-- GOSH, EUNICE!

hmm

UH... WHA-- WHAAAAAAA

WELL, BUT IT'S NATURAL TOO.

PFF

IT'S ALL BECOME SO COMMODIFIED. ARE WE REALLY THAT BASE?

HI SAM!

H-H EUN

I GUESS I SHOULD SOM SPE

69

WED JULY 27, 2011

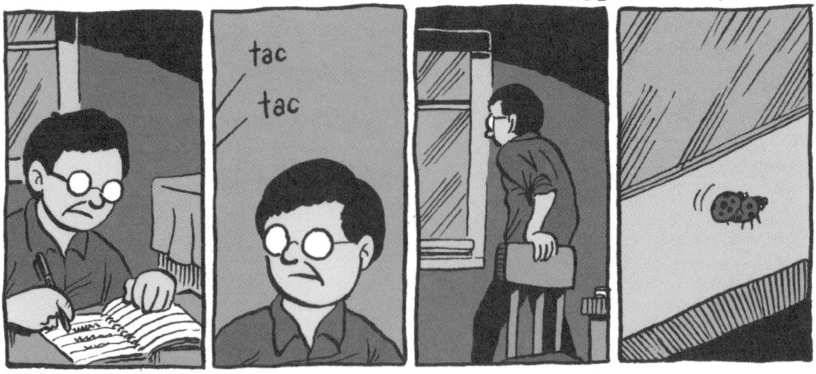
tac
tac

THU JULY 28, 2011

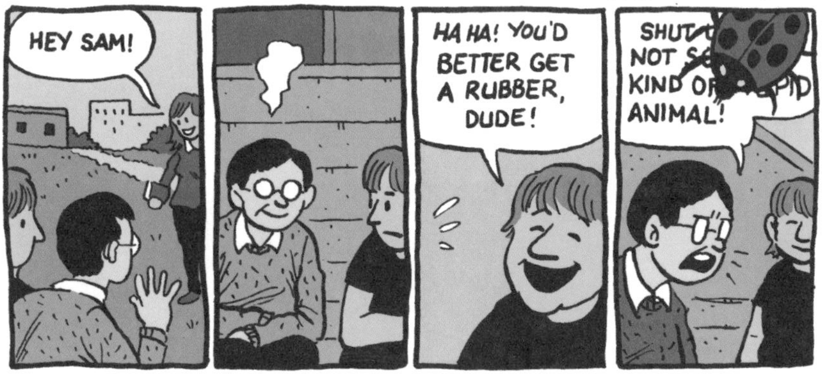
HEY SAM!
HA HA! YOU'D BETTER GET A RUBBER, DUDE!
NOT
KIND
ANIMAL!

FRI JULY 29, 2011

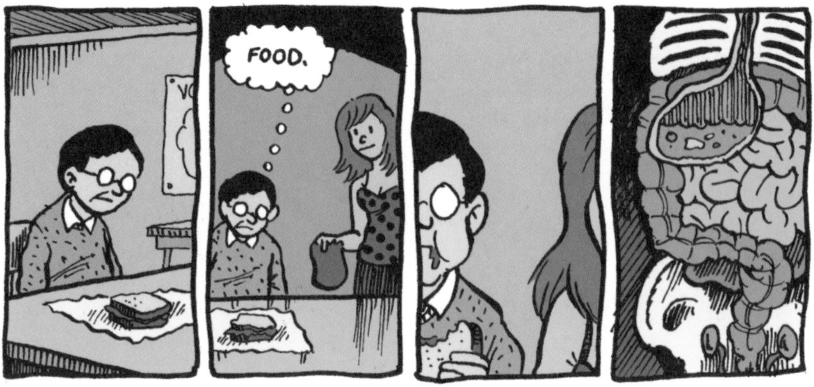
FOOD.

SAT JULY 30, 2011

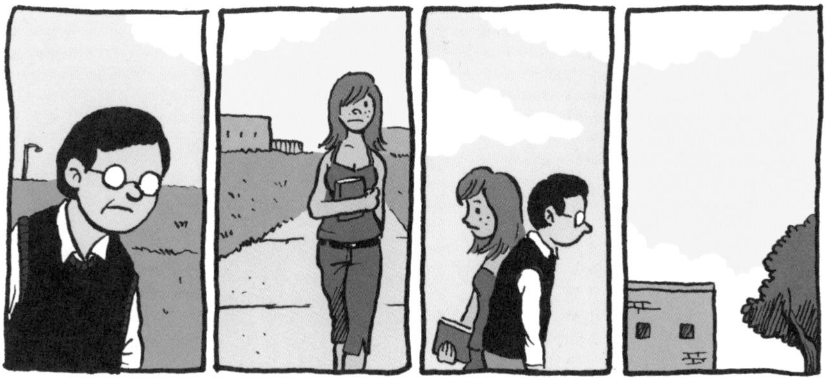

MILKY MASS

SUN JULY 31, 2011

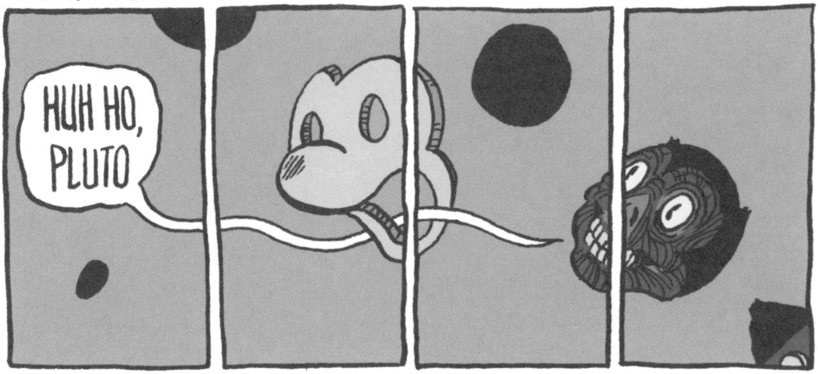
HUH HO, PLUTO

MON AUG 1, 2011

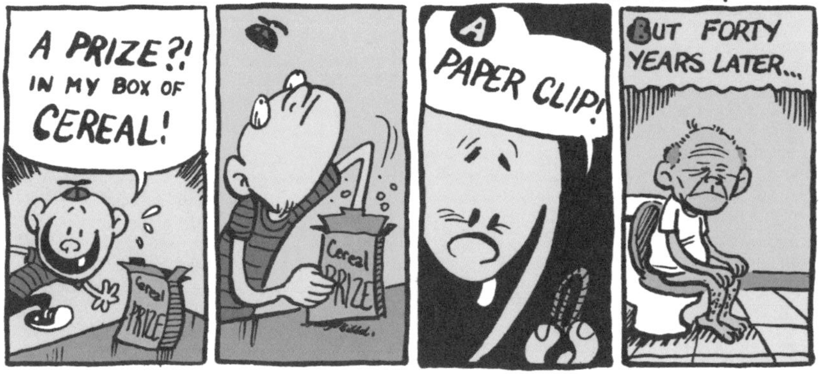
A PRIZE?! IN MY BOX OF CEREAL!
Cereal PRIZE
Cereal PRIZE
A PAPER CLIP!
BUT FORTY YEARS LATER...

TUE AUG 2, 2011

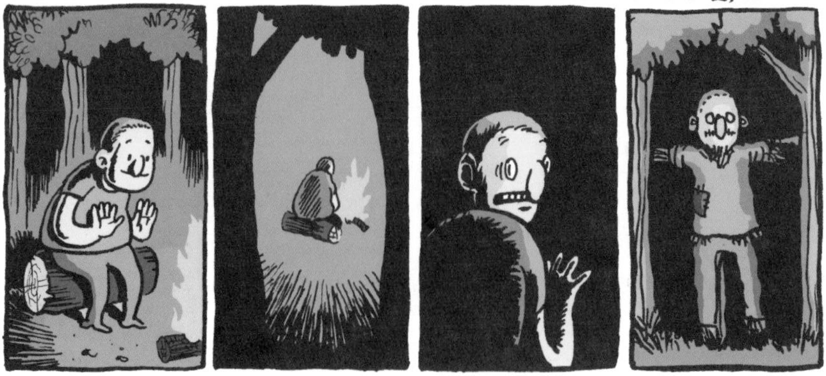

WED AUG 3, 2011

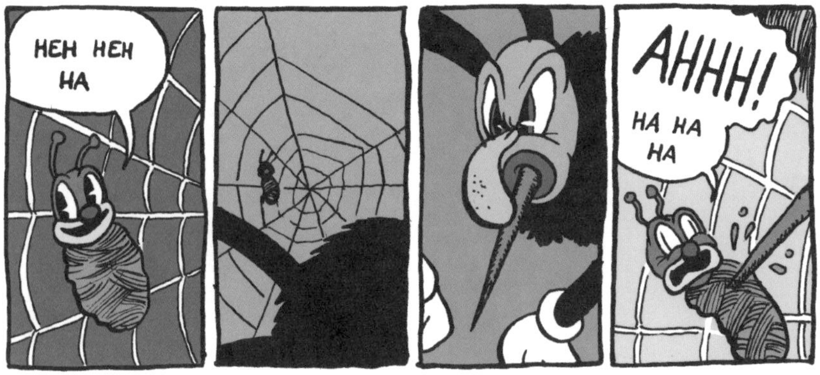
HEH HEH HA
AHHH!
HA HA HA

THU AUG 4, 2011

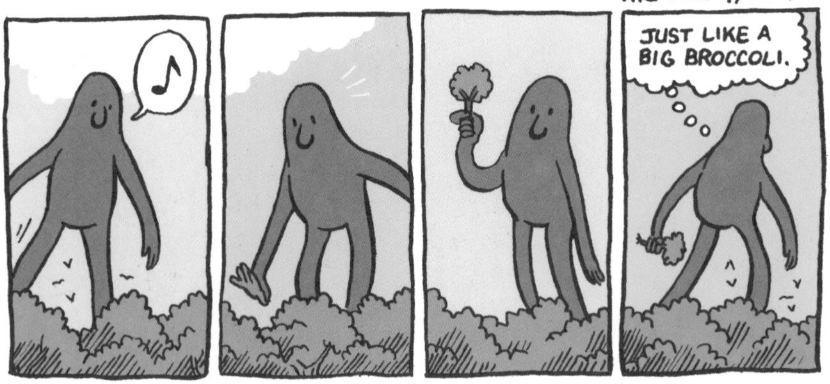
JUST LIKE A BIG BROCCOLI.

FRI AUG 5, 2011

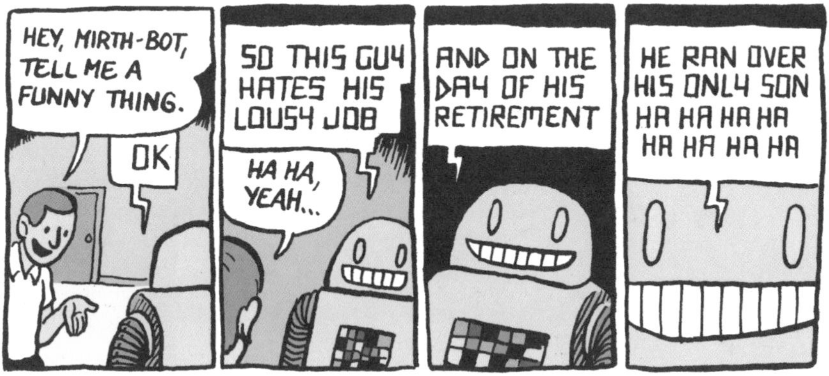
HEY, MIRTH-BOT, TELL ME A FUNNY THING.
OK
SO THIS GUY HATES HIS LOUSY JOB
HA HA, YEAH...
AND ON THE DAY OF HIS RETIREMENT
HE RAN OVER HIS ONLY SON HA HA HA HA HA HA HA HA

SAT AUG 6, 2011

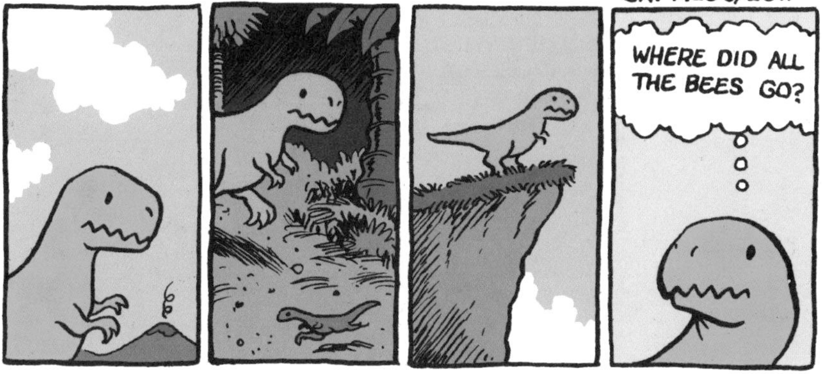
WHERE DID ALL THE BEES GO?

SUN AUG 7, 2011

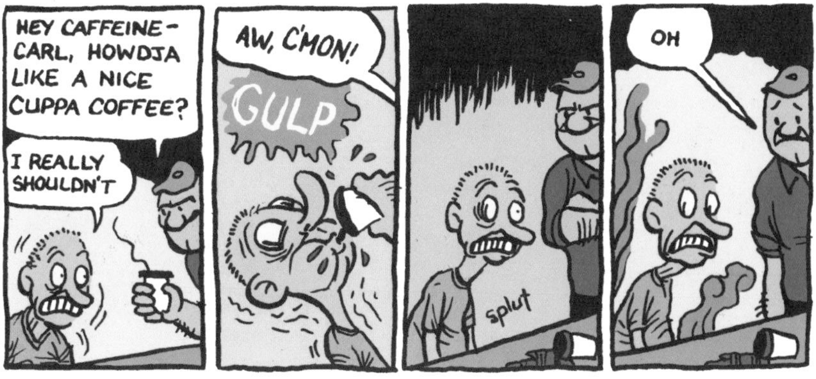
HEY CAFFEINE-CARL, HOWDJA LIKE A NICE CUPPA COFFEE?
I REALLY SHOULDN'T
AW, C'MON!
GULP
splut
OH

MON AUG 8, 2011

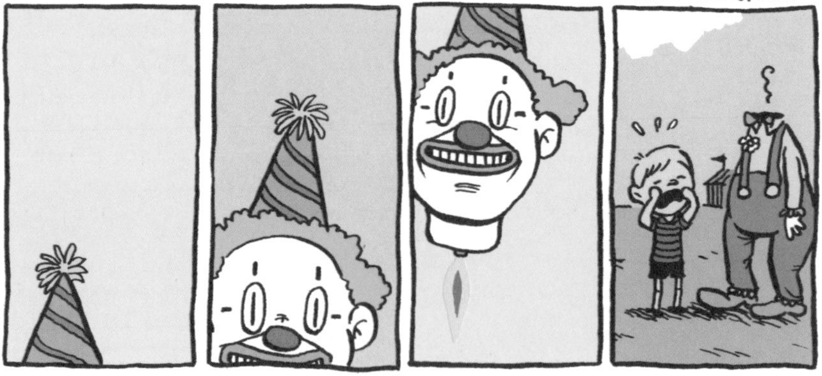

TUE AUG 9, 2011

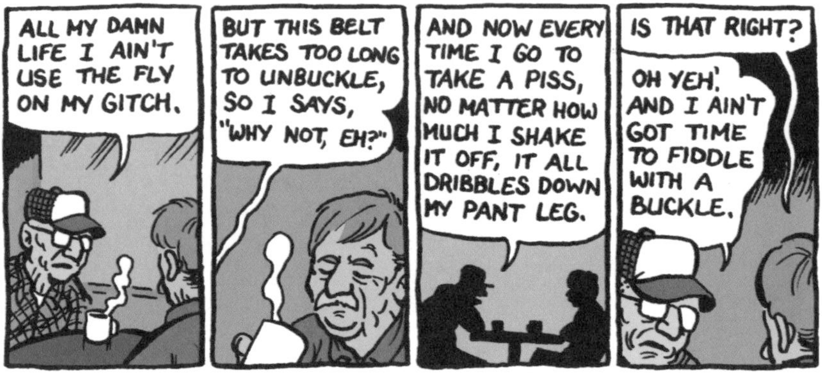
ALL MY DAMN LIFE I AIN'T USE THE FLY ON MY GITCH.
BUT THIS BELT TAKES TOO LONG TO UNBUCKLE, SO I SAYS, "WHY NOT, EH?"
AND NOW EVERY TIME I GO TO TAKE A PISS, NO MATTER HOW MUCH I SHAKE IT OFF, IT ALL DRIBBLES DOWN MY PANT LEG.
IS THAT RIGHT?
OH YEH! AND I AIN'T GOT TIME TO FIDDLE WITH A BUCKLE.

WED AUG 10, 2011

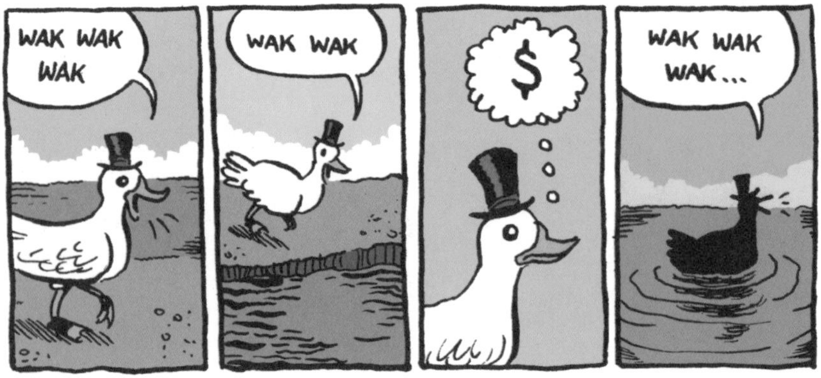
WAK WAK WAK
WAK WAK
$
WAK WAK WAK...

THU AUG 11, 2011

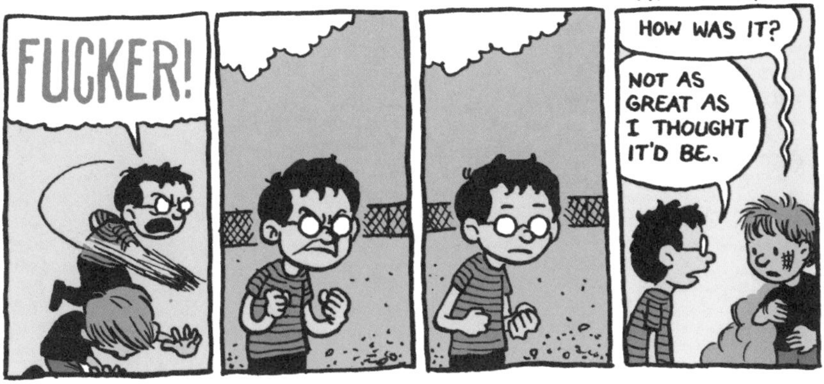
FUCKER!
HOW WAS IT?
NOT AS GREAT AS I THOUGHT IT'D BE.

FRI AUG 12, 2011

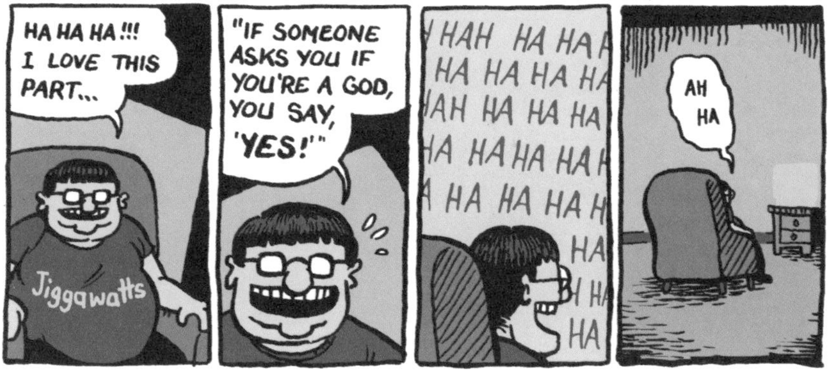
HA HA HA!!! I LOVE THIS PART...
Jiggawatts
"IF SOMEONE ASKS YOU IF YOU'RE A GOD, YOU SAY, 'YES!'"
HAH HA HA HA HA HA HA HA HAH HA HA HA HA HA HA HA HA HA HA HA HA HA HA HA HA
AH HA

SAT AUG 13, 2011

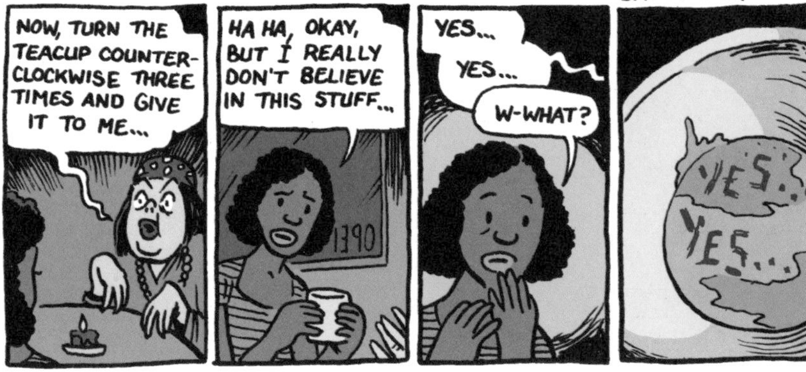
NOW, TURN THE TEACUP COUNTER-CLOCKWISE THREE TIMES AND GIVE IT TO ME...
HA HA, OKAY, BUT I REALLY DON'T BELIEVE IN THIS STUFF...
YES...
YES...
W-WHAT?
YES...
YES...

SUN AUG 14, 2011

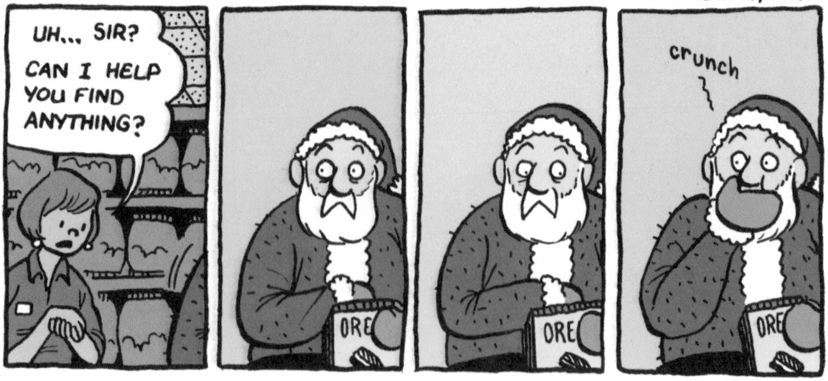
UH... SIR?
CAN I HELP YOU FIND ANYTHING?
ORE
crunch

MON AUG 15, 2011

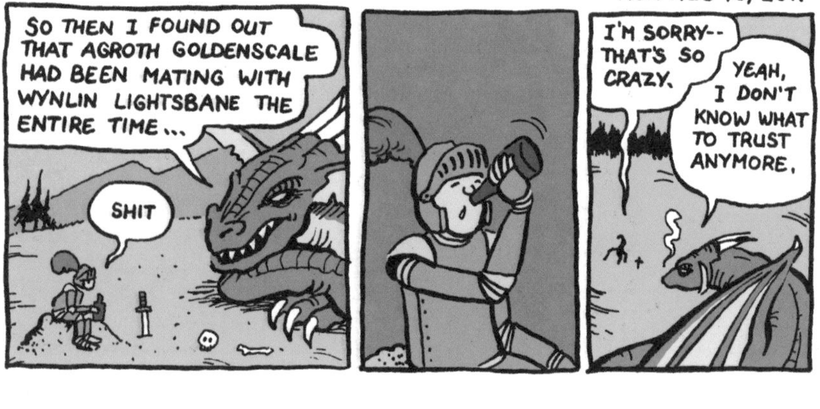
SO THEN I FOUND OUT THAT AGROTH GOLDENSCALE HAD BEEN MATING WITH WYNLIN LIGHTSBANE THE ENTIRE TIME...
SHIT
I'M SORRY-- THAT'S SO CRAZY.
YEAH, I DON'T KNOW WHAT TO TRUST ANYMORE.

TUE AUG 16, 2011

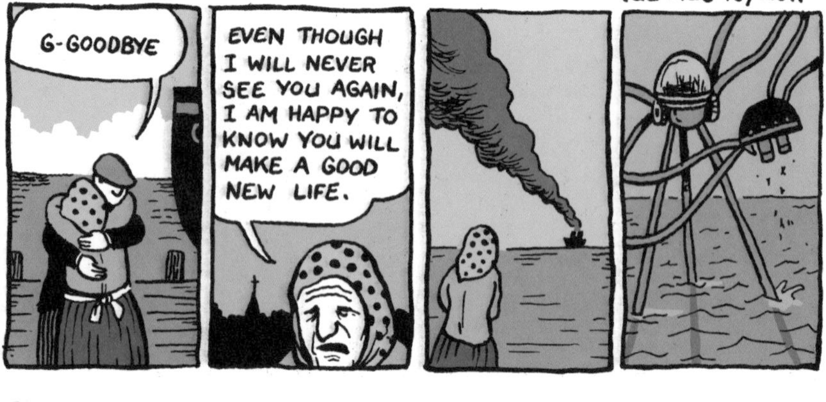
G-GOODBYE
EVEN THOUGH I WILL NEVER SEE YOU AGAIN, I AM HAPPY TO KNOW YOU WILL MAKE A GOOD NEW LIFE.

WED AUG 17, 2011

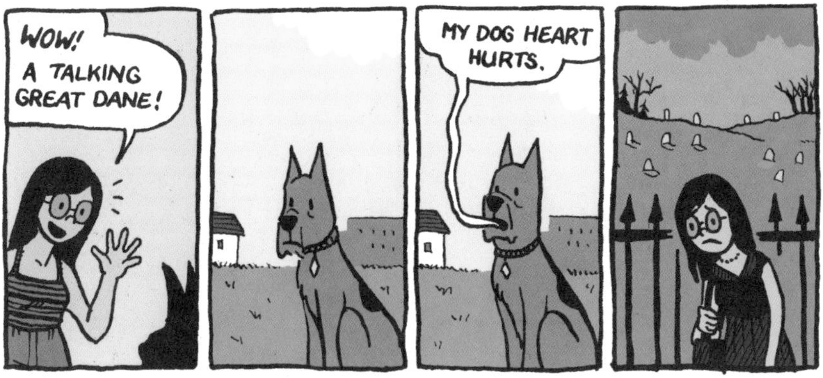
WOW!
A TALKING GREAT DANE!
MY DOG HEART HURTS.

FAN FIX!

THU AUG 18, 2011

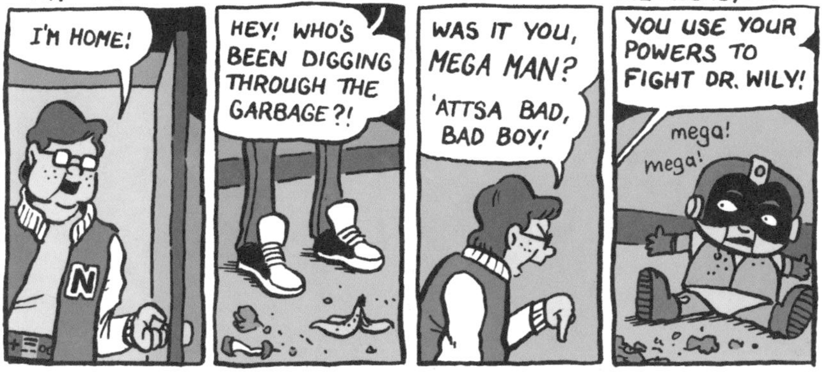
I'M HOME!
HEY! WHO'S BEEN DIGGING THROUGH THE GARBAGE?!
WAS IT YOU, MEGA MAN?
'ATTSA BAD, BAD BOY!
YOU USE YOUR POWERS TO FIGHT DR. WILY!
mega!
mega!

FRI AUG 19, 2011

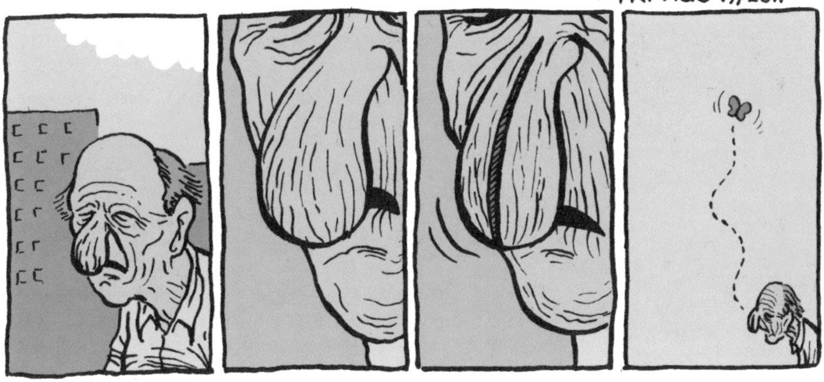

SAT AUG 20, 2011

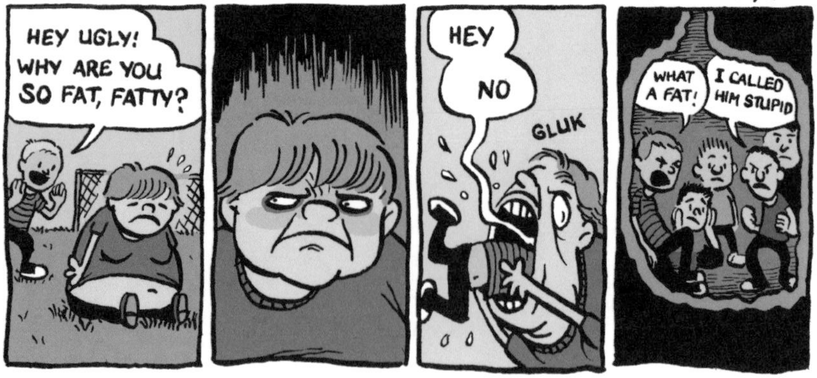
HEY UGLY! WHY ARE YOU SO FAT, FATTY?
HEY
NO
GLUK
WHAT A FAT!
I CALLED HIM STUPID

SUN AUG 21, 2011

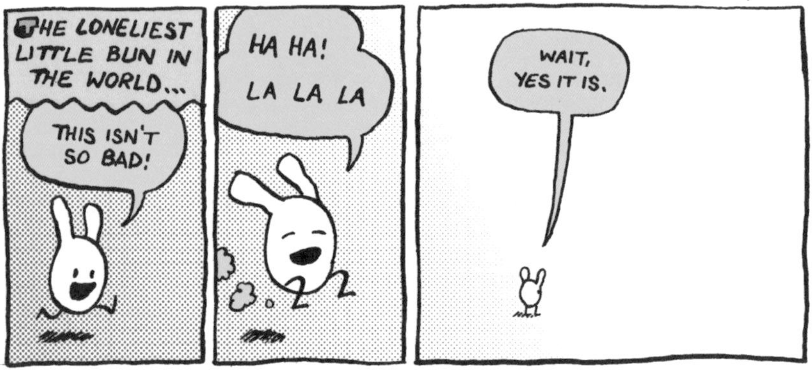
THE LONELIEST LITTLE BUN IN THE WORLD...
THIS ISN'T SO BAD!
HA HA!
LA LA LA
WAIT, YES IT IS.

SNEAKY CAT

MON AUG 22, 2011

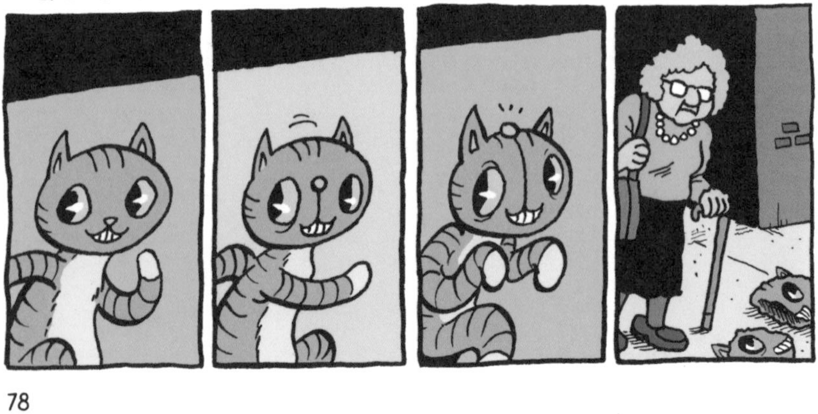

TUE AUG 23, 2011

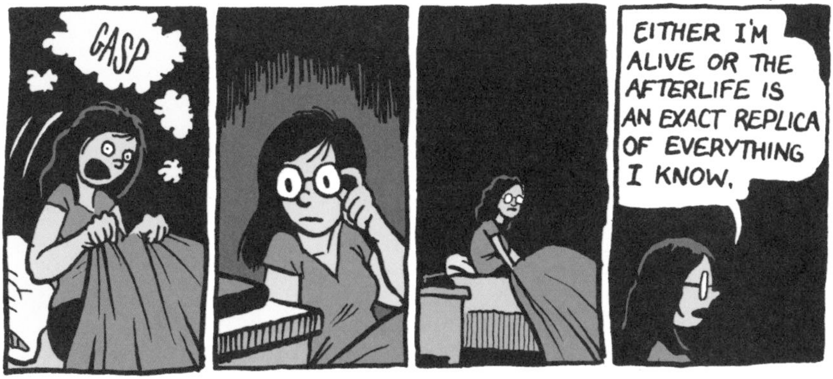
GASP
EITHER I'M ALIVE OR THE AFTERLIFE IS AN EXACT REPLICA OF EVERYTHING I KNOW.

WED AUG 24, 2011

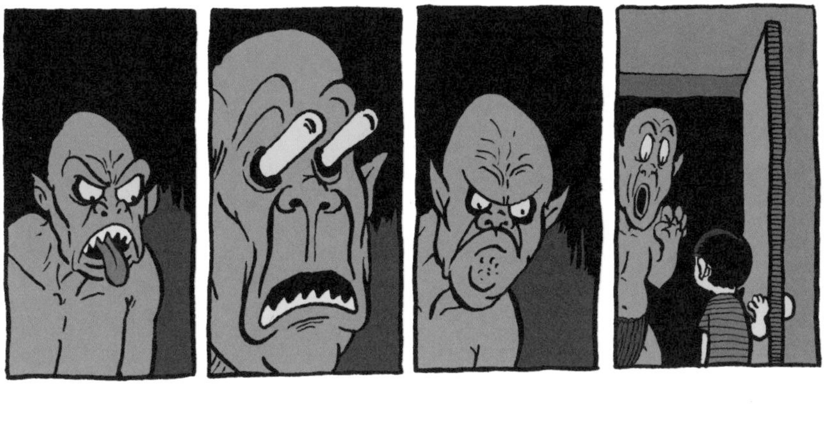

THU AUG 25, 2011

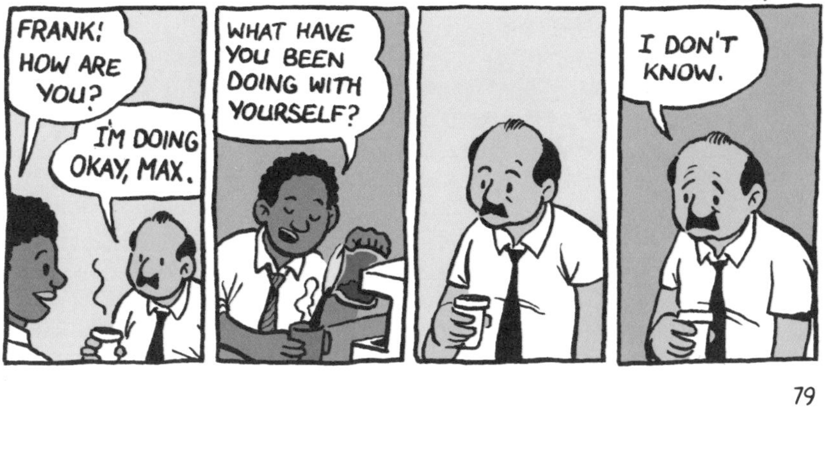
FRANK! HOW ARE YOU?
I'M DOING OKAY, MAX.
WHAT HAVE YOU BEEN DOING WITH YOURSELF?
I DON'T KNOW.

FRI AUG 26, 2011

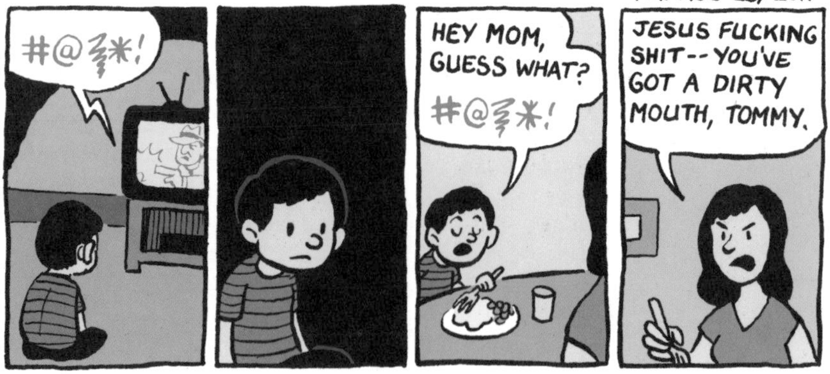
HEY MOM, GUESS WHAT?
JESUS FUCKING SHIT--YOU'VE GOT A DIRTY MOUTH, TOMMY.

SAT AUG, 27, 2011

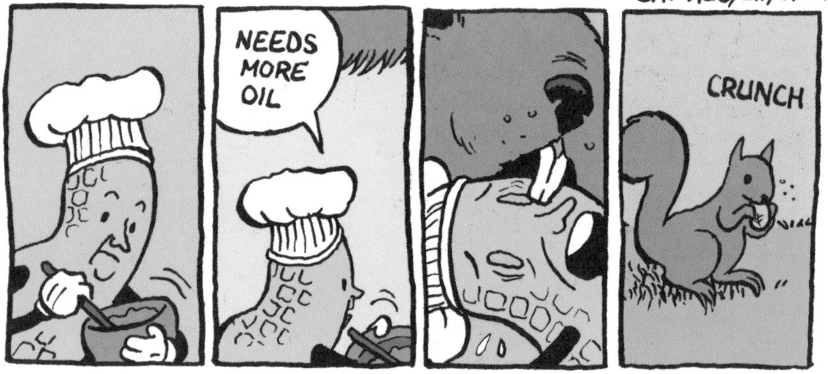
NEEDS MORE OIL
CRUNCH

SUN AUG, 28, 2011

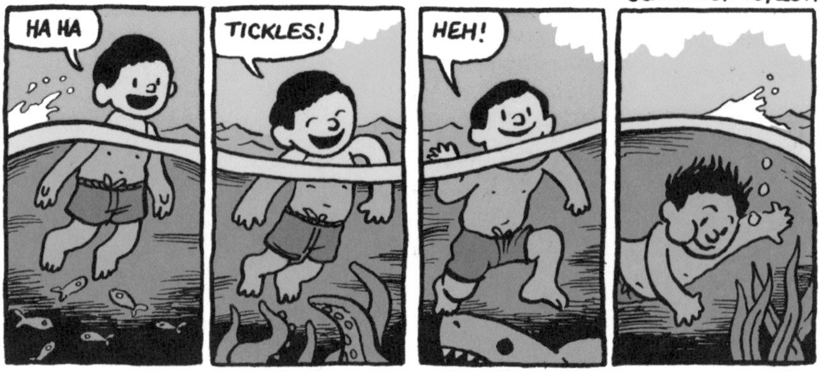
HA HA
TICKLES!
HEH!

MON AUG 29, 2011

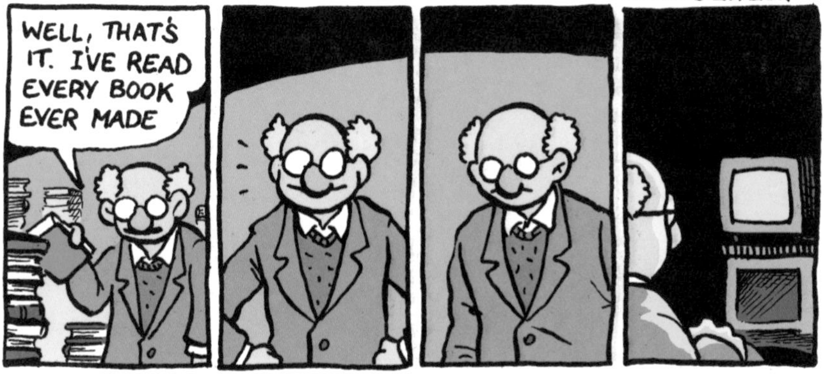
WELL, THAT'S IT. I'VE READ EVERY BOOK EVER MADE

TUE AUG 30, 2011

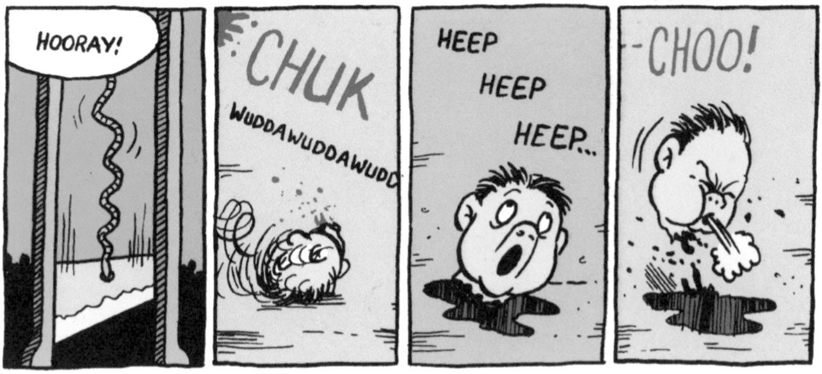
HOORAY!
CHUK
WUDDAWUDDAWUDD
HEEP
HEEP
HEEP...
-CHOO!

WED AUG 31, 2011

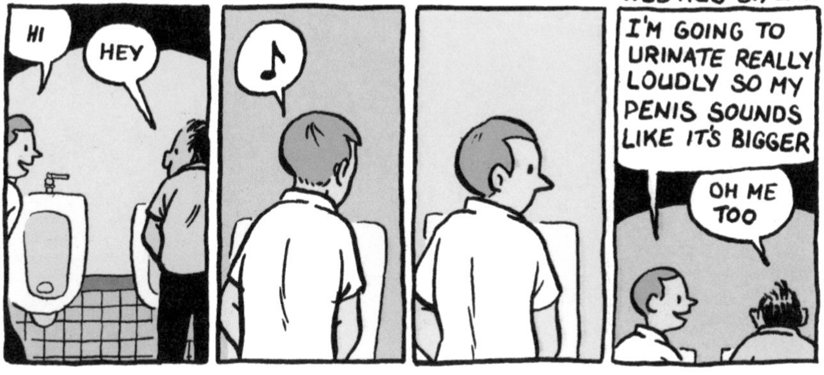
HI
HEY
I'M GOING TO URINATE REALLY LOUDLY SO MY PENIS SOUNDS LIKE IT'S BIGGER
OH ME TOO

THU SEPT 1, 2011

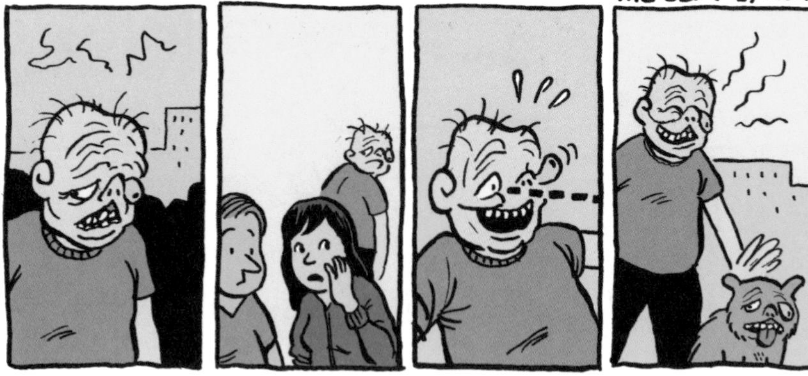

FRI SEPT 2, 2011

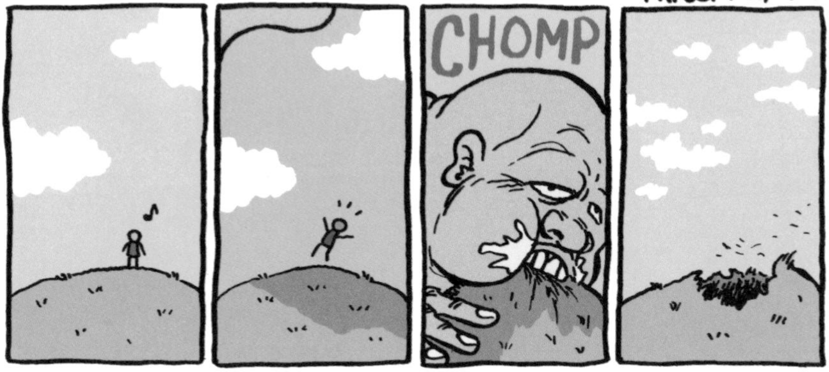
CHOMP

SAT SEPT 3, 2011

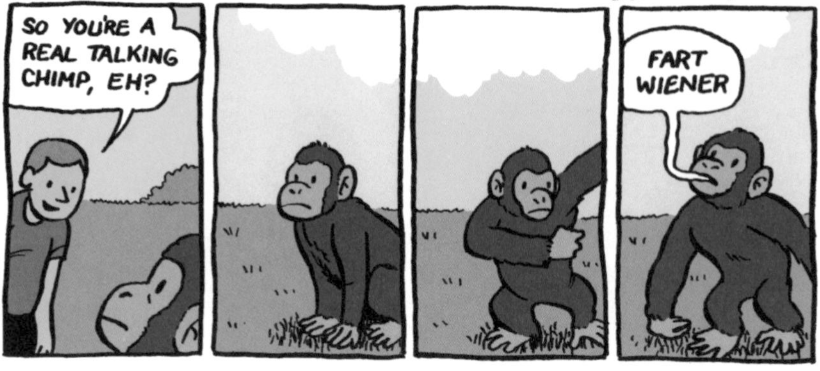
SO YOU'RE A REAL TALKING CHIMP, EH?
FART WIENER

SUN SEPT 4, 2011

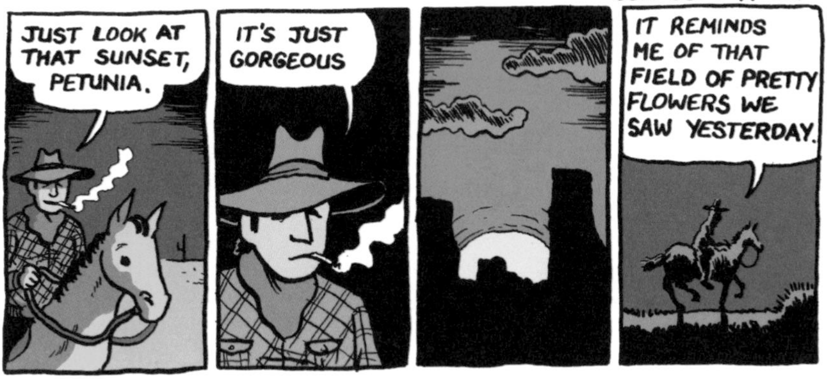
JUST LOOK AT THAT SUNSET, PETUNIA.
IT'S JUST GORGEOUS
IT REMINDS ME OF THAT FIELD OF PRETTY FLOWERS WE SAW YESTERDAY.

MON SEPT 5, 2011

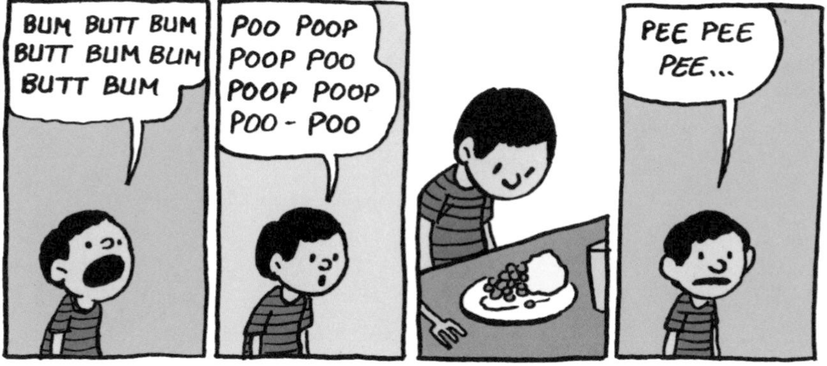
BUM BUTT BUM BUTT BUM BUM BUTT BUM
POO POOP POOP POO POOP POOP POO - POO
PEE PEE PEE...

TUE SEPT 6, 2011

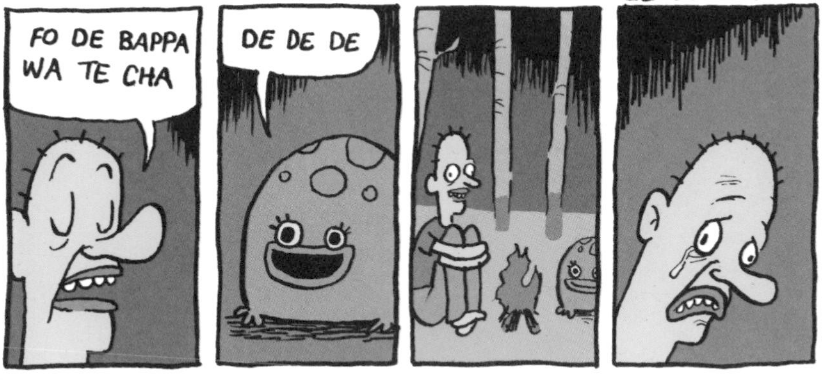
FO DE BAPPA WA TE CHA
DE DE DE

WED SEPT 7, 2011

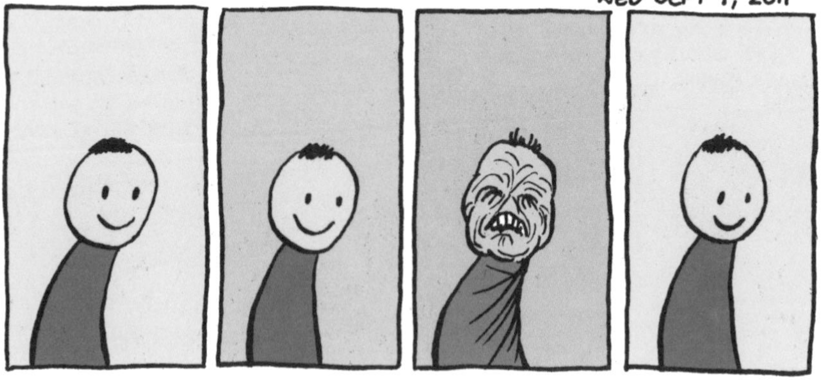

THU SEPT 8, 2011

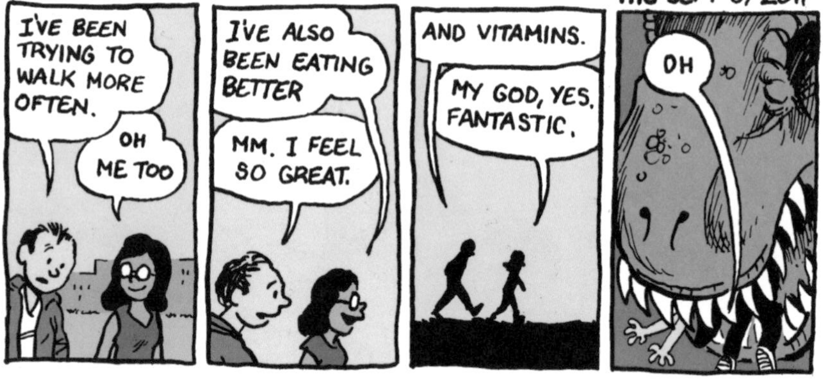
I'VE BEEN TRYING TO WALK MORE OFTEN.
OH ME TOO
I'VE ALSO BEEN EATING BETTER
MM. I FEEL SO GREAT.
AND VITAMINS.
MY GOD, YES. FANTASTIC.
OH

FRI SEPT 9, 2011

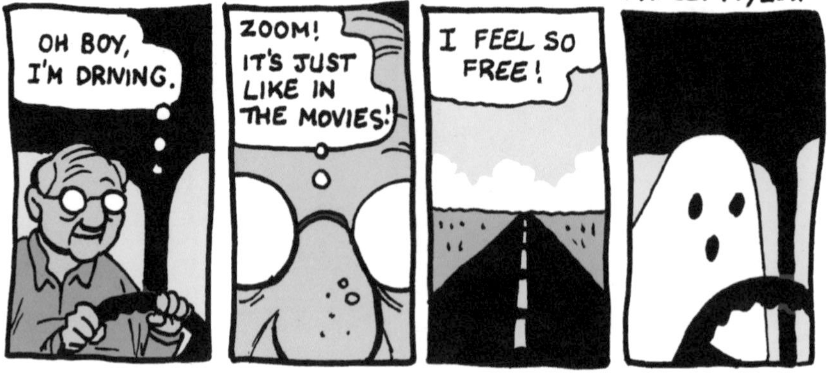
OH BOY, I'M DRIVING.
ZOOM! IT'S JUST LIKE IN THE MOVIES!
I FEEL SO FREE!

SAT SEPT 10, 2011

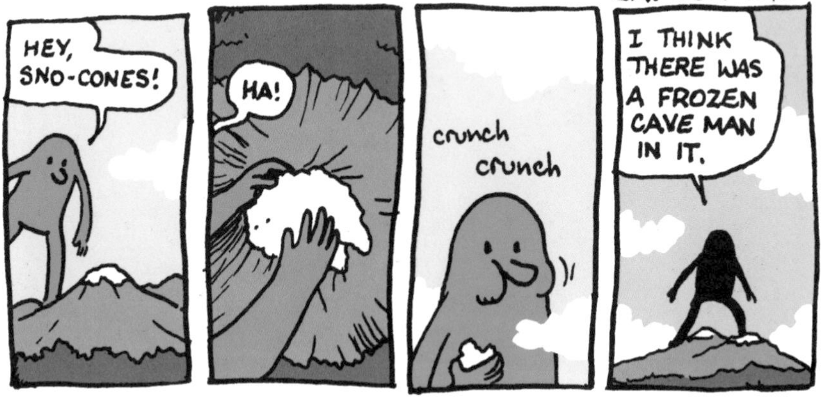
HEY, SNO-CONES!
HA!
crunch crunch
I THINK THERE WAS A FROZEN CAVE MAN IN IT.

SUN SEPT, 11, 2011

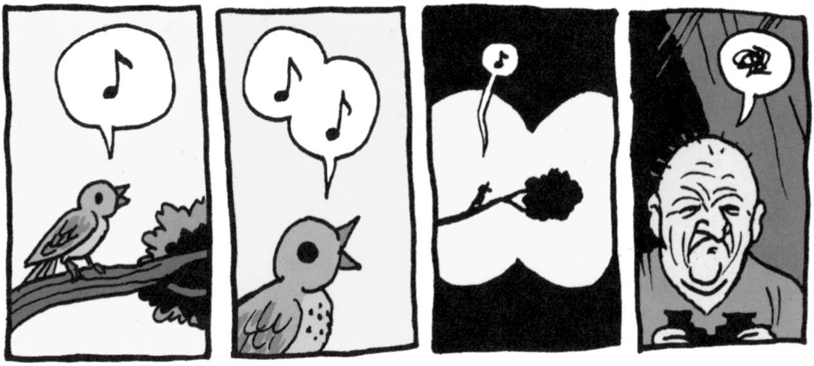

MON SEPT 12, 2011

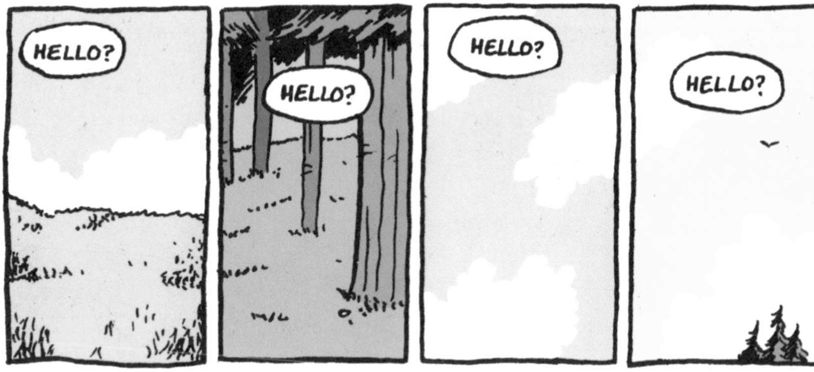
HELLO?
HELLO?
HELLO?
HELLO?

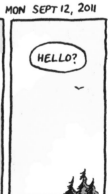

TUE SEPT 13, 2011

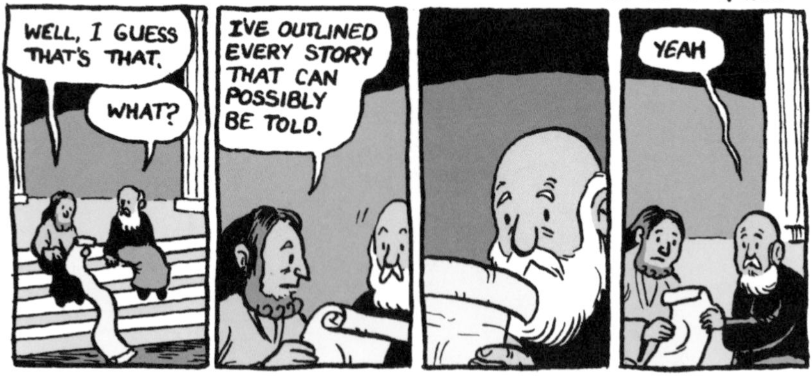
WELL, I GUESS THAT'S THAT.
WHAT?
I'VE OUTLINED EVERY STORY THAT CAN POSSIBLY BE TOLD.
YEAH

WED SEPT 14, 2011

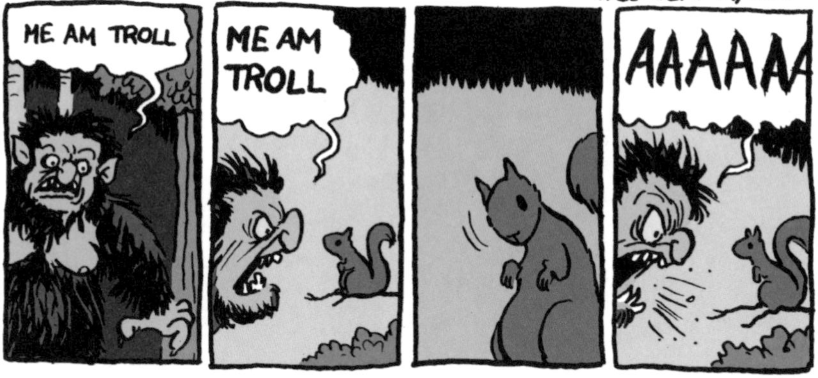
ME AM TROLL
ME AM TROLL
AAAAAA

THU SEPT 15, 2011

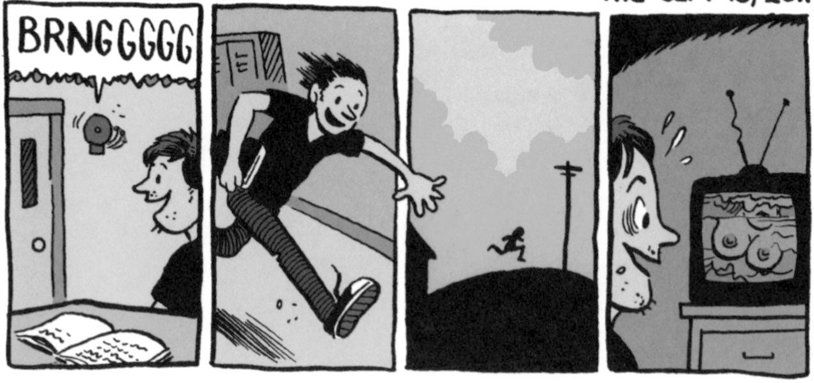
BRNGGGGG

FRI SEPT 16, 2011

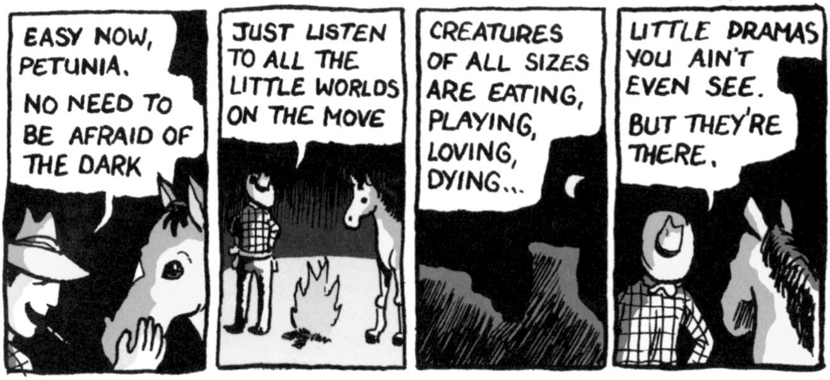
EASY NOW, PETUNIA.
NO NEED TO BE AFRAID OF THE DARK
JUST LISTEN TO ALL THE LITTLE WORLDS ON THE MOVE
CREATURES OF ALL SIZES ARE EATING, PLAYING, LOVING, DYING...
LITTLE DRAMAS YOU AIN'T EVEN SEE.
BUT THEY'RE THERE.

SAT SEPT 17, 2011

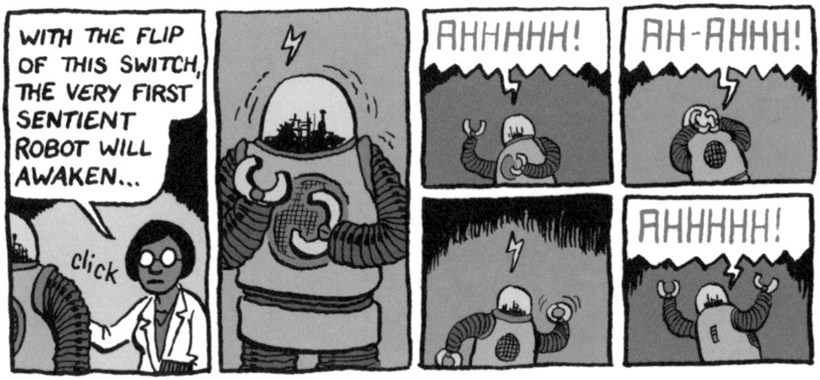
WITH THE FLIP OF THIS SWITCH, THE VERY FIRST SENTIENT ROBOT WILL AWAKEN...
click
AHHHHH!
AH-AHHH!
AHHHHH!

SUN SEPT 18, 2011

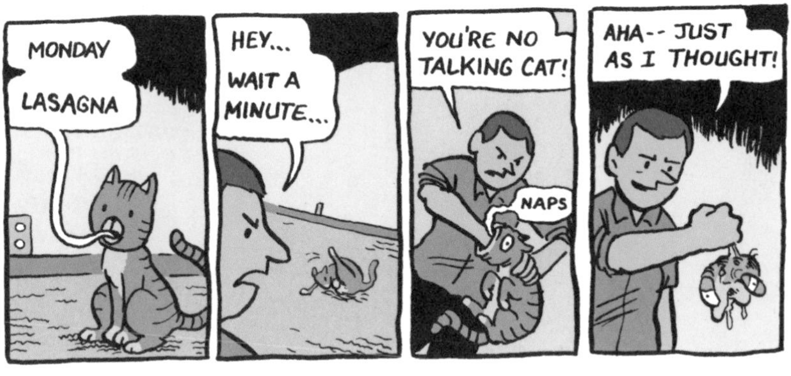
MONDAY
LASAGNA
HEY...
WAIT A MINUTE...
YOU'RE NO TALKING CAT!
NAPS
AHA-- JUST AS I THOUGHT!

MON SEPT 19, 2011

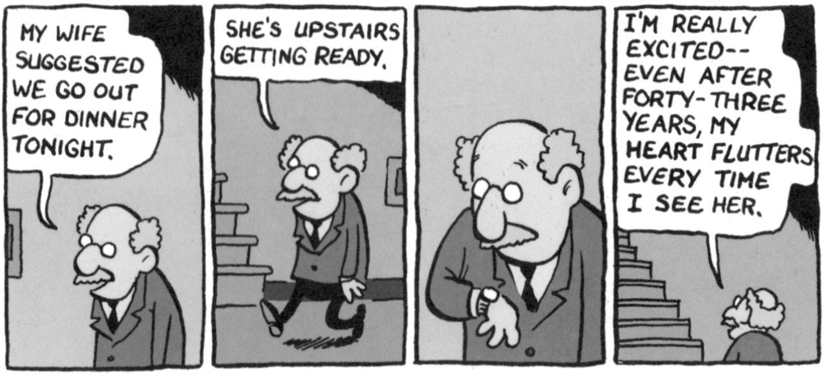

MY WIFE SUGGESTED WE GO OUT FOR DINNER TONIGHT.
SHE'S UPSTAIRS GETTING READY.
I'M REALLY EXCITED-- EVEN AFTER FORTY-THREE YEARS, MY HEART FLUTTERS EVERY TIME I SEE HER.

TUE SEPT 20, 2011

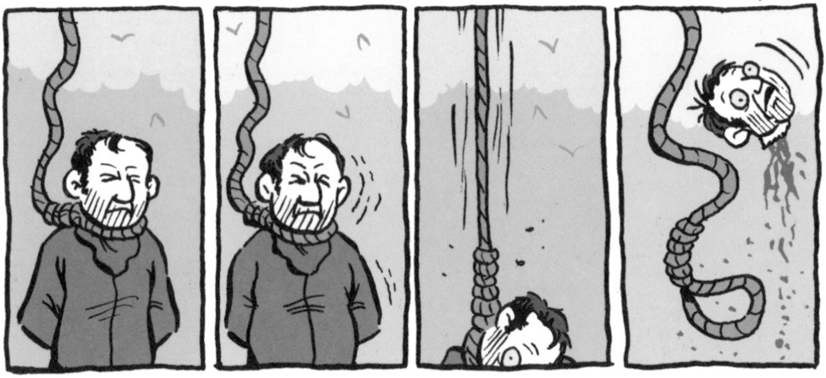

WED SEPT 21, 2011

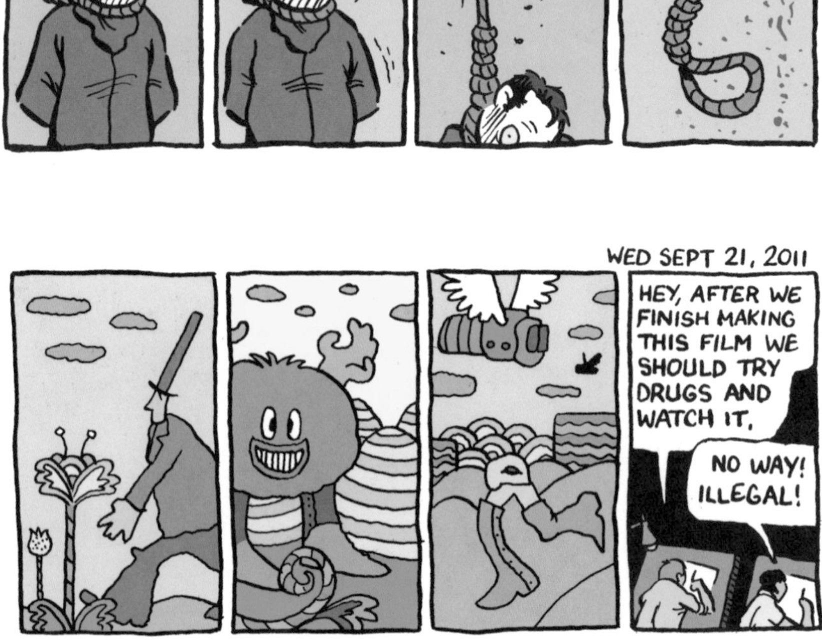

HEY, AFTER WE FINISH MAKING THIS FILM WE SHOULD TRY DRUGS AND WATCH IT.
NO WAY! ILLEGAL!

HAPPY COMICS THU SEPT 22, 2011

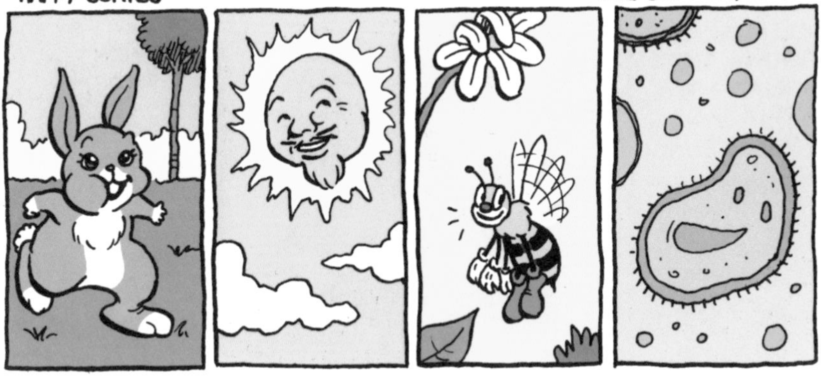

FRI SEPT 23, 2011

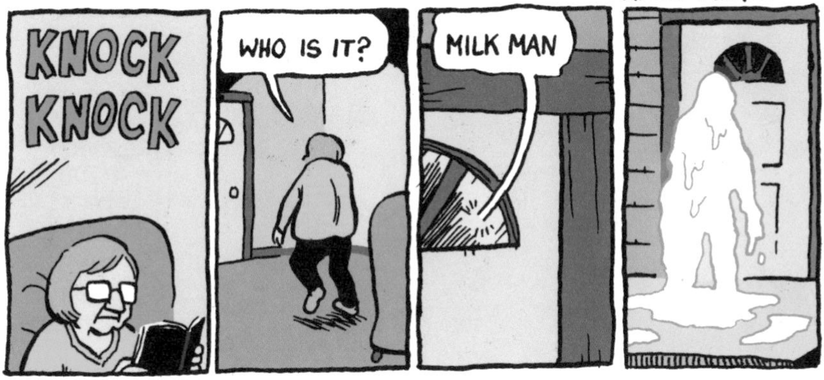
KNOCK KNOCK
WHO IS IT?
MILK MAN

SAT SEPT 24, 2011

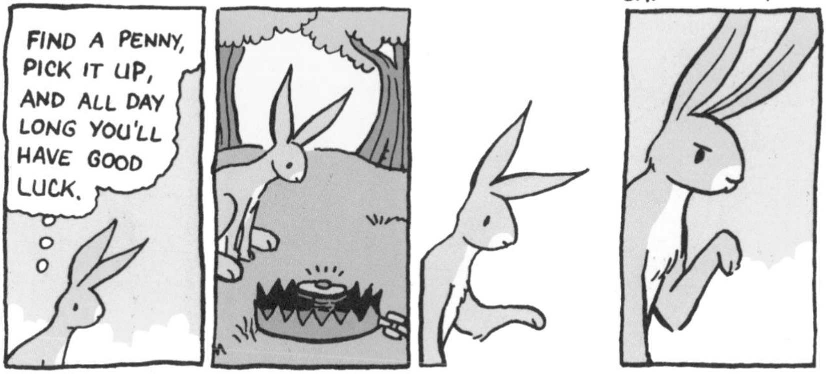
FIND A PENNY, PICK IT UP, AND ALL DAY LONG YOU'LL HAVE GOOD LUCK.

SUN SEPT 25, 2011

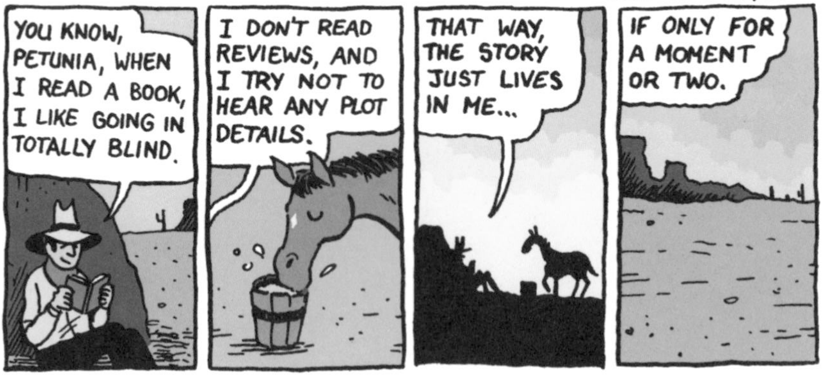
YOU KNOW, PETUNIA, WHEN I READ A BOOK, I LIKE GOING IN TOTALLY BLIND.
I DON'T READ REVIEWS, AND I TRY NOT TO HEAR ANY PLOT DETAILS.
THAT WAY, THE STORY JUST LIVES IN ME...
IF ONLY FOR A MOMENT OR TWO.

MON SEPT 26, 2011

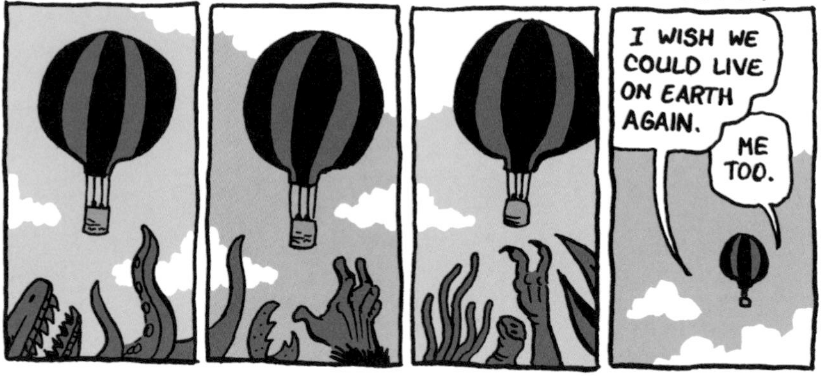
I WISH WE COULD LIVE ON EARTH AGAIN.
ME TOO.

ELEPHANT COMICS

TUE SEPT 27, 2011

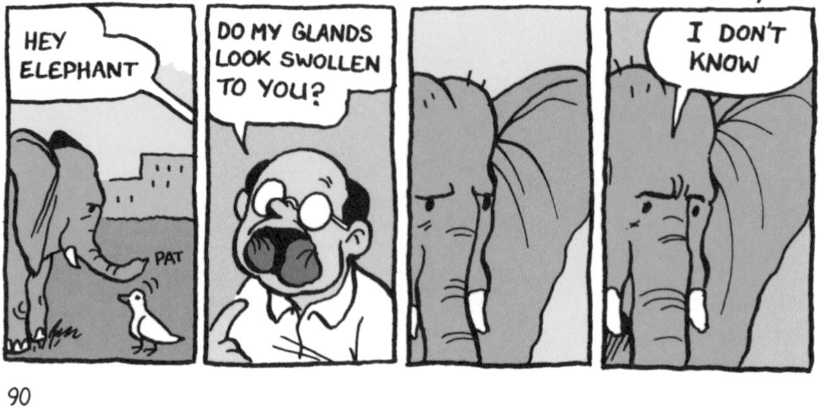
HEY ELEPHANT
PAT
DO MY GLANDS LOOK SWOLLEN TO YOU?
I DON'T KNOW

WED SEPT 28, 2011

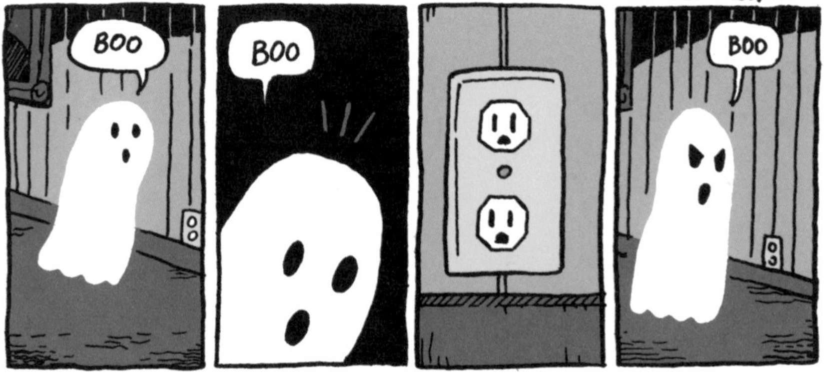

BOO
BOO
BOO

THU SEPT 29, 2011

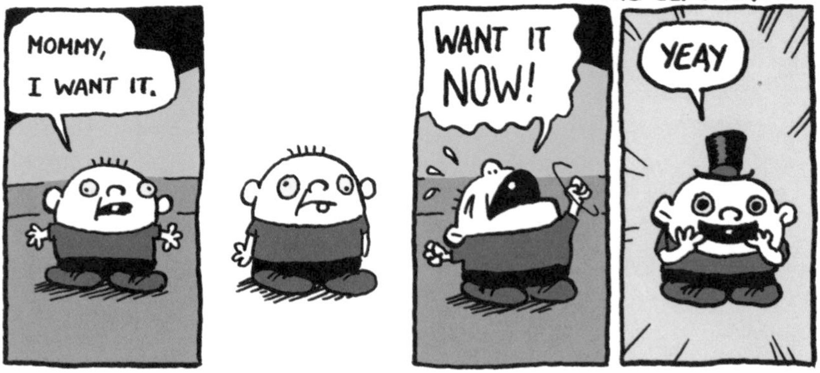

MOMMY, I WANT IT.
WANT IT NOW!
YEAY

FRI SEPT 30, 2011

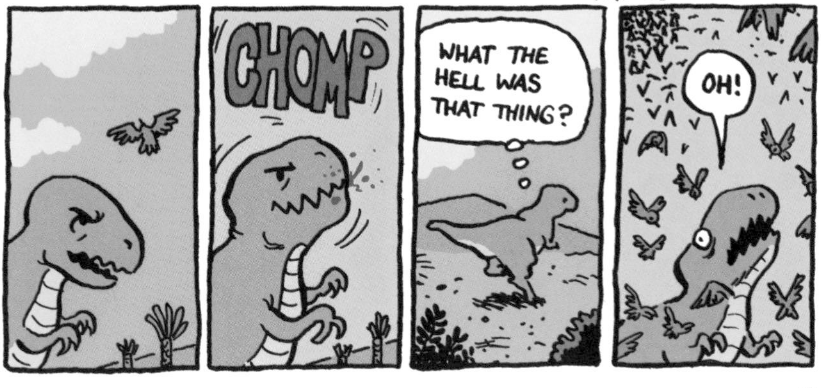

CHOMP
WHAT THE HELL WAS THAT THING?
OH!

SAT OCT 1, 2011

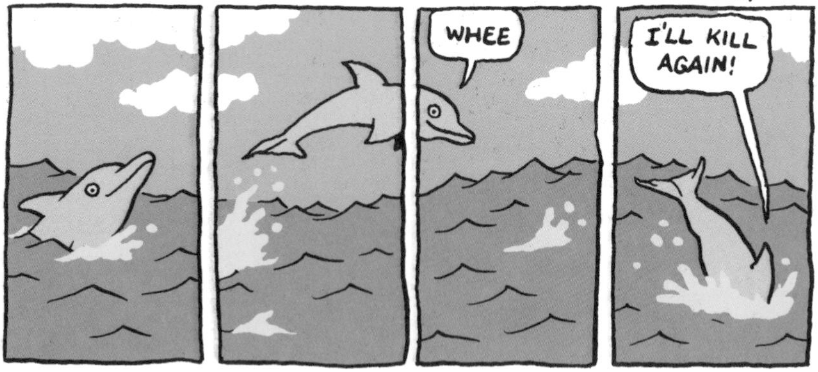
WHEE
I'LL KILL AGAIN!

SUN OCT 2, 2011

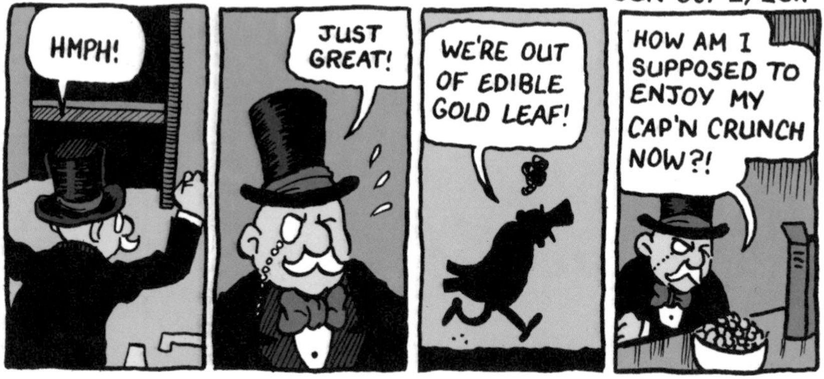
HMPH!
JUST GREAT!
WE'RE OUT OF EDIBLE GOLD LEAF!
HOW AM I SUPPOSED TO ENJOY MY CAP'N CRUNCH NOW?!

MON OCT 3, 2011

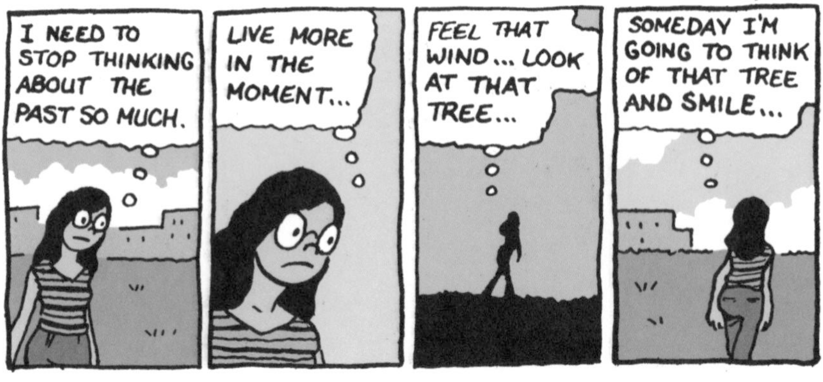
I NEED TO STOP THINKING ABOUT THE PAST SO MUCH.
LIVE MORE IN THE MOMENT...
FEEL THAT WIND... LOOK AT THAT TREE...
SOMEDAY I'M GOING TO THINK OF THAT TREE AND SMILE...

TUE OCT 4, 2011

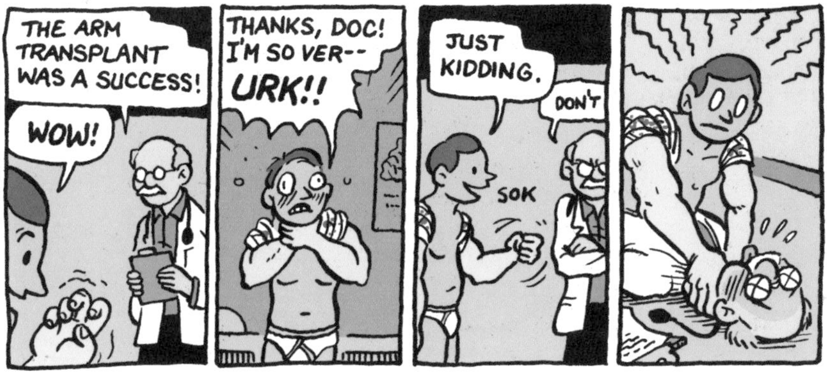
THE ARM TRANSPLANT WAS A SUCCESS!
WOW!
THANKS, DOC! I'M SO VER-- URK!!
JUST KIDDING.
DON'T
SOK

WED OCT 5, 2011

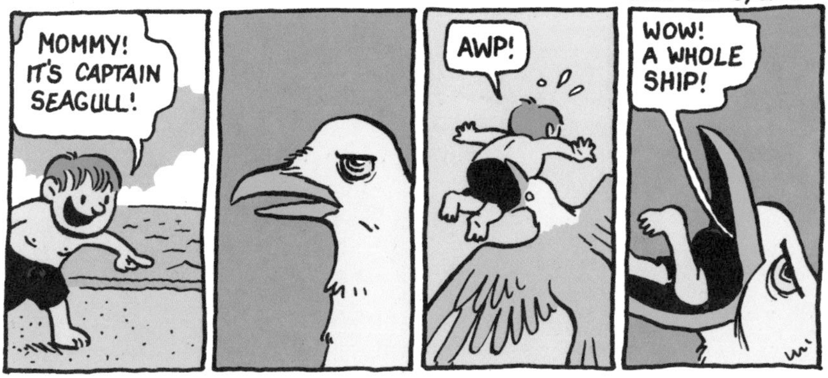
MOMMY! IT'S CAPTAIN SEAGULL!
AWP!
WOW! A WHOLE SHIP!

THU OCT 6, 2011

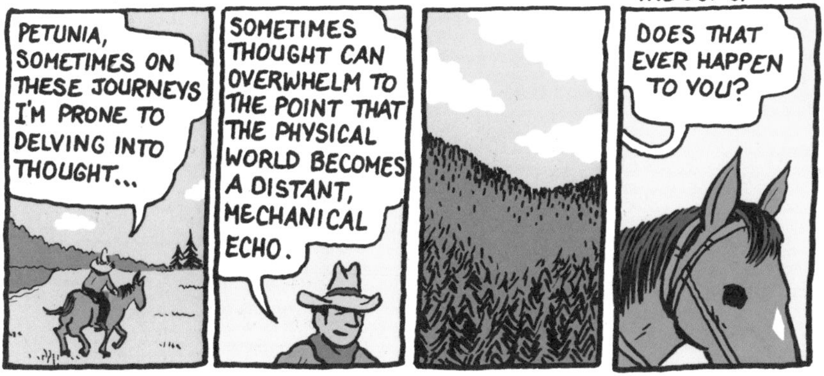
PETUNIA, SOMETIMES ON THESE JOURNEYS I'M PRONE TO DELVING INTO THOUGHT...
SOMETIMES THOUGHT CAN OVERWHELM TO THE POINT THAT THE PHYSICAL WORLD BECOMES A DISTANT, MECHANICAL ECHO.
DOES THAT EVER HAPPEN TO YOU?

FRI OCT 7, 2011

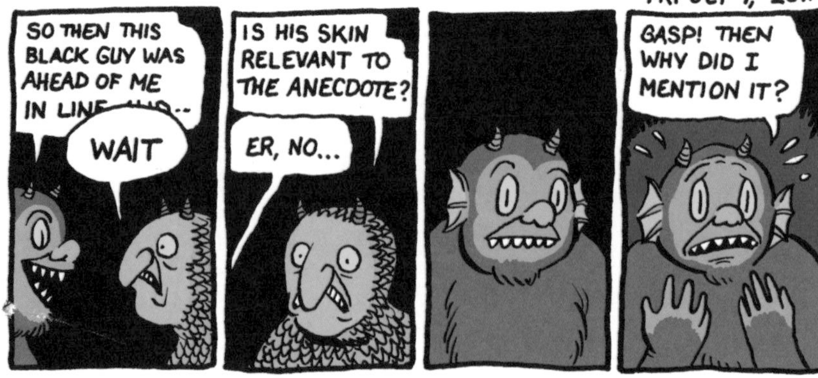
SO THEN THIS BLACK GUY WAS AHEAD OF ME IN LIN
WAIT
IS HIS SKIN RELEVANT TO THE ANECDOTE?
ER, NO...
GASP! THEN WHY DID I MENTION IT?

SAT OCT 8, 2011

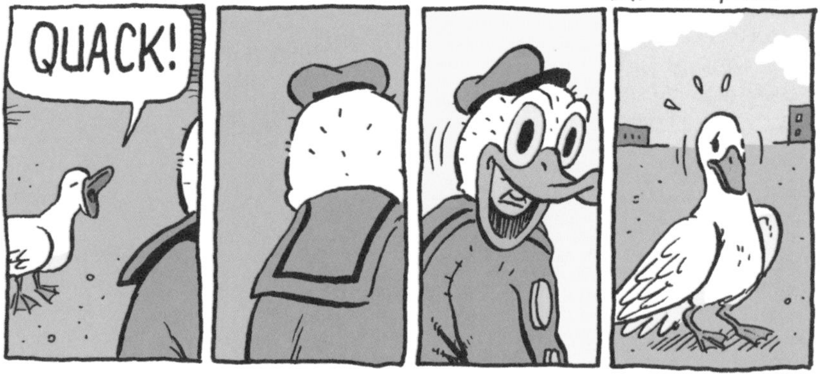
QUACK!

SUN OCT 9, 2011

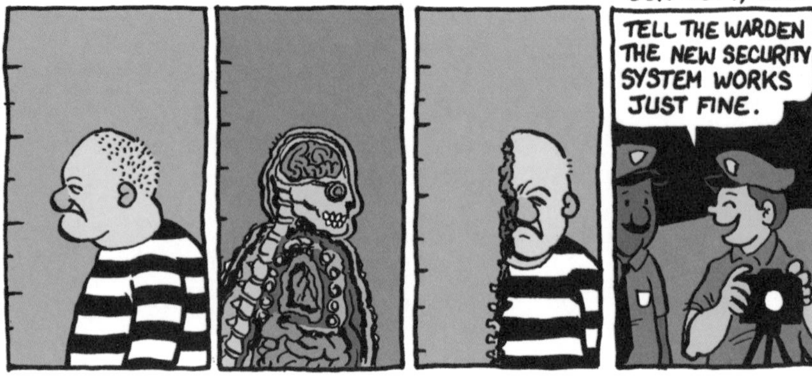
TELL THE WARDEN THE NEW SECURITY SYSTEM WORKS JUST FINE.

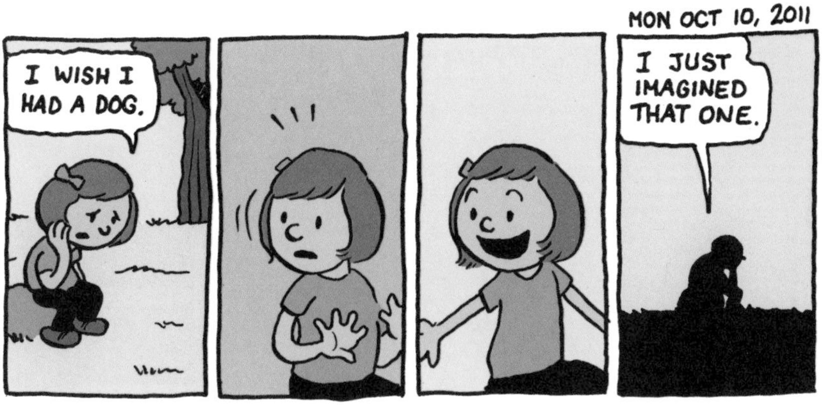
MON OCT 10, 2011
I WISH I HAD A DOG.
I JUST IMAGINED THAT ONE.

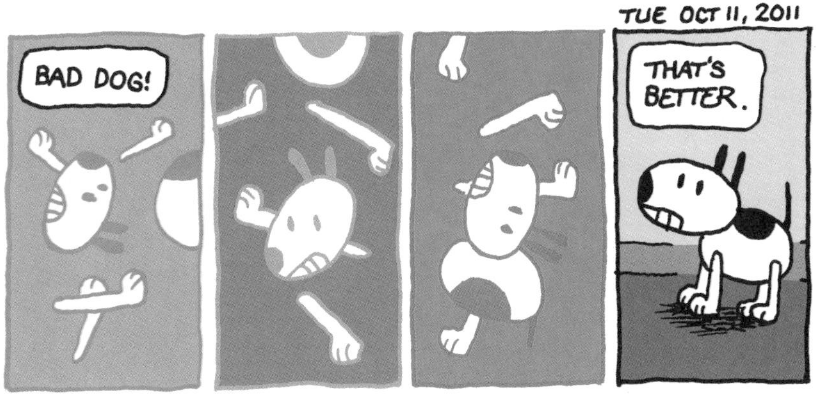
TUE OCT 11, 2011
BAD DOG!
THAT'S BETTER.

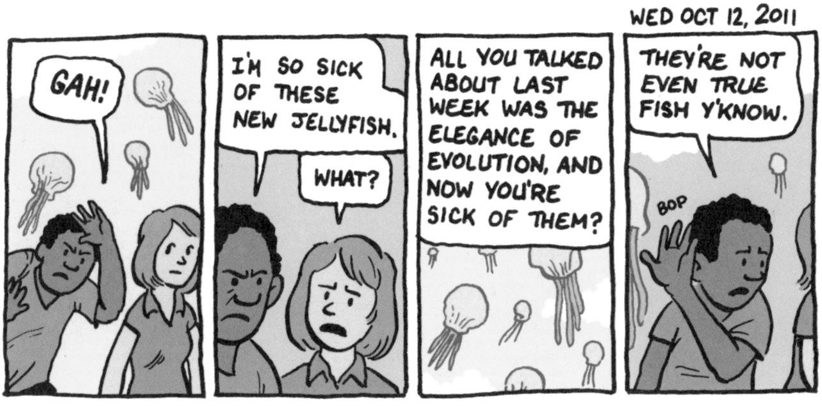
WED OCT 12, 2011
GAH!
I'M SO SICK OF THESE NEW JELLYFISH.
WHAT?
ALL YOU TALKED ABOUT LAST WEEK WAS THE ELEGANCE OF EVOLUTION, AND NOW YOU'RE SICK OF THEM?
BOP
THEY'RE NOT EVEN TRUE FISH Y'KNOW.

THU OCT 13, 2011

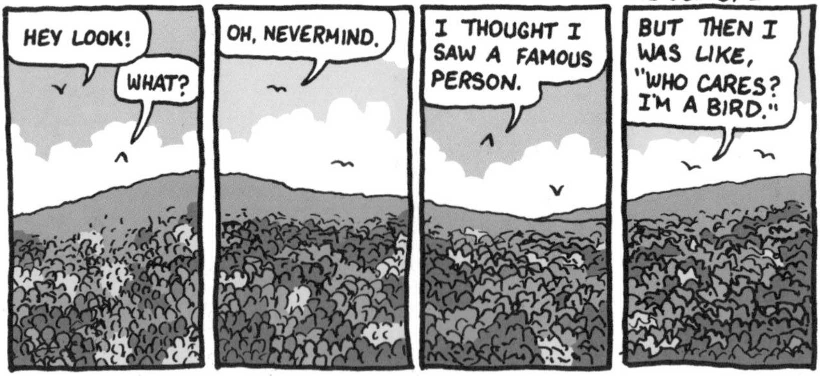
HEY LOOK!
WHAT?
OH, NEVERMIND.
I THOUGHT I SAW A FAMOUS PERSON.
BUT THEN I WAS LIKE, "WHO CARES? I'M A BIRD."

FRI OCT 14, 2011

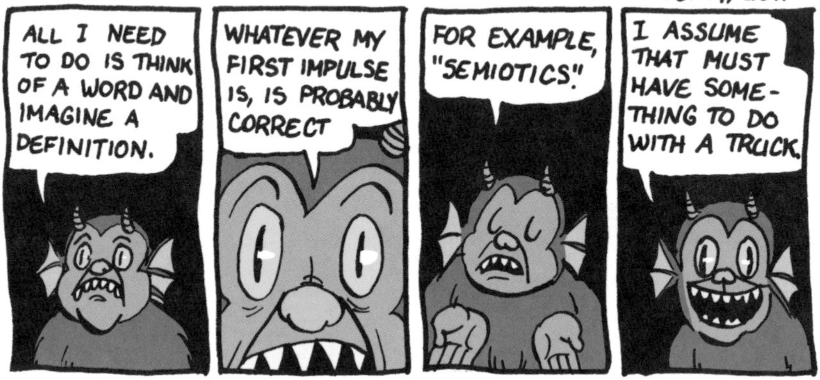
ALL I NEED TO DO IS THINK OF A WORD AND IMAGINE A DEFINITION.
WHATEVER MY FIRST IMPULSE IS, IS PROBABLY CORRECT
FOR EXAMPLE, "SEMIOTICS."
I ASSUME THAT MUST HAVE SOME-THING TO DO WITH A TRUCK.

SAT OCT 15, 2011

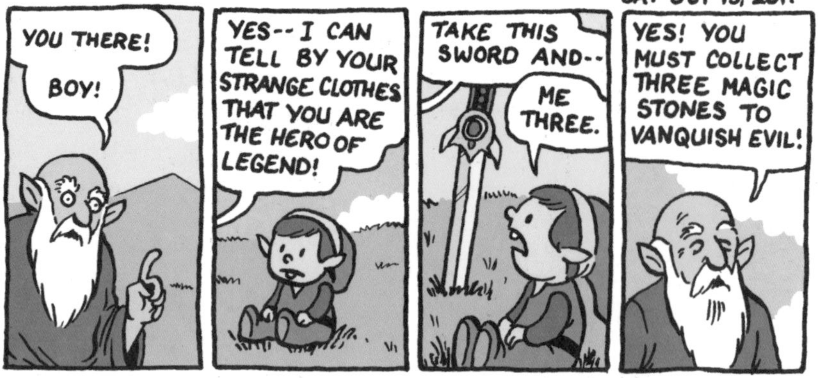
YOU THERE!
BOY!
YES-- I CAN TELL BY YOUR STRANGE CLOTHES THAT YOU ARE THE HERO OF LEGEND!
TAKE THIS SWORD AND--
ME THREE.
YES! YOU MUST COLLECT THREE MAGIC STONES TO VANQUISH EVIL!

SUN OCT 16, 2011

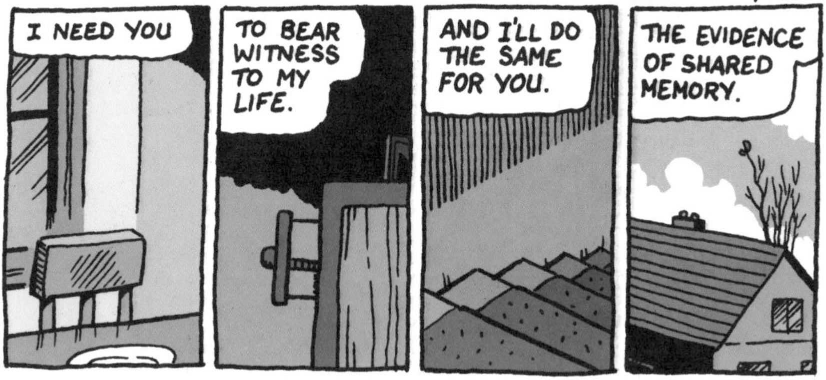
I NEED YOU
TO BEAR WITNESS TO MY LIFE.
AND I'LL DO THE SAME FOR YOU.
THE EVIDENCE OF SHARED MEMORY.

MON OCT 17, 2011

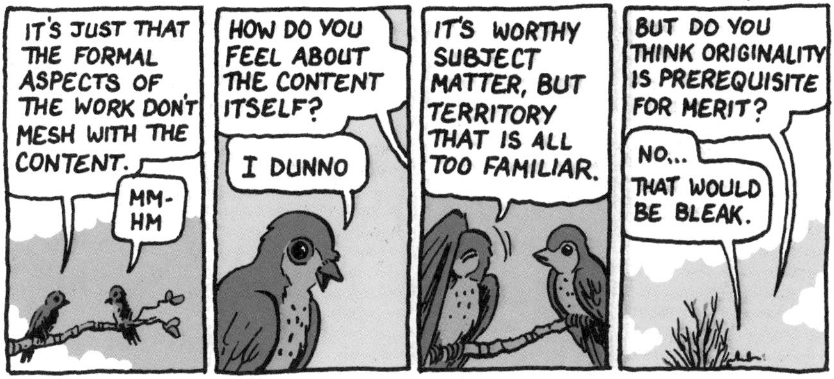
IT'S JUST THAT THE FORMAL ASPECTS OF THE WORK DON'T MESH WITH THE CONTENT.
MM-HM
HOW DO YOU FEEL ABOUT THE CONTENT ITSELF?
I DUNNO
IT'S WORTHY SUBJECT MATTER, BUT TERRITORY THAT IS ALL TOO FAMILIAR.
BUT DO YOU THINK ORIGINALITY IS PREREQUISITE FOR MERIT?
NO...
THAT WOULD BE BLEAK.

TUE OCT 18, 2011

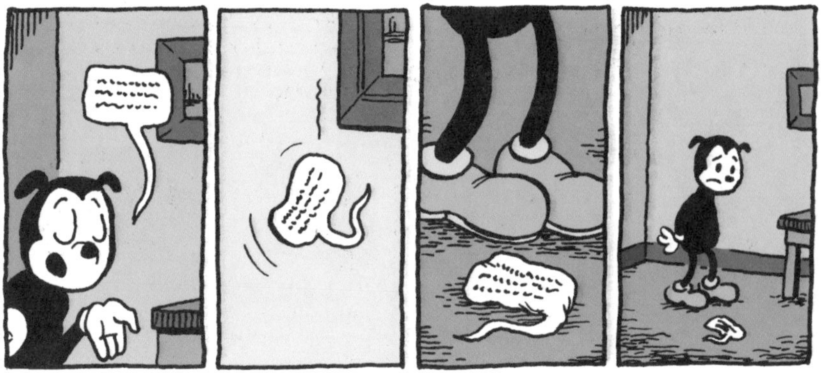

I SHOULD JUST TAKE THIS STUPID MASK OFF

WED OCT 19, 2011

THAT WOULD SHOW THEM.

THEY SAY PEOPLE START TO LOOK LIKE THEIR PETS AFTER A WHILE.

HA HA! REALLY?

THU OCT 20, 2011

WE SHOULDN'T HAVE STARTED EATING HIM.

WELL, I THOUGHT HE WAS DEAD!

cough

cough

THIS ISN'T SO BAD.

AT LEAST I DON'T HAVE TO GO TO SCHOOL.

FRI OCT 21, 2011

MOM, CAN I HAVE A GLASS OF WATER?

98

SAT OCT 22, 2011

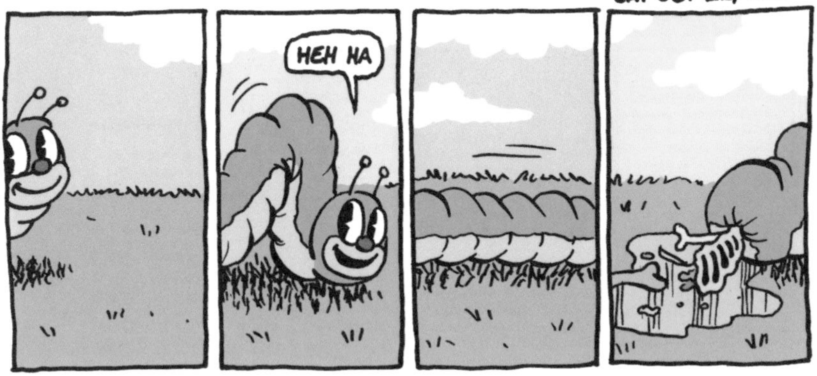
HEH HA

SUN OCT 23, 2011

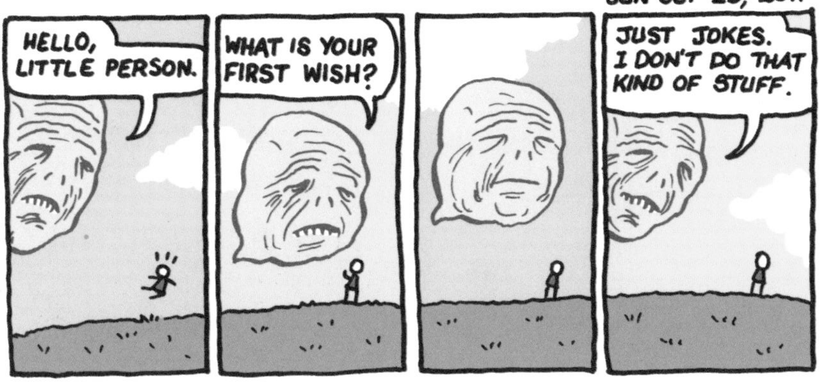
HELLO, LITTLE PERSON.
WHAT IS YOUR FIRST WISH?
JUST JOKES. I DON'T DO THAT KIND OF STUFF.

MON OCT, 24, 2011

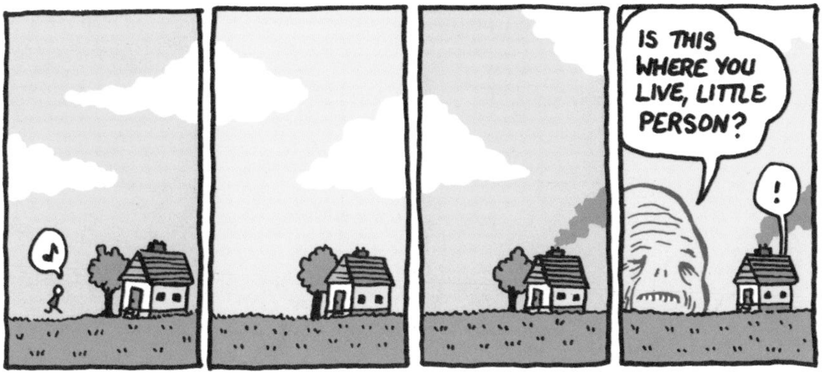
IS THIS WHERE YOU LIVE, LITTLE PERSON?
!

TUE OCT 25, 2011

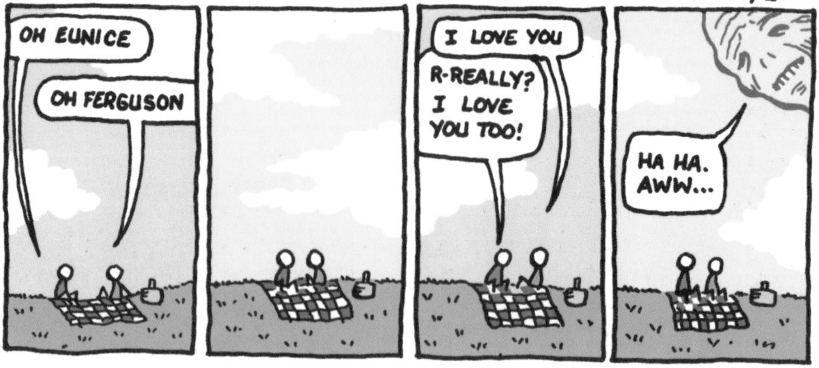
OH EUNICE
OH FERGUSON
I LOVE YOU
R-REALLY? I LOVE YOU TOO!
HA HA. AWW...

WED OCT 26, 2011

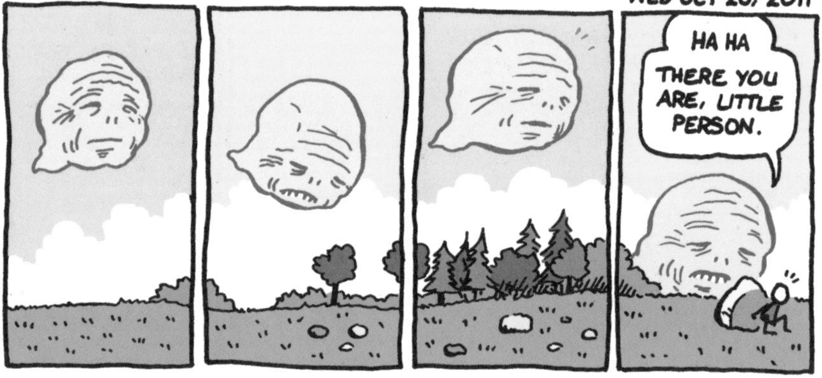
HA HA
THERE YOU ARE, LITTLE PERSON.

THU OCT 27, 2011

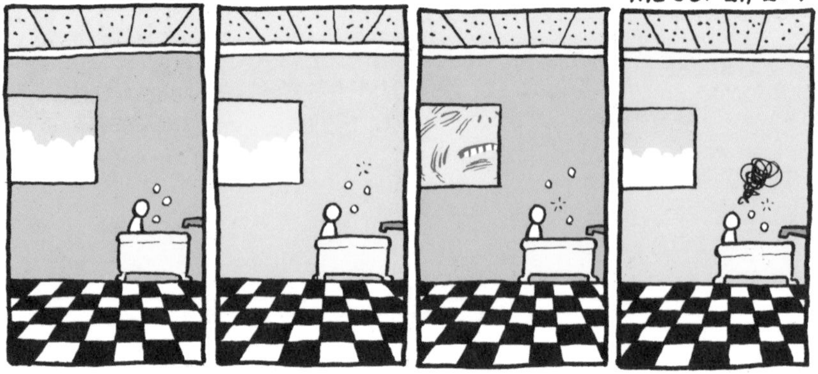

FRI OCT 28, 2011

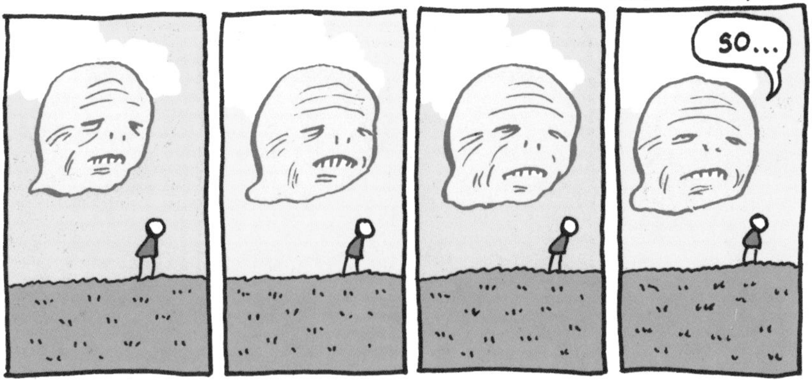
SO...

SAT OCT 29, 2011

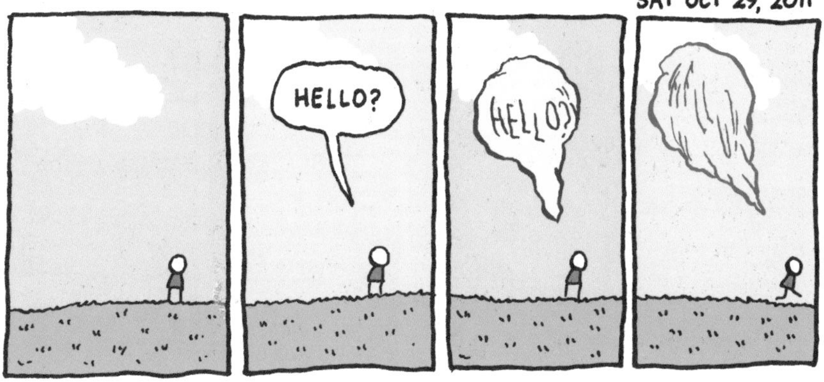
HELLO?
HELLO?

SUN OCT 30, 2011

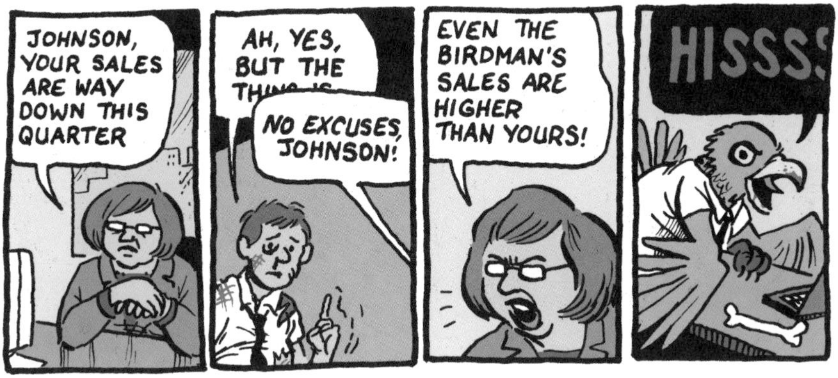
JOHNSON, YOUR SALES ARE WAY DOWN THIS QUARTER
AH, YES, BUT THE
NO EXCUSES, JOHNSON!
EVEN THE BIRDMAN'S SALES ARE HIGHER THAN YOURS!
HISSS

MON OCT 31, 2011

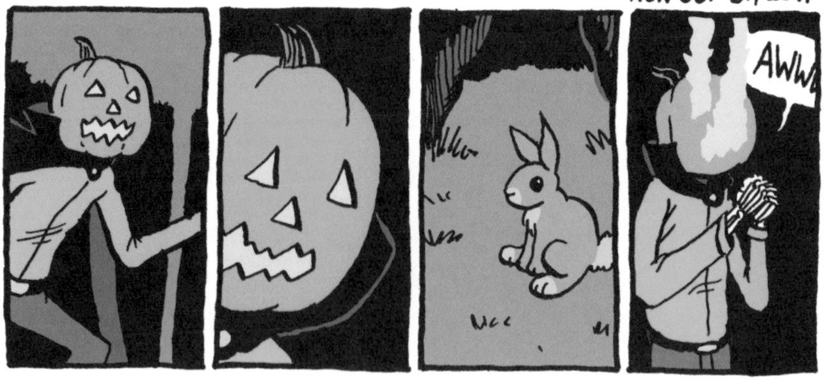
AWW

TUE NOV 1, 2011

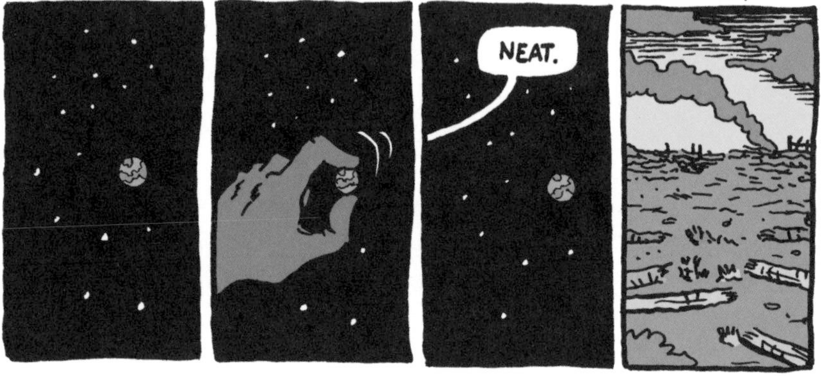
NEAT.

WED NOV 2, 2011

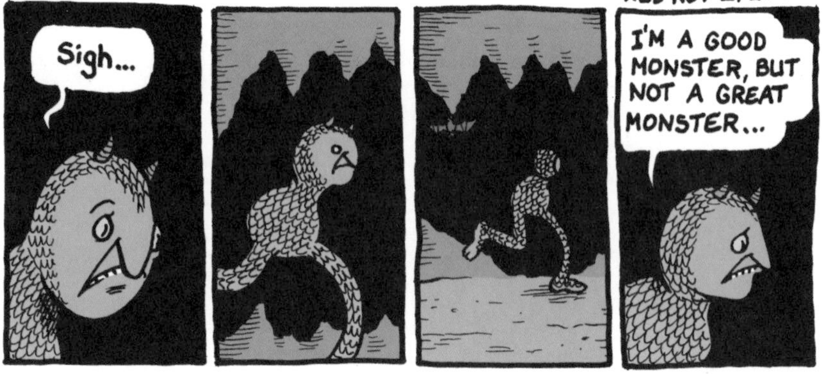
Sigh...
I'M A GOOD MONSTER, BUT NOT A GREAT MONSTER...

THU NOV 3, 2011

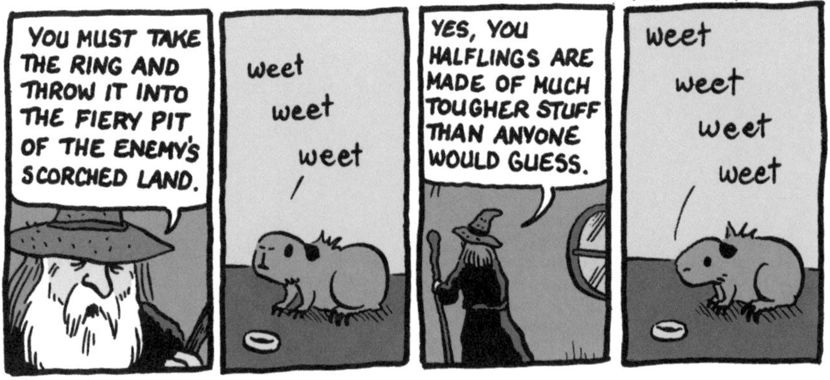
YOU MUST TAKE THE RING AND THROW IT INTO THE FIERY PIT OF THE ENEMY'S SCORCHED LAND.
weet weet weet
YES, YOU HALFLINGS ARE MADE OF MUCH TOUGHER STUFF THAN ANYONE WOULD GUESS.
weet weet weet weet

FRI NOV 4, 2011

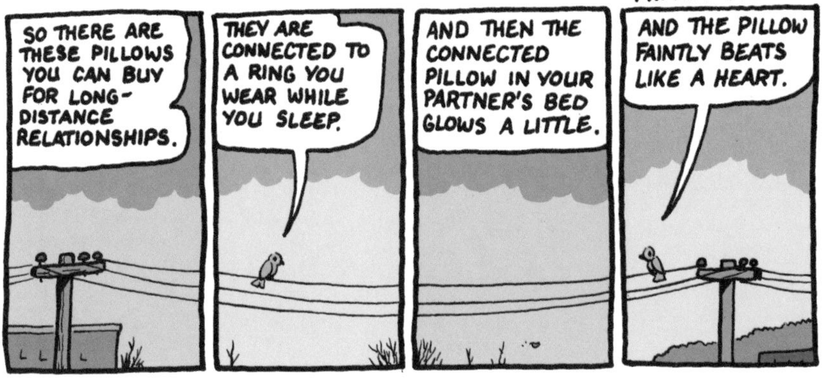
SO THERE ARE THESE PILLOWS YOU CAN BUY FOR LONG-DISTANCE RELATIONSHIPS.
THEY ARE CONNECTED TO A RING YOU WEAR WHILE YOU SLEEP.
AND THEN THE CONNECTED PILLOW IN YOUR PARTNER'S BED GLOWS A LITTLE.
AND THE PILLOW FAINTLY BEATS LIKE A HEART.

SAT NOV 5, 2011

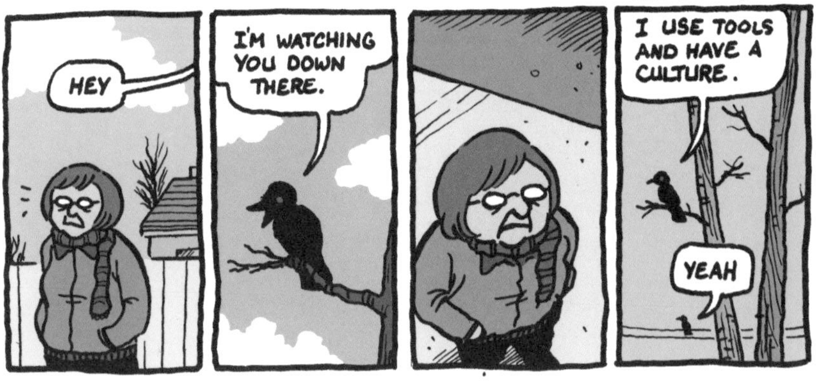
HEY
I'M WATCHING YOU DOWN THERE.
I USE TOOLS AND HAVE A CULTURE.
YEAH

SUN NOV 6, 2011

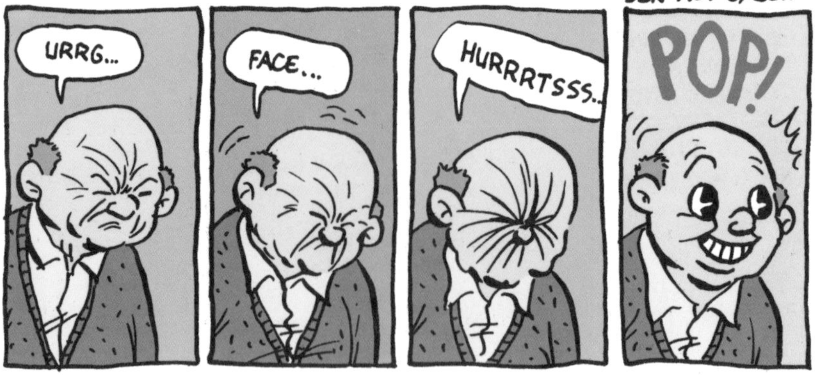
URRG...
FACE...
HURRRTSSS...
POP!

MON NOV 7, 2011

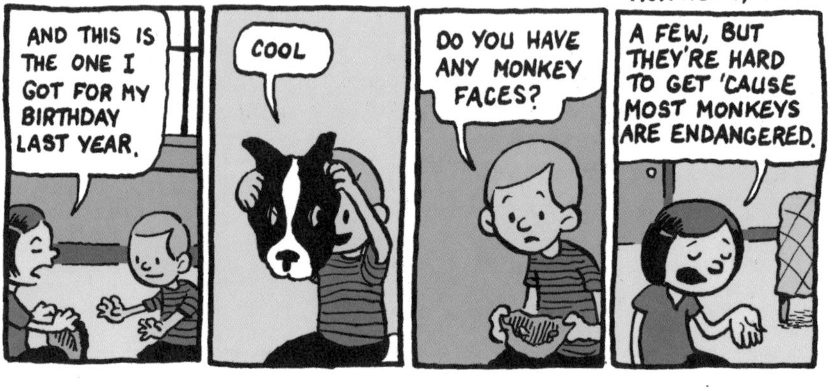
AND THIS IS THE ONE I GOT FOR MY BIRTHDAY LAST YEAR.
COOL
DO YOU HAVE ANY MONKEY FACES?
A FEW, BUT THEY'RE HARD TO GET 'CAUSE MOST MONKEYS ARE ENDANGERED.

TUE NOV 8, 2011

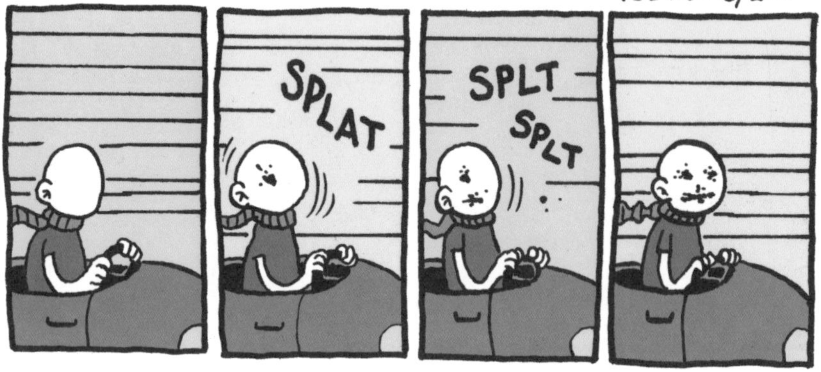
SPLAT
SPLT
SPLT

WED NOV 9, 2011

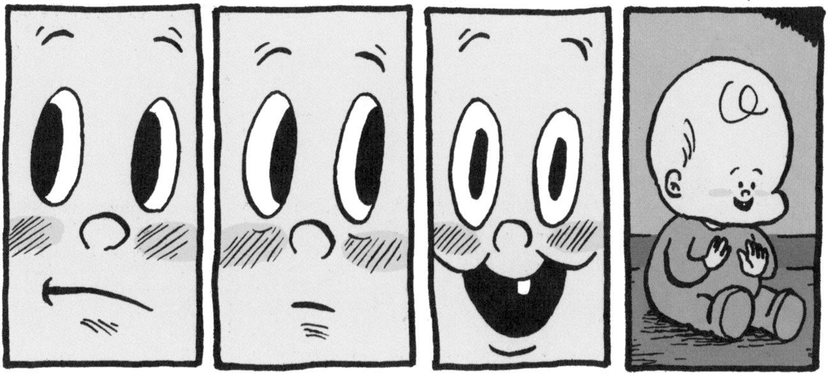

THU NOV 10, 2011

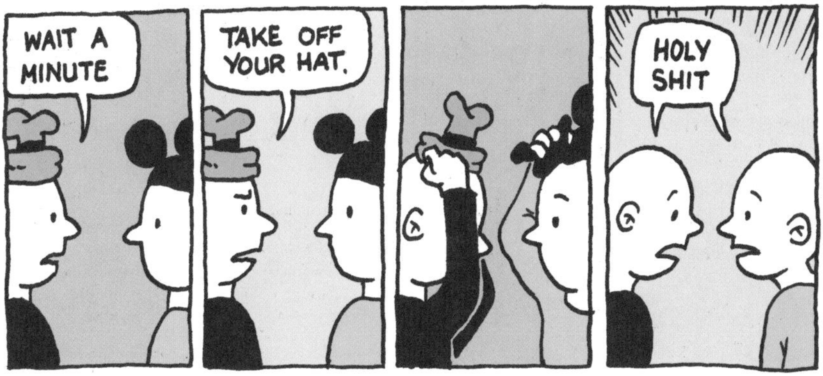
WAIT A MINUTE
TAKE OFF YOUR HAT.
HOLY SHIT

FRI NOV 11, 2011

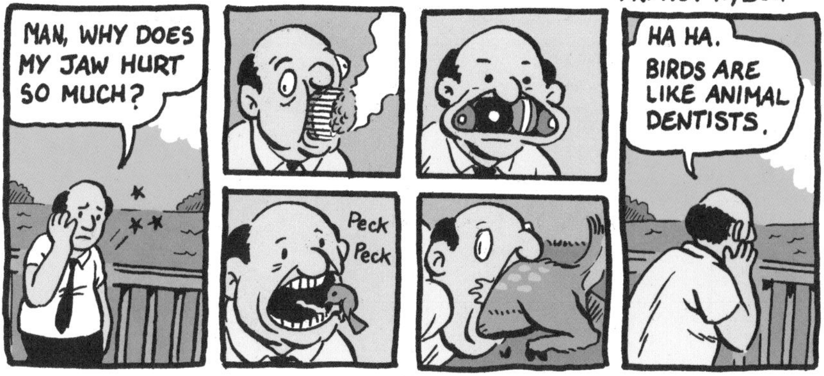
MAN, WHY DOES MY JAW HURT SO MUCH?
Peck Peck
HA HA.
BIRDS ARE LIKE ANIMAL DENTISTS.

SAT NOV 12, 2011

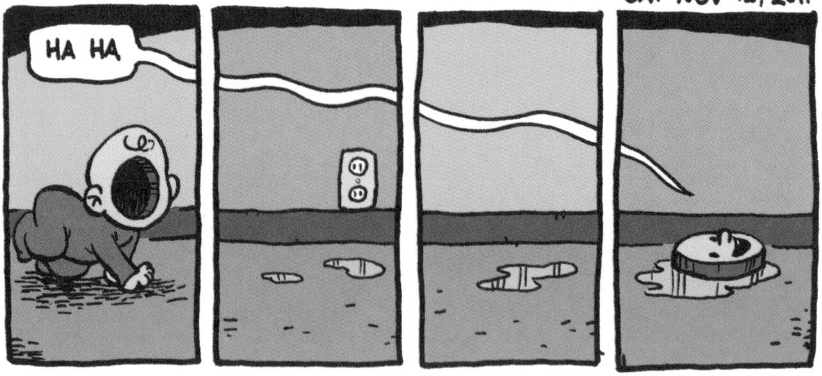
HA HA

SUN NOV 13, 2011

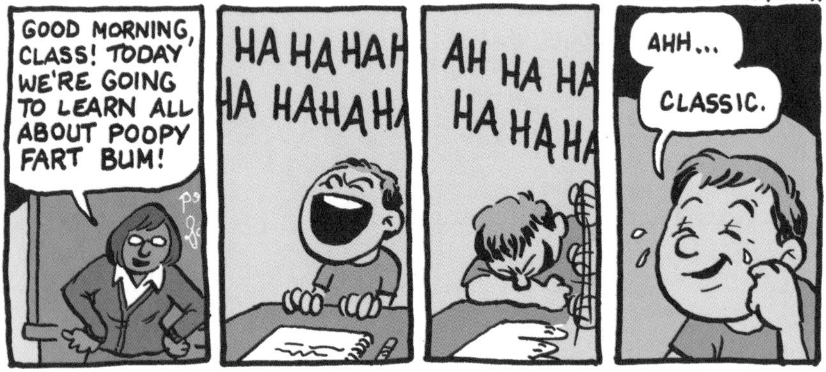
GOOD MORNING, CLASS! TODAY WE'RE GOING TO LEARN ALL ABOUT POOPY FART BUM!
HA HA HAH
HA HAHAH
AH HA HA
HA HA HA
AHH...
CLASSIC.

MON NOV 14, 2011

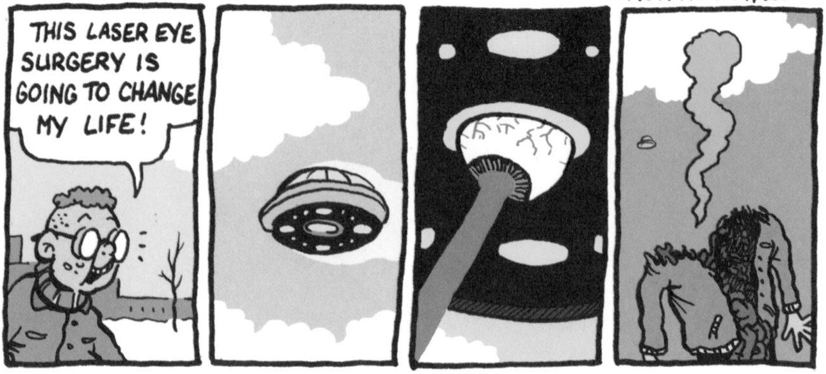
THIS LASER EYE SURGERY IS GOING TO CHANGE MY LIFE!

TUE NOV 15, 2011

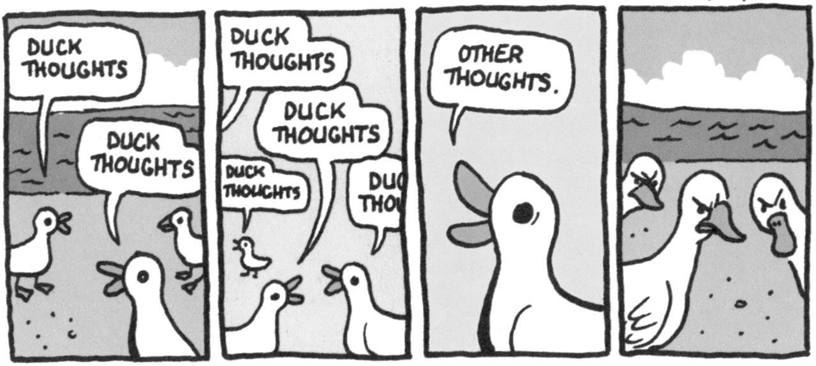
DUCK THOUGHTS
DUCK THOUGHTS
DUCK THOUGHTS
DUCK THOUGHTS
DUCK THOUGHTS
OTHER THOUGHTS.

WED NOV 16, 2011

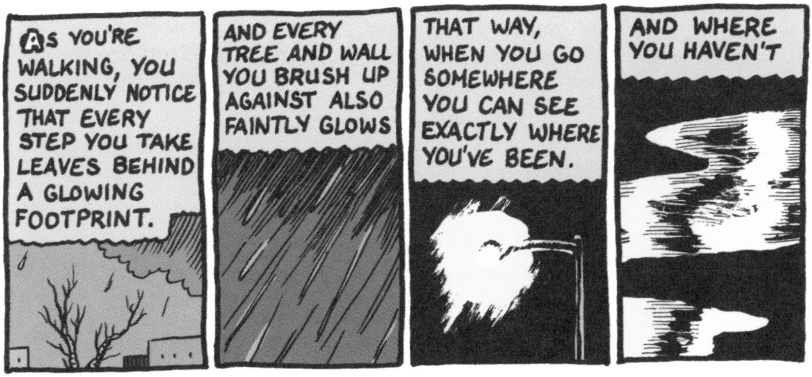
AS YOU'RE WALKING, YOU SUDDENLY NOTICE THAT EVERY STEP YOU TAKE LEAVES BEHIND A GLOWING FOOTPRINT.
AND EVERY TREE AND WALL YOU BRUSH UP AGAINST ALSO FAINTLY GLOWS
THAT WAY, WHEN YOU GO SOMEWHERE YOU CAN SEE EXACTLY WHERE YOU'VE BEEN.
AND WHERE YOU HAVEN'T

THU NOV 17, 2011

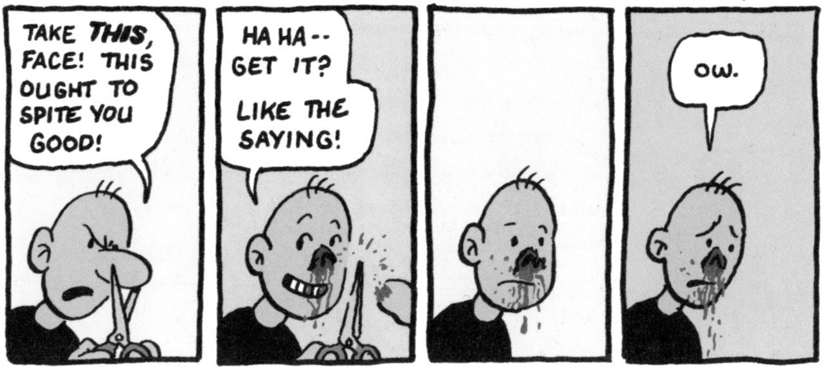
TAKE THIS, FACE! THIS OUGHT TO SPITE YOU GOOD!
HA HA -- GET IT?
LIKE THE SAYING!
OW.

FRI NOV 18, 2011

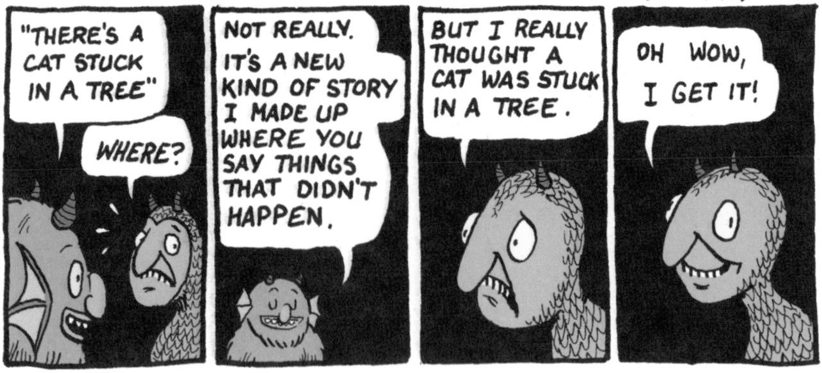
"THERE'S A CAT STUCK IN A TREE"
WHERE?
NOT REALLY. IT'S A NEW KIND OF STORY I MADE UP WHERE YOU SAY THINGS THAT DIDN'T HAPPEN.
BUT I REALLY THOUGHT A CAT WAS STUCK IN A TREE.
OH WOW, I GET IT!

SAT NOV 19, 2011

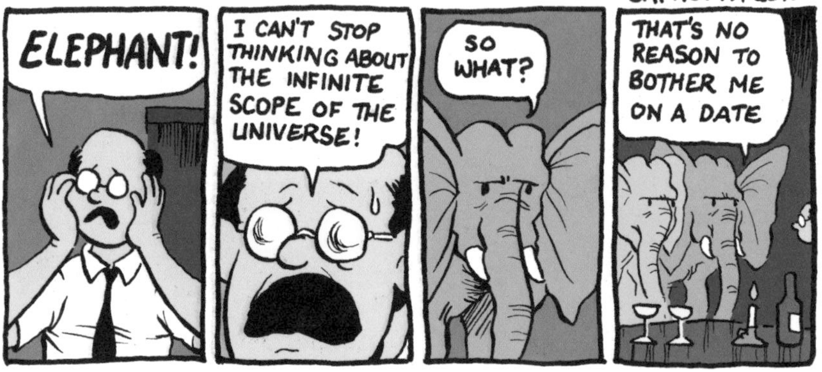
ELEPHANT!
I CAN'T STOP THINKING ABOUT THE INFINITE SCOPE OF THE UNIVERSE!
SO WHAT?
THAT'S NO REASON TO BOTHER ME ON A DATE

SUN NOV 20, 2011

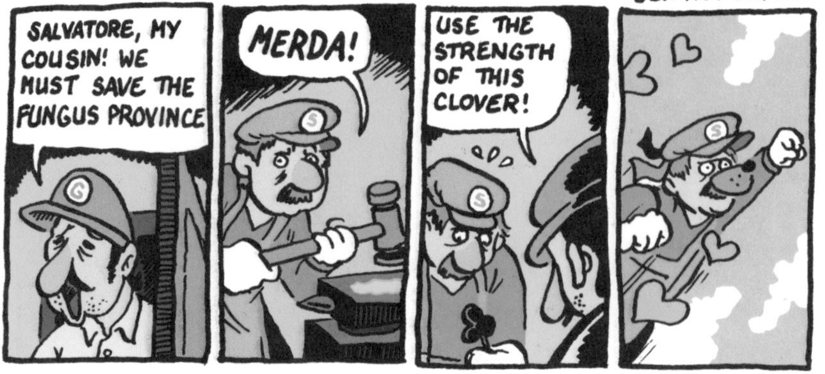
SALVATORE, MY COUSIN! WE MUST SAVE THE FUNGUS PROVINCE
MERDA!
USE THE STRENGTH OF THIS CLOVER!

MON NOV 21, 2011

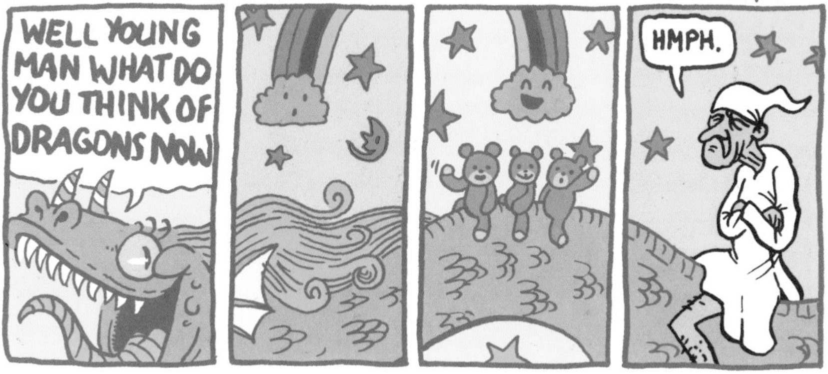
WELL YOUNG MAN WHAT DO YOU THINK OF DRAGONS NOW
HMPH.

TUE NOV 22, 2011

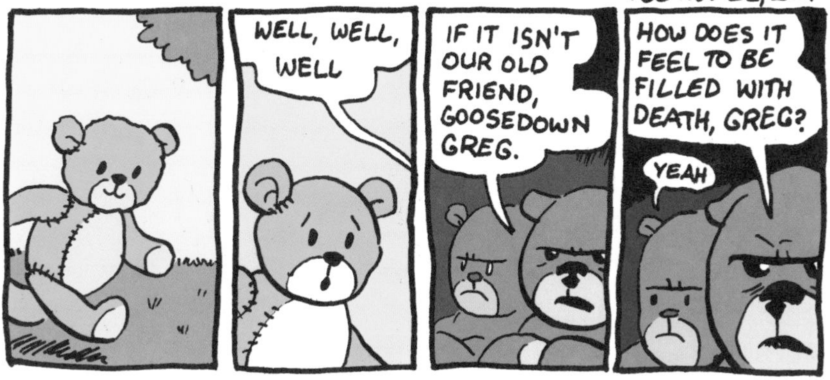
WELL, WELL, WELL
IF IT ISN'T OUR OLD FRIEND, GOOSEDOWN GREG.
HOW DOES IT FEEL TO BE FILLED WITH DEATH, GREG?
YEAH

WED NOV 23, 2011

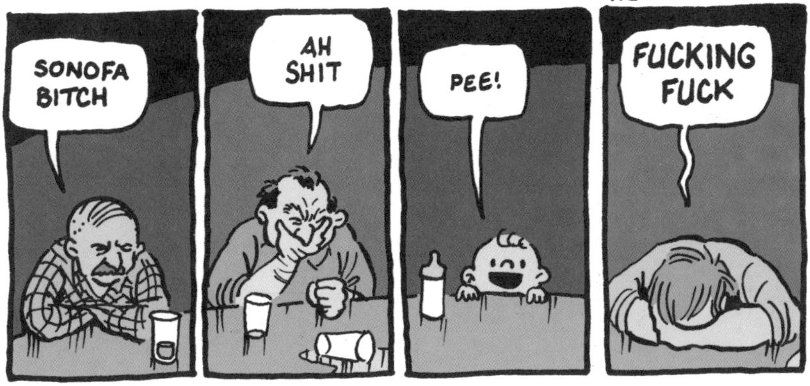
SONOFA BITCH
AH SHIT
PEE!
FUCKING FUCK

THU NOV 24, 2011

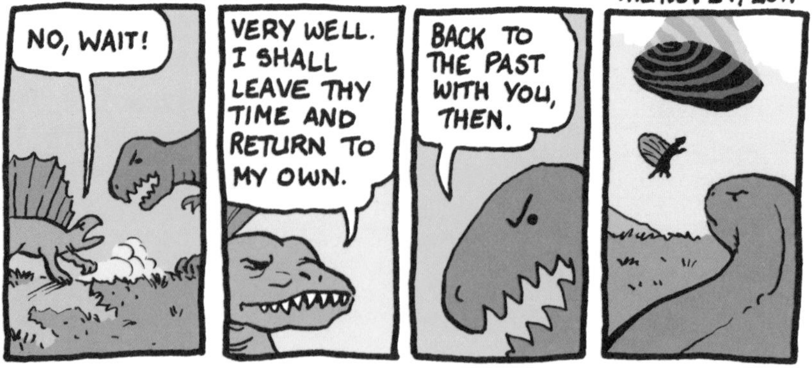
NO, WAIT!
VERY WELL. I SHALL LEAVE THY TIME AND RETURN TO MY OWN.
BACK TO THE PAST WITH YOU, THEN.

FRI NOV 25, 2011

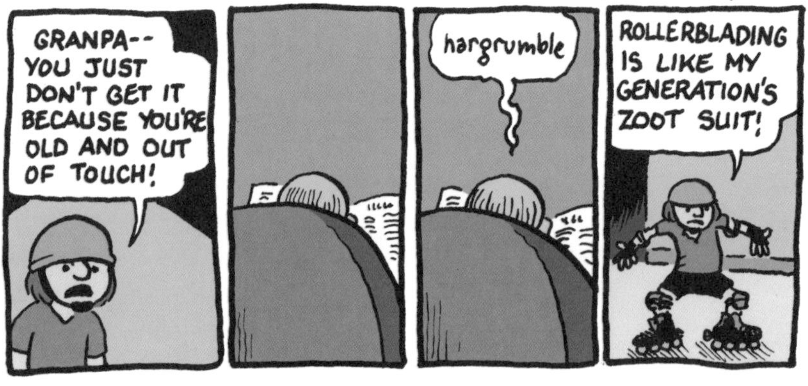
GRANPA-- YOU JUST DON'T GET IT BECAUSE YOU'RE OLD AND OUT OF TOUCH!
hargrumble
ROLLERBLADING IS LIKE MY GENERATION'S ZOOT SUIT!

SAT NOV 26, 2011

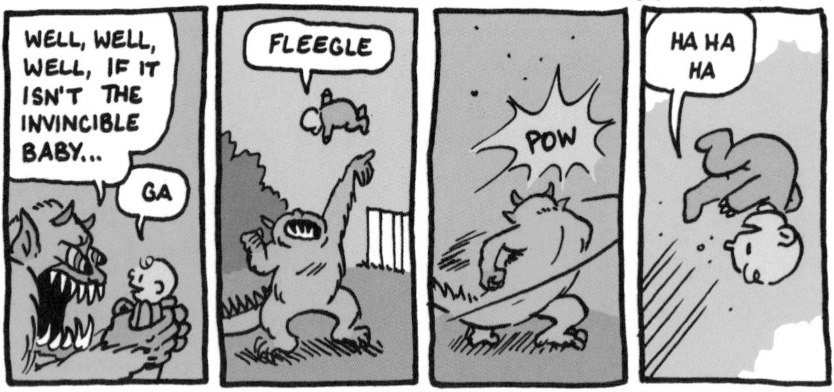
WELL, WELL, WELL, IF IT ISN'T THE INVINCIBLE BABY...
GA
FLEEGLE
POW
HA HA HA

SUN NOV 27, 2011

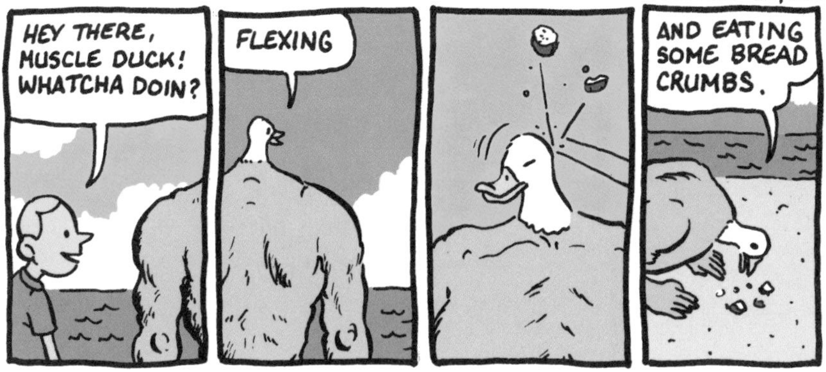
HEY THERE, MUSCLE DUCK! WHATCHA DOIN?
FLEXING
AND EATING SOME BREAD CRUMBS.

MAMMALS

MON NOV 28, 2011

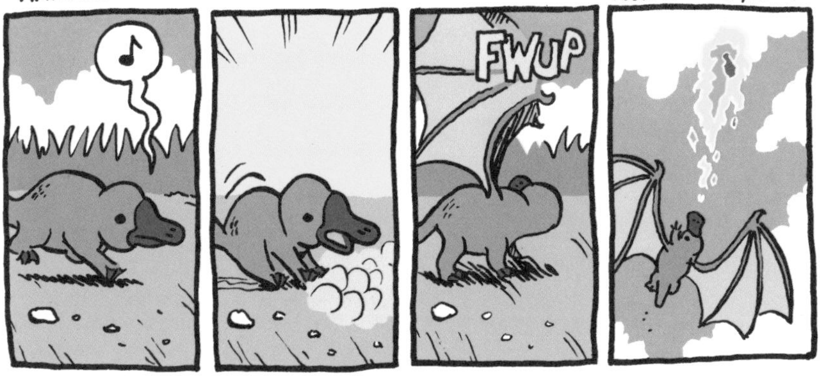
FWUP

TUE NOV 29, 2011

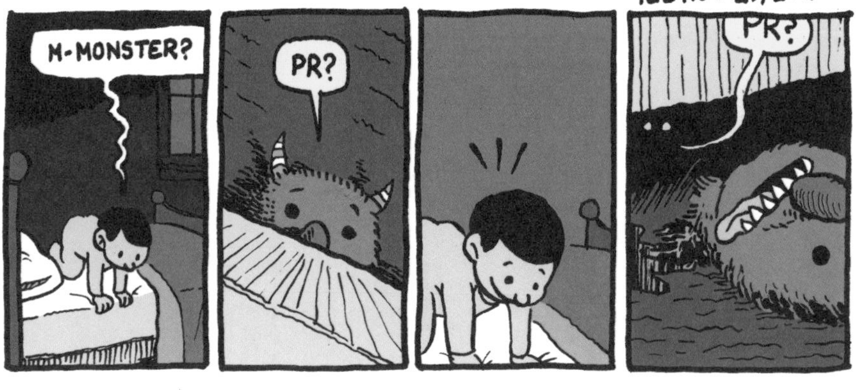
M-MONSTER?
PR?
PR?

WED NOV 30, 2011

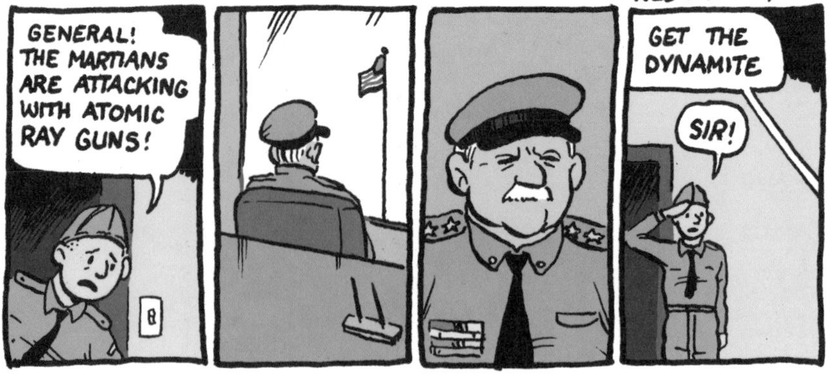
GENERAL! THE MARTIANS ARE ATTACKING WITH ATOMIC RAY GUNS!
GET THE DYNAMITE
SIR!

THU DEC 1, 2011

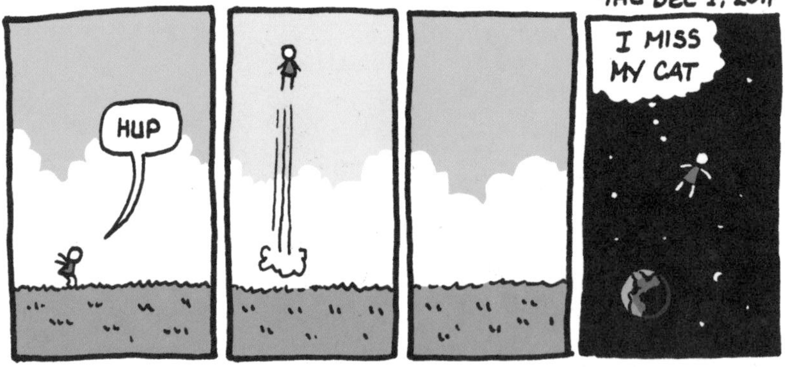
HUP
I MISS MY CAT

FRI DEC 2, 2011

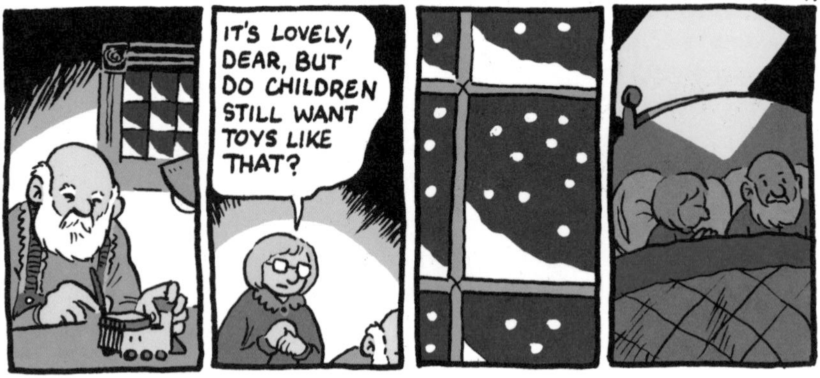
IT'S LOVELY, DEAR, BUT DO CHILDREN STILL WANT TOYS LIKE THAT?

SAT DEC 3, 2011

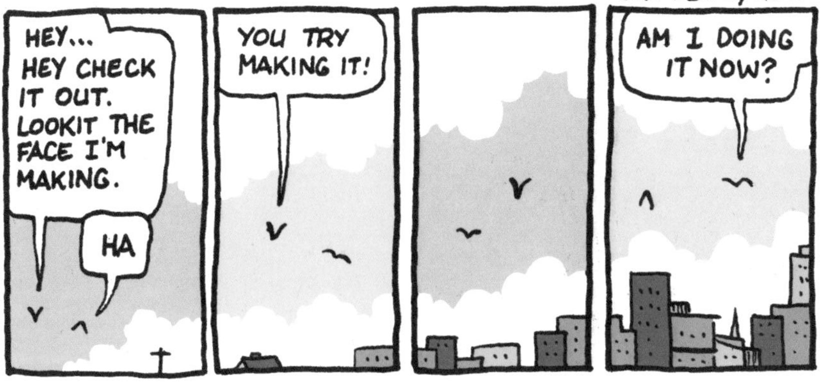
HEY... HEY CHECK IT OUT. LOOKIT THE FACE I'M MAKING.
HA
YOU TRY MAKING IT!
AM I DOING IT NOW?

SUN DEC 4, 2011

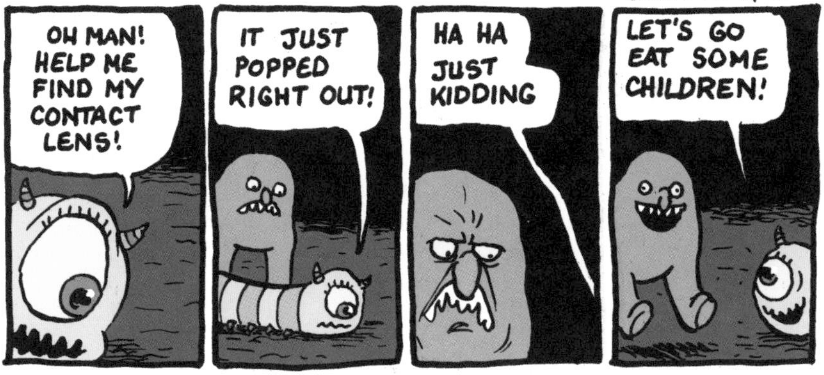
OH MAN! HELP ME FIND MY CONTACT LENS!
IT JUST POPPED RIGHT OUT!
HA HA JUST KIDDING
LET'S GO EAT SOME CHILDREN!

MON DEC 5, 2011

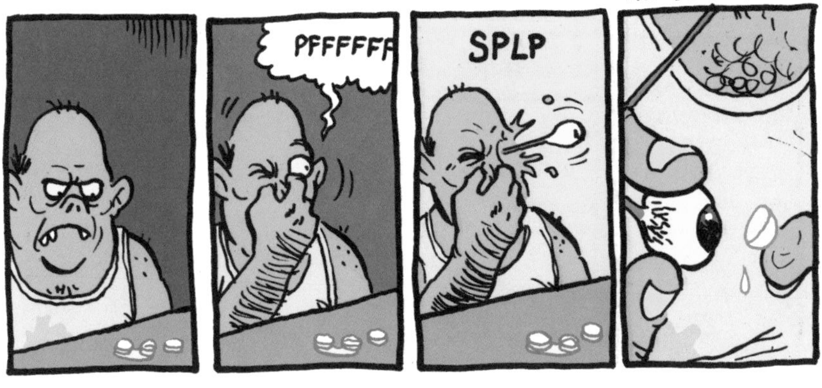
PFFFFFF
SPLP

TUE DEC 6, 2011

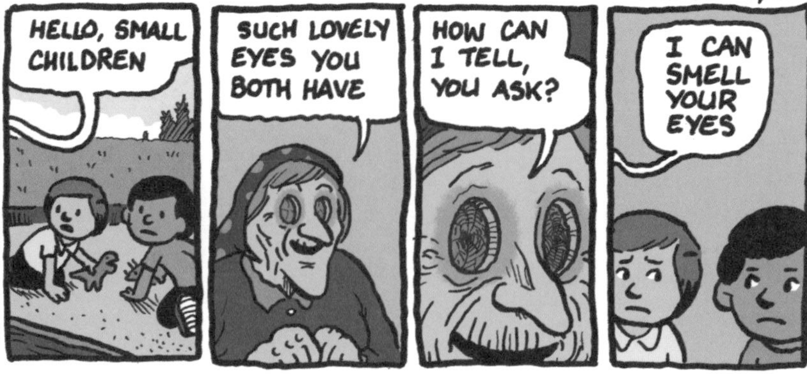
HELLO, SMALL CHILDREN
SUCH LOVELY EYES YOU BOTH HAVE
HOW CAN I TELL, YOU ASK?
I CAN SMELL YOUR EYES

RAIN

WED DEC 7, 2011

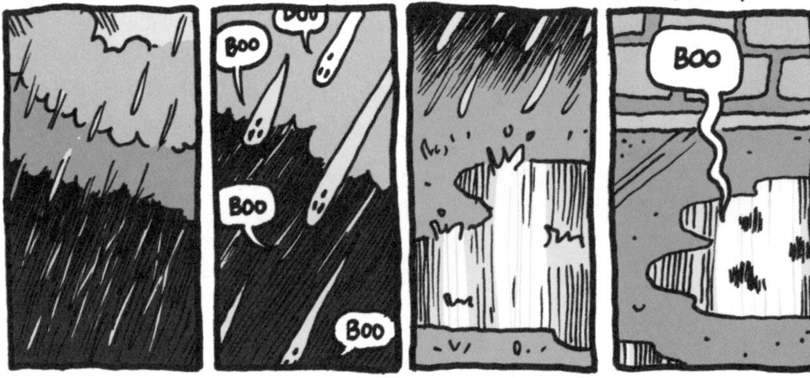
BOO
BOO
BOO
BOO

THU DEC 8, 2011

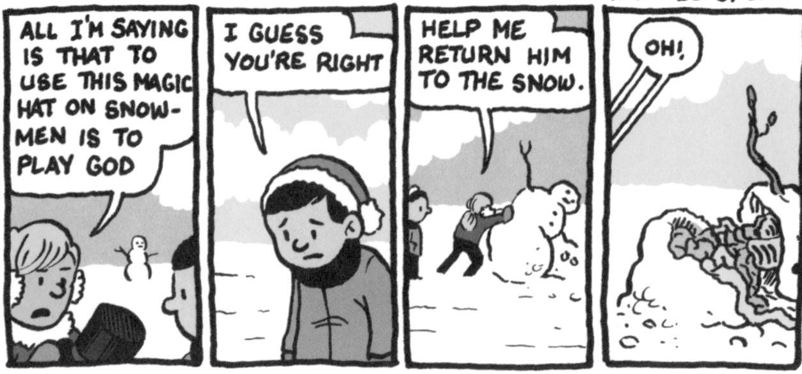
ALL I'M SAYING IS THAT TO USE THIS MAGIC HAT ON SNOW-MEN IS TO PLAY GOD
I GUESS YOU'RE RIGHT
HELP ME RETURN HIM TO THE SNOW.
OH!

FIREMAN

FRI DEC 9, 2011

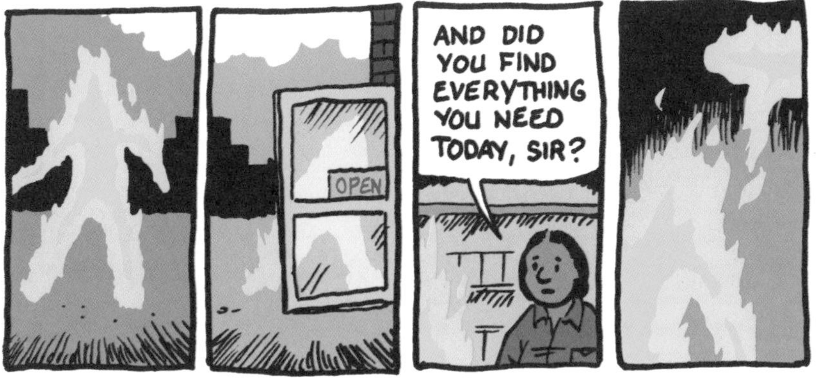
OPEN
AND DID YOU FIND EVERYTHING YOU NEED TODAY, SIR?

SAT DEC 10, 2011

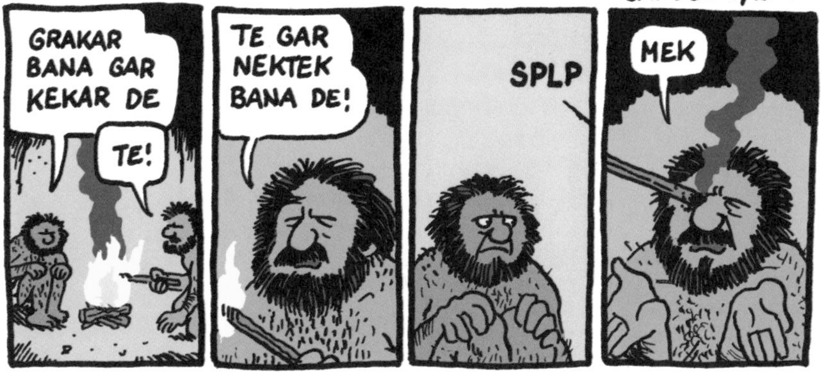
GRAKAR BANA GAR KEKAR DE
TE!
TE GAR NEKTEK BANA DE!
SPLP
MEK

SUN DEC 11, 2011

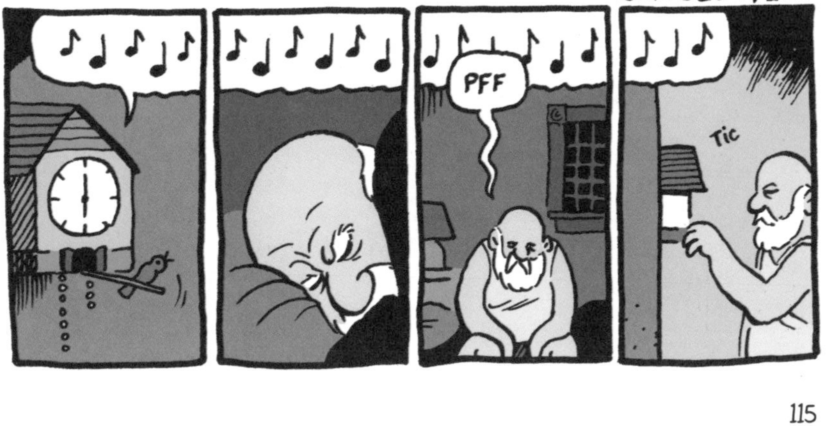
PFF
Tic

MON DEC 12, 2011

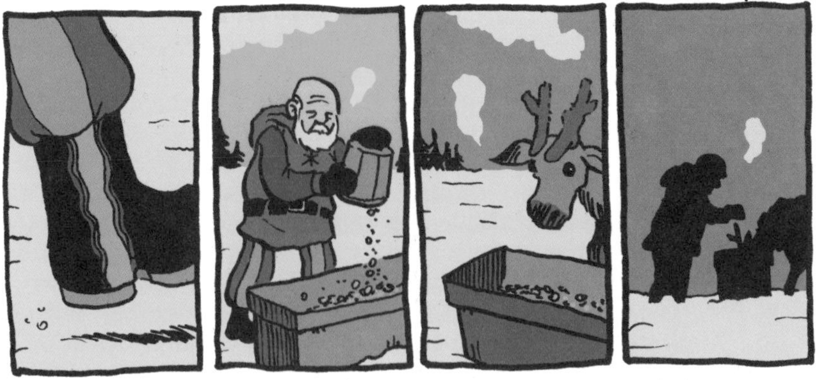

TUE DEC 13, 2011

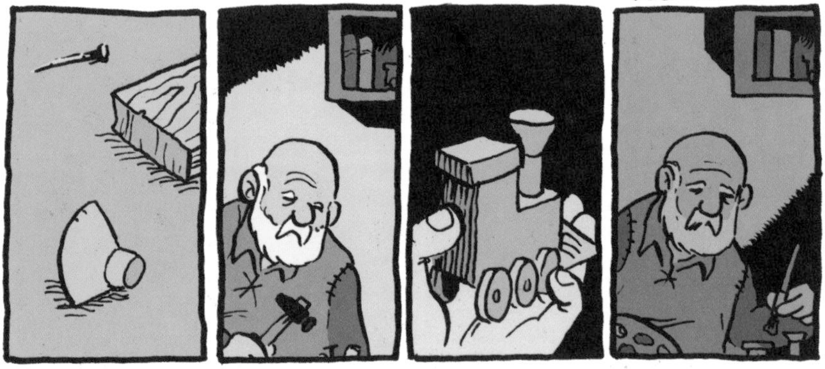

WED DEC 14, 2011

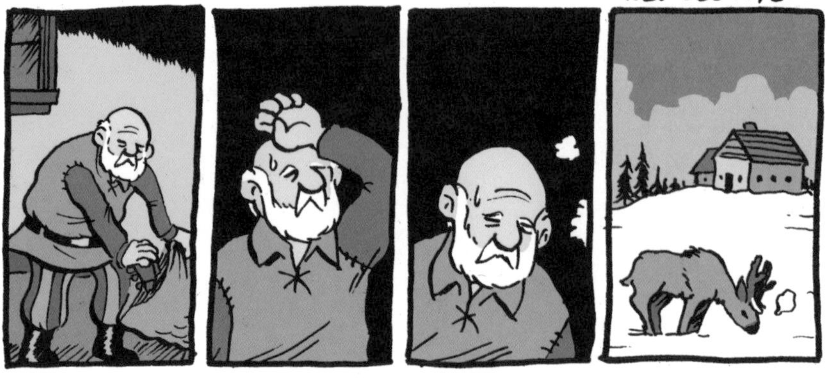

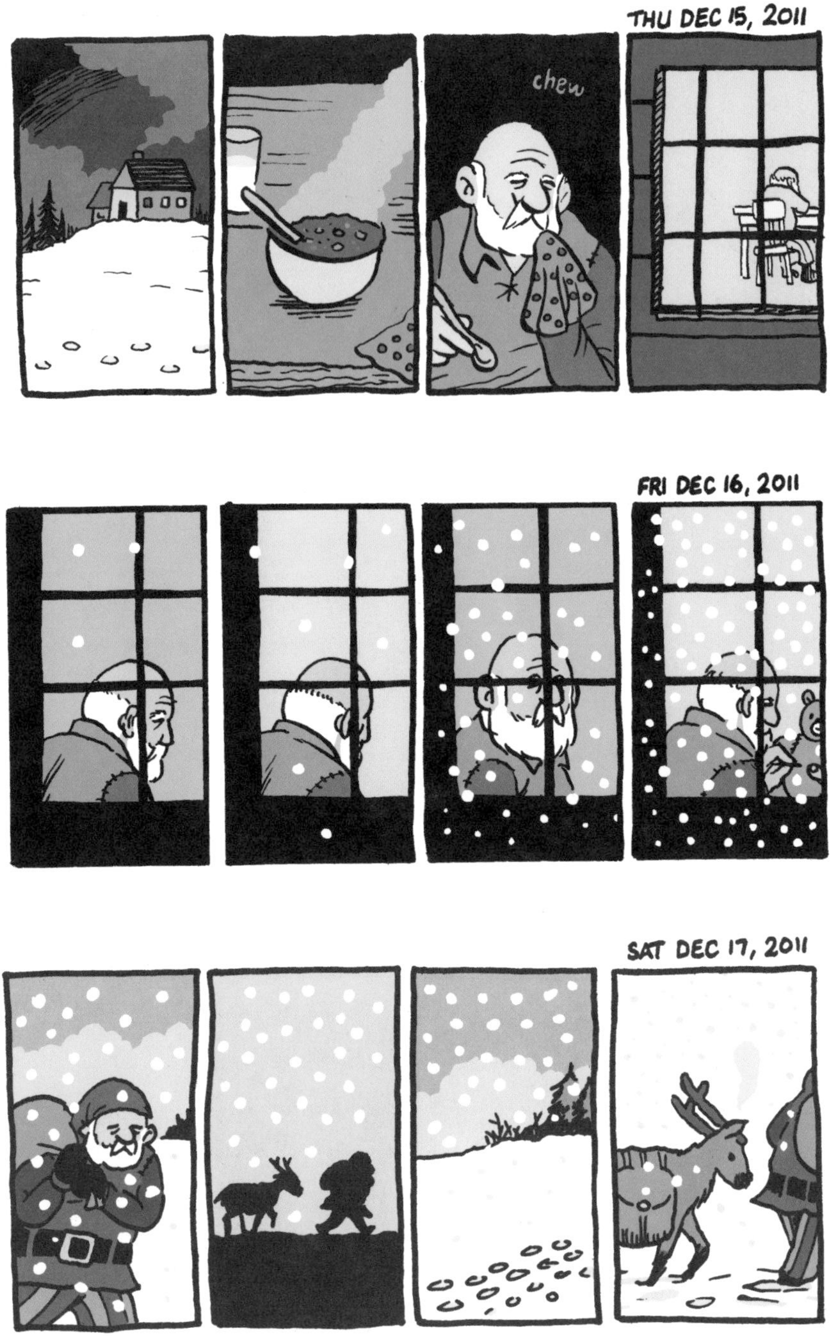
THU DEC 15, 2011
chew
FRI DEC 16, 2011
SAT DEC 17, 2011

SUN DEC 18, 2011

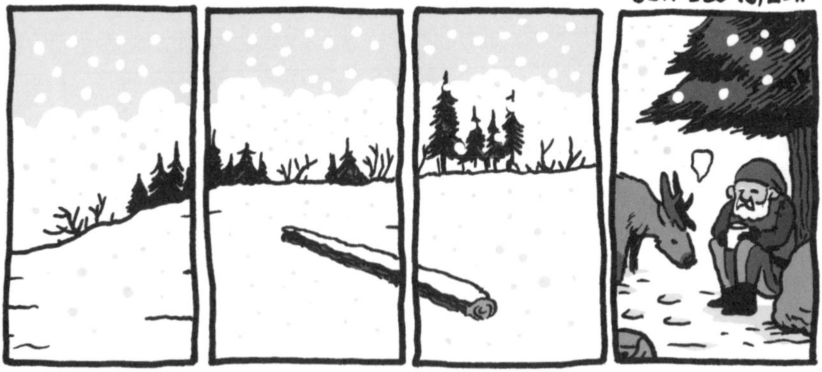

MON DEC 19, 2011

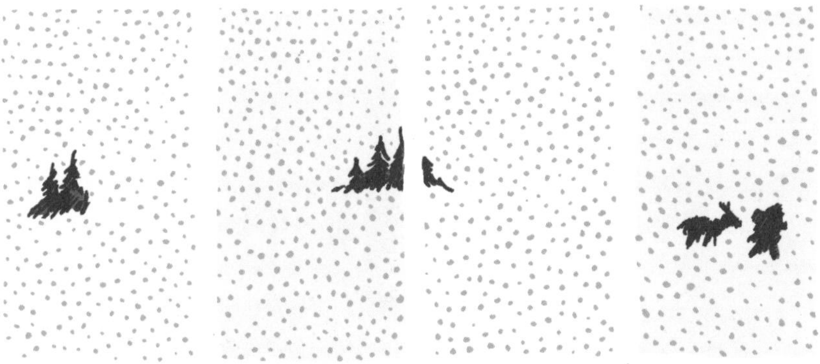

TUE DEC 20, 2011

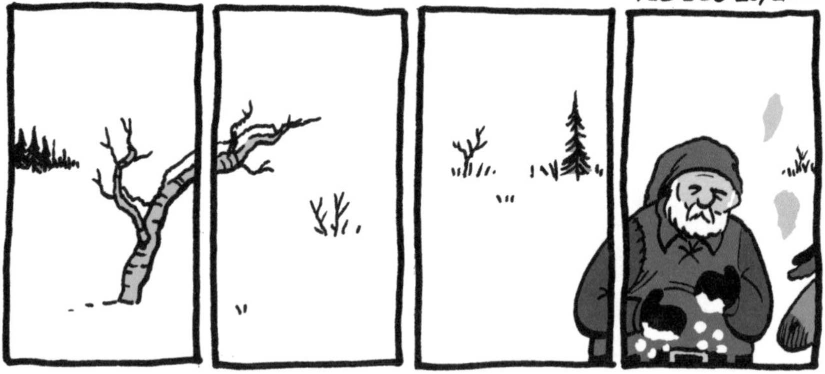

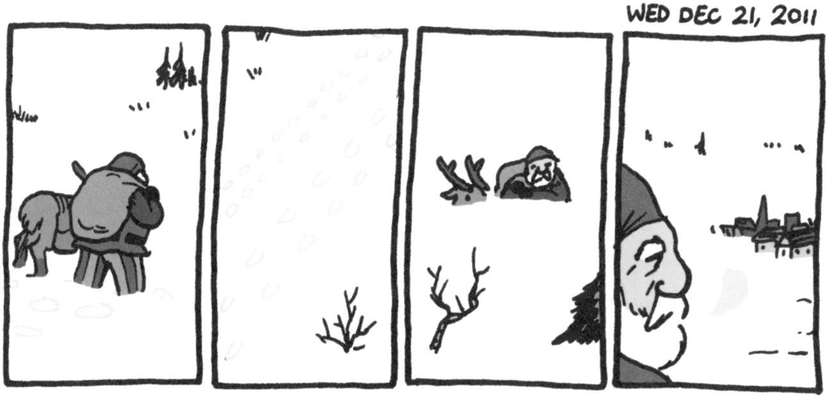
WED DEC 21, 2011

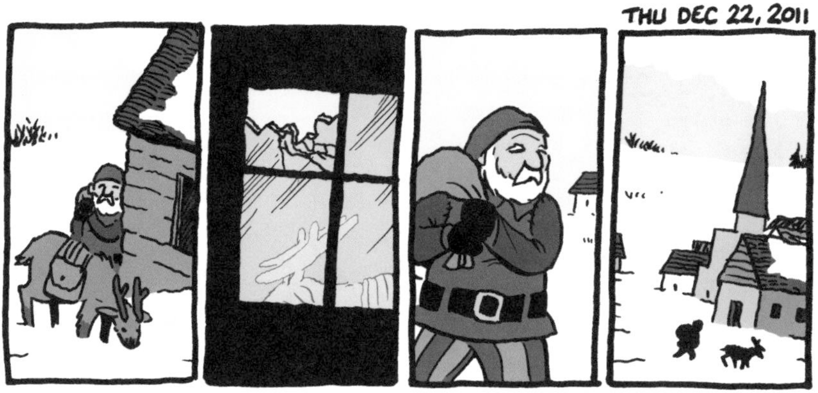
THU DEC 22, 2011

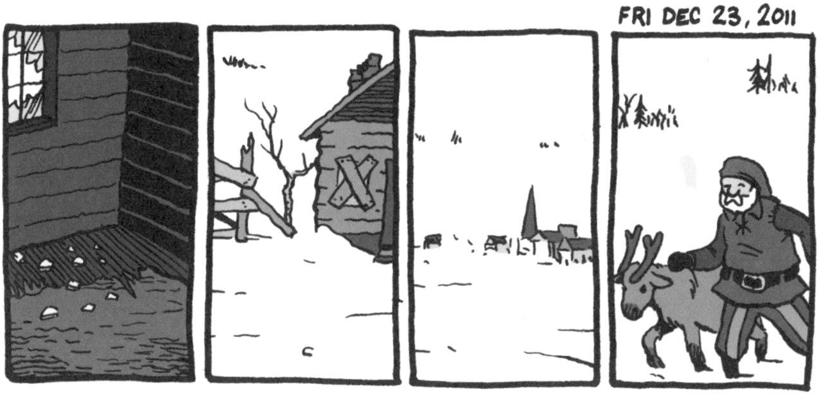
FRI DEC 23, 2011

SAT DEC 24, 2011

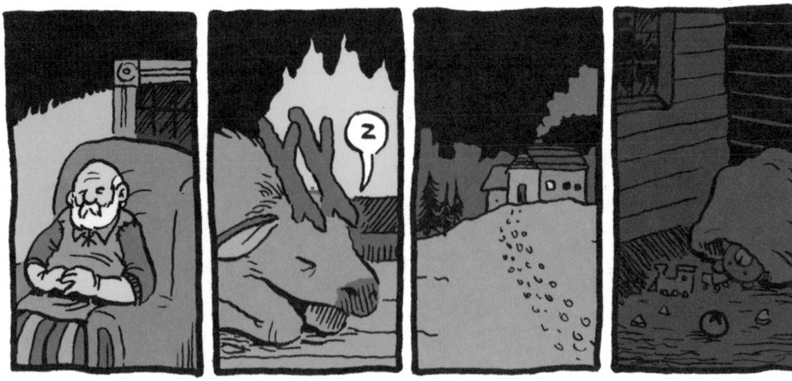
Z

SUN DEC 25, 2011

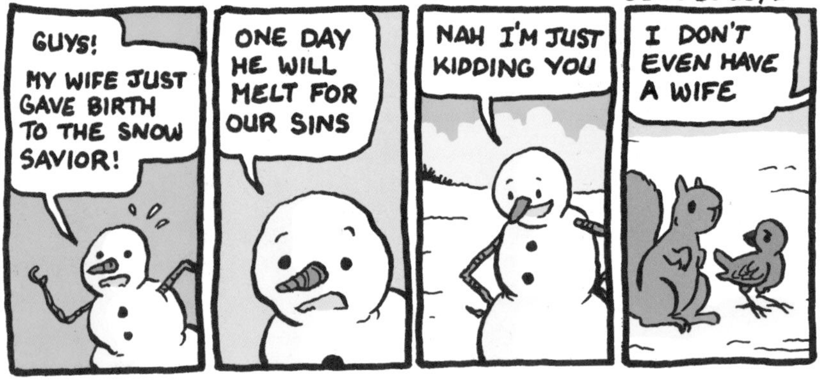
GUYS! MY WIFE JUST GAVE BIRTH TO THE SNOW SAVIOR!
ONE DAY HE WILL MELT FOR OUR SINS
NAH I'M JUST KIDDING YOU
I DON'T EVEN HAVE A WIFE

MON DEC 26, 2011

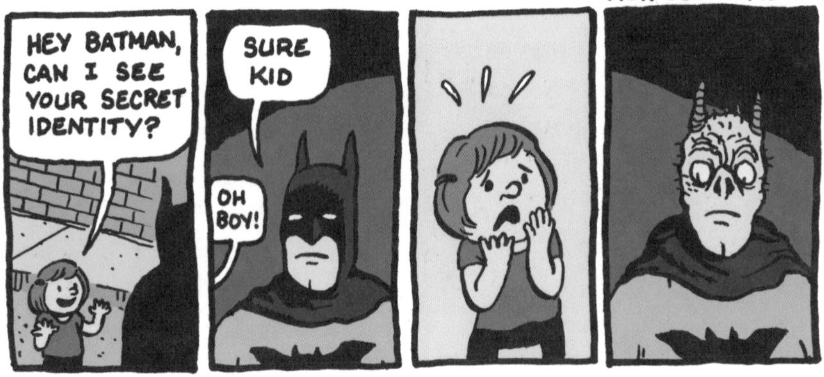
HEY BATMAN, CAN I SEE YOUR SECRET IDENTITY?
SURE KID
OH BOY!

TUE DEC 27, 2011

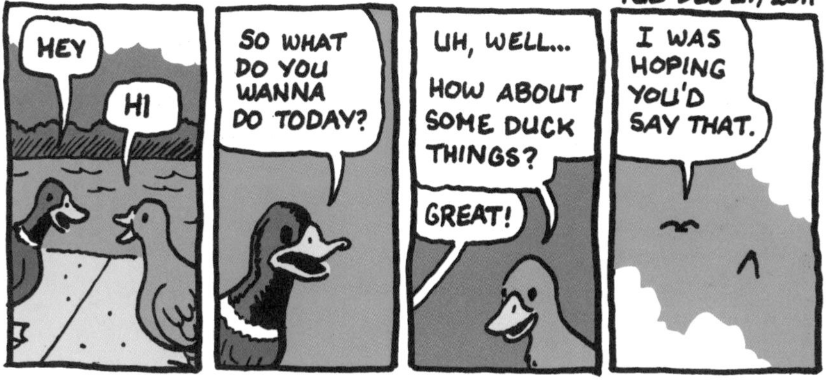
HEY
HI
SO WHAT DO YOU WANNA DO TODAY?
UH, WELL...
HOW ABOUT SOME DUCK THINGS?
GREAT!
I WAS HOPING YOU'D SAY THAT.

WED DEC 28, 2011

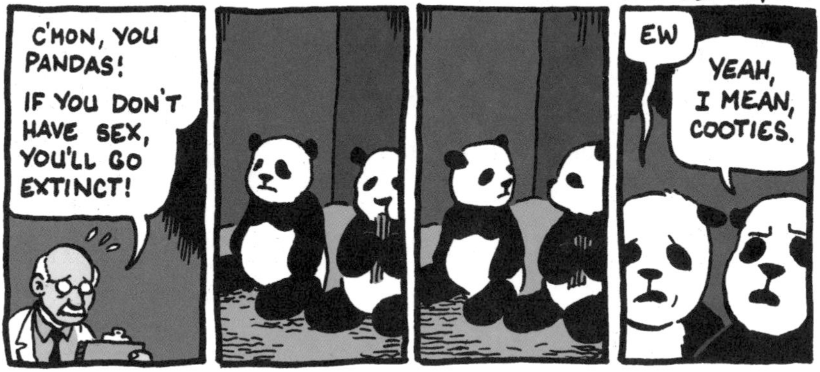
C'MON, YOU PANDAS!
IF YOU DON'T HAVE SEX, YOU'LL GO EXTINCT!
EW
YEAH, I MEAN, COOTIES.

THU DEC 29, 2011

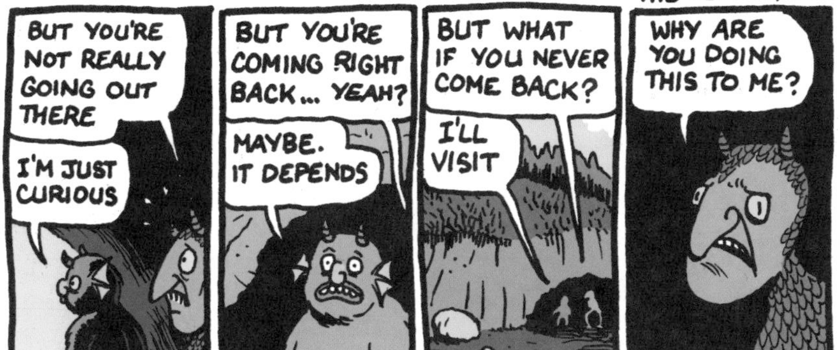
BUT YOU'RE NOT REALLY GOING OUT THERE
I'M JUST CURIOUS
BUT YOU'RE COMING RIGHT BACK... YEAH?
MAYBE. IT DEPENDS
BUT WHAT IF YOU NEVER COME BACK?
I'LL VISIT
WHY ARE YOU DOING THIS TO ME?

FRI DEC 30, 2011

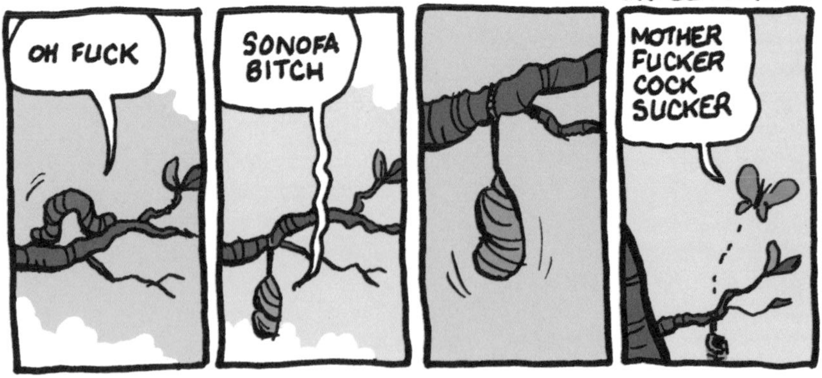
OH FUCK
SONOFA BITCH
MOTHER FUCKER COCK SUCKER

SAT DEC 31, 2011

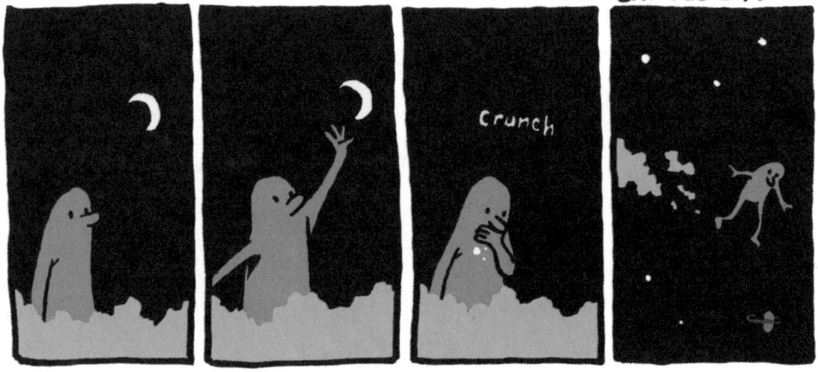
crunch

SUN JAN 1, 2012

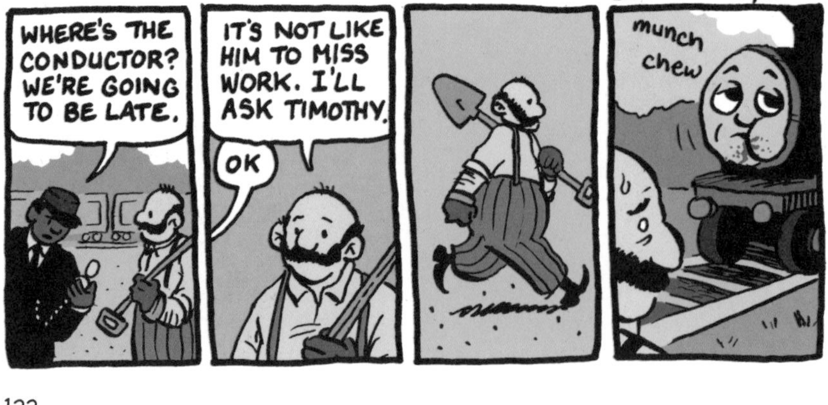
WHERE'S THE CONDUCTOR? WE'RE GOING TO BE LATE.
IT'S NOT LIKE HIM TO MISS WORK. I'LL ASK TIMOTHY.
OK
munch
chew

MON JAN 2, 2012

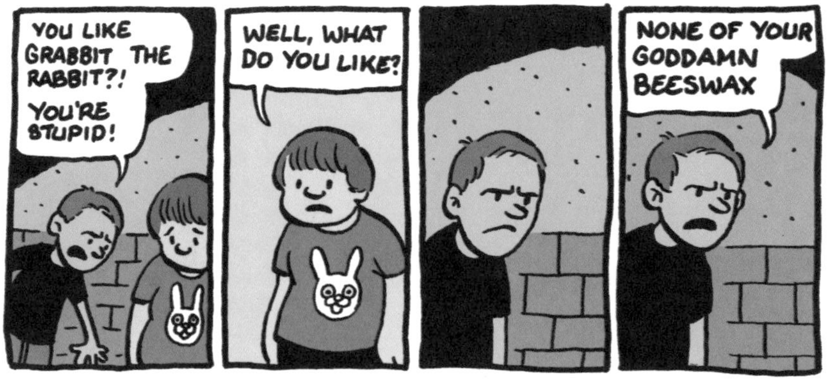
YOU LIKE GRABBIT THE RABBIT?!
YOU'RE STUPID!
WELL, WHAT DO YOU LIKE?
NONE OF YOUR GODDAMN BEESWAX

TUE JAN 3, 2012

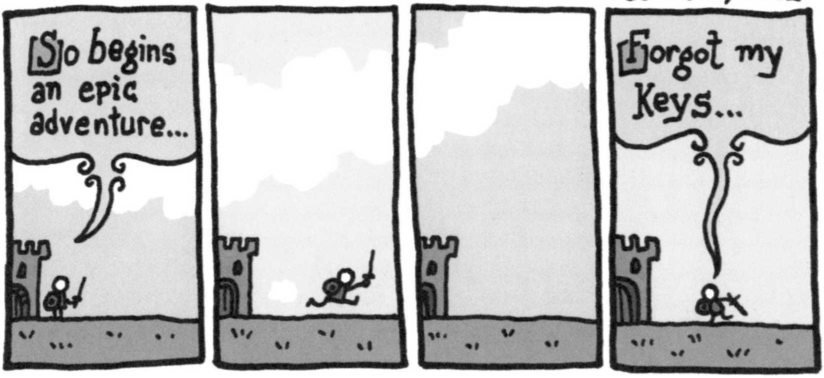
So begins an epic adventure...
Forgot my Keys...

WED JAN 4, 2012

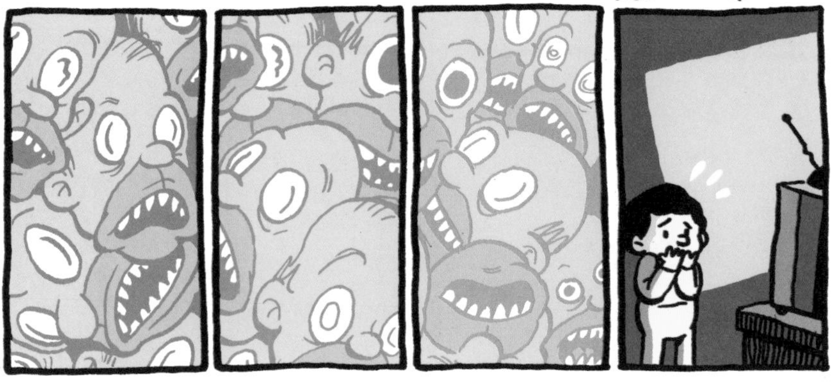

THU JAN 5, 2012

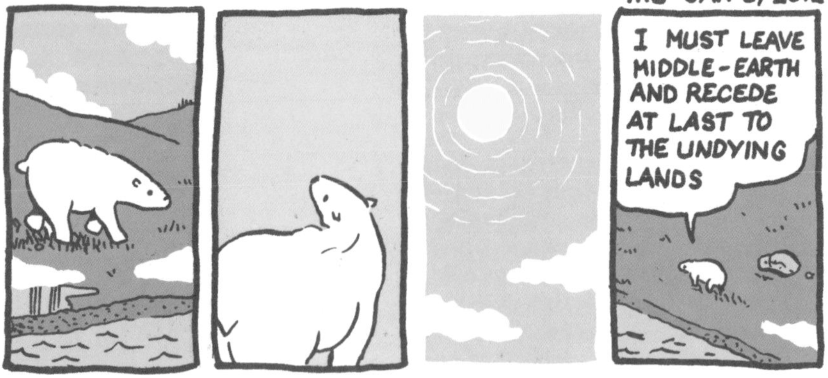
I MUST LEAVE MIDDLE-EARTH AND RECEDE AT LAST TO THE UNDYING LANDS

FRI JAN 6, 2012

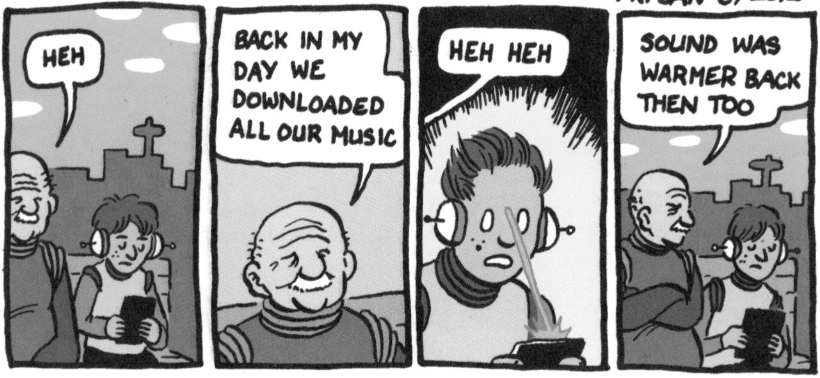
HEH
BACK IN MY DAY WE DOWNLOADED ALL OUR MUSIC
HEH HEH
SOUND WAS WARMER BACK THEN TOO

SAT JAN 7, 2012

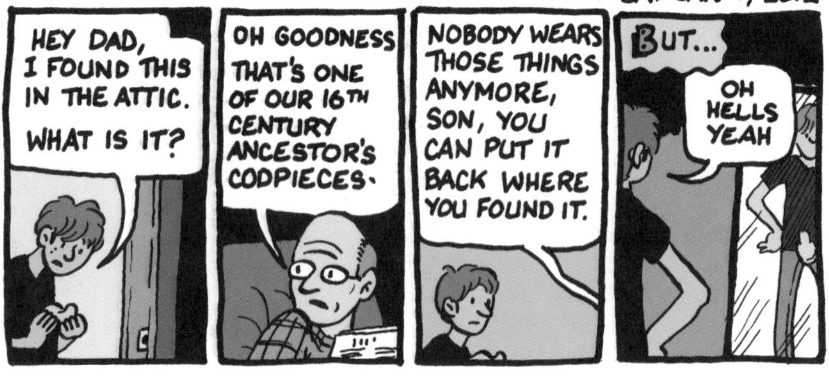
HEY DAD, I FOUND THIS IN THE ATTIC. WHAT IS IT?
OH GOODNESS THAT'S ONE OF OUR 16TH CENTURY ANCESTOR'S CODPIECES.
NOBODY WEARS THOSE THINGS ANYMORE, SON, YOU CAN PUT IT BACK WHERE YOU FOUND IT.
BUT...
OH HELLS YEAH

SUN JAN 8, 2012

HEY, GRABBIT THE RABBIT-- WHAT DO YOU LIKE?
SPARKLES

MON JAN 9, 2012

DO YA LIKE THE SPARKLES OVER HERE, GRABBIT?
YES
HOW ABOUT THESE ONES?
SURE
I DON'T HAVE TO TAKE THIS.

TUE JAN 10, 2012

EN GARDE!
SWISH! PARRY!

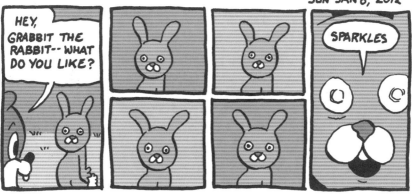

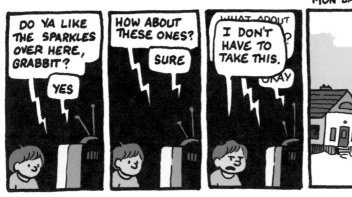

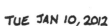

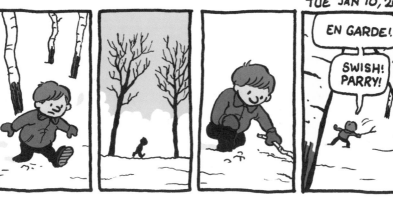

WED JAN 11, 2012

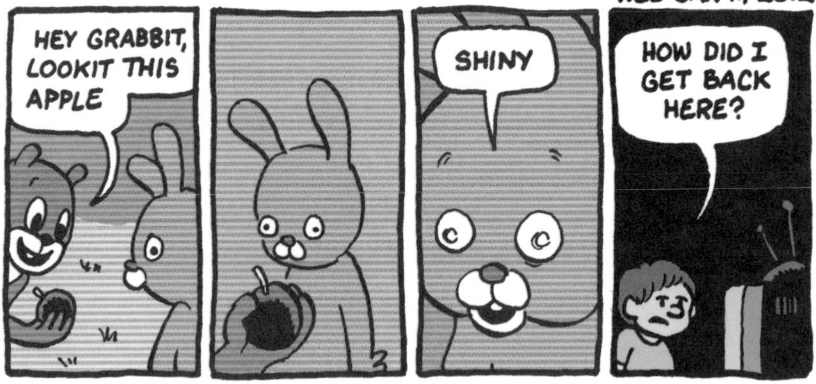
HEY GRABBIT, LOOKIT THIS APPLE
SHINY
HOW DID I GET BACK HERE?

THU JAN 12, 2012

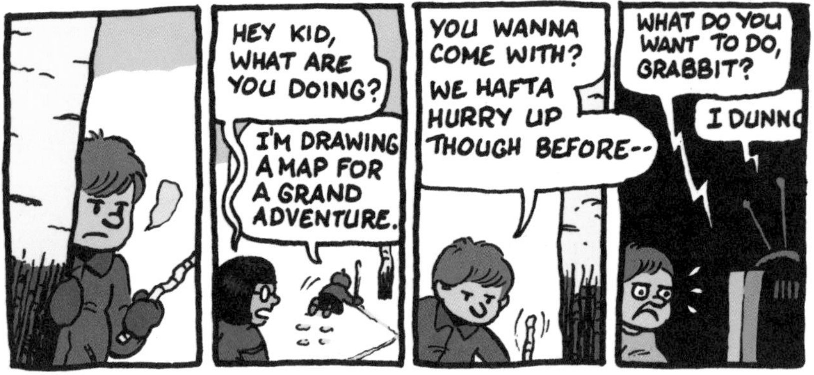
HEY KID, WHAT ARE YOU DOING?
I'M DRAWING A MAP FOR A GRAND ADVENTURE.
YOU WANNA COME WITH? WE HAFTA HURRY UP THOUGH BEFORE--
WHAT DO YOU WANT TO DO, GRABBIT?
I DUNNO

FRI JAN 13, 2012

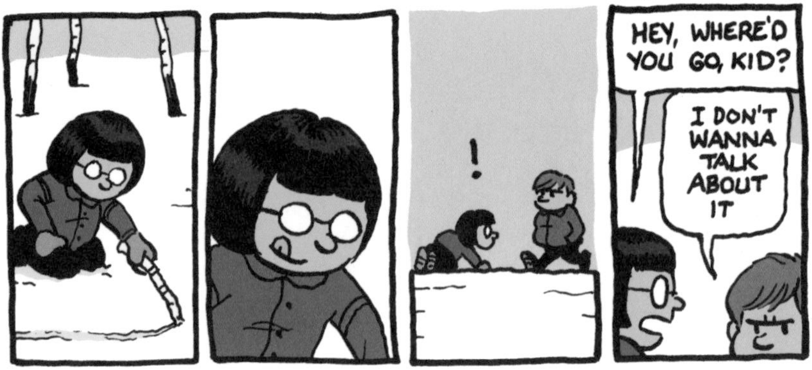
!
HEY, WHERE'D YOU GO, KID?
I DON'T WANNA TALK ABOUT IT

SAT JAN 14, 2012

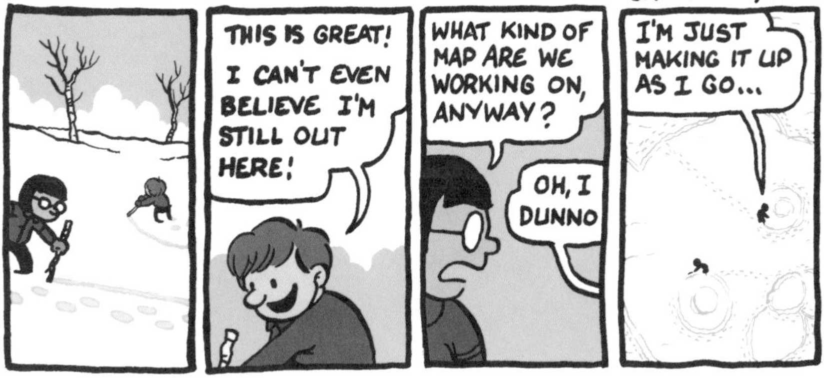
THIS IS GREAT!
I CAN'T EVEN BELIEVE I'M STILL OUT HERE!
WHAT KIND OF MAP ARE WE WORKING ON, ANYWAY?
OH, I DUNNO
I'M JUST MAKING IT UP AS I GO...

SUN JAN 15, 2012

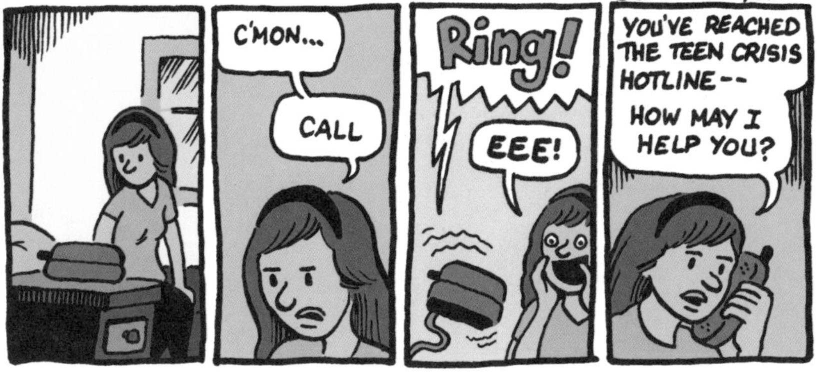
C'MON...
CALL
Ring!
EEE!
YOU'VE REACHED THE TEEN CRISIS HOTLINE--
HOW MAY I HELP YOU?

MON JAN 16, 2012

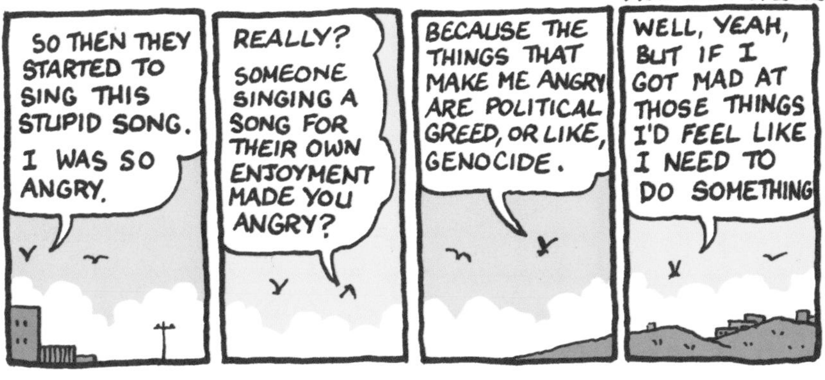
SO THEN THEY STARTED TO SING THIS STUPID SONG.
I WAS SO ANGRY.
REALLY?
SOMEONE SINGING A SONG FOR THEIR OWN ENJOYMENT MADE YOU ANGRY?
BECAUSE THE THINGS THAT MAKE ME ANGRY ARE POLITICAL GREED, OR LIKE, GENOCIDE.
WELL, YEAH, BUT IF I GOT MAD AT THOSE THINGS I'D FEEL LIKE I NEED TO DO SOMETHING

TUE JAN 17, 2012

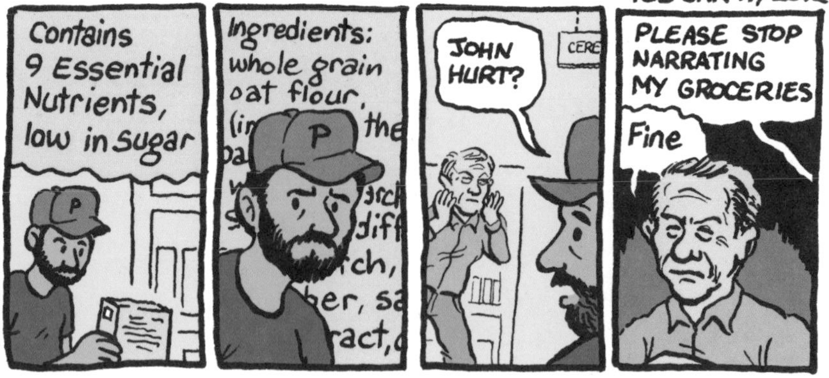

Contains 9 Essential Nutrients, low in sugar
Ingredients: whole grain oat flour,
JOHN HURT?
PLEASE STOP NARRATING MY GROCERIES
Fine

WED JAN 18, 2012

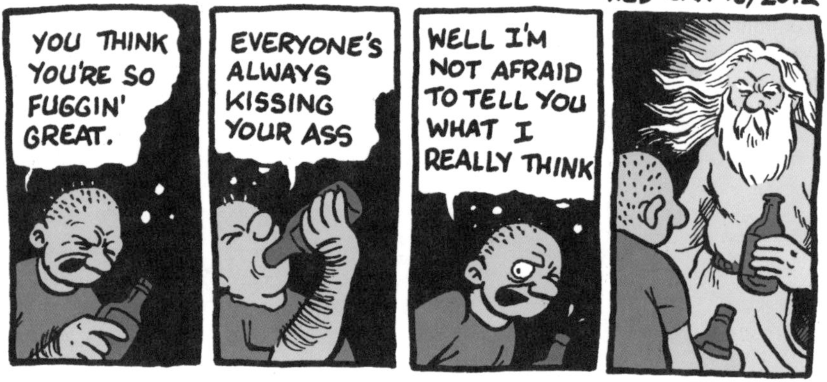

YOU THINK YOU'RE SO FUGGIN' GREAT.
EVERYONE'S ALWAYS KISSING YOUR ASS
WELL I'M NOT AFRAID TO TELL YOU WHAT I REALLY THINK

THU JAN 19, 2012

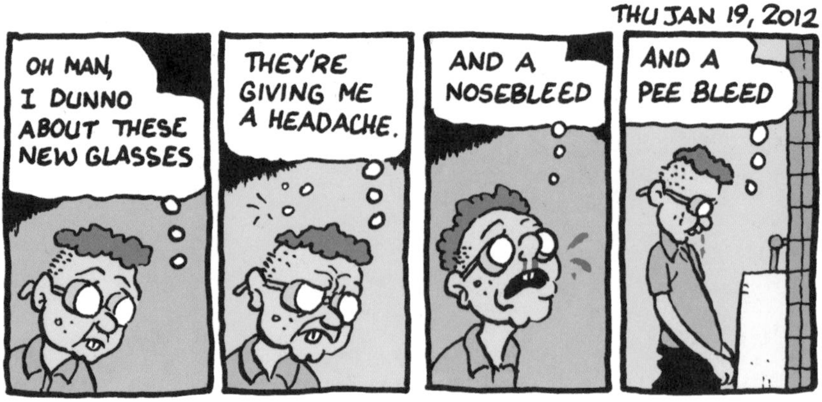

OH MAN, I DUNNO ABOUT THESE NEW GLASSES
THEY'RE GIVING ME A HEADACHE.
AND A NOSEBLEED
AND A PEE BLEED

FRI JAN 20, 2012

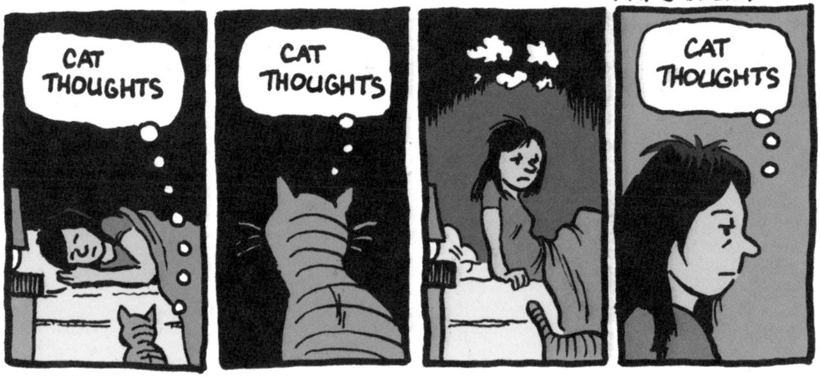
CAT THOUGHTS
CAT THOUGHTS
CAT THOUGHTS

SAT JAN 21, 2012

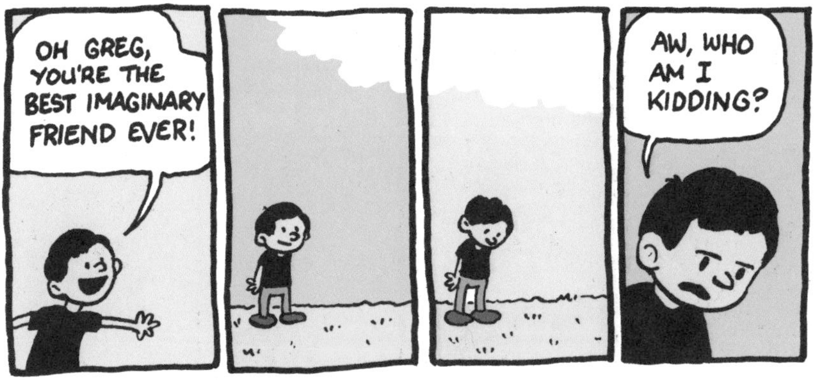
OH GREG, YOU'RE THE BEST IMAGINARY FRIEND EVER!
AW, WHO AM I KIDDING?

SUN JAN 22, 2012

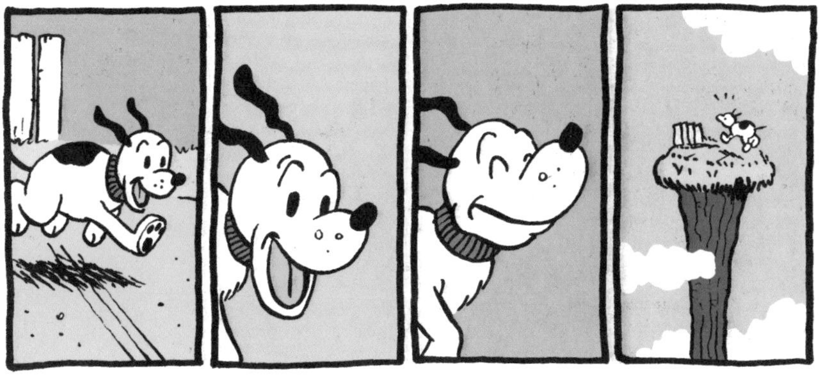

MON JAN 23, 2012

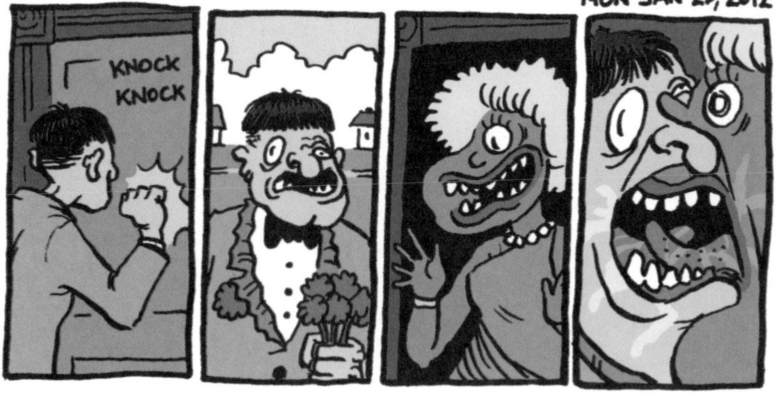
KNOCK
KNOCK

TUE JAN 24, 2012

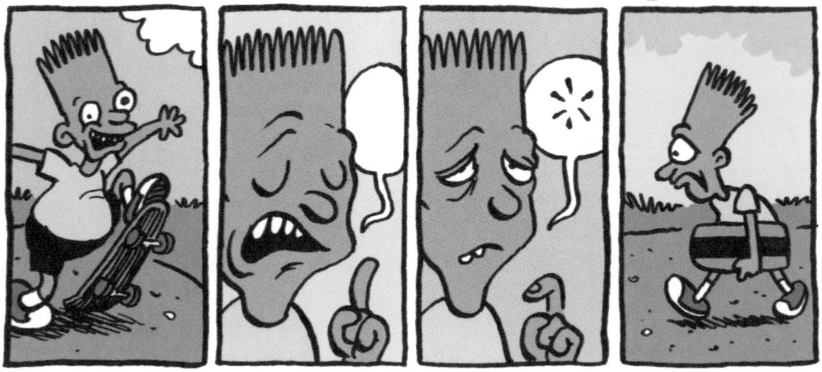

WED JAN 25, 2012

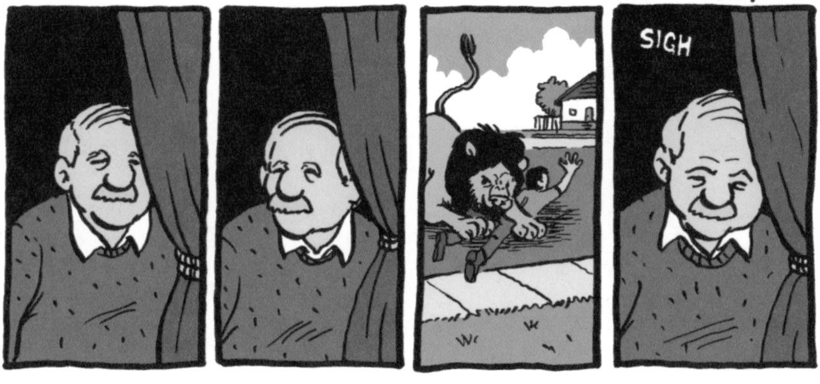
SIGH

THU JAN 26 2012

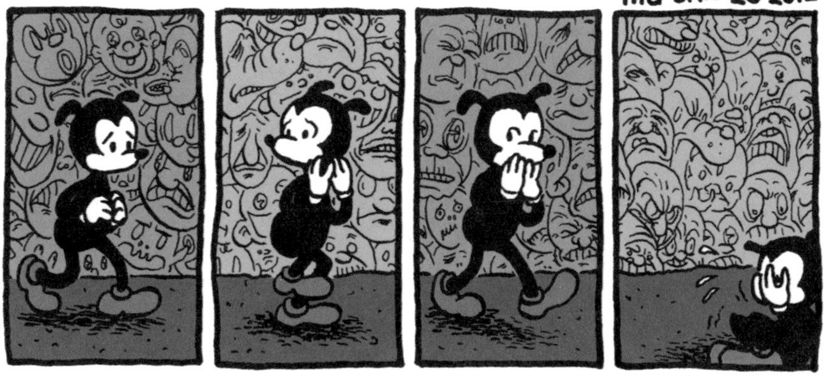

FRI JAN 27, 2012

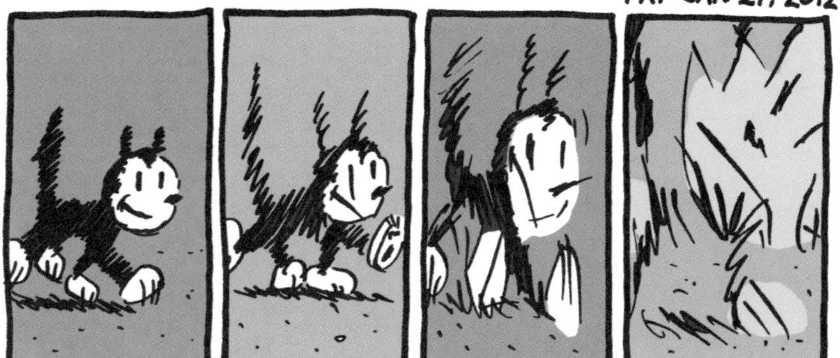

SAT JAN 28, 2012

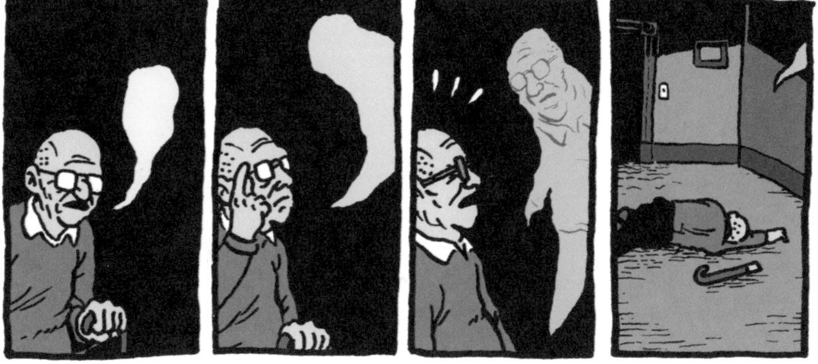

SUN JAN 29, 2012

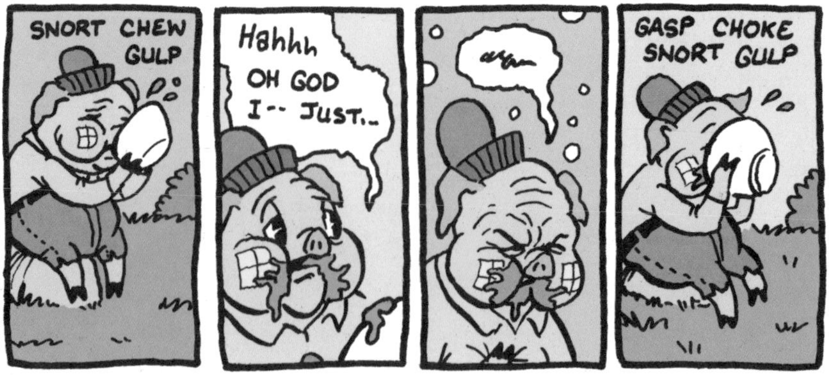
SNORT CHEW GULP
Hahhh OH GOD I-- JUST...
GASP CHOKE SNORT GULP

MON JAN 30, 2012

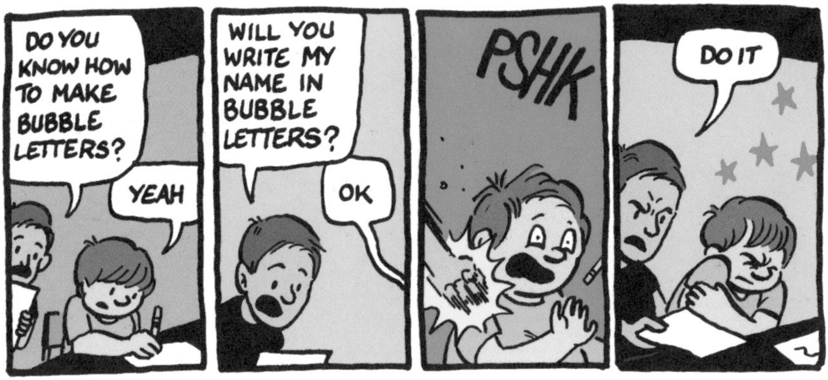
DO YOU KNOW HOW TO MAKE BUBBLE LETTERS?
YEAH
WILL YOU WRITE MY NAME IN BUBBLE LETTERS?
OK
PSHK
DO IT

TUE JAN 31, 2012

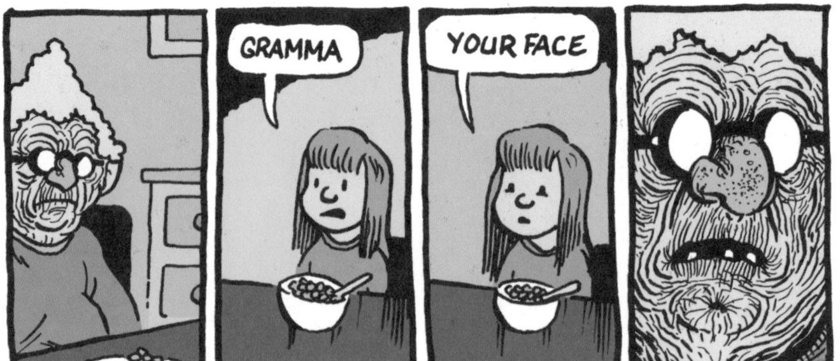
GRAMMA
YOUR FACE

WED FEB 1, 2012

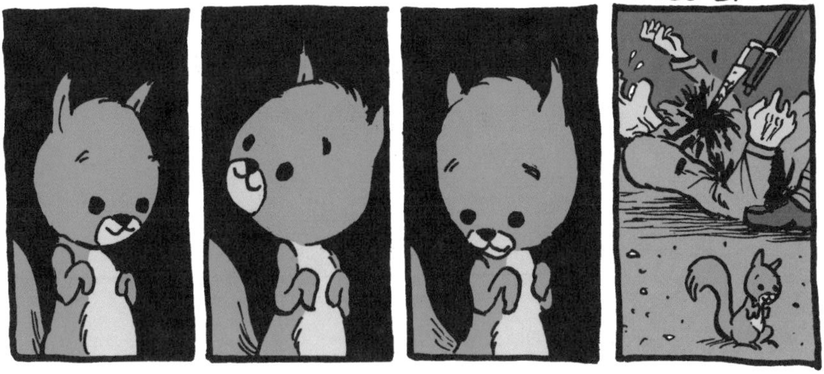

THU FEB 2, 2012

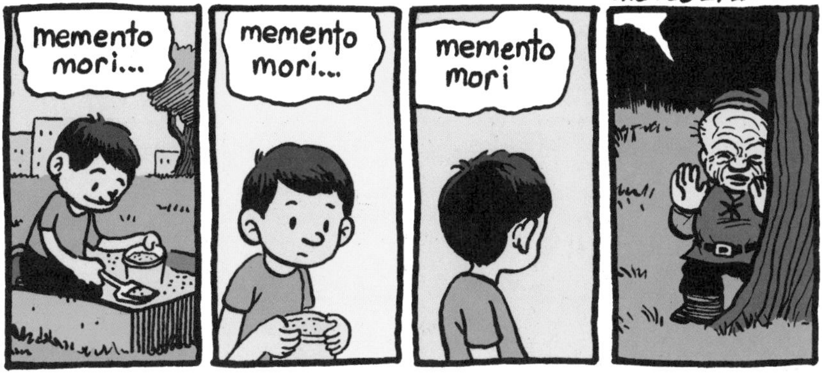
memento mori...
memento mori...
memento mori

FRI FEB 3, 2012

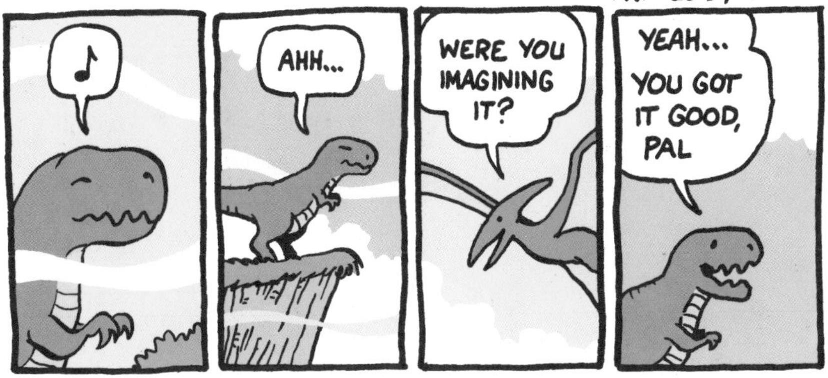
♪
AHH...
WERE YOU IMAGINING IT?
YEAH...
YOU GOT IT GOOD, PAL

SAT FEB 4, 2012

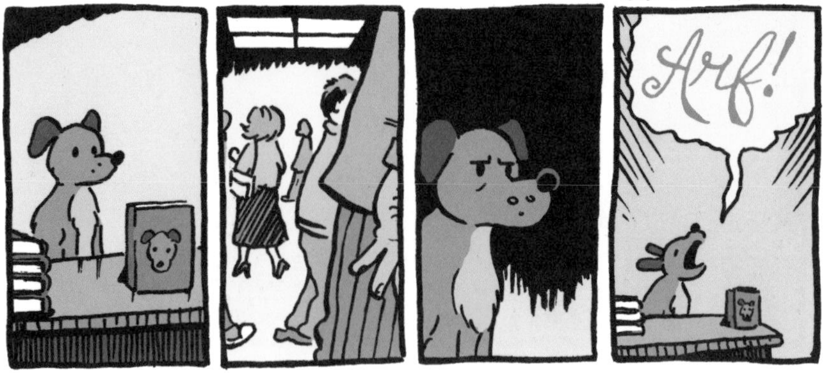
Arf!

SUN FEB 5, 2012

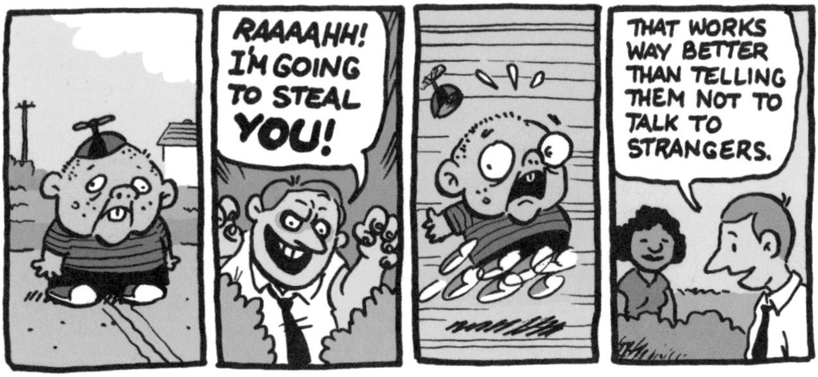
RAAAAHH! I'M GOING TO STEAL YOU!
THAT WORKS WAY BETTER THAN TELLING THEM NOT TO TALK TO STRANGERS.

MON FEB 6, 2012

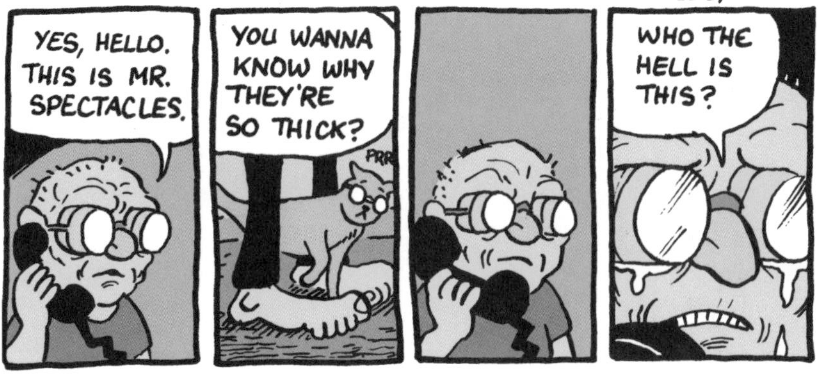
YES, HELLO. THIS IS MR. SPECTACLES.
YOU WANNA KNOW WHY THEY'RE SO THICK?
PRR
WHO THE HELL IS THIS?

TUE FEB 7, 2012

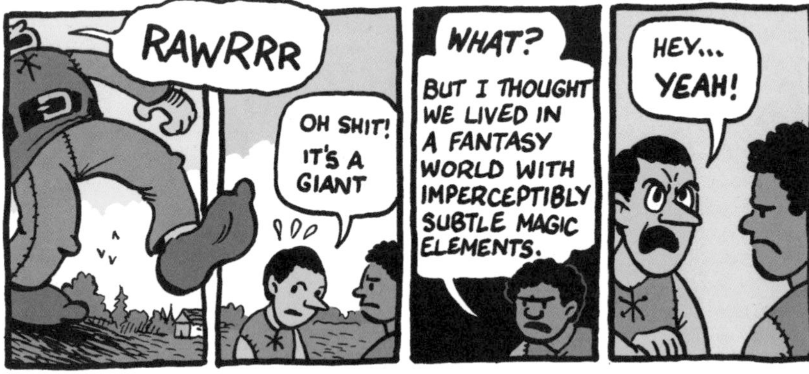
RAWRRR
OH SHIT! IT'S A GIANT
WHAT?
BUT I THOUGHT WE LIVED IN A FANTASY WORLD WITH IMPERCEPTIBLY SUBTLE MAGIC ELEMENTS.
HEY... YEAH!

WED FEB 8, 2012

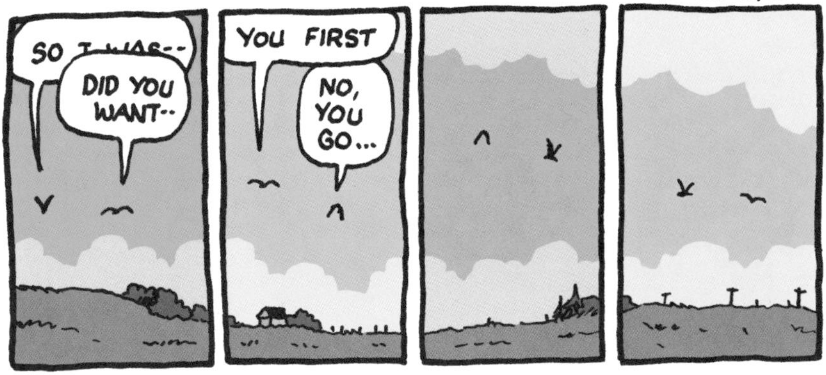
SO
DID YOU WANT--
YOU FIRST
NO, YOU GO...

THU FEB 9, 2012

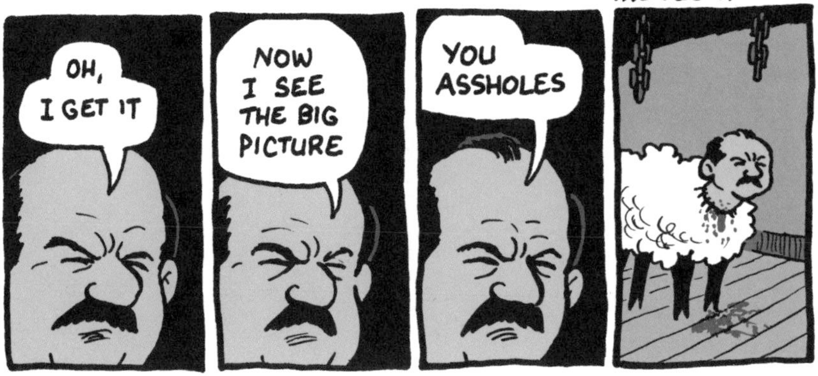
OH, I GET IT
NOW I SEE THE BIG PICTURE
YOU ASSHOLES

FRI FEB 10, 2012

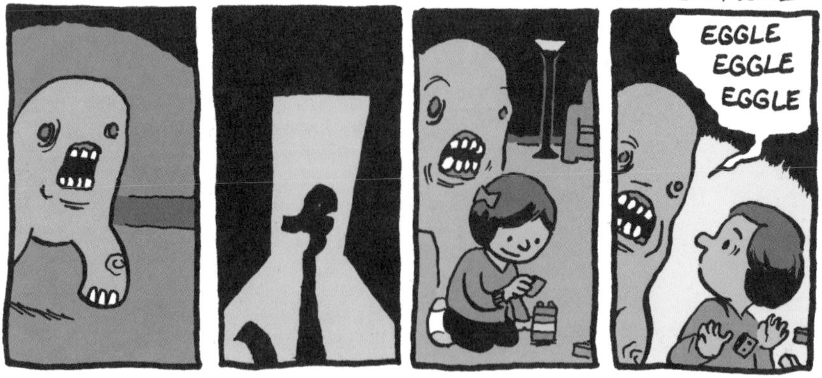
EGGLE EGGLE EGGLE

SAT FEB 11, 2012

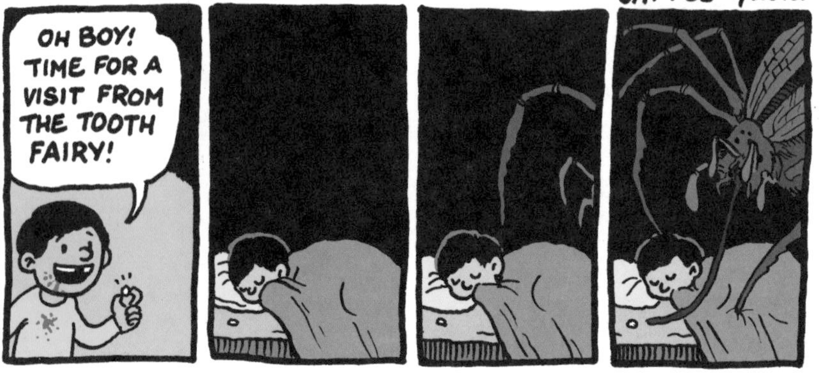
OH BOY! TIME FOR A VISIT FROM THE TOOTH FAIRY!

SUN FEB 12, 2012

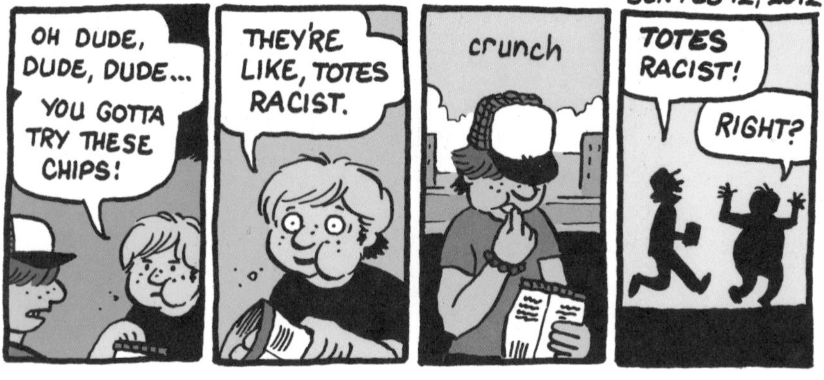
OH DUDE, DUDE, DUDE...
YOU GOTTA TRY THESE CHIPS!
THEY'RE LIKE, TOTES RACIST.
crunch
TOTES RACIST!
RIGHT?

MON FEB 13, 2012

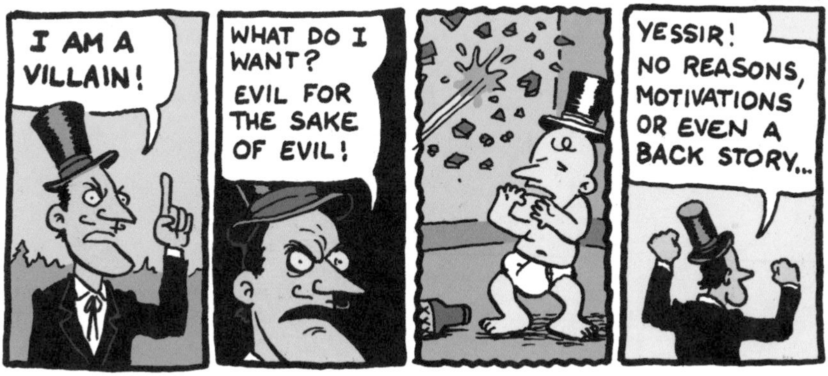
I AM A VILLAIN!
WHAT DO I WANT? EVIL FOR THE SAKE OF EVIL!
YESSIR! NO REASONS, MOTIVATIONS OR EVEN A BACK STORY...

TUE FEB 14, 2012

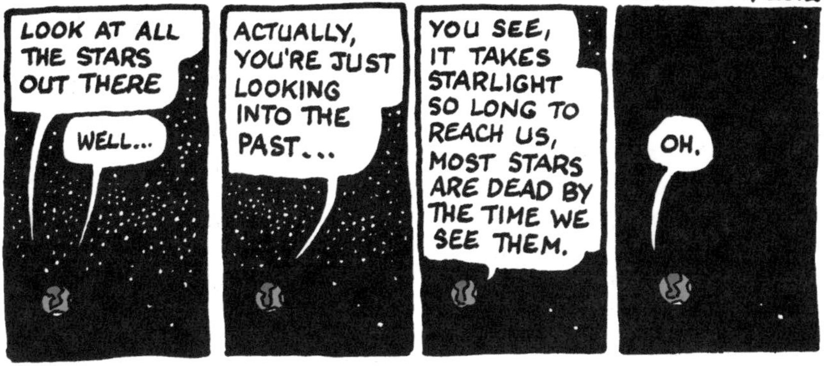
LOOK AT ALL THE STARS OUT THERE
WELL...
ACTUALLY, YOU'RE JUST LOOKING INTO THE PAST...
YOU SEE, IT TAKES STARLIGHT SO LONG TO REACH US, MOST STARS ARE DEAD BY THE TIME WE SEE THEM.
OH.

WED FEB 15, 2012

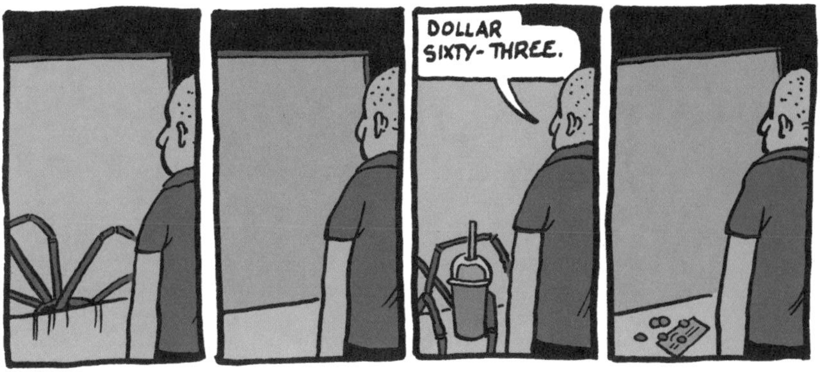
DOLLAR SIXTY-THREE.

THU FEB 16, 2012

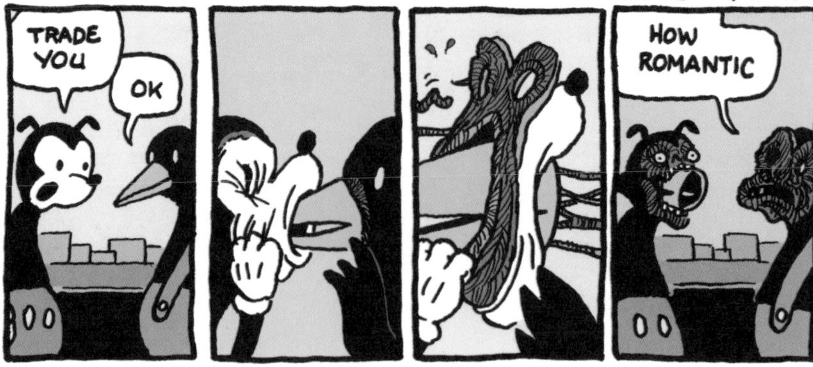
TRADE YOU
OK
HOW ROMANTIC

FRI FEB 17, 2012

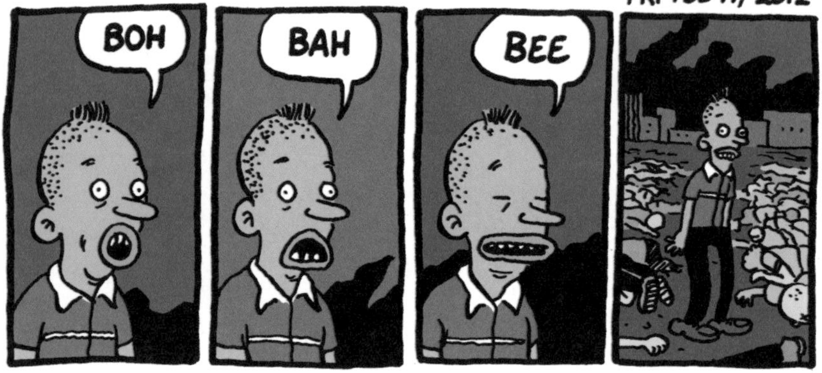
BOH
BAH
BEE

SAT FEB 18, 2012

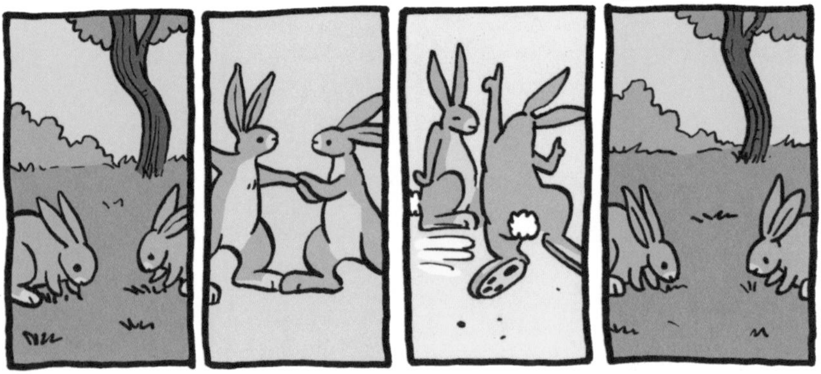

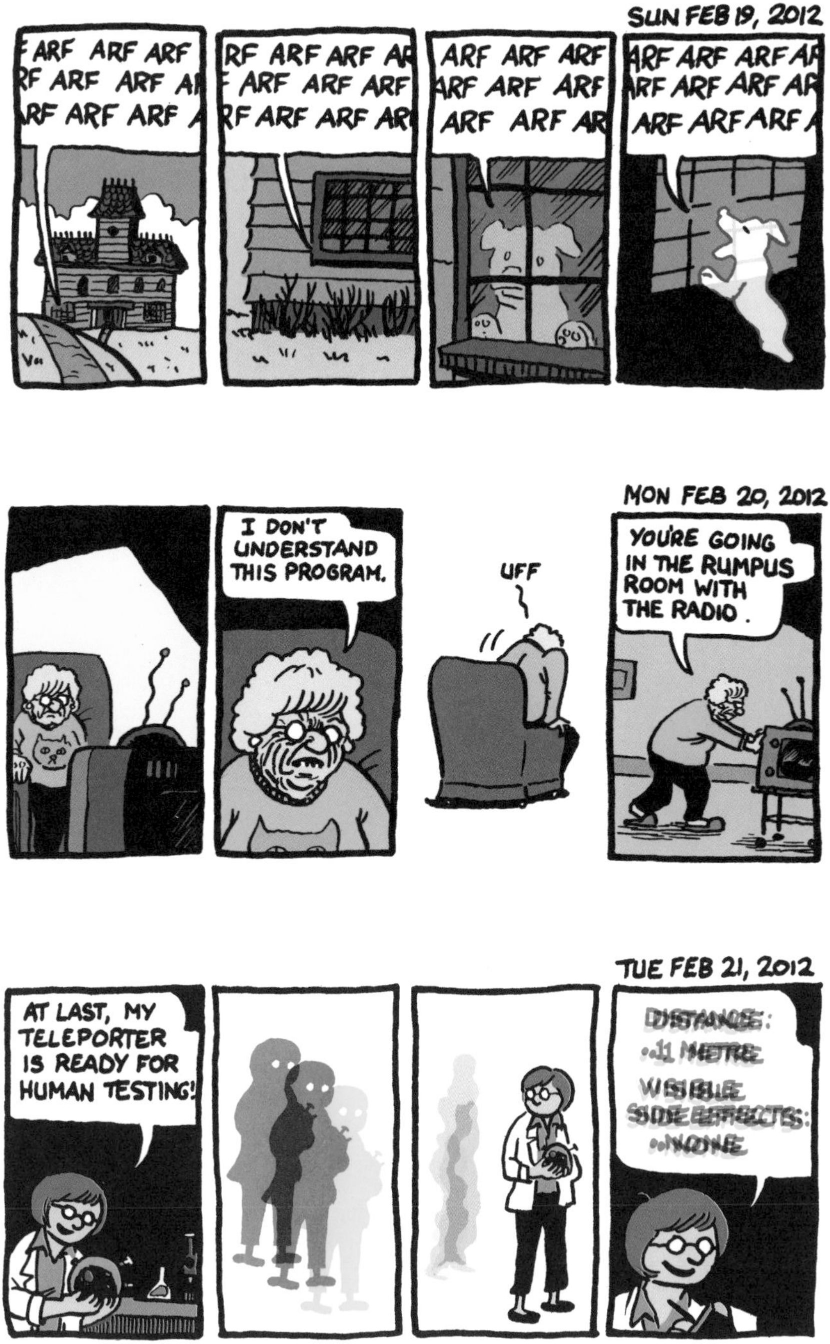

ARF ARF ARF ARF ARF ARF ARF ARF ARF
ARF ARF ARF ARF ARF ARF ARF ARF
ARF ARF ARF ARF ARF ARF ARF ARF
SUN FEB 19, 2012
ARF ARF ARF ARF ARF ARF ARF ARF ARF
MON FEB 20, 2012
I DON'T UNDERSTAND THIS PROGRAM.
UFF
YOU'RE GOING IN THE RUMPUS ROOM WITH THE RADIO.
TUE FEB 21, 2012
AT LAST, MY TELEPORTER IS READY FOR HUMAN TESTING!
DISTANCE: •1 METRE
VISIBLE SIDE EFFECTS: •NONE

WED FEB 22, 2012

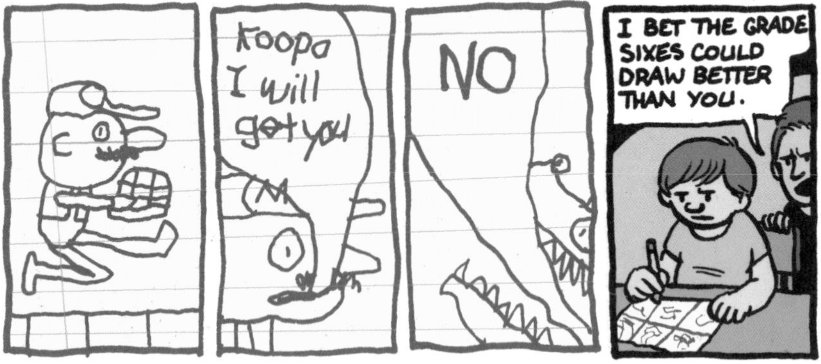
koopa
I will
get you
NO
I BET THE GRADE SIXES COULD DRAW BETTER THAN YOU.

THU FEB 23, 2012

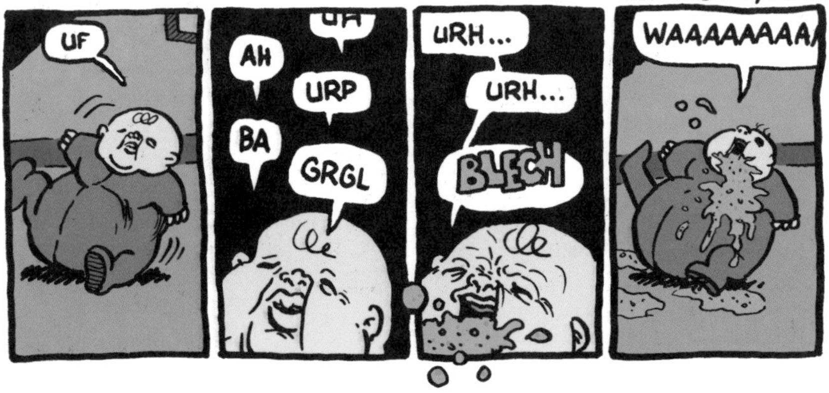
UF
AH
URP
BA
GRGL
URH...
URH...
BLECH
WAAAAAAAA

FRI FEB 24, 2012

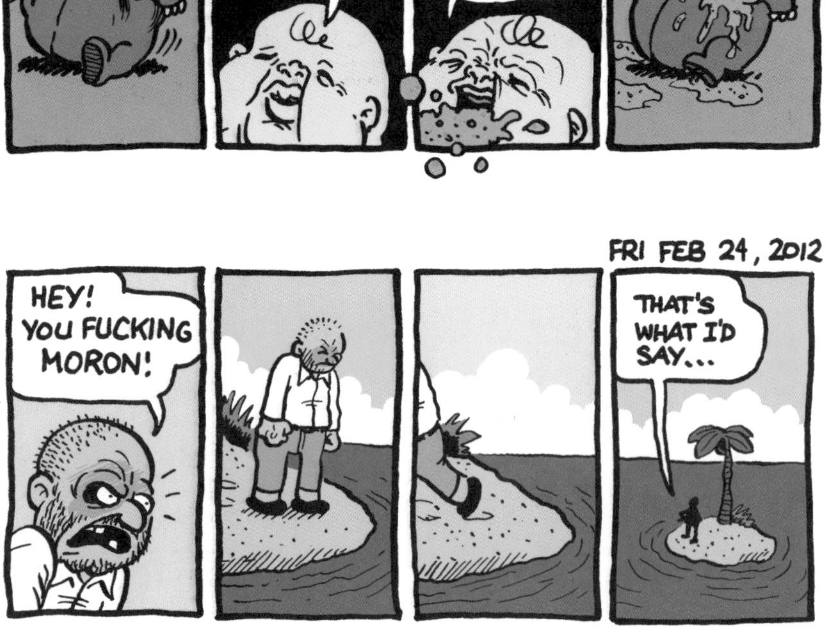
HEY! YOU FUCKING MORON!
THAT'S WHAT I'D SAY...

SAT FEB 25, 2012

SUN FEB 26, 2012

GOD COMICS

MON FEB 27, 2012

crinkle

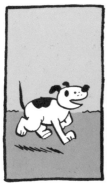

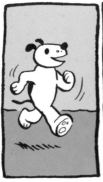

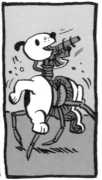

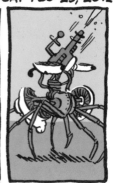

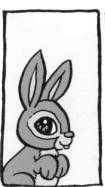

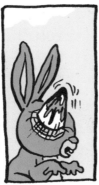

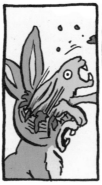

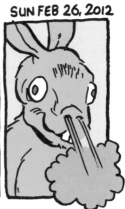

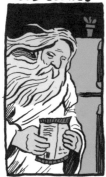

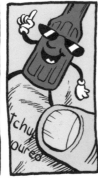

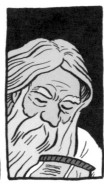

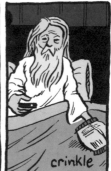

TUE FEB 28, 2012

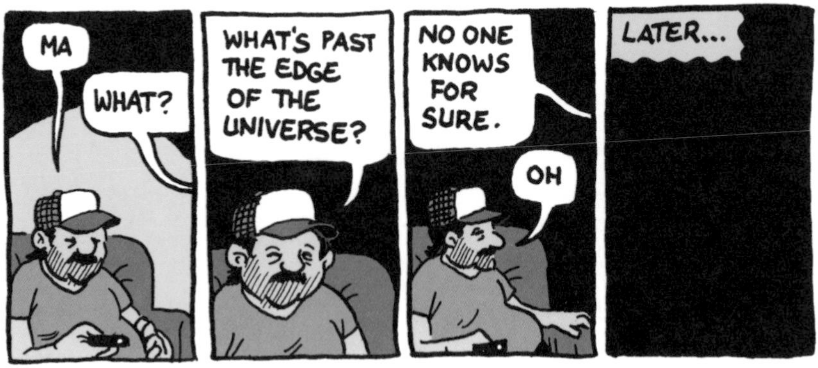
MA
WHAT?
WHAT'S PAST THE EDGE OF THE UNIVERSE?
NO ONE KNOWS FOR SURE.
OH
LATER...

WED FEB 29, 2012

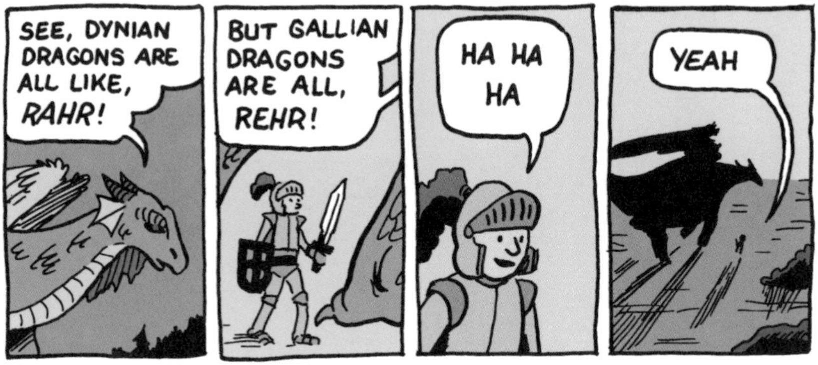
SEE, DYNIAN DRAGONS ARE ALL LIKE, RAHR!
BUT GALLIAN DRAGONS ARE ALL, REHR!
HA HA HA
YEAH

THU MAR 1, 2012

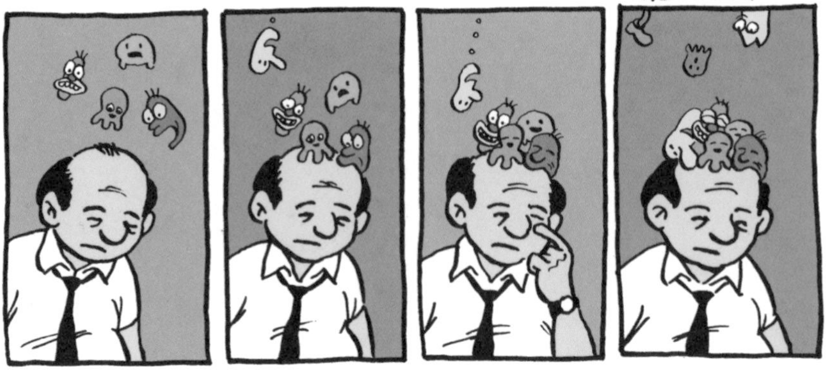

FRI MAR 2, 2012

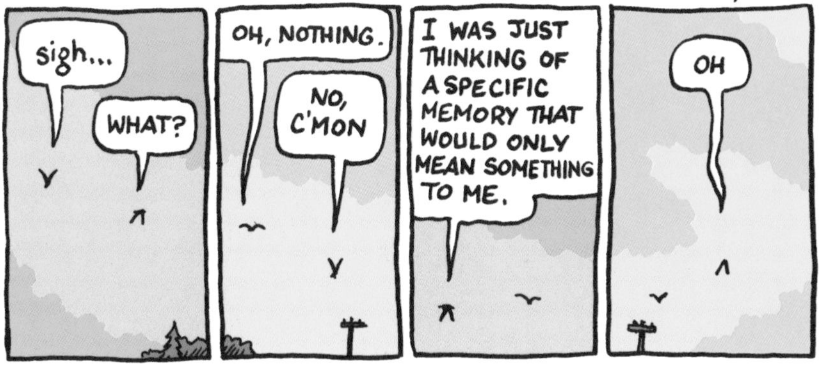

sigh...
WHAT?
OH, NOTHING.
NO, C'MON
I WAS JUST THINKING OF A SPECIFIC MEMORY THAT WOULD ONLY MEAN SOMETHING TO ME.
OH

SAT MAR 3, 2012

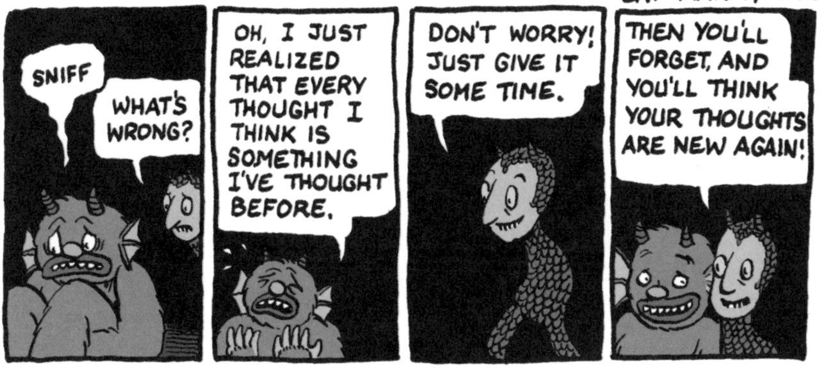

SNIFF
WHAT'S WRONG?
OH, I JUST REALIZED THAT EVERY THOUGHT I THINK IS SOMETHING I'VE THOUGHT BEFORE.
DON'T WORRY! JUST GIVE IT SOME TIME.
THEN YOU'LL FORGET, AND YOU'LL THINK YOUR THOUGHTS ARE NEW AGAIN!

SUN MAR 4, 2012

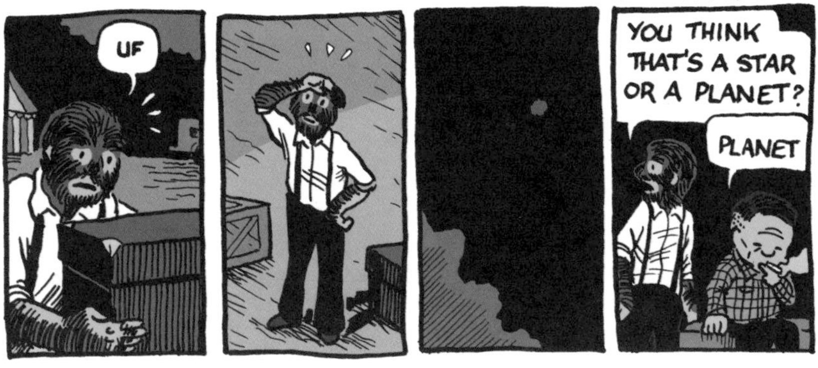

UF
YOU THINK THAT'S A STAR OR A PLANET?
PLANET

MON MAR 5, 2012

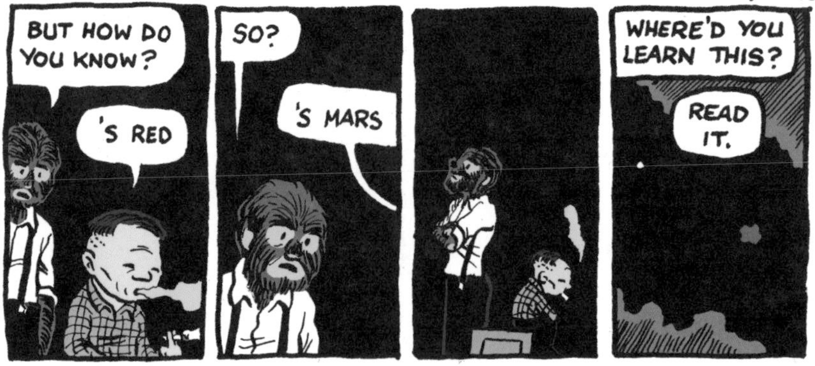
BUT HOW DO YOU KNOW?
'S RED
SO?
'S MARS
WHERE'D YOU LEARN THIS?
READ IT.

TUE MAR 6, 2012

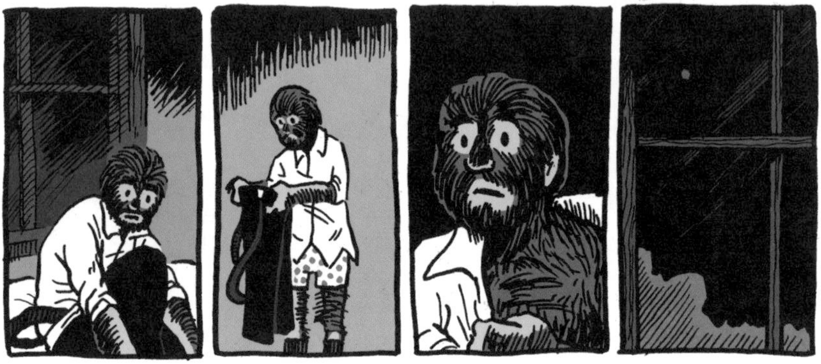

WED MAR 7, 2012

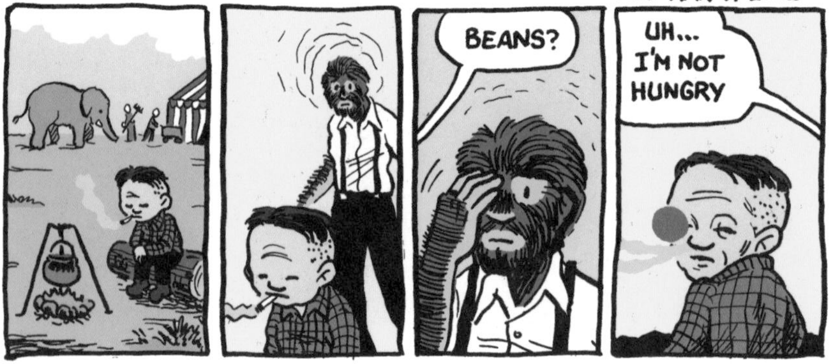
BEANS?
UH... I'M NOT HUNGRY

THU MAR 8, 2012

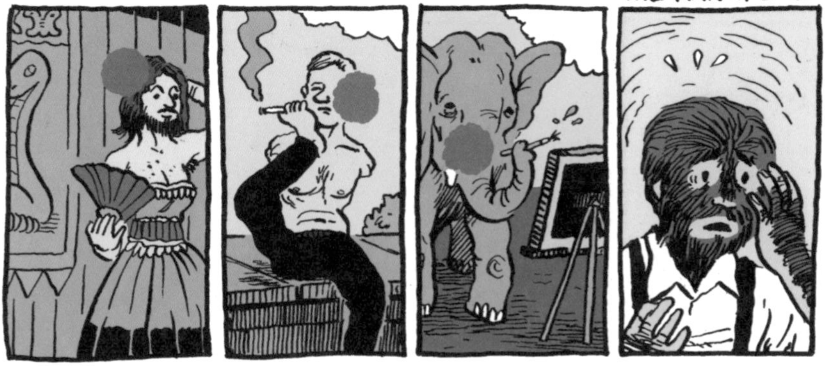

FRI MAR 9, 2012

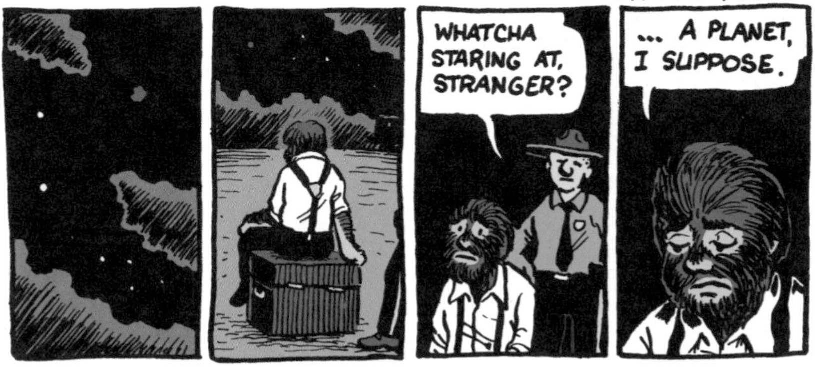
WHATCHA STARING AT, STRANGER?
... A PLANET, I SUPPOSE.

SAT MAR 10, 2012

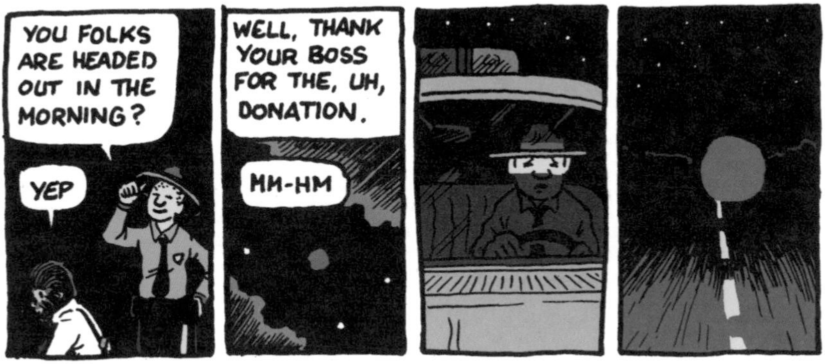
YOU FOLKS ARE HEADED OUT IN THE MORNING?
YEP
WELL, THANK YOUR BOSS FOR THE, UH, DONATION.
MM-HM

SUN MAR 11, 2012

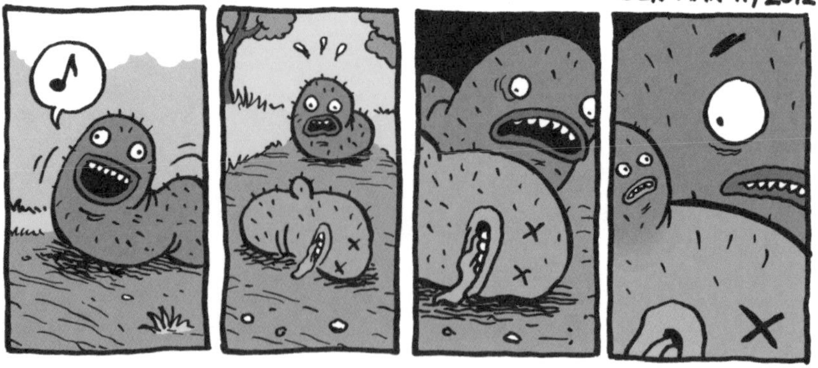

MON MAR 12, 2012

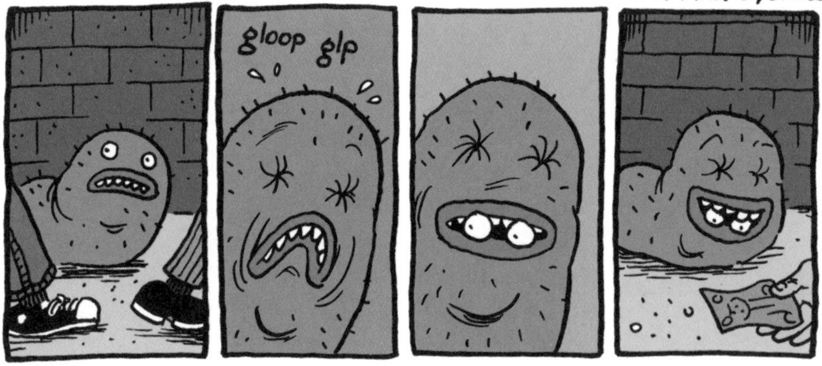
gloop glp

TUE MAR 13, 2012

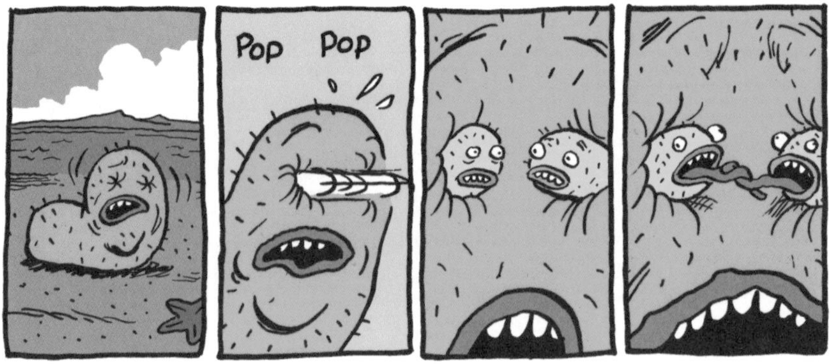
Pop Pop

WED MAR 14, 2012

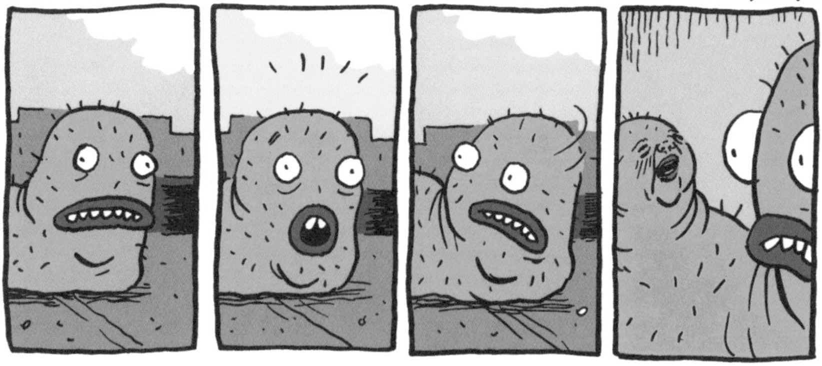

THU MAR 15, 2012

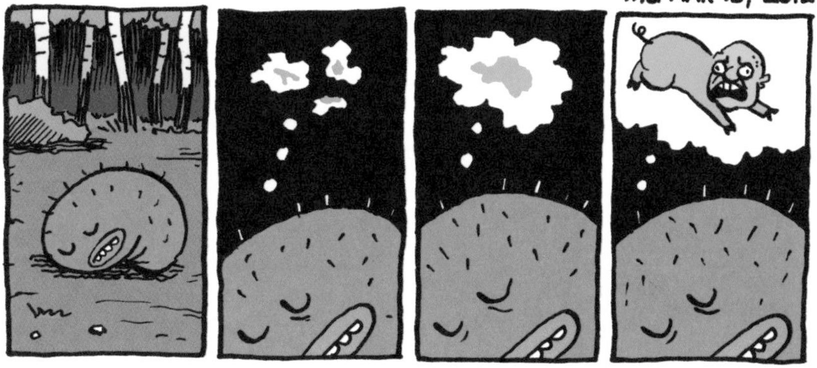

FRI MAR 16, 2012

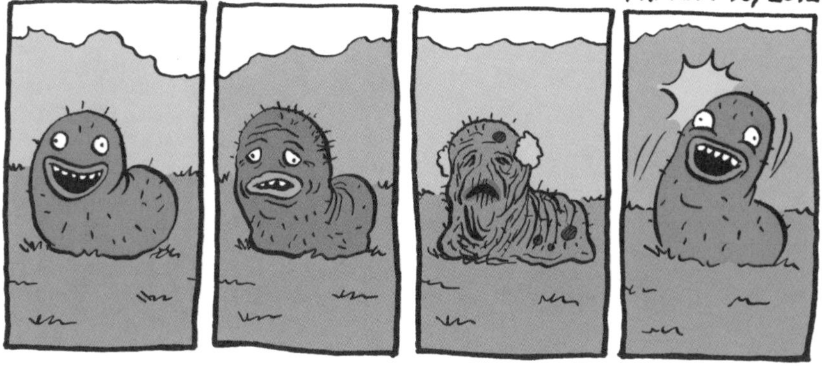

SAT MAR 17, 2012

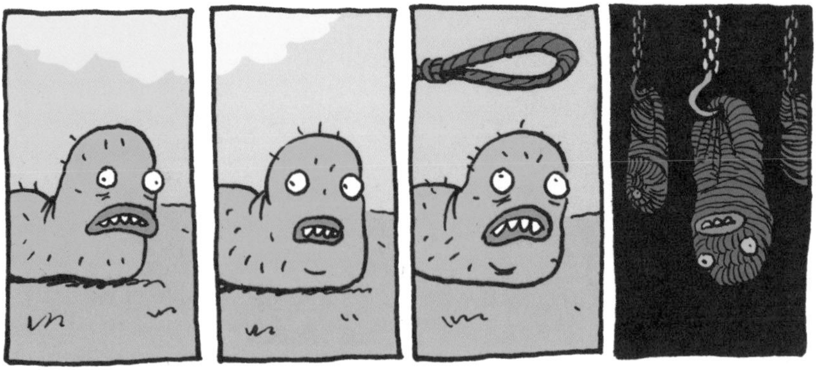

SUN MAR 18, 2012

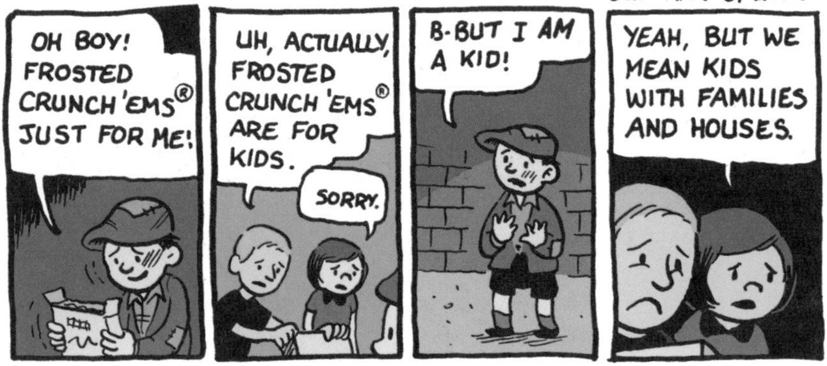
OH BOY! FROSTED CRUNCH 'EMS® JUST FOR ME!
UH, ACTUALLY, FROSTED CRUNCH 'EMS® ARE FOR KIDS.
SORRY.
B-BUT I AM A KID!
YEAH, BUT WE MEAN KIDS WITH FAMILIES AND HOUSES.

MON MAR 19, 2012

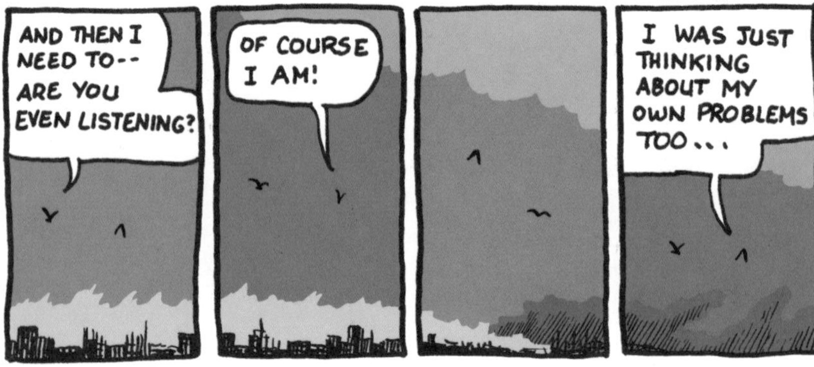
AND THEN I NEED TO-- ARE YOU EVEN LISTENING?
OF COURSE I AM!
I WAS JUST THINKING ABOUT MY OWN PROBLEMS TOO...

TUE MAR 20, 2012

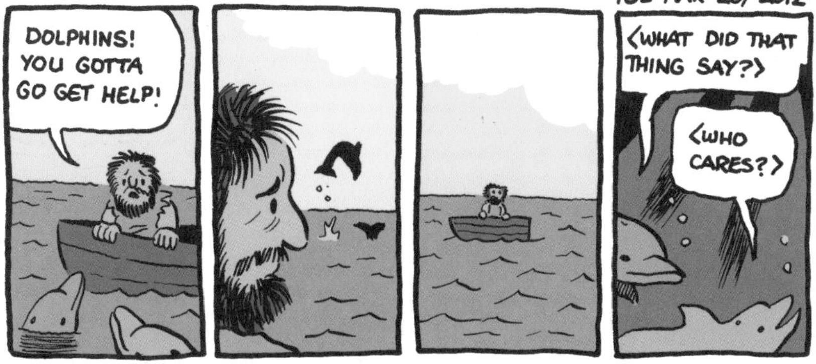
DOLPHINS! YOU GOTTA GO GET HELP!
<WHAT DID THAT THING SAY?>
<WHO CARES?>

WED MAR 21, 2012

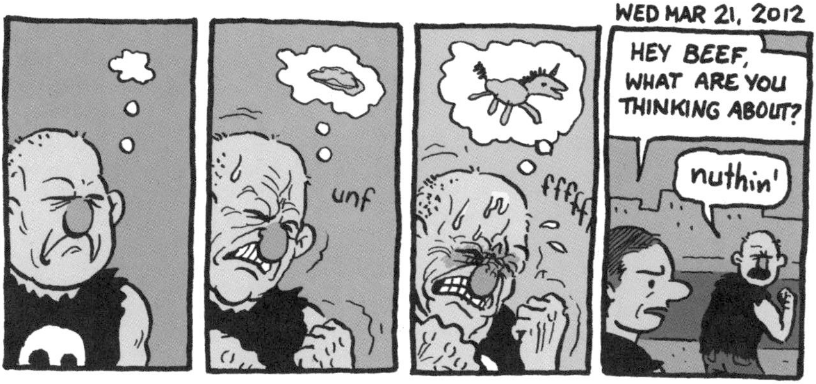
unf
ffffff
HEY BEEF, WHAT ARE YOU THINKING ABOUT?
nuthin'

THU MAR 22, 2012

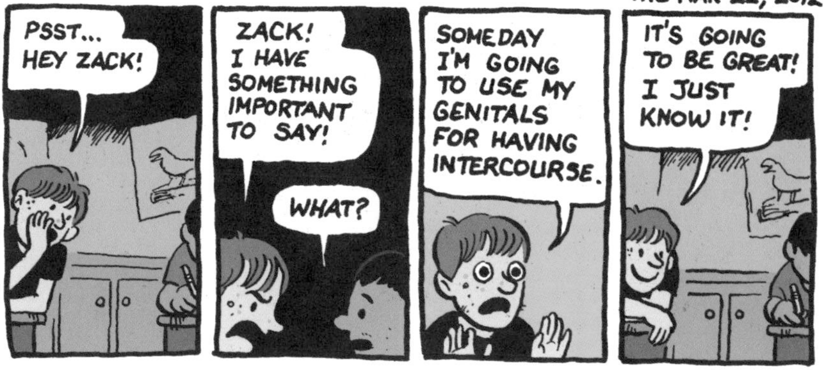
PSST... HEY ZACK!
ZACK! I HAVE SOMETHING IMPORTANT TO SAY!
WHAT?
SOMEDAY I'M GOING TO USE MY GENITALS FOR HAVING INTERCOURSE.
IT'S GOING TO BE GREAT! I JUST KNOW IT!

FRI MAR 23, 2012

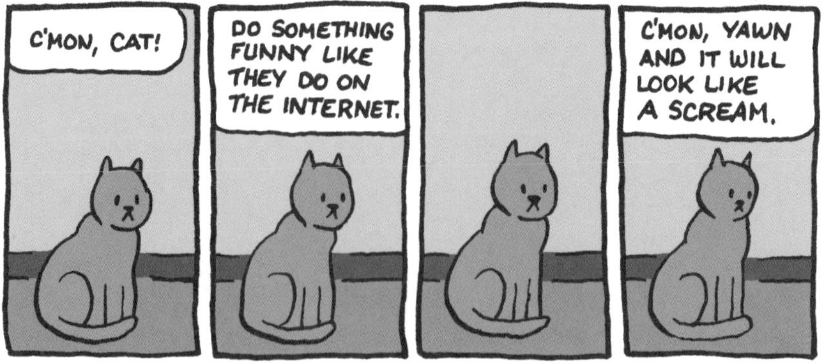
C'MON, CAT!
DO SOMETHING FUNNY LIKE THEY DO ON THE INTERNET.
C'MON, YAWN AND IT WILL LOOK LIKE A SCREAM.

SAT MAR 24, 2012

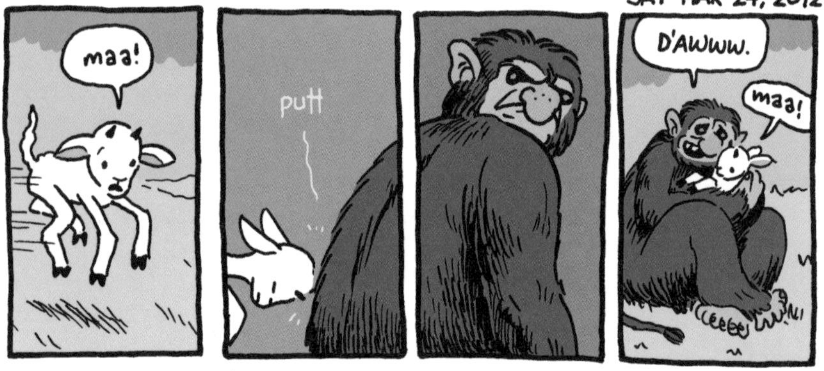
maa!
putt
D'AWWW.
maa!

SUN MAR 25, 2012

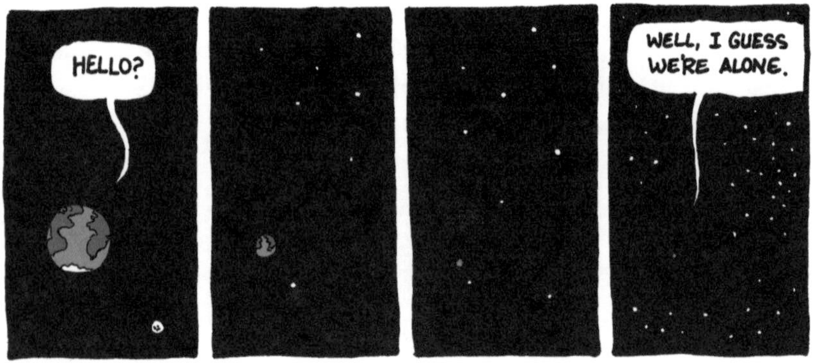
HELLO?
WELL, I GUESS WE'RE ALONE.

MON MAR 26, 2012

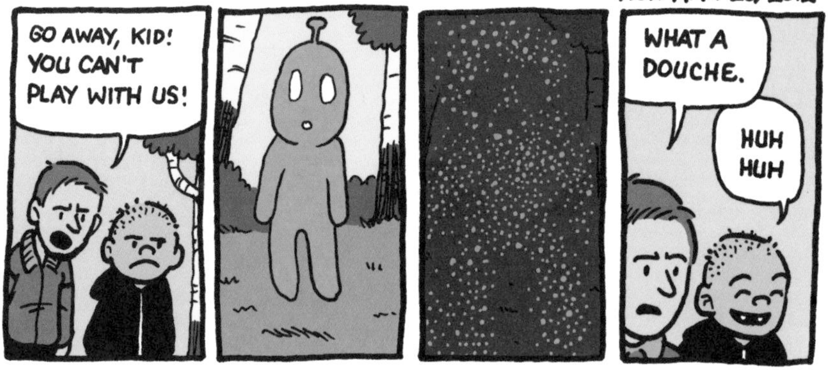
GO AWAY, KID! YOU CAN'T PLAY WITH US!
WHAT A DOUCHE.
HUH HUH

TUE MAR 27, 2012

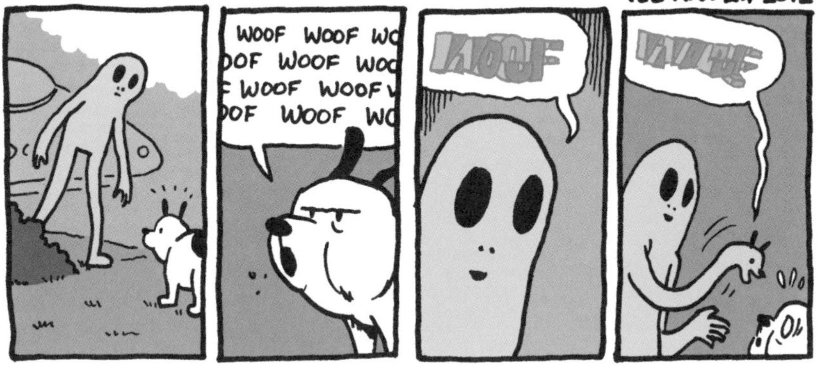
WOOF WOOF WO
OF WOOF WOO
WOOF WOOF
OF WOOF WO

WED MAR 28, 2012

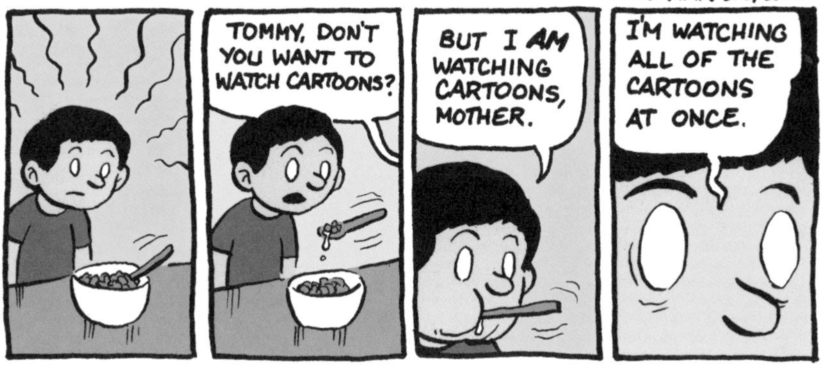
TOMMY, DON'T YOU WANT TO WATCH CARTOONS?
BUT I *AM* WATCHING CARTOONS, MOTHER.
I'M WATCHING ALL OF THE CARTOONS AT ONCE.

THU MAR 29, 2012

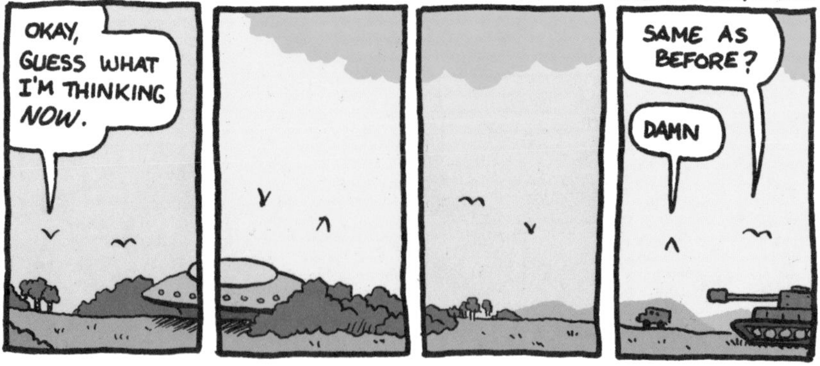
OKAY, GUESS WHAT I'M THINKING *NOW*.
SAME AS BEFORE?
DAMN

FRI MAR 30, 2012

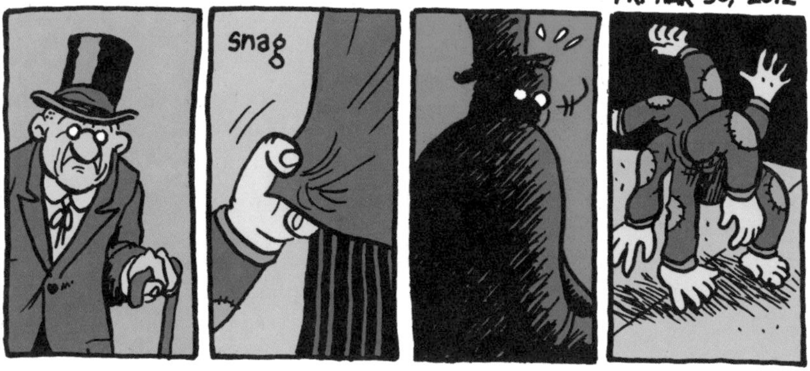
snag

SAT MAR 31, 2012

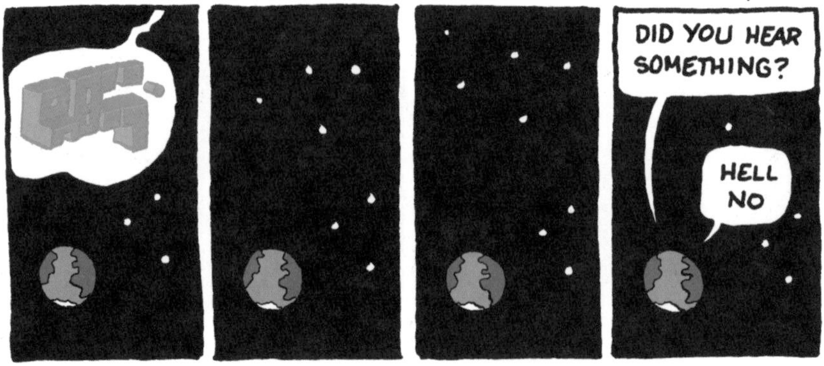
DID YOU HEAR SOMETHING?
HELL NO

SUN APR 1 2012

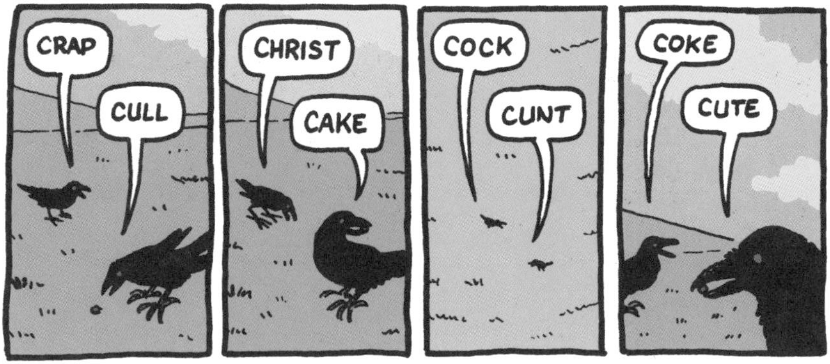
CRAP
CULL
CHRIST
CAKE
COCK
CUNT
COKE
CUTE

MON ARR 2, 2012

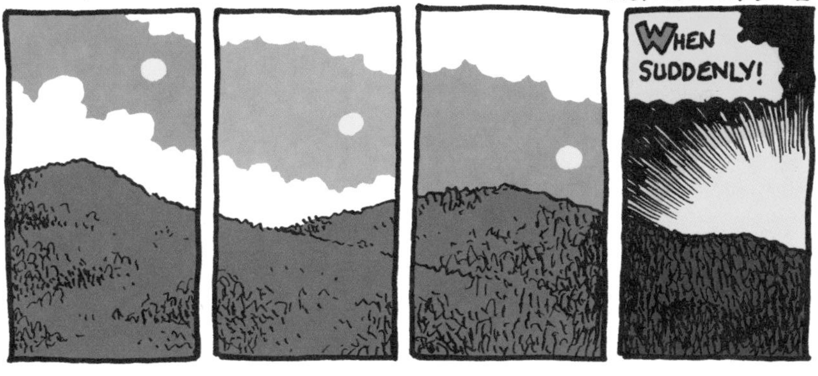
WHEN SUDDENLY!

TUE APR 3, 2012

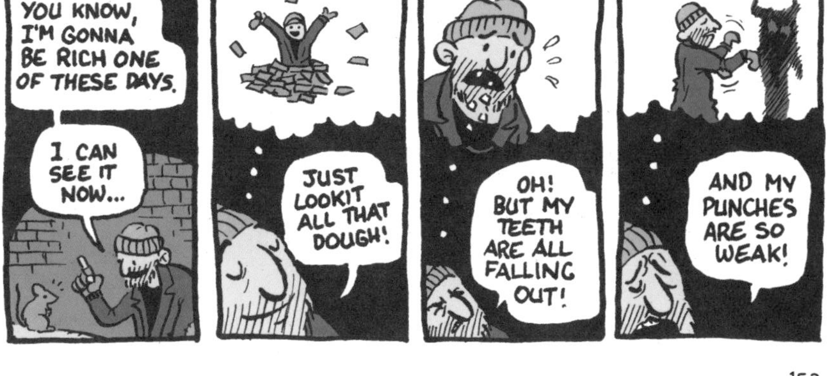
YOU KNOW, I'M GONNA BE RICH ONE OF THESE DAYS.
I CAN SEE IT NOW...
JUST LOOKIT ALL THAT DOUGH!
OH! BUT MY TEETH ARE ALL FALLING OUT!
AND MY PUNCHES ARE SO WEAK!

WED APR 4, 2012

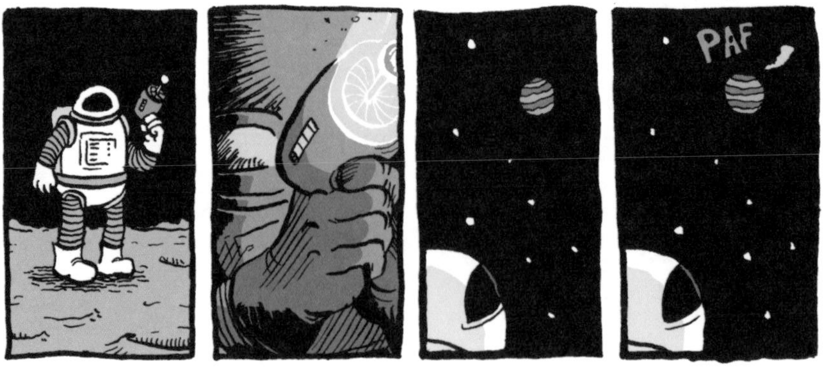
PAF

THU APR 5, 2012

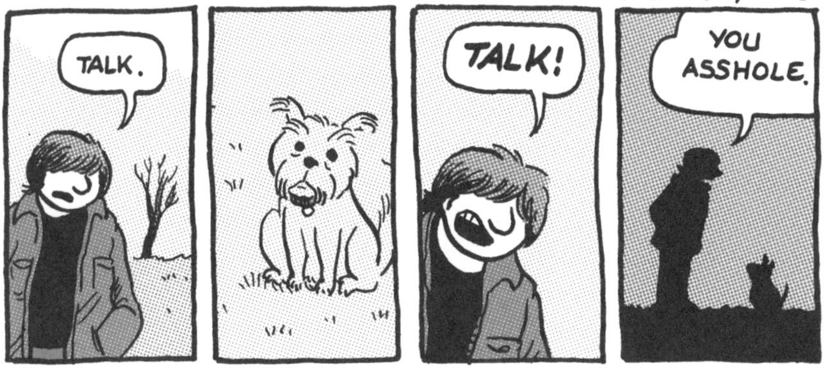
TALK.
TALK!
YOU ASSHOLE.

FRI APR 6, 2012

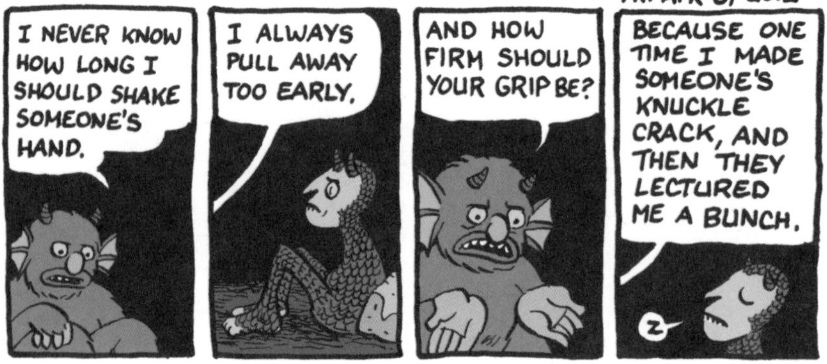
I NEVER KNOW HOW LONG I SHOULD SHAKE SOMEONE'S HAND.
I ALWAYS PULL AWAY TOO EARLY.
AND HOW FIRM SHOULD YOUR GRIP BE?
BECAUSE ONE TIME I MADE SOMEONE'S KNUCKLE CRACK, AND THEN THEY LECTURED ME A BUNCH.
Z

BOB PIT

SAT APR 7, 2012

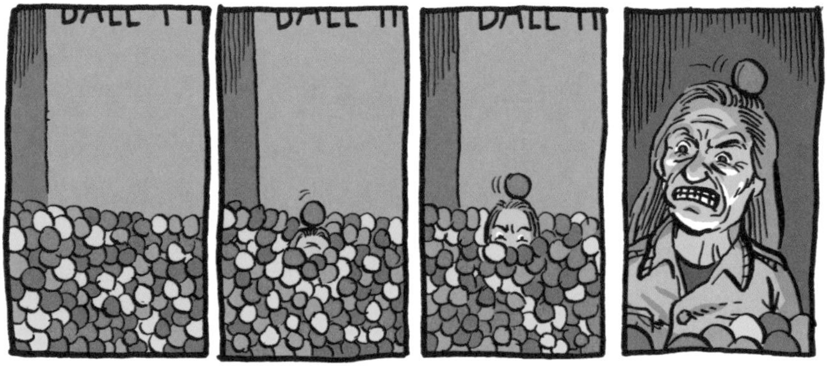

SUN APR 8, 2012

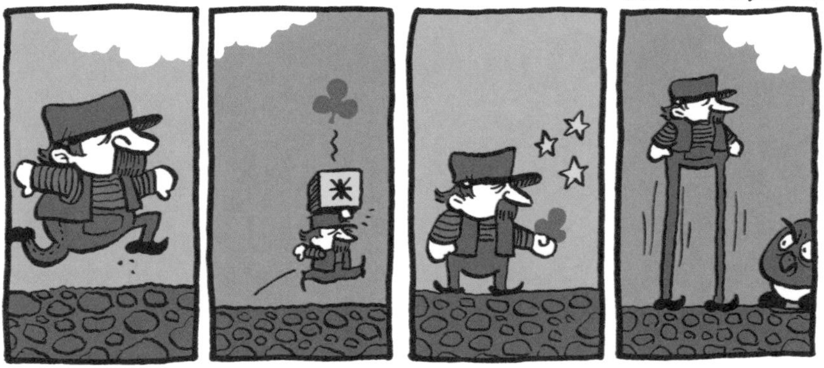

MON APR 9, 2012

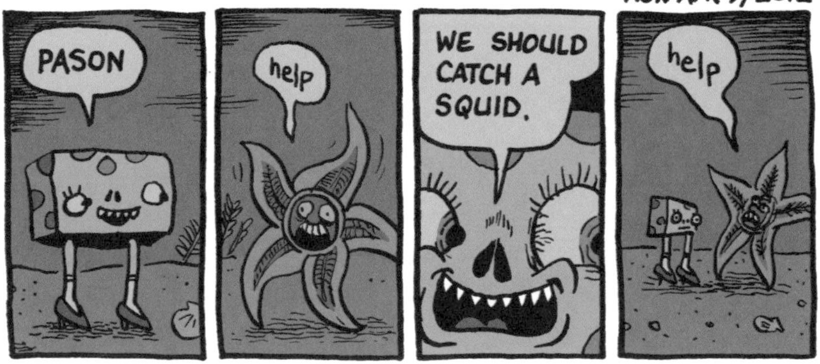
PASON
help
WE SHOULD CATCH A SQUID.
help

TUE APR 10, 2012

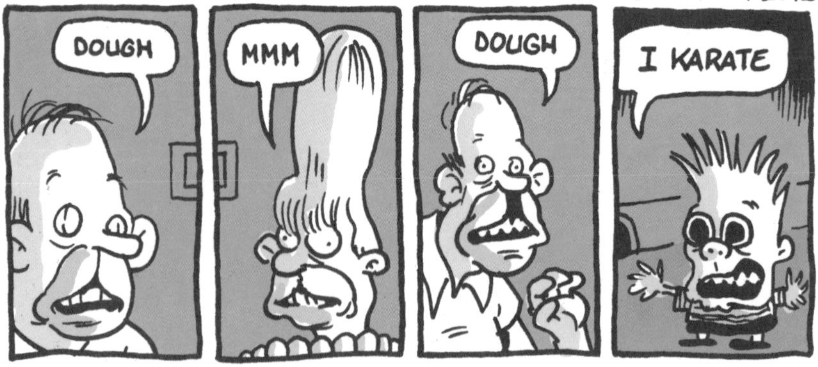
DOUGH
MMM
DOUGH
I KARATE

WED APR 11, 2012

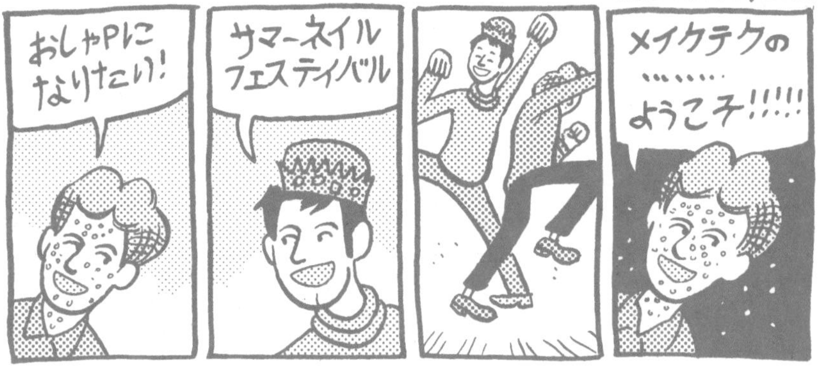
おしゃPになりたい!
サマーネイルフェスティバル
メイクテクの……… ようこ子!!!!!

THU APR 12, 2012

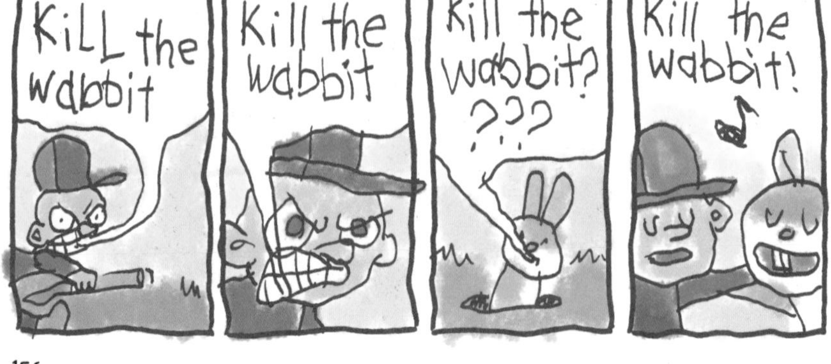
KiLL the wabbit
Kill the wabbit
Kill the wabbit? ???
Kill the wabbit!

FRI APR 13, 2012

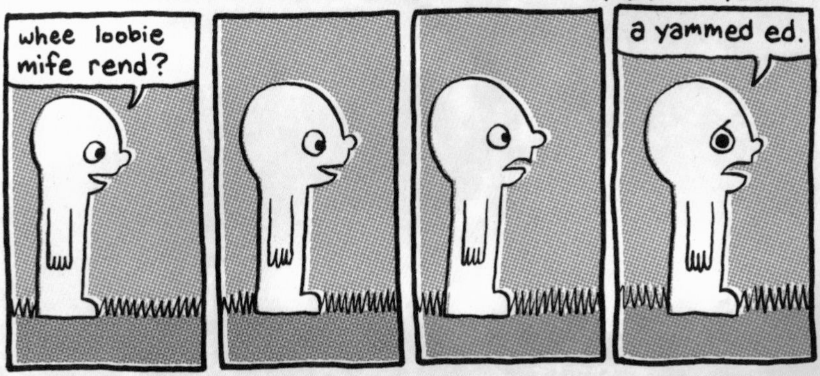
whee loobie mife rend?
a yammed ed.

SAT APR 14, 2012

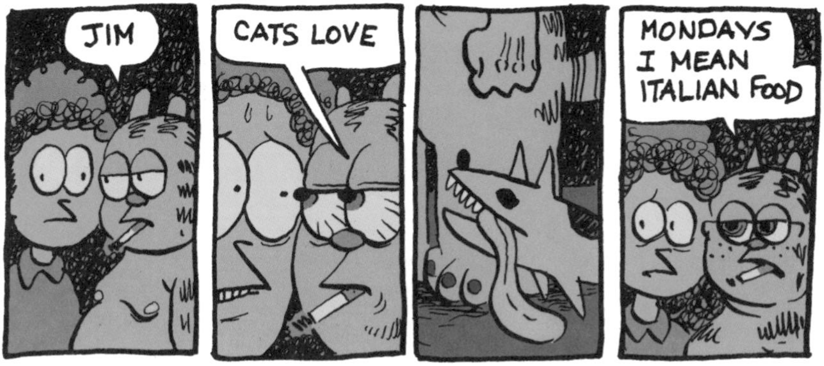
JIM
CATS LOVE
MONDAYS I MEAN ITALIAN FOOD

SUN APR 15, 2012

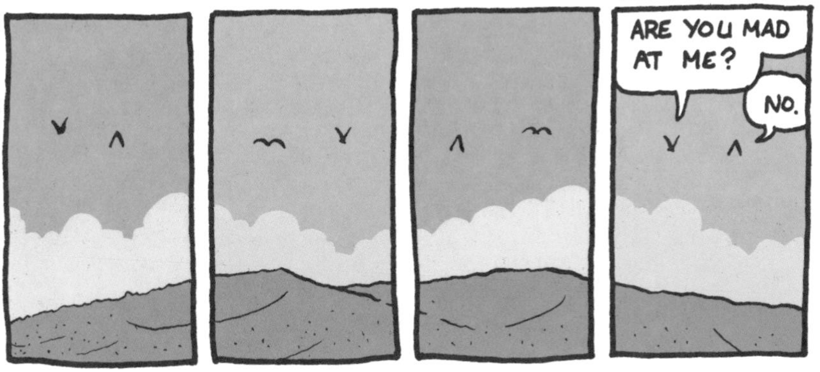
ARE YOU MAD AT ME?
NO.

MON APR 16, 2012

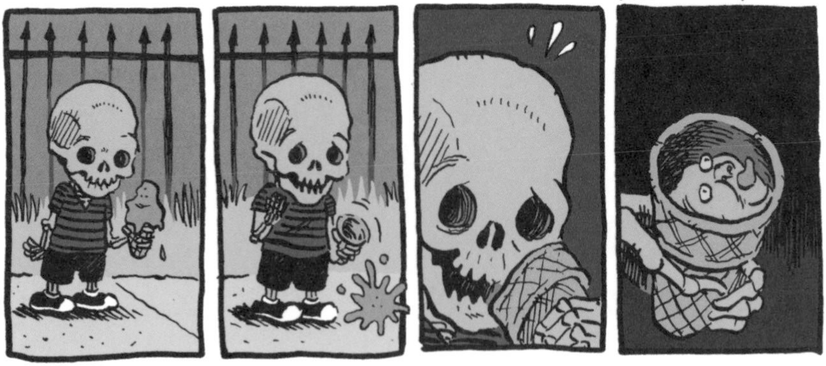

TUE APR 17, 2012

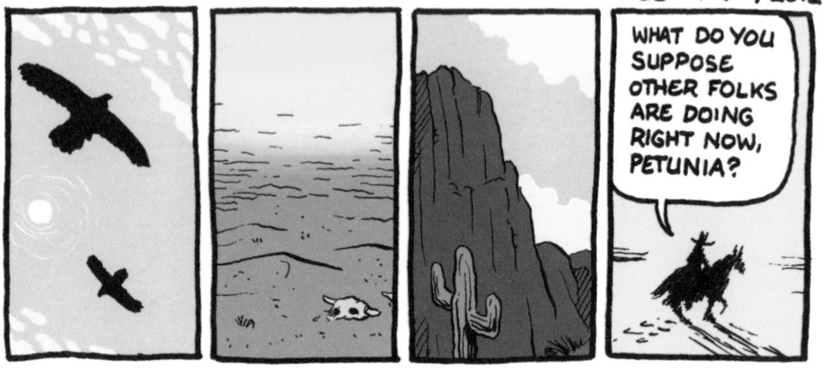
WHAT DO YOU SUPPOSE OTHER FOLKS ARE DOING RIGHT NOW, PETUNIA?

WED APR 18, 2012

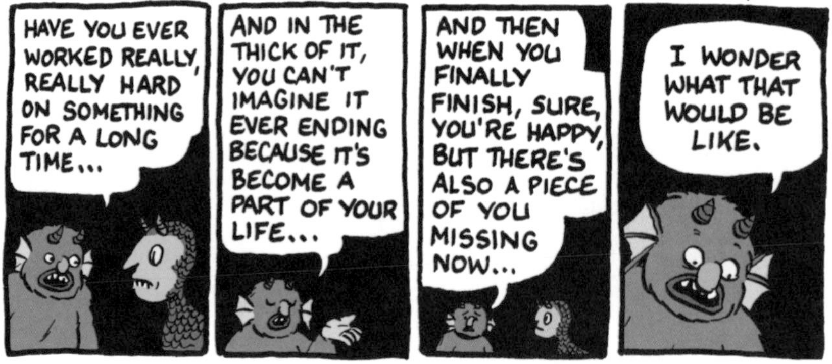
HAVE YOU EVER WORKED REALLY, REALLY HARD ON SOMETHING FOR A LONG TIME...
AND IN THE THICK OF IT, YOU CAN'T IMAGINE IT EVER ENDING BECAUSE IT'S BECOME A PART OF YOUR LIFE...
AND THEN WHEN YOU FINALLY FINISH, SURE, YOU'RE HAPPY, BUT THERE'S ALSO A PIECE OF YOU MISSING NOW...
I WONDER WHAT THAT WOULD BE LIKE.

THU APR 19, 2012

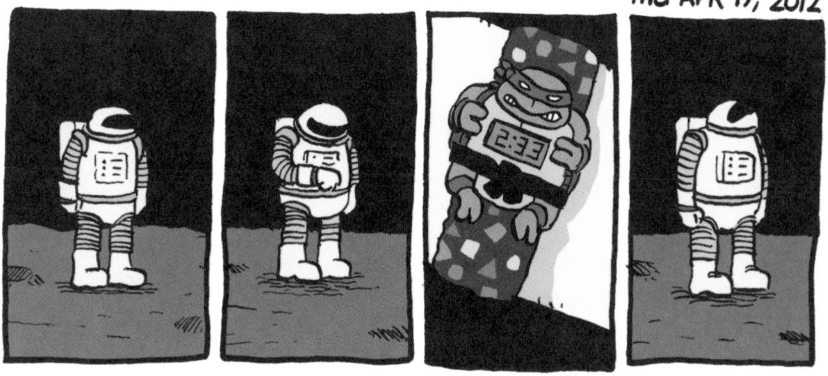
2:33

FRI APR 20, 2012

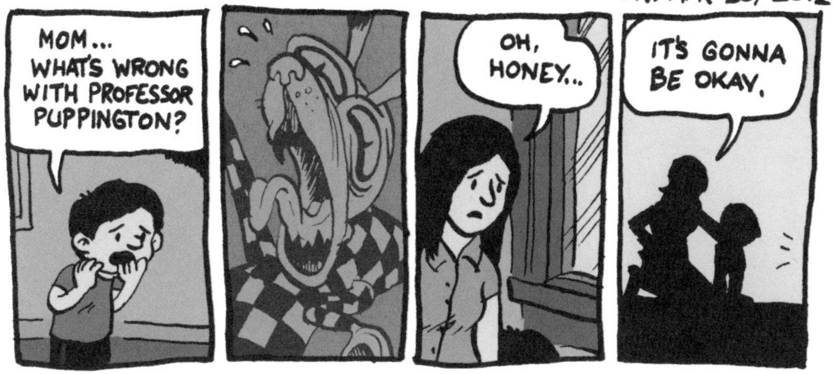
MOM... WHAT'S WRONG WITH PROFESSOR PUPPINGTON?
OH, HONEY...
IT'S GONNA BE OKAY.

SAT APR 21, 2012

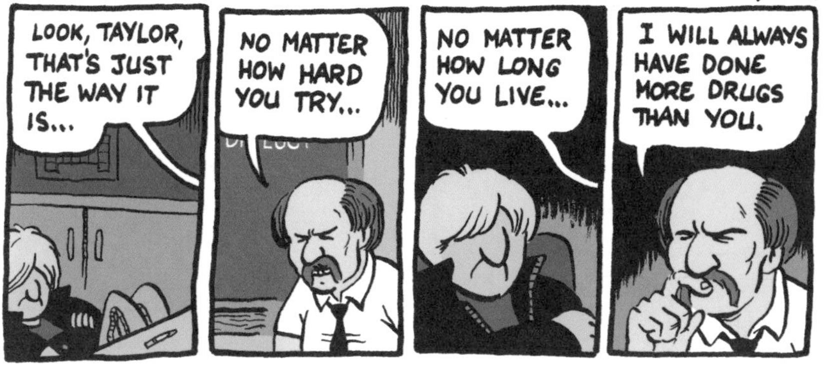
LOOK, TAYLOR, THAT'S JUST THE WAY IT IS...
NO MATTER HOW HARD YOU TRY...
NO MATTER HOW LONG YOU LIVE...
I WILL ALWAYS HAVE DONE MORE DRUGS THAN YOU.

SUN APR 22, 2012

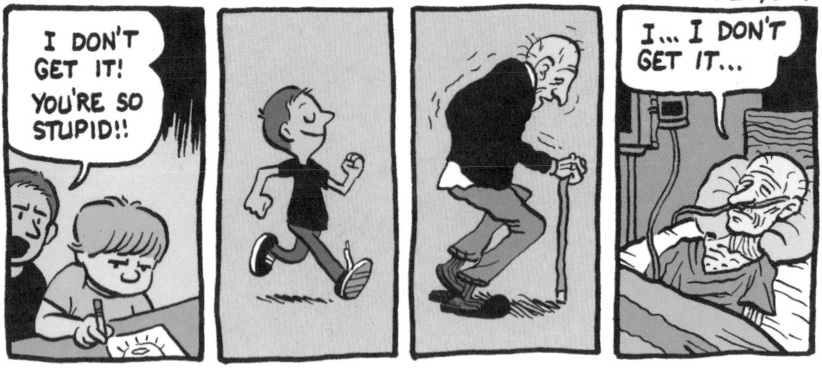

I DON'T GET IT! YOU'RE SO STUPID!!
I... I DON'T GET IT...

MON APR 23, 2012

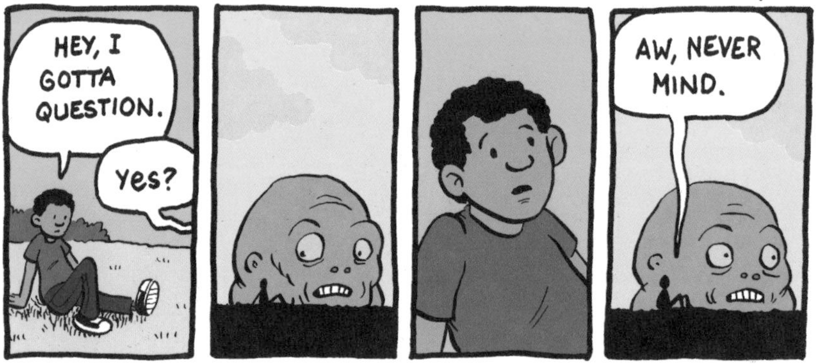

HEY, I GOTTA QUESTION.
Yes?
AW, NEVER MIND.

TUE APR 24, 2012

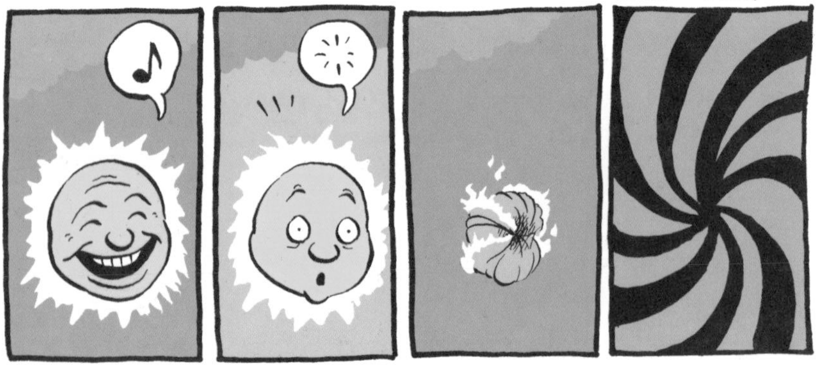

WED APR 25, 2012

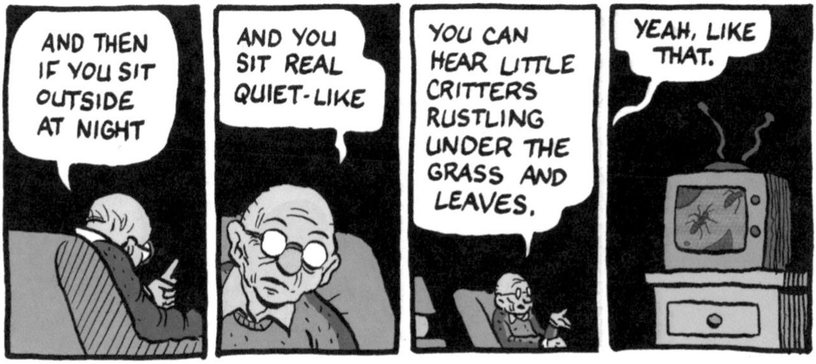
AND THEN IF YOU SIT OUTSIDE AT NIGHT
AND YOU SIT REAL QUIET-LIKE
YOU CAN HEAR LITTLE CRITTERS RUSTLING UNDER THE GRASS AND LEAVES.
YEAH, LIKE THAT.

THU APR 26, 2012

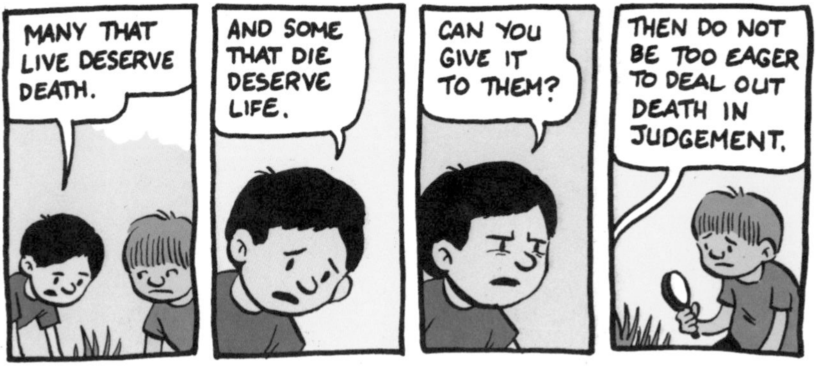
MANY THAT LIVE DESERVE DEATH.
AND SOME THAT DIE DESERVE LIFE.
CAN YOU GIVE IT TO THEM?
THEN DO NOT BE TOO EAGER TO DEAL OUT DEATH IN JUDGEMENT.

FRI APR 27, 2012

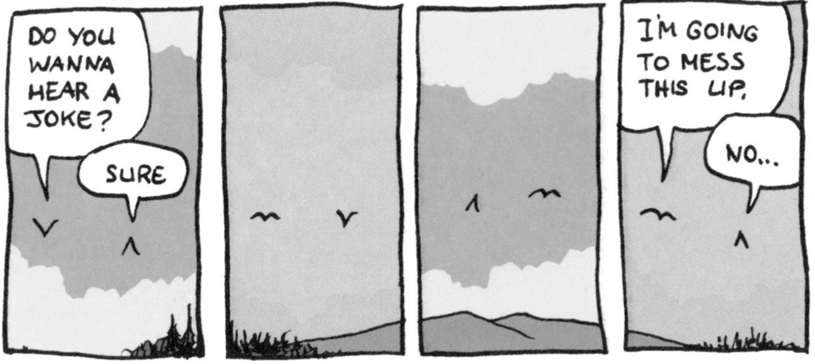
DO YOU WANNA HEAR A JOKE?
SURE
I'M GOING TO MESS THIS UP.
NO...

SAT APR 28, 2012

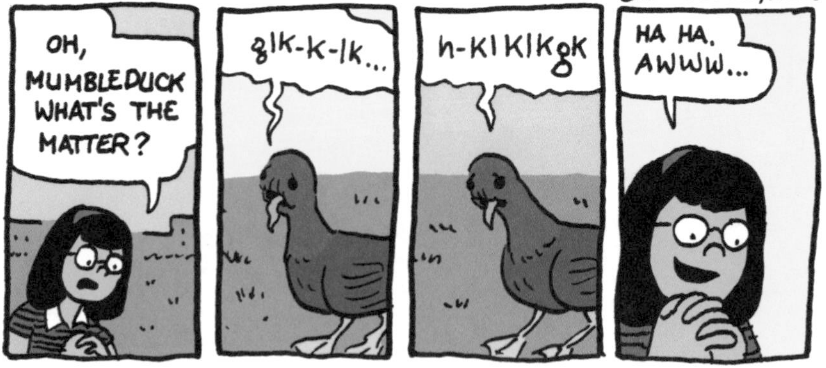
OH, MUMBLEDUCK WHAT'S THE MATTER?
glk-k-lk...
h-KlKlKgK
HA HA. AWWW...

SUN APR 29, 2012

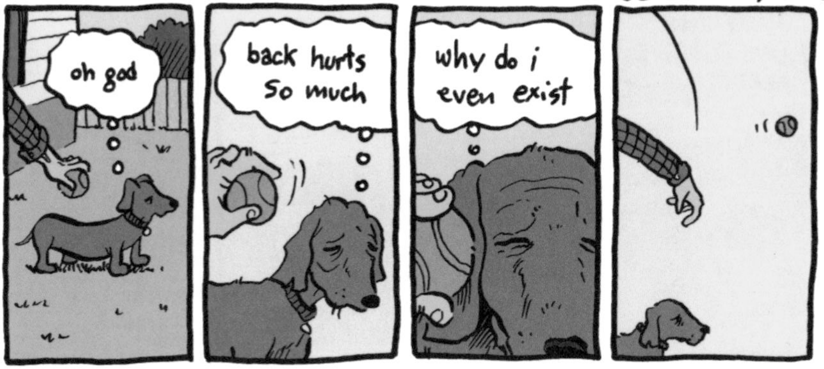
oh god
back hurts so much
why do i even exist

MON APR 30, 2012

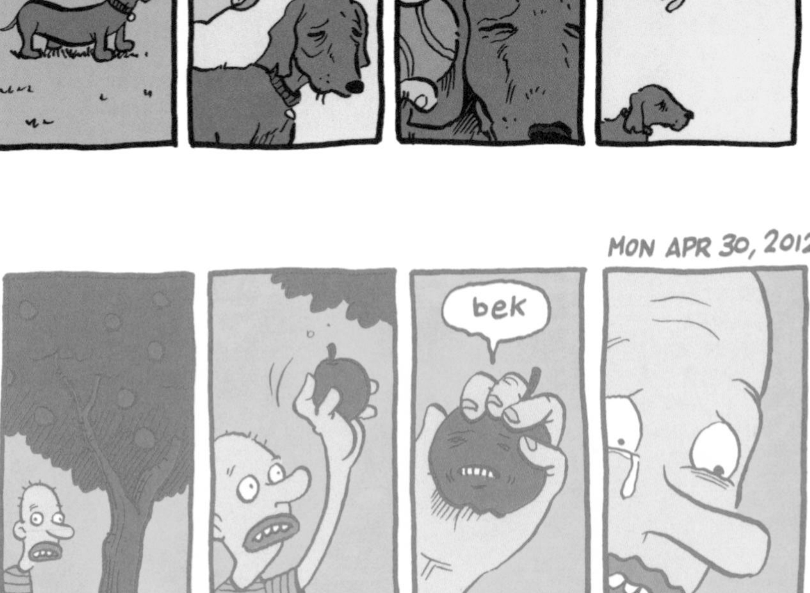
bek

TUE MAY 1, 2012

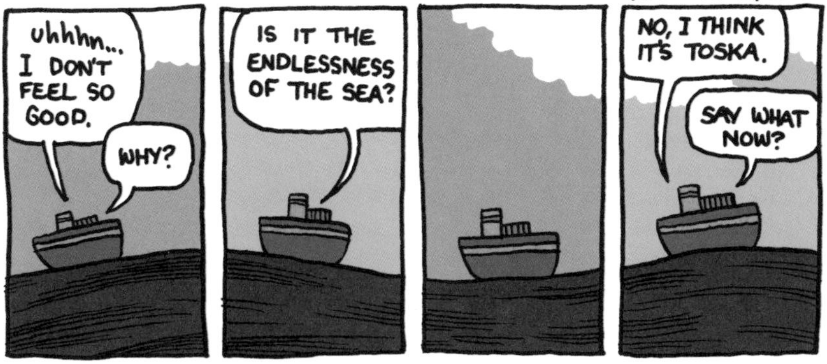
uhhhn... I DON'T FEEL SO GOOD.
WHY?
IS IT THE ENDLESSNESS OF THE SEA?
NO, I THINK IT'S TOSKA.
SAY WHAT NOW?

WED MAY 2, 2012

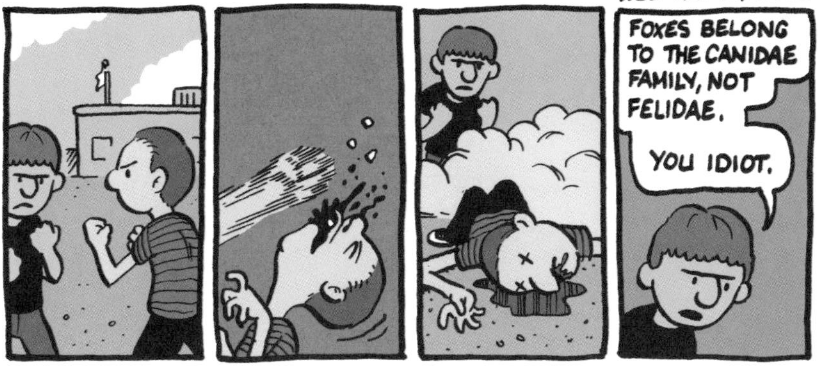
FOXES BELONG TO THE CANIDAE FAMILY, NOT FELIDAE.
YOU IDIOT.

THU MAY 3, 2012

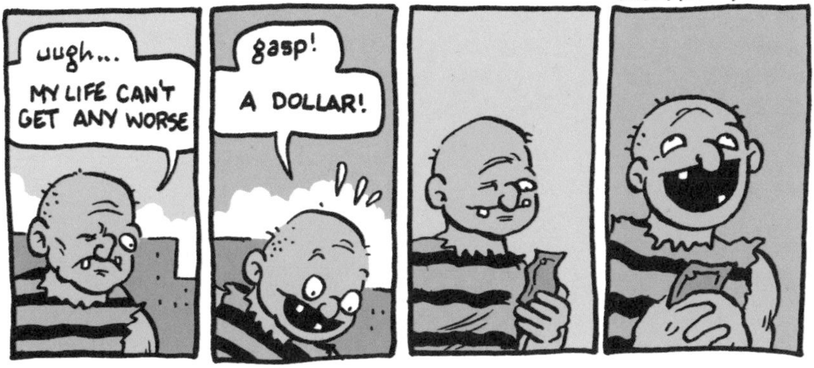
uugh... MY LIFE CAN'T GET ANY WORSE
gasp!
A DOLLAR!

FRI MAY 4, 2012

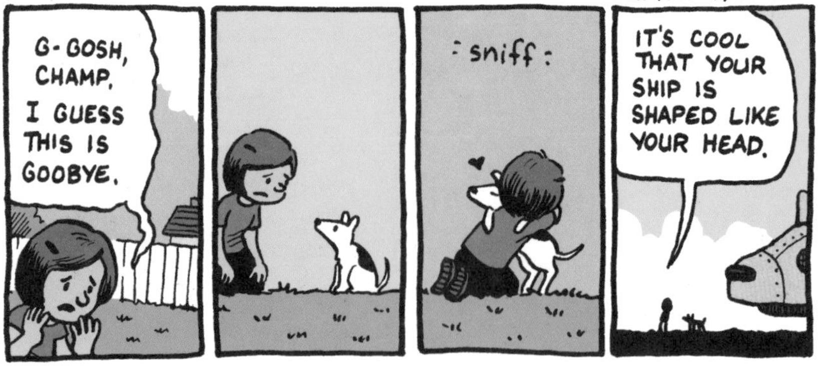
G-GOSH, CHAMP. I GUESS THIS IS GOOBYE.
: sniff :
IT'S COOL THAT YOUR SHIP IS SHAPED LIKE YOUR HEAD.

SAT MAY 5, 2012

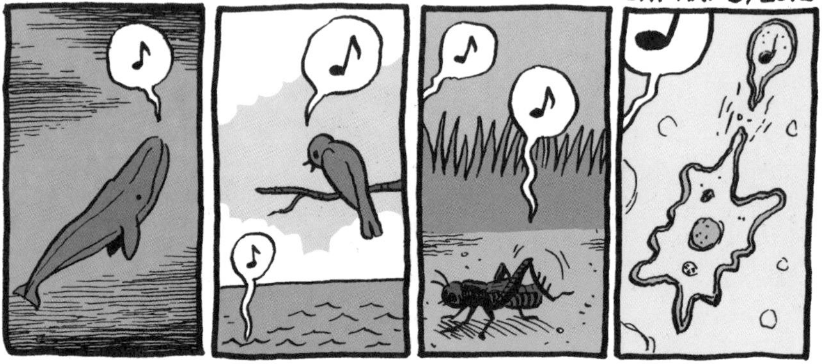

SUN MAY 6, 2012

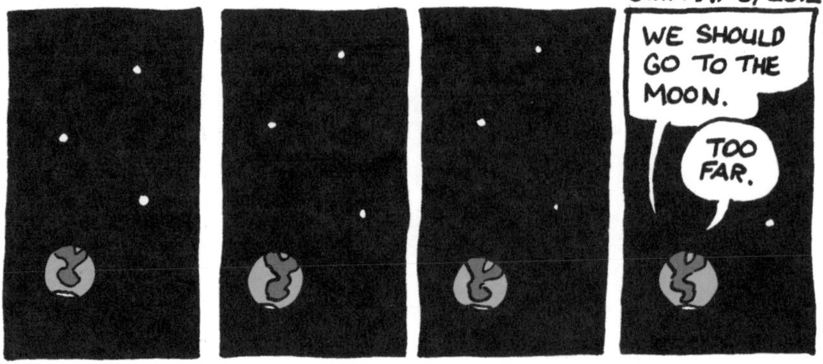
WE SHOULD GO TO THE MOON.
TOO FAR.

MON MAY 7, 2012

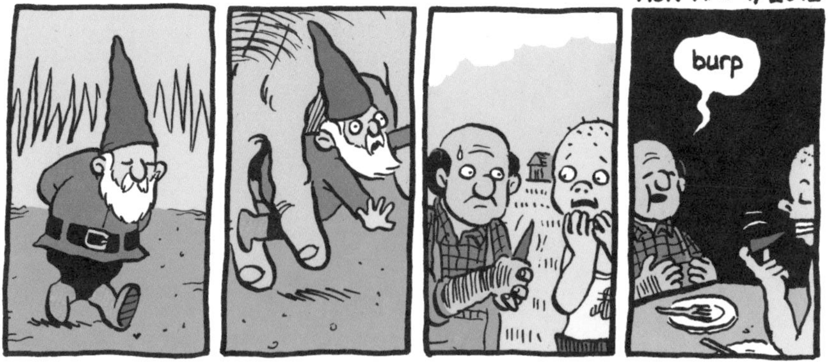
burp

TUE MAY 8, 2012

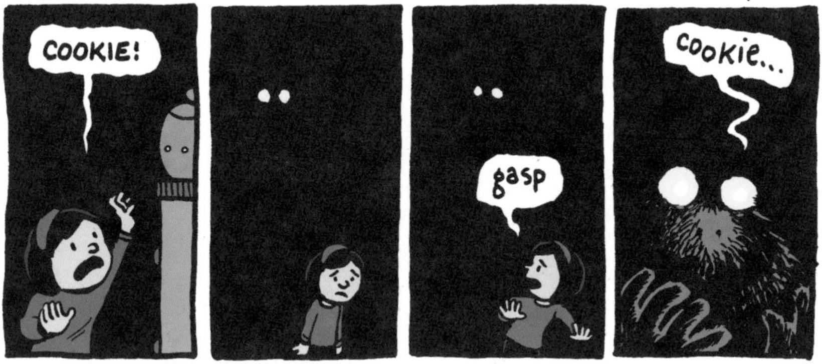
COOKIE!
gasp
cookie...

WED MAY 9, 2012

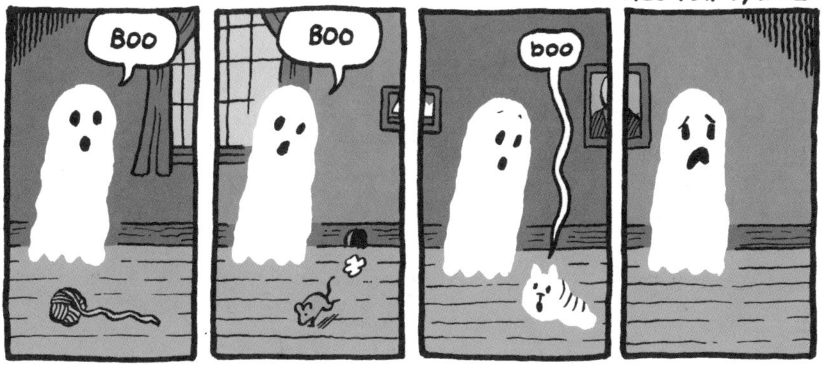
BOO
BOO
boo

THU MAY 10, 2012

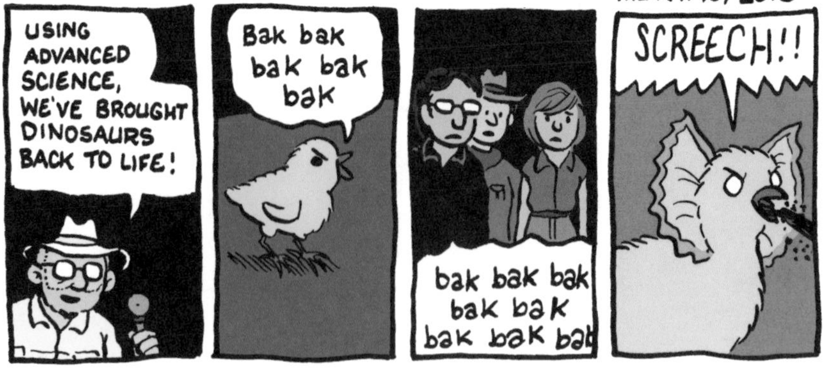
USING ADVANCED SCIENCE, WE'VE BROUGHT DINOSAURS BACK TO LIFE!
Bak bak bak bak bak
bak bak bak bak bak bak bak bat
SCREECH!!

FRI MAY 11, 2012

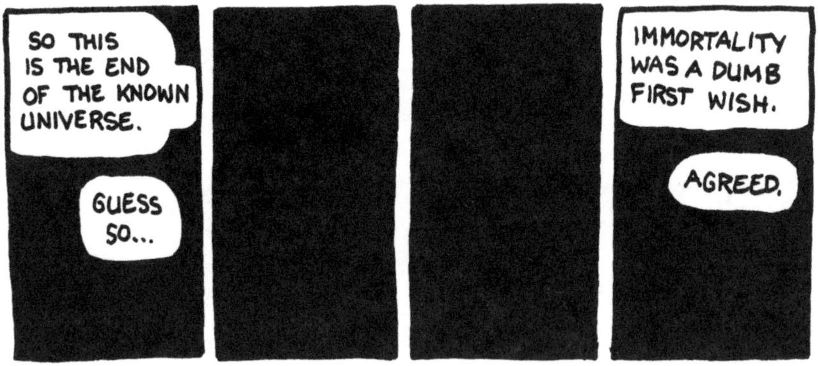
SO THIS IS THE END OF THE KNOWN UNIVERSE.
GUESS SO...
IMMORTALITY WAS A DUMB FIRST WISH.
AGREED.

SAT MAY 12, 2012

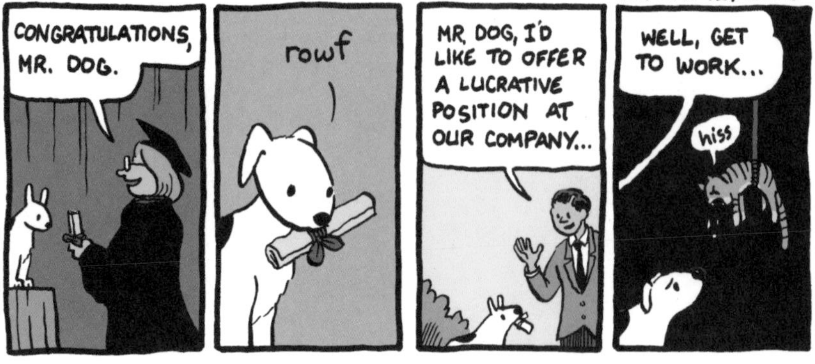
CONGRATULATIONS, MR. DOG.
rowf
MR. DOG, I'D LIKE TO OFFER A LUCRATIVE POSITION AT OUR COMPANY...
WELL, GET TO WORK...
hiss

SUN MAY 13, 2012

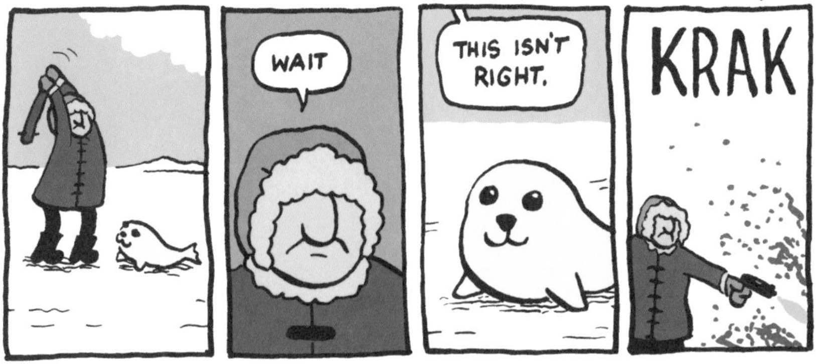
WAIT
THIS ISN'T RIGHT.
KRAK

MON MAY 14, 2012

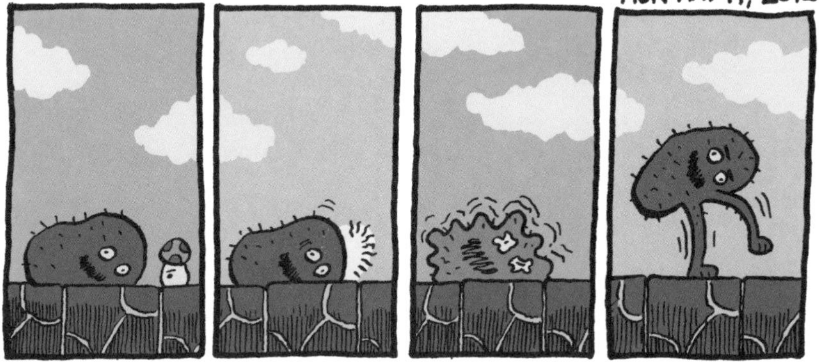

TUE MAY 15, 2012

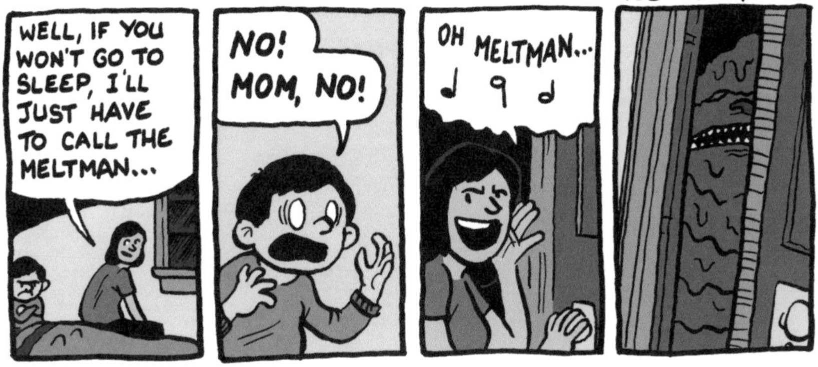
WELL, IF YOU WON'T GO TO SLEEP, I'LL JUST HAVE TO CALL THE MELTMAN...
NO! MOM, NO!
OH MELTMAN...

WED MAY 16, 2012

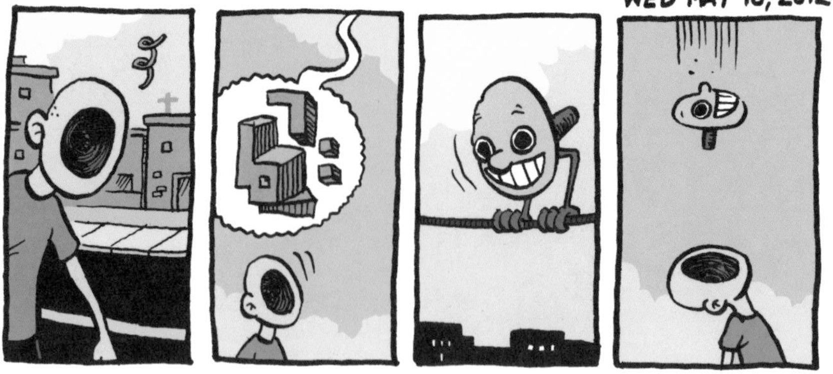

THU MAY 17, 2012

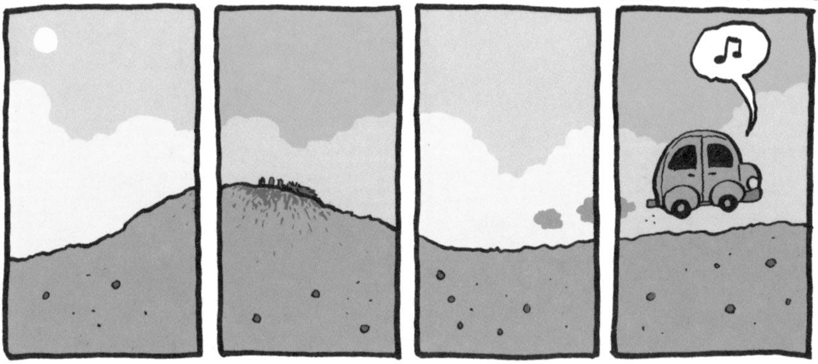

FRI MAY 18, 2012

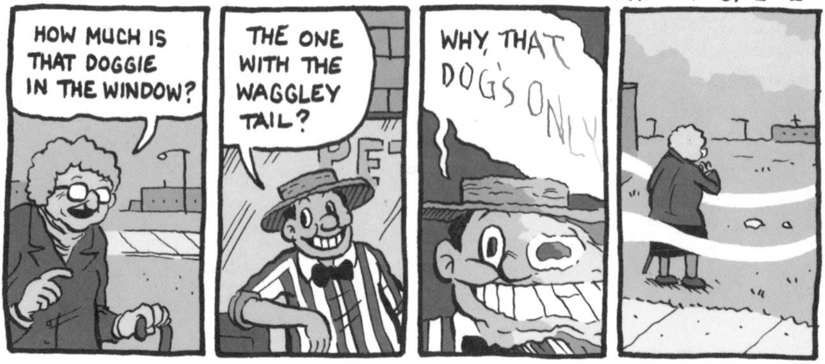
HOW MUCH IS THAT DOGGIE IN THE WINDOW?
THE ONE WITH THE WAGGLEY TAIL?
WHY, THAT DOG'S ONLY

SAT MAY 19, 2012

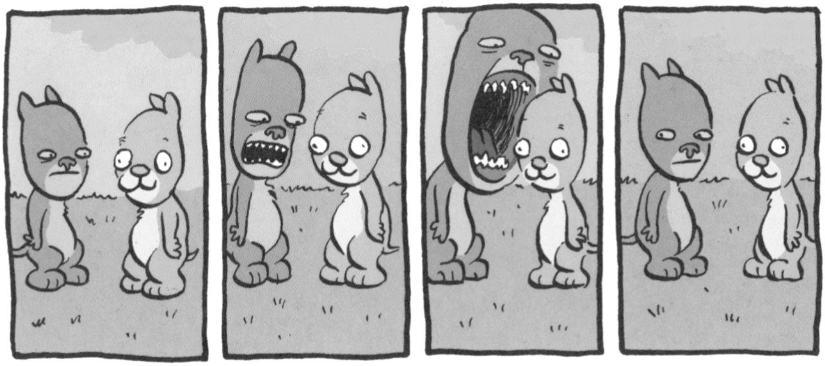

SUN MAY 20, 2012

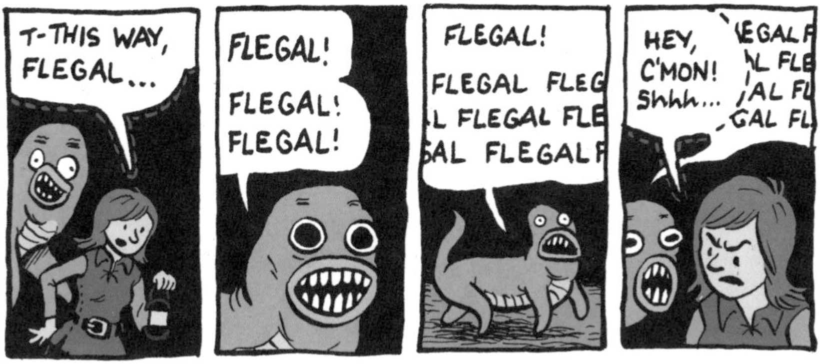
T-THIS WAY, FLEGAL...
FLEGAL!
FLEGAL! FLEGAL!
FLEGAL!
FLEGAL FLEG
L FLEGAL FLE
AL FLEGAL F
HEY, C'MON! Shhh...

MON MAY 21, 2012

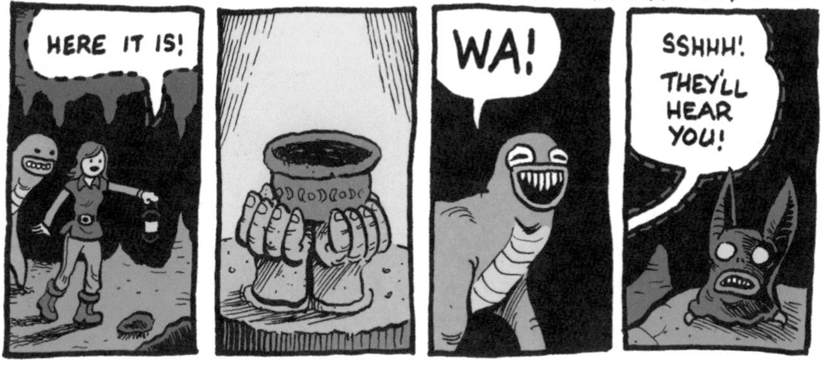
HERE IT IS!
WA!
SSHHH! THEY'LL HEAR YOU!

TUE MAY 22, 2012

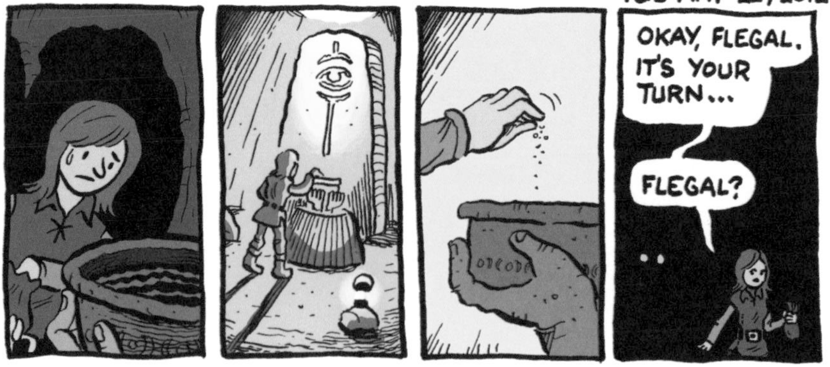
OKAY, FLEGAL. IT'S YOUR TURN...
FLEGAL?

WED MAY 23, 2012

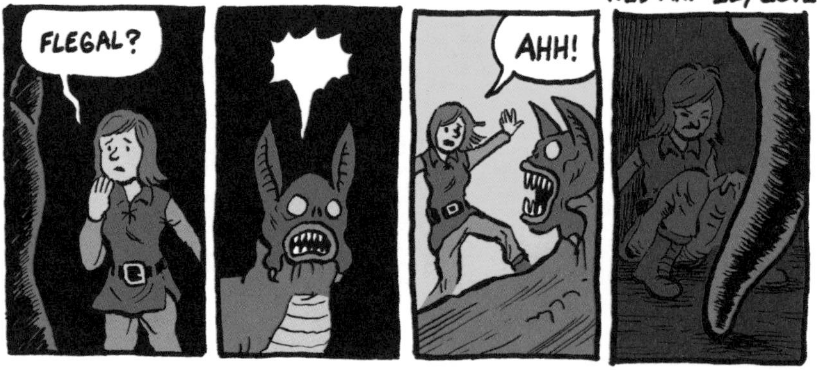
FLEGAL?
AHH!

THU MAY 24, 2012

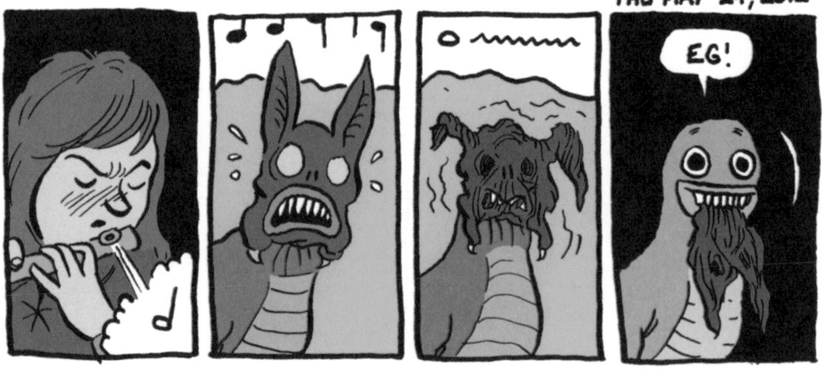
EG!

FRI MAY 25, 2012

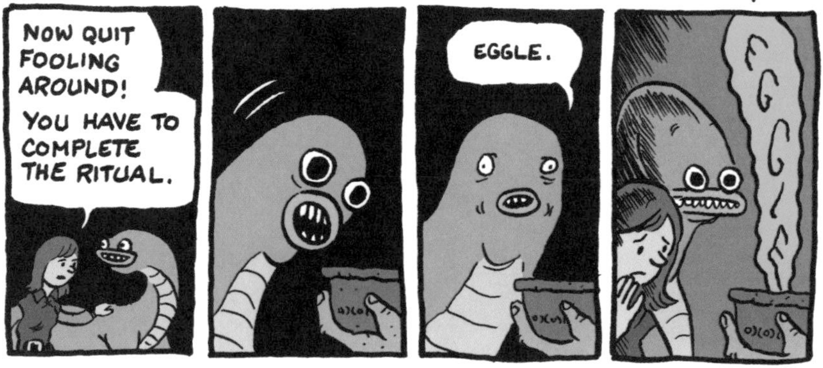
NOW QUIT FOOLING AROUND!
YOU HAVE TO COMPLETE THE RITUAL.
EGGLE.

SAT MAY 26, 2012

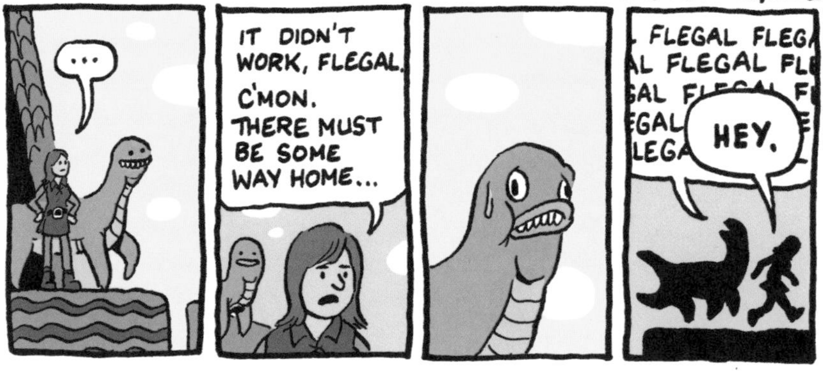
...
IT DIDN'T WORK, FLEGAL.
C'MON. THERE MUST BE SOME WAY HOME...
FLEGAL FLEG
L FLEGAL FL
HEY.

SUN MAY 27, 2012

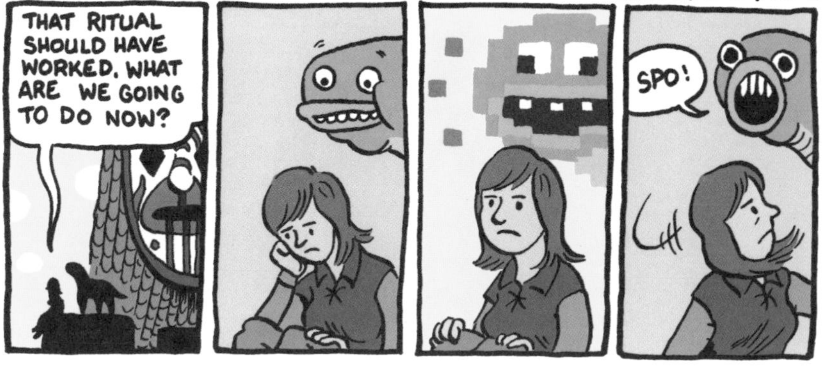
THAT RITUAL SHOULD HAVE WORKED. WHAT ARE WE GOING TO DO NOW?
SPO!

MON MAY 28, 2012

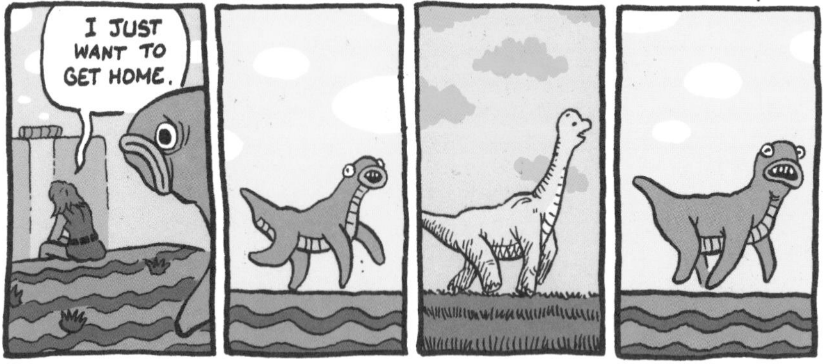
I JUST WANT TO GET HOME.

TUE MAY 29, 2012

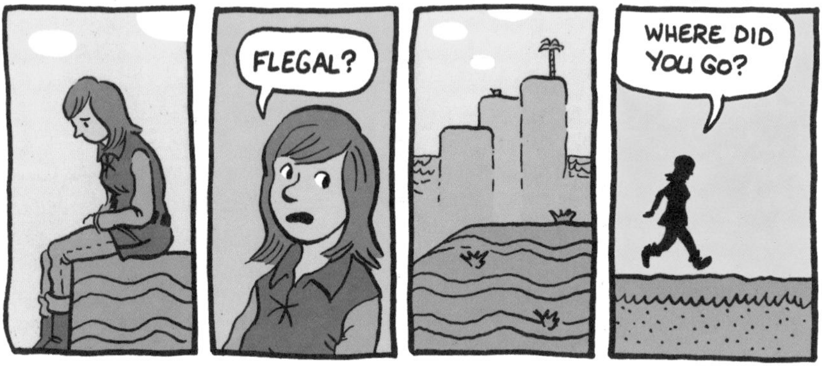
FLEGAL?
WHERE DID YOU GO?

WED MAY 30, 2012

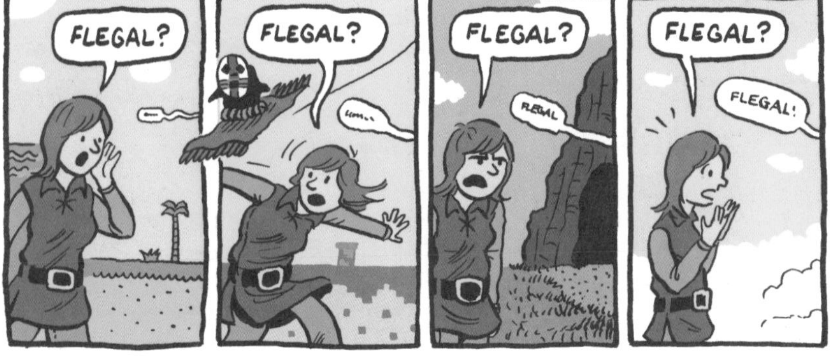
FLEGAL?
FLEGAL?
FLEGAL?
FLEGAL
FLEGAL?
FLEGAL!

THU MAY 31, 2012

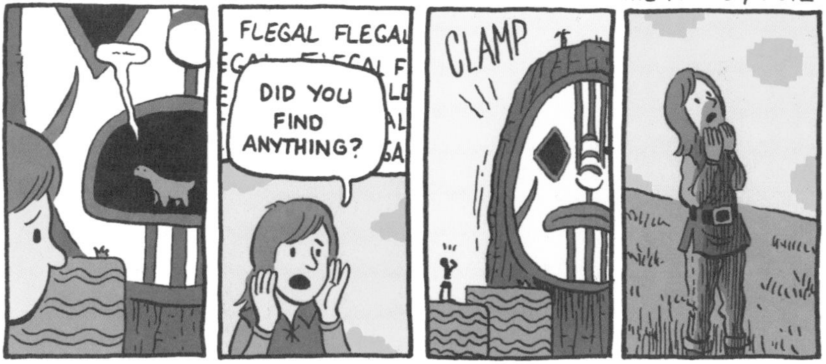
FLEGAL FLEGAL
DID YOU FIND ANYTHING?
CLAMP

FRI JUNE 1, 2012

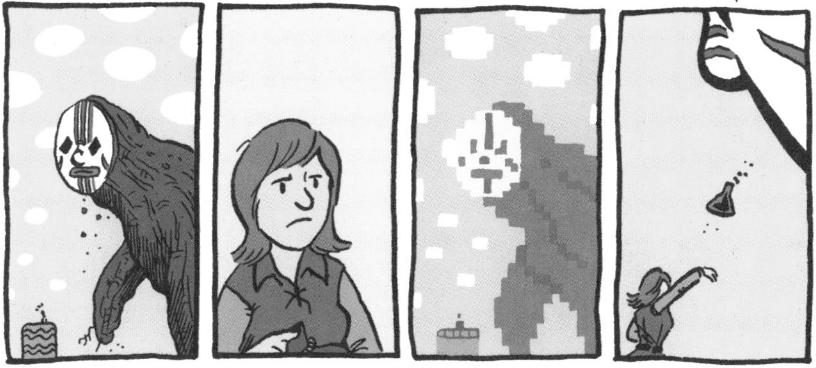

SAT JUNE 2, 2012

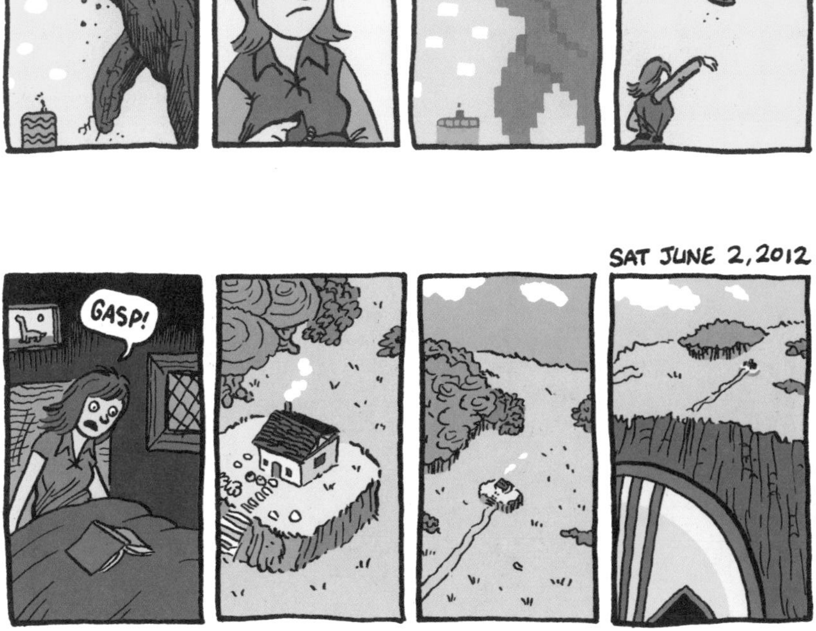
GASP!

SUN JUNE 3, 2012

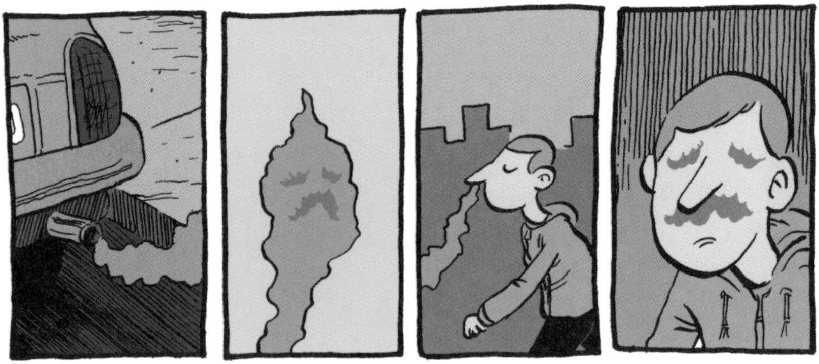

MON JUNE 4, 2012

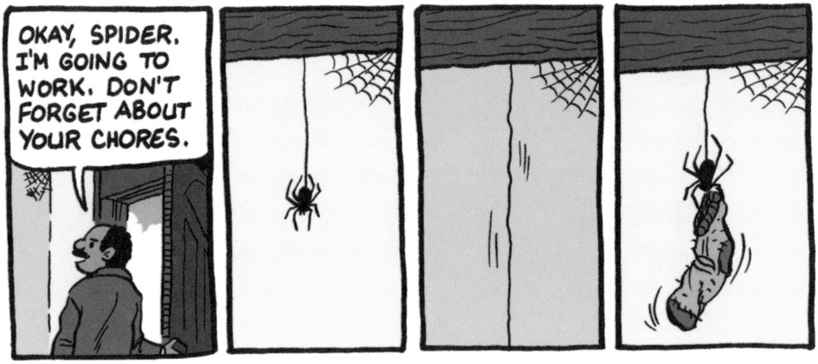
OKAY, SPIDER. I'M GOING TO WORK. DON'T FORGET ABOUT YOUR CHORES.

TUE JUNE 5, 2012

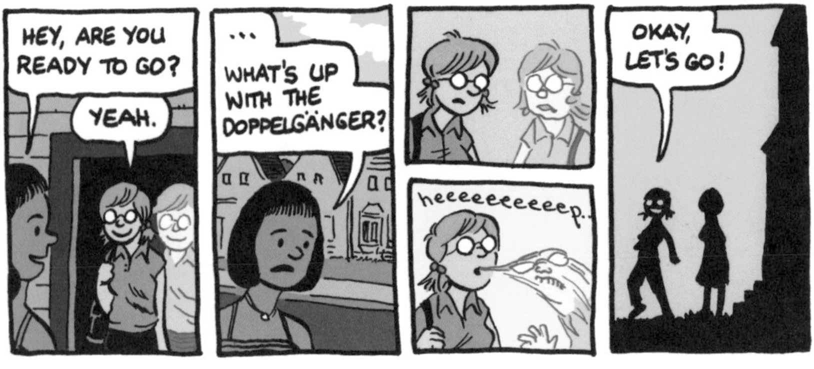
HEY, ARE YOU READY TO GO?
YEAH.
...
WHAT'S UP WITH THE DOPPELGÄNGER?
heeeeeeeeeeep..
OKAY, LET'S GO!

WED JUNE 6, 2012

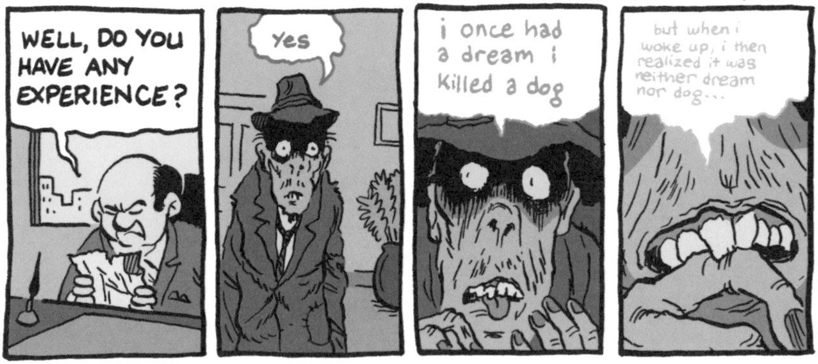
WELL, DO YOU HAVE ANY EXPERIENCE?
Yes
i once had a dream i killed a dog
but when i woke up, i then realized it was neither dream nor dog...

THU JUNE 7, 2012

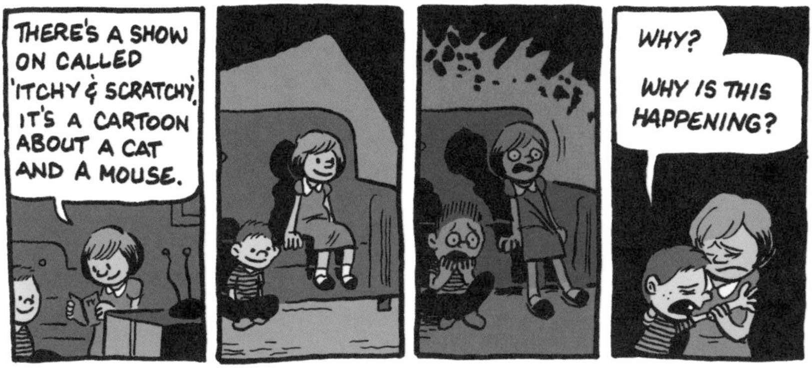
THERE'S A SHOW ON CALLED 'ITCHY & SCRATCHY'. IT'S A CARTOON ABOUT A CAT AND A MOUSE.
WHY?
WHY IS THIS HAPPENING?

FRI JUNE 8, 2012

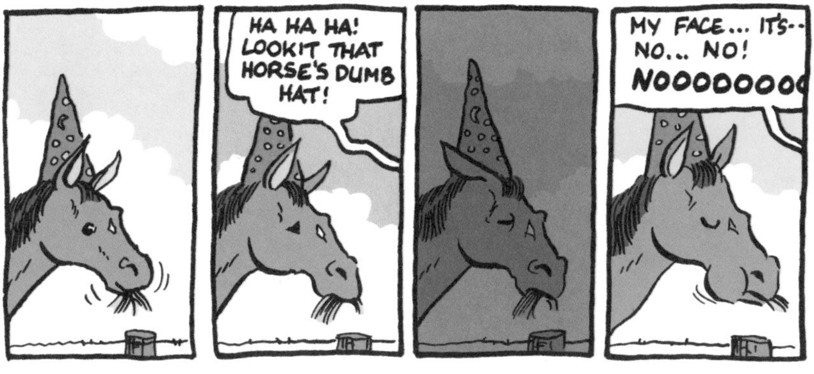
HA HA HA! LOOKIT THAT HORSE'S DUMB HAT!
MY FACE... IT'S--
NO... NO!
NOOOOOOOO

SAT JUNE 9, 2012

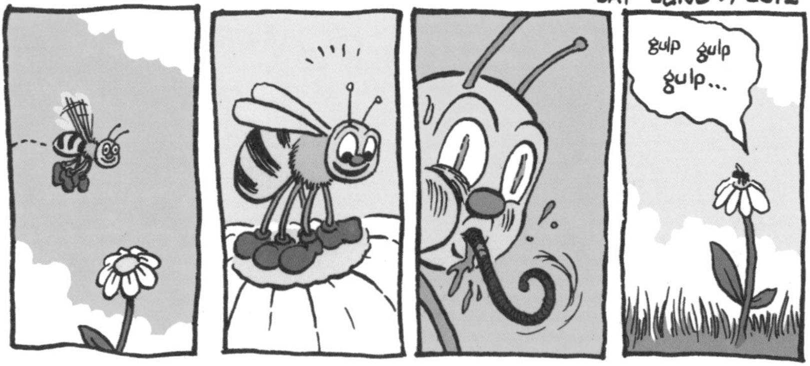
gulp gulp gulp...

SUN JUNE 10, 2012

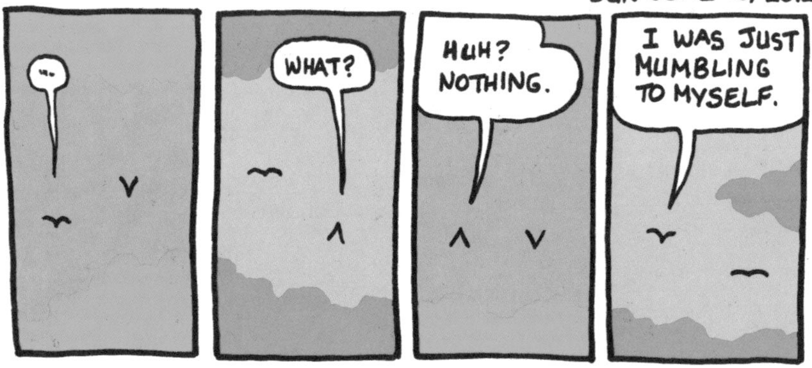
WHAT?
HUH? NOTHING.
I WAS JUST MUMBLING TO MYSELF.

MON JUNE 11, 2012

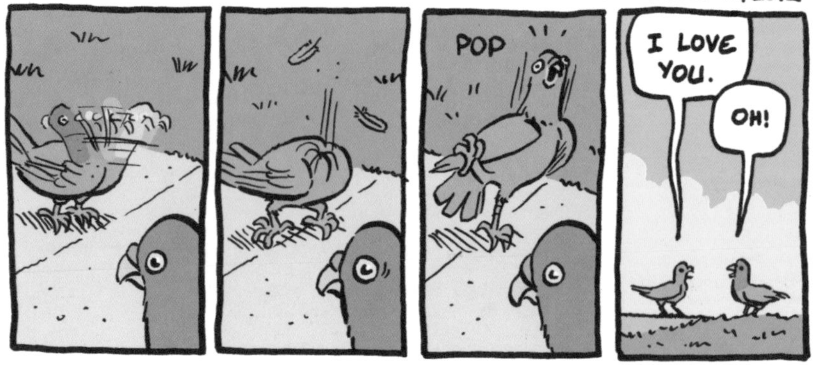
POP
I LOVE YOU.
OH!

TUE JUNE 12, 2012

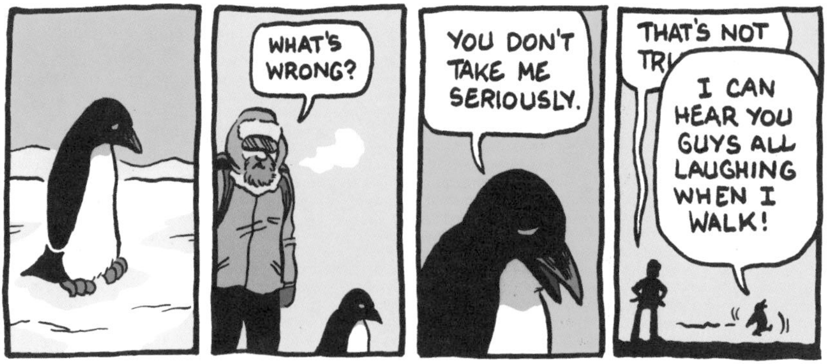
WHAT'S WRONG?
YOU DON'T TAKE ME SERIOUSLY.
THAT'S NOT
I CAN HEAR YOU GUYS ALL LAUGHING WHEN I WALK!

WED JUNE 13, 2012

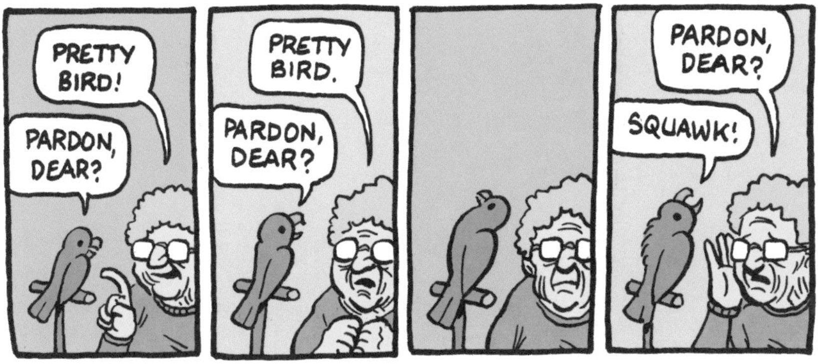
PRETTY BIRD!
PARDON, DEAR?
PRETTY BIRD.
PARDON, DEAR?
PARDON, DEAR?
SQUAWK!

THU JUNE 14, 2012

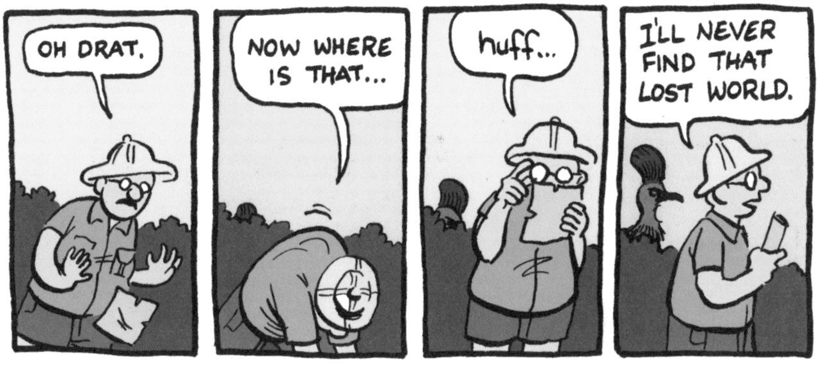
OH DRAT.
NOW WHERE IS THAT...
huff...
I'LL NEVER FIND THAT LOST WORLD.

FRI JUNE 15, 2012

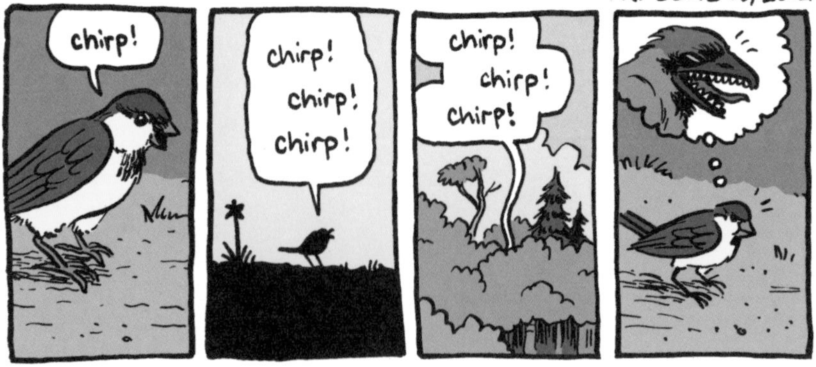
chirp!
chirp! chirp! chirp!
chirp! chirp! chirp!

SAT JUNE 16, 2012

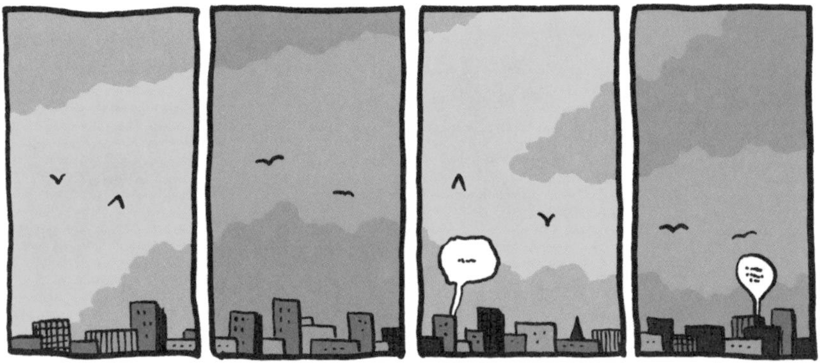

SUN JUNE 17, 2012

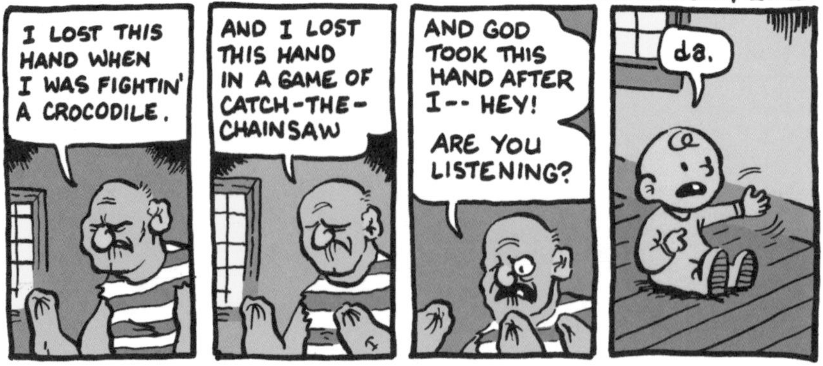
I LOST THIS HAND WHEN I WAS FIGHTIN' A CROCODILE.
AND I LOST THIS HAND IN A GAME OF CATCH-THE-CHAINSAW
AND GOD TOOK THIS HAND AFTER I-- HEY!
ARE YOU LISTENING?
da.

MON JUNE 18, 2012

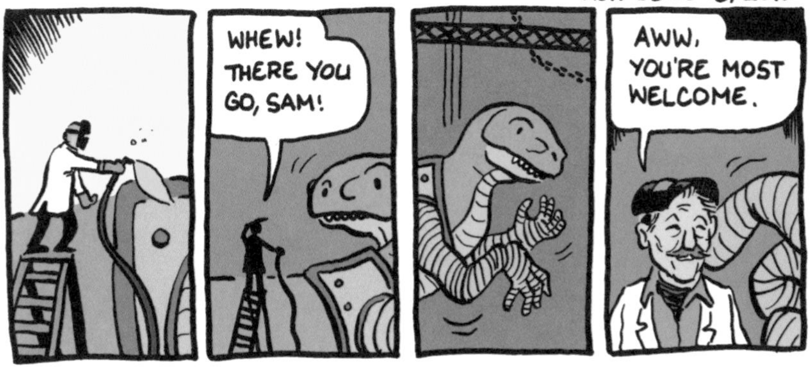
WHEW! THERE YOU GO, SAM!
AWW, YOU'RE MOST WELCOME.

TUE JUNE 19, 2012

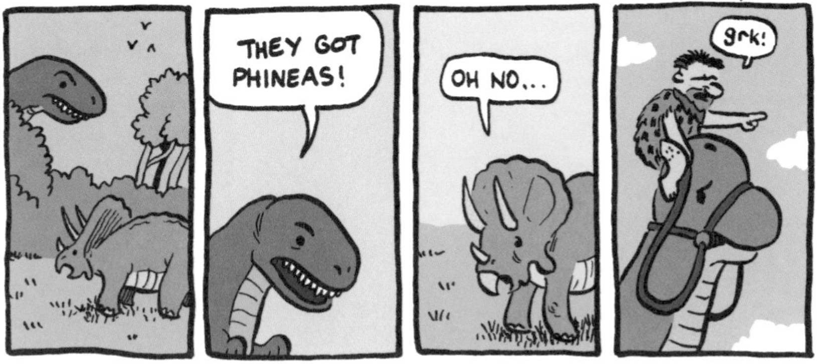
THEY GOT PHINEAS!
OH NO...
grk!

WED JUNE 20, 2012

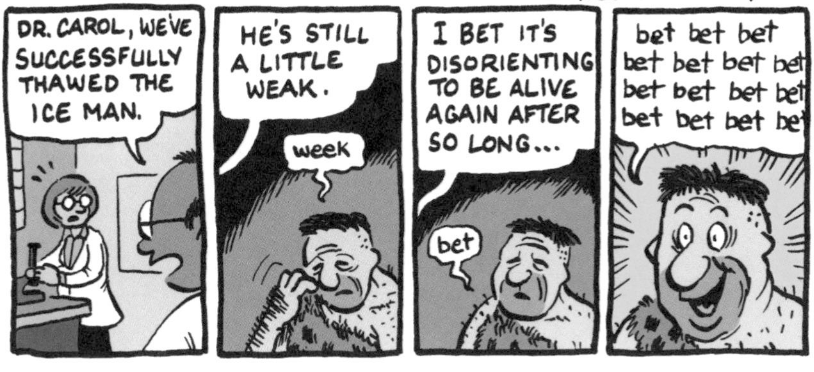
DR. CAROL, WE'VE SUCCESSFULLY THAWED THE ICE MAN.
HE'S STILL A LITTLE WEAK.
week
I BET IT'S DISORIENTING TO BE ALIVE AGAIN AFTER SO LONG...
bet
bet bet bet bet bet bet bet bet bet bet bet bet bet bet bet

THU JUNE 21, 2012

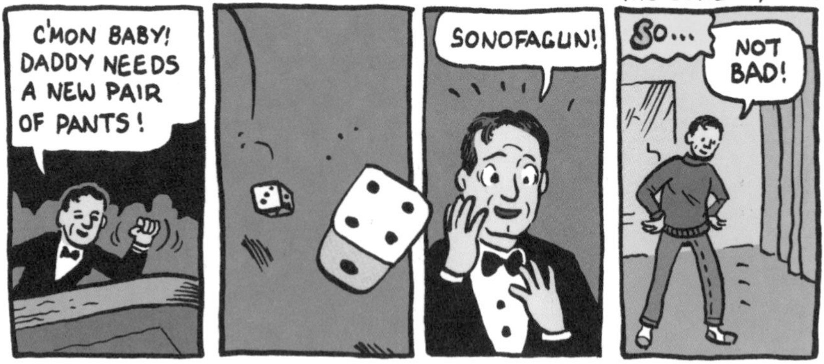

C'MON BABY! DADDY NEEDS A NEW PAIR OF PANTS!
SONOFAGUN!
SO...
NOT BAD!

FRI JUNE 22, 2012

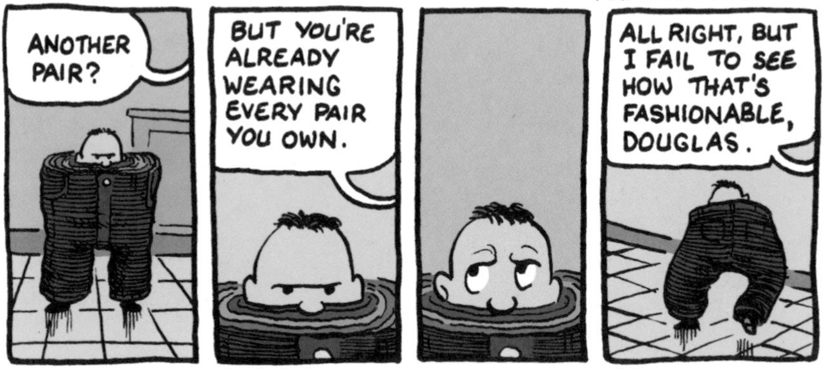

ANOTHER PAIR?
BUT YOU'RE ALREADY WEARING EVERY PAIR YOU OWN.
ALL RIGHT, BUT I FAIL TO SEE HOW THAT'S FASHIONABLE, DOUGLAS.

SAT JUNE 23, 2012

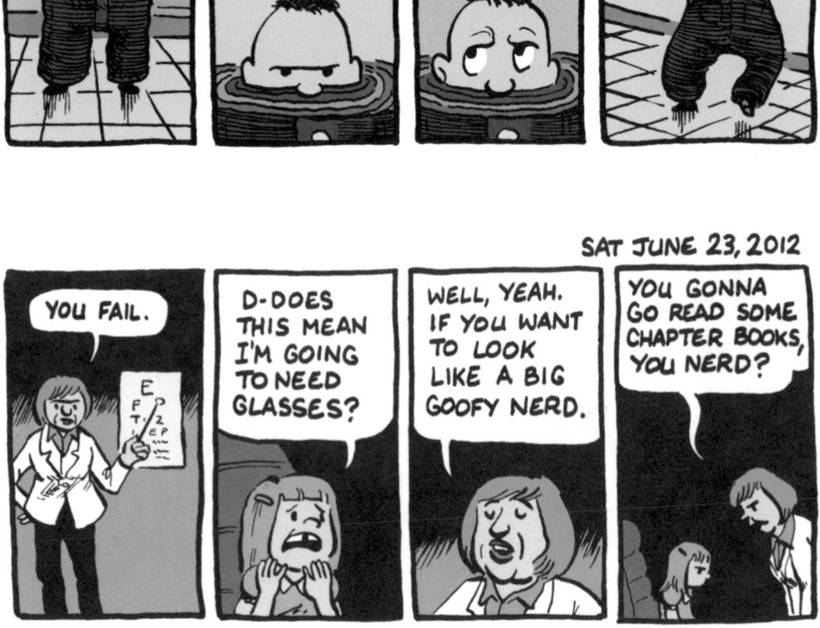

YOU FAIL.
D-DOES THIS MEAN I'M GOING TO NEED GLASSES?
WELL, YEAH. IF YOU WANT TO LOOK LIKE A BIG GOOFY NERD.
YOU GONNA GO READ SOME CHAPTER BOOKS, YOU NERD?

SUN JUNE 24, 2012

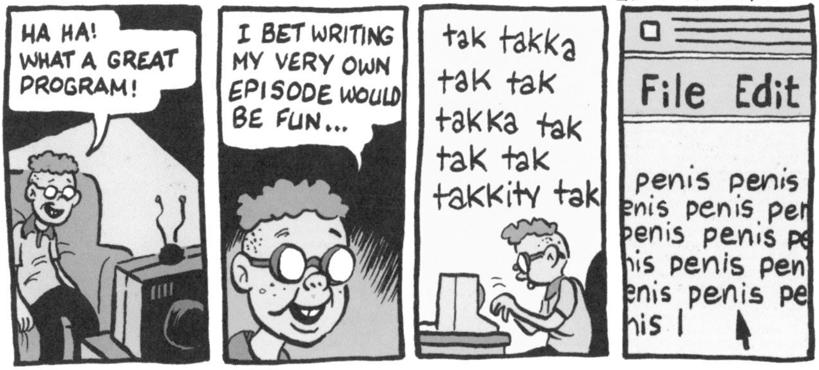
HA HA! WHAT A GREAT PROGRAM!
I BET WRITING MY VERY OWN EPISODE WOULD BE FUN...
tak takka tak tak takka tak tak tak takkity tak
File Edit
penis penis
enis penis pe
penis penis p
nis penis pen
enis penis pe
nis

MON JUNE 25, 2012

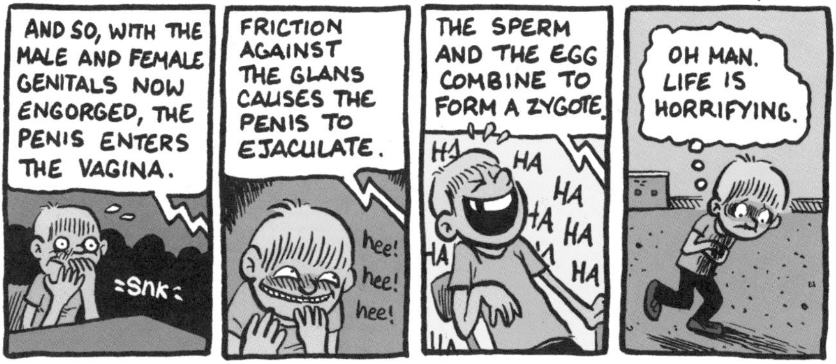
AND SO, WITH THE MALE AND FEMALE GENITALS NOW ENGORGED, THE PENIS ENTERS THE VAGINA.
SNK
FRICTION AGAINST THE GLANS CAUSES THE PENIS TO EJACULATE.
hee! hee! hee!
THE SPERM AND THE EGG COMBINE TO FORM A ZYGOTE.
HA HA HA HA HA HA
OH MAN. LIFE IS HORRIFYING.

TUE JUNE 26, 2012.

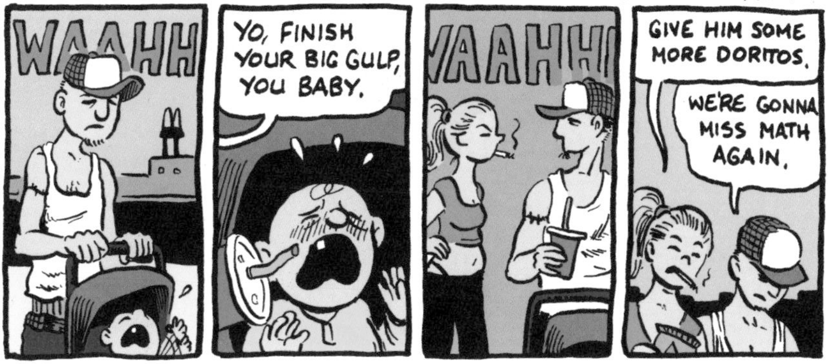
WAAHH
YO, FINISH YOUR BIG GULP, YOU BABY.
GIVE HIM SOME MORE DORITOS.
WE'RE GONNA MISS MATH AGAIN.

WED JUNE 27, 2012

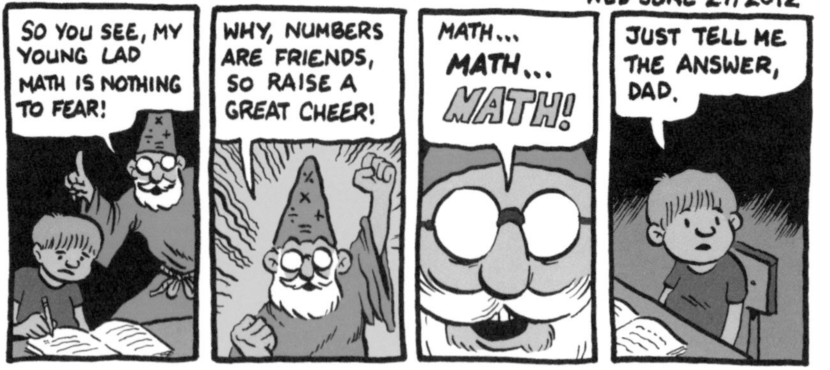
SO YOU SEE, MY YOUNG LAD MATH IS NOTHING TO FEAR!
WHY, NUMBERS ARE FRIENDS, SO RAISE A GREAT CHEER!
MATH... MATH... MATH!
JUST TELL ME THE ANSWER, DAD.

THU JUNE 28, 2012

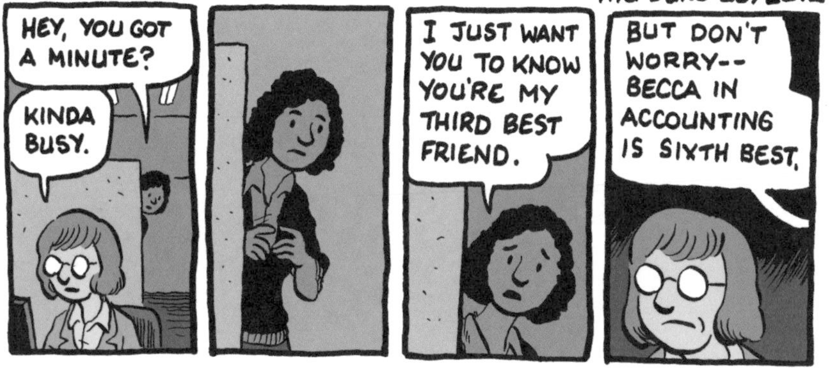
HEY, YOU GOT A MINUTE?
KINDA BUSY.
I JUST WANT YOU TO KNOW YOU'RE MY THIRD BEST FRIEND.
BUT DON'T WORRY-- BECCA IN ACCOUNTING IS SIXTH BEST.

FRI JUNE 29, 2012

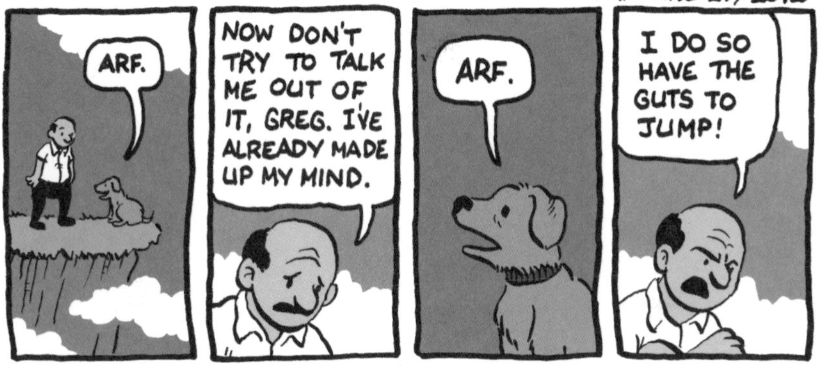
ARF.
NOW DON'T TRY TO TALK ME OUT OF IT, GREG. I'VE ALREADY MADE UP MY MIND.
ARF.
I DO SO HAVE THE GUTS TO JUMP!

SAT JUNE 30, 2012

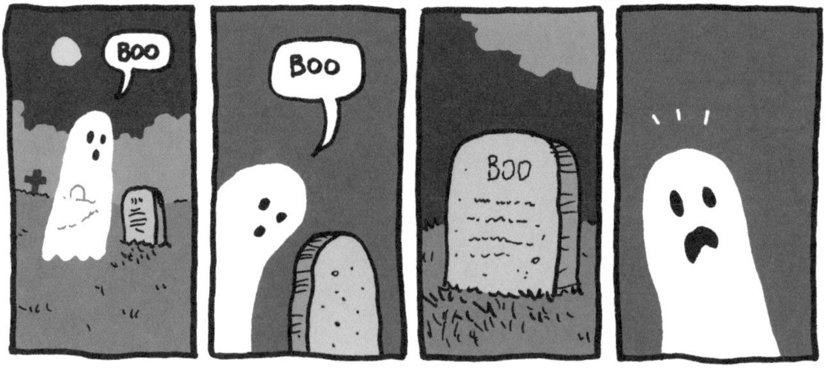
BOO
BOO
BOO

SUN JULY 1, 2012

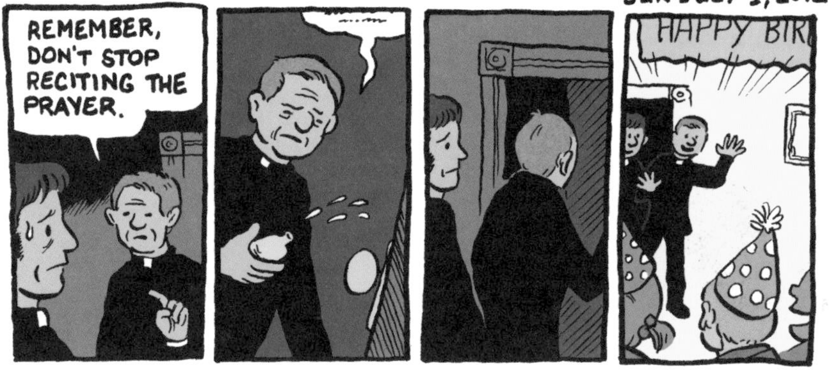
REMEMBER, DON'T STOP RECITING THE PRAYER.
HAPPY BIR

MON JULY 2, 2012

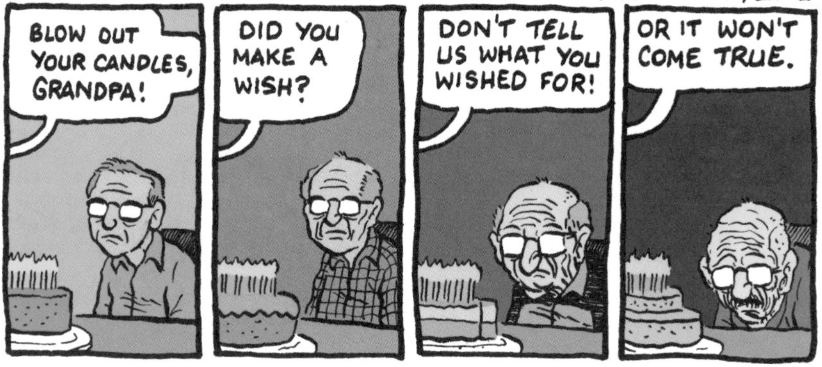
BLOW OUT YOUR CANDLES, GRANDPA!
DID YOU MAKE A WISH?
DON'T TELL US WHAT YOU WISHED FOR!
OR IT WON'T COME TRUE.

TUE JULY 3, 2012

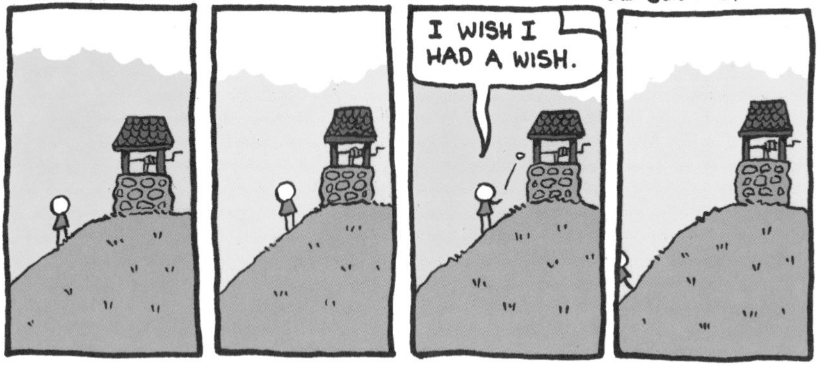
I WISH I HAD A WISH.

WED JULY 4, 2012

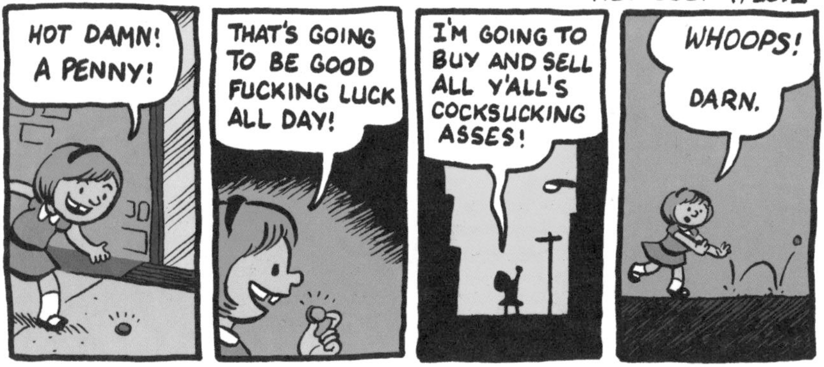
HOT DAMN! A PENNY!
THAT'S GOING TO BE GOOD FUCKING LUCK ALL DAY!
I'M GOING TO BUY AND SELL ALL Y'ALL'S COCKSUCKING ASSES!
WHOOPS!
DARN.

THU JULY 5, 2012

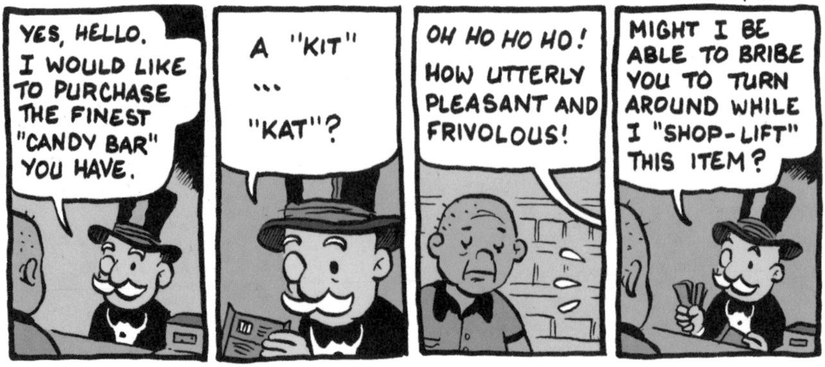
YES, HELLO. I WOULD LIKE TO PURCHASE THE FINEST "CANDY BAR" YOU HAVE.
A "KIT" ... "KAT"?
OH HO HO HO! HOW UTTERLY PLEASANT AND FRIVOLOUS!
MIGHT I BE ABLE TO BRIBE YOU TO TURN AROUND WHILE I "SHOP-LIFT" THIS ITEM?

FRI JULY 6, 2012

SAT JULY 7, 2012

SUN JULY 8, 2012

BA

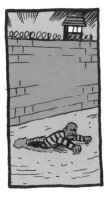

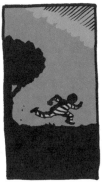

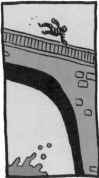

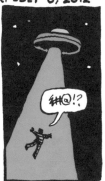

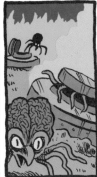

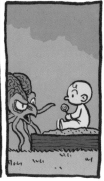

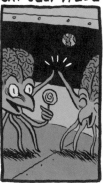

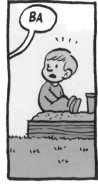

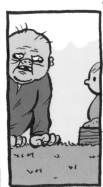

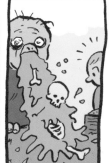

MON JULY 9, 2012

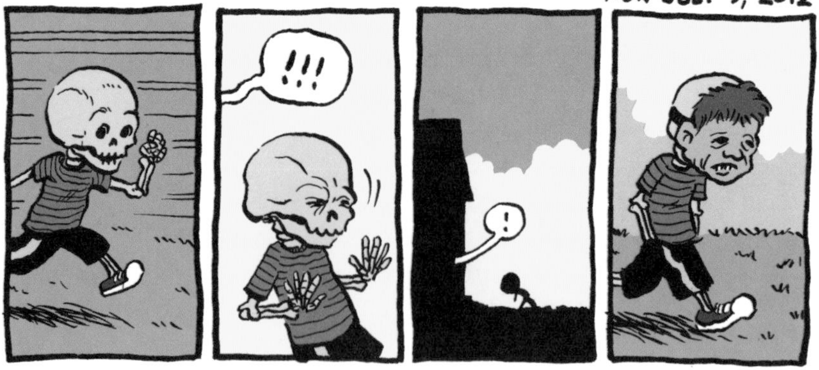
!!!
!

TUE JULY 10, 2012

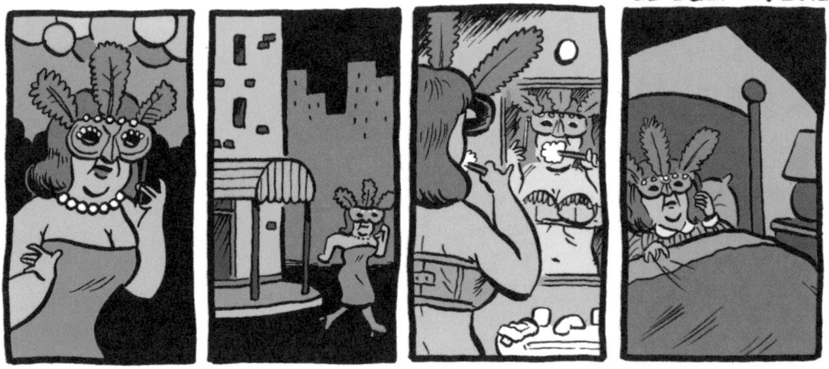

WED JULY 11, 2012

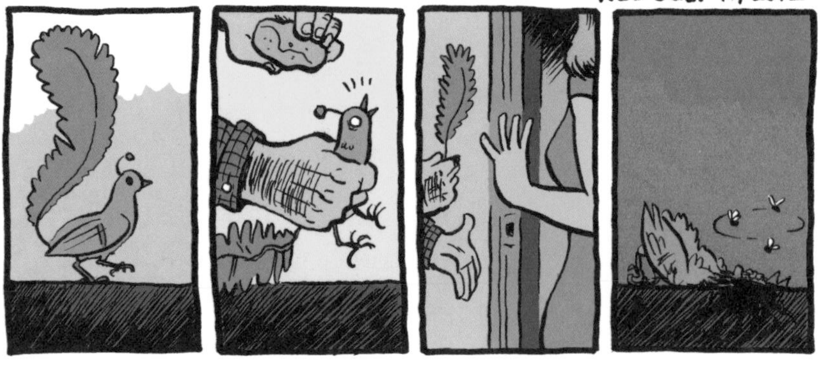

THU JULY 12, 2012

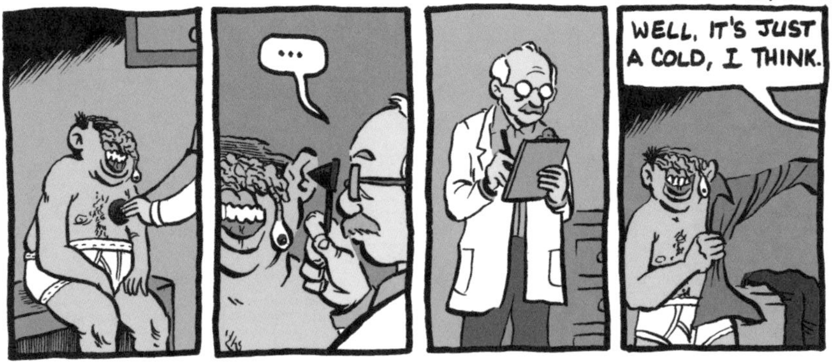
...
WELL, IT'S JUST A COLD, I THINK.

FRI JULY 13, 2012

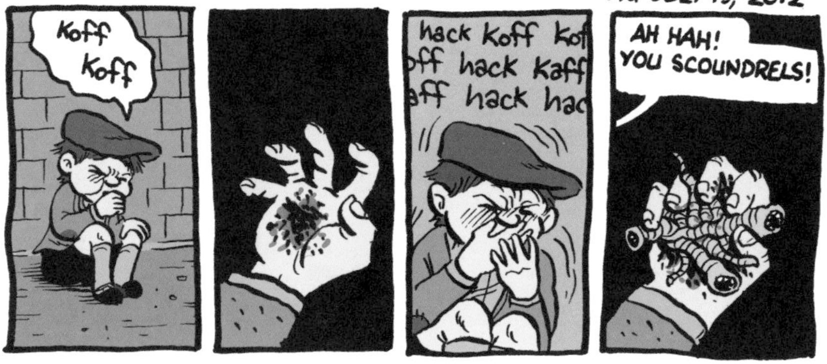
Koff Koff
hack koff kof
off hack kaff
aff hack hac
AH HAH! YOU SCOUNDRELS!

SAT JULY 14, 2012

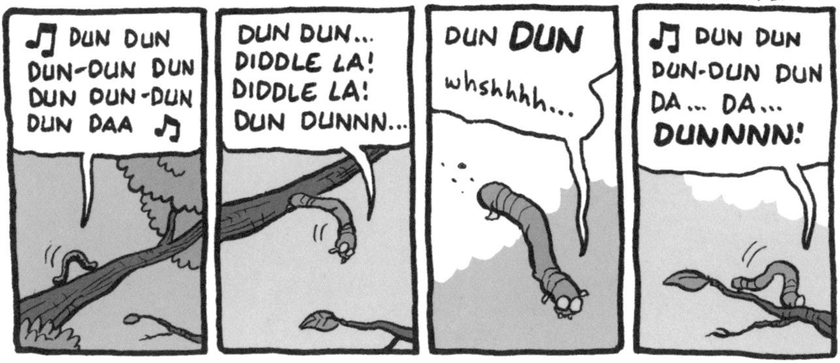
♫ DUN DUN DUN-DUN DUN DUN DUN-DUN DUN DAA ♫
DUN DUN... DIDDLE LA! DIDDLE LA! DUN DUNNN...
DUN DUN
whshhhh...
♫ DUN DUN DUN-DUN DUN DA... DA... DUNNNN!

SUN JULY 15, 2012

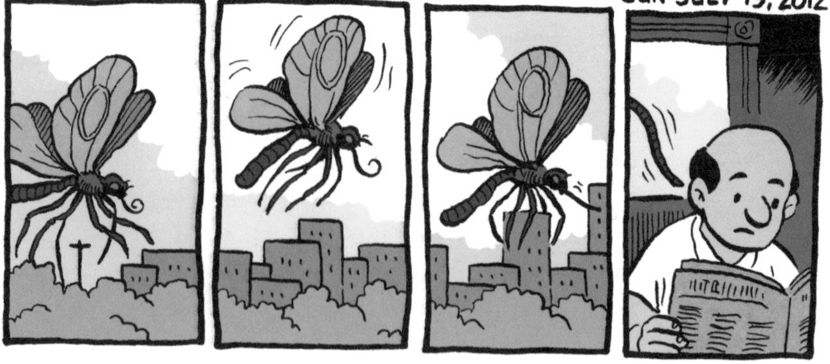

MON JULY 16, 2012

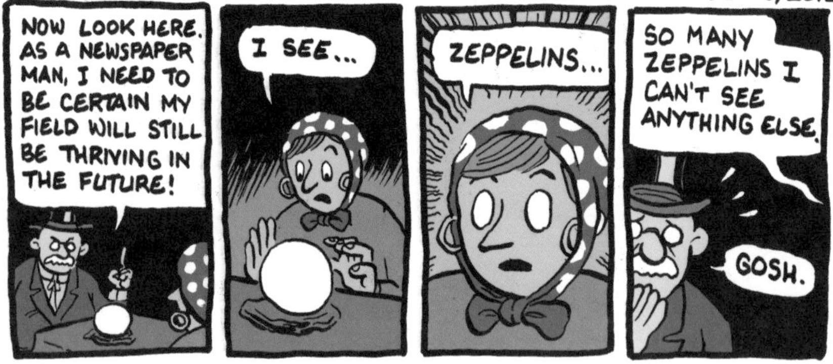
NOW LOOK HERE. AS A NEWSPAPER MAN, I NEED TO BE CERTAIN MY FIELD WILL STILL BE THRIVING IN THE FUTURE!
I SEE...
ZEPPELINS...
SO MANY ZEPPELINS I CAN'T SEE ANYTHING ELSE.
GOSH.

TUE JULY 17, 2012

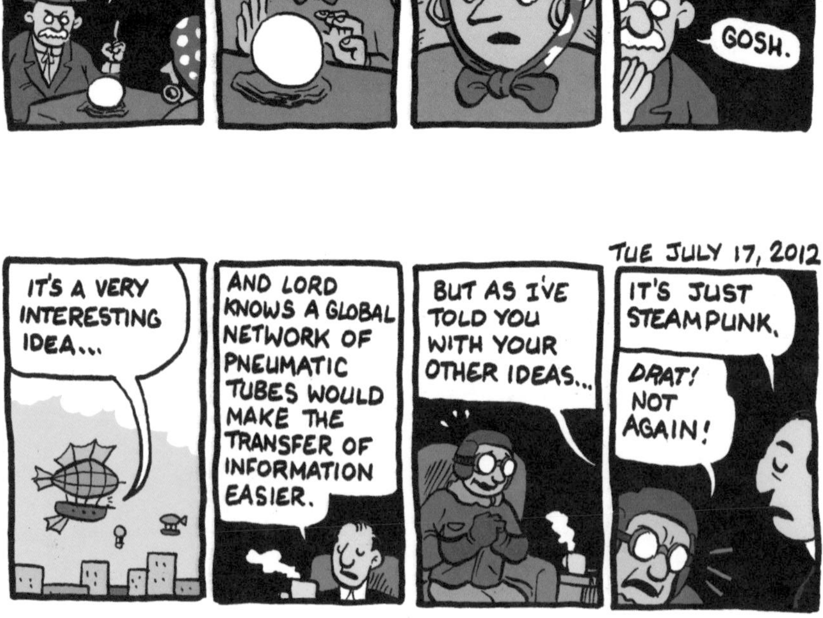
IT'S A VERY INTERESTING IDEA...
AND LORD KNOWS A GLOBAL NETWORK OF PNEUMATIC TUBES WOULD MAKE THE TRANSFER OF INFORMATION EASIER.
BUT AS I'VE TOLD YOU WITH YOUR OTHER IDEAS...
IT'S JUST STEAMPUNK.
DRAT! NOT AGAIN!

WED JULY 18, 2012

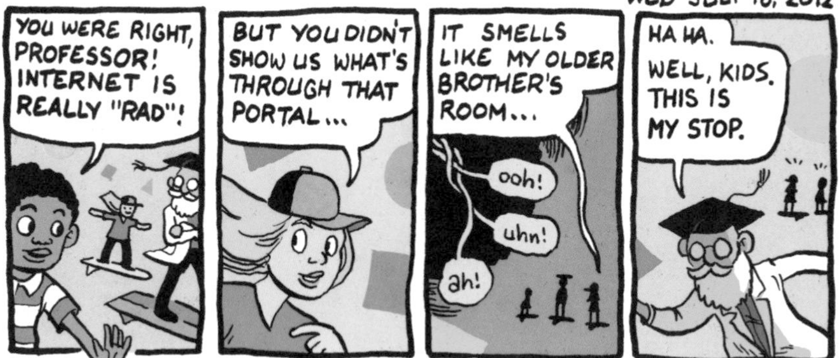
YOU WERE RIGHT, PROFESSOR! INTERNET IS REALLY "RAD"!
BUT YOU DIDN'T SHOW US WHAT'S THROUGH THAT PORTAL...
IT SMELLS LIKE MY OLDER BROTHER'S ROOM...
ooh!
uhn!
ah!
HA HA.
WELL, KIDS. THIS IS MY STOP.

THU JULY 19, 2012

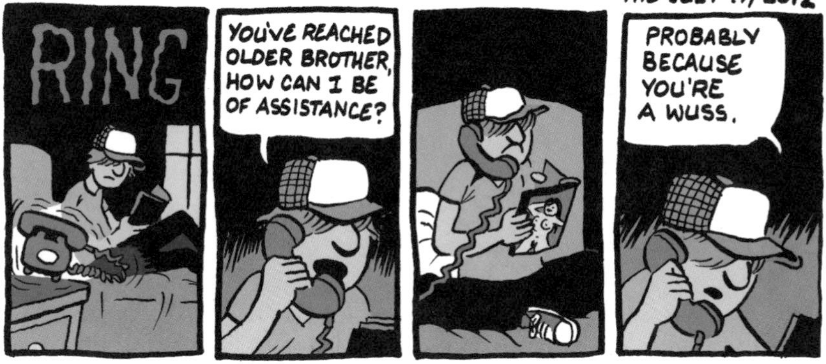
RING
YOU'VE REACHED OLDER BROTHER, HOW CAN I BE OF ASSISTANCE?
PROBABLY BECAUSE YOU'RE A WUSS.

FRI JULY 20, 2012

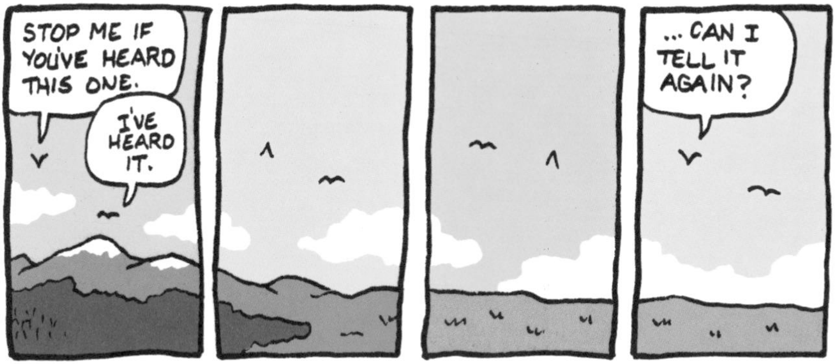
STOP ME IF YOU'VE HEARD THIS ONE.
I'VE HEARD IT.
... CAN I TELL IT AGAIN?

SAT JULY 21, 2012

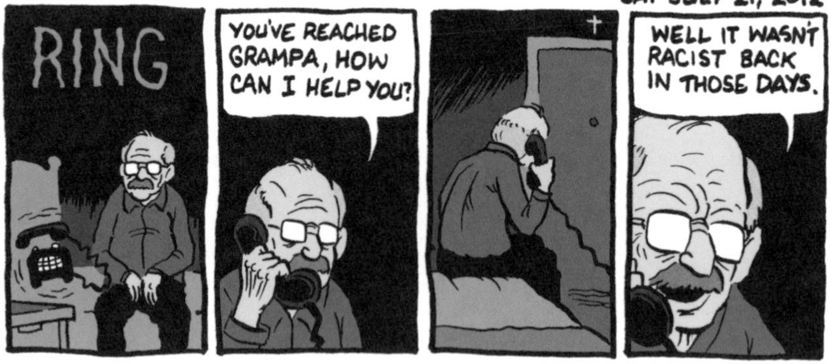
RING
YOU'VE REACHED GRAMPA, HOW CAN I HELP YOU?
WELL IT WASN'T RACIST BACK IN THOSE DAYS.

SUN JULY 22, 2012

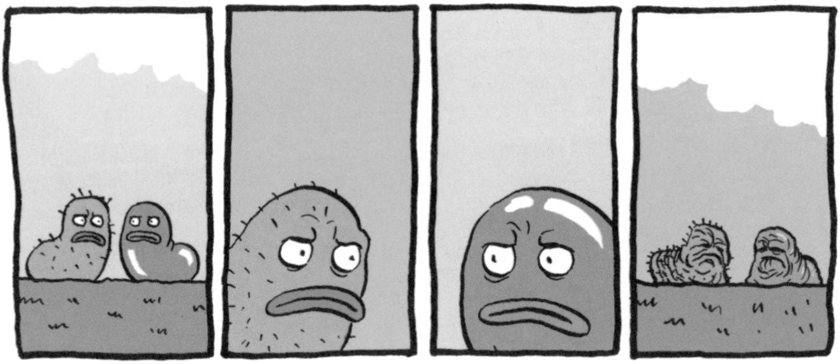

MON JULY 23, 2012

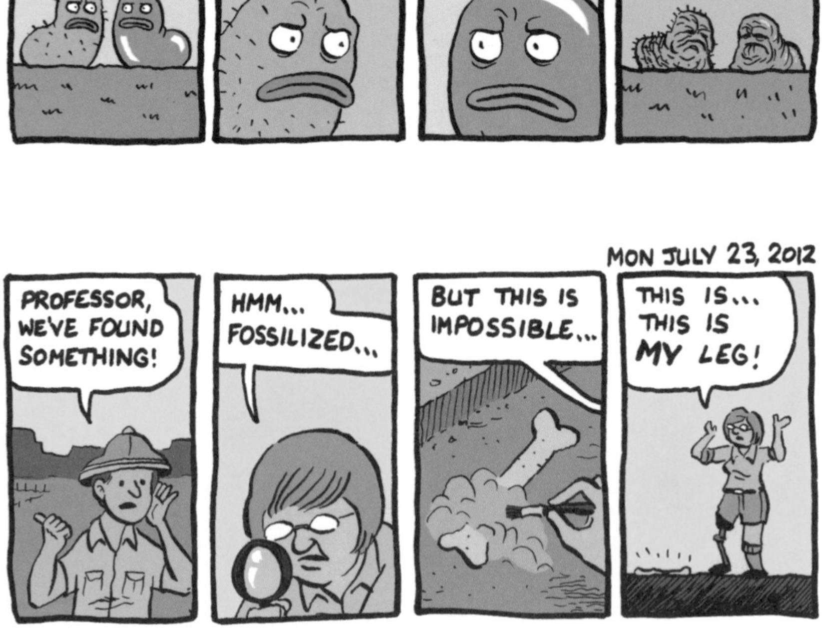
PROFESSOR, WE'VE FOUND SOMETHING!
HMM... FOSSILIZED...
BUT THIS IS IMPOSSIBLE...
THIS IS... THIS IS MY LEG!

TUE JULY 24, 2012

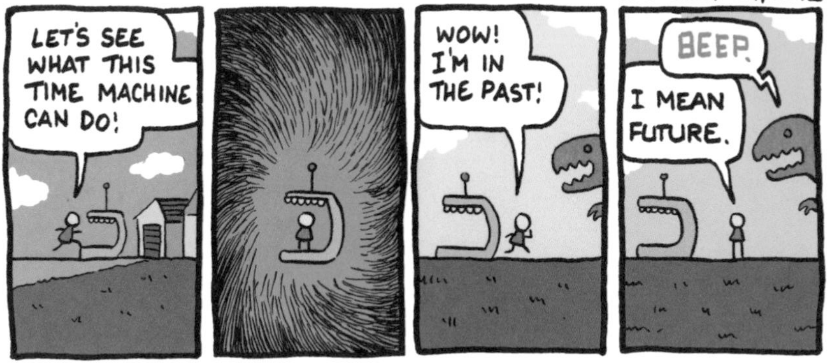
LET'S SEE WHAT THIS TIME MACHINE CAN DO!
WOW! I'M IN THE PAST!
BEEP.
I MEAN FUTURE.

WED JULY 25, 2012

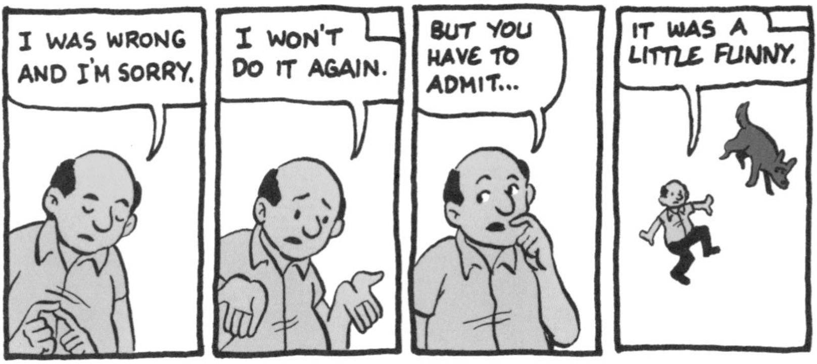
I WAS WRONG AND I'M SORRY.
I WON'T DO IT AGAIN.
BUT YOU HAVE TO ADMIT...
IT WAS A LITTLE FUNNY.

THU JULY 26, 2012

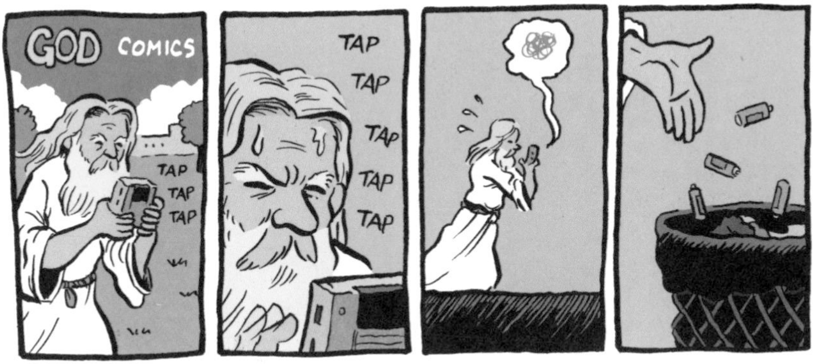
GOD COMICS
TAP
TAP
TAP
TAP
TAP
TAP
TAP
TAP
TAP

FRI JULY 27, 2012

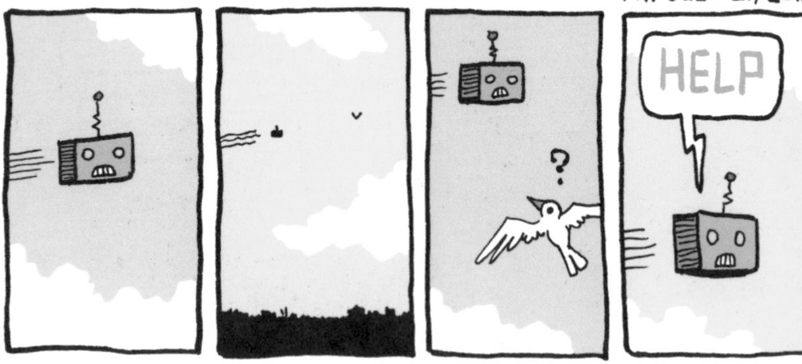
?
HELP

SAT JULY 28, 2012

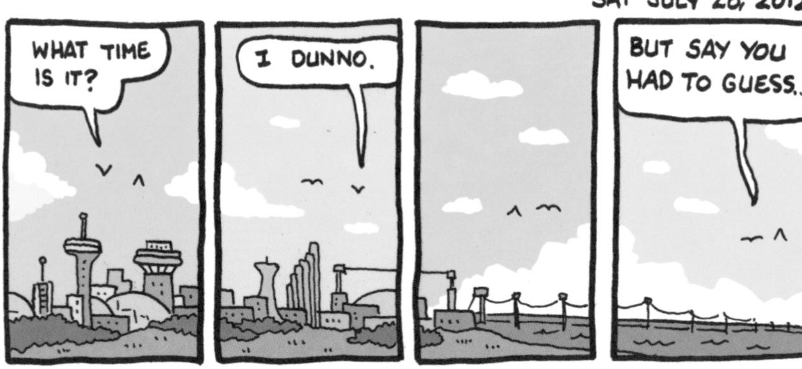
WHAT TIME IS IT?
I DUNNO.
BUT SAY YOU HAD TO GUESS...

SUN JULY 29, 2012

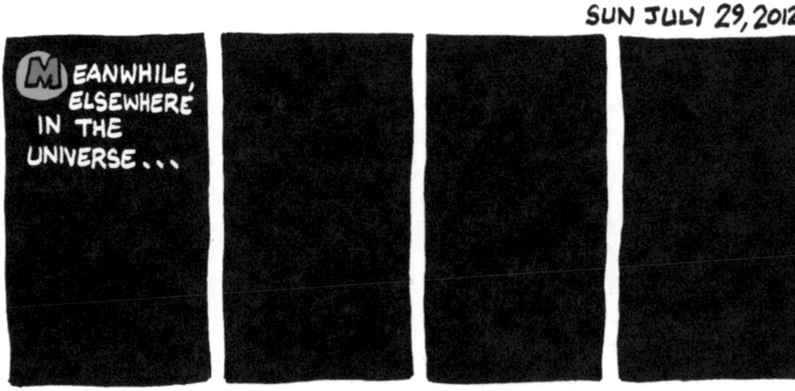
MEANWHILE, ELSEWHERE IN THE UNIVERSE...

MON JULY 30, 2012

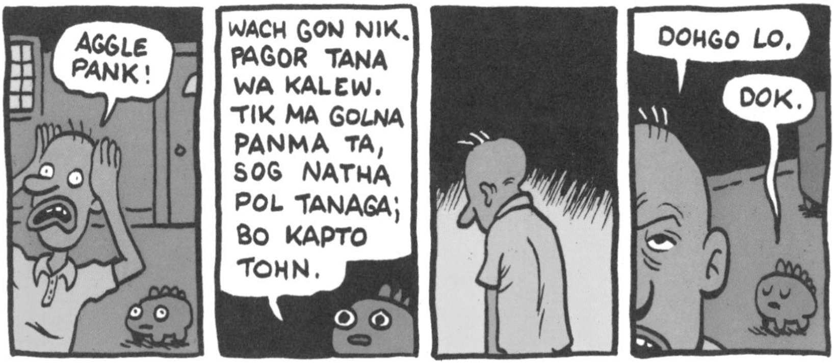
AGGLE PANK!
WACH GON NIK. PAGOR TANA WA KALEW. TIK MA GOLNA PANMA TA, SOG NATHA POL TANAGA; BO KAPTO TOHN.
DOHGO LO.
DOK.

TUE JULY 31, 2012

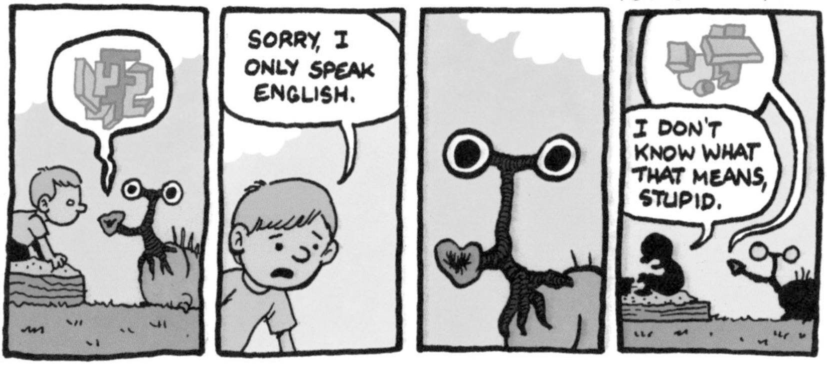
SORRY, I ONLY SPEAK ENGLISH.
I DON'T KNOW WHAT THAT MEANS, STUPID.

WED AUG 1, 2012

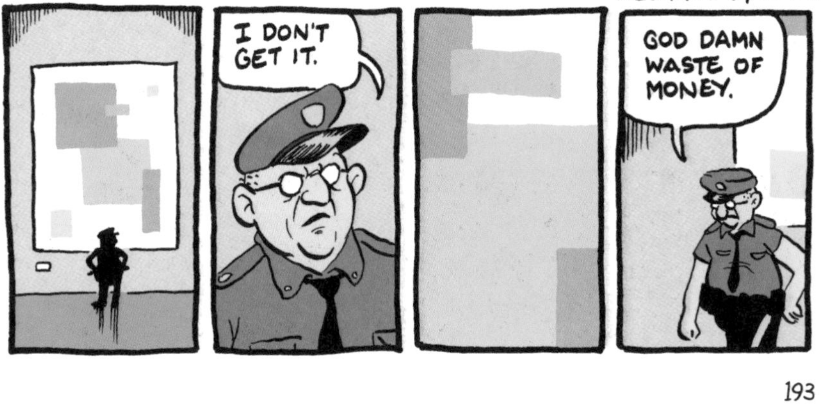
I DON'T GET IT.
GOD DAMN WASTE OF MONEY.

THU AUG 2, 2012

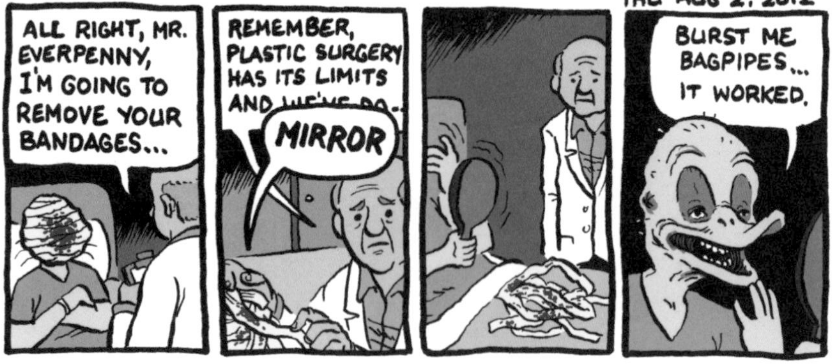
ALL RIGHT, MR. EVERPENNY, I'M GOING TO REMOVE YOUR BANDAGES...
REMEMBER, PLASTIC SURGERY HAS ITS LIMITS AND
MIRROR
BURST ME BAGPIPES... IT WORKED.

FRI AUG 3, 2012

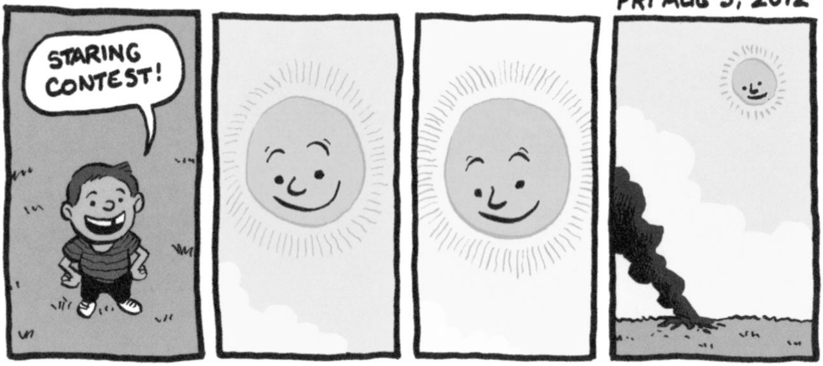
STARING CONTEST!

SAT AUG 4, 2012

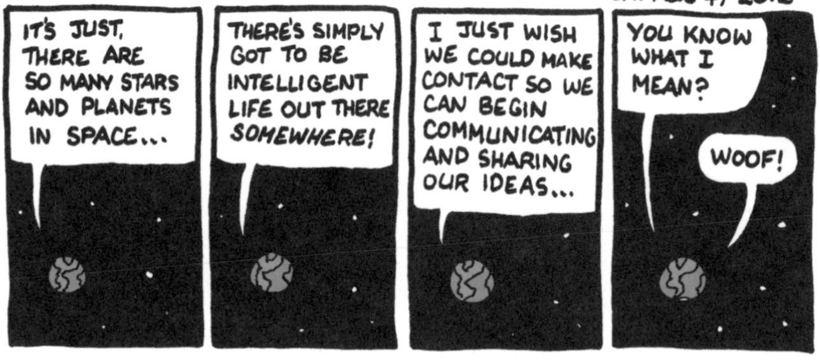
IT'S JUST, THERE ARE SO MANY STARS AND PLANETS IN SPACE...
THERE'S SIMPLY GOT TO BE INTELLIGENT LIFE OUT THERE *SOMEWHERE!*
I JUST WISH WE COULD MAKE CONTACT SO WE CAN BEGIN COMMUNICATING AND SHARING OUR IDEAS...
YOU KNOW WHAT I MEAN?
WOOF!

SUN AUG 5, 2012

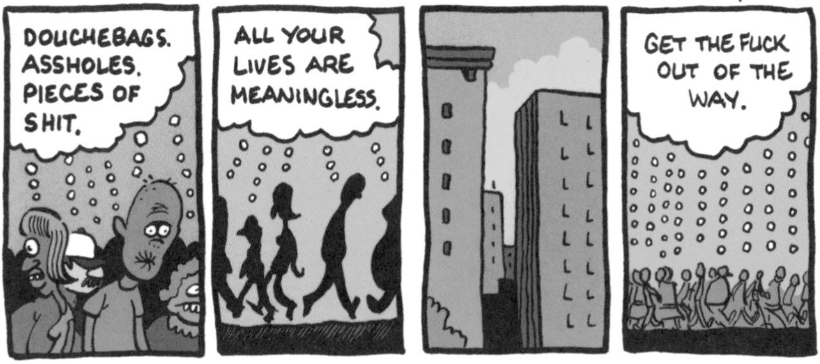
DOUCHEBAGS. ASSHOLES. PIECES OF SHIT.
ALL YOUR LIVES ARE MEANINGLESS.
GET THE FUCK OUT OF THE WAY.

MON AUG 6, 2012

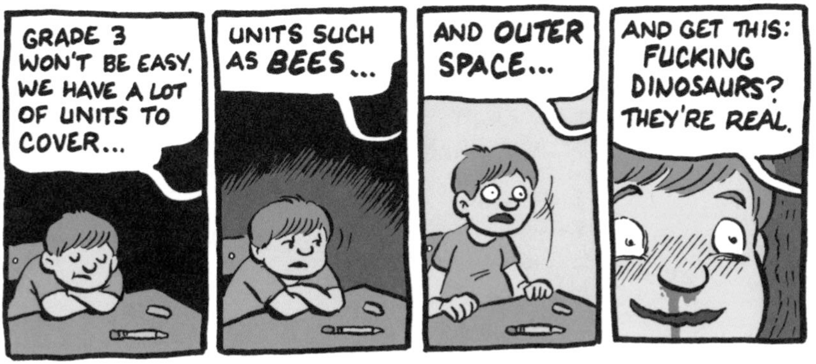
GRADE 3 WON'T BE EASY. WE HAVE A LOT OF UNITS TO COVER...
UNITS SUCH AS BEES...
AND OUTER SPACE...
AND GET THIS: FUCKING DINOSAURS? THEY'RE REAL.

TUE AUG 7, 2012

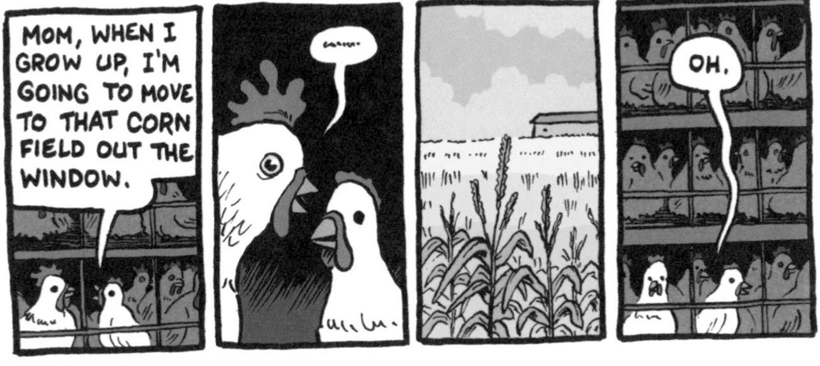
MOM, WHEN I GROW UP, I'M GOING TO MOVE TO THAT CORN FIELD OUT THE WINDOW.
OH.

WED AUG 8, 2012

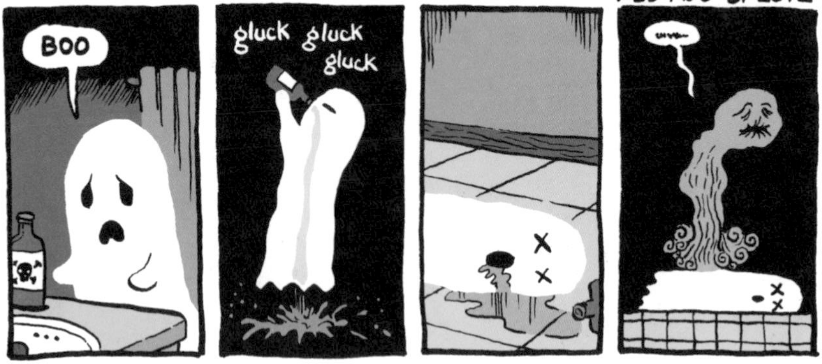
BOO
gluck gluck gluck

THU AUG 9, 2012

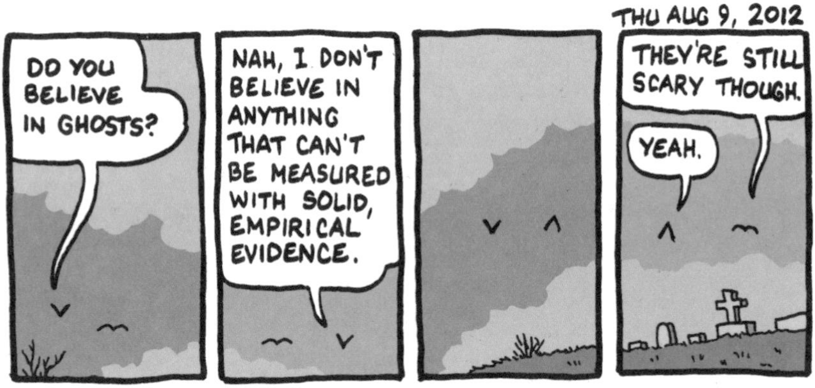
DO YOU BELIEVE IN GHOSTS?
NAH, I DON'T BELIEVE IN ANYTHING THAT CAN'T BE MEASURED WITH SOLID, EMPIRICAL EVIDENCE.
THEY'RE STILL SCARY THOUGH.
YEAH.

FRI AUG 10, 2012

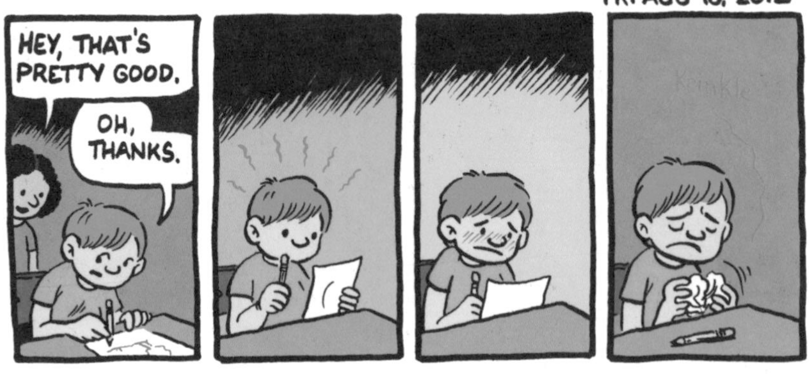
HEY, THAT'S PRETTY GOOD.
OH, THANKS.

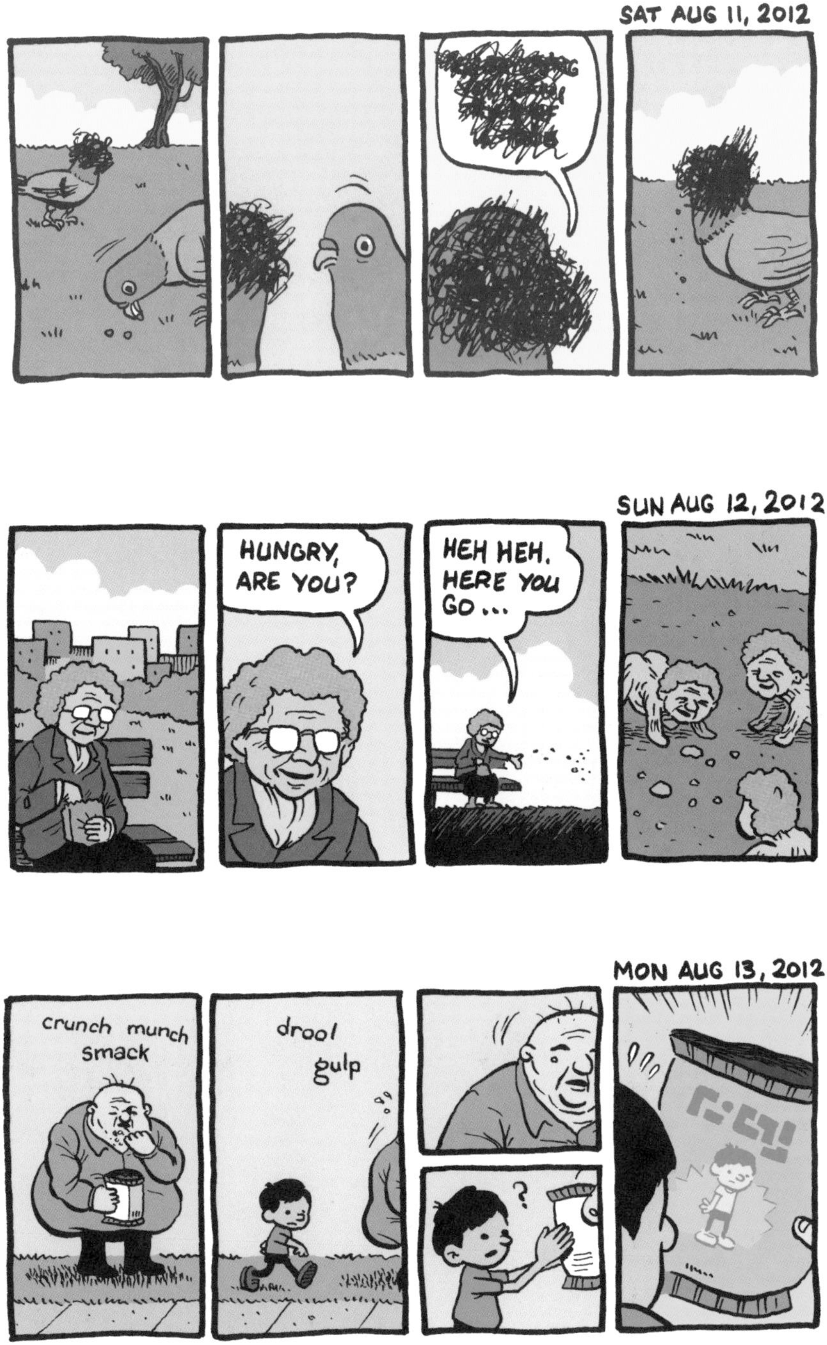
SAT AUG 11, 2012
SUN AUG 12, 2012
HUNGRY, ARE YOU?
HEH HEH. HERE YOU GO...
MON AUG 13, 2012
crunch munch smack
drool gulp
?

TUE AUG 14, 2012

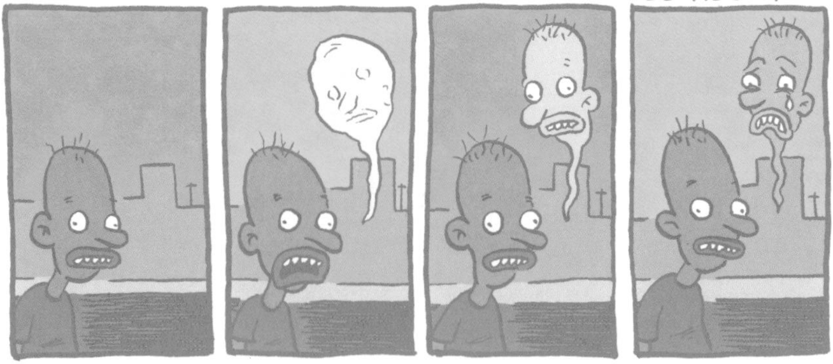

WED AUG 15, 2012

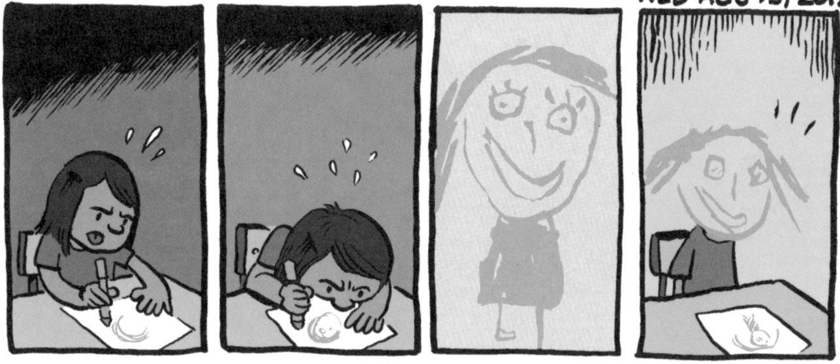

THU AUG 16, 2012

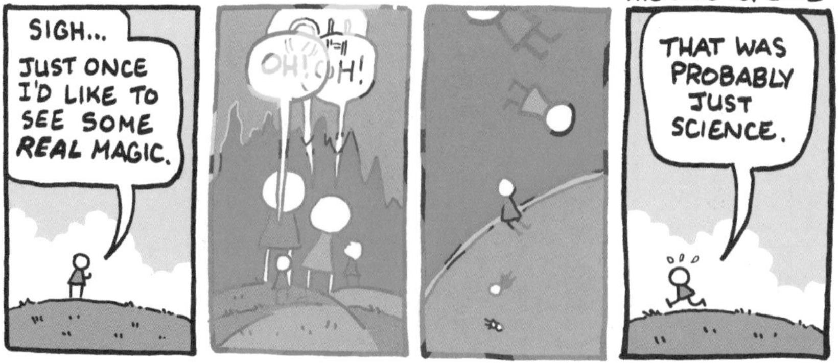
SIGH... JUST ONCE I'D LIKE TO SEE SOME REAL MAGIC.
OH!
OH!
THAT WAS PROBABLY JUST SCIENCE.

FRI AUG 17, 2012

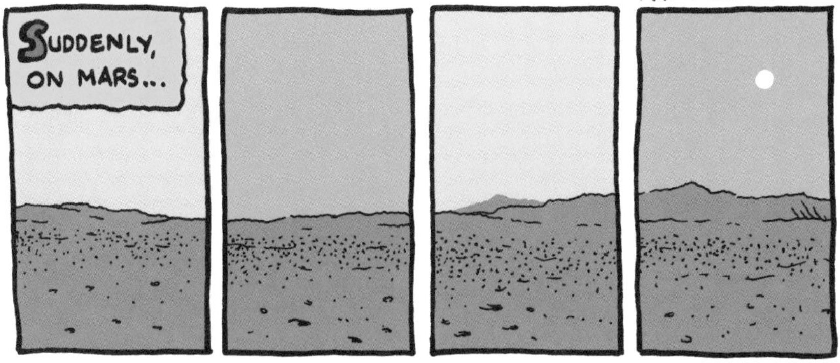
SUDDENLY, ON MARS...

SAT AUG 18, 2012

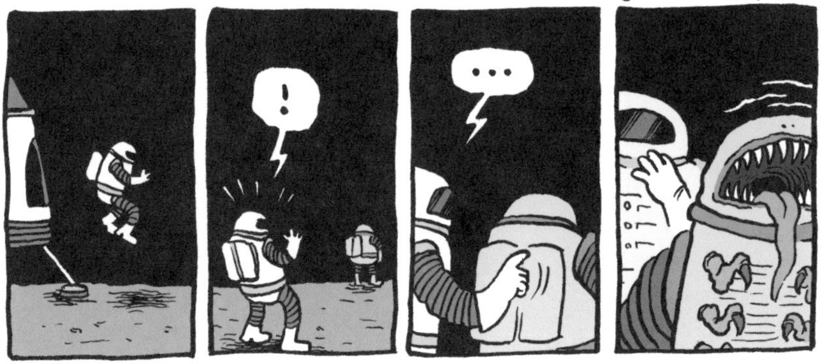
!
...

SUN AUG 19, 2012

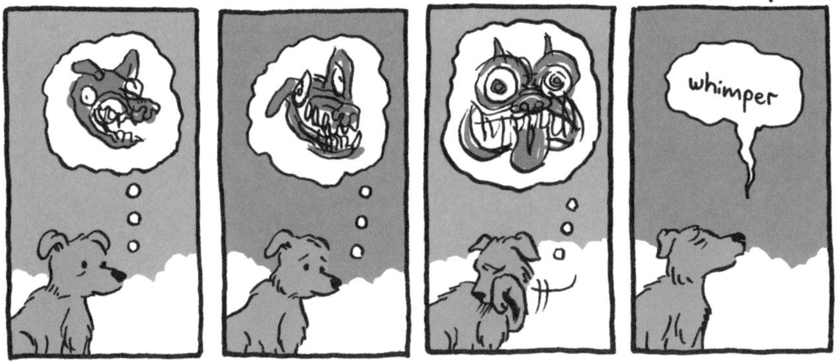
whimper

MON AUG 20, 2012

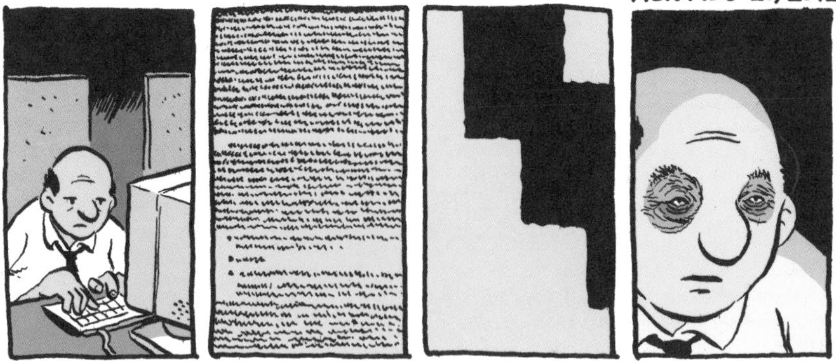

TUE AUG 21, 2012

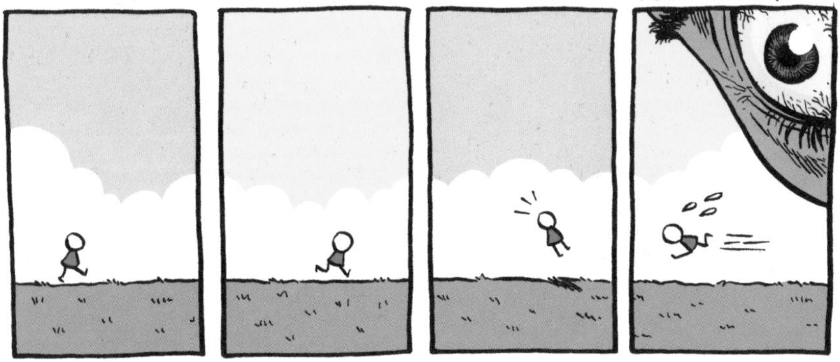

WED AUG 22, 2012

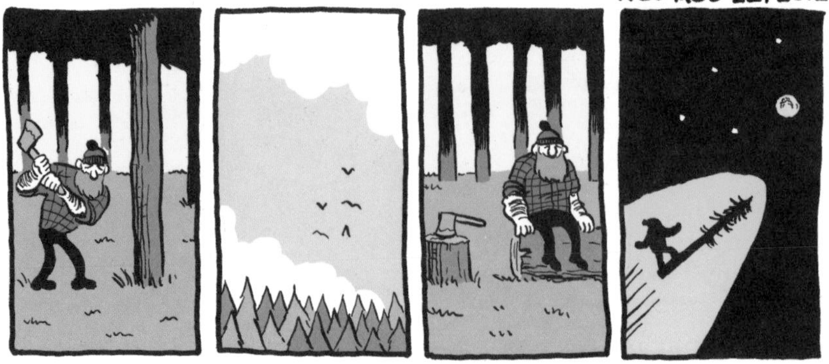

THU AUG 23, 2012

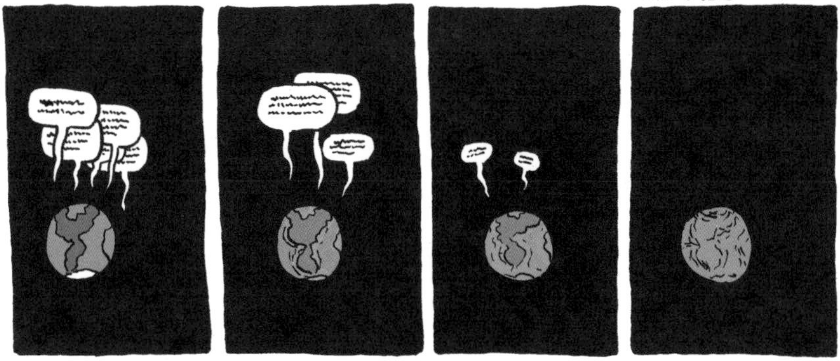

FRI AUG 24, 2012

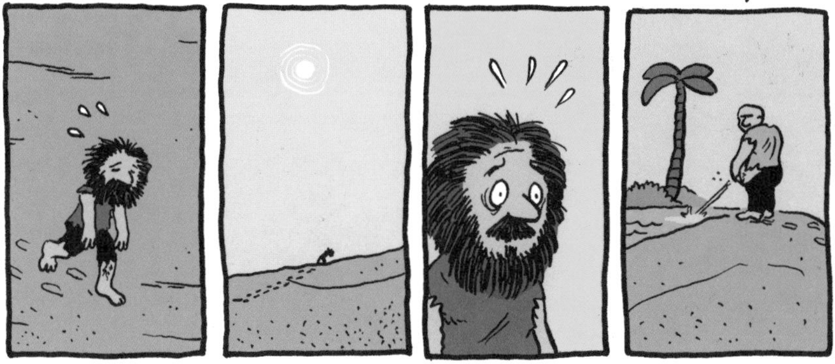

SAT AUG, 25, 2012

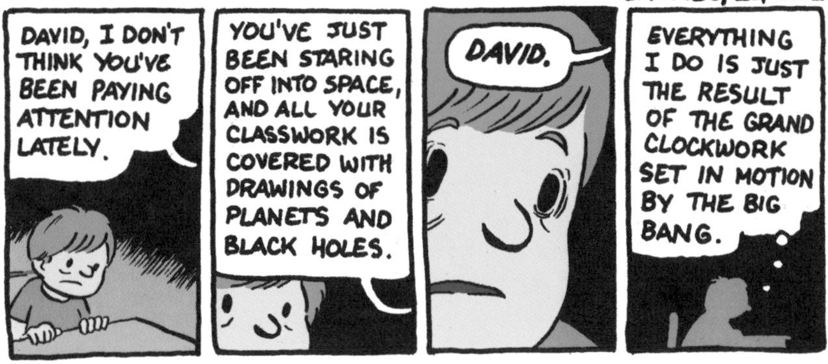
DAVID, I DON'T THINK YOU'VE BEEN PAYING ATTENTION LATELY.
YOU'VE JUST BEEN STARING OFF INTO SPACE, AND ALL YOUR CLASSWORK IS COVERED WITH DRAWINGS OF PLANETS AND BLACK HOLES.
DAVID.
EVERYTHING I DO IS JUST THE RESULT OF THE GRAND CLOCKWORK SET IN MOTION BY THE BIG BANG.

SUN AUG 26, 2012

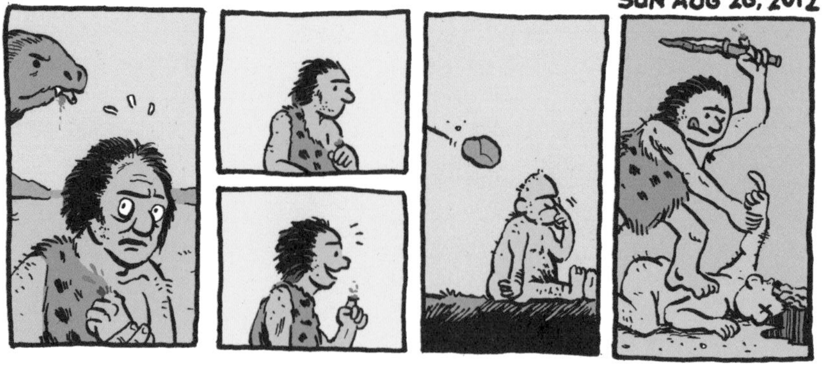

MON AUG 27, 2012

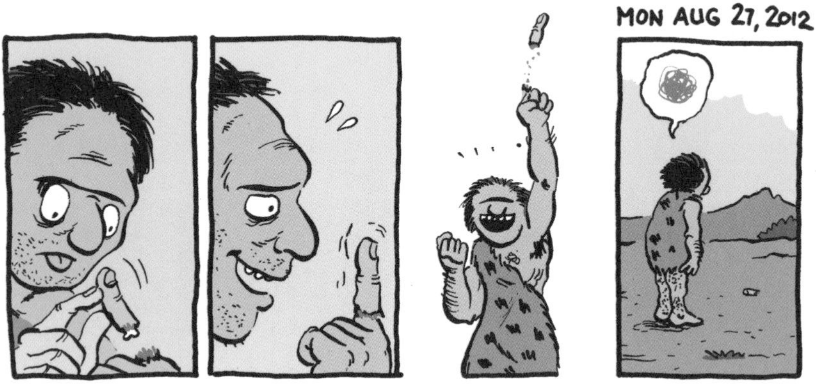

TUE AUG 28, 2012

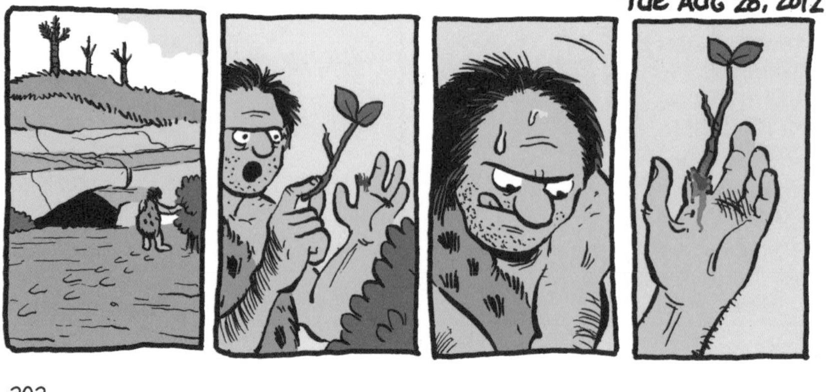

WED AUG 29, 2012

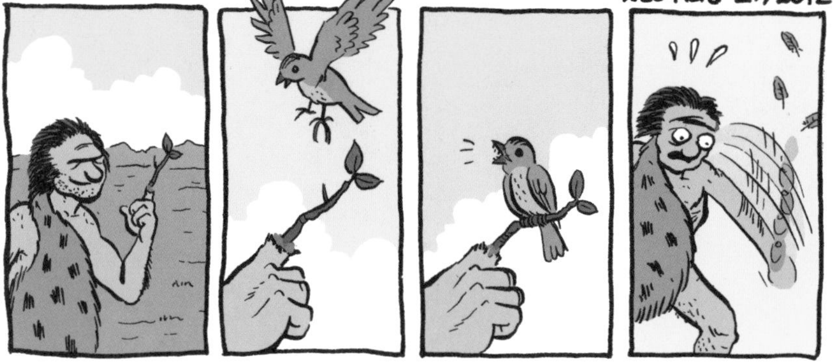

THU AUG 30, 2012

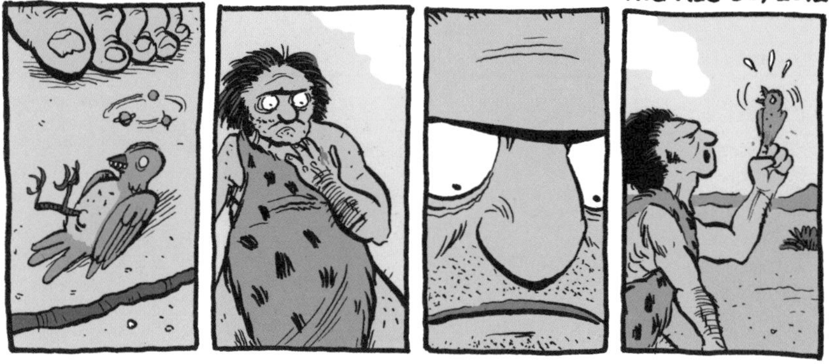

FRI AUG 31, 2012

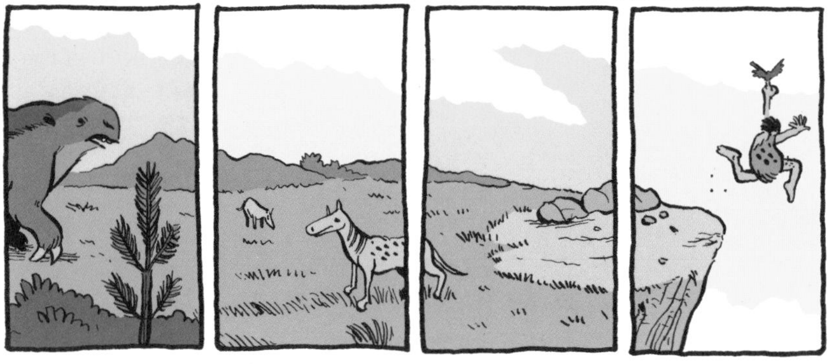

SAT SEPT 1 2012

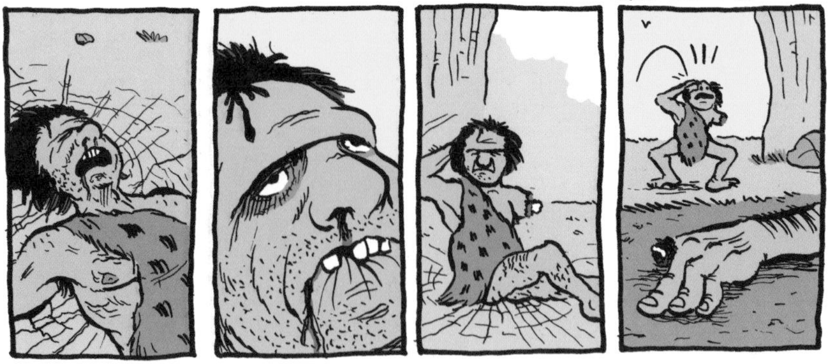

SUN SEPT 2, 2012

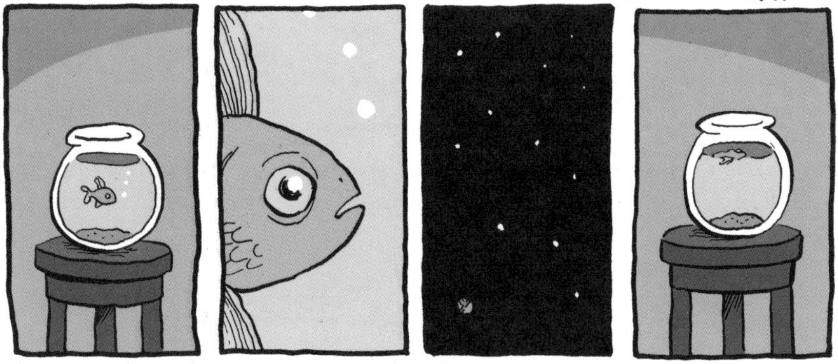

MON SEPT 3, 2012

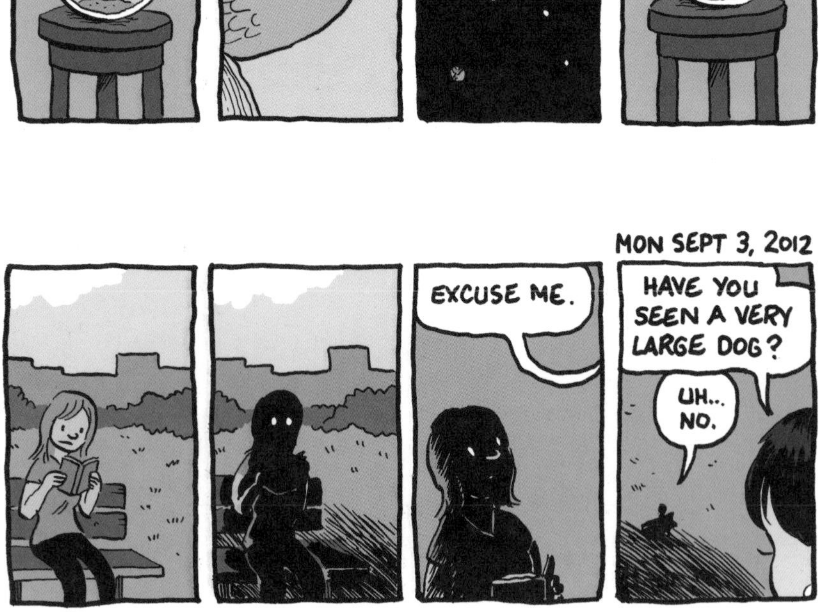
EXCUSE ME.
HAVE YOU SEEN A VERY LARGE DOG?
UH... NO.

TUE SEPT 4, 2012

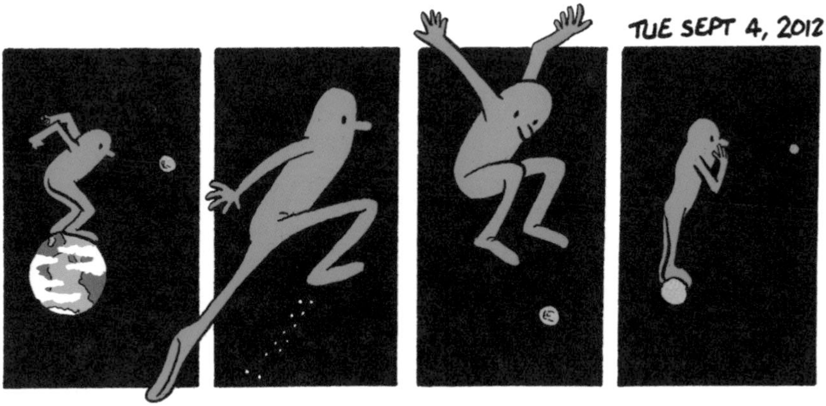

WED SEPT 5, 2012

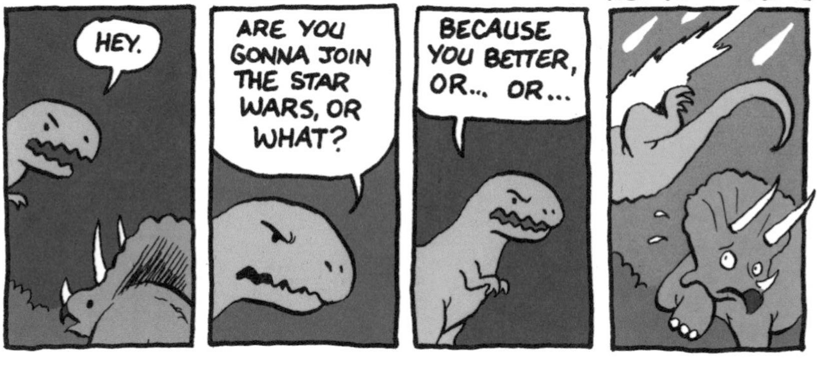
HEY.
ARE YOU GONNA JOIN THE STAR WARS, OR WHAT?
BECAUSE YOU BETTER, OR... OR...

THU SEPT 6, 2012

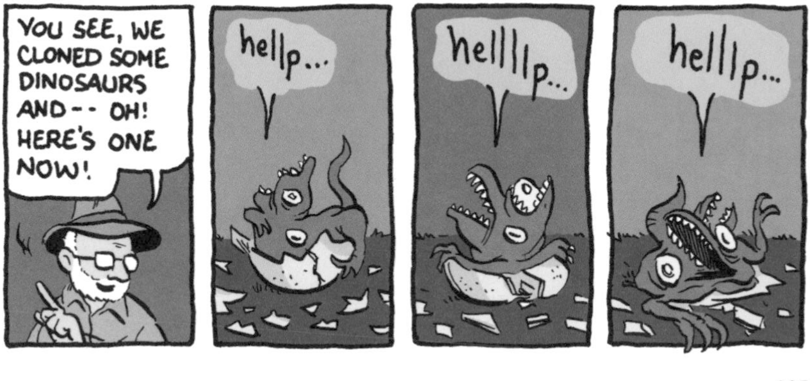
YOU SEE, WE CLONED SOME DINOSAURS AND-- OH! HERE'S ONE NOW!
hellp...
hellllp...
helllp...

FRI SEPT 7, 2012

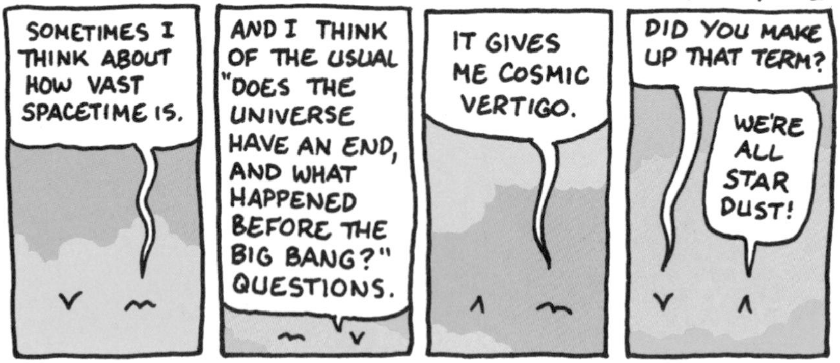
SOMETIMES I THINK ABOUT HOW VAST SPACETIME IS.
AND I THINK OF THE USUAL "DOES THE UNIVERSE HAVE AN END, AND WHAT HAPPENED BEFORE THE BIG BANG?" QUESTIONS.
IT GIVES ME COSMIC VERTIGO.
DID YOU MAKE UP THAT TERM?
WE'RE ALL STAR DUST!

SAT SEPT 8, 2012

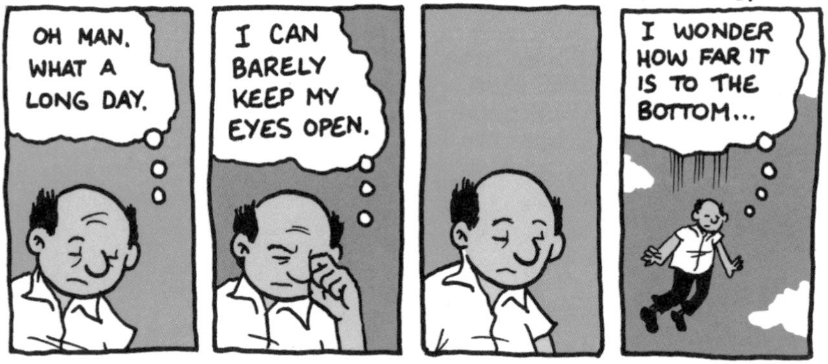
OH MAN. WHAT A LONG DAY.
I CAN BARELY KEEP MY EYES OPEN.
I WONDER HOW FAR IT IS TO THE BOTTOM...

SUN SEPT 9, 2012

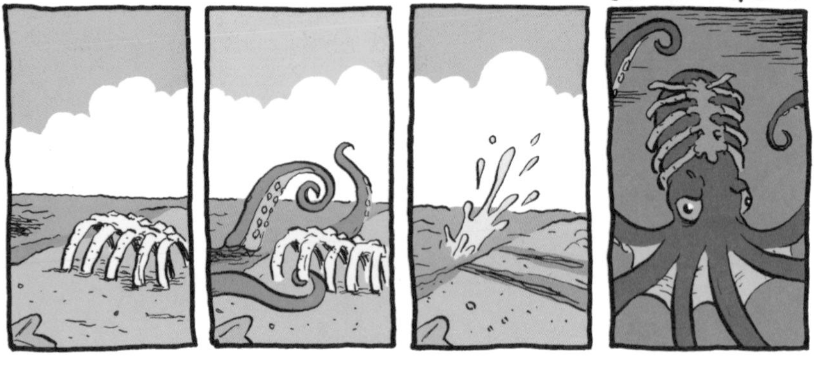

MON SEPT 10, 2012

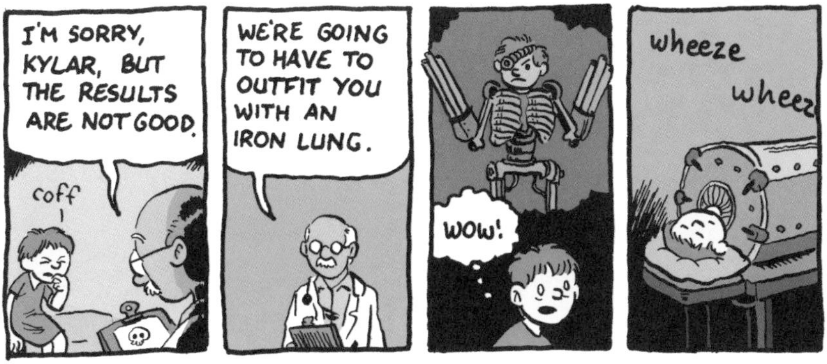
I'M SORRY, KYLAR, BUT THE RESULTS ARE NOT GOOD.
coff
WE'RE GOING TO HAVE TO OUTFIT YOU WITH AN IRON LUNG.
WOW!
wheeze
wheez

TUE SEPT 11, 2012

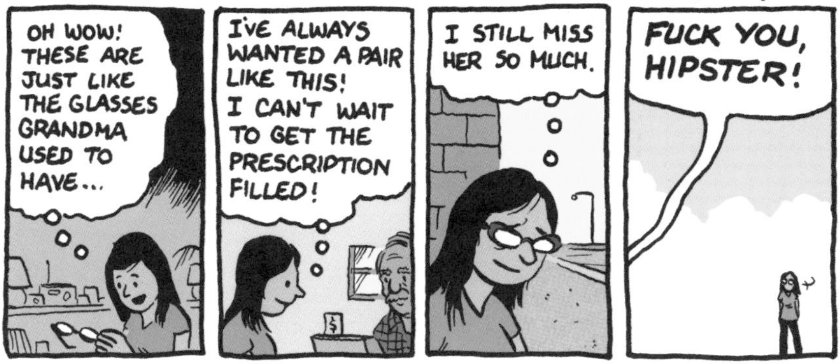
OH WOW! THESE ARE JUST LIKE THE GLASSES GRANDMA USED TO HAVE...
I'VE ALWAYS WANTED A PAIR LIKE THIS! I CAN'T WAIT TO GET THE PRESCRIPTION FILLED!
I STILL MISS HER SO MUCH.
FUCK YOU, HIPSTER!

WED SEPT 12, 2012

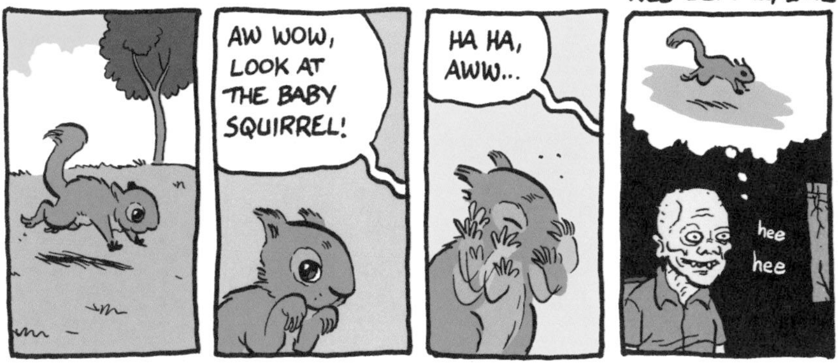
AW WOW, LOOK AT THE BABY SQUIRREL!
HA HA, AWW...
hee
hee

THU SEPT 13, 2012

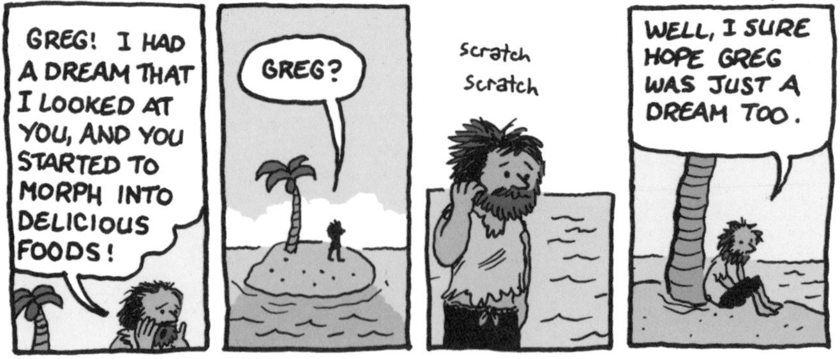

GREG! I HAD A DREAM THAT I LOOKED AT YOU, AND YOU STARTED TO MORPH INTO DELICIOUS FOODS!
GREG?
scratch
scratch
WELL, I SURE HOPE GREG WAS JUST A DREAM TOO.

FRI SEPT 14, 2012

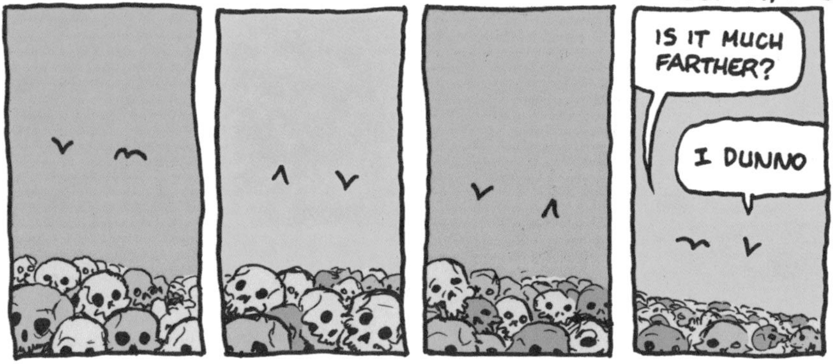

IS IT MUCH FARTHER?
I DUNNO

SAT SEPT 15, 2012

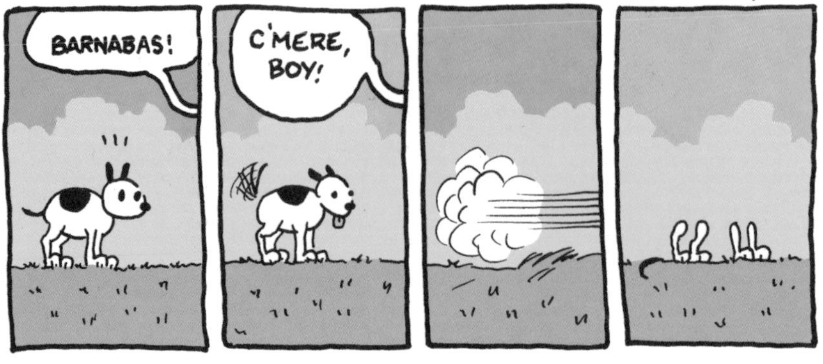

BARNABAS!
C'MERE, BOY!

SUN SEPT 16, 2012

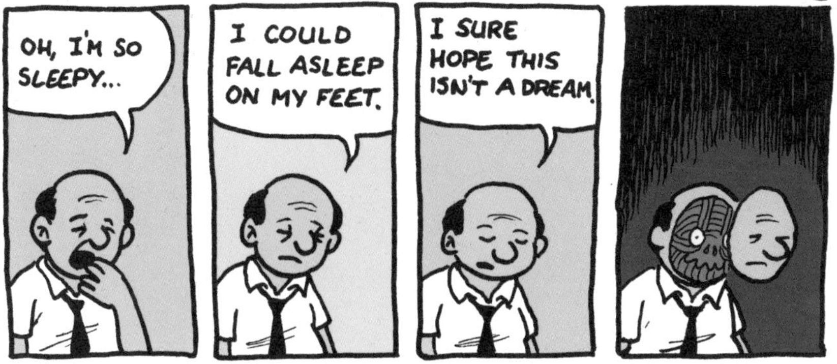
OH, I'M SO SLEEPY...
I COULD FALL ASLEEP ON MY FEET.
I SURE HOPE THIS ISN'T A DREAM!

MON SEPT 17, 2012

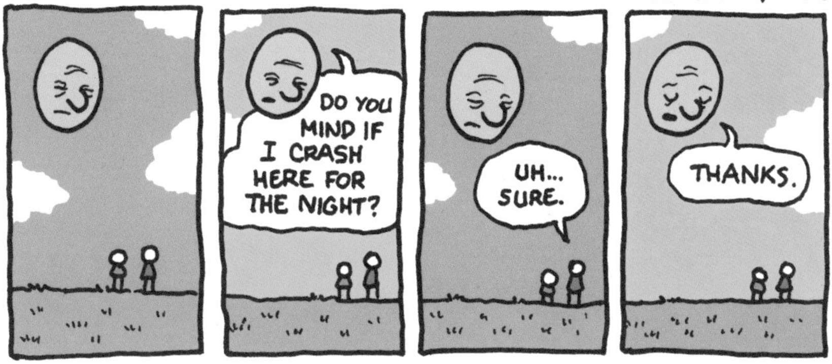
DO YOU MIND IF I CRASH HERE FOR THE NIGHT?
UH... SURE.
THANKS.

TUE SEPT 18, 2012

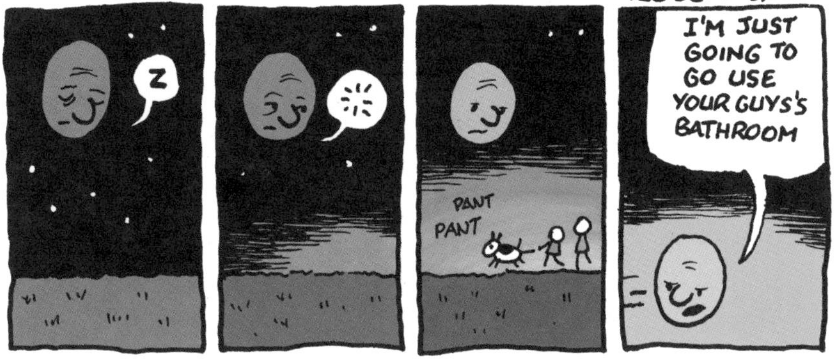
Z
PANT PANT
I'M JUST GOING TO GO USE YOUR GUYS'S BATHROOM

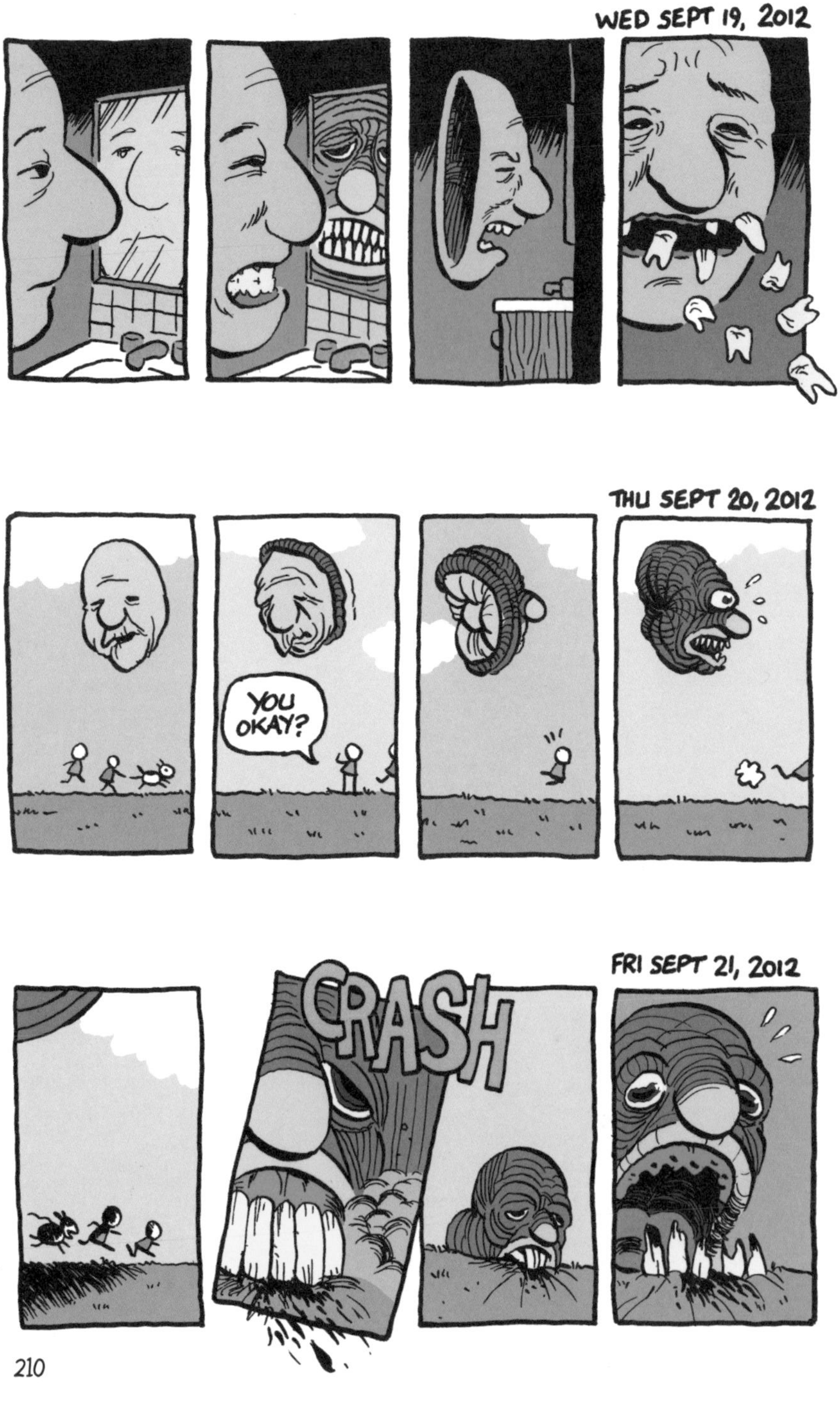
WED SEPT 19, 2012
THU SEPT 20, 2012
YOU OKAY?
FRI SEPT 21, 2012
CRASH

SAT SEPT 22, 2012

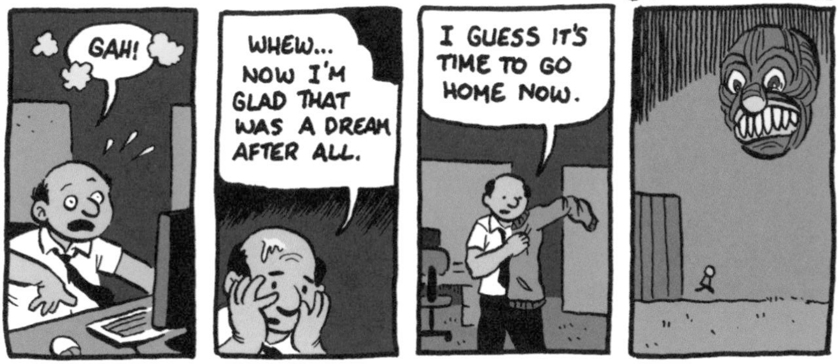
GAH!
WHEW... NOW I'M GLAD THAT WAS A DREAM AFTER ALL.
I GUESS IT'S TIME TO GO HOME NOW.

SUN SEPT 23, 2012

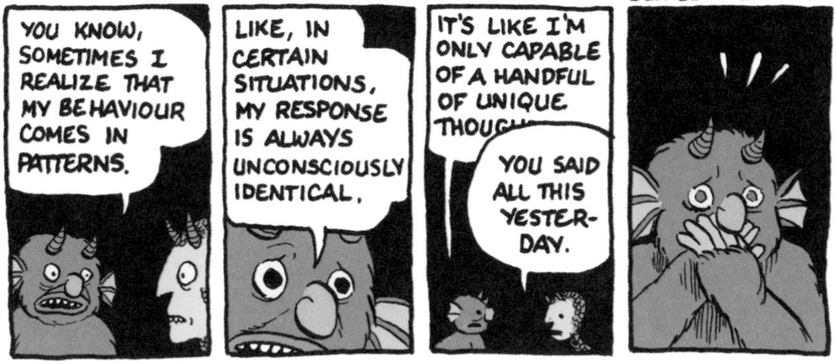
YOU KNOW, SOMETIMES I REALIZE THAT MY BEHAVIOUR COMES IN PATTERNS.
LIKE, IN CERTAIN SITUATIONS, MY RESPONSE IS ALWAYS UNCONSCIOUSLY IDENTICAL.
IT'S LIKE I'M ONLY CAPABLE OF A HANDFUL OF UNIQUE
YOU SAID ALL THIS YESTER-DAY.

MON SEPT 24, 2012

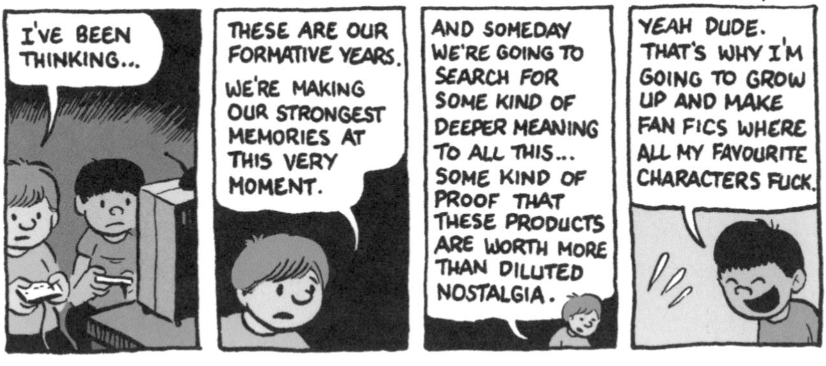
I'VE BEEN THINKING...
THESE ARE OUR FORMATIVE YEARS.
WE'RE MAKING OUR STRONGEST MEMORIES AT THIS VERY MOMENT.
AND SOMEDAY WE'RE GOING TO SEARCH FOR SOME KIND OF DEEPER MEANING TO ALL THIS... SOME KIND OF PROOF THAT THESE PRODUCTS ARE WORTH MORE THAN DILUTED NOSTALGIA.
YEAH DUDE. THAT'S WHY I'M GOING TO GROW UP AND MAKE FAN FICS WHERE ALL MY FAVOURITE CHARACTERS FUCK.

TUE SEPT 25, 2012

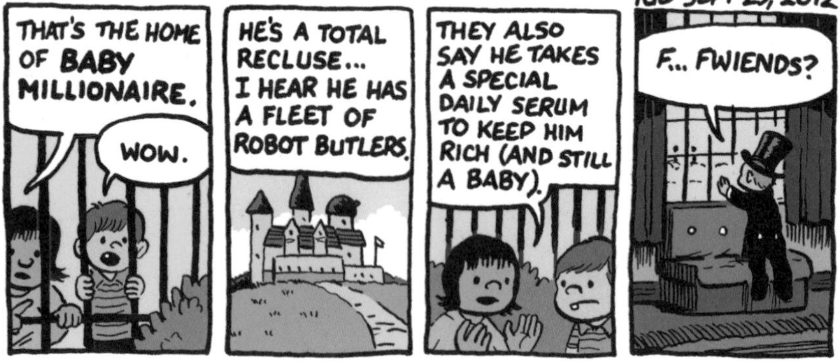
THAT'S THE HOME OF BABY MILLIONAIRE.
WOW.
HE'S A TOTAL RECLUSE... I HEAR HE HAS A FLEET OF ROBOT BUTLERS.
THEY ALSO SAY HE TAKES A SPECIAL DAILY SERUM TO KEEP HIM RICH (AND STILL A BABY).
F... FWIENDS?

WED SEPT 26, 2012

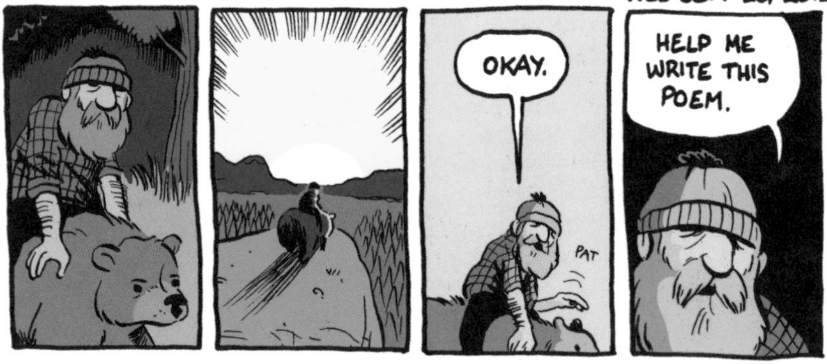
OKAY.
PAT
HELP ME WRITE THIS POEM.

THU SEPT 27, 2012

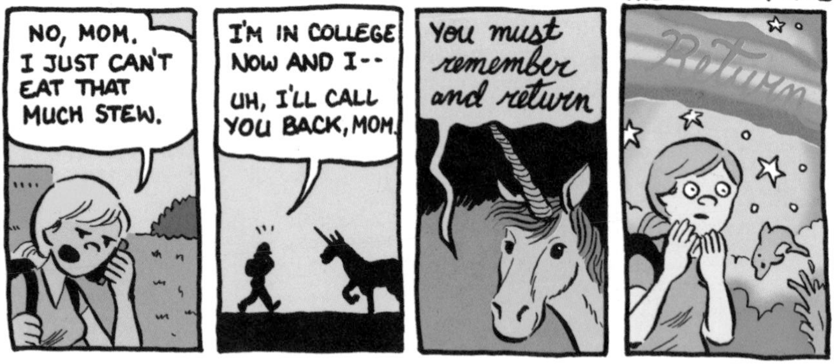
NO, MOM. I JUST CAN'T EAT THAT MUCH STEW.
I'M IN COLLEGE NOW AND I--
UH, I'LL CALL YOU BACK, MOM.
You must remember and return
Return

FRI SEPT 28, 2012

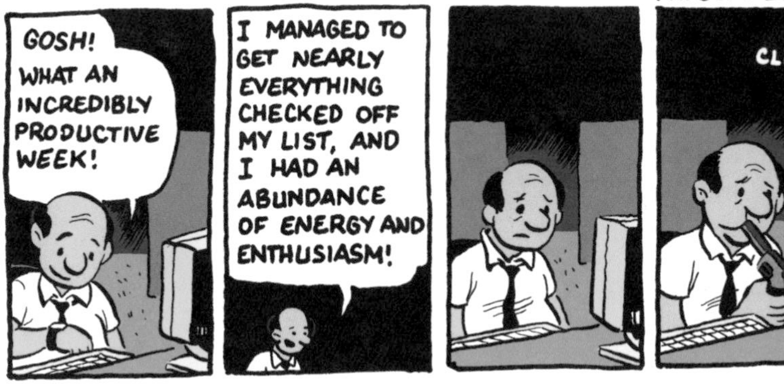
GOSH! WHAT AN INCREDIBLY PRODUCTIVE WEEK!
I MANAGED TO GET NEARLY EVERYTHING CHECKED OFF MY LIST, AND I HAD AN ABUNDANCE OF ENERGY AND ENTHUSIASM!
CLICK

SAT SEPT 29, 2012

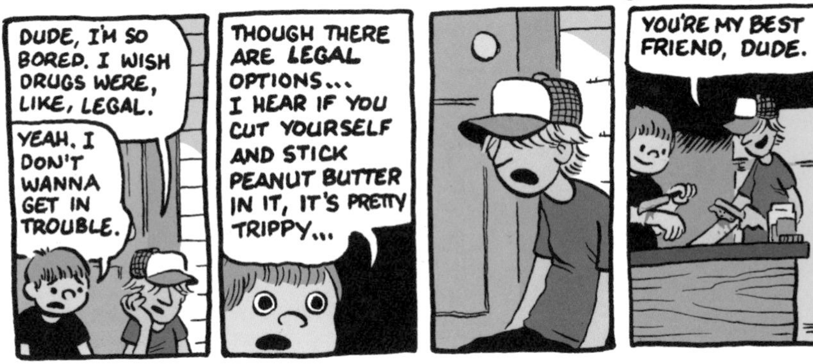
DUDE, I'M SO BORED. I WISH DRUGS WERE, LIKE, LEGAL.
YEAH. I DON'T WANNA GET IN TROUBLE.
THOUGH THERE ARE LEGAL OPTIONS... I HEAR IF YOU CUT YOURSELF AND STICK PEANUT BUTTER IN IT, IT'S PRETTY TRIPPY...
YOU'RE MY BEST FRIEND, DUDE.

SUN SEPT 30, 2012

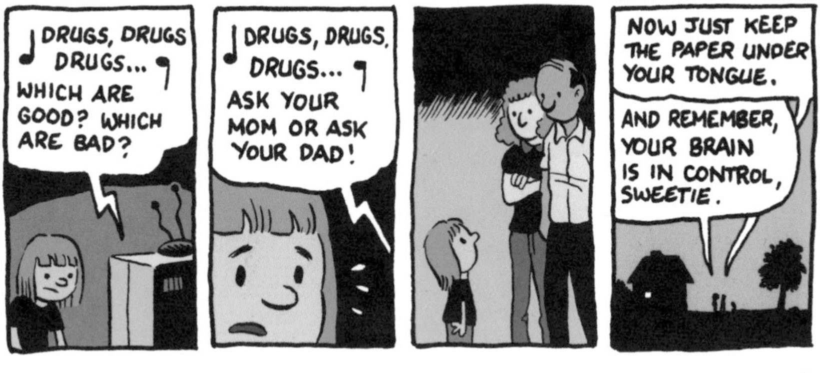
♩ DRUGS, DRUGS DRUGS... ♪ WHICH ARE GOOD? WHICH ARE BAD?
♩ DRUGS, DRUGS, DRUGS... ♪ ASK YOUR MOM OR ASK YOUR DAD!
NOW JUST KEEP THE PAPER UNDER YOUR TONGUE.
AND REMEMBER, YOUR BRAIN IS IN CONTROL, SWEETIE.

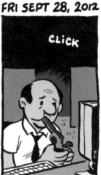

MON OCT 1, 2012

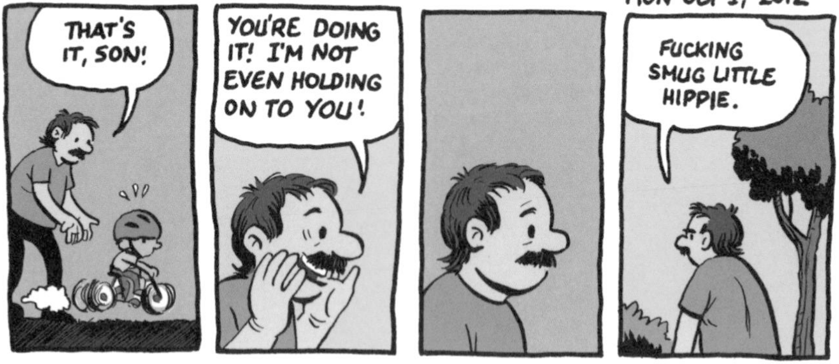
THAT'S IT, SON!
YOU'RE DOING IT! I'M NOT EVEN HOLDING ON TO YOU!
FUCKING SMUG LITTLE HIPPIE.

TUE OCT 2, 2012

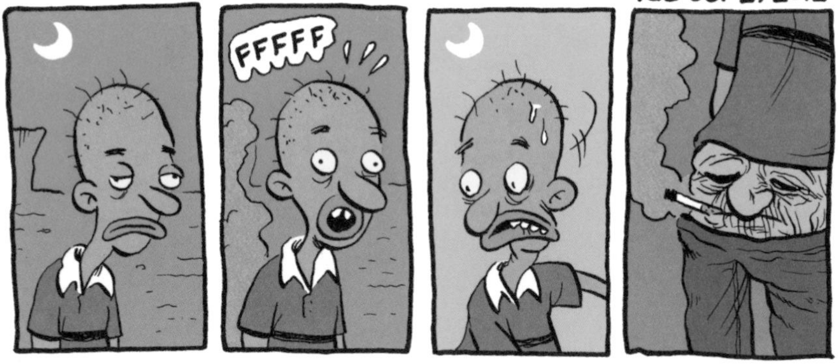
FFFFF

WED OCT 3, 2012

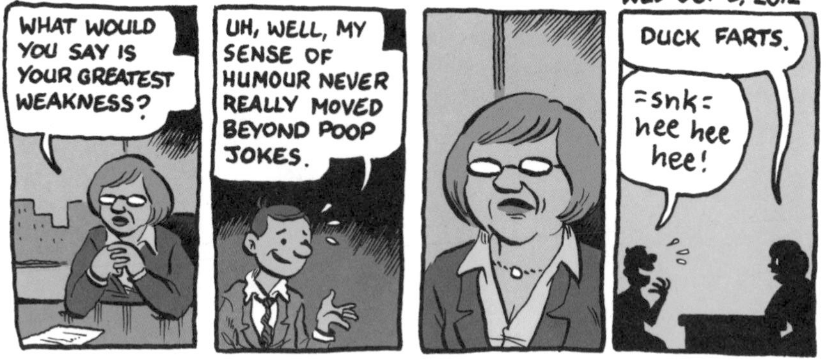
WHAT WOULD YOU SAY IS YOUR GREATEST WEAKNESS?
UH, WELL, MY SENSE OF HUMOUR NEVER REALLY MOVED BEYOND POOP JOKES.
DUCK FARTS.
=snk= hee hee hee!

THU OCT 4, 2012

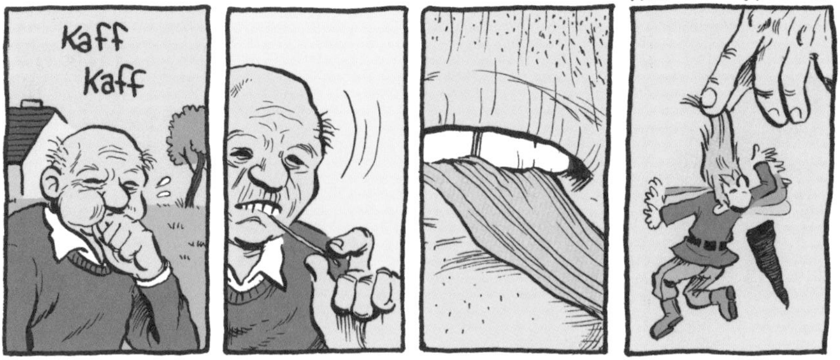
Kaff
Kaff

FRI OCT 5, 2012

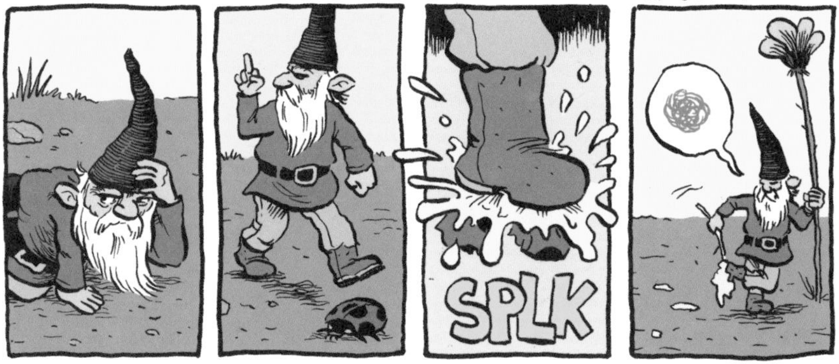
SPLK

SAT OCT 6, 2012

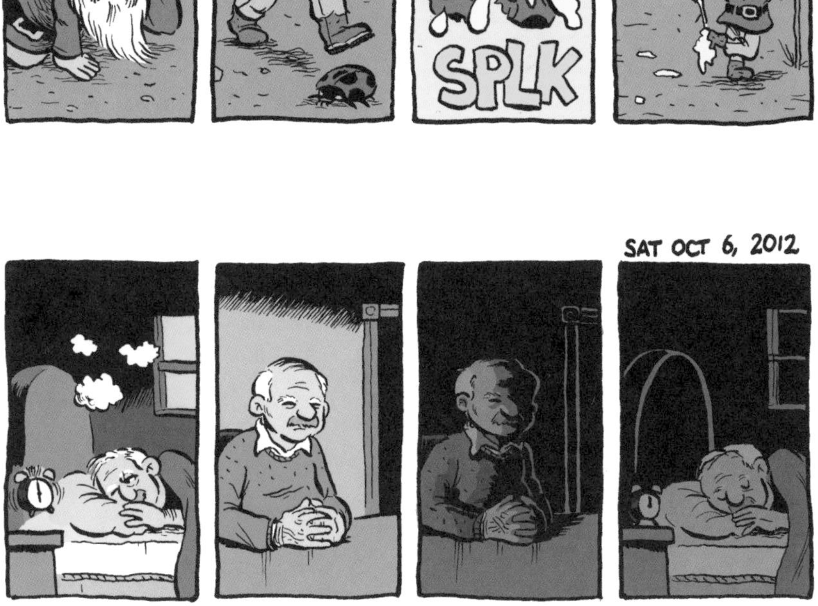

SUN OCT 7, 2012

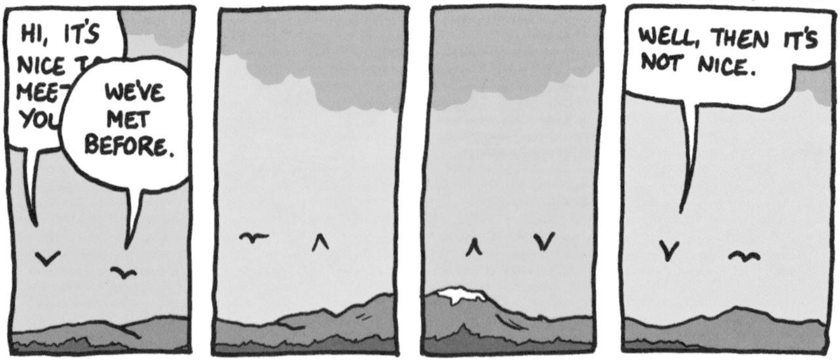
HI, IT'S NICE
WE'VE MET BEFORE.
WELL, THEN IT'S NOT NICE.

INVINCIBLE BABY

MON OCT 8, 2012

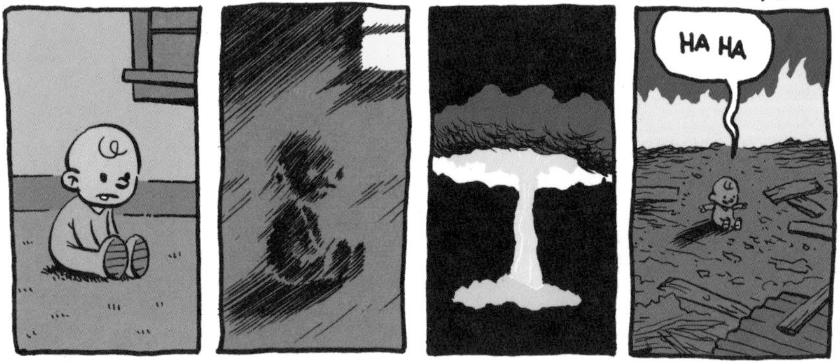
HA HA

TUE OCT 9, 2012

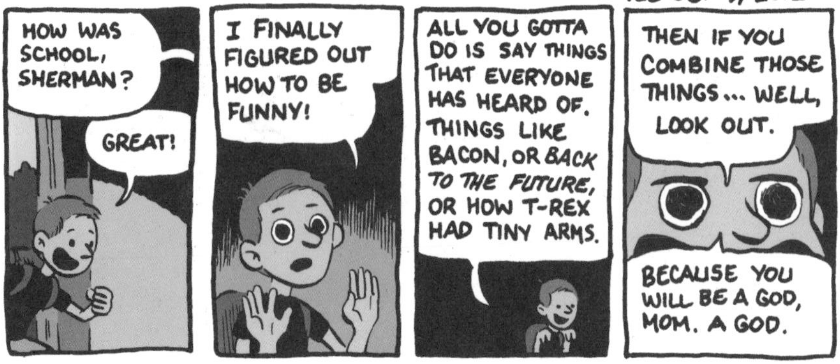
HOW WAS SCHOOL, SHERMAN?
GREAT!
I FINALLY FIGURED OUT HOW TO BE FUNNY!
ALL YOU GOTTA DO IS SAY THINGS THAT EVERYONE HAS HEARD OF. THINGS LIKE BACON, OR *BACK TO THE FUTURE*, OR HOW T-REX HAD TINY ARMS.
THEN IF YOU COMBINE THOSE THINGS... WELL, LOOK OUT.
BECAUSE YOU WILL BE A GOD, MOM. A GOD.

WED OCT 10, 2012

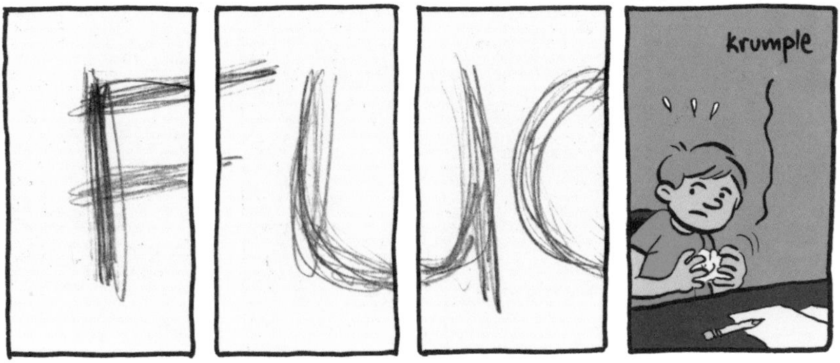
FUC
krumple

THU OCT 11, 2012

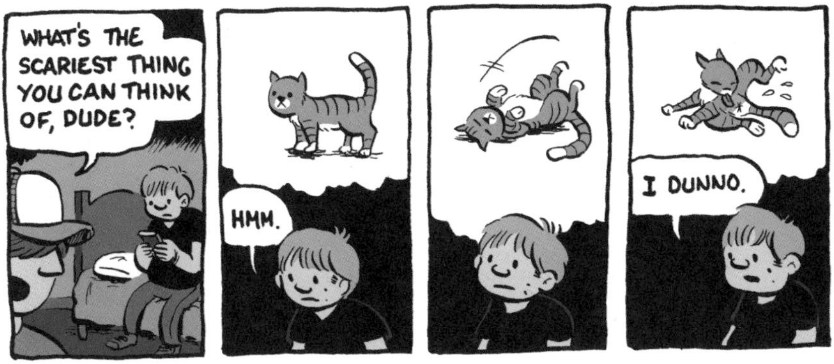
WHAT'S THE SCARIEST THING YOU CAN THINK OF, DUDE?
HMM.
I DUNNO.

FRI OCT 12, 2012

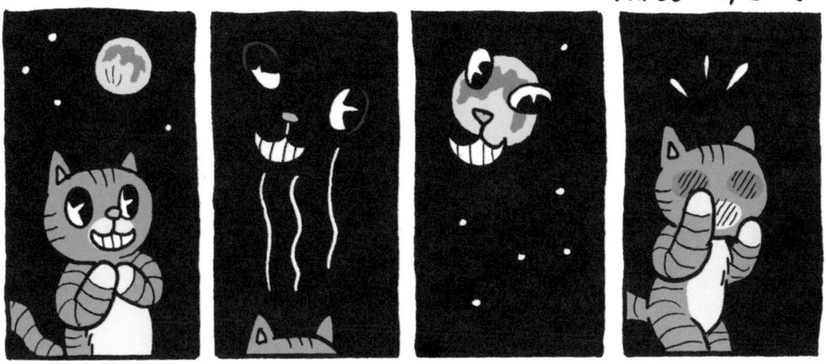

SAT OCT 13, 2012

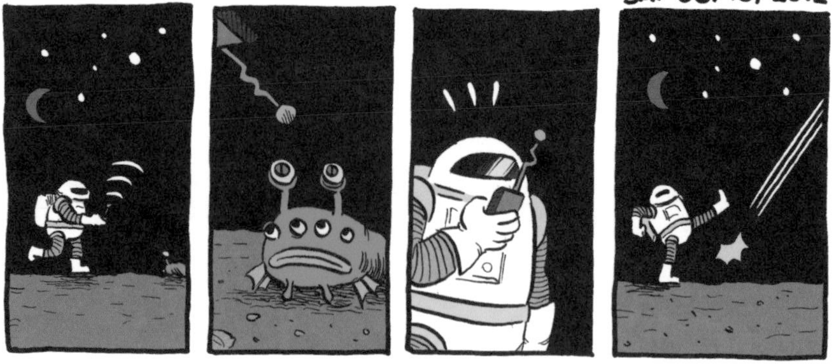

SUN OCT 14, 2012

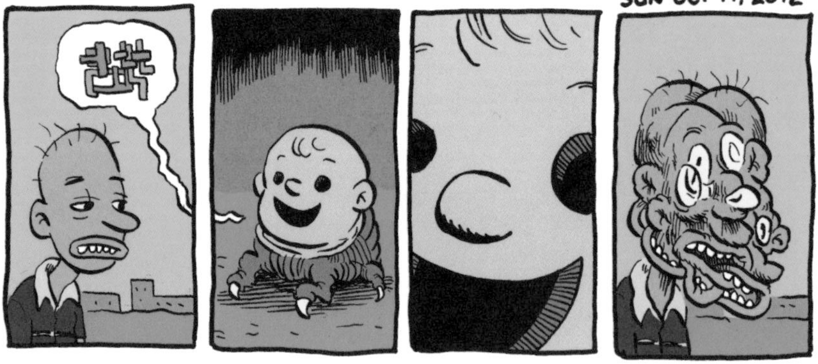

MON OCT 15 2012

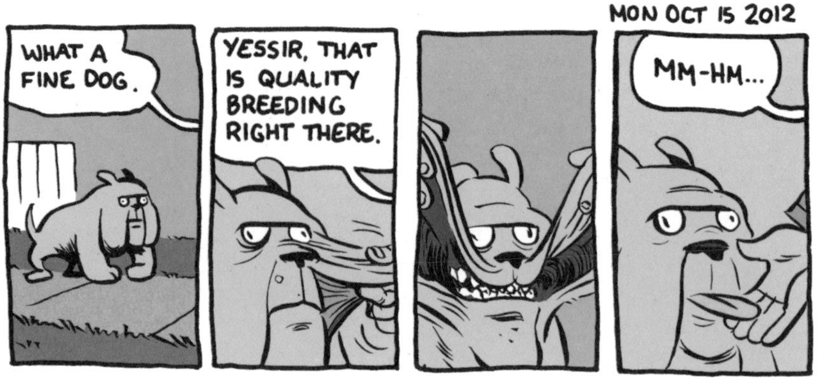

WHAT A FINE DOG.
YESSIR, THAT IS QUALITY BREEDING RIGHT THERE.
MM-HM...

TUE OCT 16, 2012

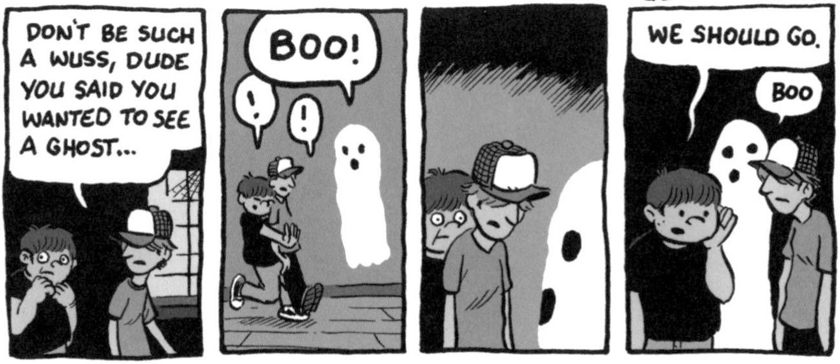
DON'T BE SUCH A WUSS, DUDE YOU SAID YOU WANTED TO SEE A GHOST...
BOO!
!
!
WE SHOULD GO.
BOO

WED OCT 17, 2012

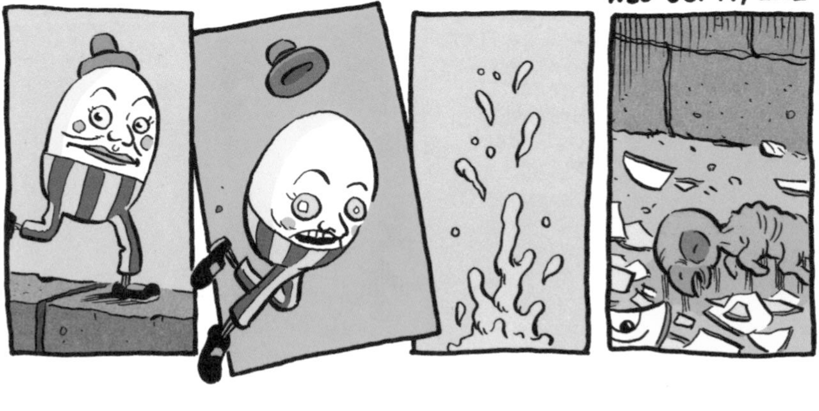

THU OCT 18, 2012

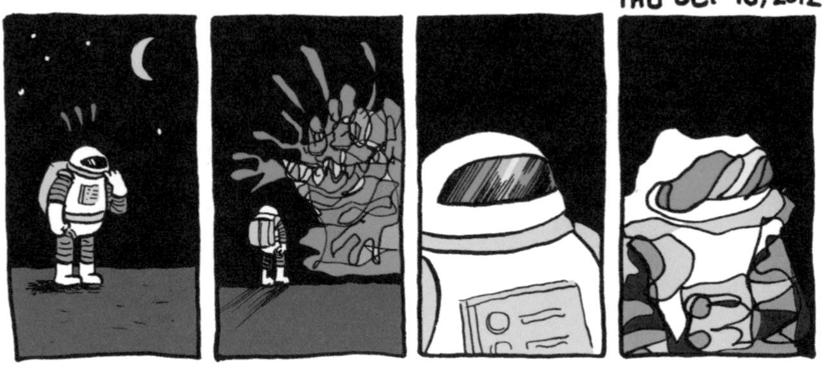

FRI OCT 19, 2012

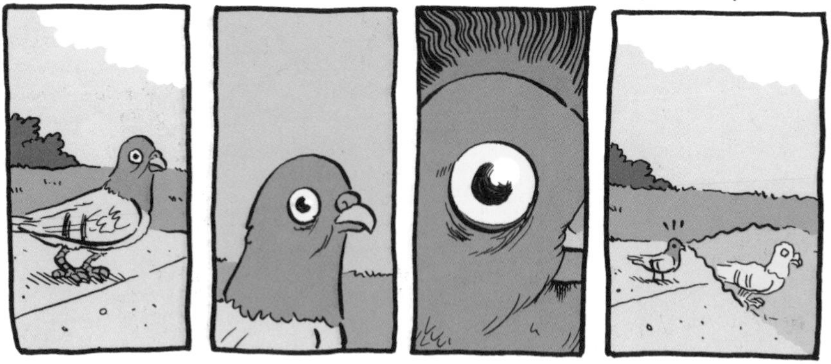

SAT OCT 20, 2012

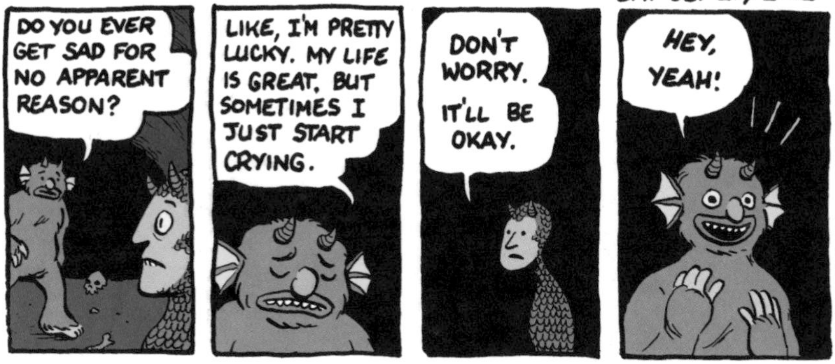
DO YOU EVER GET SAD FOR NO APPARENT REASON?
LIKE, I'M PRETTY LUCKY. MY LIFE IS GREAT, BUT SOMETIMES I JUST START CRYING.
DON'T WORRY.
IT'LL BE OKAY.
HEY, YEAH!

SUN OCT 21, 2012

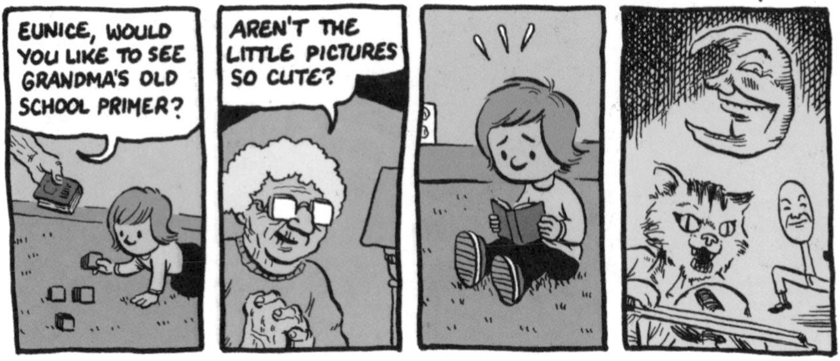
EUNICE, WOULD YOU LIKE TO SEE GRANDMA'S OLD SCHOOL PRIMER?
AREN'T THE LITTLE PICTURES SO CUTE?

MON OCT 22, 2012

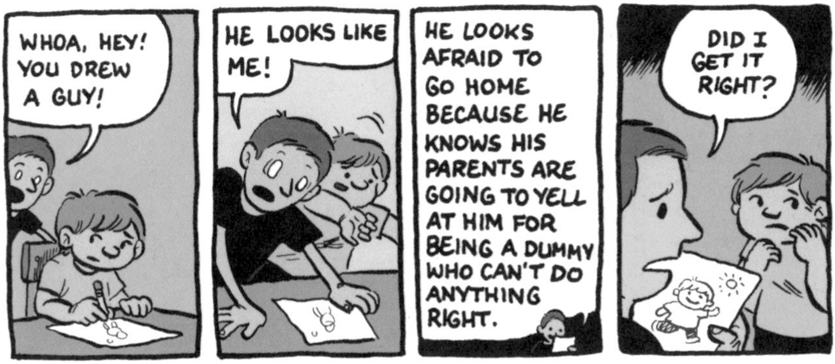

WHOA, HEY! YOU DREW A GUY!
HE LOOKS LIKE ME!
HE LOOKS AFRAID TO GO HOME BECAUSE HE KNOWS HIS PARENTS ARE GOING TO YELL AT HIM FOR BEING A DUMMY WHO CAN'T DO ANYTHING RIGHT.
DID I GET IT RIGHT?

TUE OCT 23, 2012

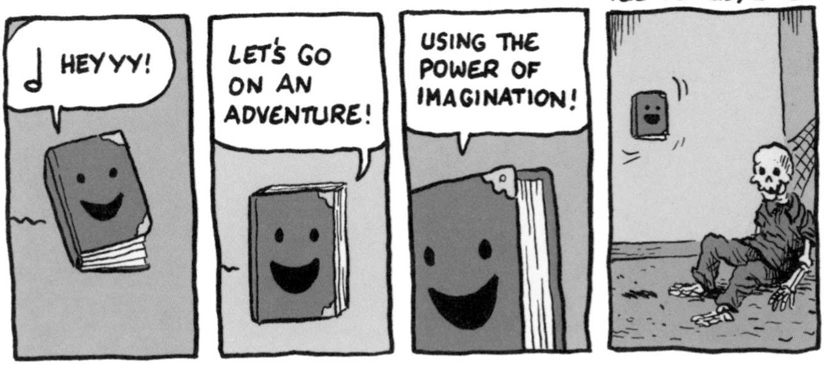

HEYYY!
LET'S GO ON AN ADVENTURE!
USING THE POWER OF IMAGINATION!

WED OCT 24, 2012

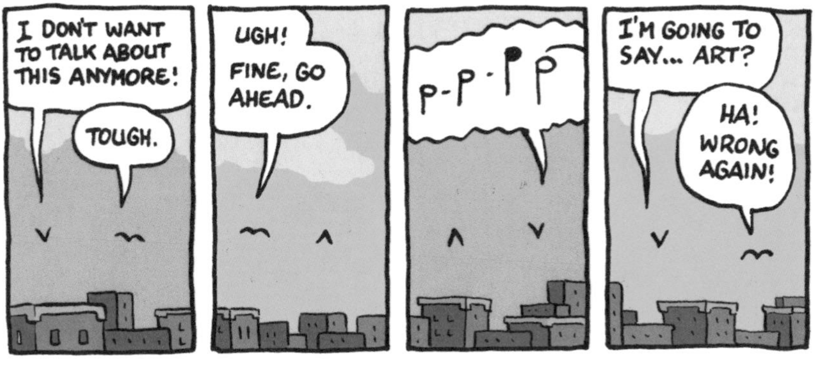

I DON'T WANT TO TALK ABOUT THIS ANYMORE!
TOUGH.
UGH! FINE, GO AHEAD.
P-P-PP
I'M GOING TO SAY... ART?
HA! WRONG AGAIN!

THU OCT 25, 2012

FRI OCT 26, 2012

SUDDENLY, THE UNIVERSE ENDS...

SAT OCT 27, 2012

C'MON, BABY, I THOUGHT YOU WANTED THIS.
I THOUGHT I DID TOO.
IT JUST SEEMS WRONG TO DO IT HERE.
SHOULD I STILL SACRIFICE THE GOAT?
NAH, LET HIM GO.
BAA

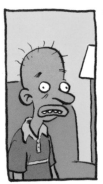

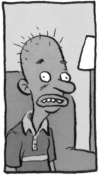

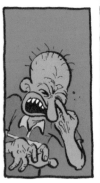

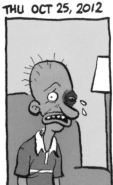

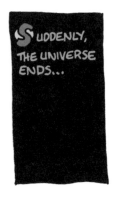

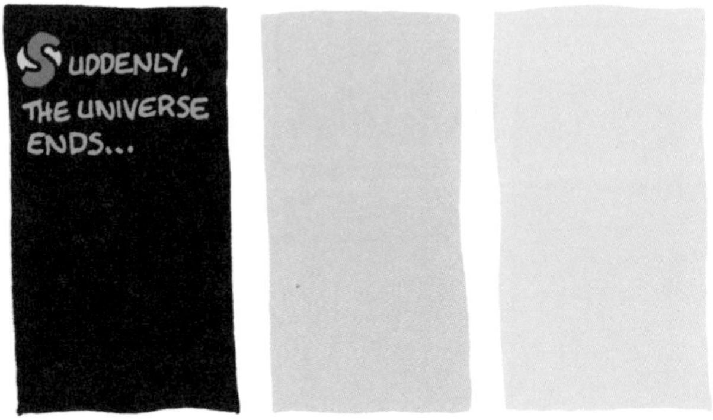

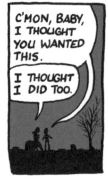

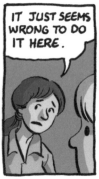

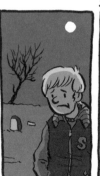

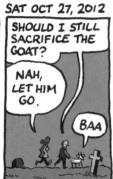

SUN OCT 28, 2012

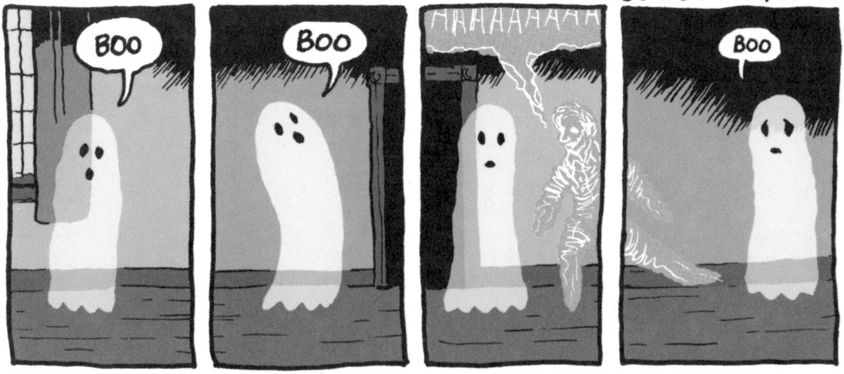
BOO
BOO
AHHHHHHHHH
BOO

MON OCT 29, 2012

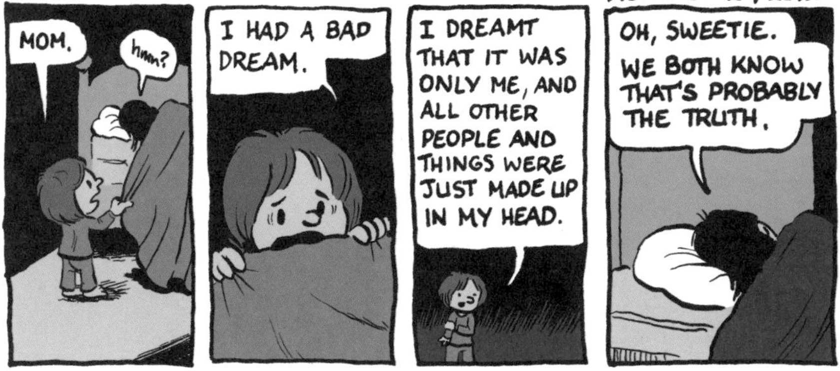
MOM.
hmm?
I HAD A BAD DREAM.
I DREAMT THAT IT WAS ONLY ME, AND ALL OTHER PEOPLE AND THINGS WERE JUST MADE UP IN MY HEAD.
OH, SWEETIE.
WE BOTH KNOW THAT'S PROBABLY THE TRUTH.

TUE OCT 30, 2012

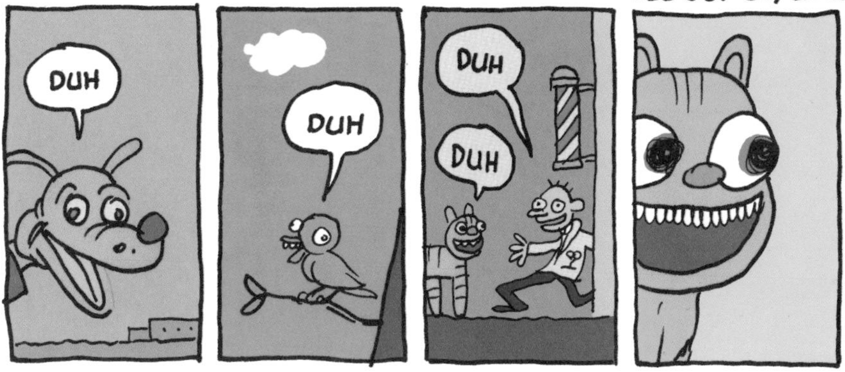
DUH
DUH
DUH
DUH

WED OCT 31, 2012

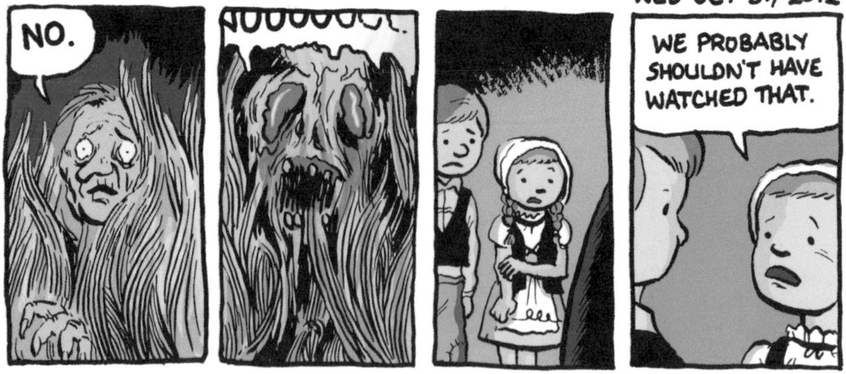

NO.
WE PROBABLY SHOULDN'T HAVE WATCHED THAT.

THU NOV 1, 2012

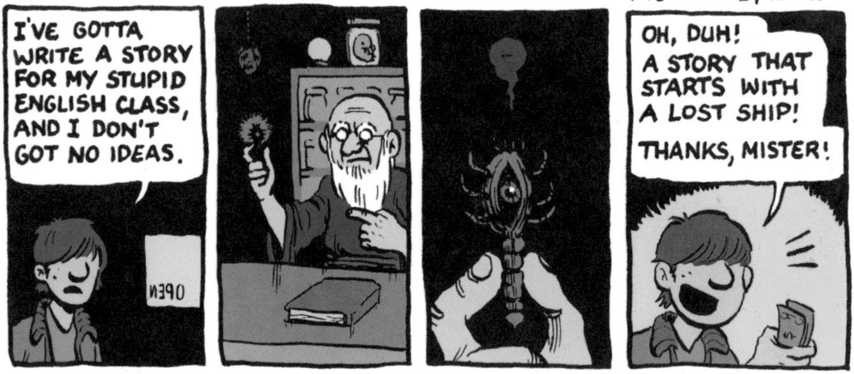

I'VE GOTTA WRITE A STORY FOR MY STUPID ENGLISH CLASS, AND I DON'T GOT NO IDEAS.
OH, DUH! A STORY THAT STARTS WITH A LOST SHIP!
THANKS, MISTER!

FRI NOV 2, 2012

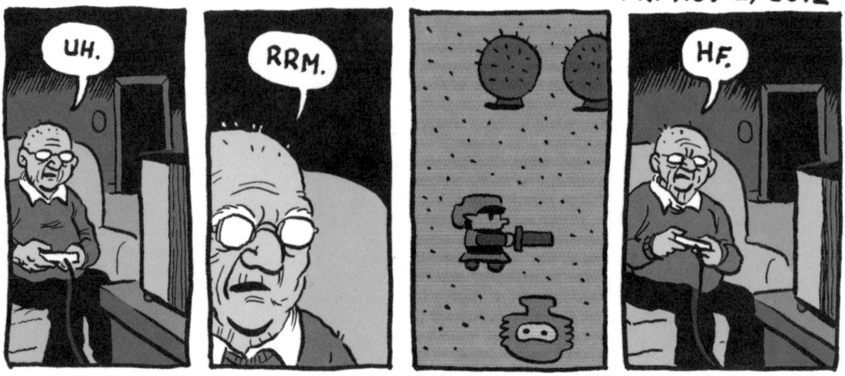

UH.
RRM.
HF.

SAT NOV 3, 2012

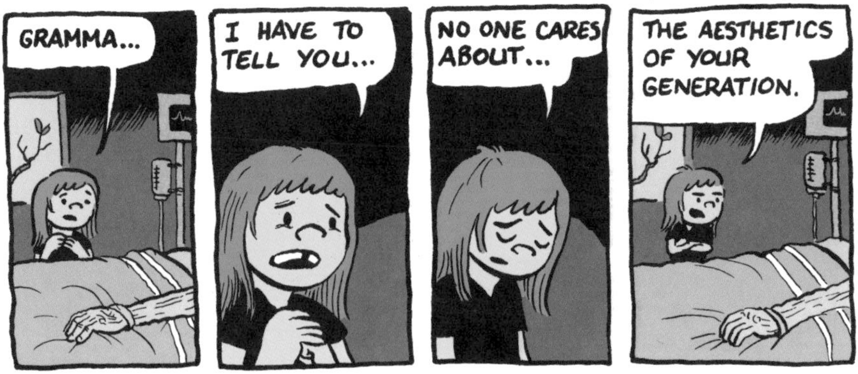
GRAMMA...
I HAVE TO TELL YOU...
NO ONE CARES ABOUT...
THE AESTHETICS OF YOUR GENERATION.

SUN NOV 4, 2012

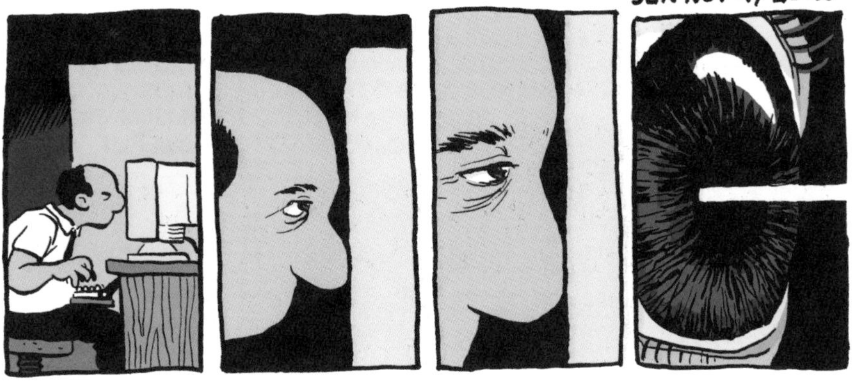

MON NOV 5, 2012

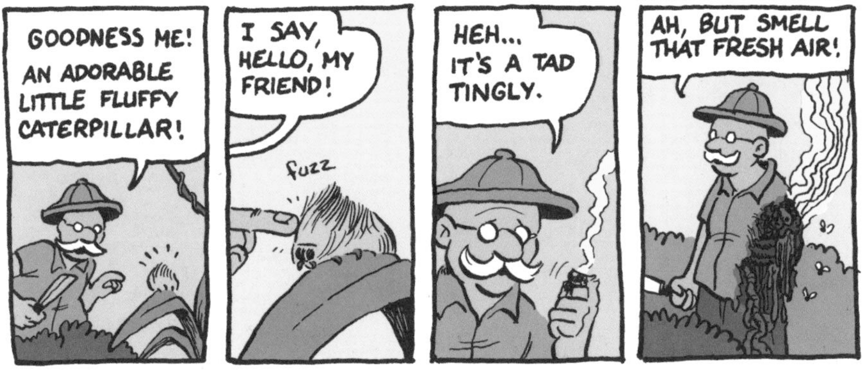
GOODNESS ME! AN ADORABLE LITTLE FLUFFY CATERPILLAR!
I SAY, HELLO, MY FRIEND!
fuzz
HEH... IT'S A TAD TINGLY.
AH, BUT SMELL THAT FRESH AIR!

TUE NOV 6, 2012

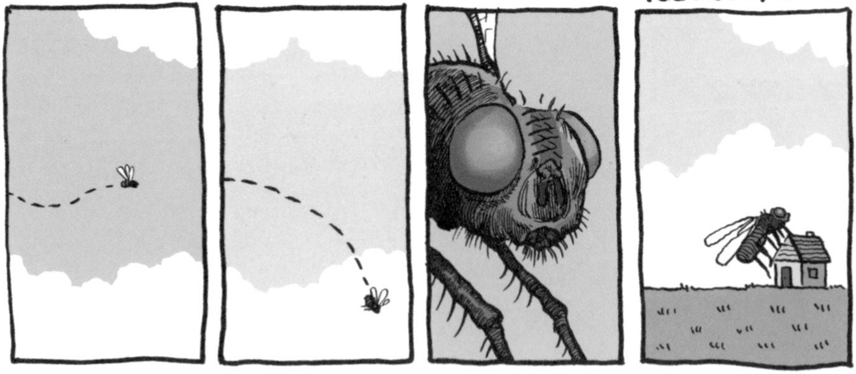

WED NOV 7 2012

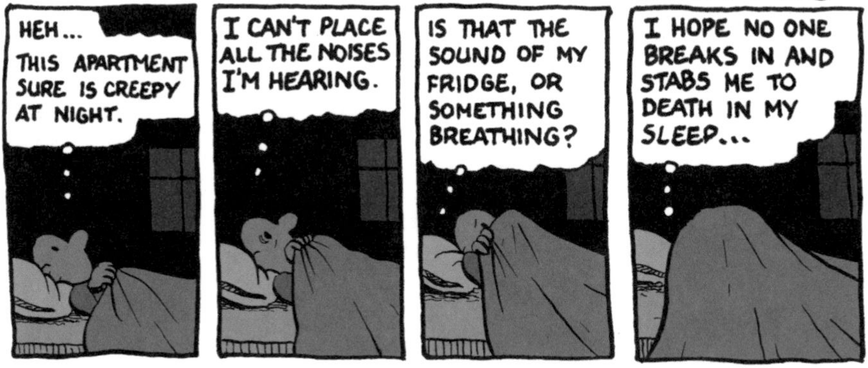
HEH...
THIS APARTMENT SURE IS CREEPY AT NIGHT.
I CAN'T PLACE ALL THE NOISES I'M HEARING.
IS THAT THE SOUND OF MY FRIDGE, OR SOMETHING BREATHING?
I HOPE NO ONE BREAKS IN AND STABS ME TO DEATH IN MY SLEEP...

THU NOV 8, 2012

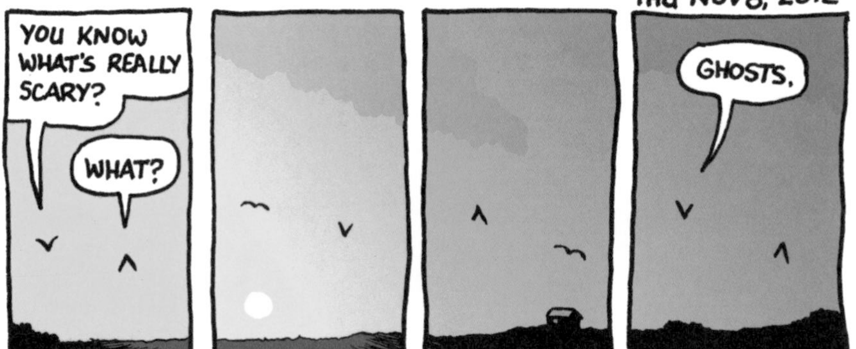
YOU KNOW WHAT'S REALLY SCARY?
WHAT?
GHOSTS.

FRI NOV 9, 2012

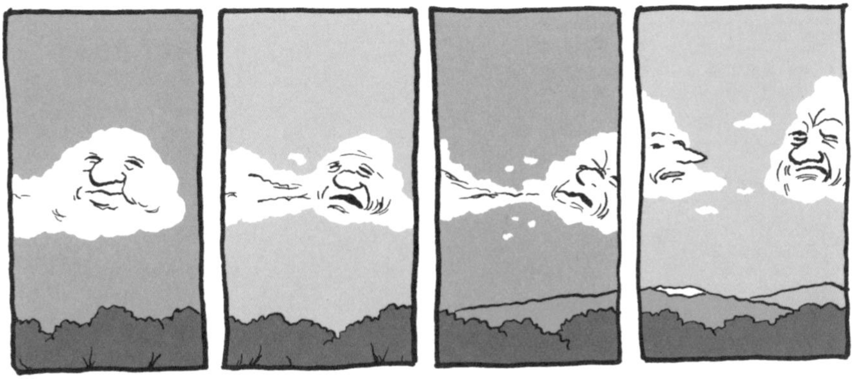

SAT NOV 10, 2012

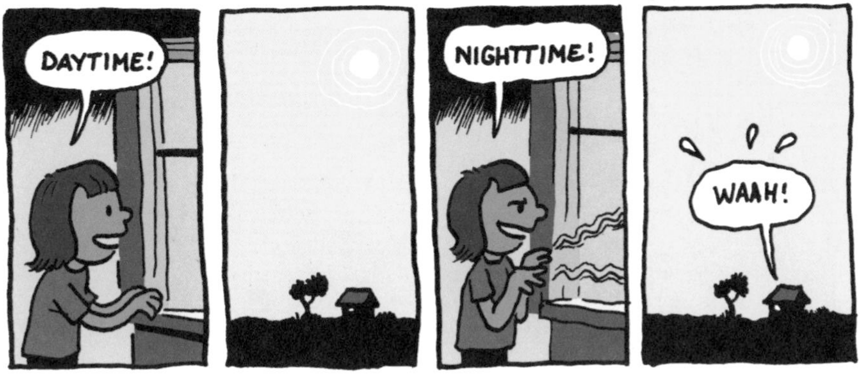
DAYTIME!
NIGHTTIME!
WAAH!

SUN NOV 11, 2012

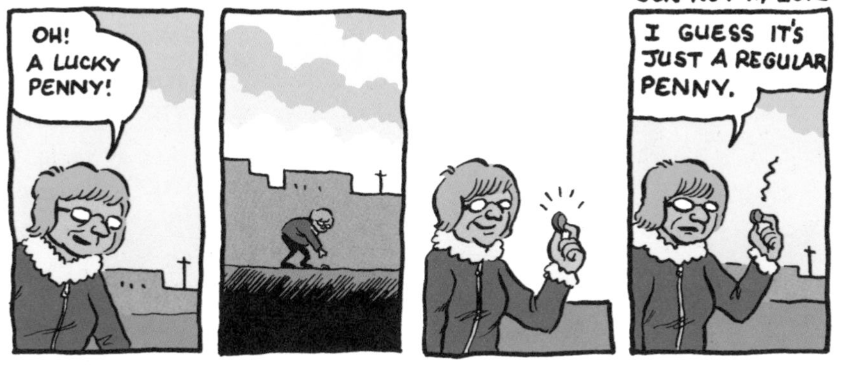
OH! A LUCKY PENNY!
I GUESS IT'S JUST A REGULAR PENNY.

MON NOV 12, 2012

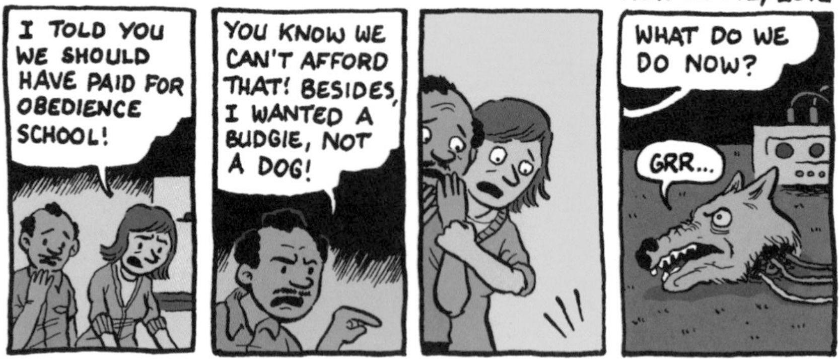
I TOLD YOU WE SHOULD HAVE PAID FOR OBEDIENCE SCHOOL!
YOU KNOW WE CAN'T AFFORD THAT! BESIDES, I WANTED A BUDGIE, NOT A DOG!
WHAT DO WE DO NOW?
GRR...

TUE NOV 13, 2012

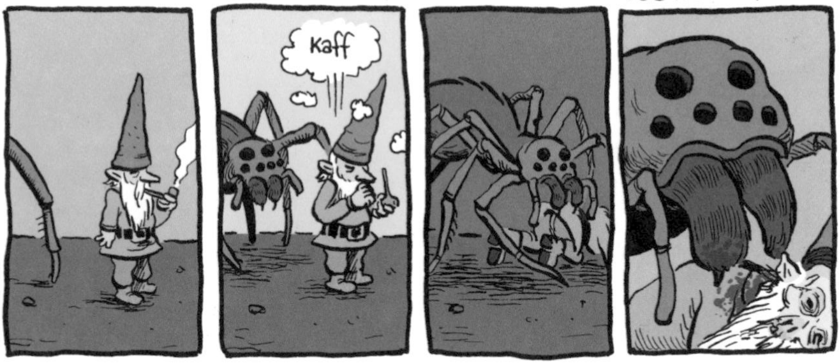
Kaff

WED NOV 14, 2012

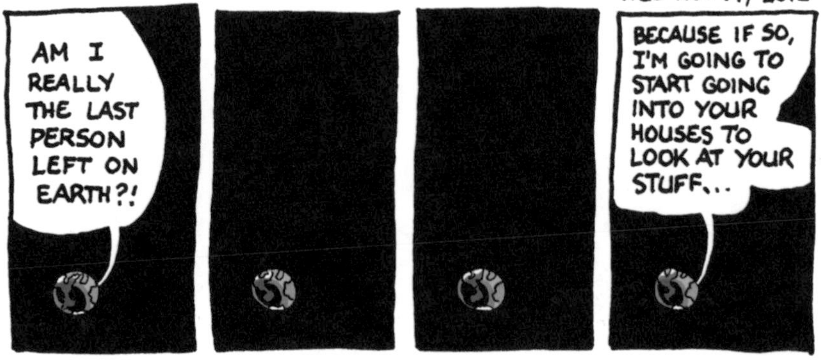
AM I REALLY THE LAST PERSON LEFT ON EARTH?!
BECAUSE IF SO, I'M GOING TO START GOING INTO YOUR HOUSES TO LOOK AT YOUR STUFF...

THU NOV 15, 2012

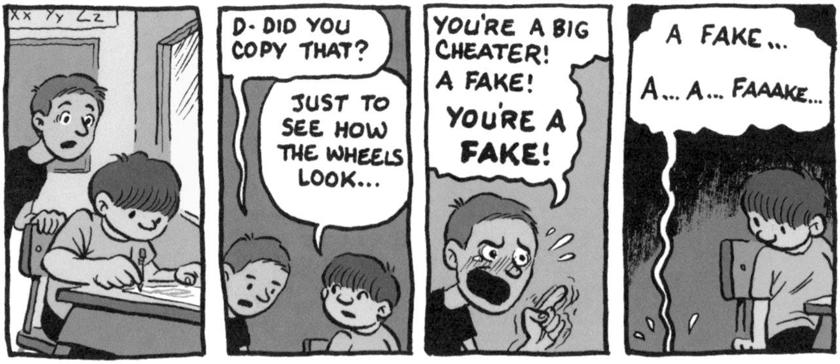
Xx Yy Zz
D- DID YOU COPY THAT?
JUST TO SEE HOW THE WHEELS LOOK...
YOU'RE A BIG CHEATER! A FAKE! YOU'RE A FAKE!
A FAKE...
A... A... FAAAKE...

FRI NOV 16, 2012

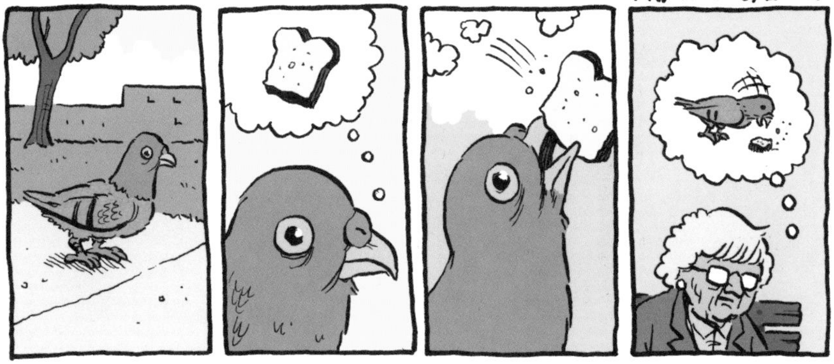

SAT NOV 17, 2012

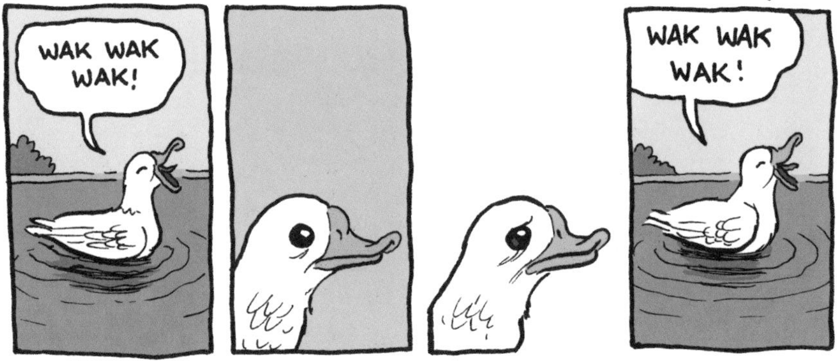
WAK WAK WAK!
WAK WAK WAK!

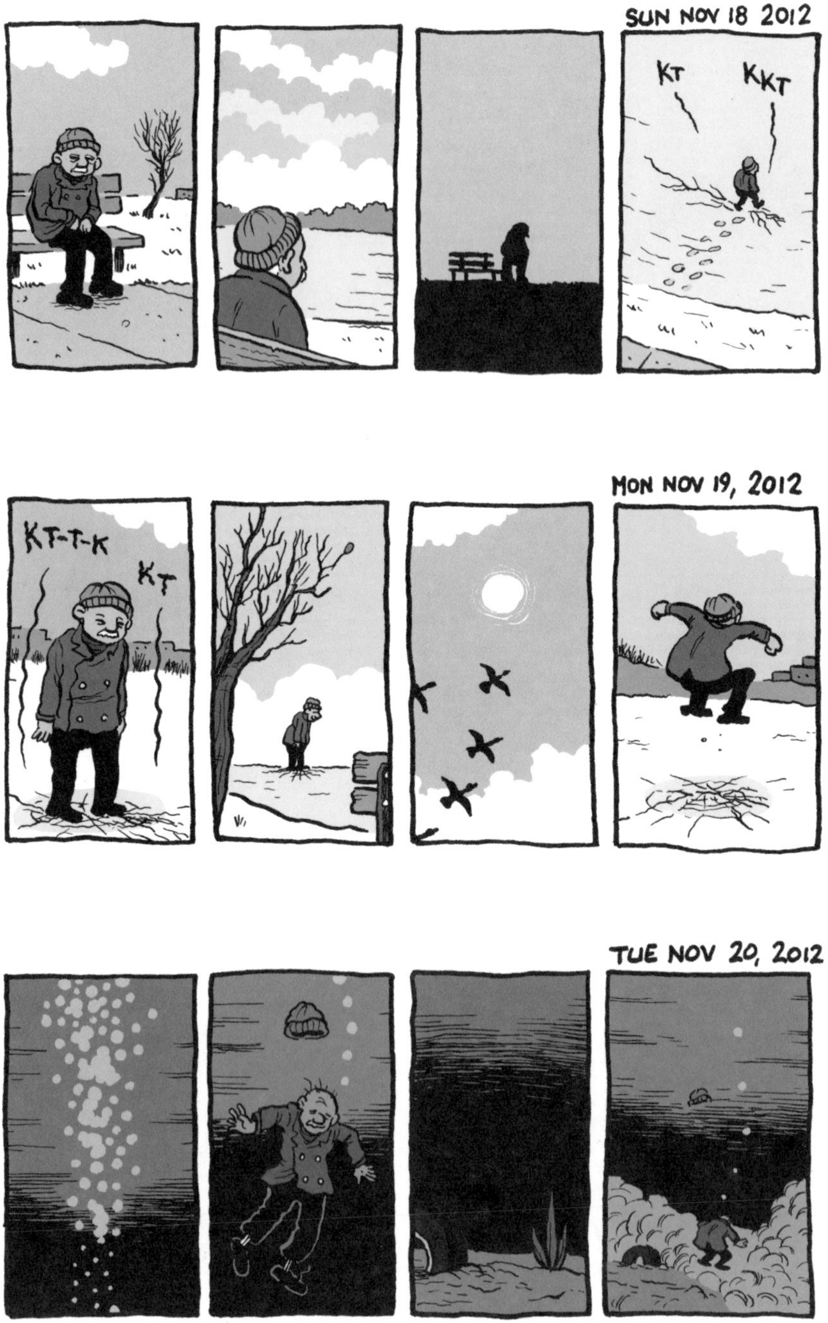
SUN NOV 18 2012
KT
KKT
MON NOV 19, 2012
KT-T-K
KT
TUE NOV 20, 2012

WED NOV 21, 2012

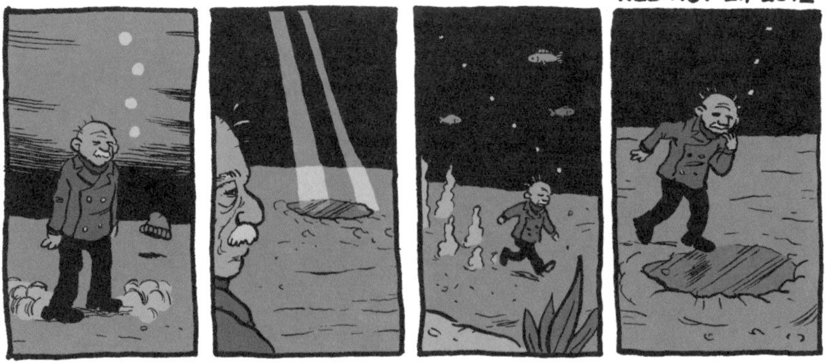

THU NOV 22, 2012

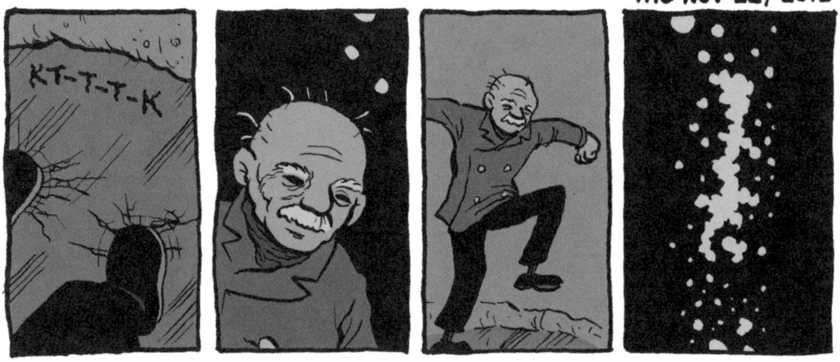
KT-T-T-K

FRI NOV 23, 2012

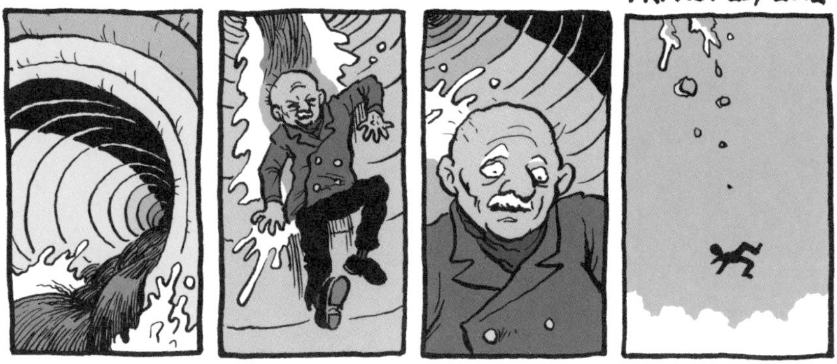

SAT NOV 24, 2012

SUN NOV 25, 2012

OH, WOW!
WHAT A HUGE BUG!
HA HA HA
HA...
AW MAN. NOT AGAIN.

MON NOV 26, 2012

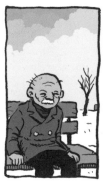

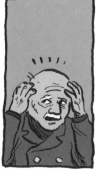

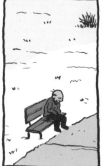

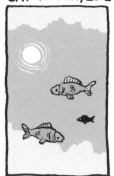

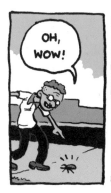

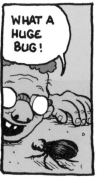

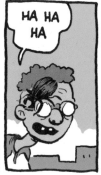

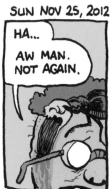

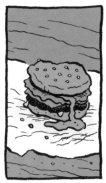

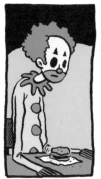

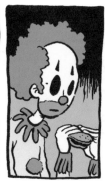

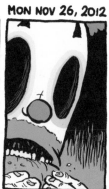

TUE NOV 27, 2012

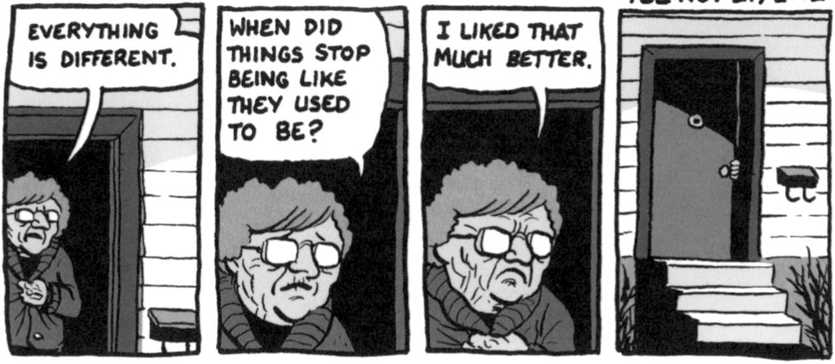

EVERYTHING IS DIFFERENT.
WHEN DID THINGS STOP BEING LIKE THEY USED TO BE?
I LIKED THAT MUCH BETTER.

WED NOV 28, 2012

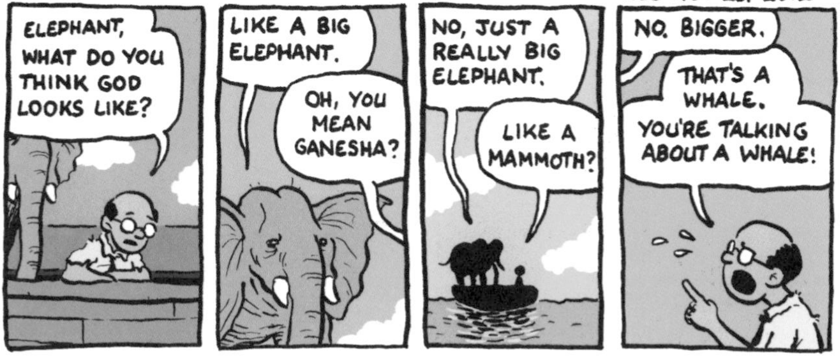

ELEPHANT, WHAT DO YOU THINK GOD LOOKS LIKE?
LIKE A BIG ELEPHANT.
OH, YOU MEAN GANESHA?
NO, JUST A REALLY BIG ELEPHANT.
LIKE A MAMMOTH?
NO. BIGGER.
THAT'S A WHALE. YOU'RE TALKING ABOUT A WHALE!

THU NOV 29, 2012

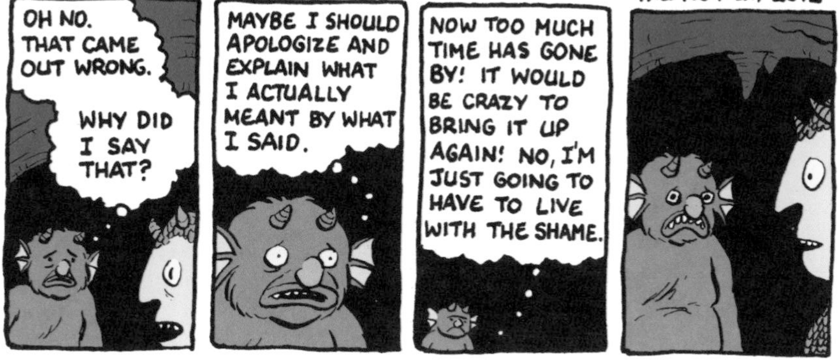

OH NO. THAT CAME OUT WRONG.
WHY DID I SAY THAT?
MAYBE I SHOULD APOLOGIZE AND EXPLAIN WHAT I ACTUALLY MEANT BY WHAT I SAID.
NOW TOO MUCH TIME HAS GONE BY! IT WOULD BE CRAZY TO BRING IT UP AGAIN! NO, I'M JUST GOING TO HAVE TO LIVE WITH THE SHAME.

INVINCIBLE BABY

FRI NOV 30, 2012

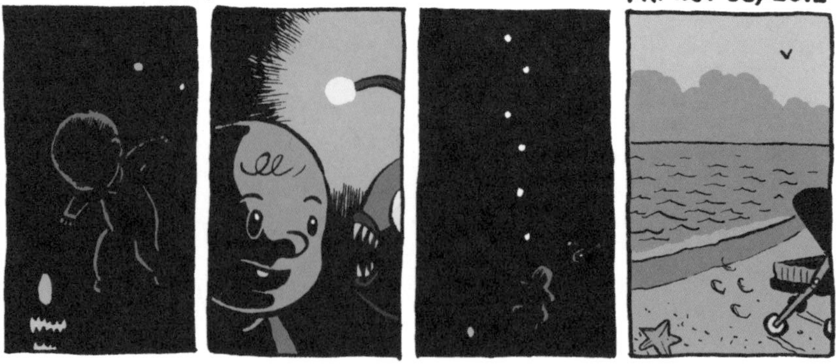

SAT DEC 1, 2012

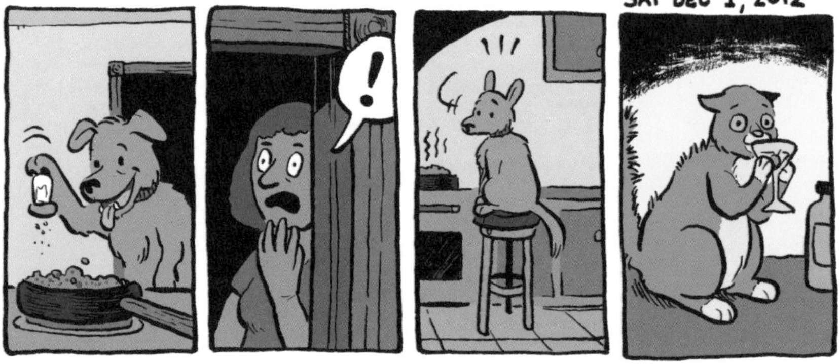
!

SUN DEC 2, 2012

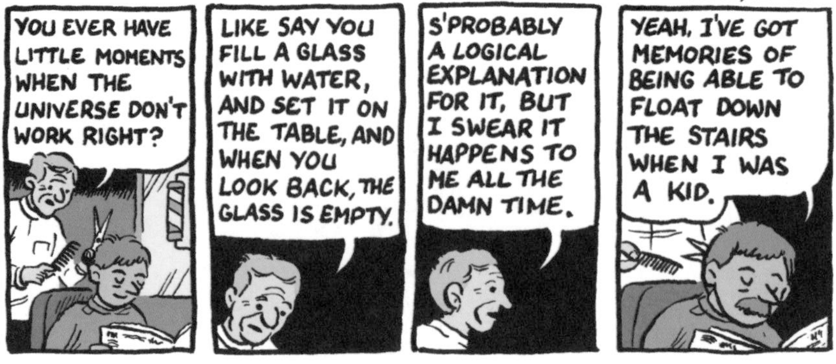
YOU EVER HAVE LITTLE MOMENTS WHEN THE UNIVERSE DON'T WORK RIGHT?
LIKE SAY YOU FILL A GLASS WITH WATER, AND SET IT ON THE TABLE, AND WHEN YOU LOOK BACK, THE GLASS IS EMPTY.
S'PROBABLY A LOGICAL EXPLANATION FOR IT, BUT I SWEAR IT HAPPENS TO ME ALL THE DAMN TIME.
YEAH, I'VE GOT MEMORIES OF BEING ABLE TO FLOAT DOWN THE STAIRS WHEN I WAS A KID.

MON DEC 3, 2012

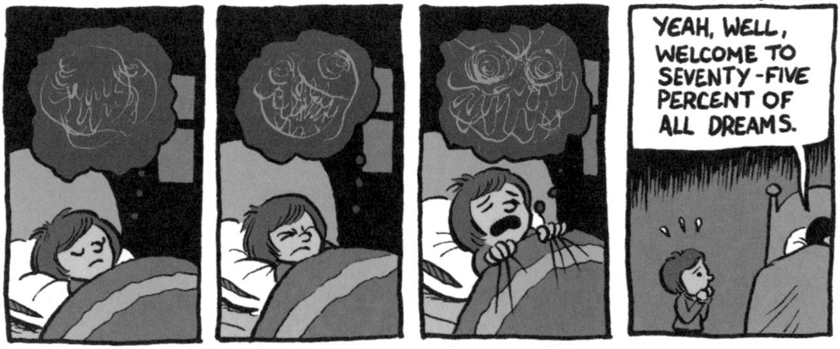
YEAH, WELL, WELCOME TO SEVENTY-FIVE PERCENT OF ALL DREAMS.

TUE DEC 4, 2012

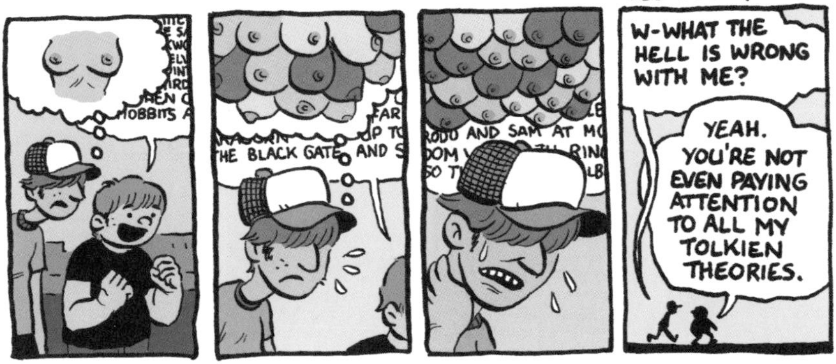
W-WHAT THE HELL IS WRONG WITH ME?
YEAH. YOU'RE NOT EVEN PAYING ATTENTION TO ALL MY TOLKIEN THEORIES.

WED DEC 5, 2012

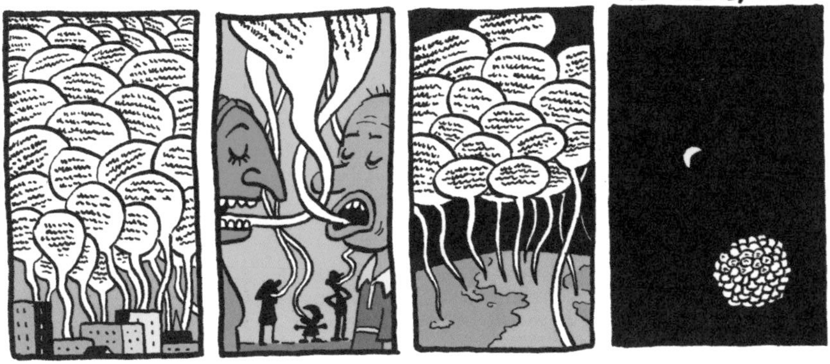

THU DEC 6, 2012

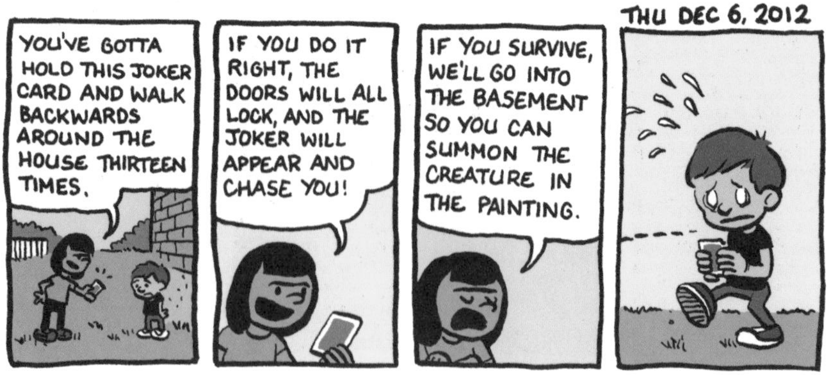

YOU'VE GOTTA HOLD THIS JOKER CARD AND WALK BACKWARDS AROUND THE HOUSE THIRTEEN TIMES.
IF YOU DO IT RIGHT, THE DOORS WILL ALL LOCK, AND THE JOKER WILL APPEAR AND CHASE YOU!
IF YOU SURVIVE, WE'LL GO INTO THE BASEMENT SO YOU CAN SUMMON THE CREATURE IN THE PAINTING.

FRI DEC 7, 2012

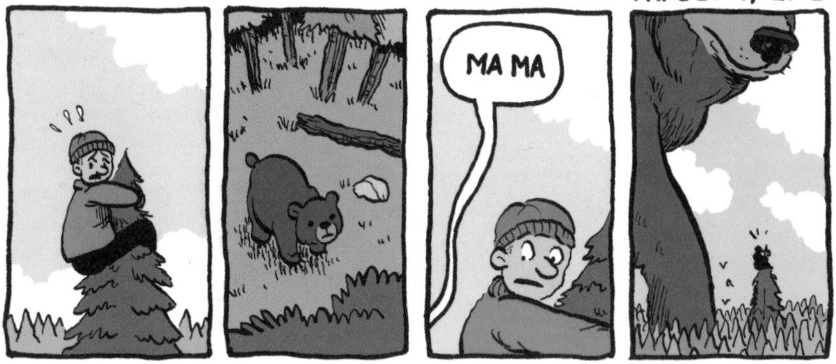

MA MA

SAT DEC 8, 2012

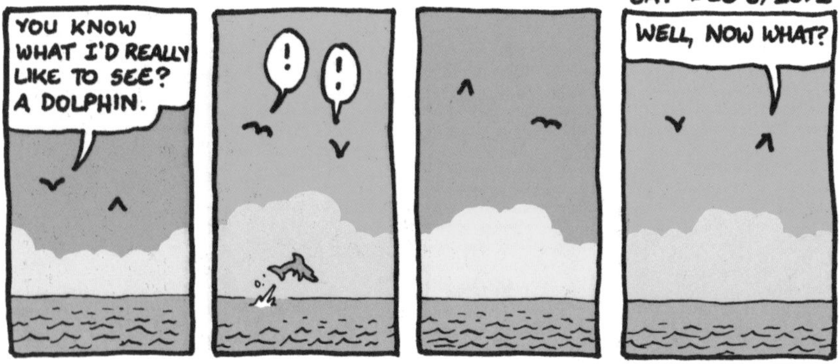

YOU KNOW WHAT I'D REALLY LIKE TO SEE? A DOLPHIN.
!
!
WELL, NOW WHAT?

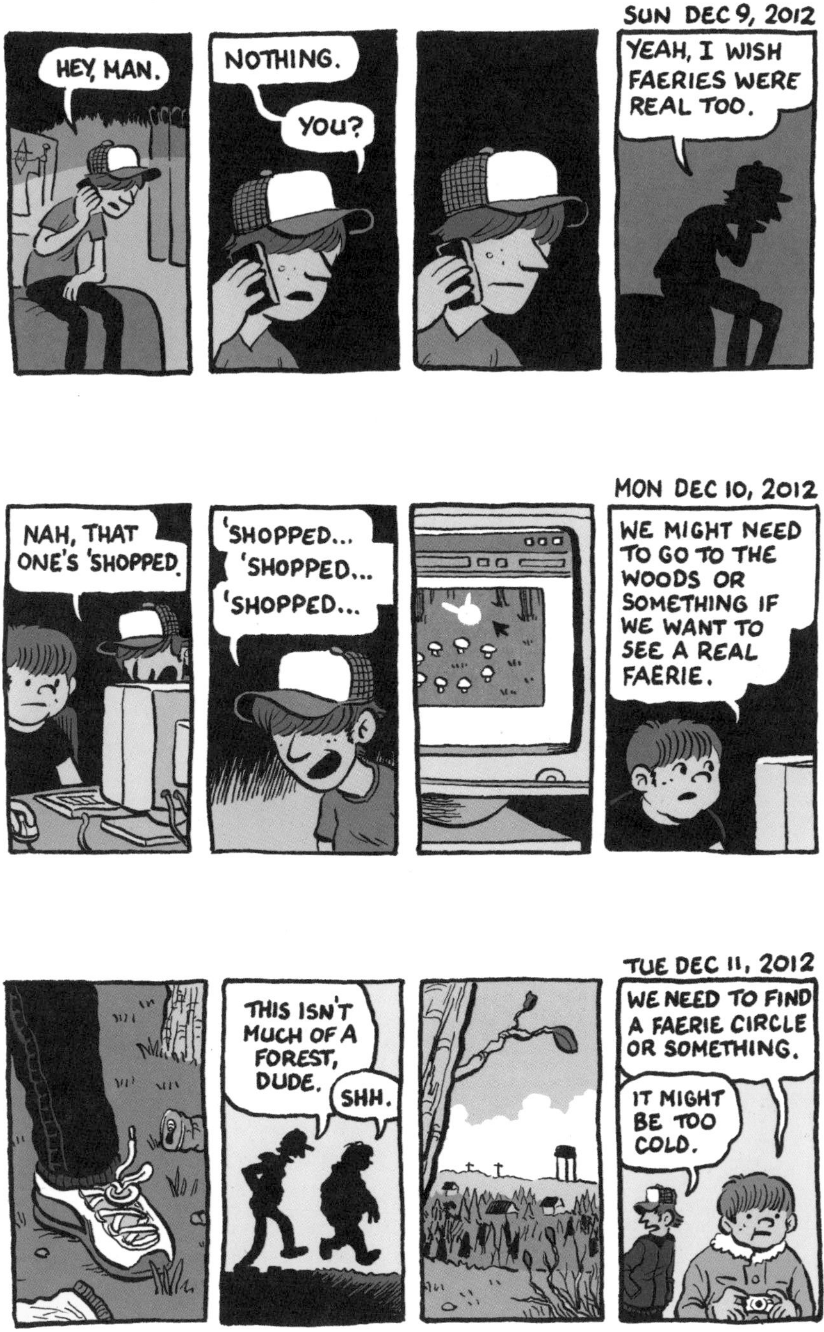
HEY, MAN.
NOTHING.
YOU?
SUN DEC 9, 2012
YEAH, I WISH FAERIES WERE REAL TOO.
NAH, THAT ONE'S 'SHOPPED.
'SHOPPED... 'SHOPPED... 'SHOPPED...
MON DEC 10, 2012
WE MIGHT NEED TO GO TO THE WOODS OR SOMETHING IF WE WANT TO SEE A REAL FAERIE.
THIS ISN'T MUCH OF A FOREST, DUDE.
SHH.
TUE DEC 11, 2012
WE NEED TO FIND A FAERIE CIRCLE OR SOMETHING.
IT MIGHT BE TOO COLD.

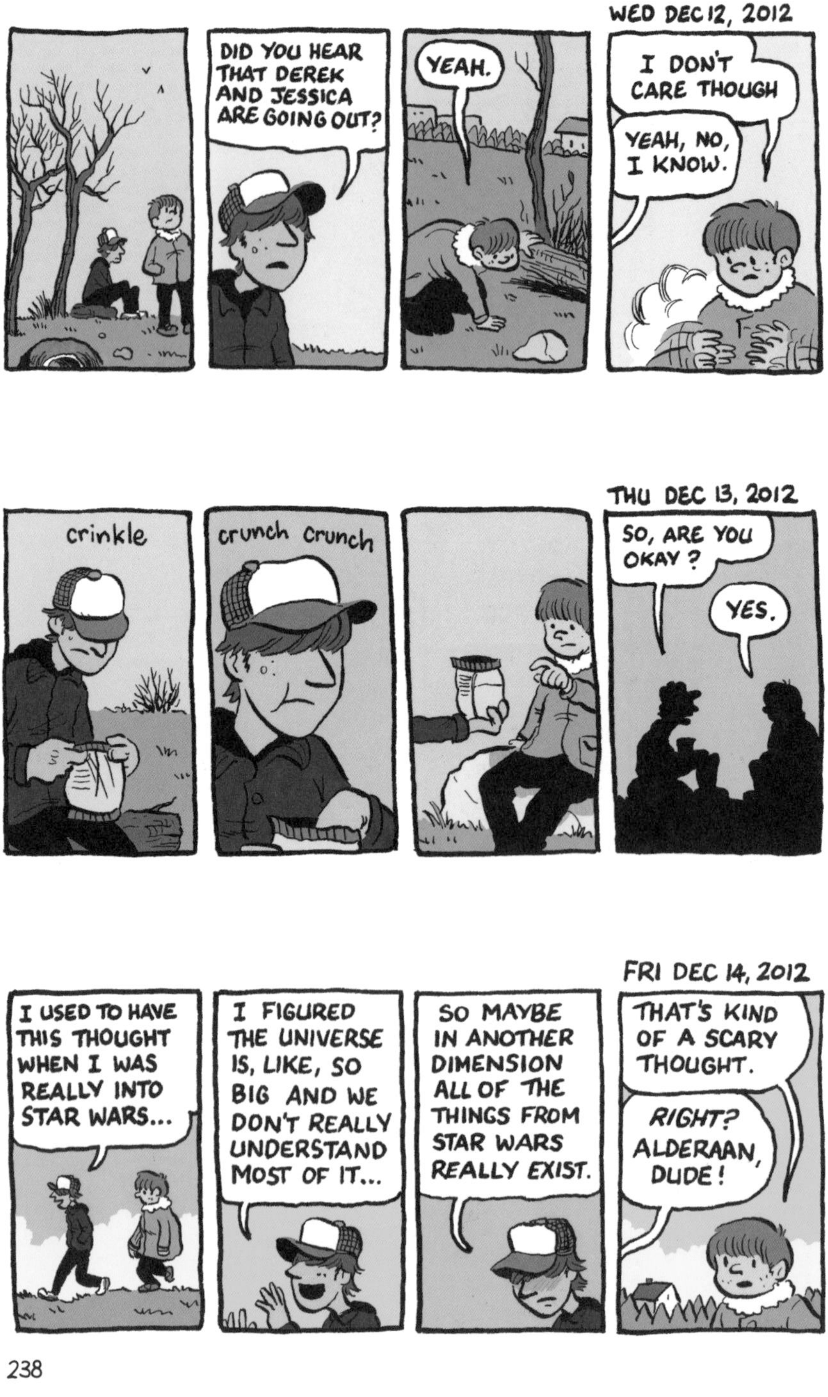

WED DEC 12, 2012
DID YOU HEAR THAT DEREK AND JESSICA ARE GOING OUT?
YEAH.
I DON'T CARE THOUGH
YEAH, NO, I KNOW.
THU DEC 13, 2012
crinkle
crunch crunch
SO, ARE YOU OKAY ?
YES.
FRI DEC 14, 2012
I USED TO HAVE THIS THOUGHT WHEN I WAS REALLY INTO STAR WARS...
I FIGURED THE UNIVERSE IS, LIKE, SO BIG AND WE DON'T REALLY UNDERSTAND MOST OF IT...
SO MAYBE IN ANOTHER DIMENSION ALL OF THE THINGS FROM STAR WARS REALLY EXIST.
THAT'S KIND OF A SCARY THOUGHT.
RIGHT? ALDERAAN, DUDE!

SAT DEC 15, 2012

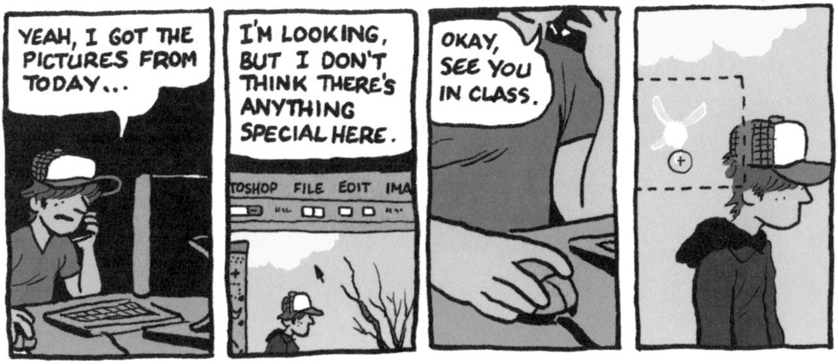
YEAH, I GOT THE PICTURES FROM TODAY...
I'M LOOKING, BUT I DON'T THINK THERE'S ANYTHING SPECIAL HERE.
TOSHOP FILE EDIT IMA
OKAY, SEE YOU IN CLASS.

SUN DEC 16, 2012

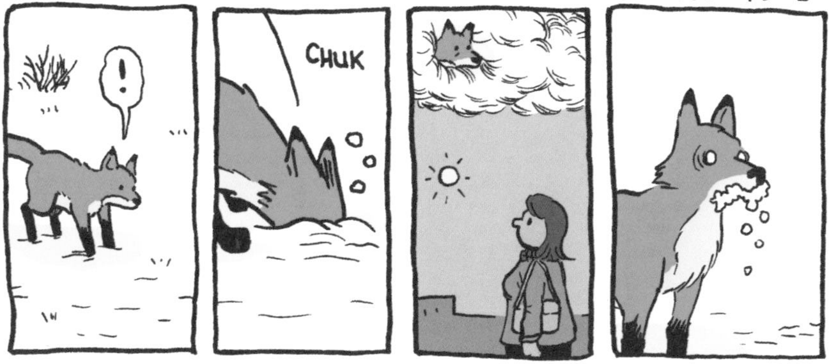
!
CHUK

MON DEC 17, 2012

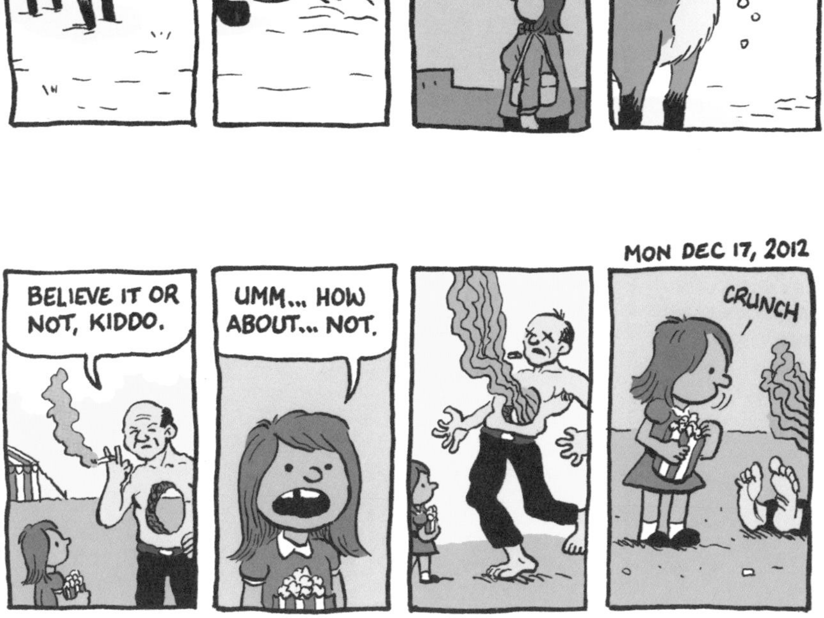
BELIEVE IT OR NOT, KIDDO.
UMM... HOW ABOUT... NOT.
CRUNCH

TUE DEC 18, 2012

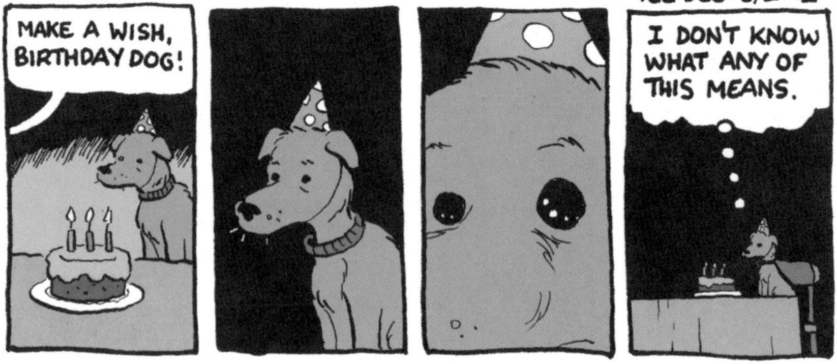
MAKE A WISH, BIRTHDAY DOG!
I DON'T KNOW WHAT ANY OF THIS MEANS.

WED DEC 19, 2012

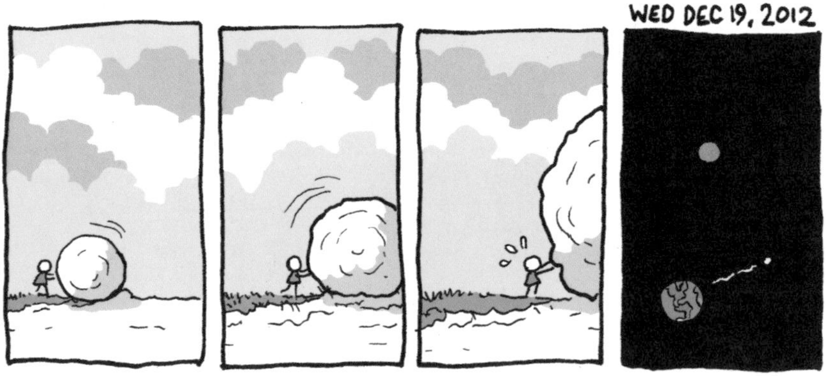

THU DEC 20, 2012

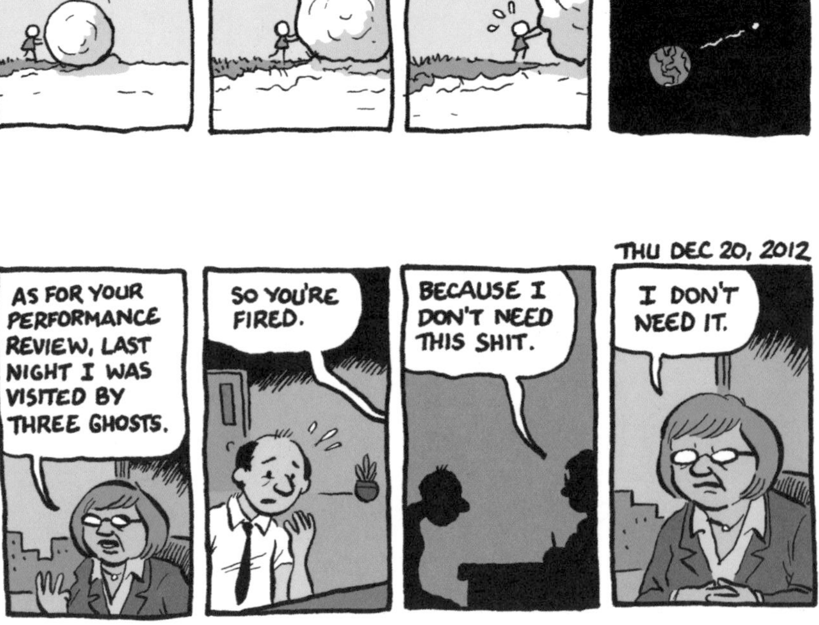
AS FOR YOUR PERFORMANCE REVIEW, LAST NIGHT I WAS VISITED BY THREE GHOSTS.
SO YOU'RE FIRED.
BECAUSE I DON'T NEED THIS SHIT.
I DON'T NEED IT.

FRI DEC 21, 2012

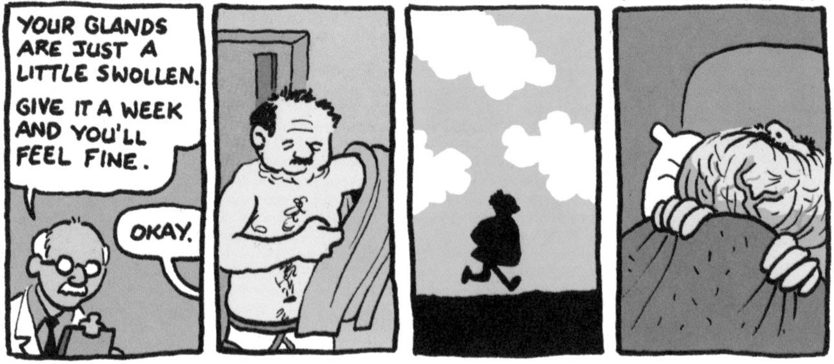
YOUR GLANDS ARE JUST A LITTLE SWOLLEN.
GIVE IT A WEEK AND YOU'LL FEEL FINE.
OKAY.

SAT DEC 22, 2012

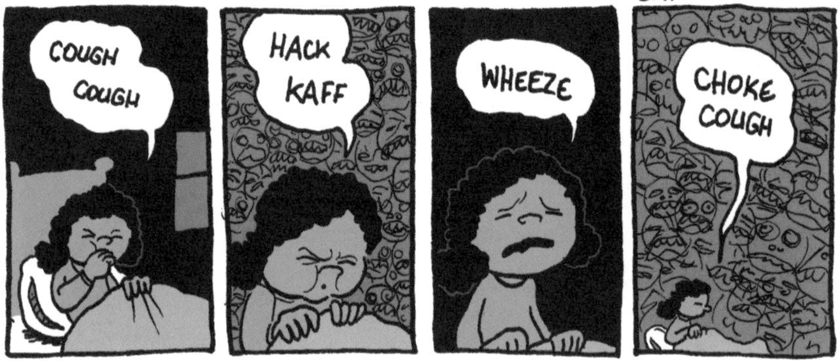
COUGH COUGH
HACK KAFF
WHEEZE
CHOKE COUGH

SUN DEC 23, 2012

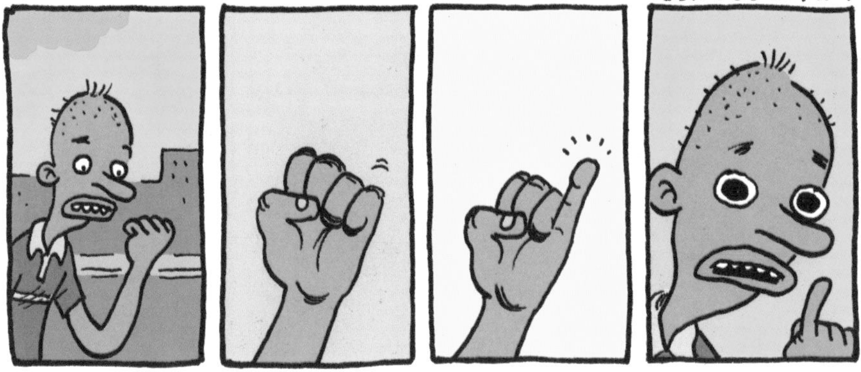

MON DEC 24, 2012

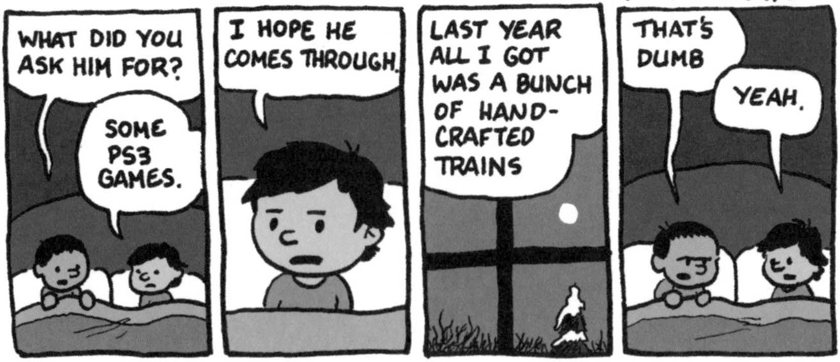
WHAT DID YOU ASK HIM FOR?
SOME PS3 GAMES.
I HOPE HE COMES THROUGH.
LAST YEAR ALL I GOT WAS A BUNCH OF HAND-CRAFTED TRAINS
THAT'S DUMB
YEAH.

TUE DEC 25, 2012

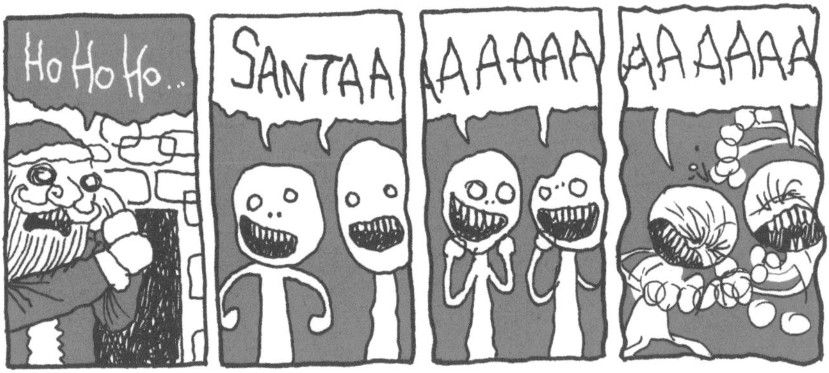
Ho Ho Ho...
SANTAA
AAAAAA
AAAAAA

WED DEC 26, 2012

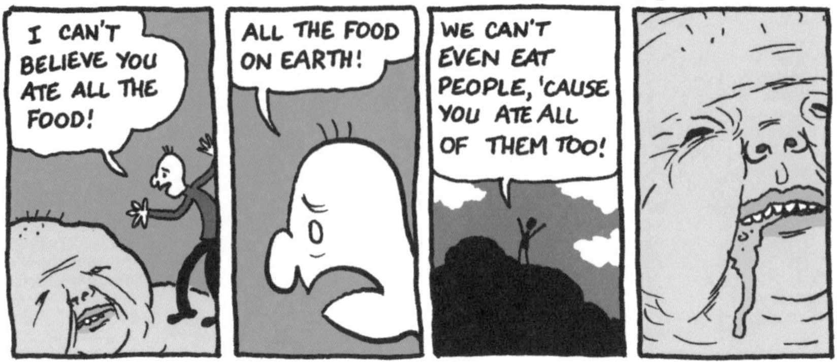
I CAN'T BELIEVE YOU ATE ALL THE FOOD!
ALL THE FOOD ON EARTH!
WE CAN'T EVEN EAT PEOPLE, 'CAUSE YOU ATE ALL OF THEM TOO!

THU DEC 27, 2012

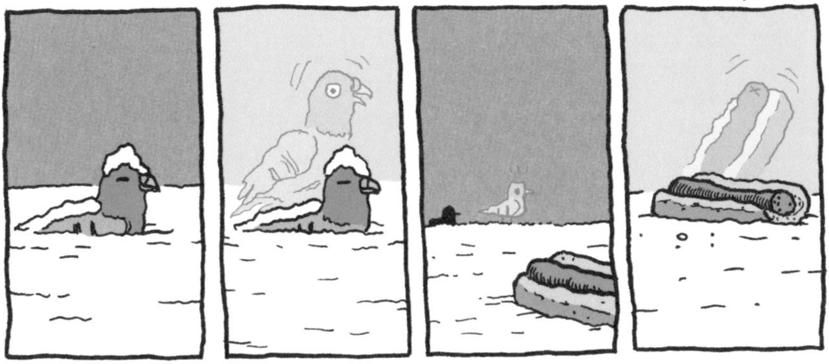

FRI DEC 28, 2012

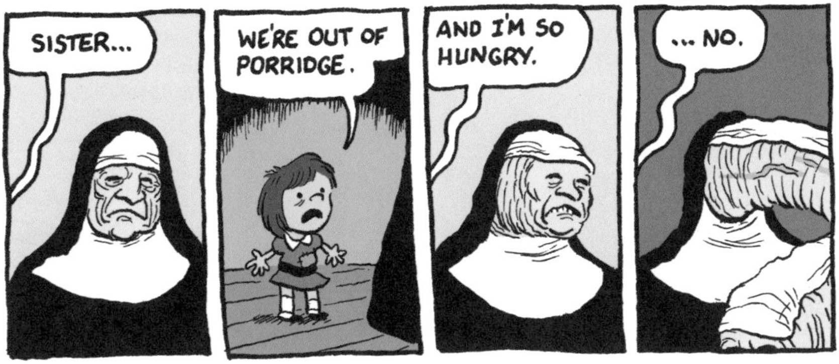
SISTER...
WE'RE OUT OF PORRIDGE.
AND I'M SO HUNGRY.
... NO.

SAT DEC 29, 2012

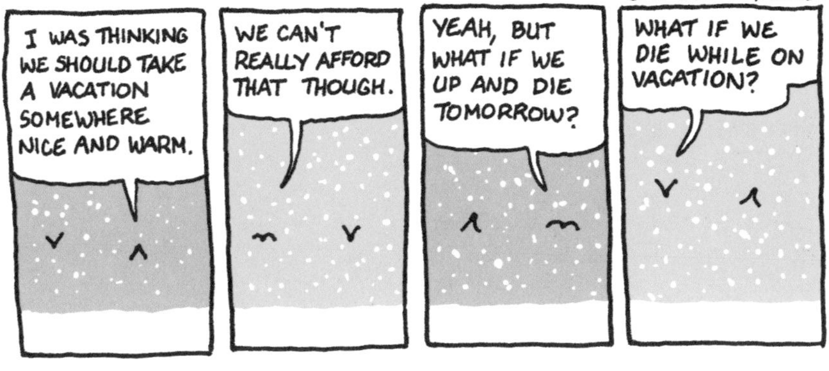
I WAS THINKING WE SHOULD TAKE A VACATION SOMEWHERE NICE AND WARM.
WE CAN'T REALLY AFFORD THAT THOUGH.
YEAH, BUT WHAT IF WE UP AND DIE TOMORROW?
WHAT IF WE DIE WHILE ON VACATION?

SUN DEC 30, 2012

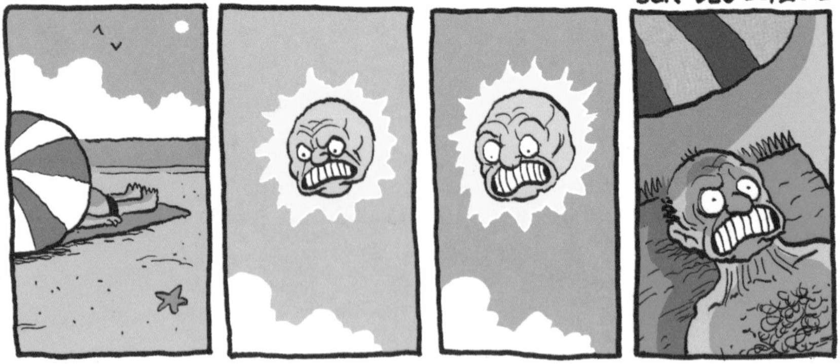

MON DEC 31, 2012

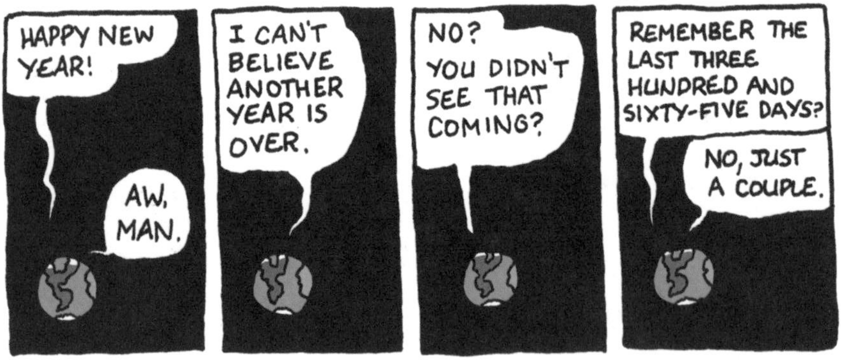
HAPPY NEW YEAR!
AW, MAN.
I CAN'T BELIEVE ANOTHER YEAR IS OVER.
NO?
YOU DIDN'T SEE THAT COMING?
REMEMBER THE LAST THREE HUNDRED AND SIXTY-FIVE DAYS?
NO, JUST A COUPLE.

TUE JAN 1, 2013

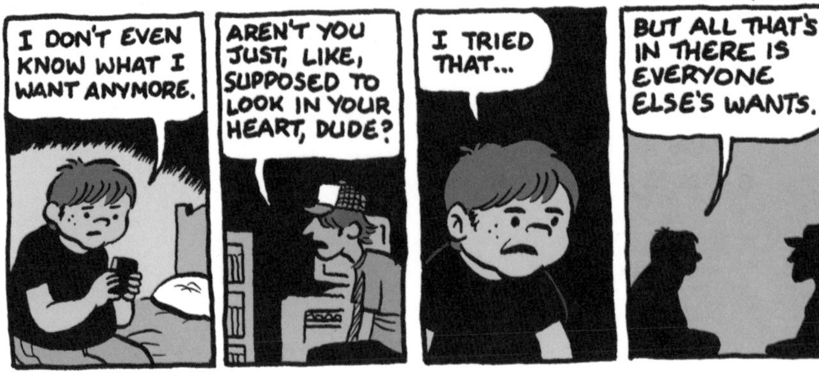
I DON'T EVEN KNOW WHAT I WANT ANYMORE.
AREN'T YOU JUST, LIKE, SUPPOSED TO LOOK IN YOUR HEART, DUDE?
I TRIED THAT...
BUT ALL THAT'S IN THERE IS EVERYONE ELSE'S WANTS.

WED JAN 2, 2013

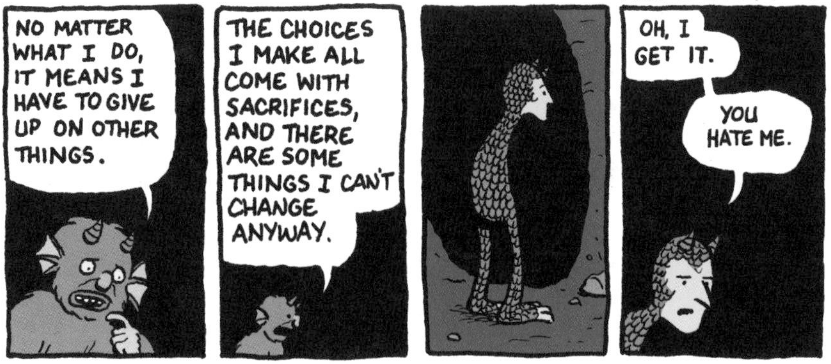
NO MATTER WHAT I DO, IT MEANS I HAVE TO GIVE UP ON OTHER THINGS.
THE CHOICES I MAKE ALL COME WITH SACRIFICES, AND THERE ARE SOME THINGS I CAN'T CHANGE ANYWAY.
OH, I GET IT.
YOU HATE ME.

THU JAN 3, 2013

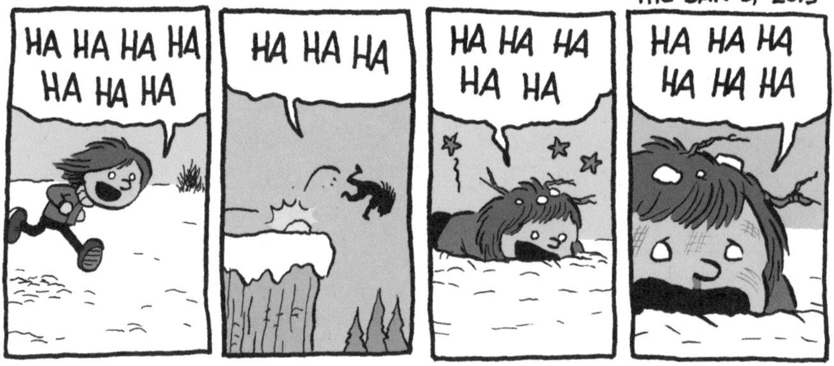
HA HA HA HA HA HA HA
HA HA HA
HA HA HA HA HA
HA HA HA HA HA HA

FRI JAN 4, 2013

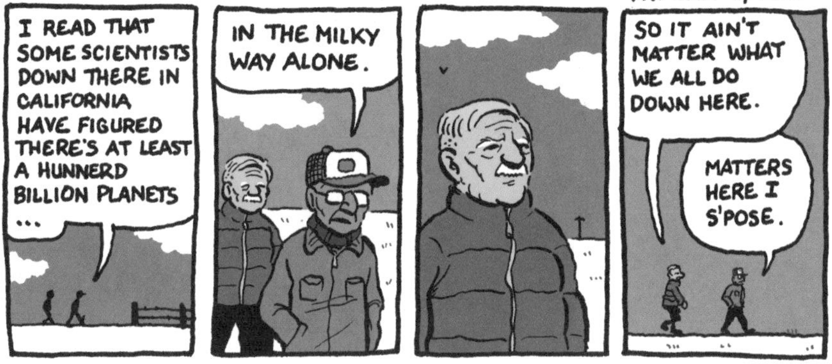
I READ THAT SOME SCIENTISTS DOWN THERE IN CALIFORNIA HAVE FIGURED THERE'S AT LEAST A HUNNERD BILLION PLANETS ...
IN THE MILKY WAY ALONE.
SO IT AIN'T MATTER WHAT WE ALL DO DOWN HERE.
MATTERS HERE I S'POSE.

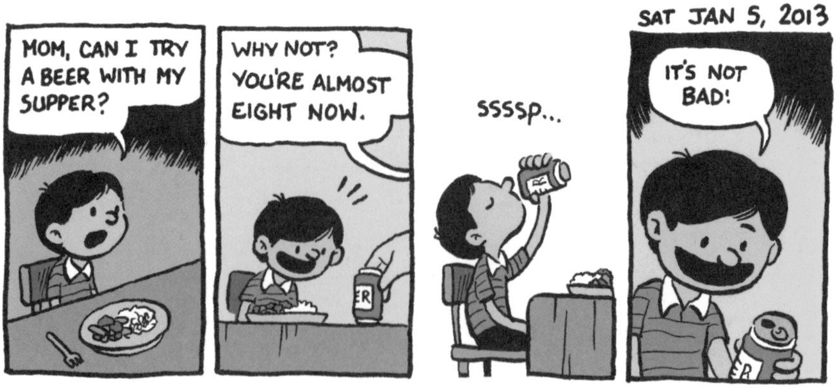
SAT JAN 5, 2013
MOM, CAN I TRY A BEER WITH MY SUPPER?
WHY NOT? YOU'RE ALMOST EIGHT NOW.
SSSSP...
IT'S NOT BAD!

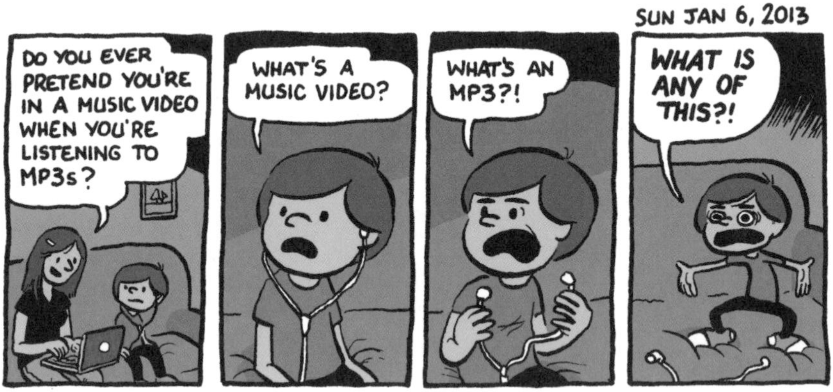
SUN JAN 6, 2013
DO YOU EVER PRETEND YOU'RE IN A MUSIC VIDEO WHEN YOU'RE LISTENING TO MP3s?
WHAT'S A MUSIC VIDEO?
WHAT'S AN MP3?!
WHAT IS ANY OF THIS?!

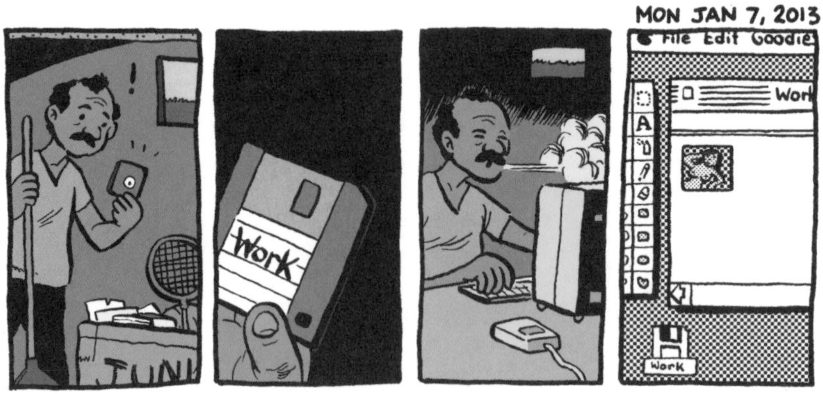
MON JAN 7, 2013
Work
File Edit Goodie
Work

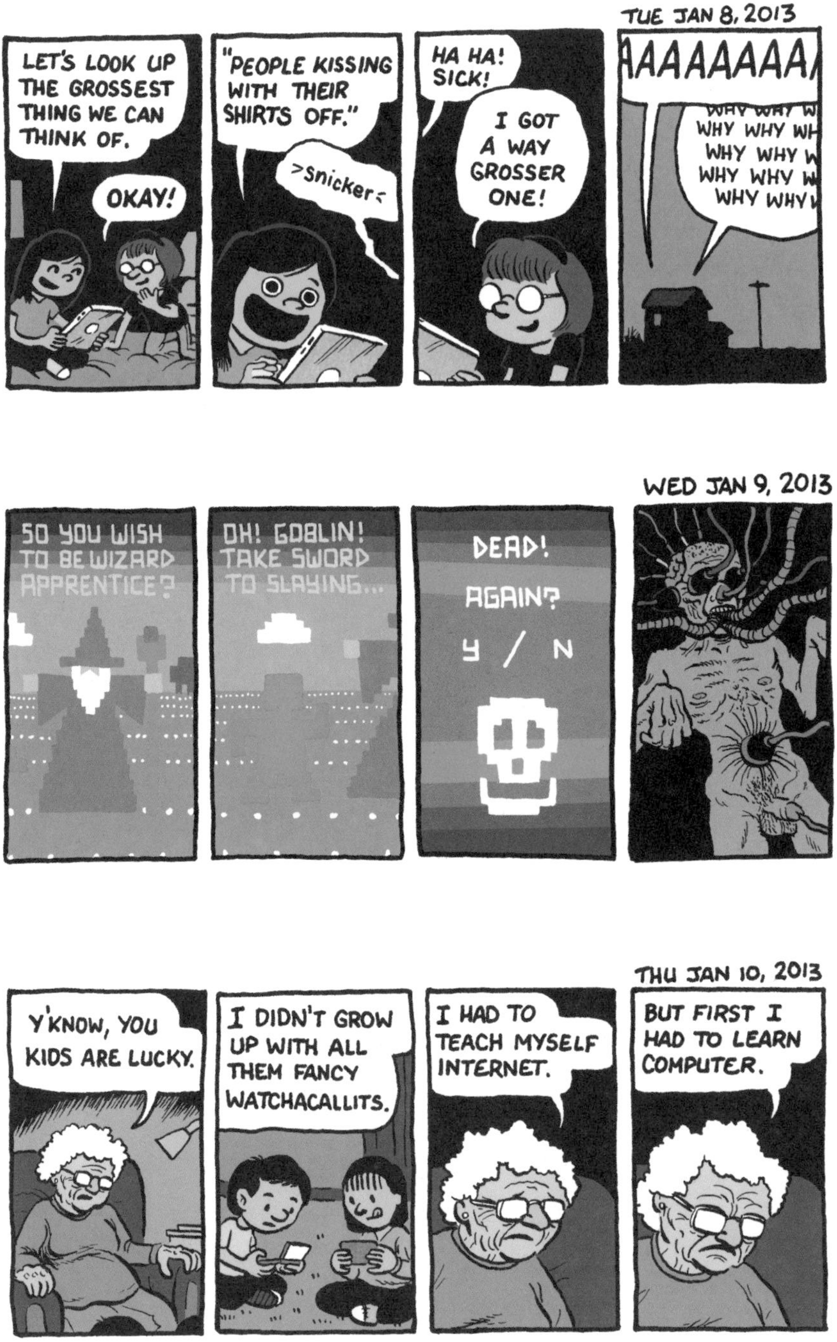
LET'S LOOK UP THE GROSSEST THING WE CAN THINK OF.
OKAY!
"PEOPLE KISSING WITH THEIR SHIRTS OFF."
>Snicker<
HA HA! SICK!
I GOT A WAY GROSSER ONE!
TUE JAN 8, 2013
AAAAAAAA
WHY WHY WH
WHY WHY W
WHY WHY W
WHY WHY
WED JAN 9, 2013
SO YOU WISH TO BE WIZARD APPRENTICE?
OH! GOBLIN! TAKE SWORD TO SLAYING...
DEAD!
AGAIN?
Y / N
THU JAN 10, 2013
Y'KNOW, YOU KIDS ARE LUCKY.
I DIDN'T GROW UP WITH ALL THEM FANCY WATCHACALLITS.
I HAD TO TEACH MYSELF INTERNET.
BUT FIRST I HAD TO LEARN COMPUTER.

GOD COMICS

FRI JAN 11, 2013

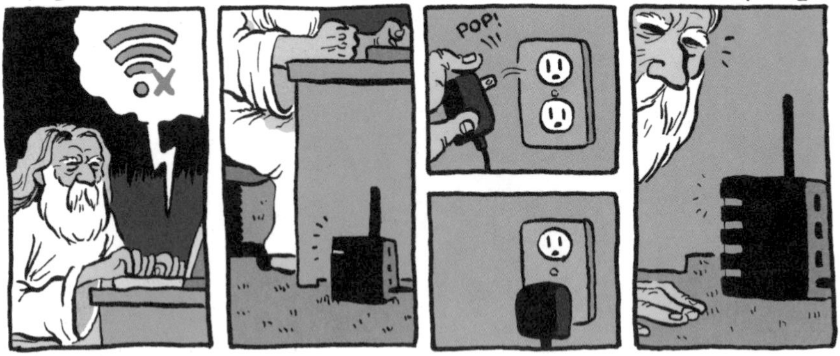
POP!

SAT JAN 12, 2013

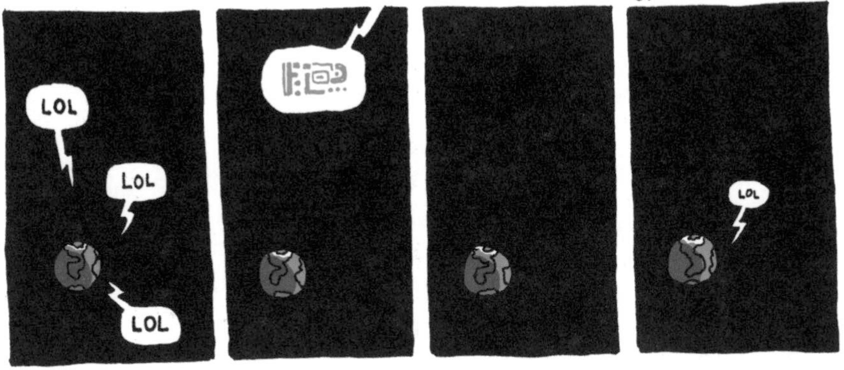
LOL
LOL
LOL
LOL

SUN JAN 13, 2013

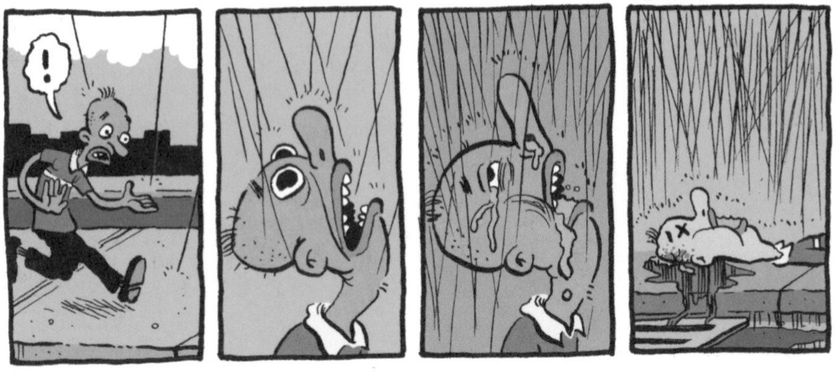
!

MON JAN 14, 2013

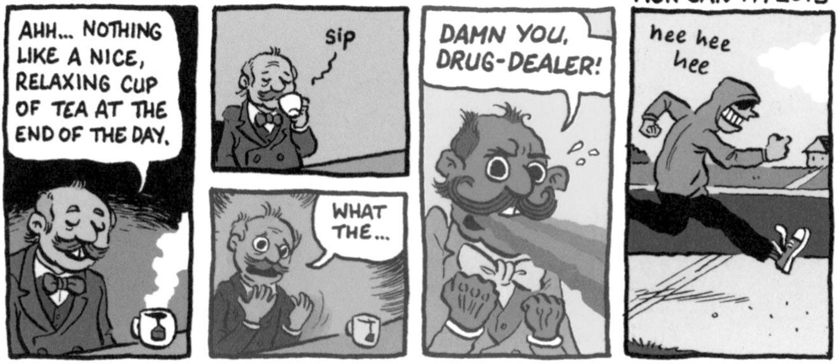
AHH... NOTHING LIKE A NICE, RELAXING CUP OF TEA AT THE END OF THE DAY.
sip
WHAT THE...
DAMN YOU, DRUG-DEALER!
hee hee hee

TUE JAN 15, 2013

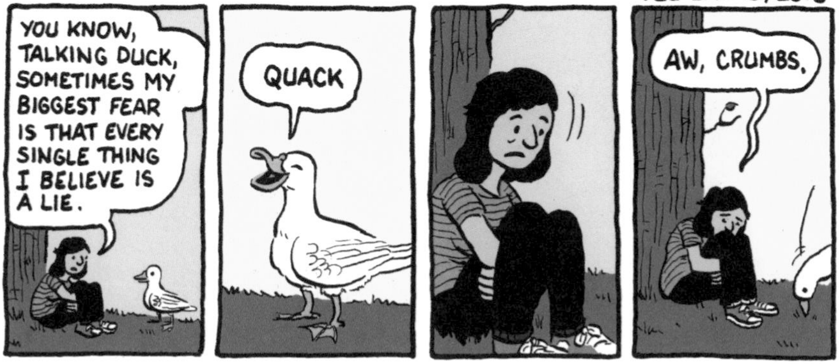
YOU KNOW, TALKING DUCK, SOMETIMES MY BIGGEST FEAR IS THAT EVERY SINGLE THING I BELIEVE IS A LIE.
QUACK
AW, CRUMBS.

WED JAN 16, 2013

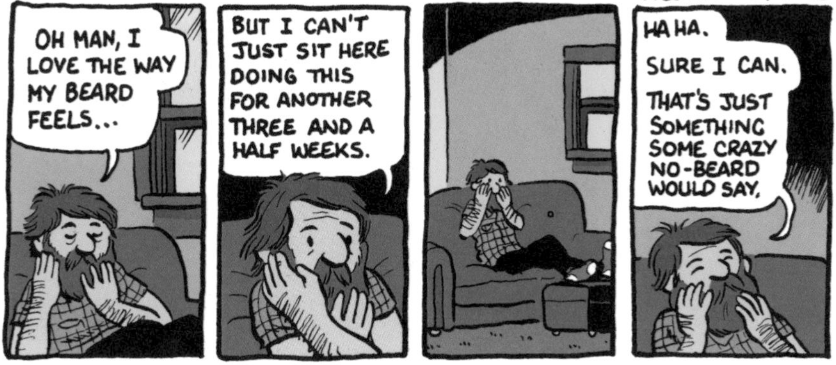
OH MAN, I LOVE THE WAY MY BEARD FEELS...
BUT I CAN'T JUST SIT HERE DOING THIS FOR ANOTHER THREE AND A HALF WEEKS.
HA HA.
SURE I CAN.
THAT'S JUST SOMETHING SOME CRAZY NO-BEARD WOULD SAY.

THU JAN 17, 2013

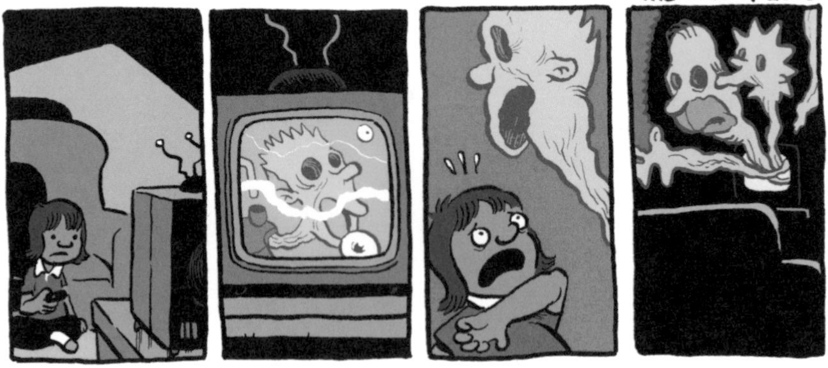

FRI JAN 18, 2013

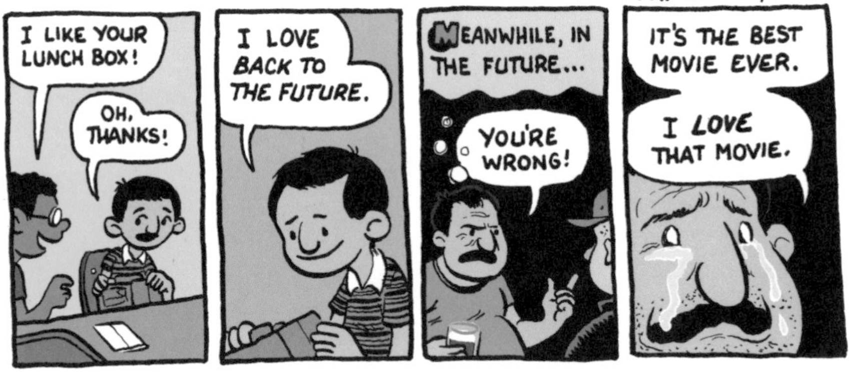
I LIKE YOUR LUNCH BOX!
OH, THANKS!
I LOVE *BACK TO THE FUTURE*.
MEANWHILE, IN THE FUTURE...
YOU'RE WRONG!
IT'S THE BEST MOVIE EVER.
I *LOVE* THAT MOVIE.

SAT JAN 19, 2013

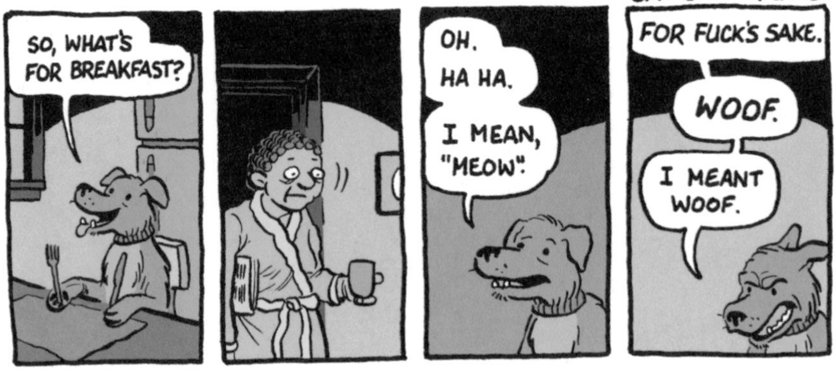
SO, WHAT'S FOR BREAKFAST?
OH.
HA HA.
I MEAN, "MEOW".
FOR FUCK'S SAKE.
WOOF.
I MEANT WOOF.

INVINCIBLE BABY

SUN JAN 20, 2013

*
* THE SOUND OF CHILDREN'S LAUGHTER IN A VACUUM.

MON JAN 21, 2013

THESE ARE MY NEW AUGMENTED REALITY GLASSES.
A COMPUTER CHIP READS MY MOOD AND IF I'M NOT HAPPY, THE GLASSES MAKE REALITY BETTER.
THAT SOUNDS LIKE A STUPID WASTE OF MONEY.
MOOD:

TUE JAN 22, 2013

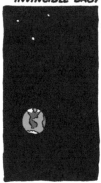

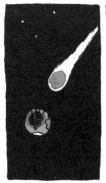

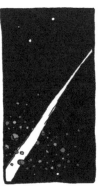

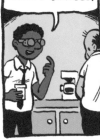

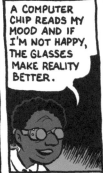

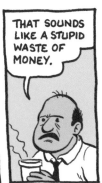

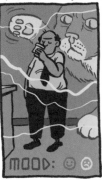

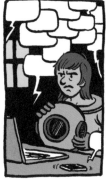

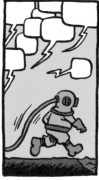

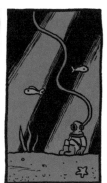

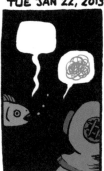

WED JAN 23, 2013

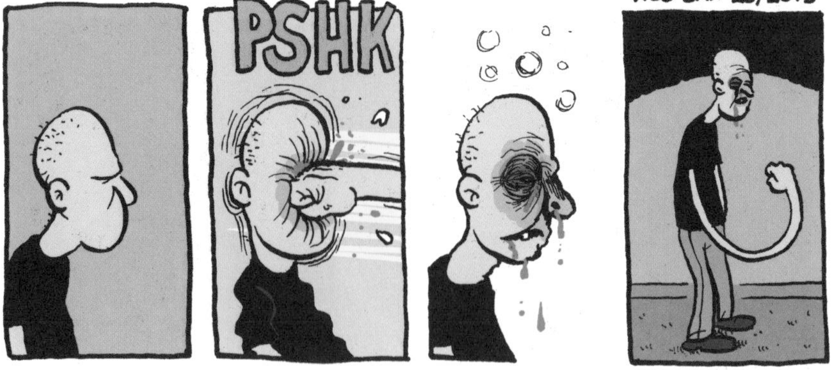
PSHK

THU JAN 24, 2013

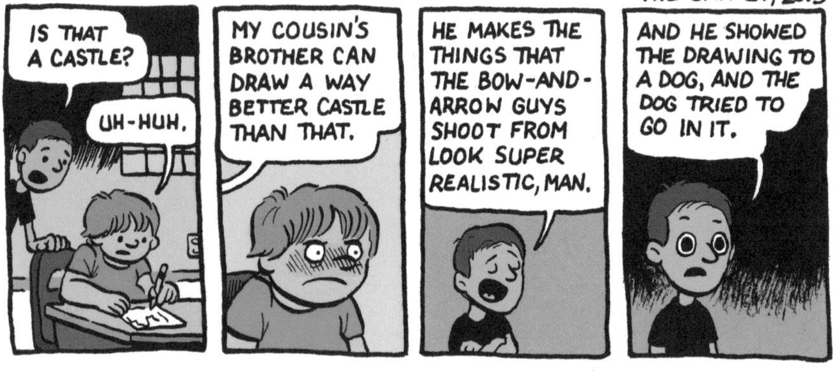
IS THAT A CASTLE?
UH-HUH.
MY COUSIN'S BROTHER CAN DRAW A WAY BETTER CASTLE THAN THAT.
HE MAKES THE THINGS THAT THE BOW-AND-ARROW GUYS SHOOT FROM LOOK SUPER REALISTIC, MAN.
AND HE SHOWED THE DRAWING TO A DOG, AND THE DOG TRIED TO GO IN IT.

FRI JAN 25, 2013

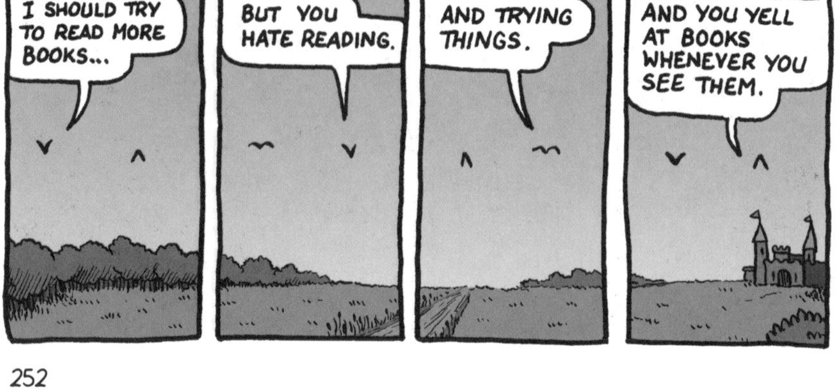
I SHOULD TRY TO READ MORE BOOKS...
BUT YOU HATE READING.
AND TRYING THINGS.
AND YOU YELL AT BOOKS WHENEVER YOU SEE THEM.

SAT JAN 26, 2013

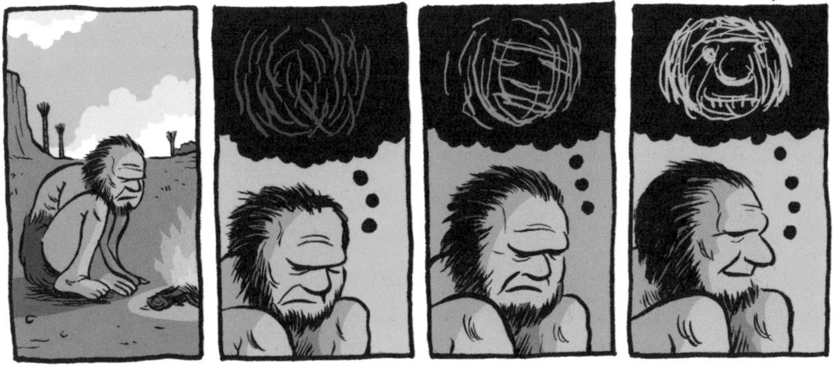

SUN JAN 27, 2013

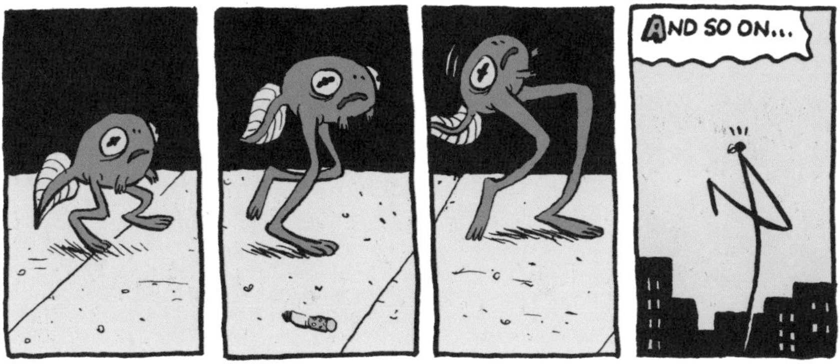
AND SO ON...

MON JAN 28, 2013

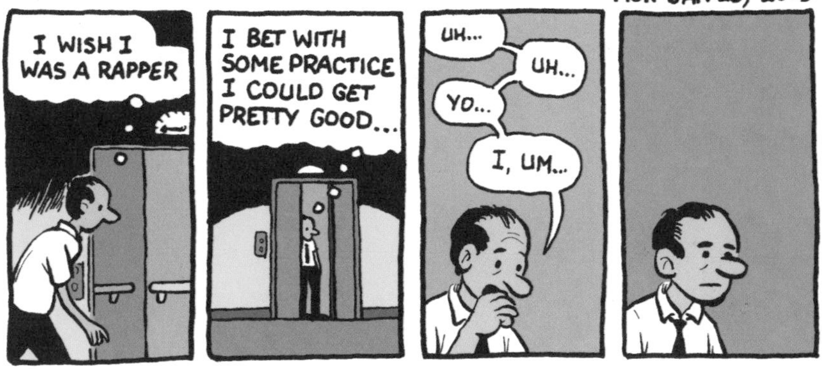
I WISH I WAS A RAPPER
I BET WITH SOME PRACTICE I COULD GET PRETTY GOOD...
UH...
UH...
YO...
I, UM...

TUE JAN 29, 2013

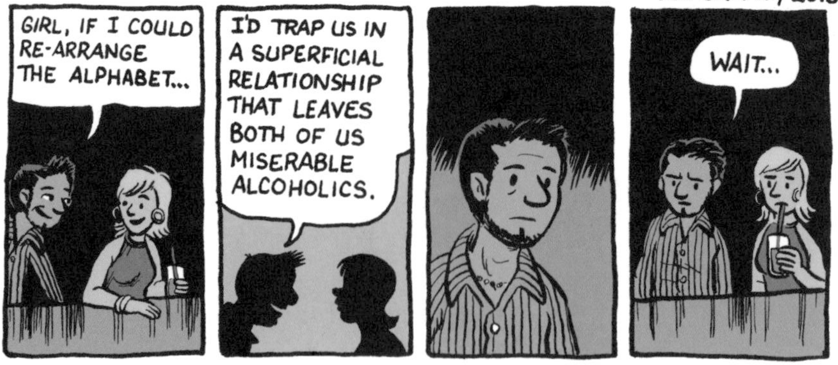

GIRL, IF I COULD RE-ARRANGE THE ALPHABET...
I'D TRAP US IN A SUPERFICIAL RELATIONSHIP THAT LEAVES BOTH OF US MISERABLE ALCOHOLICS.
WAIT...

WED JAN 30, 2013

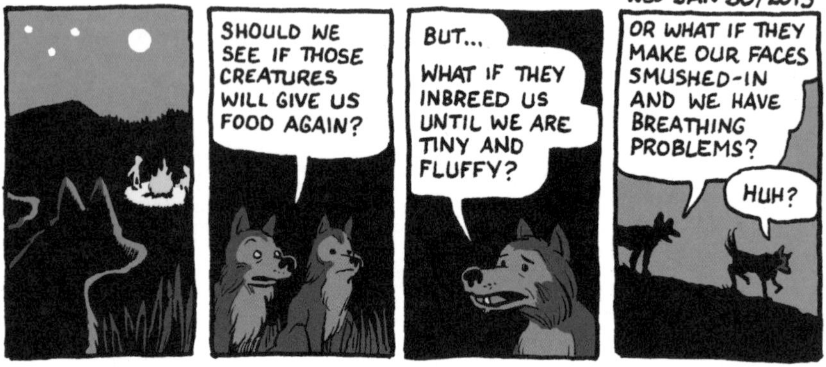

SHOULD WE SEE IF THOSE CREATURES WILL GIVE US FOOD AGAIN?
BUT...
WHAT IF THEY INBREED US UNTIL WE ARE TINY AND FLUFFY?
OR WHAT IF THEY MAKE OUR FACES SMUSHED-IN AND WE HAVE BREATHING PROBLEMS?
HUH?

THU JAN 31, 2013

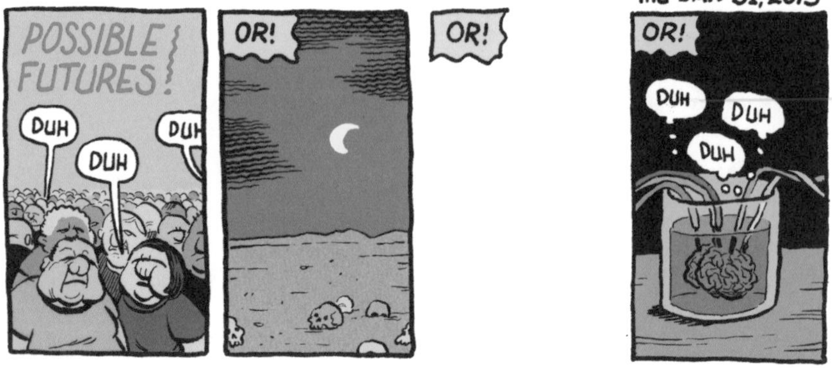

POSSIBLE FUTURES!
DUH
DUH
DUH
OR!
OR!
OR!
DUH
DUH
DUH

FRI FEB 1, 2013

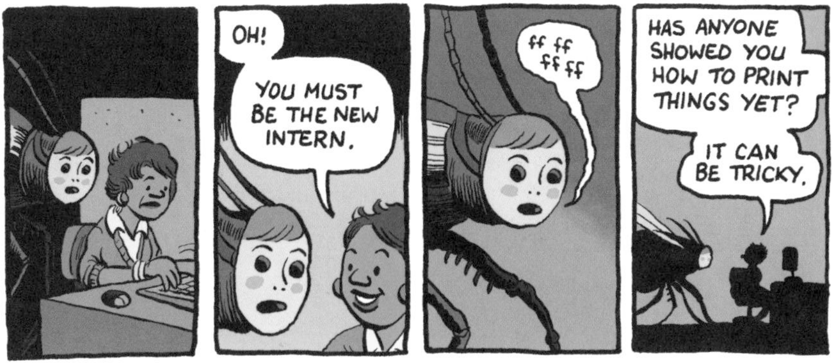
OH!
YOU MUST BE THE NEW INTERN.
ff ff ff ff
HAS ANYONE SHOWED YOU HOW TO PRINT THINGS YET?
IT CAN BE TRICKY.

SAT FEB 2, 2013

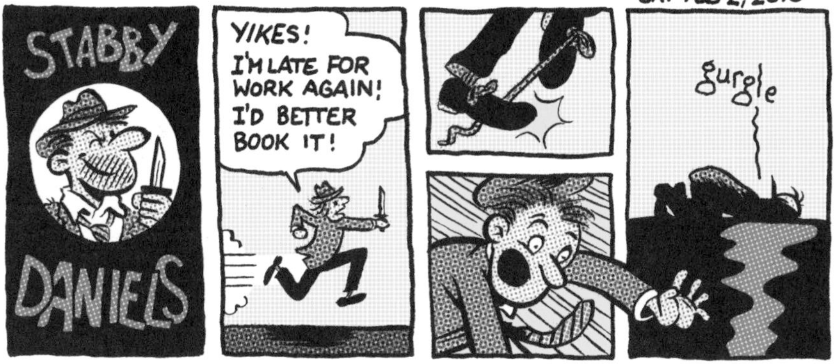
STABBY DANIELS
YIKES! I'M LATE FOR WORK AGAIN! I'D BETTER BOOK IT!
gurgle

SUN FEB 3, 2013

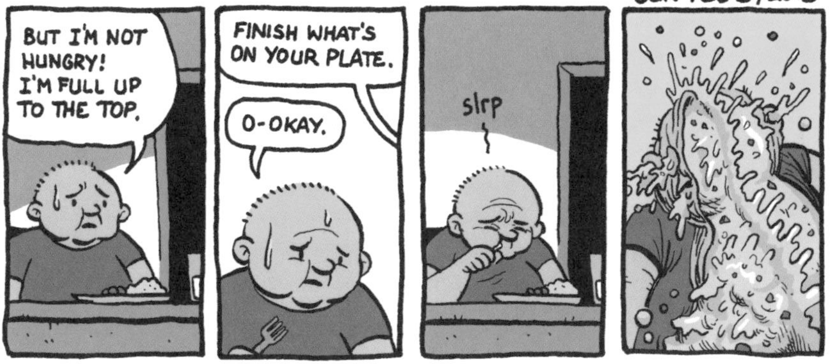
BUT I'M NOT HUNGRY! I'M FULL UP TO THE TOP.
FINISH WHAT'S ON YOUR PLATE.
O-OKAY.
slrp

MON FEB 4, 2013

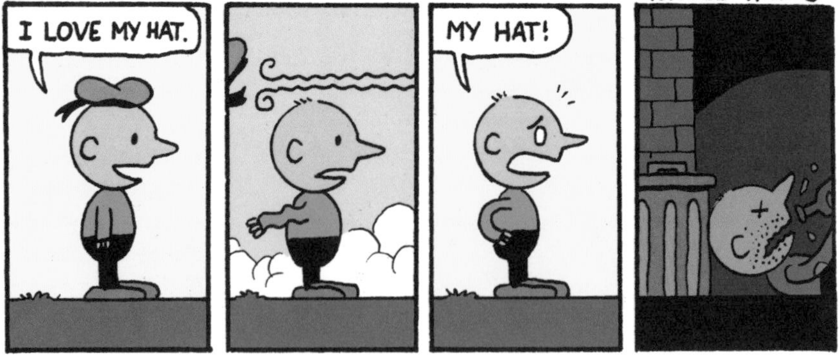
I LOVE MY HAT.
MY HAT!

TUE FEB 5, 2013

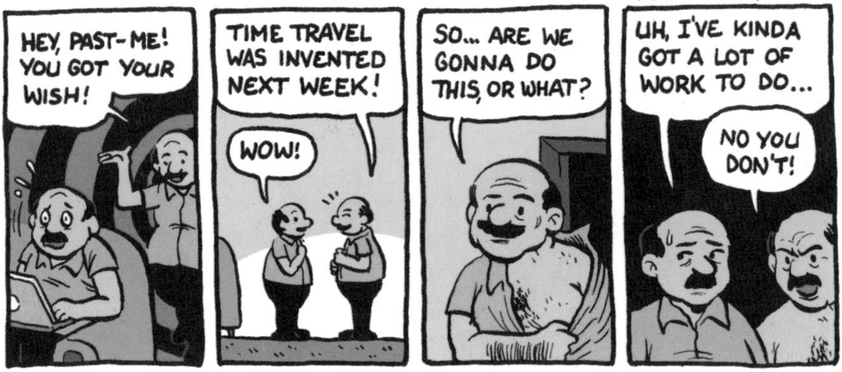
HEY, PAST-ME! YOU GOT YOUR WISH!
TIME TRAVEL WAS INVENTED NEXT WEEK!
WOW!
SO... ARE WE GONNA DO THIS, OR WHAT?
UH, I'VE KINDA GOT A LOT OF WORK TO DO...
NO YOU DON'T!

WED FEB 6, 2013

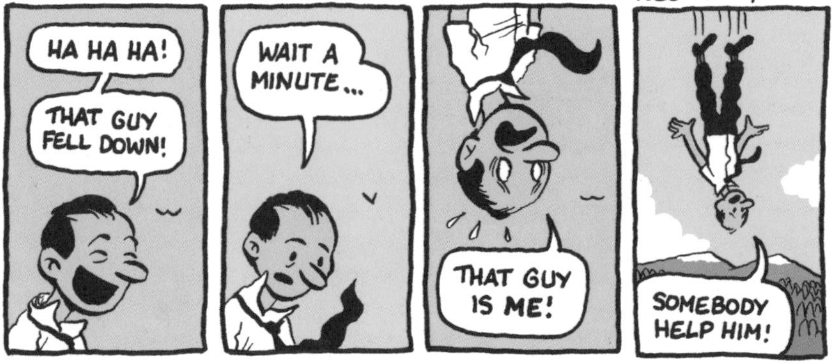
HA HA HA!
THAT GUY FELL DOWN!
WAIT A MINUTE...
THAT GUY IS ME!
SOMEBODY HELP HIM!

THU FEB 7, 2013

DO YOU HAVE A QUESTION, STEPHANIE?
SPA
YEAH. YOU SAID WE DON'T KNOW HOW BIG SPACE IS OR IF IT HAS AN END...
BUT HOW CAN WE NOT KNOW ALL THAT?
AND DON'T GIVE ME THAT GOD STUFF.
HOW CAN WE NOT KNOW?!
AAAAAAHH

FRI FEB 8, 2013

DON'T GET EATEN BY ANYTHING...
DON'T GET EATEN BY ANYTHING...
DON'T GET EATEN BY ANYTHING...
DON'T GET EATEN BY ANYTHING...
DON'T GET EATEN BY ANYTHING...
DON'T GET EATEN BY ANYTHING...

SAT FEB 9, 2013

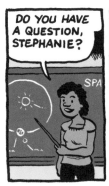

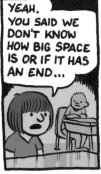

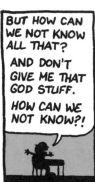

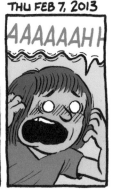

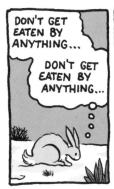

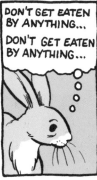

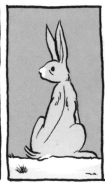

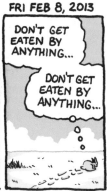

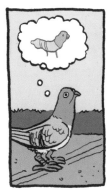

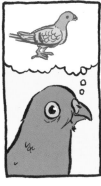

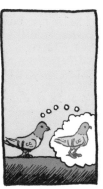

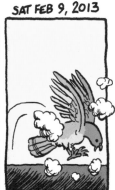

SUN FEB 10, 2013

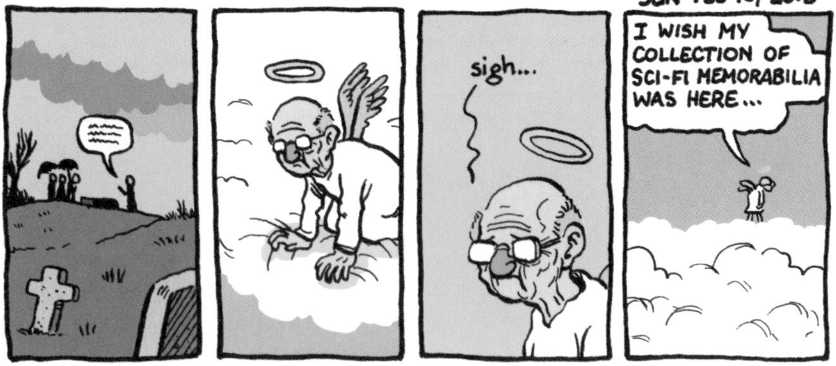

sigh...
I WISH MY COLLECTION OF SCI-FI MEMORABILIA WAS HERE...

MON FEB 11, 2013

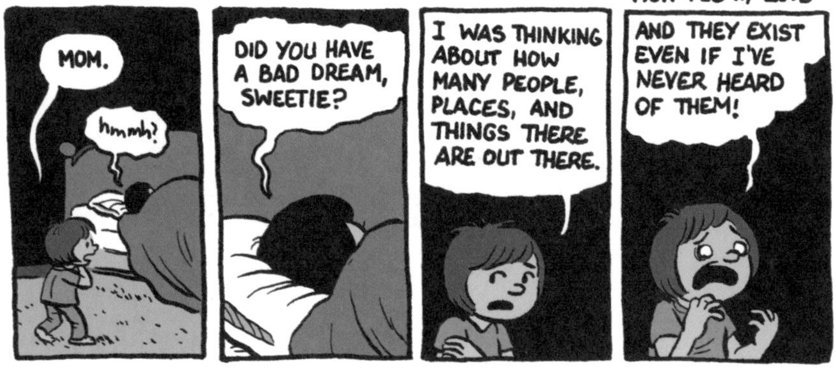

MOM.
hmmh?
DID YOU HAVE A BAD DREAM, SWEETIE?
I WAS THINKING ABOUT HOW MANY PEOPLE, PLACES, AND THINGS THERE ARE OUT THERE.
AND THEY EXIST EVEN IF I'VE NEVER HEARD OF THEM!

TUE FEB 12, 2013

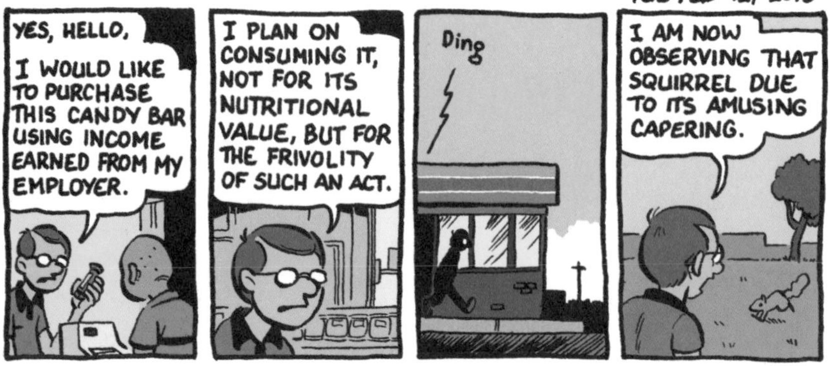

YES, HELLO.
I WOULD LIKE TO PURCHASE THIS CANDY BAR USING INCOME EARNED FROM MY EMPLOYER.
I PLAN ON CONSUMING IT, NOT FOR ITS NUTRITIONAL VALUE, BUT FOR THE FRIVOLITY OF SUCH AN ACT.
Ding
I AM NOW OBSERVING THAT SQUIRREL DUE TO ITS AMUSING CAPERING.

WED FEB 13, 2013

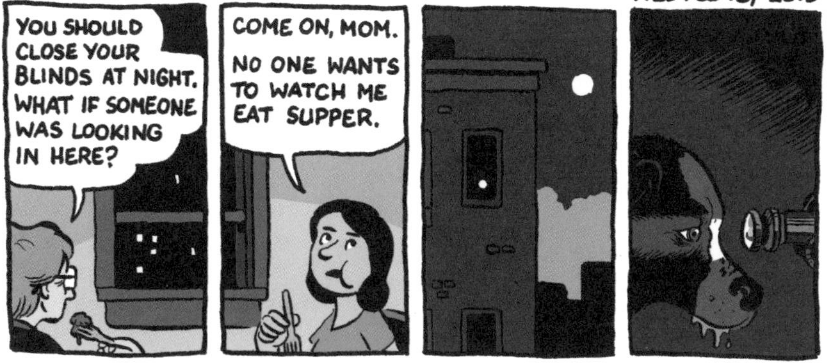
YOU SHOULD CLOSE YOUR BLINDS AT NIGHT. WHAT IF SOMEONE WAS LOOKING IN HERE?
COME ON, MOM.
NO ONE WANTS TO WATCH ME EAT SUPPER.

THU FEB 14, 2013

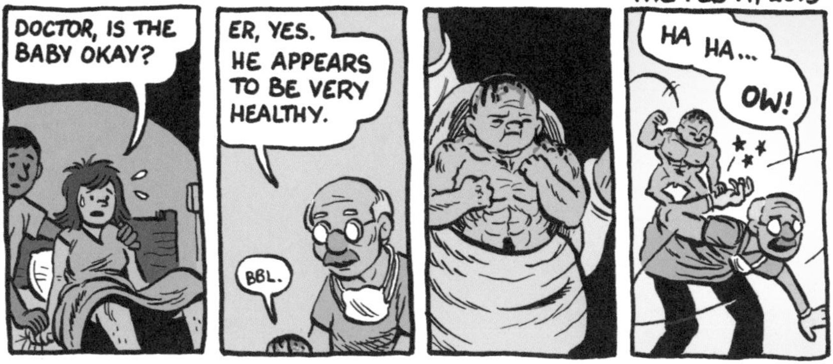
DOCTOR, IS THE BABY OKAY?
ER, YES.
HE APPEARS TO BE VERY HEALTHY.
BBL.
HA HA...
OW!

FRI FEB 15, 2013

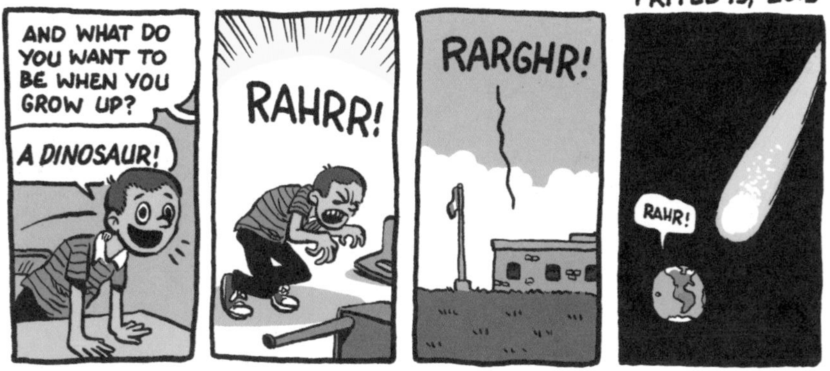
AND WHAT DO YOU WANT TO BE WHEN YOU GROW UP?
A DINOSAUR!
RAHRR!
RARGHR!
RAHR!

SAT FEB 16, 2013

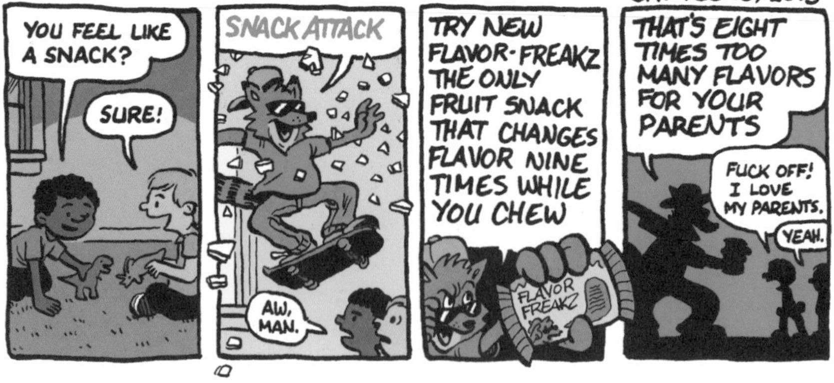

YOU FEEL LIKE A SNACK?
SURE!
SNACK ATTACK
AW, MAN.
TRY NEW FLAVOR-FREAKZ THE ONLY FRUIT SNACK THAT CHANGES FLAVOR NINE TIMES WHILE YOU CHEW
FLAVOR FREAKZ
THAT'S EIGHT TIMES TOO MANY FLAVORS FOR YOUR PARENTS
FUCK OFF! I LOVE MY PARENTS.
YEAH.

SUN FEB 17, 2013

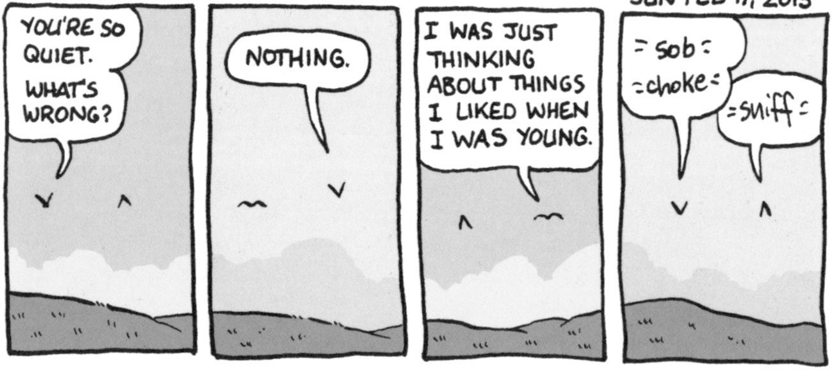

YOU'RE SO QUIET. WHAT'S WRONG?
NOTHING.
I WAS JUST THINKING ABOUT THINGS I LIKED WHEN I WAS YOUNG.
=sob=
=choke=
=sniff=

MON FEB 18, 2013

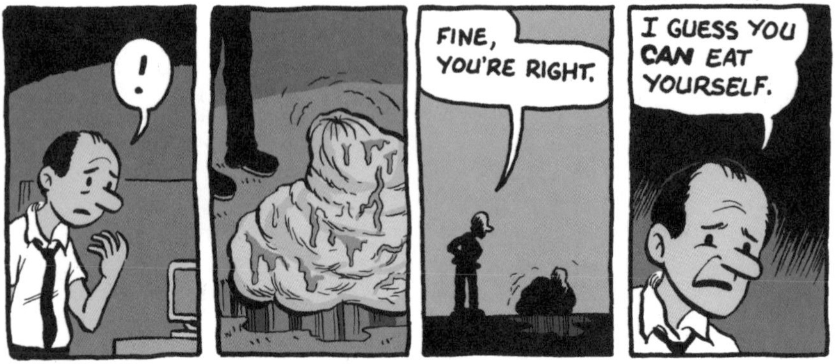

!
FINE, YOU'RE RIGHT.
I GUESS YOU **CAN** EAT YOURSELF.

TUE FEB 19, 2013

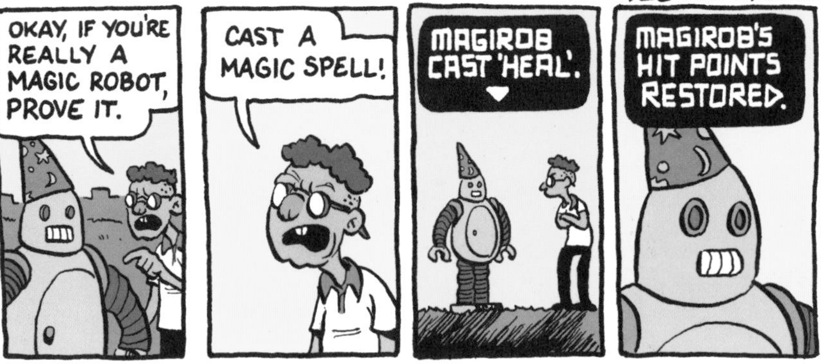
OKAY, IF YOU'RE REALLY A MAGIC ROBOT, PROVE IT.
CAST A MAGIC SPELL!
MAGIROB CAST 'HEAL'.
MAGIROB'S HIT POINTS RESTORED.

WED FEB 20, 2013

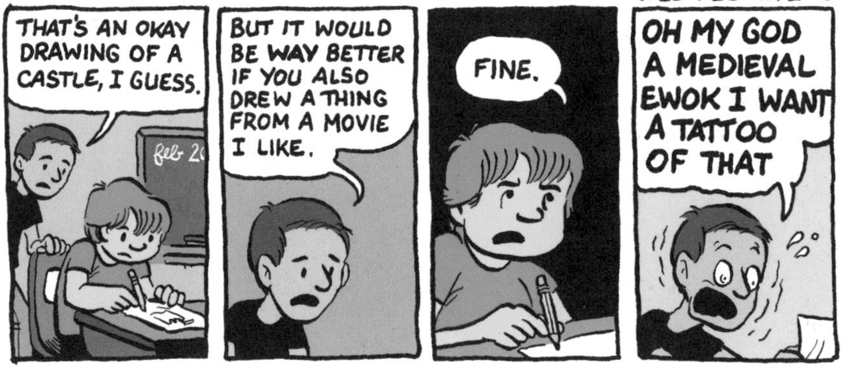
THAT'S AN OKAY DRAWING OF A CASTLE, I GUESS.
feb 20
BUT IT WOULD BE WAY BETTER IF YOU ALSO DREW A THING FROM A MOVIE I LIKE.
FINE.
OH MY GOD A MEDIEVAL EWOK I WANT A TATTOO OF THAT

THU FEB 21, 2013

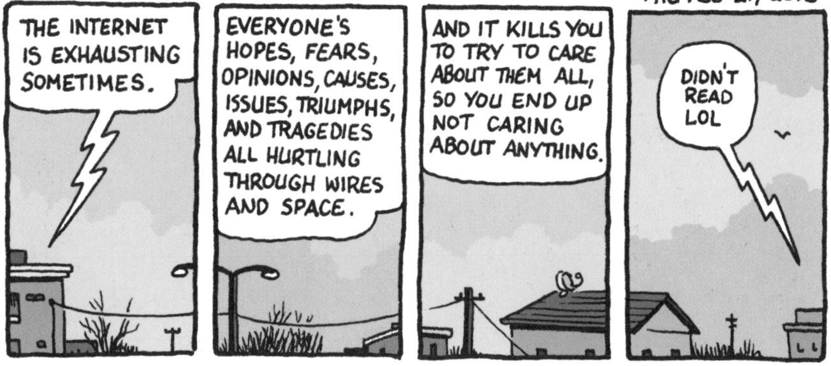
THE INTERNET IS EXHAUSTING SOMETIMES.
EVERYONE'S HOPES, FEARS, OPINIONS, CAUSES, ISSUES, TRIUMPHS, AND TRAGEDIES ALL HURTLING THROUGH WIRES AND SPACE.
AND IT KILLS YOU TO TRY TO CARE ABOUT THEM ALL, SO YOU END UP NOT CARING ABOUT ANYTHING.
DIDN'T READ LOL

FRI FEB 22, 2013

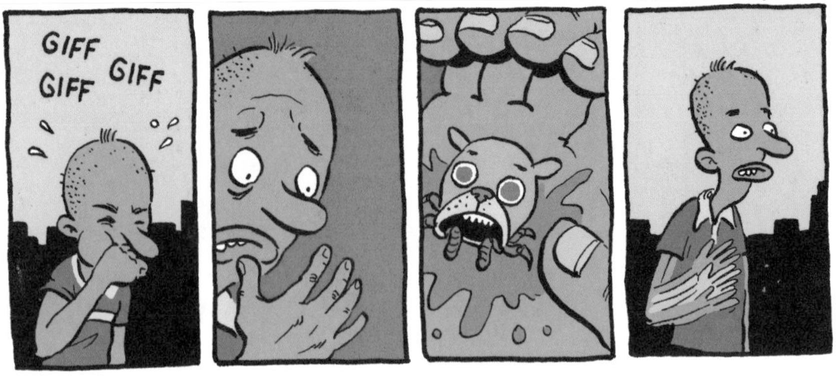
GIFF
GIFF
GIFF

SAT FEB 23, 2013

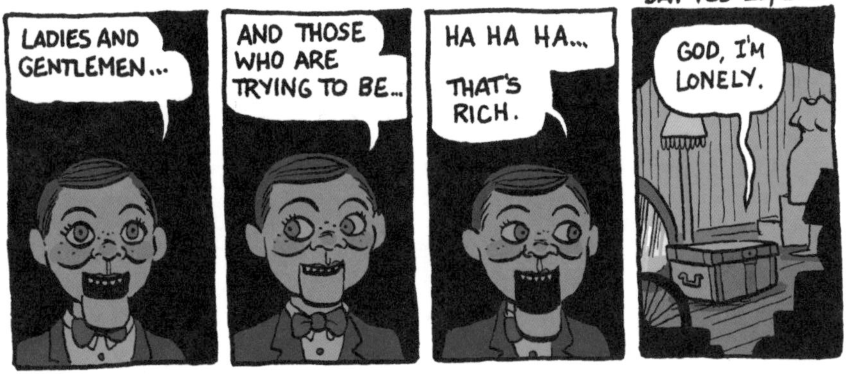
LADIES AND GENTLEMEN...
AND THOSE WHO ARE TRYING TO BE...
HA HA HA...
THAT'S RICH.
GOD, I'M LONELY.

SUN FEB 24, 2013

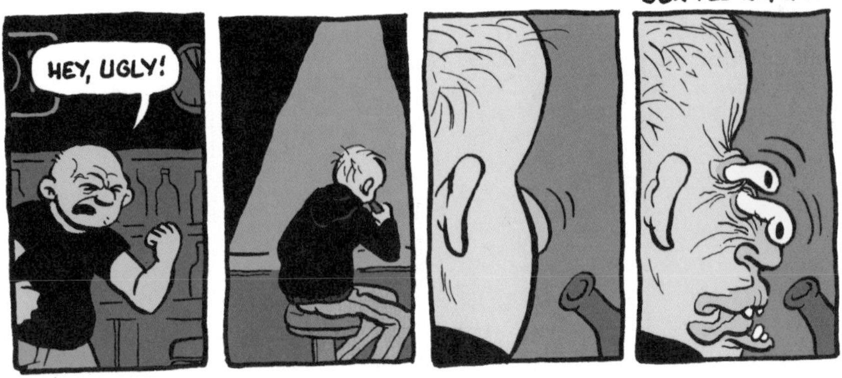
HEY, UGLY!

MON FEB 25, 2013

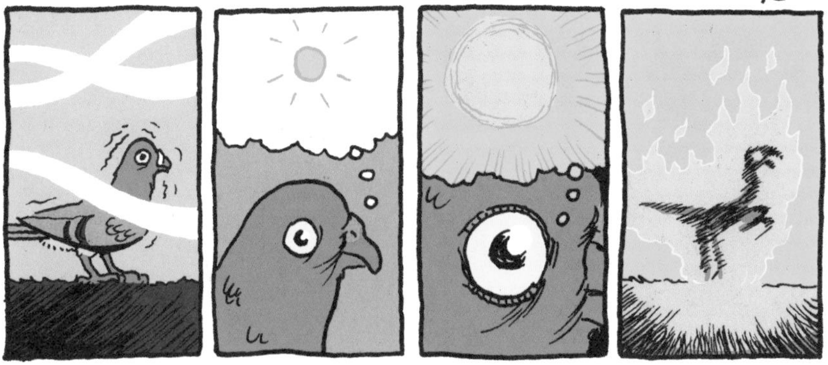

TUE FEB 26, 2013

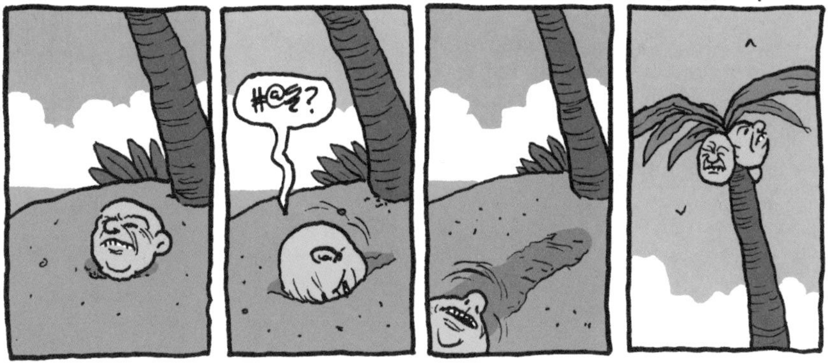

WED FEB 27, 2013

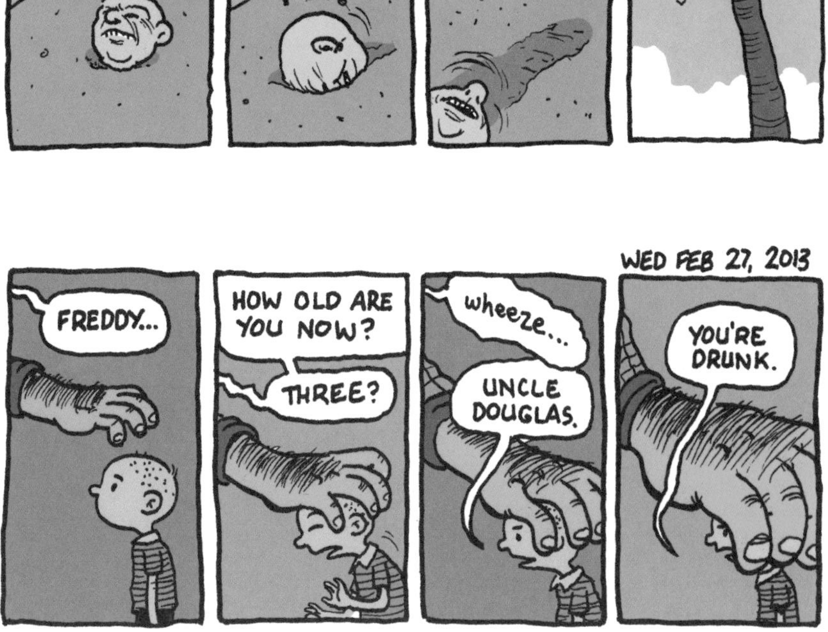

FREDDY...
HOW OLD ARE YOU NOW?
THREE?
wheeze...
UNCLE DOUGLAS.
YOU'RE DRUNK.

THU FEB 28, 2013

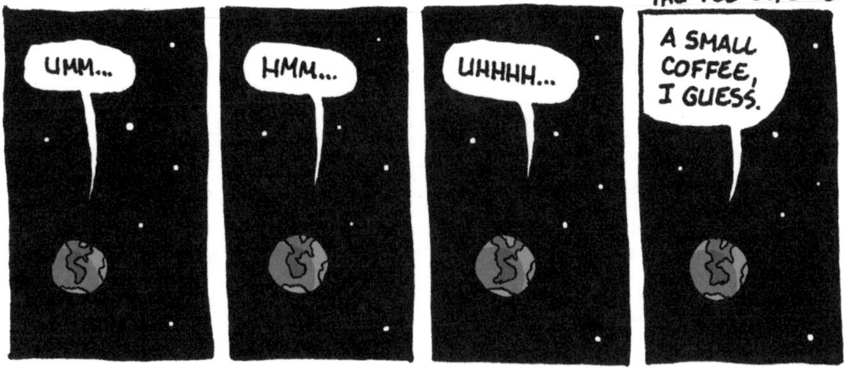
UMM...
HMM...
UHHHH...
A SMALL COFFEE, I GUESS.

FRI MAR 1, 2013

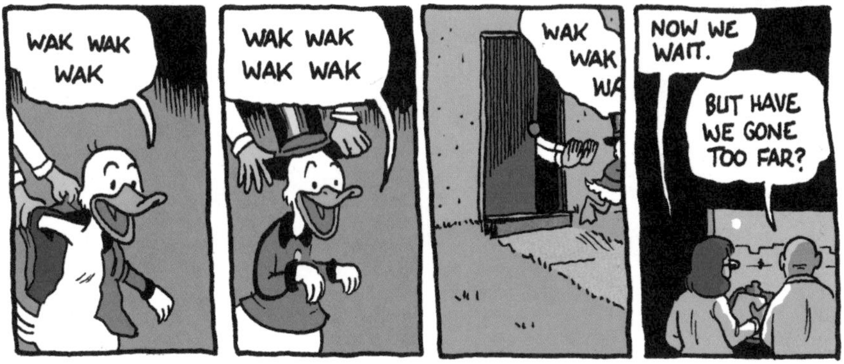
WAK WAK WAK
WAK WAK WAK WAK
WAK WAK WA
NOW WE WAIT.
BUT HAVE WE GONE TOO FAR?

SAT MAR 2, 2013

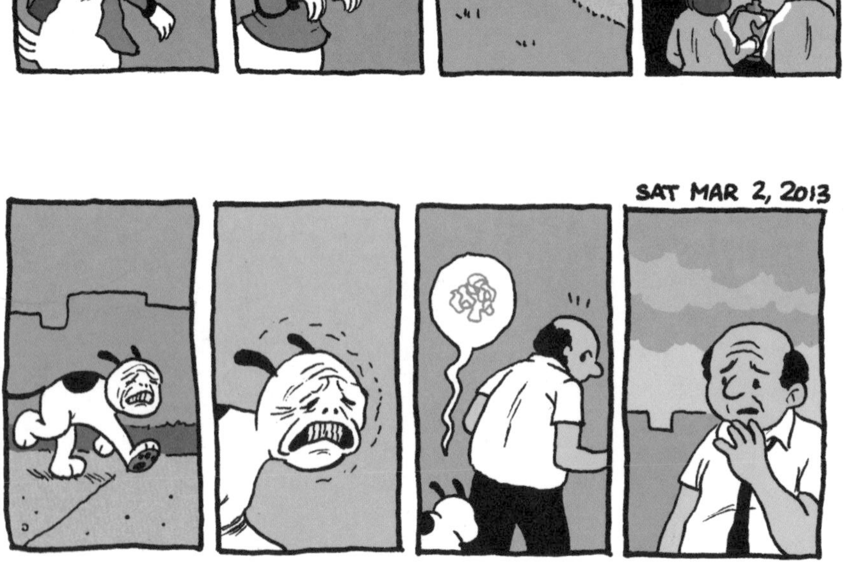

SUN MAR 3, 2013

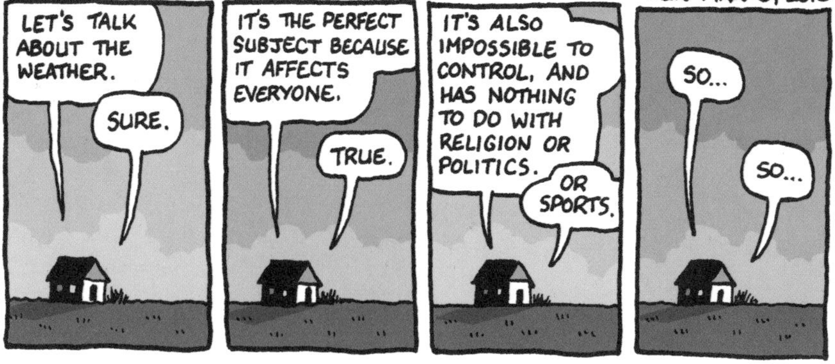
LET'S TALK ABOUT THE WEATHER.
SURE.
IT'S THE PERFECT SUBJECT BECAUSE IT AFFECTS EVERYONE.
TRUE.
IT'S ALSO IMPOSSIBLE TO CONTROL, AND HAS NOTHING TO DO WITH RELIGION OR POLITICS.
OR SPORTS.
SO...
SO...

MON MAR 4, 2013

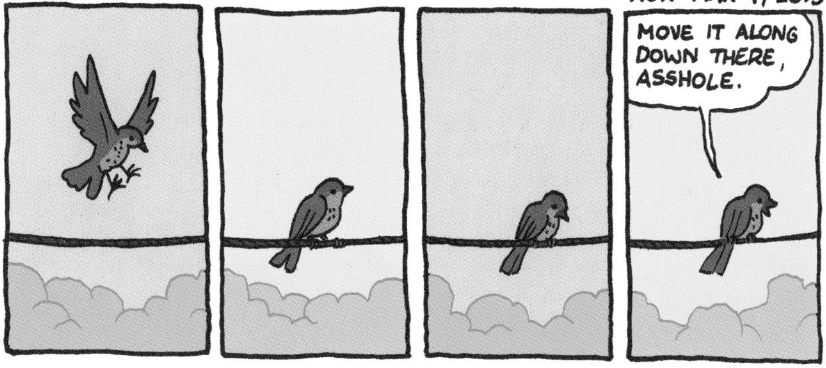
MOVE IT ALONG DOWN THERE, ASSHOLE.

TUE MAR 5, 2013

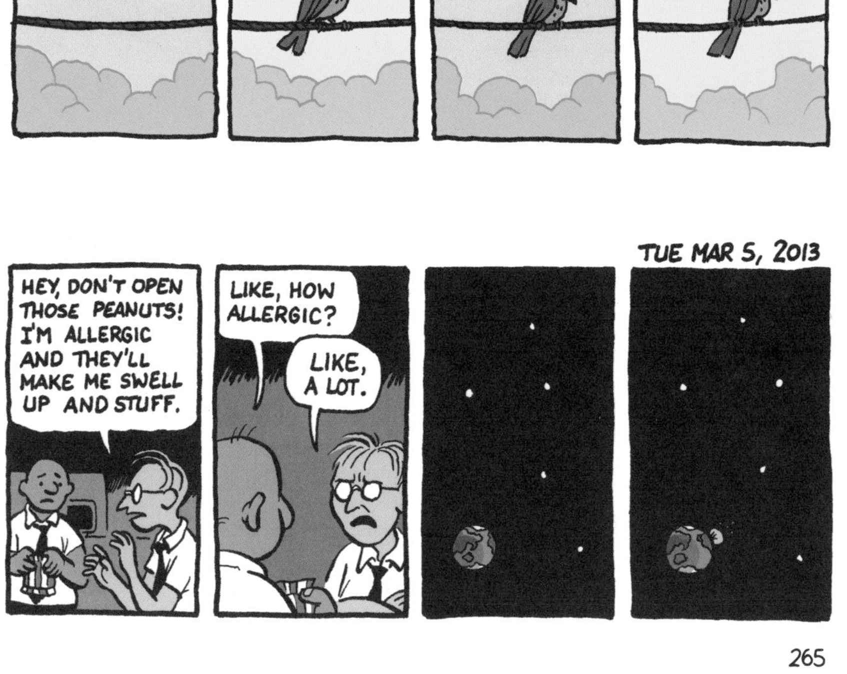
HEY, DON'T OPEN THOSE PEANUTS! I'M ALLERGIC AND THEY'LL MAKE ME SWELL UP AND STUFF.
LIKE, HOW ALLERGIC?
LIKE, A LOT.

WED MAR 6, 2013

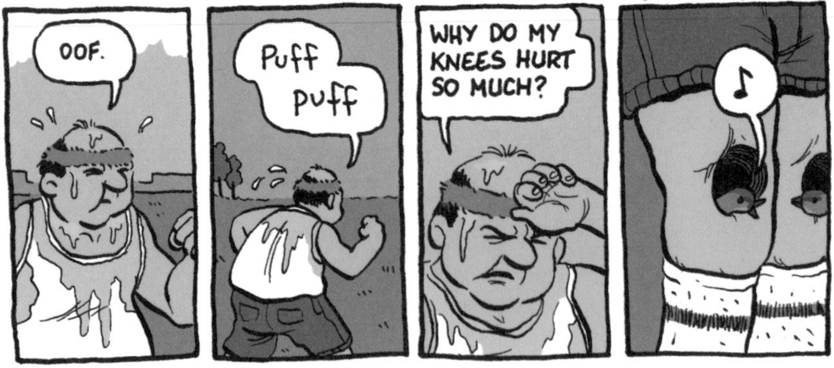
OOF.
Puff puff
WHY DO MY KNEES HURT SO MUCH?
♪

THU MAR 7, 2013

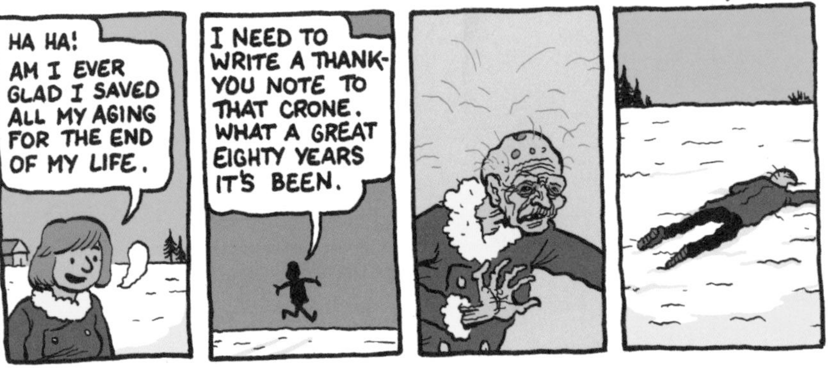
HA HA! AM I EVER GLAD I SAVED ALL MY AGING FOR THE END OF MY LIFE.
I NEED TO WRITE A THANK-YOU NOTE TO THAT CRONE. WHAT A GREAT EIGHTY YEARS IT'S BEEN.

FRI MAR 8, 2013

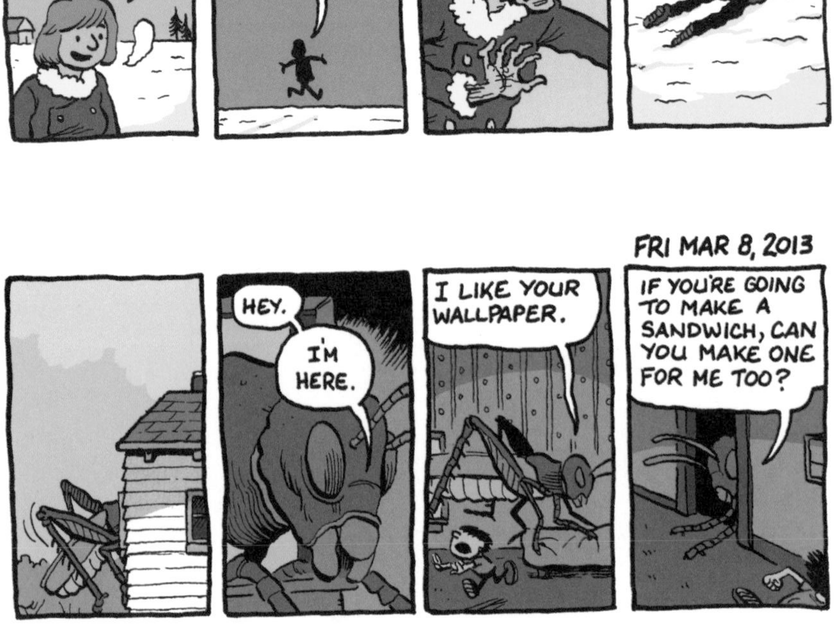
HEY.
I'M HERE.
I LIKE YOUR WALLPAPER.
IF YOU'RE GOING TO MAKE A SANDWICH, CAN YOU MAKE ONE FOR ME TOO?

OH NO! SOMEBODY TOOK MY KIDNEY!

GOTTA TRY TO REMEMBER LAST NIGHT. PIECE IT ALL TOGETHER...

MMM! KIDNEY!

smack chew

HA HA! OH YEAH!

GOTTA MAKE SOME MONEY SOMEHOW...

WAIT! IF I GO INTO A BUSINESS AND SHOW REAL GUMPTION, THEN MAYBE THEY'LL HIRE ME AND I CAN FINALLY PUT MY LIFE BACK TOGETHER.

HELLO! I WOULD LIKE A JOB!

G-GET AWAY!

=POP=

QUITTING TIME.

OH BOY!

WHAT ARE YOU SO EXCITED FOR? YOU KNOW WE'RE ALL GOING TO WASTE THE WEEKEND IN FRONT OF A SCREEN JUST LIKE THE REST OF THE WEEK.

NOT ALL OF US.

HA HA HA HA HA HA HA HA HA HA HA HA HA HA HA HA HA HA HA HA HA HA HA HA HA HA HA HA

267

TUE MAR 12, 2013

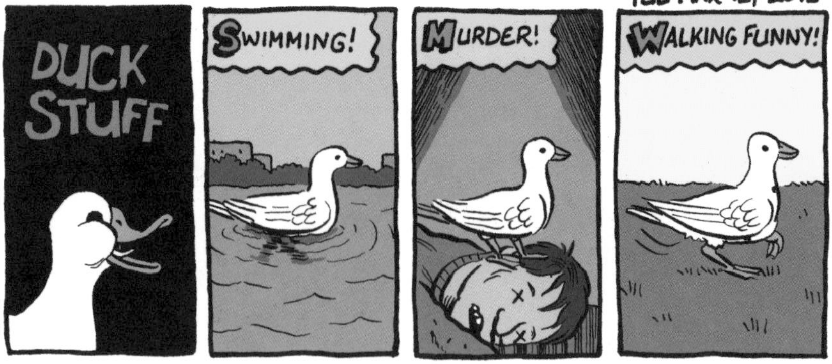
DUCK STUFF
SWIMMING!
MURDER!
WALKING FUNNY!

WED MAR 13, 2013

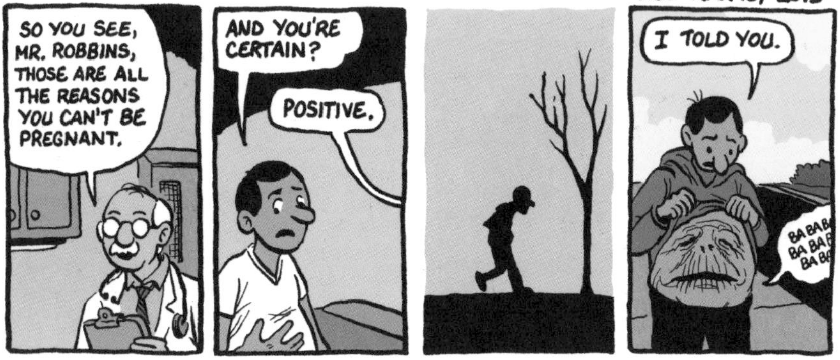
SO YOU SEE, MR. ROBBINS, THOSE ARE ALL THE REASONS YOU CAN'T BE PREGNANT.
AND YOU'RE CERTAIN?
POSITIVE.
I TOLD YOU.

THU MAR 14, 2013

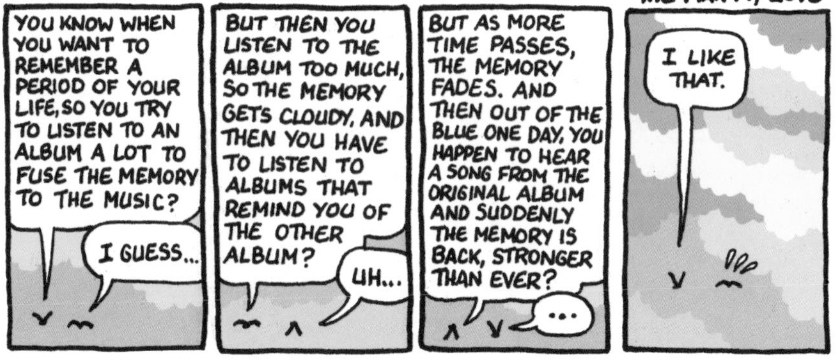
YOU KNOW WHEN YOU WANT TO REMEMBER A PERIOD OF YOUR LIFE, SO YOU TRY TO LISTEN TO AN ALBUM A LOT TO FUSE THE MEMORY TO THE MUSIC?
I GUESS...
BUT THEN YOU LISTEN TO THE ALBUM TOO MUCH, SO THE MEMORY GETS CLOUDY, AND THEN YOU HAVE TO LISTEN TO ALBUMS THAT REMIND YOU OF THE OTHER ALBUM?
UH...
BUT AS MORE TIME PASSES, THE MEMORY FADES. AND THEN OUT OF THE BLUE ONE DAY, YOU HAPPEN TO HEAR A SONG FROM THE ORIGINAL ALBUM AND SUDDENLY THE MEMORY IS BACK, STRONGER THAN EVER?
...
I LIKE THAT.

FRI MAR 15, 2013

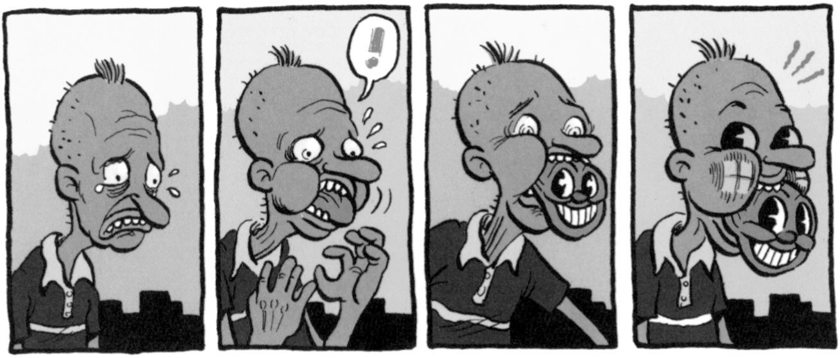
!

SAT MAR 16, 2013

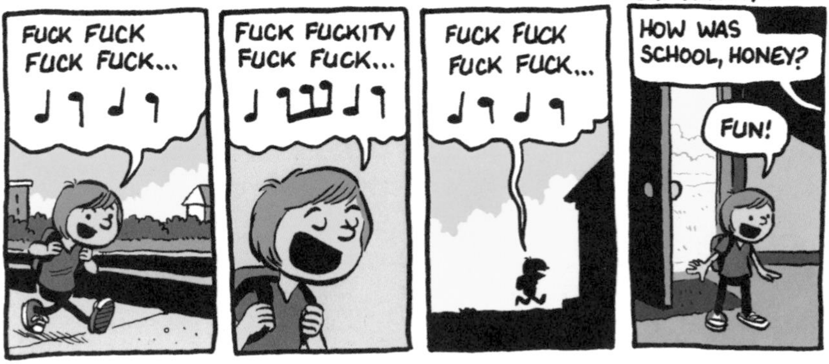
FUCK FUCK
FUCK FUCK...
FUCK FUCKITY
FUCK FUCK...
FUCK FUCK
FUCK FUCK...
HOW WAS
SCHOOL, HONEY?
FUN!

SUN MAR 17, 2013

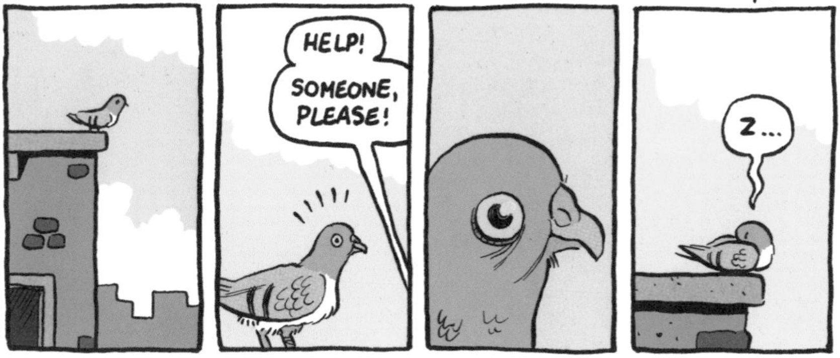
HELP!
SOMEONE,
PLEASE!
Z...

MON MAR 18, 2013

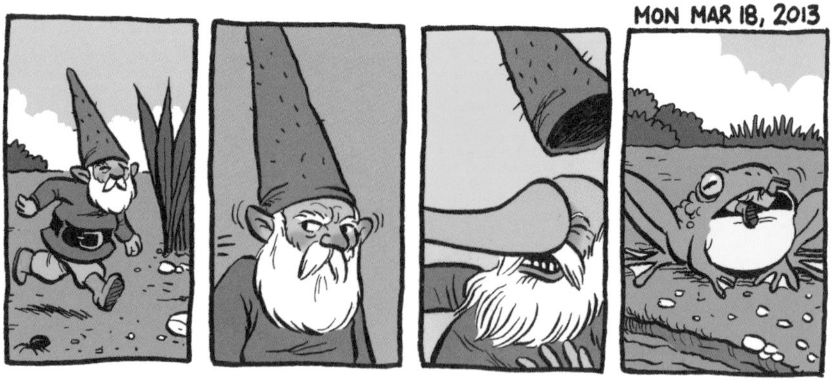

TUE MAR, 19, 2013

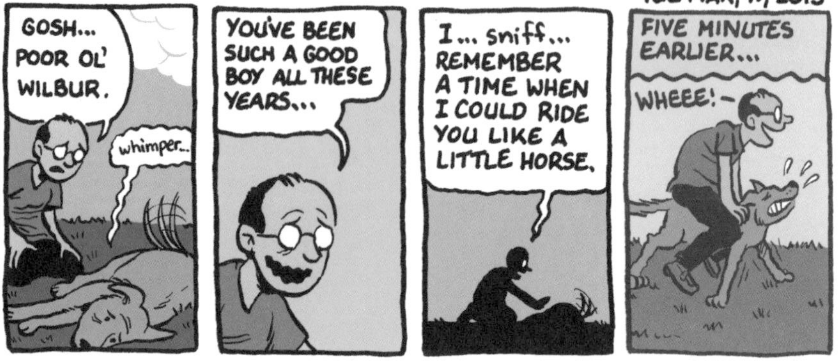
GOSH... POOR OL' WILBUR.
whimper...
YOU'VE BEEN SUCH A GOOD BOY ALL THESE YEARS...
I... sniff... REMEMBER A TIME WHEN I COULD RIDE YOU LIKE A LITTLE HORSE.
FIVE MINUTES EARLIER...
WHEEE!

WED MAR 20, 2013

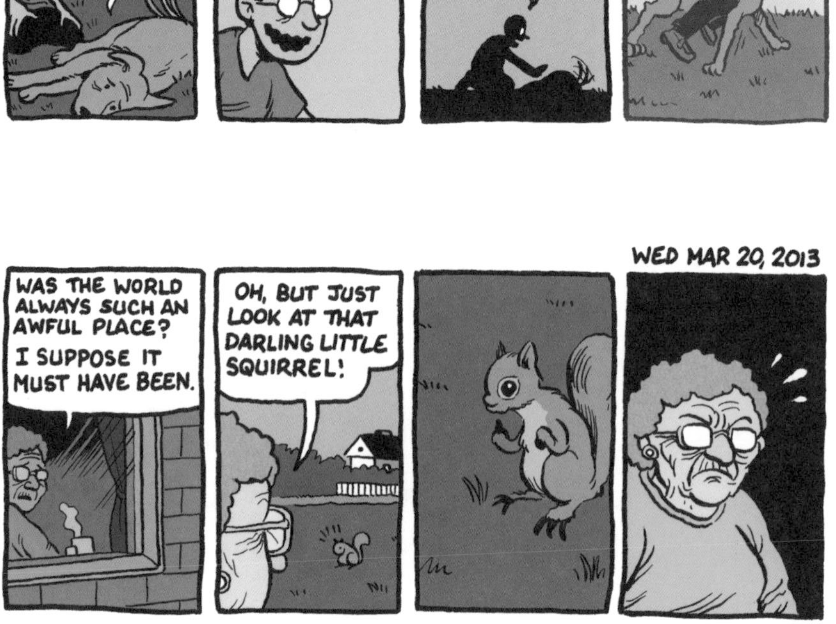
WAS THE WORLD ALWAYS SUCH AN AWFUL PLACE?
I SUPPOSE IT MUST HAVE BEEN.
OH, BUT JUST LOOK AT THAT DARLING LITTLE SQUIRREL!

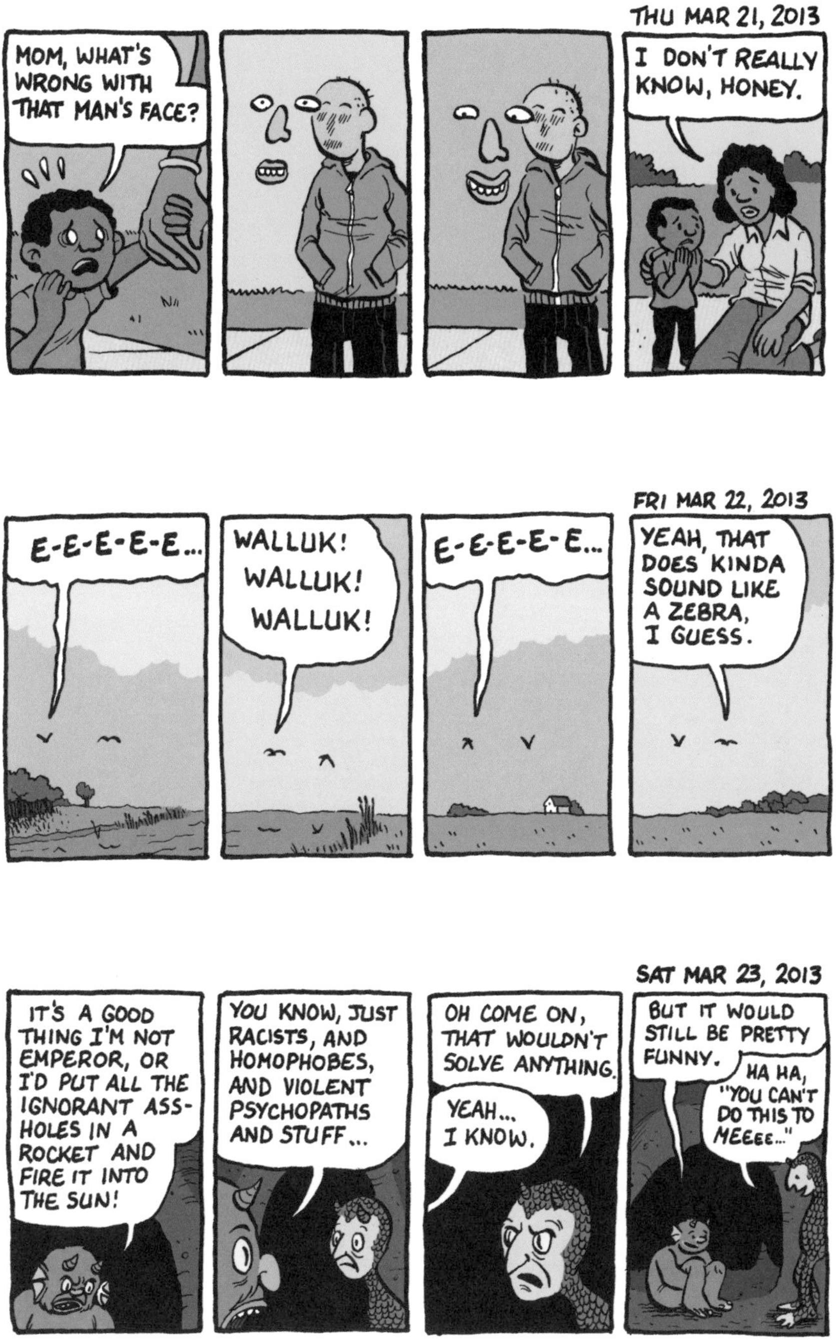
THU MAR 21, 2013
MOM, WHAT'S WRONG WITH THAT MAN'S FACE?
I DON'T REALLY KNOW, HONEY.
FRI MAR 22, 2013
E-E-E-E-E...
WALLUK! WALLUK! WALLUK!
E-E-E-E-E...
YEAH, THAT DOES KINDA SOUND LIKE A ZEBRA, I GUESS.
SAT MAR 23, 2013
IT'S A GOOD THING I'M NOT EMPEROR, OR I'D PUT ALL THE IGNORANT ASS-HOLES IN A ROCKET AND FIRE IT INTO THE SUN!
YOU KNOW, JUST RACISTS, AND HOMOPHOBES, AND VIOLENT PSYCHOPATHS AND STUFF...
OH COME ON, THAT WOULDN'T SOLVE ANYTHING.
YEAH... I KNOW.
BUT IT WOULD STILL BE PRETTY FUNNY.
HA HA, "YOU CAN'T DO THIS TO MEEEE..."

SUN MAR 24, 2013

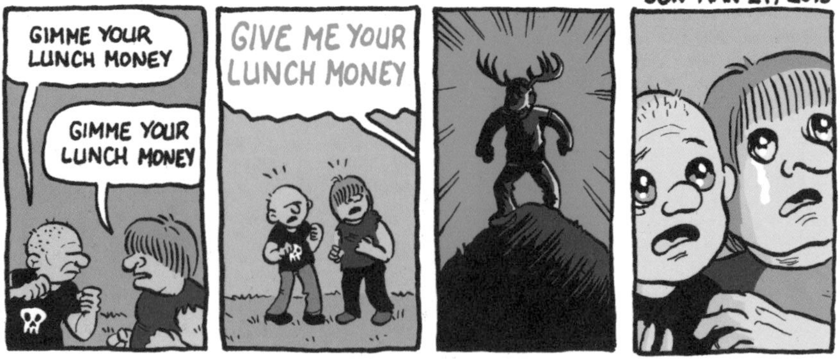
GIMME YOUR LUNCH MONEY
GIMME YOUR LUNCH MONEY
GIVE ME YOUR LUNCH MONEY

MON MAR 25, 2013

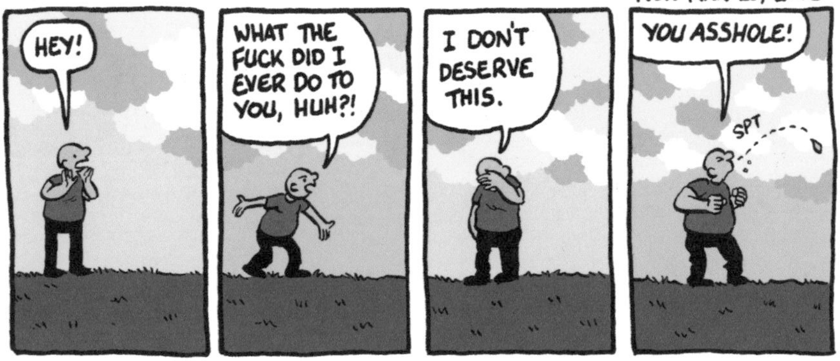
HEY!
WHAT THE FUCK DID I EVER DO TO YOU, HUH?!
I DON'T DESERVE THIS.
YOU ASSHOLE!
SPT

TUE MAR 26, 2013

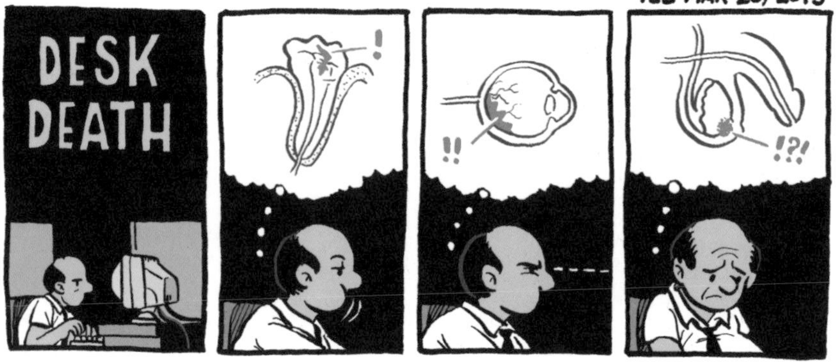
DESK DEATH
!
!!
!?!

WED MAR 27, 2013

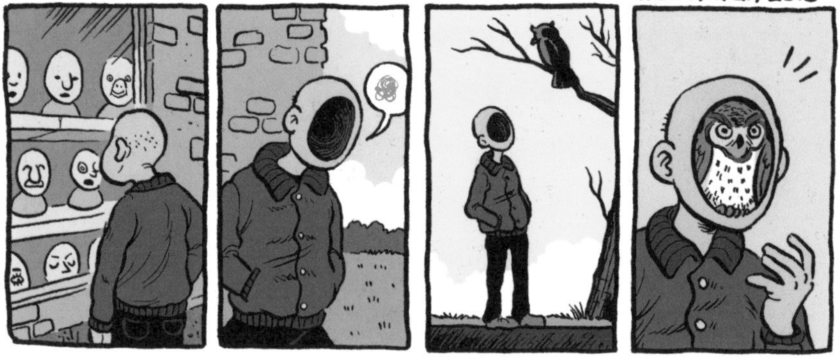

THU MAR 28, 2013

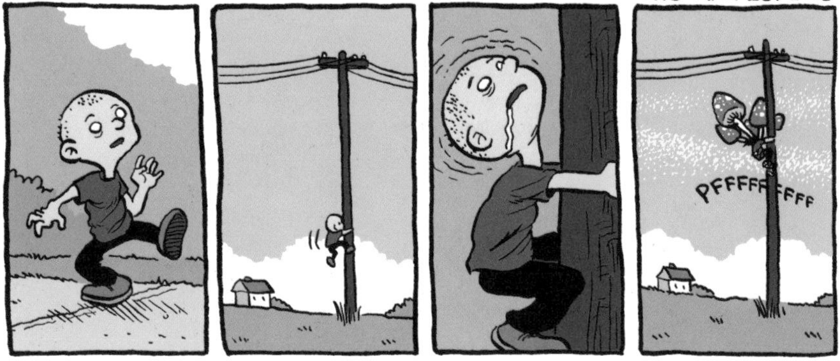
PFFFFF FFFF

FRI MAR 29, 2013

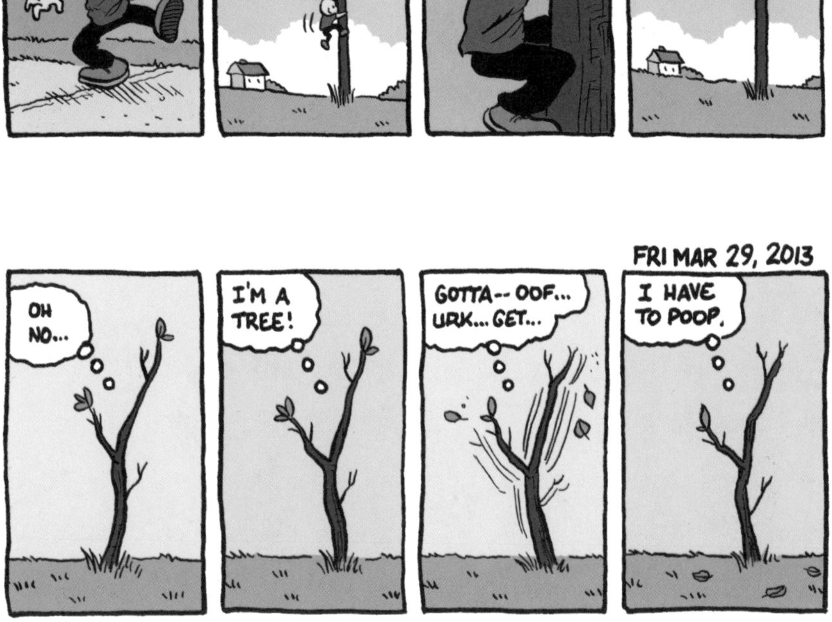
OH NO...
I'M A TREE!
GOTTA-- OOF... URK... GET...
I HAVE TO POOP.

SAT MAR 30, 2013

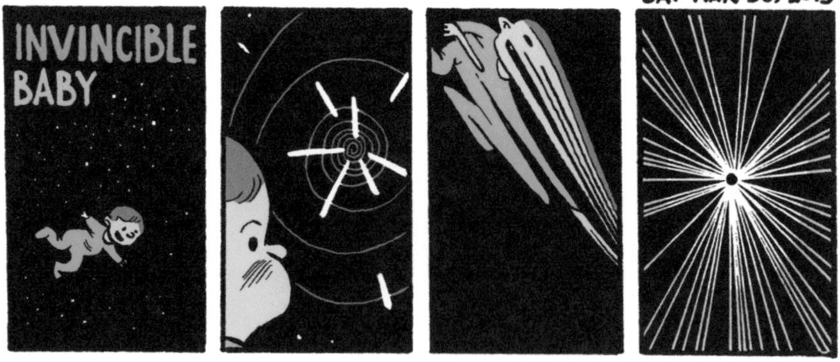
INVINCIBLE BABY

SUN MAR 31, 2013

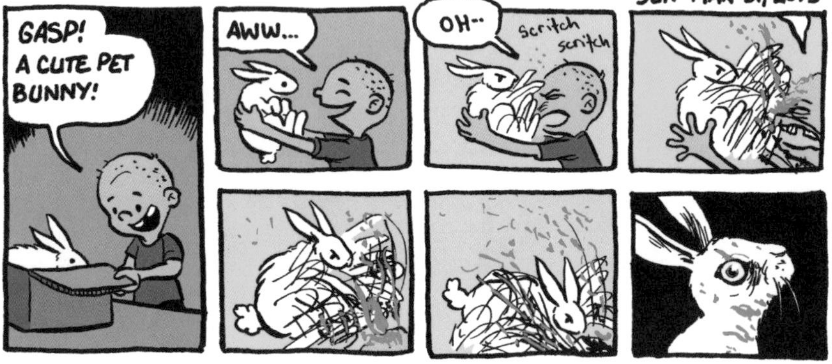
GASP!
A CUTE PET BUNNY!
AWW...
OH--
scritch scritch

MON APR 1, 2013

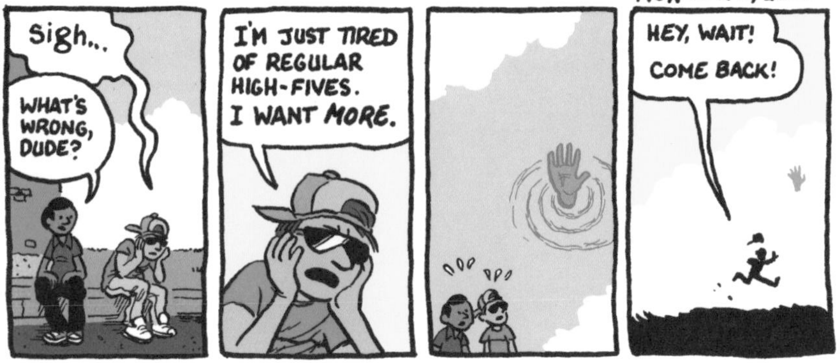
Sigh...
WHAT'S WRONG, DUDE?
I'M JUST TIRED OF REGULAR HIGH-FIVES. I WANT MORE.
HEY, WAIT! COME BACK!

TUE APR 2, 2013

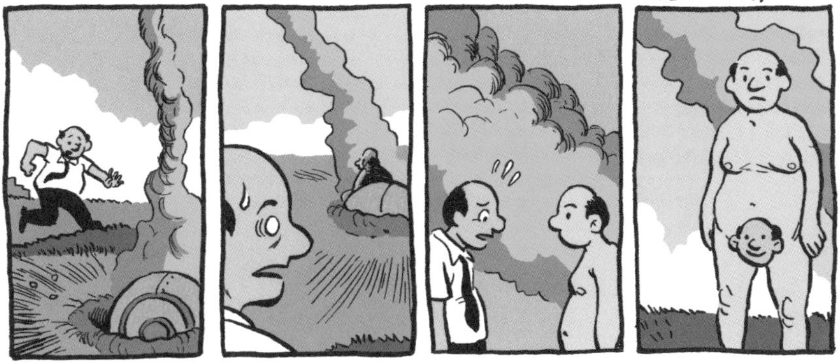

WED APR 3, 2013

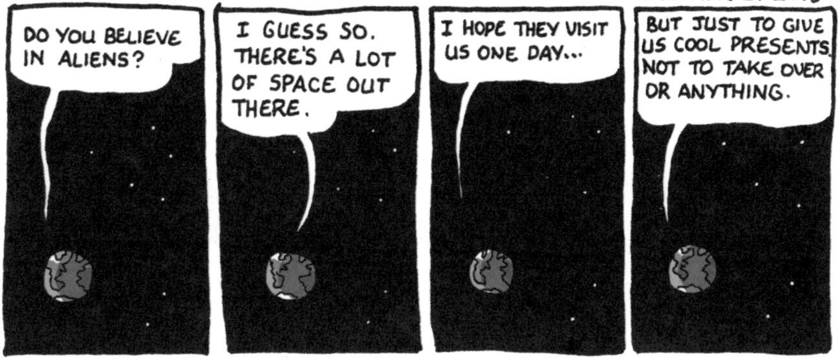
DO YOU BELIEVE IN ALIENS?
I GUESS SO. THERE'S A LOT OF SPACE OUT THERE.
I HOPE THEY VISIT US ONE DAY...
BUT JUST TO GIVE US COOL PRESENTS. NOT TO TAKE OVER OR ANYTHING.

THU APR 4, 2013

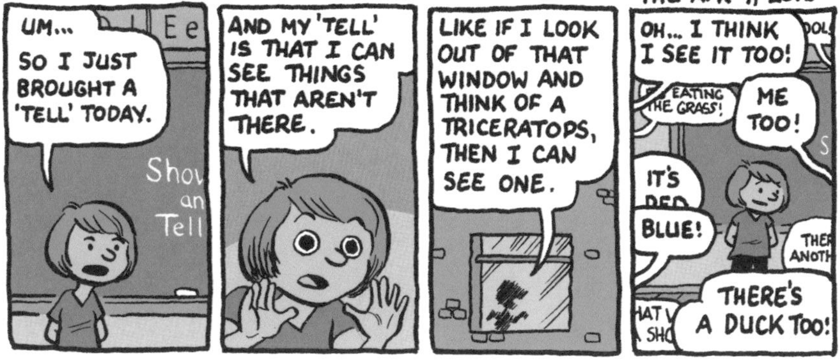
UM...
SO I JUST BROUGHT A 'TELL' TODAY.
AND MY 'TELL' IS THAT I CAN SEE THINGS THAT AREN'T THERE.
LIKE IF I LOOK OUT OF THAT WINDOW AND THINK OF A TRICERATOPS, THEN I CAN SEE ONE.
OH... I THINK I SEE IT TOO!
ME TOO!
BLUE!
THERE'S A DUCK TOO!

FRI APR 5, 2013

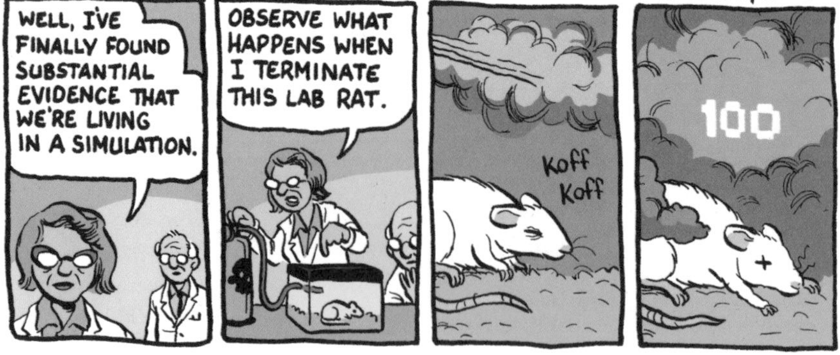
WELL, I'VE FINALLY FOUND SUBSTANTIAL EVIDENCE THAT WE'RE LIVING IN A SIMULATION.
OBSERVE WHAT HAPPENS WHEN I TERMINATE THIS LAB RAT.
Koff Koff
100

SAT APR 6, 2013

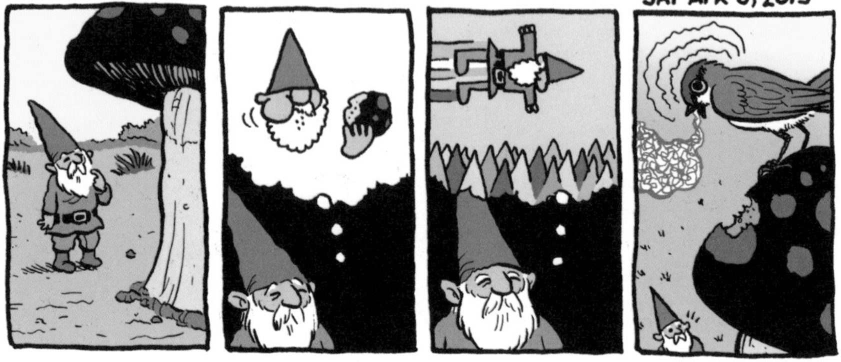

SUN APR 7, 2013

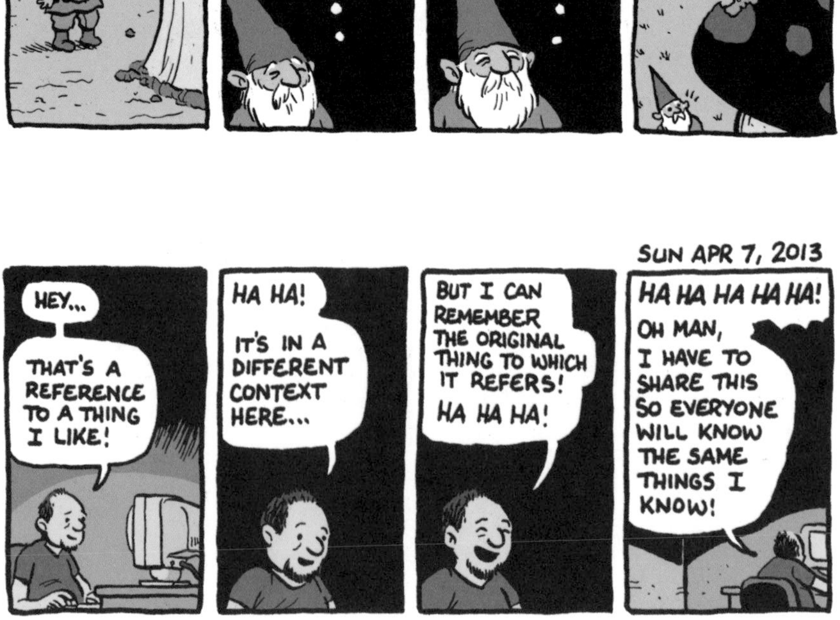
HEY...
THAT'S A REFERENCE TO A THING I LIKE!
HA HA!
IT'S IN A DIFFERENT CONTEXT HERE...
BUT I CAN REMEMBER THE ORIGINAL THING TO WHICH IT REFERS!
HA HA HA!
HA HA HA HA HA!
OH MAN, I HAVE TO SHARE THIS SO EVERYONE WILL KNOW THE SAME THINGS I KNOW!

MON APR 8, 2013

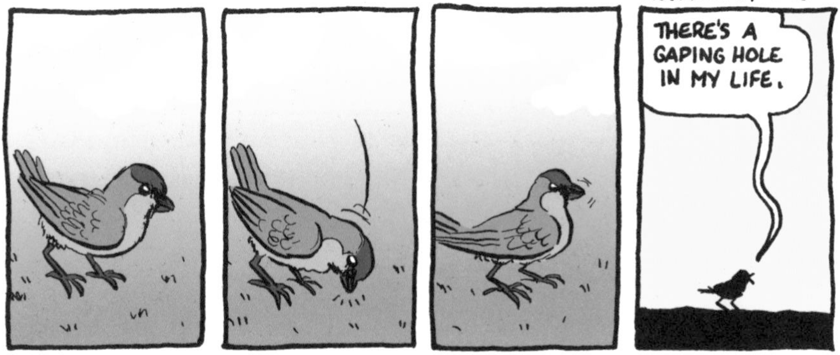
THERE'S A GAPING HOLE IN MY LIFE.

TUE APR 9, 2013

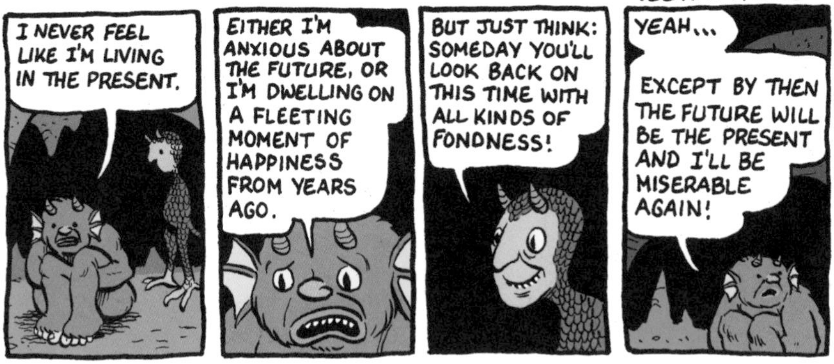
I NEVER FEEL LIKE I'M LIVING IN THE PRESENT.
EITHER I'M ANXIOUS ABOUT THE FUTURE, OR I'M DWELLING ON A FLEETING MOMENT OF HAPPINESS FROM YEARS AGO.
BUT JUST THINK: SOMEDAY YOU'LL LOOK BACK ON THIS TIME WITH ALL KINDS OF FONDNESS!
YEAH...
EXCEPT BY THEN THE FUTURE WILL BE THE PRESENT AND I'LL BE MISERABLE AGAIN!

WED APR 10, 2013

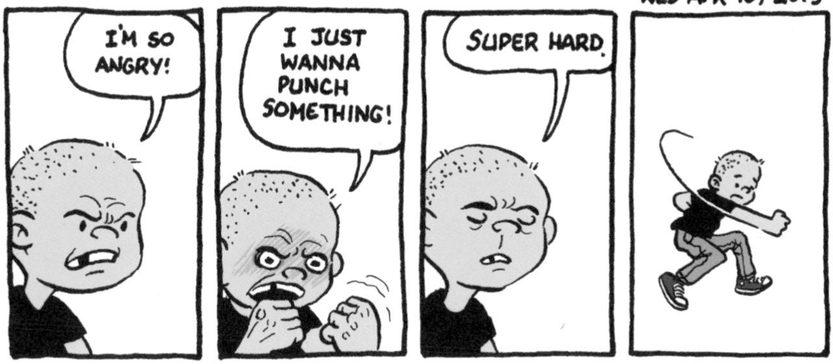
I'M SO ANGRY!
I JUST WANNA PUNCH SOMETHING!
SUPER HARD.

THU APR 11, 2013

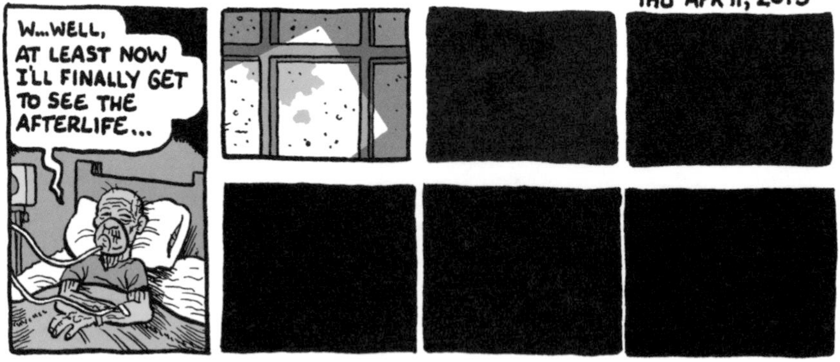
W...WELL, AT LEAST NOW I'LL FINALLY GET TO SEE THE AFTERLIFE...

FRI APR 12, 2013

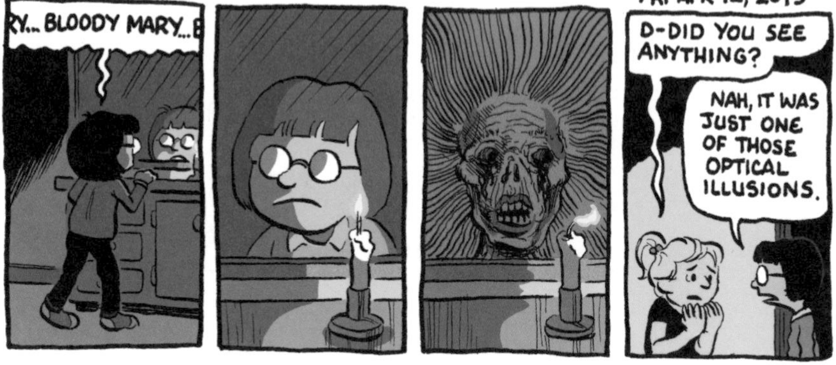
RY... BLOODY MARY... B
D-DID YOU SEE ANYTHING?
NAH, IT WAS JUST ONE OF THOSE OPTICAL ILLUSIONS.

SAT APR 13, 2013

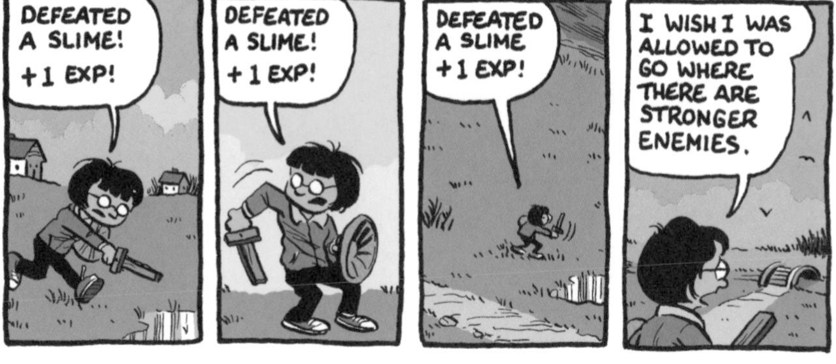
DEFEATED A SLIME! +1 EXP!
DEFEATED A SLIME! +1 EXP!
DEFEATED A SLIME +1 EXP!
I WISH I WAS ALLOWED TO GO WHERE THERE ARE STRONGER ENEMIES.

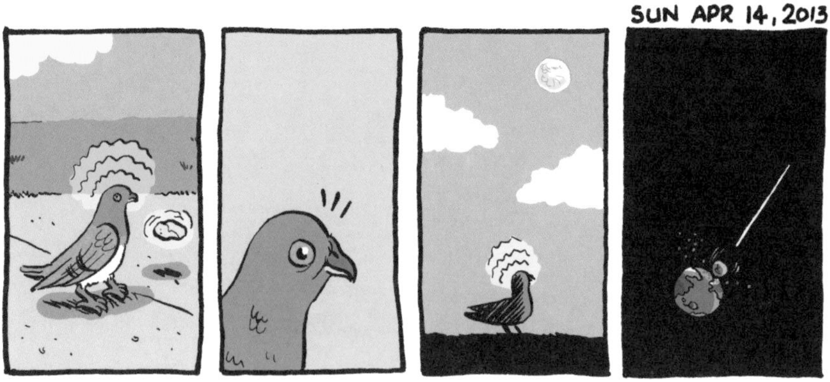
SUN APR 14, 2013

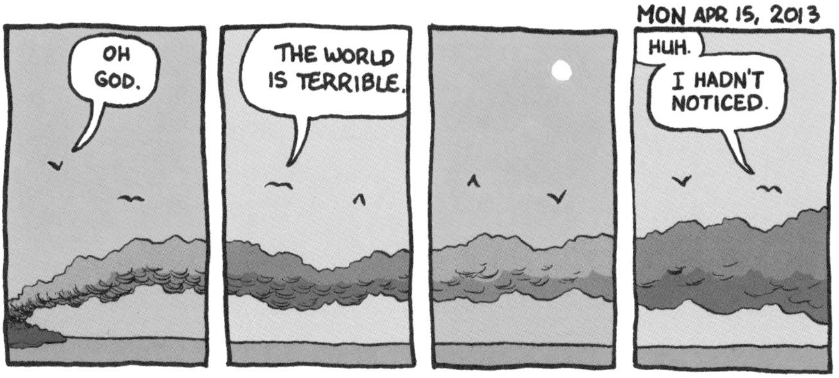
MON APR 15, 2013
OH GOD.
THE WORLD IS TERRIBLE.
HUH.
I HADN'T NOTICED.

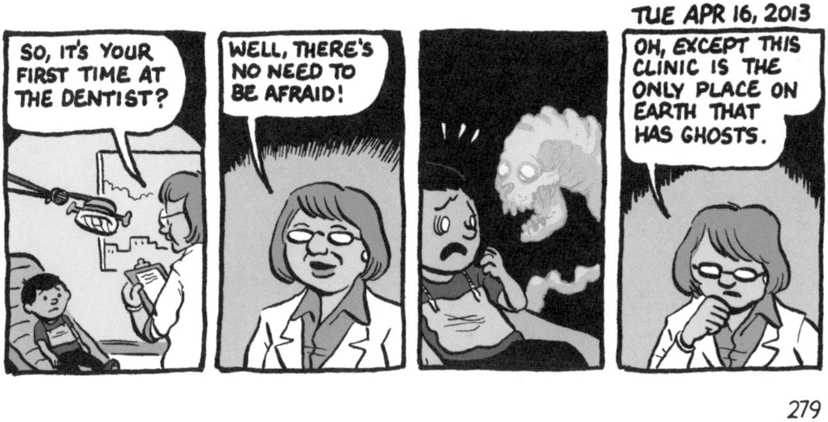
TUE APR 16, 2013
SO, IT'S YOUR FIRST TIME AT THE DENTIST?
WELL, THERE'S NO NEED TO BE AFRAID!
OH, EXCEPT THIS CLINIC IS THE ONLY PLACE ON EARTH THAT HAS GHOSTS.

WED APR 17, 2013

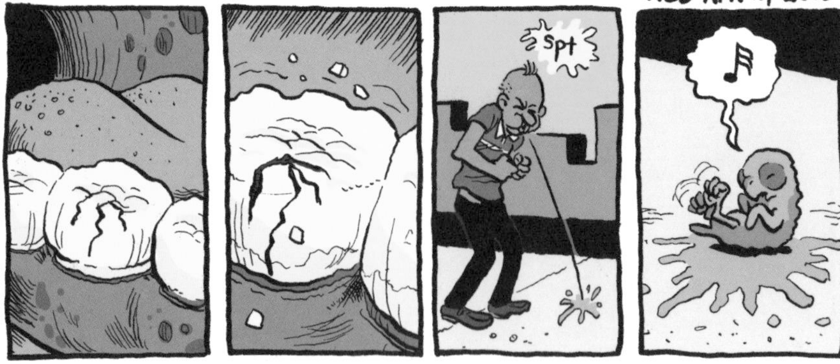
Spt

THU APR 18, 2013

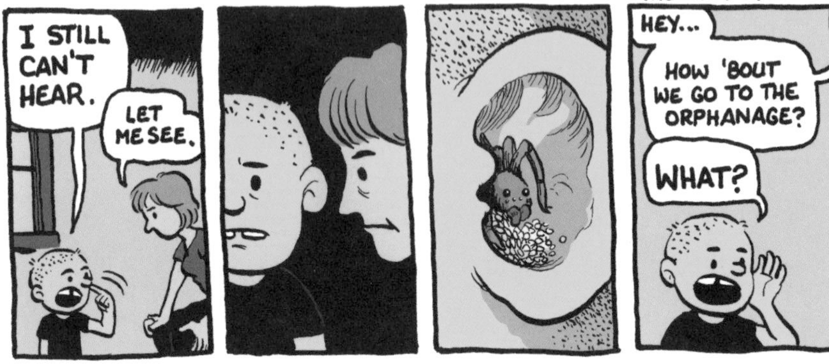
I STILL CAN'T HEAR.
LET ME SEE.
HEY...
HOW 'BOUT WE GO TO THE ORPHANAGE?
WHAT?

FRI APR 19, 2013

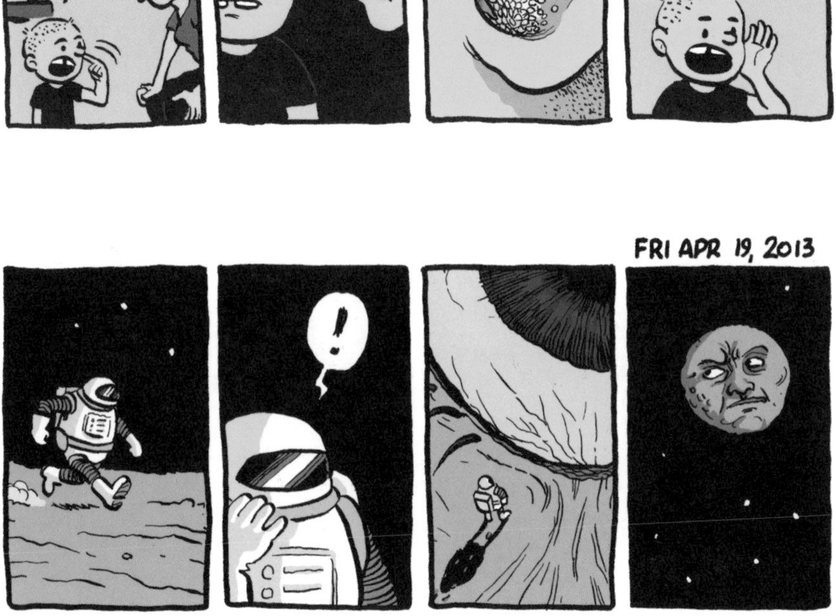
!

SAT APR 20, 2013

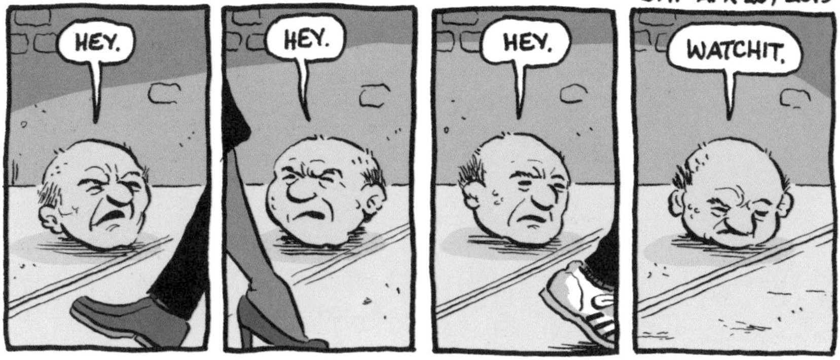
HEY.
HEY.
HEY.
WATCHIT.

SUN APR 21, 2013

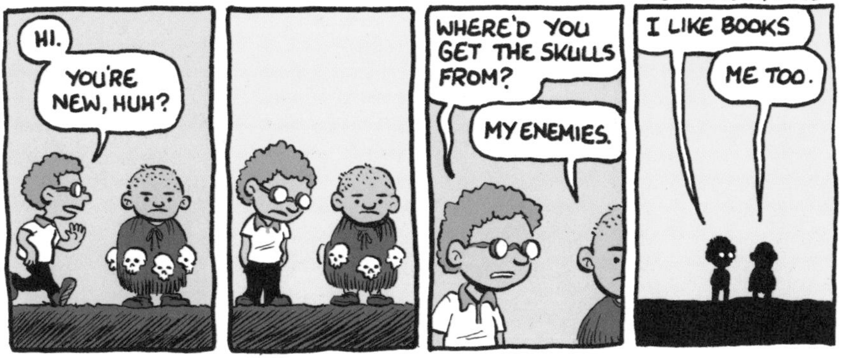
HI.
YOU'RE NEW, HUH?
WHERE'D YOU GET THE SKULLS FROM?
MY ENEMIES.
I LIKE BOOKS
ME TOO.

MON APR 22, 2013

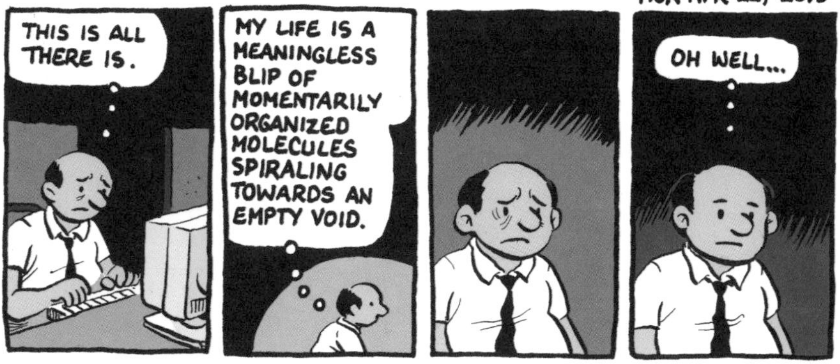
THIS IS ALL THERE IS.
MY LIFE IS A MEANINGLESS BLIP OF MOMENTARILY ORGANIZED MOLECULES SPIRALING TOWARDS AN EMPTY VOID.
OH WELL...

TUE APR 23, 2013

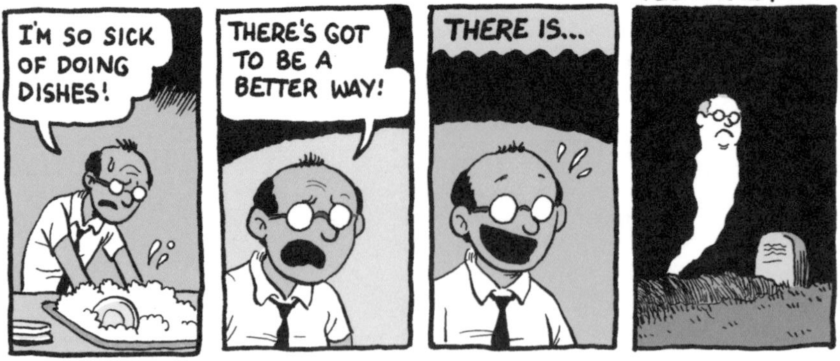
I'M SO SICK OF DOING DISHES!
THERE'S GOT TO BE A BETTER WAY!
THERE IS...

WED APR 24, 2013

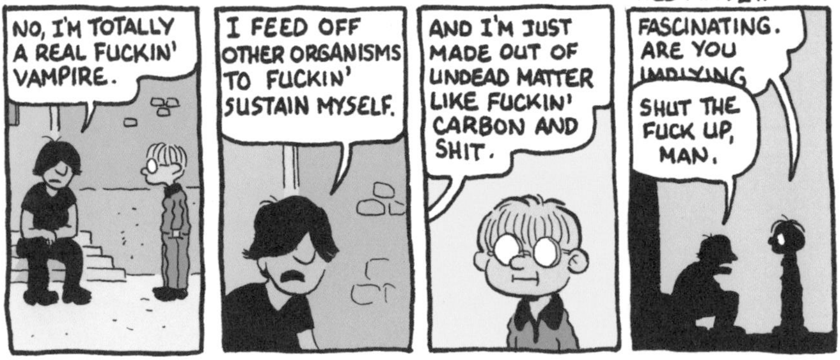
NO, I'M TOTALLY A REAL FUCKIN' VAMPIRE.
I FEED OFF OTHER ORGANISMS TO FUCKIN' SUSTAIN MYSELF.
AND I'M JUST MADE OUT OF UNDEAD MATTER LIKE FUCKIN' CARBON AND SHIT.
FASCINATING. ARE YOU
SHUT THE FUCK UP, MAN.

THU APR 25, 2013

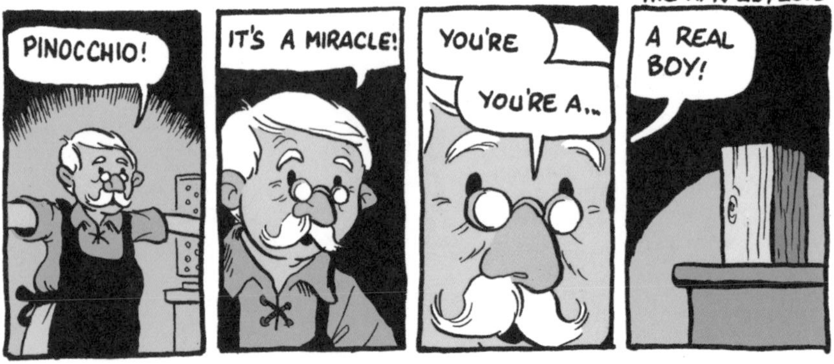
PINOCCHIO!
IT'S A MIRACLE!
YOU'RE
YOU'RE A...
A REAL BOY!

HOW WOULD I HANDLE A CONFLICT IN THE WORKPLACE?

ba ba ba ba ba ba ba

THAT'S A GOOD QUESTION. I THINK I'M VERY GOOD AT CONSIDERING OTHER'S POINTS OF VIEW.

ba ba ba ba ba ba ba ba ba ba

I ALSO TEND TO BE PRETTY EVEN-TEMPERED, SO THAT DEFUSES TENSION BEFORE IT GETS OUT OF HAND.

BUT I CAN ALSO BE QUITE DIRECT, WITHOUT BEING RUDE, WHEN I HAVE TO BE.

bo bo bo bo bo bo bo bo

I DON'T WANT TO DO HOMEWORK!

IT'S THE WEEKEND!

I DO WORK AT SCHOOL ALL WEEK!

MY LIFE IS SLIPPING AWAY FROM ME. I WANT TO LIVE!

NO.

WHAT WOULD YOU DO IF YOU WERE RICH?

HMM...

I WOULD GO ALL. OUT.

LIKE I WOULD GET BRAND NAME CEREAL SOMETIMES.

IT WOULD BE TOTALLY CRAZY. EVERYONE WOULD BE LIKE, "YOU'VE CHANGED..."

283

MON APR 29, 2013

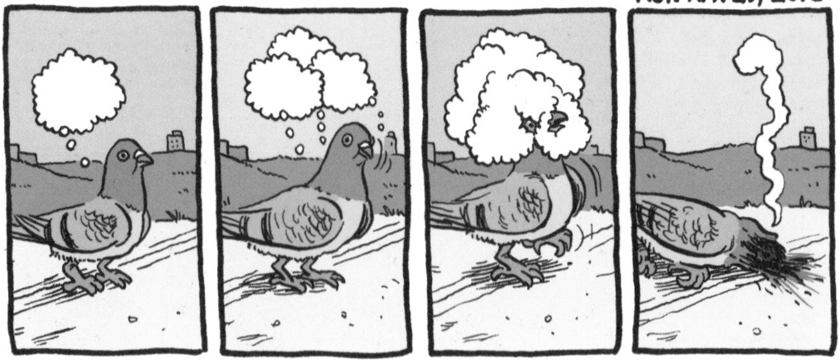

TUE APR 30, 2013

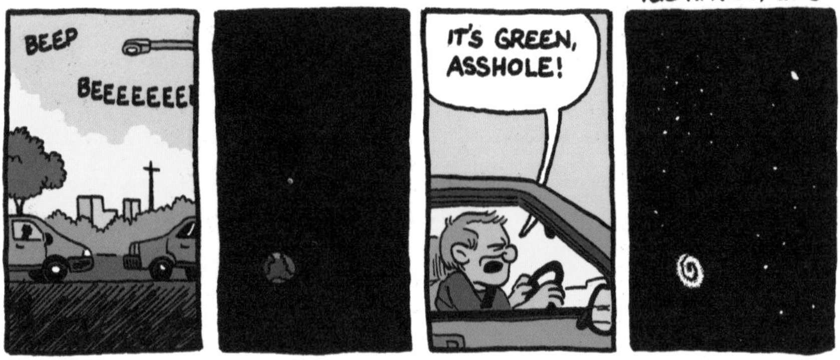
BEEP
BEEEEEEEE
IT'S GREEN, ASSHOLE!

WED MAY 1, 2013

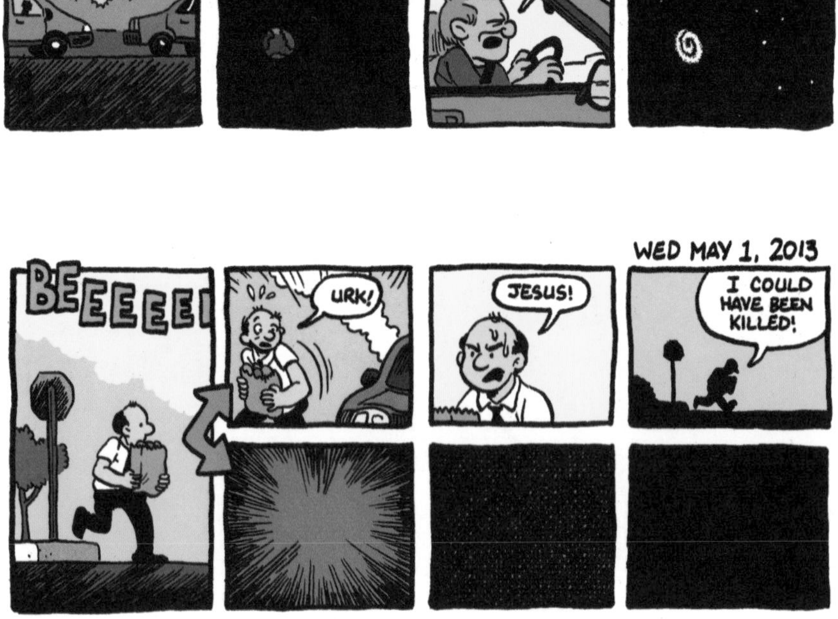
BEEEEEE
URK!
JESUS!
I COULD HAVE BEEN KILLED!

THU MAY 2, 2013

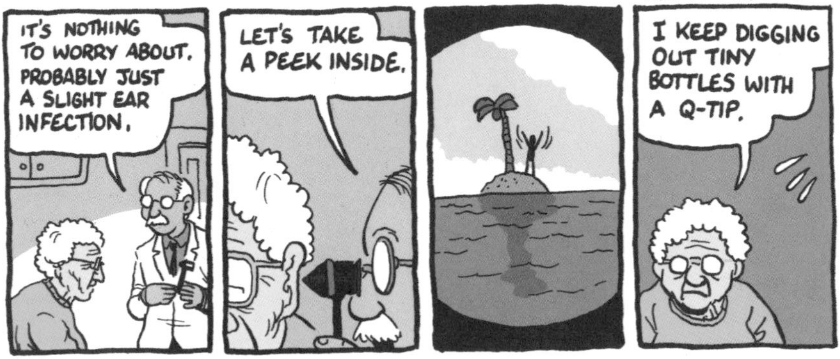
IT'S NOTHING TO WORRY ABOUT. PROBABLY JUST A SLIGHT EAR INFECTION.
LET'S TAKE A PEEK INSIDE.
I KEEP DIGGING OUT TINY BOTTLES WITH A Q-TIP.

FRI MAY 3, 2013

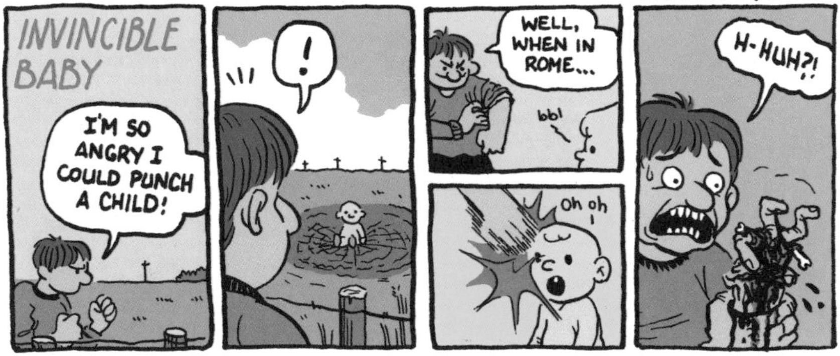
INVINCIBLE BABY
I'M SO ANGRY I COULD PUNCH A CHILD!
!
WELL, WHEN IN ROME...
bbl
Oh oh
H-HUH?!

SAT MAY 4, 2013

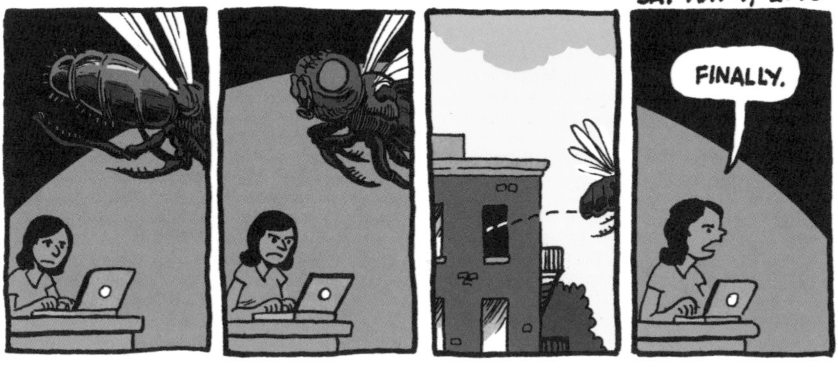
FINALLY.

SUN MAY 5, 2013

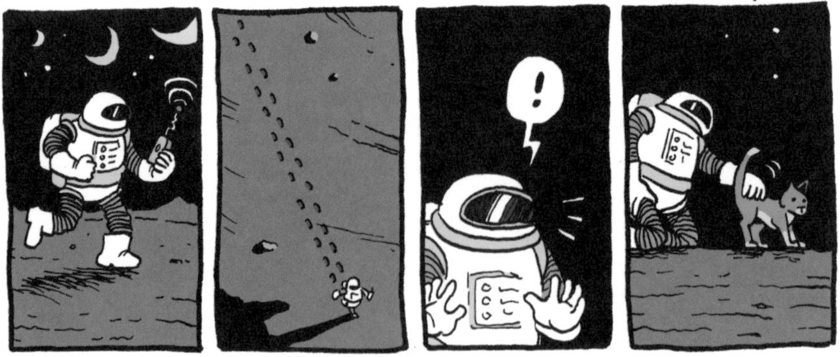
!

MON MAY 6, 2013

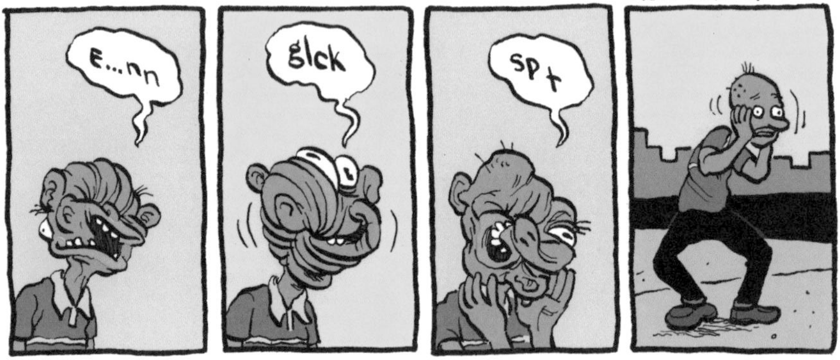
E...nn
glck
spt

TUE MAY 7, 2013

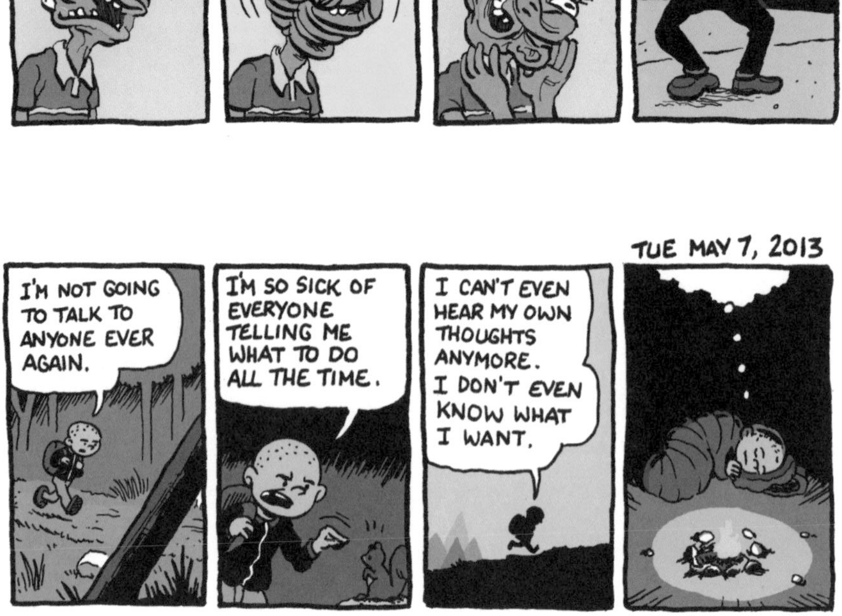
I'M NOT GOING TO TALK TO ANYONE EVER AGAIN.
I'M SO SICK OF EVERYONE TELLING ME WHAT TO DO ALL THE TIME.
I CAN'T EVEN HEAR MY OWN THOUGHTS ANYMORE. I DON'T EVEN KNOW WHAT I WANT.

WED MAY 8, 2013

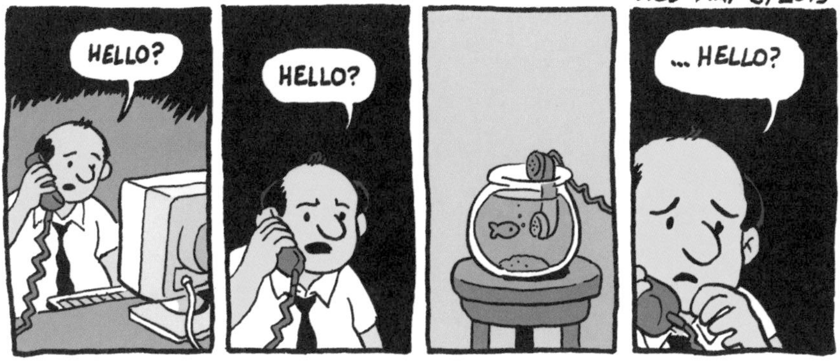
HELLO?
HELLO?
... HELLO?

THU MAY 9, 2013

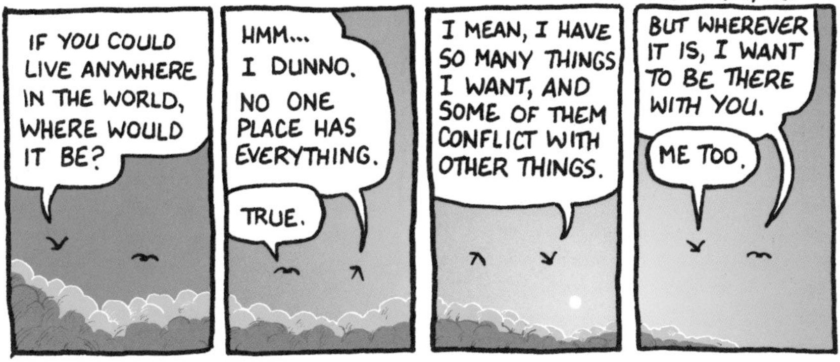
IF YOU COULD LIVE ANYWHERE IN THE WORLD, WHERE WOULD IT BE?
HMM... I DUNNO. NO ONE PLACE HAS EVERYTHING.
TRUE.
I MEAN, I HAVE SO MANY THINGS I WANT, AND SOME OF THEM CONFLICT WITH OTHER THINGS.
BUT WHEREVER IT IS, I WANT TO BE THERE WITH YOU.
ME TOO.

FRI MAY 10, 2013

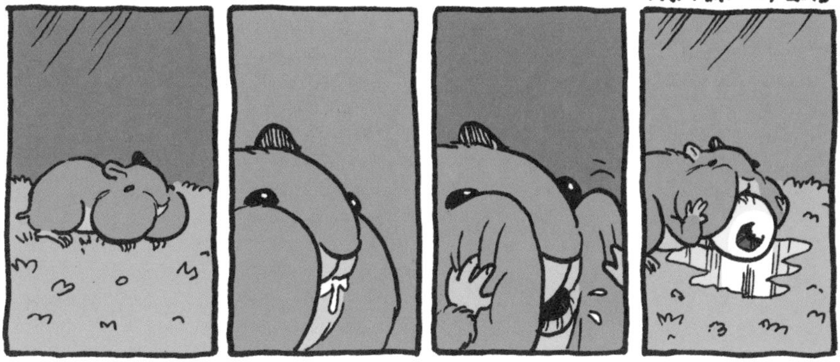

SAT MAY 11, 2013

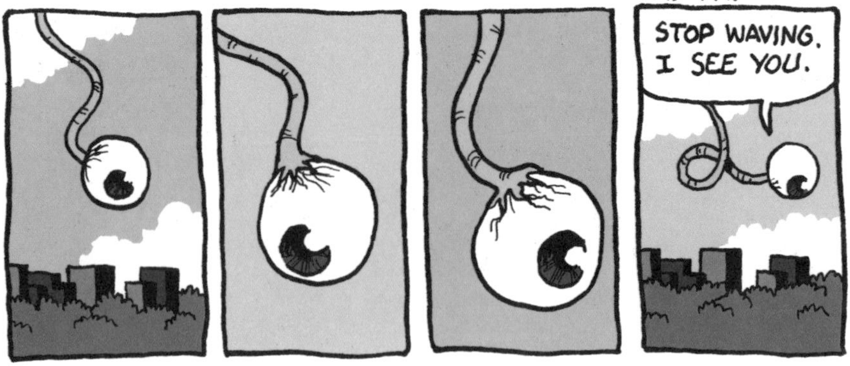
STOP WAVING. I SEE YOU.

SUN MAY 12, 2013

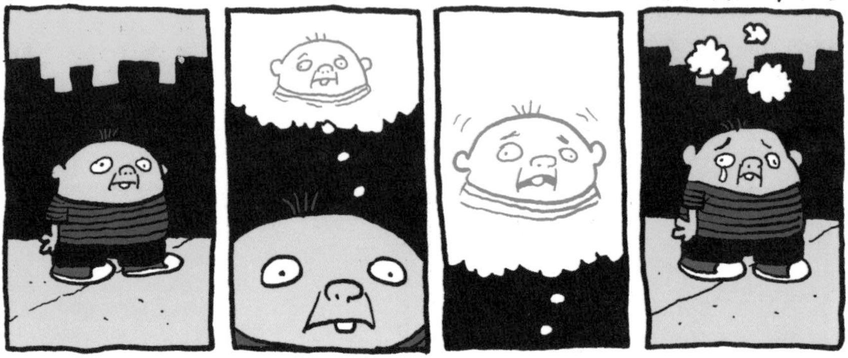

MON MAY 13, 2013

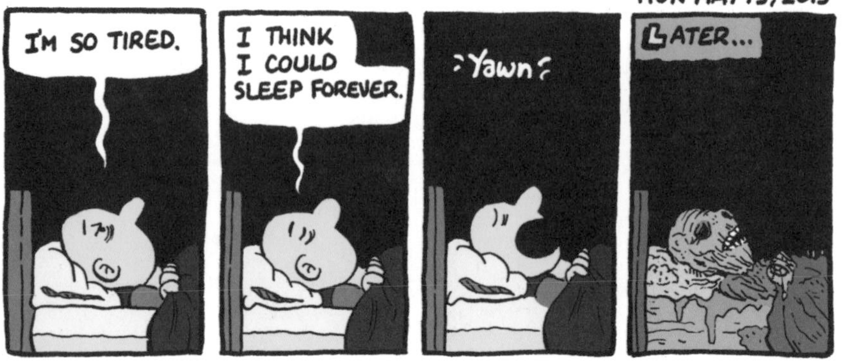
I'M SO TIRED.
I THINK I COULD SLEEP FOREVER.
Yawn
LATER...

TUE MAY 14, 2013

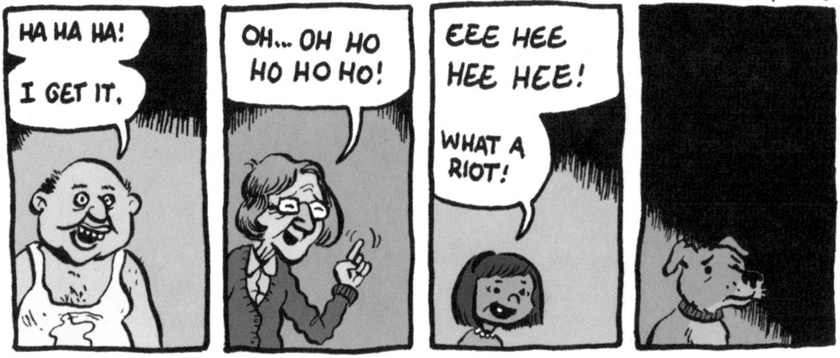
HA HA HA!
I GET IT.
OH... OH HO HO HO HO!
EEE HEE HEE HEE!
WHAT A RIOT!

WED MAY 15, 2013

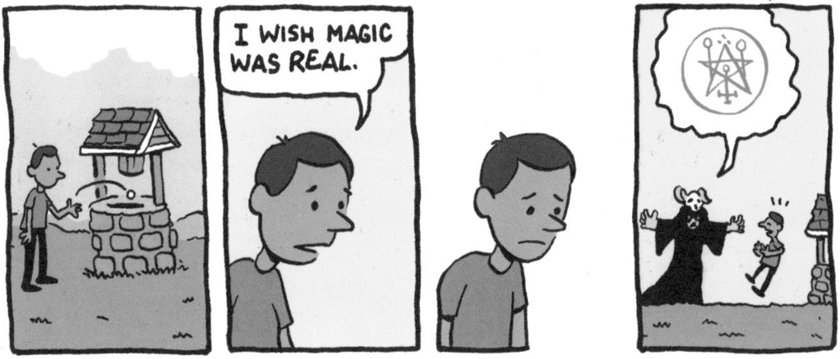
I WISH MAGIC WAS REAL.

THU MAY 16, 2013

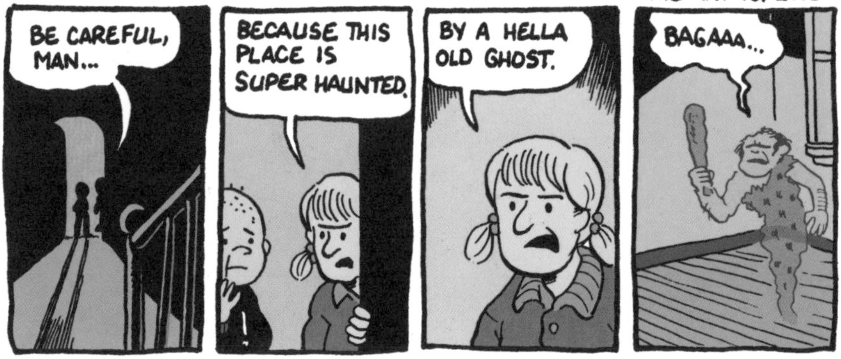
BE CAREFUL, MAN...
BECAUSE THIS PLACE IS SUPER HAUNTED.
BY A HELLA OLD GHOST.
BAGAAA...

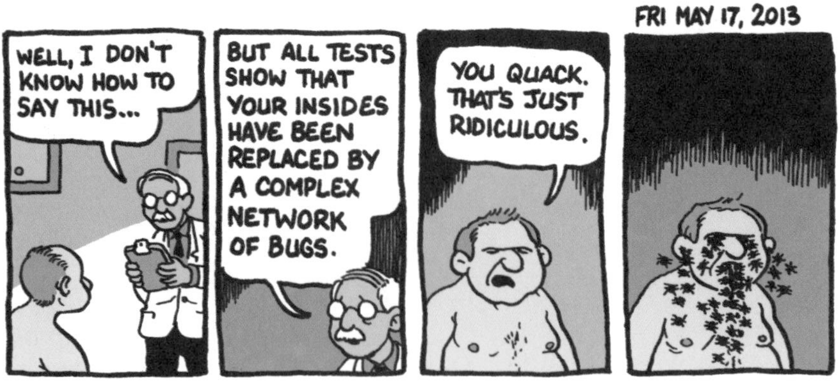
FRI MAY 17, 2013
WELL, I DON'T KNOW HOW TO SAY THIS...
BUT ALL TESTS SHOW THAT YOUR INSIDES HAVE BEEN REPLACED BY A COMPLEX NETWORK OF BUGS.
YOU QUACK. THAT'S JUST RIDICULOUS.

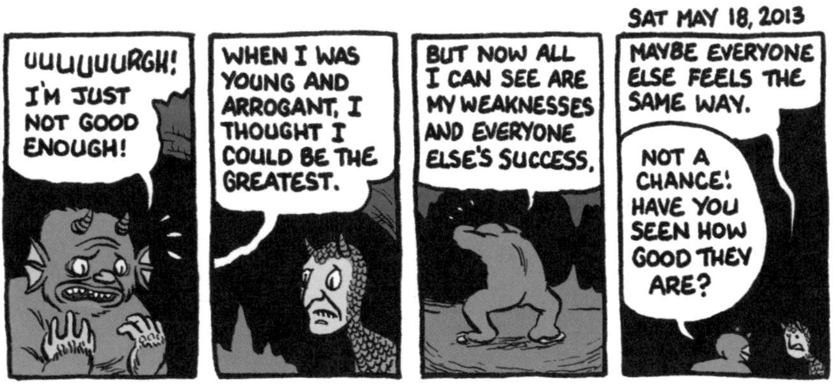
SAT MAY 18, 2013
UUUUUUURGH! I'M JUST NOT GOOD ENOUGH!
WHEN I WAS YOUNG AND ARROGANT, I THOUGHT I COULD BE THE GREATEST.
BUT NOW ALL I CAN SEE ARE MY WEAKNESSES AND EVERYONE ELSE'S SUCCESS.
MAYBE EVERYONE ELSE FEELS THE SAME WAY.
NOT A CHANCE! HAVE YOU SEEN HOW GOOD THEY ARE?

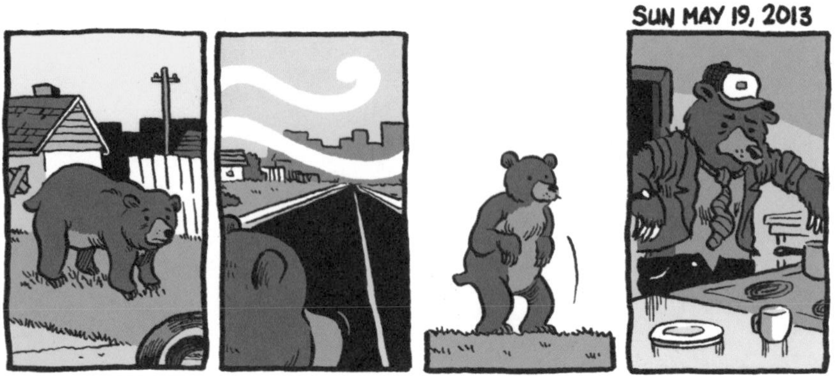
SUN MAY 19, 2013

MON MAY 20, 2013

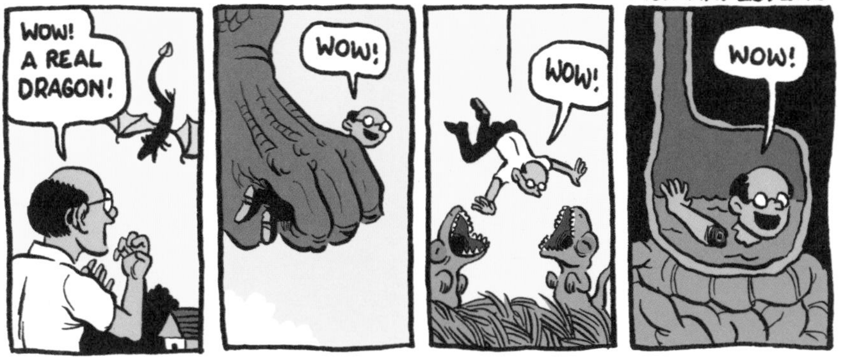

WOW! A REAL DRAGON!
WOW!
WOW!
WOW!

TUE MAY 21, 2013

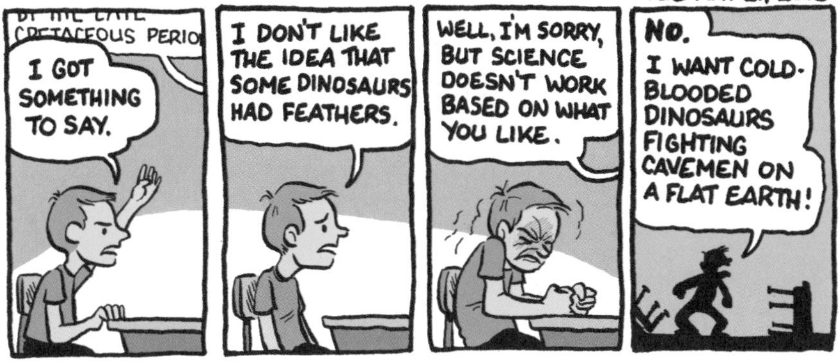

CRETACEOUS PERIO
I GOT SOMETHING TO SAY.
I DON'T LIKE THE IDEA THAT SOME DINOSAURS HAD FEATHERS.
WELL, I'M SORRY, BUT SCIENCE DOESN'T WORK BASED ON WHAT YOU LIKE.
NO.
I WANT COLD-BLOODED DINOSAURS FIGHTING CAVEMEN ON A FLAT EARTH!

WED MAY 22, 2013

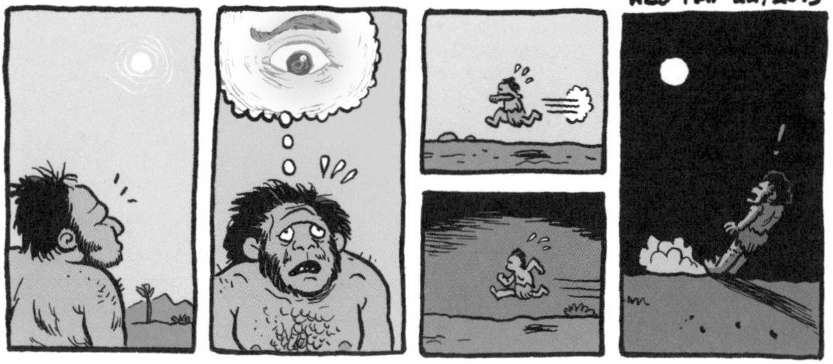

THU MAY 23, 2013

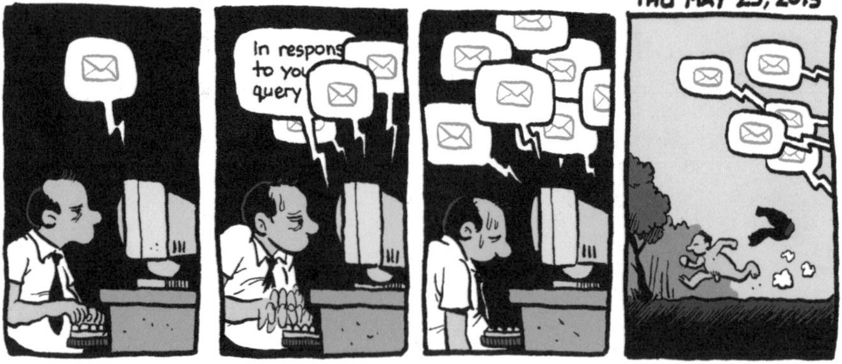

In respons
to you
query

FRI MAY 24, 2013

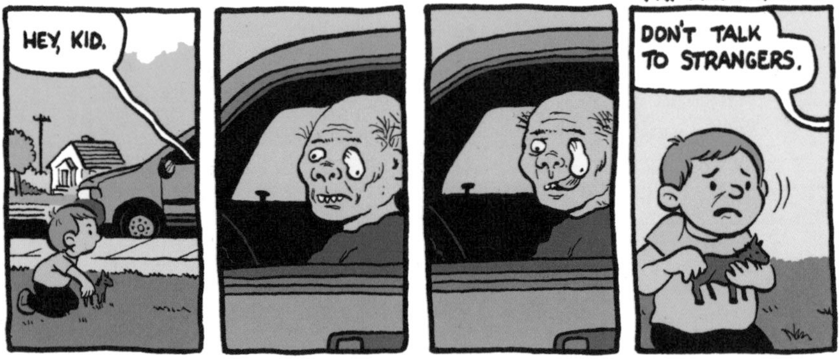

HEY, KID.
DON'T TALK TO STRANGERS.

SAT MAY 25, 2013

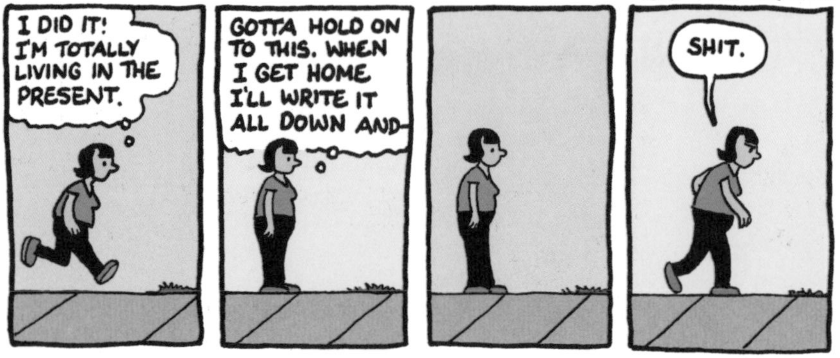

I DID IT! I'M TOTALLY LIVING IN THE PRESENT.
GOTTA HOLD ON TO THIS. WHEN I GET HOME I'LL WRITE IT ALL DOWN AND-
SHIT.

SUN MAY 26, 2013

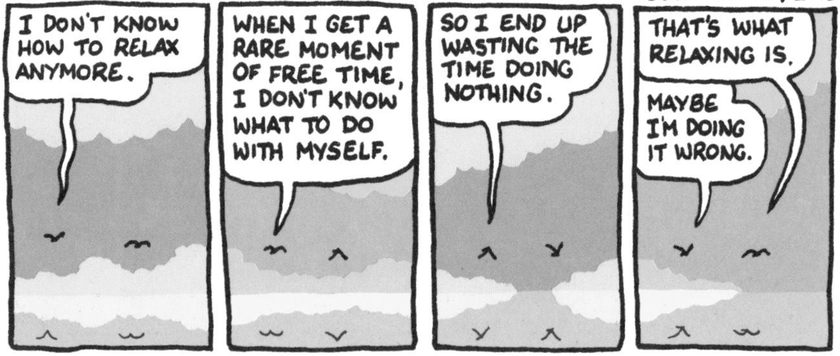
I DON'T KNOW HOW TO RELAX ANYMORE.
WHEN I GET A RARE MOMENT OF FREE TIME, I DON'T KNOW WHAT TO DO WITH MYSELF.
SO I END UP WASTING THE TIME DOING NOTHING.
THAT'S WHAT RELAXING IS.
MAYBE I'M DOING IT WRONG.

MON MAY 27, 2013

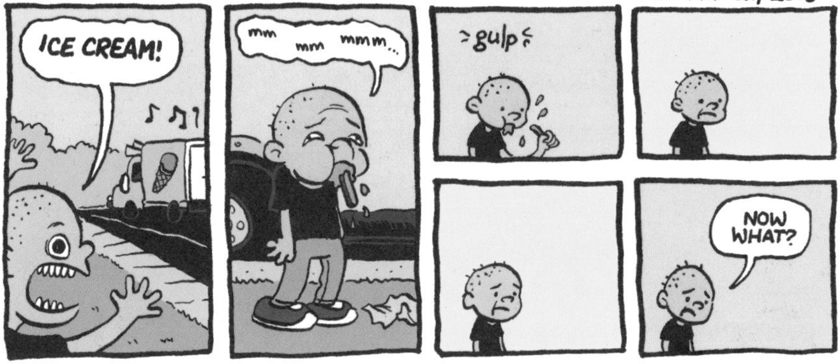
ICE CREAM!
mm mm mmm...
>gulp<
NOW WHAT?

TUE MAY 28, 2013

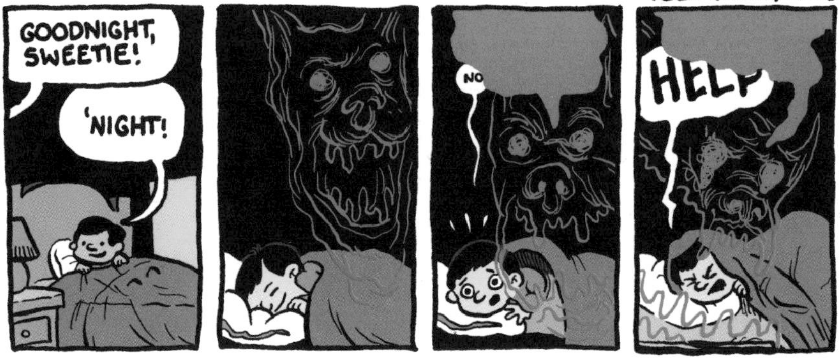
GOODNIGHT, SWEETIE!
'NIGHT!
NO
HELP

WED MAY 29, 2013

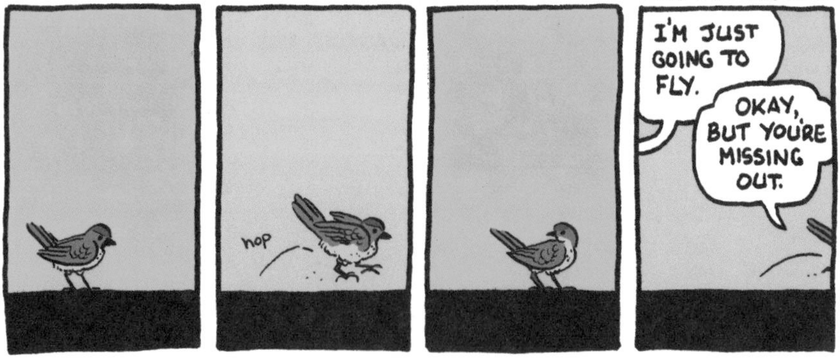
hop
I'M JUST GOING TO FLY.
OKAY, BUT YOU'RE MISSING OUT.

THU MAY 30, 2013

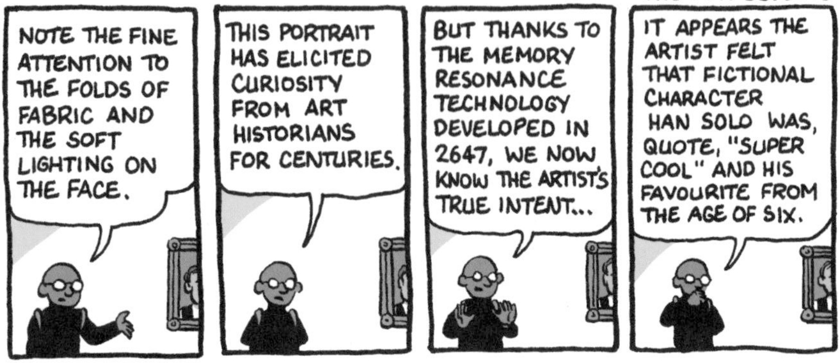
NOTE THE FINE ATTENTION TO THE FOLDS OF FABRIC AND THE SOFT LIGHTING ON THE FACE.
THIS PORTRAIT HAS ELICITED CURIOSITY FROM ART HISTORIANS FOR CENTURIES.
BUT THANKS TO THE MEMORY RESONANCE TECHNOLOGY DEVELOPED IN 2647, WE NOW KNOW THE ARTIST'S TRUE INTENT...
IT APPEARS THE ARTIST FELT THAT FICTIONAL CHARACTER HAN SOLO WAS, QUOTE, "SUPER COOL" AND HIS FAVOURITE FROM THE AGE OF SIX.

FRI MAY 31, 2013

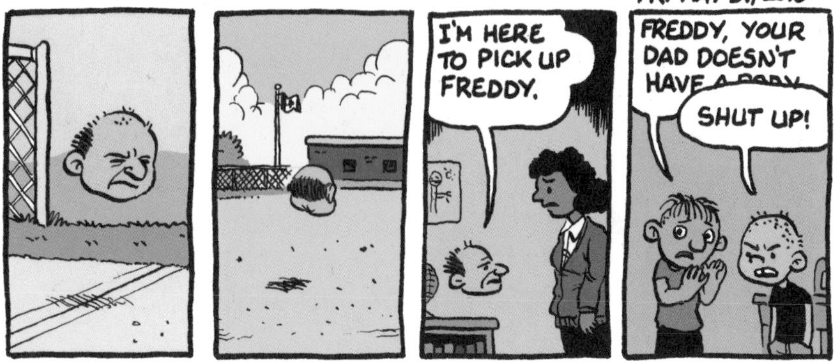
I'M HERE TO PICK UP FREDDY.
FREDDY, YOUR DAD DOESN'T HAVE
SHUT UP!

SAT JUNE 1 2013

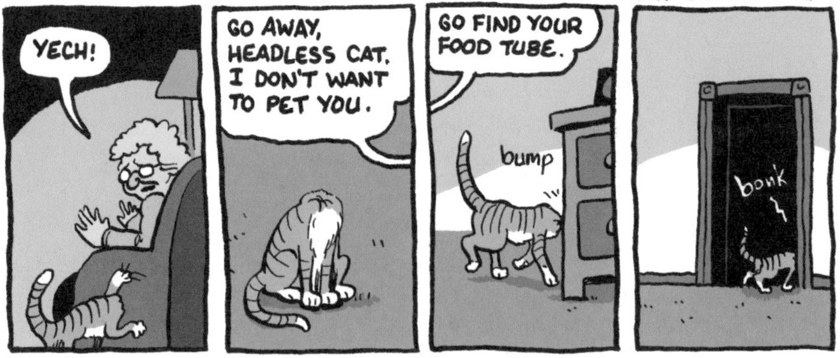
YECH!
GO AWAY, HEADLESS CAT. I DON'T WANT TO PET YOU.
GO FIND YOUR FOOD TUBE.
bump
bonk

SUN JUNE 2, 2013

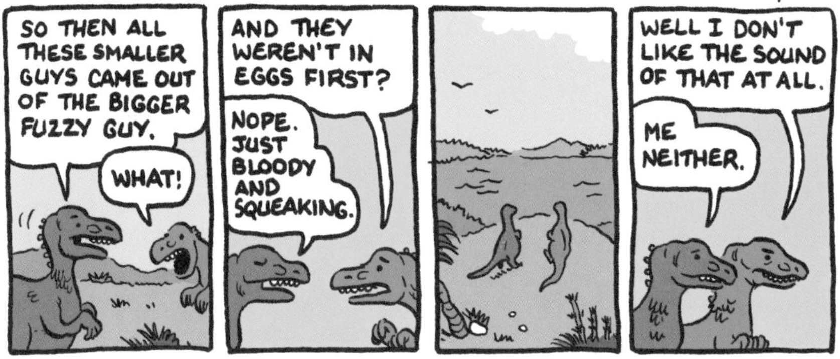
SO THEN ALL THESE SMALLER GUYS CAME OUT OF THE BIGGER FUZZY GUY.
WHAT!
AND THEY WEREN'T IN EGGS FIRST?
NOPE. JUST BLOODY AND SQUEAKING.
WELL I DON'T LIKE THE SOUND OF THAT AT ALL.
ME NEITHER.

MON JUNE 3, 2013

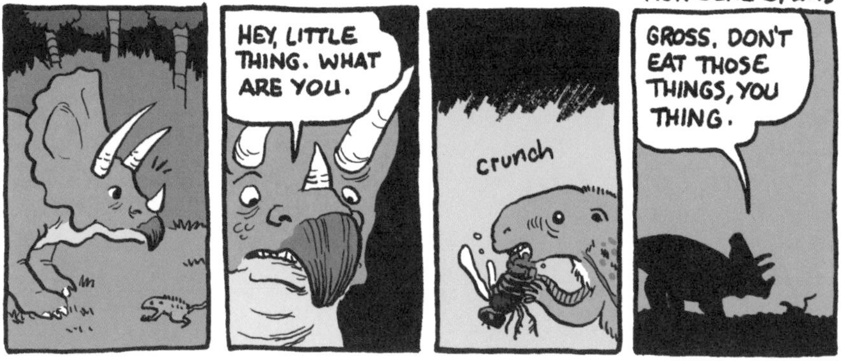
HEY, LITTLE THING. WHAT ARE YOU.
crunch
GROSS. DON'T EAT THOSE THINGS, YOU THING.

TUE JUNE 4, 2013

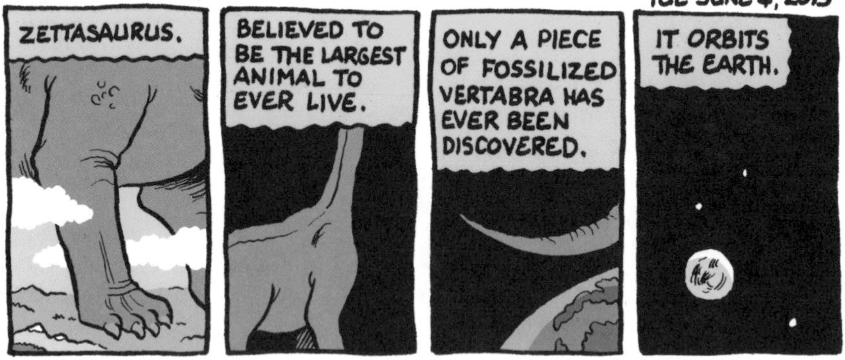
ZETTASAURUS.
BELIEVED TO BE THE LARGEST ANIMAL TO EVER LIVE.
ONLY A PIECE OF FOSSILIZED VERTABRA HAS EVER BEEN DISCOVERED.
IT ORBITS THE EARTH.

WED JUNE 5, 2013

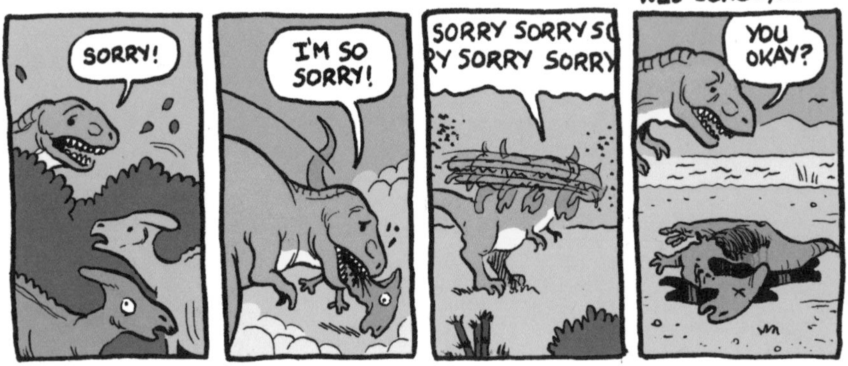
SORRY!
I'M SO SORRY!
SORRY SORRY SO
RY SORRY SORRY
YOU OKAY?

THU JUNE 6, 2013

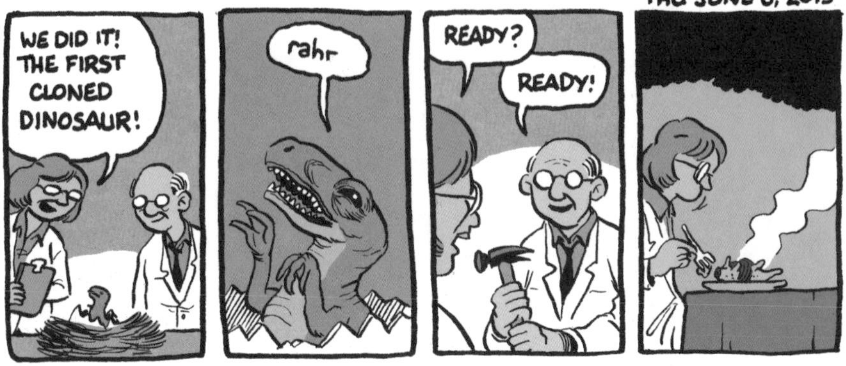
WE DID IT! THE FIRST CLONED DINOSAUR!
rahr
READY?
READY!

FRI JUNE 7, 2013

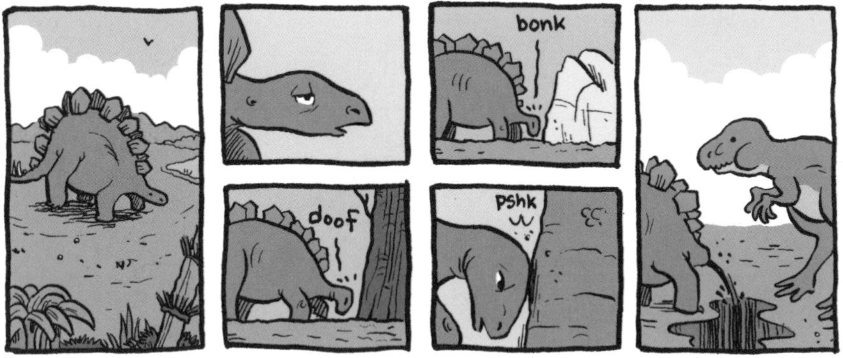
bonk
doof
pshk

SAT JUNE 8, 2013

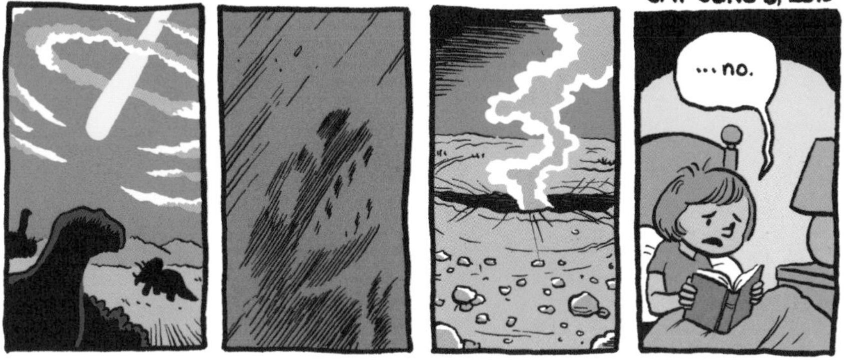
...no.

SUN JUNE 9, 2013

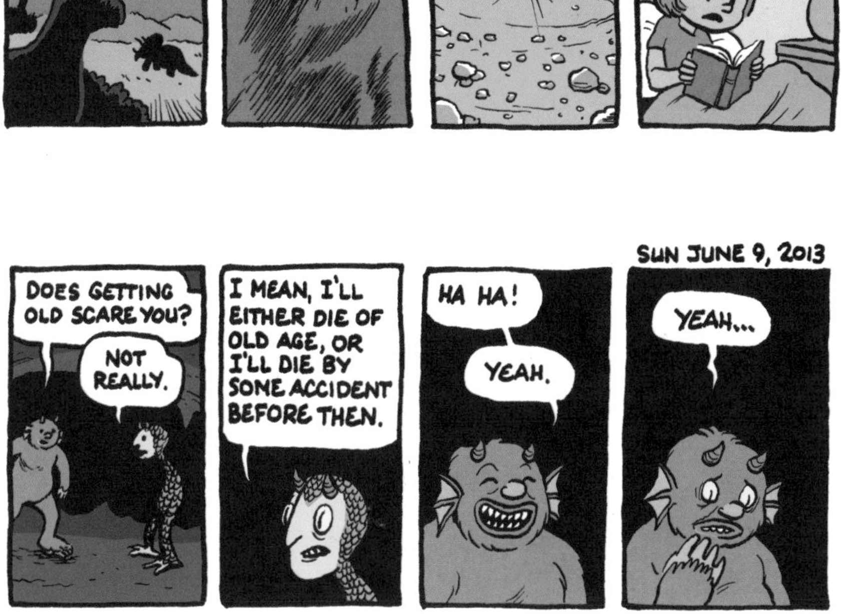
DOES GETTING OLD SCARE YOU?
NOT REALLY.
I MEAN, I'LL EITHER DIE OF OLD AGE, OR I'LL DIE BY SOME ACCIDENT BEFORE THEN.
HA HA!
YEAH.
YEAH...

MON JUNE 10, 2013

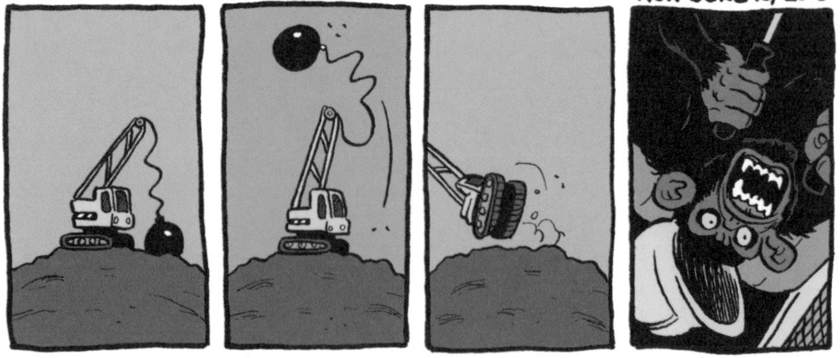

TUE JUNE 11, 2013

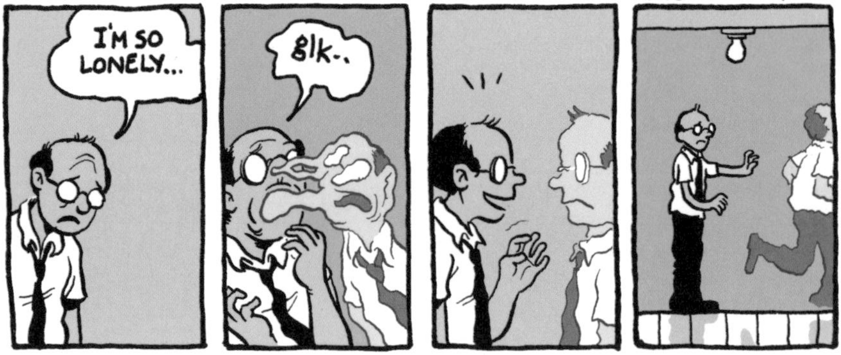
I'M SO LONELY...
glk-.

WED JUNE 12, 2013

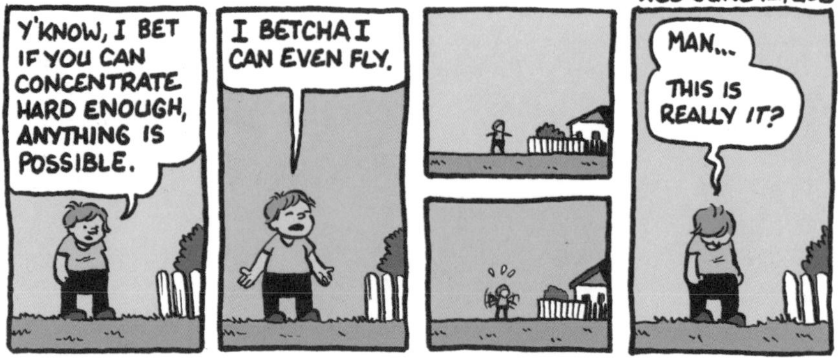
Y'KNOW, I BET IF YOU CAN CONCENTRATE HARD ENOUGH, ANYTHING IS POSSIBLE.
I BETCHA I CAN EVEN FLY.
MAN...
THIS IS REALLY IT?

THU JUNE 13, 2013

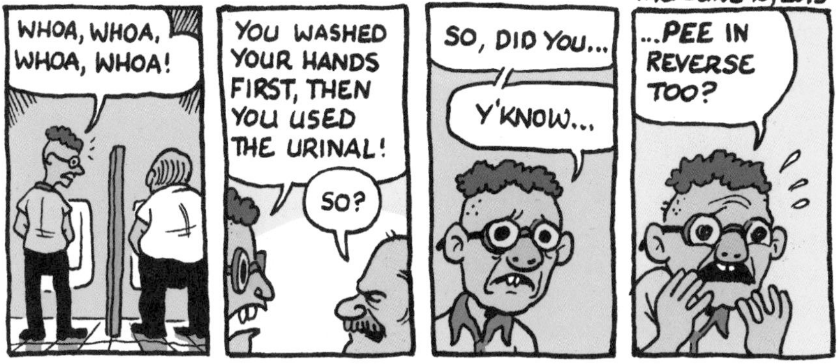
WHOA, WHOA, WHOA, WHOA!
YOU WASHED YOUR HANDS FIRST, THEN YOU USED THE URINAL!
SO?
SO, DID YOU...
Y'KNOW...
...PEE IN REVERSE TOO?

FRI JUNE 14, 2013

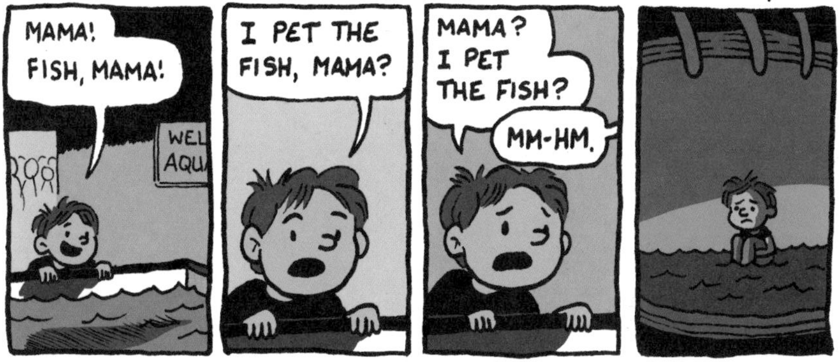
MAMA! FISH, MAMA!
WEL
AQU
I PET THE FISH, MAMA?
MAMA? I PET THE FISH?
MM-HM.

SAT JUNE 15, 2013

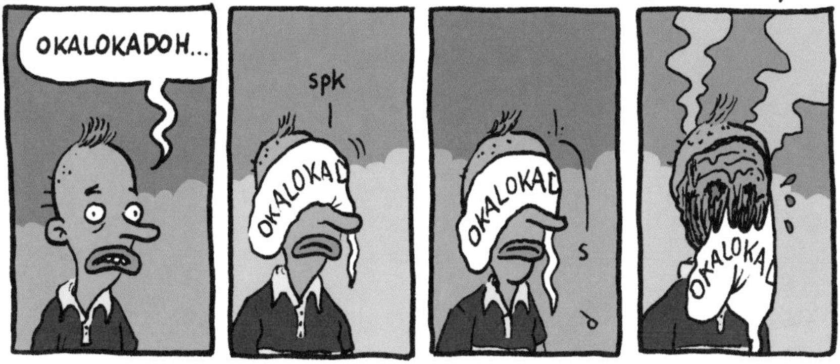
OKALOKADOH...
spk
OKALOKAD
OKALOKAD
OKALOKAD

SUN JUNE 16, 2013

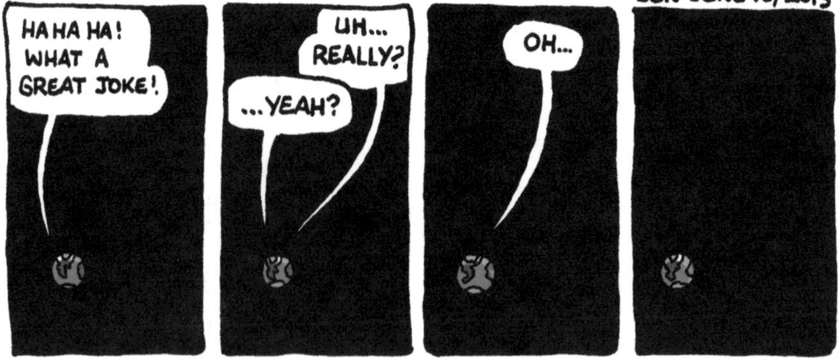
HA HA HA! WHAT A GREAT JOKE!
UH... REALLY?
...YEAH?
OH...

MON JUNE 17, 2013

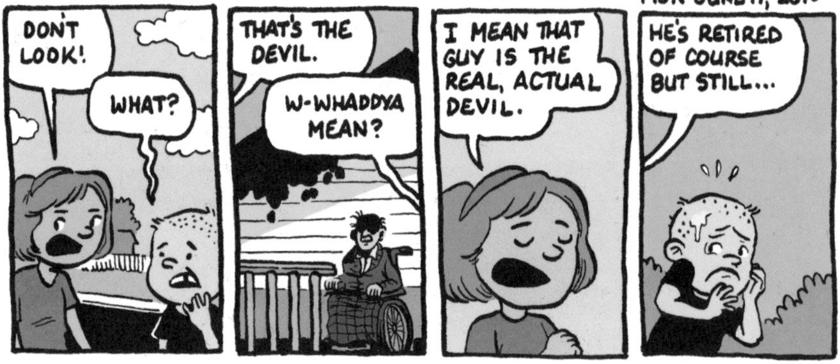
DON'T LOOK!
WHAT?
THAT'S THE DEVIL.
W-WHADDYA MEAN?
I MEAN THAT GUY IS THE REAL, ACTUAL DEVIL.
HE'S RETIRED OF COURSE BUT STILL...

TUE JUNE 18, 2013

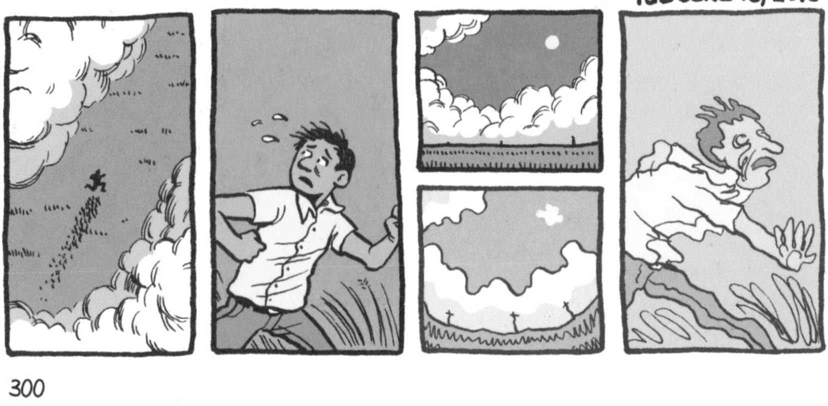

WED JUNE 19, 2013

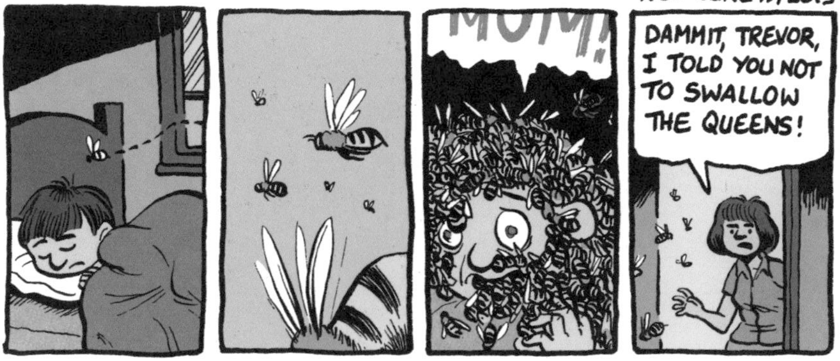
MOM!
DAMMIT, TREVOR, I TOLD YOU NOT TO SWALLOW THE QUEENS!

THU JUNE 20, 2013

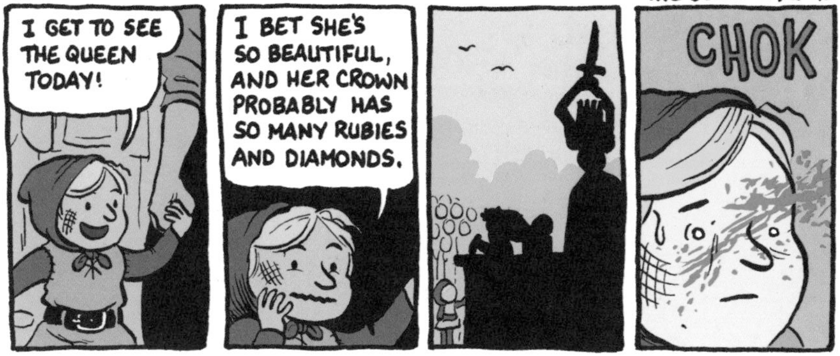
I GET TO SEE THE QUEEN TODAY!
I BET SHE'S SO BEAUTIFUL, AND HER CROWN PROBABLY HAS SO MANY RUBIES AND DIAMONDS.
CHOK

FRI JUNE 21, 2013

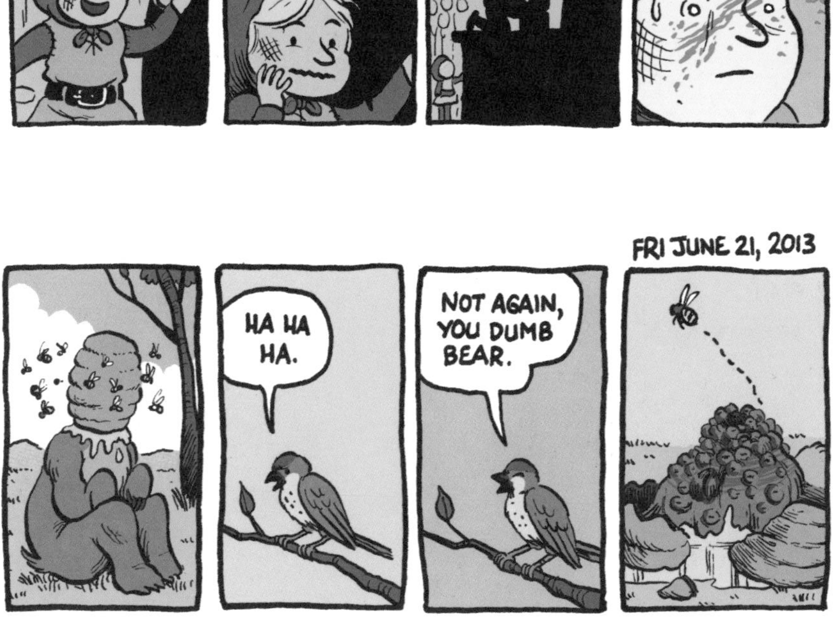
HA HA HA.
NOT AGAIN, YOU DUMB BEAR.

SAT JUNE 22, 2013

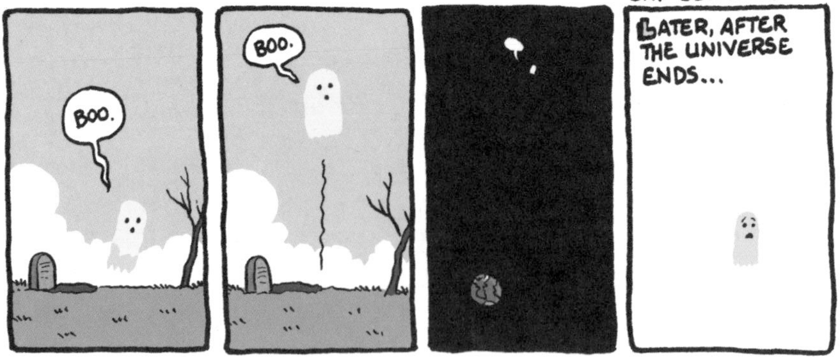
BOO.
BOO.
LATER, AFTER THE UNIVERSE ENDS...

MON JUNE 23, 2013

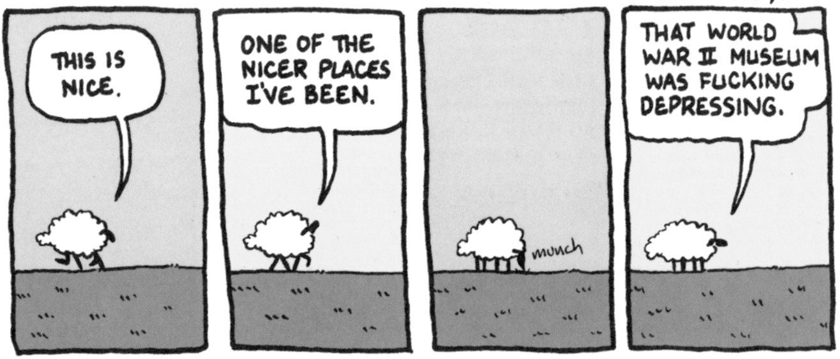
THIS IS NICE.
ONE OF THE NICER PLACES I'VE BEEN.
munch
THAT WORLD WAR II MUSEUM WAS FUCKING DEPRESSING.

MON, JUNE 24, 2013

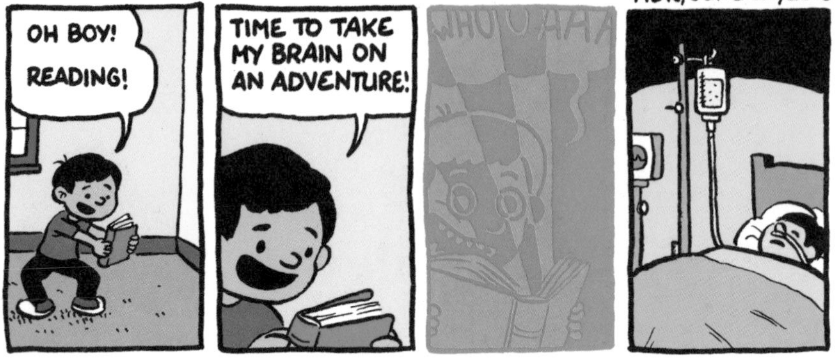
OH BOY! READING!
TIME TO TAKE MY BRAIN ON AN ADVENTURE!

TUE JUNE 25, 2013

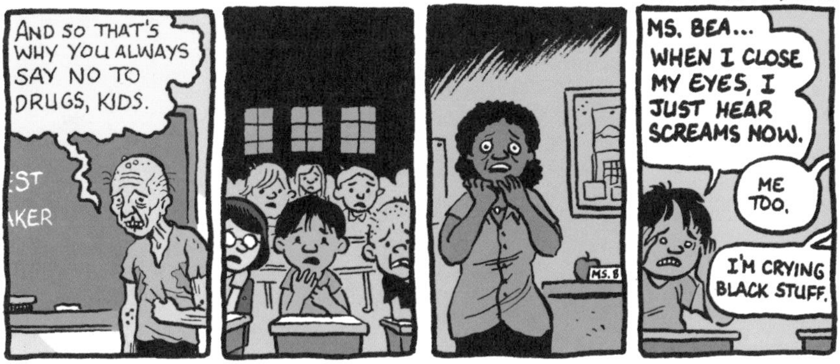
AND SO THAT'S WHY YOU ALWAYS SAY NO TO DRUGS, KIDS.
MS. BEA...
WHEN I CLOSE MY EYES, I JUST HEAR SCREAMS NOW.
ME TOO.
I'M CRYING BLACK STUFF.

WED JUNE 26, 2013

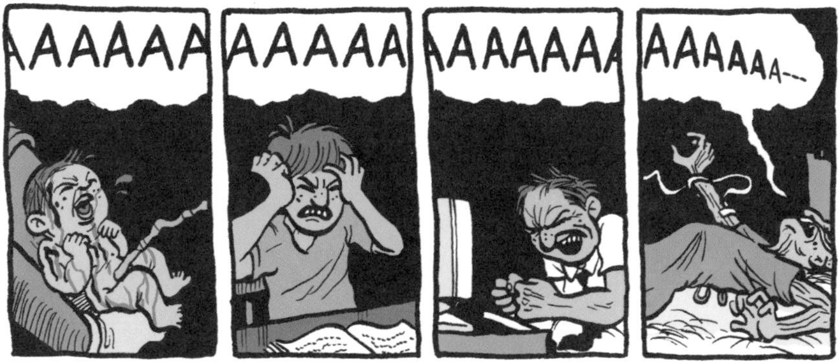
AAAAAA
AAAAAA
AAAAAAA
AAAAAA---

THU JUNE 27, 2013

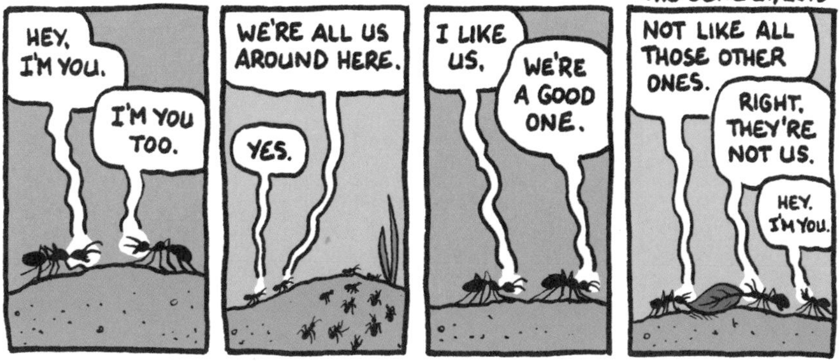
HEY, I'M YOU.
I'M YOU TOO.
WE'RE ALL US AROUND HERE.
YES.
I LIKE US.
WE'RE A GOOD ONE.
NOT LIKE ALL THOSE OTHER ONES.
RIGHT. THEY'RE NOT US.
HEY. I'M YOU.

FRI JUNE 28, 2013

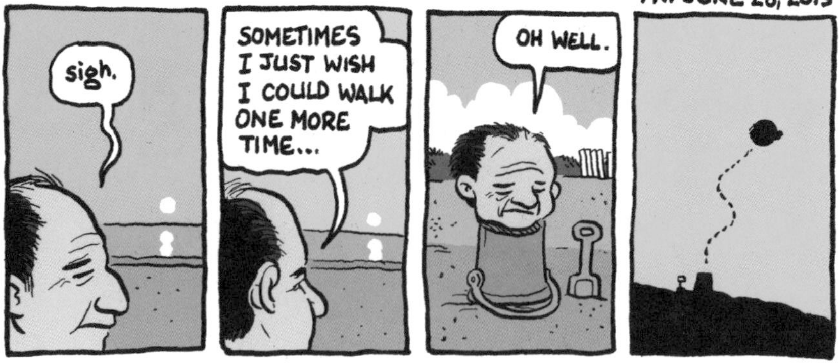
sigh.
SOMETIMES I JUST WISH I COULD WALK ONE MORE TIME...
OH WELL.

SAT JUNE 29, 2013

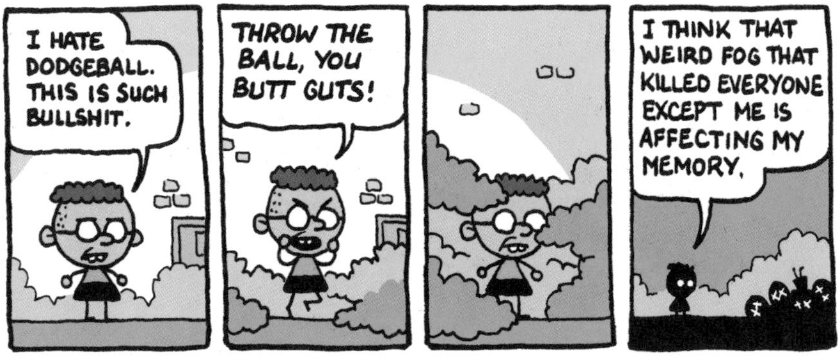
I HATE DODGEBALL. THIS IS SUCH BULLSHIT.
THROW THE BALL, YOU BUTT GUTS!
I THINK THAT WEIRD FOG THAT KILLED EVERYONE EXCEPT ME IS AFFECTING MY MEMORY.

SUN JUNE 30, 2013

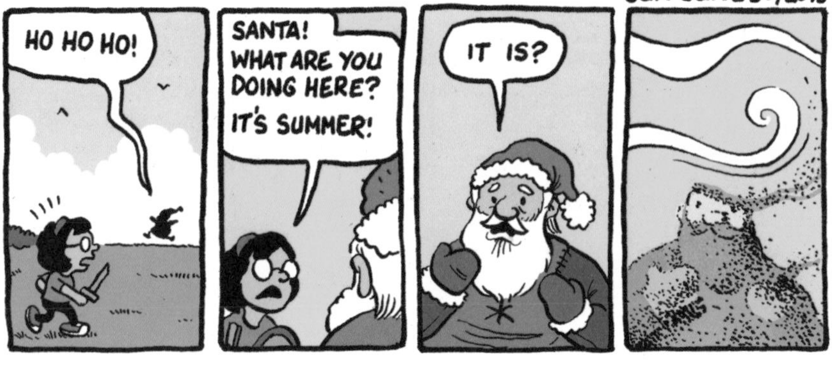
HO HO HO!
SANTA! WHAT ARE YOU DOING HERE? IT'S SUMMER!
IT IS?

MON JULY 1, 2013

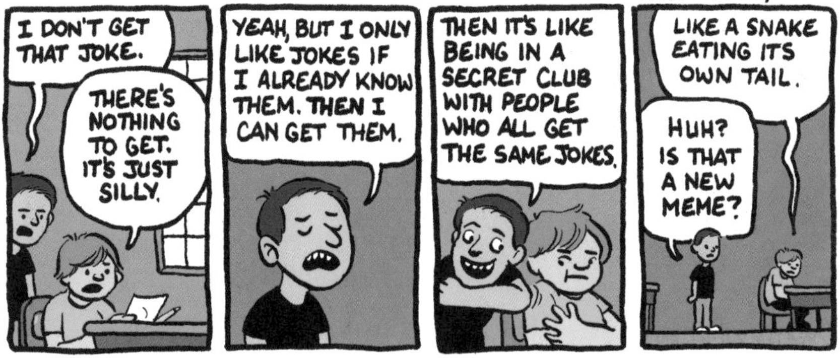
I DON'T GET THAT JOKE.
THERE'S NOTHING TO GET. IT'S JUST SILLY.
YEAH, BUT I ONLY LIKE JOKES IF I ALREADY KNOW THEM. THEN I CAN GET THEM.
THEN IT'S LIKE BEING IN A SECRET CLUB WITH PEOPLE WHO ALL GET THE SAME JOKES.
LIKE A SNAKE EATING ITS OWN TAIL.
HUH? IS THAT A NEW MEME?

TUE JULY 2, 2013

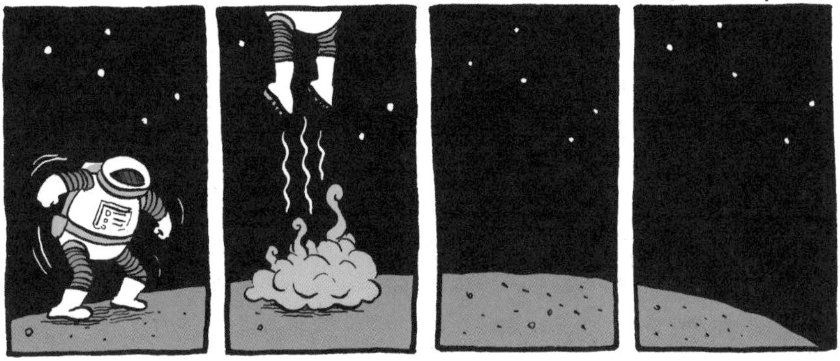

WED JULY 3, 2013

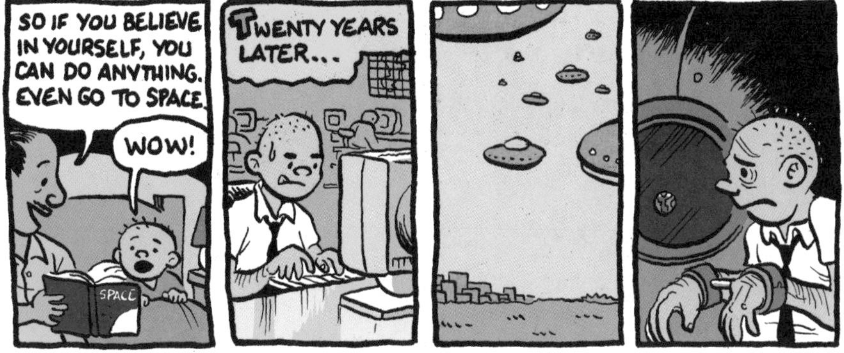
SO IF YOU BELIEVE IN YOURSELF, YOU CAN DO ANYTHING. EVEN GO TO SPACE.
WOW!
SPACE
TWENTY YEARS LATER...

THU JULY 4, 2013

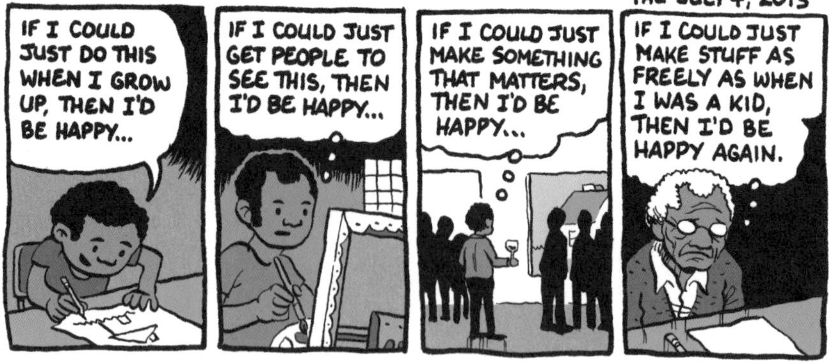
IF I COULD JUST DO THIS WHEN I GROW UP, THEN I'D BE HAPPY...
IF I COULD JUST GET PEOPLE TO SEE THIS, THEN I'D BE HAPPY...
IF I COULD JUST MAKE SOMETHING THAT MATTERS, THEN I'D BE HAPPY...
IF I COULD JUST MAKE STUFF AS FREELY AS WHEN I WAS A KID, THEN I'D BE HAPPY AGAIN.

FRI JULY 5, 2013

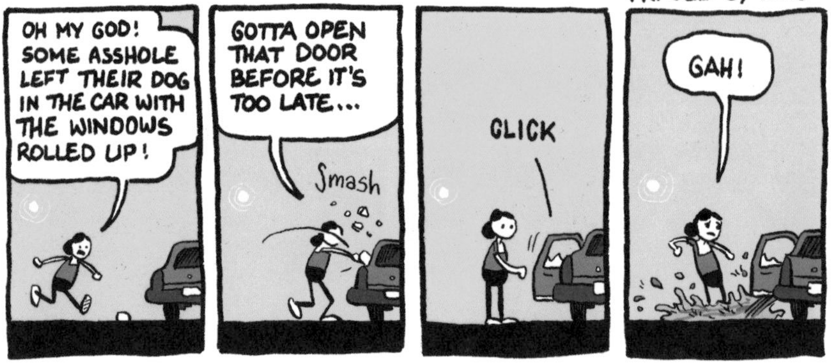
OH MY GOD! SOME ASSHOLE LEFT THEIR DOG IN THE CAR WITH THE WINDOWS ROLLED UP!
GOTTA OPEN THAT DOOR BEFORE IT'S TOO LATE...
Smash
CLICK
GAH!

SAT JULY 6, 2013

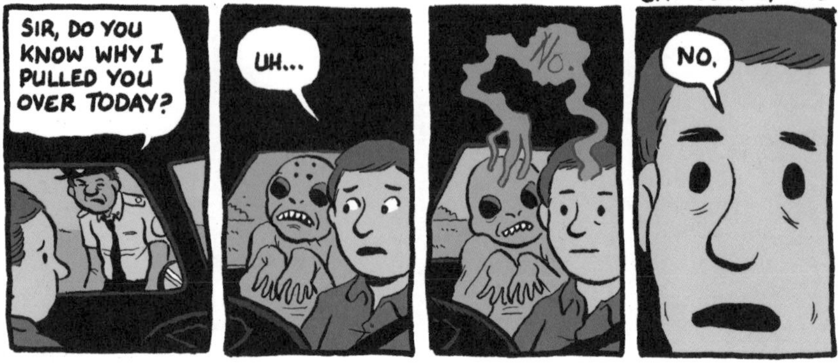
SIR, DO YOU KNOW WHY I PULLED YOU OVER TODAY?
UH...
No.
NO.

SUN JULY 7, 2013

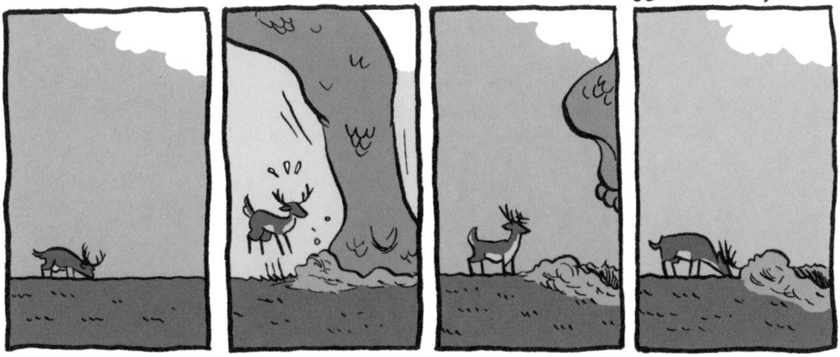

MON JULY 8, 2013

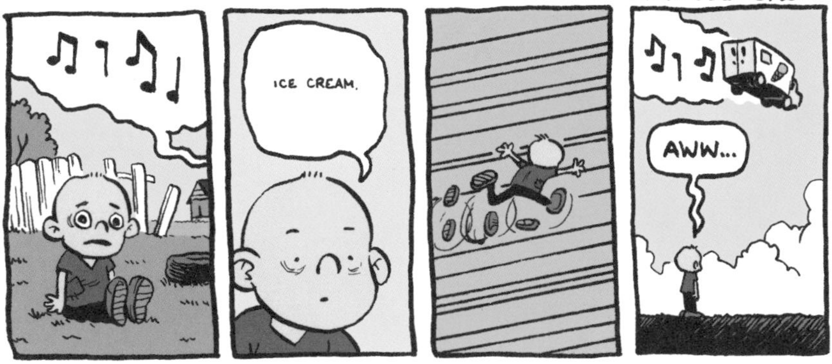
ICE CREAM.
AWW...

TUE JULY 9, 2013

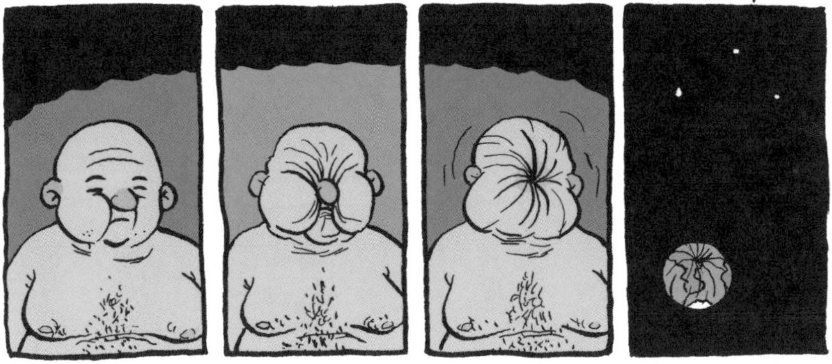

WED JULY 10, 2013

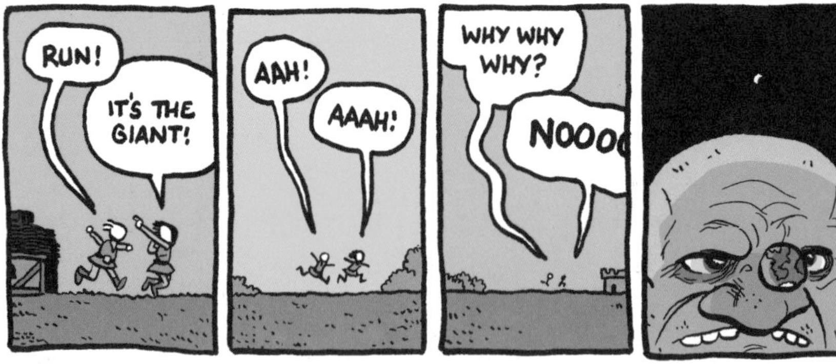
RUN!
IT'S THE GIANT!
AAH!
AAAH!
WHY WHY WHY?
NOOO

THU JULY 11, 2013

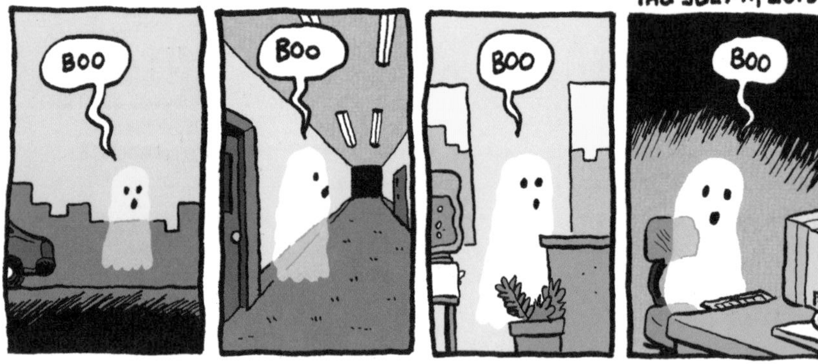
BOO
BOO
BOO
BOO

FRI JULY 12, 2013

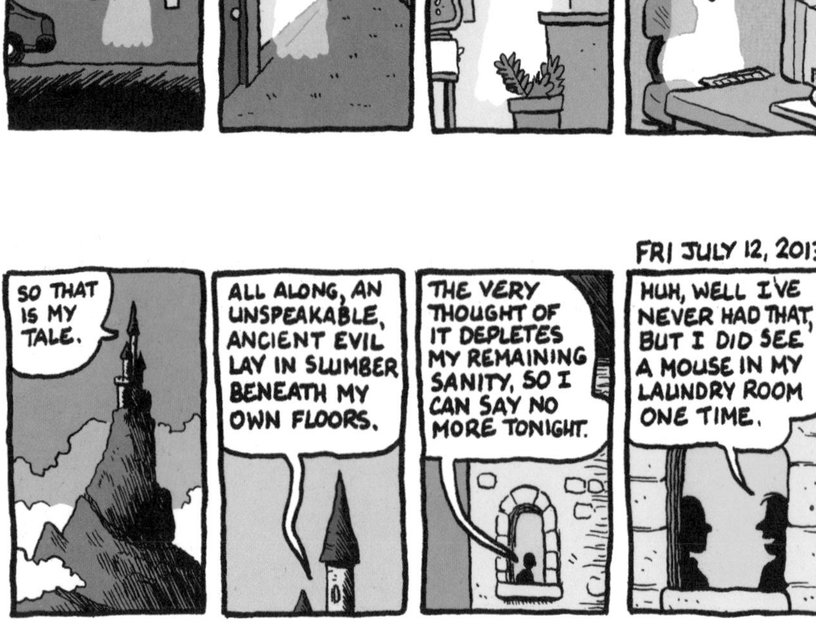
SO THAT IS MY TALE.
ALL ALONG, AN UNSPEAKABLE, ANCIENT EVIL LAY IN SLUMBER BENEATH MY OWN FLOORS.
THE VERY THOUGHT OF IT DEPLETES MY REMAINING SANITY, SO I CAN SAY NO MORE TONIGHT.
HUH, WELL I'VE NEVER HAD THAT, BUT I DID SEE A MOUSE IN MY LAUNDRY ROOM ONE TIME.

SAT JULY 13, 2013

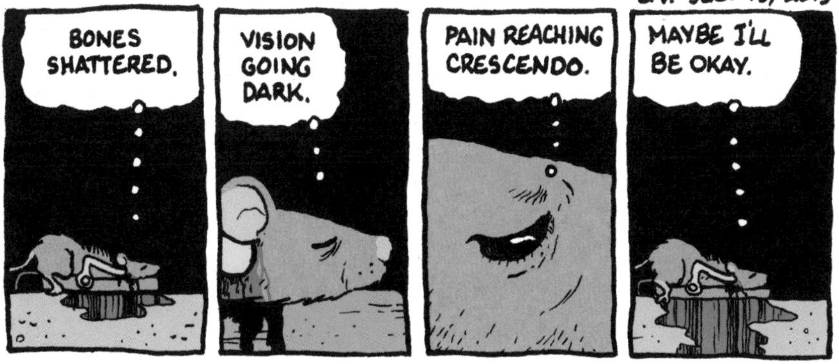

BONES SHATTERED.
VISION GOING DARK.
PAIN REACHING CRESCENDO.
MAYBE I'LL BE OKAY.

SUN JULY 14, 2013

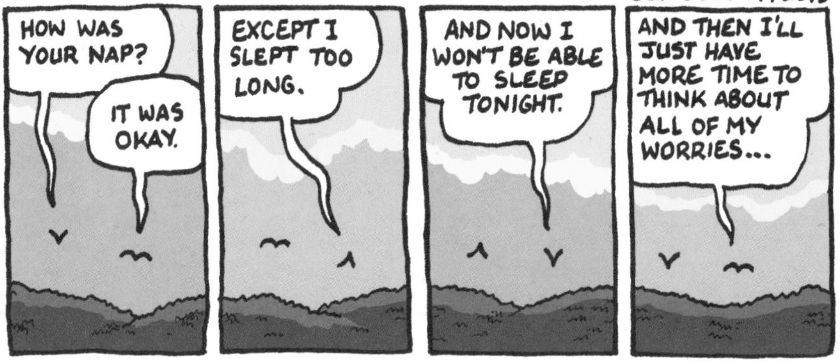

HOW WAS YOUR NAP?
IT WAS OKAY.
EXCEPT I SLEPT TOO LONG.
AND NOW I WON'T BE ABLE TO SLEEP TONIGHT.
AND THEN I'LL JUST HAVE MORE TIME TO THINK ABOUT ALL OF MY WORRIES...

MON JULY 15, 2013

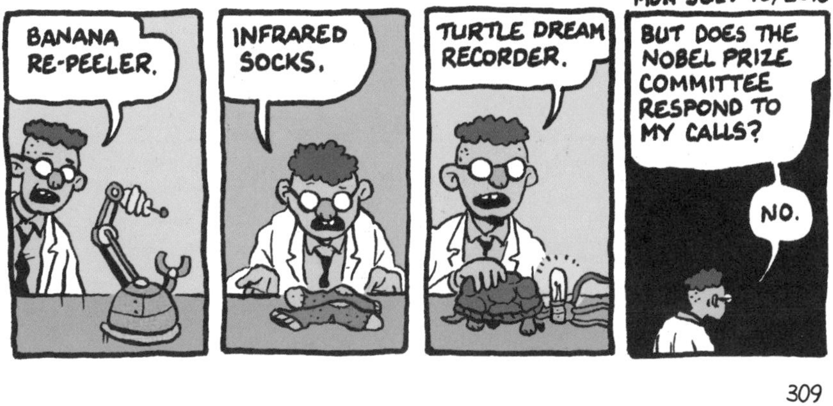

BANANA RE-PEELER.
INFRARED SOCKS.
TURTLE DREAM RECORDER.
BUT DOES THE NOBEL PRIZE COMMITTEE RESPOND TO MY CALLS?
NO.

TUE JULY 16, 2013

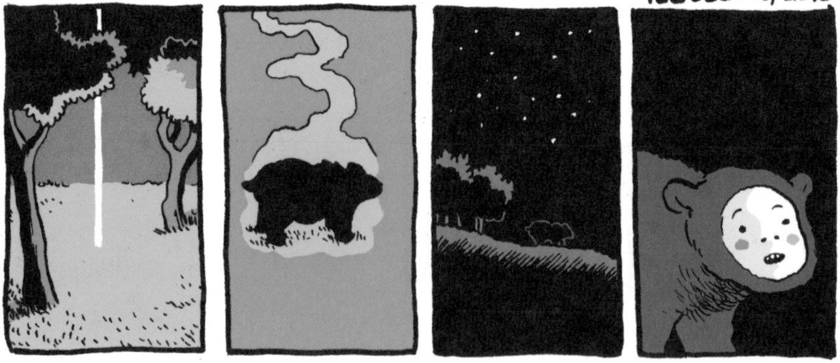

WED JULY 17, 2013

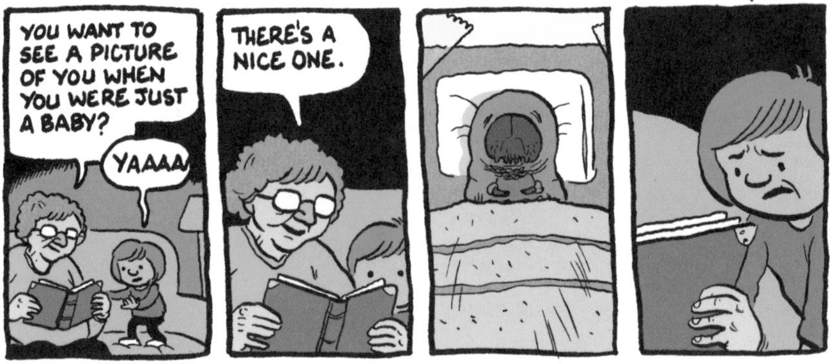
YOU WANT TO SEE A PICTURE OF YOU WHEN YOU WERE JUST A BABY?
YAAAA
THERE'S A NICE ONE.

THU JULY 18, 2013

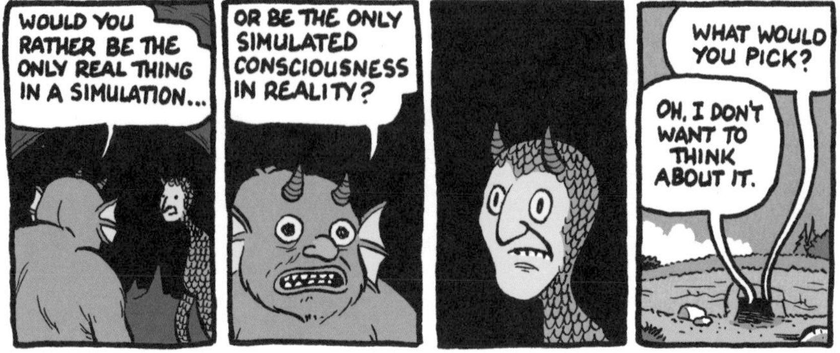
WOULD YOU RATHER BE THE ONLY REAL THING IN A SIMULATION...
OR BE THE ONLY SIMULATED CONSCIOUSNESS IN REALITY?
WHAT WOULD YOU PICK?
OH, I DON'T WANT TO THINK ABOUT IT.

FRI JULY 19, 2013

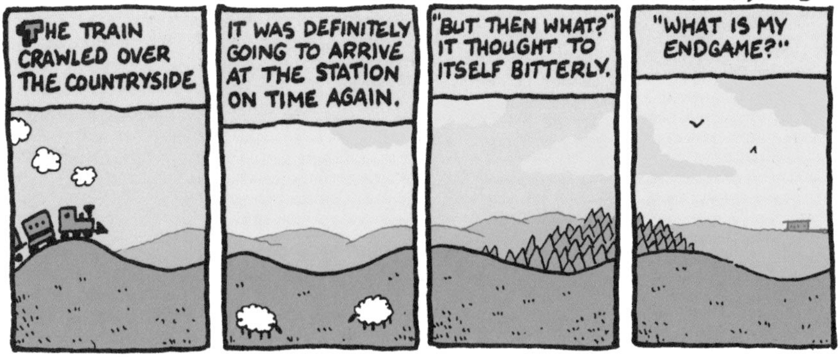
THE TRAIN CRAWLED OVER THE COUNTRYSIDE
IT WAS DEFINITELY GOING TO ARRIVE AT THE STATION ON TIME AGAIN.
"BUT THEN WHAT?" IT THOUGHT TO ITSELF BITTERLY.
"WHAT IS MY ENDGAME?"

SAT JULY 20, 2013

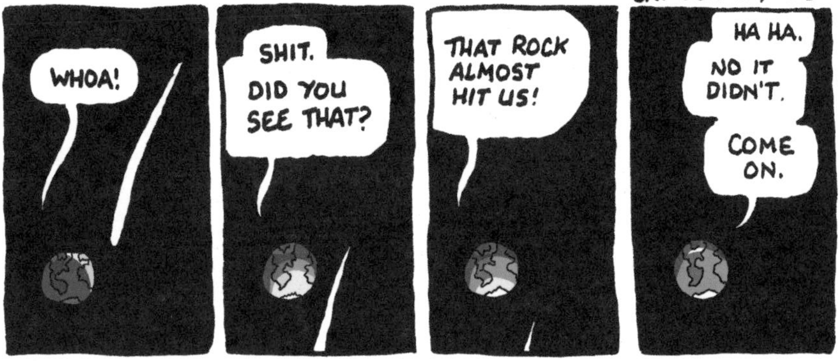
WHOA!
SHIT.
DID YOU SEE THAT?
THAT ROCK ALMOST HIT US!
HA HA.
NO IT DIDN'T.
COME ON.

SUN JULY 21, 2013

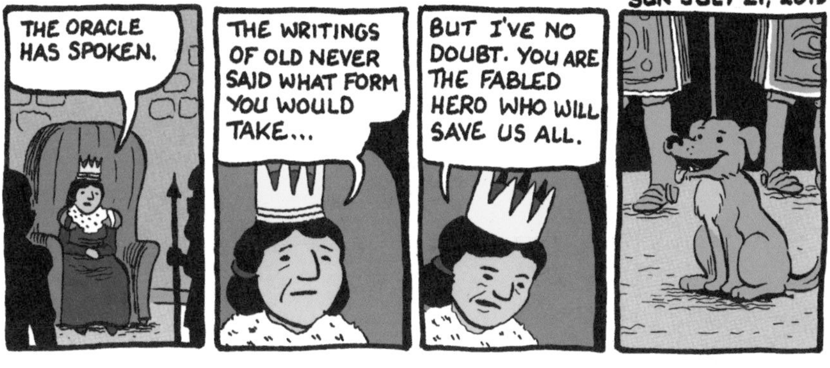
THE ORACLE HAS SPOKEN.
THE WRITINGS OF OLD NEVER SAID WHAT FORM YOU WOULD TAKE...
BUT I'VE NO DOUBT. YOU ARE THE FABLED HERO WHO WILL SAVE US ALL.

MON JULY 22, 2013

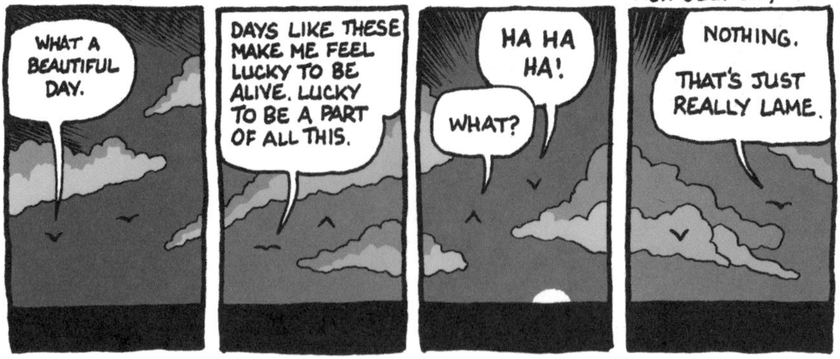
WHAT A BEAUTIFUL DAY.
DAYS LIKE THESE MAKE ME FEEL LUCKY TO BE ALIVE. LUCKY TO BE A PART OF ALL THIS.
HA HA HA!
WHAT?
NOTHING.
THAT'S JUST REALLY LAME.

TUE JULY 23, 2013

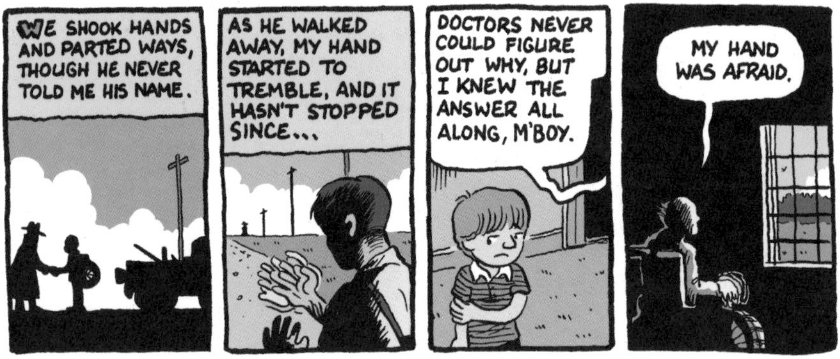
WE SHOOK HANDS AND PARTED WAYS, THOUGH HE NEVER TOLD ME HIS NAME.
AS HE WALKED AWAY, MY HAND STARTED TO TREMBLE, AND IT HASN'T STOPPED SINCE...
DOCTORS NEVER COULD FIGURE OUT WHY, BUT I KNEW THE ANSWER ALL ALONG, M'BOY.
MY HAND WAS AFRAID.

WED JULY 24, 2013

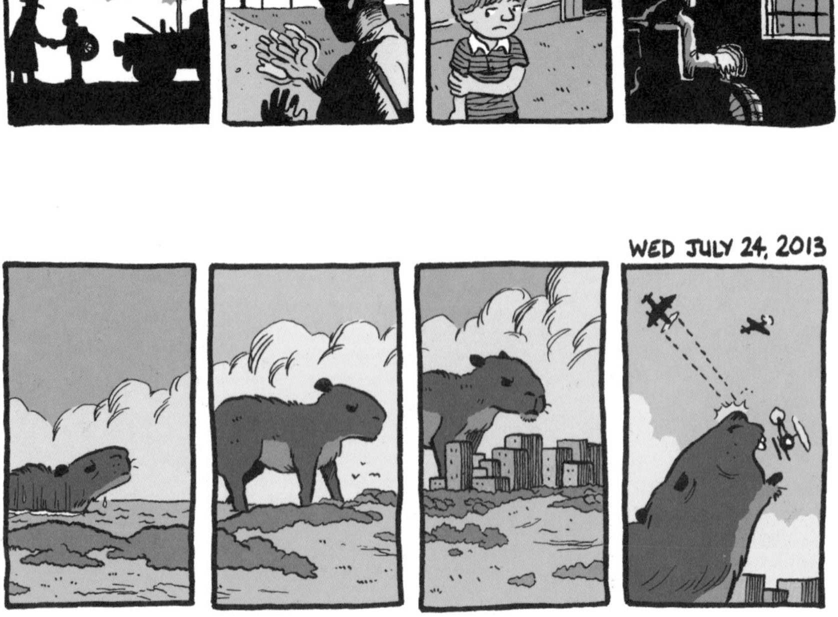

THU JULY 25, 2013

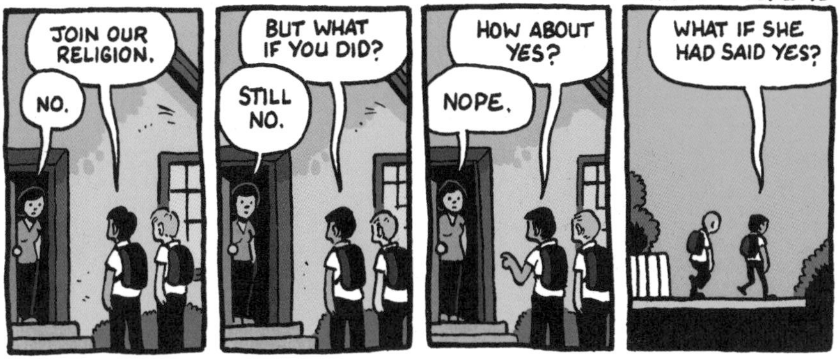
JOIN OUR RELIGION.
NO.
BUT WHAT IF YOU DID?
STILL NO.
HOW ABOUT YES?
NOPE.
WHAT IF SHE HAD SAID YES?

FRI JULY 26, 2013

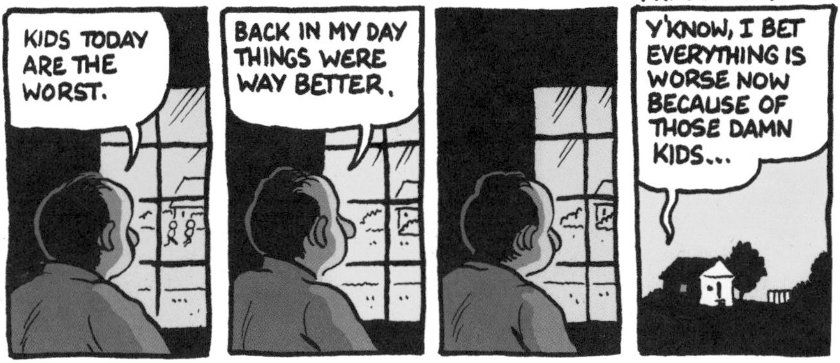
KIDS TODAY ARE THE WORST.
BACK IN MY DAY THINGS WERE WAY BETTER.
Y'KNOW, I BET EVERYTHING IS WORSE NOW BECAUSE OF THOSE DAMN KIDS...

SAT JULY 27, 2013

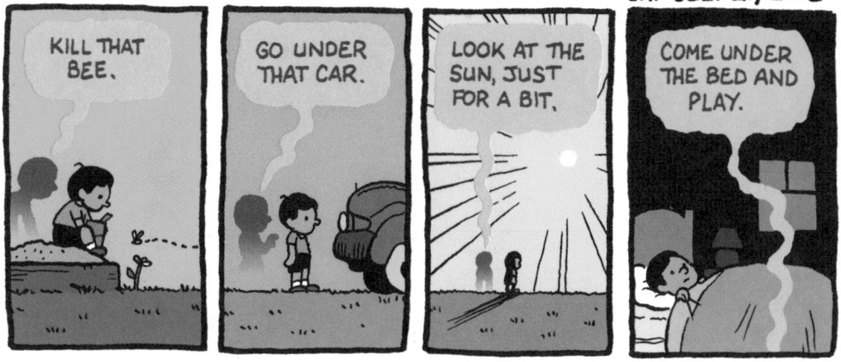
KILL THAT BEE.
GO UNDER THAT CAR.
LOOK AT THE SUN, JUST FOR A BIT.
COME UNDER THE BED AND PLAY.

SUN JULY 28, 2013

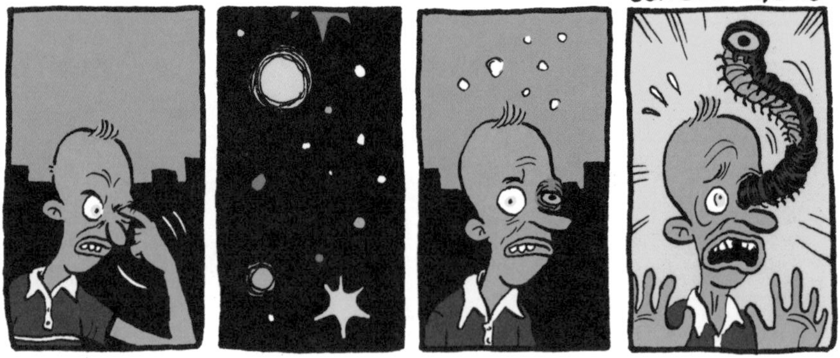

MON JULY 29, 2013

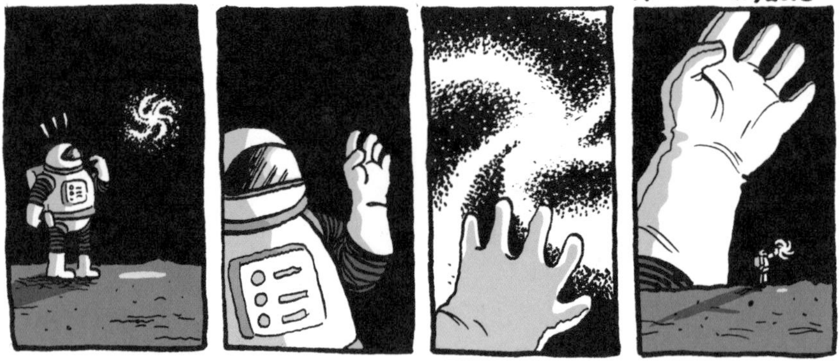

TUE JULY 30, 2013

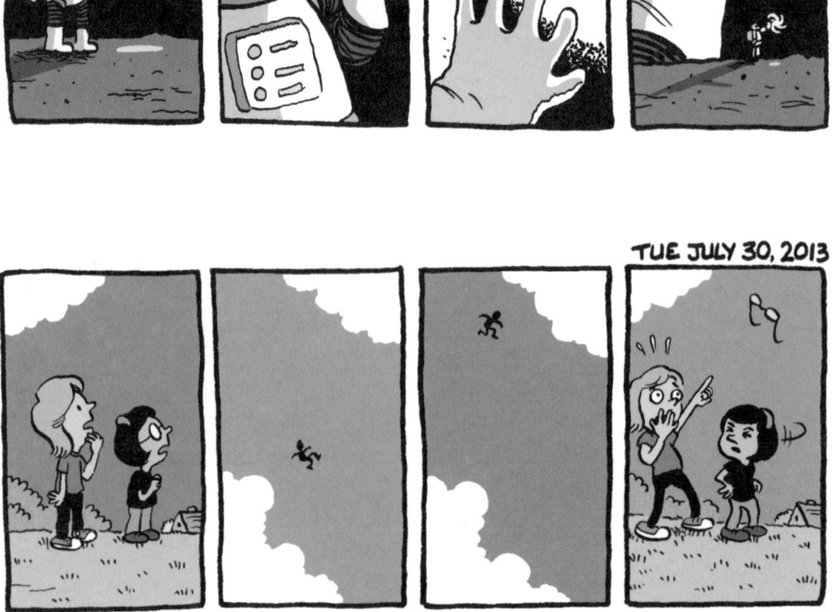

WED JULY 31, 2013

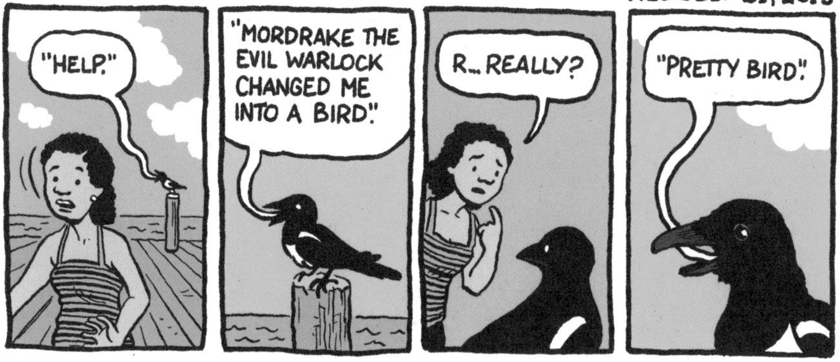
"HELP."
"MORDRAKE THE EVIL WARLOCK CHANGED ME INTO A BIRD."
R... REALLY?
"PRETTY BIRD."

THU AUG 1, 2013

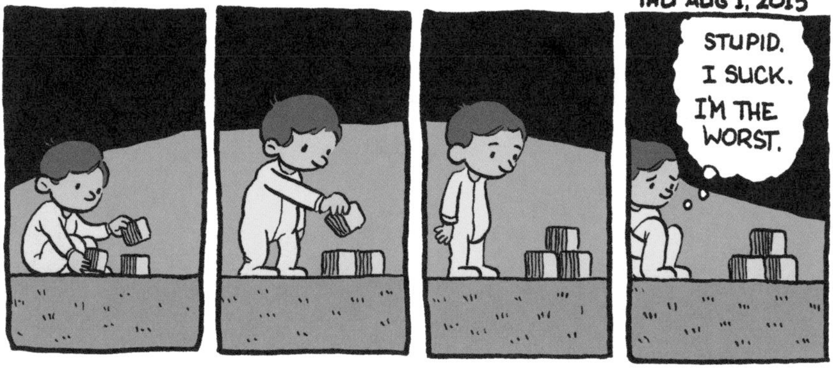
STUPID.
I SUCK.
I'M THE WORST.

FRI AUG 2, 2013

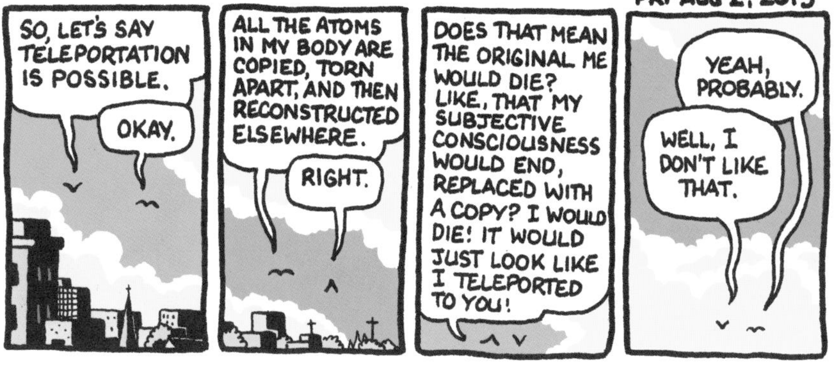
SO, LET'S SAY TELEPORTATION IS POSSIBLE.
OKAY.
ALL THE ATOMS IN MY BODY ARE COPIED, TORN APART, AND THEN RECONSTRUCTED ELSEWHERE.
RIGHT.
DOES THAT MEAN THE ORIGINAL ME WOULD DIE? LIKE, THAT MY SUBJECTIVE CONSCIOUSNESS WOULD END, REPLACED WITH A COPY? I WOULD DIE! IT WOULD JUST LOOK LIKE I TELEPORTED TO YOU!
YEAH, PROBABLY.
WELL, I DON'T LIKE THAT.

SAT AUG 3, 2013

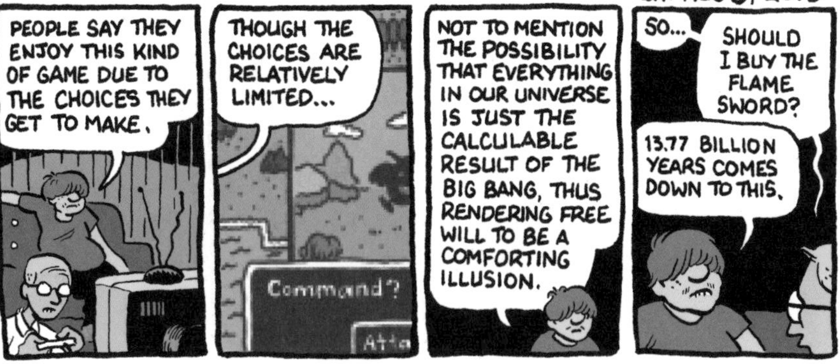
PEOPLE SAY THEY ENJOY THIS KIND OF GAME DUE TO THE CHOICES THEY GET TO MAKE.
THOUGH THE CHOICES ARE RELATIVELY LIMITED...
Command?
NOT TO MENTION THE POSSIBILITY THAT EVERYTHING IN OUR UNIVERSE IS JUST THE CALCULABLE RESULT OF THE BIG BANG, THUS RENDERING FREE WILL TO BE A COMFORTING ILLUSION.
SO...
SHOULD I BUY THE FLAME SWORD?
13.77 BILLION YEARS COMES DOWN TO THIS.

SUN AUG, 4, 2013

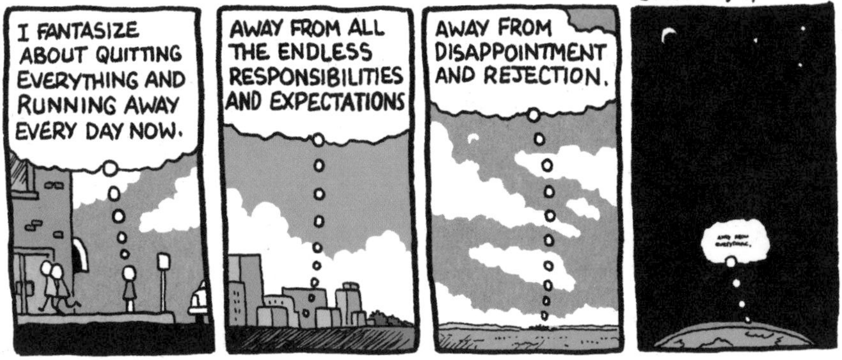
I FANTASIZE ABOUT QUITTING EVERYTHING AND RUNNING AWAY EVERY DAY NOW.
AWAY FROM ALL THE ENDLESS RESPONSIBILITIES AND EXPECTATIONS
AWAY FROM DISAPPOINTMENT AND REJECTION.

MON AUG 5, 2013

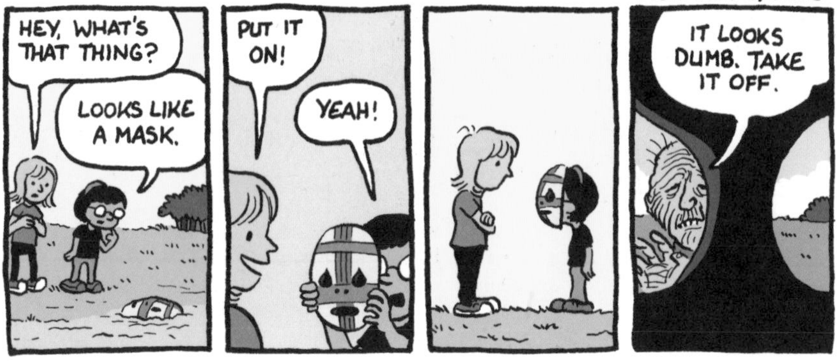
HEY, WHAT'S THAT THING?
LOOKS LIKE A MASK.
PUT IT ON!
YEAH!
IT LOOKS DUMB. TAKE IT OFF.

TUE AUG 6, 2013

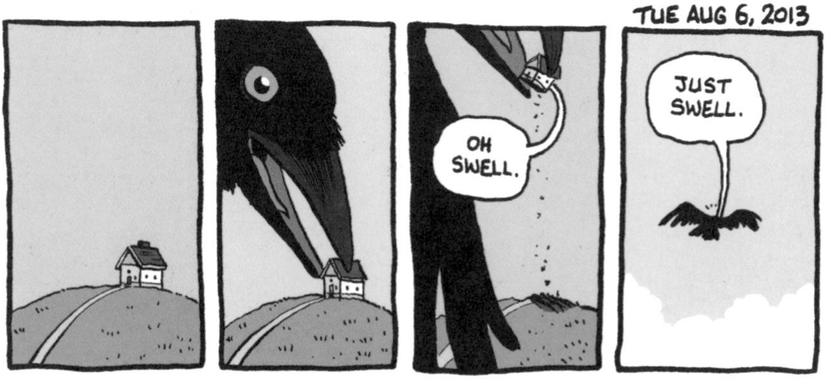
OH SWELL.
JUST SWELL.

WED AUG 7, 2013

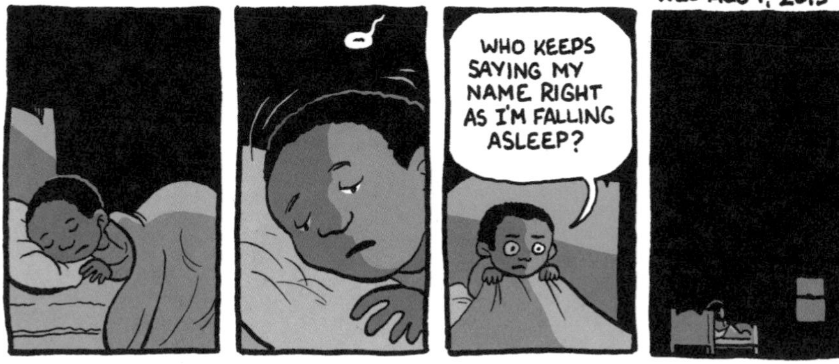
WHO KEEPS SAYING MY NAME RIGHT AS I'M FALLING ASLEEP?

THU AUG 8, 2013

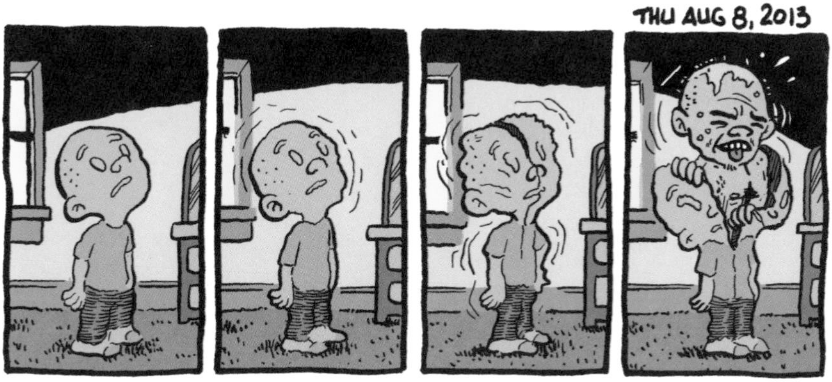

FRI AUG, 9, 2013

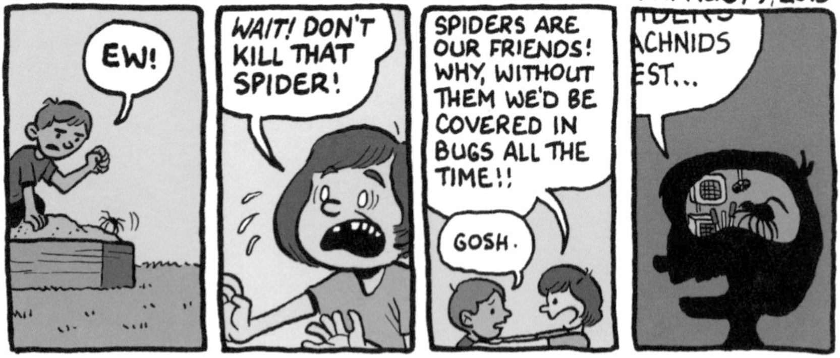
EW!
WAIT! DON'T KILL THAT SPIDER!
SPIDERS ARE OUR FRIENDS! WHY, WITHOUT THEM WE'D BE COVERED IN BUGS ALL THE TIME!!
GOSH.
ACHNIDS
EST...

SAT AUG 10, 2013

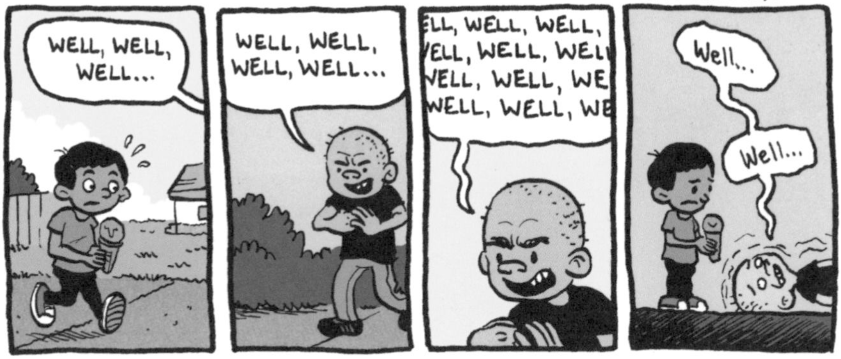
WELL, WELL, WELL...
WELL, WELL, WELL, WELL...
LL, WELL, WELL,
ELL, WELL, WEL
VELL, WELL, WE
WELL, WELL, WE
Well...
Well...

SUN AUG 11, 2013

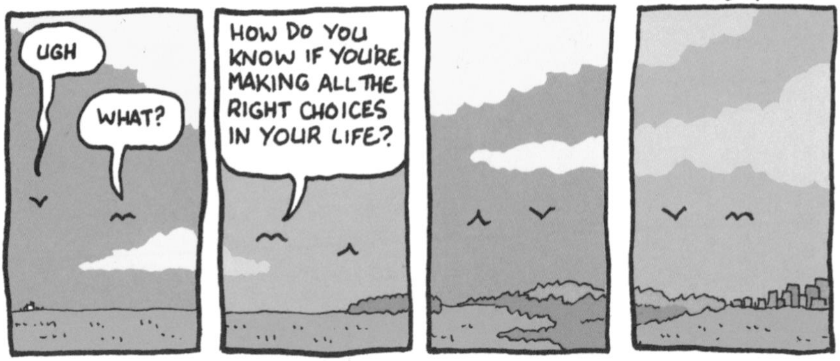
UGH
WHAT?
HOW DO YOU KNOW IF YOU'RE MAKING ALL THE RIGHT CHOICES IN YOUR LIFE?

MON AUG 12, 2013

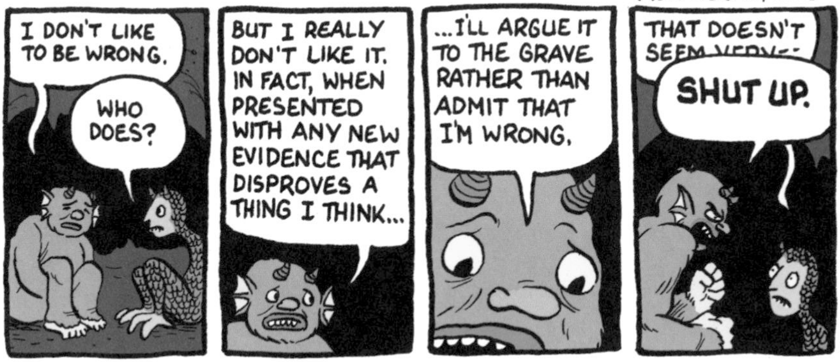
I DON'T LIKE TO BE WRONG.
WHO DOES?
BUT I REALLY DON'T LIKE IT. IN FACT, WHEN PRESENTED WITH ANY NEW EVIDENCE THAT DISPROVES A THING I THINK...
...I'LL ARGUE IT TO THE GRAVE RATHER THAN ADMIT THAT I'M WRONG.
THAT DOESN'T
SHUT UP.

TUE AUG 13, 2013

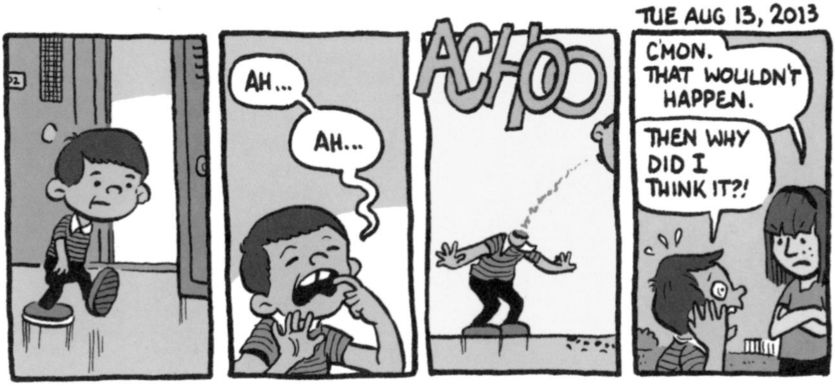
AH...
AH...
ACHOO
C'MON. THAT WOULDN'T HAPPEN.
THEN WHY DID I THINK IT?!

WED AUG 14, 2013

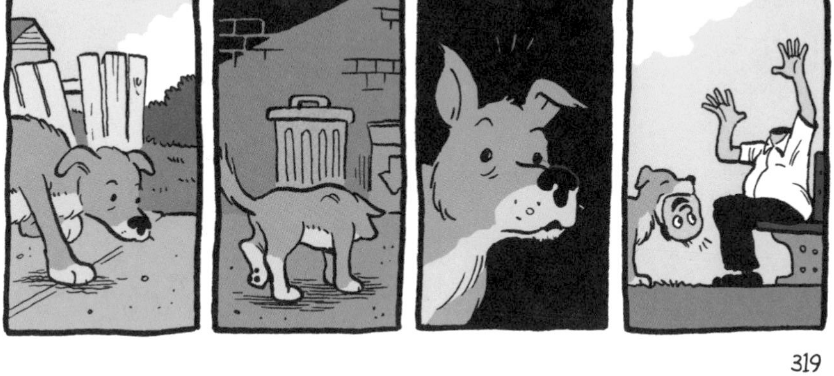

THU AUG 15, 2013

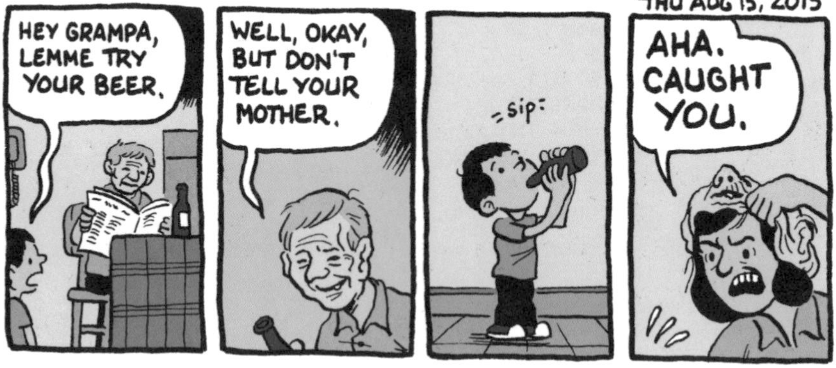
HEY GRAMPA, LEMME TRY YOUR BEER.
WELL, OKAY, BUT DON'T TELL YOUR MOTHER.
=sip=
AHA. CAUGHT YOU.

FRI AUG 16, 2013

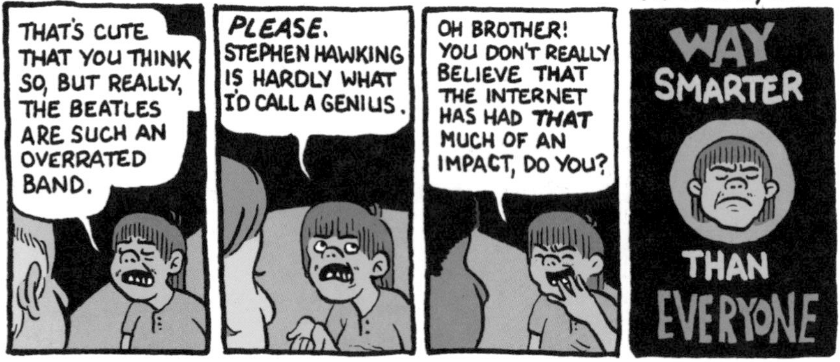
THAT'S CUTE THAT YOU THINK SO, BUT REALLY, THE BEATLES ARE SUCH AN OVERRATED BAND.
PLEASE. STEPHEN HAWKING IS HARDLY WHAT I'D CALL A GENIUS.
OH BROTHER! YOU DON'T REALLY BELIEVE THAT THE INTERNET HAS HAD *THAT* MUCH OF AN IMPACT, DO YOU?
WAY SMARTER
THAN EVERYONE

SAT AUG 17, 2013

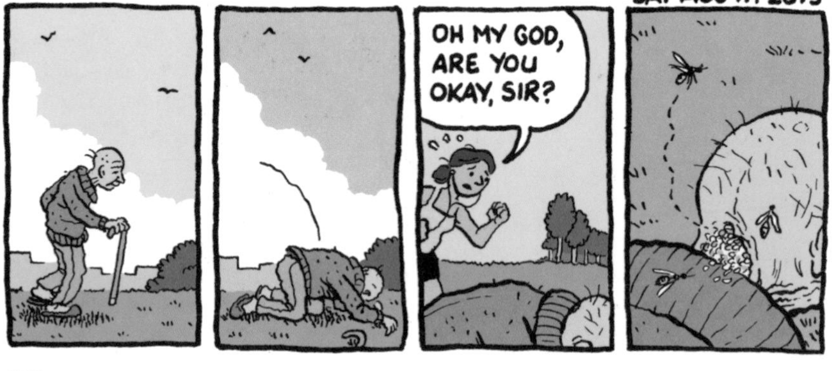
OH MY GOD, ARE YOU OKAY, SIR?

SUN AUG 18, 2013

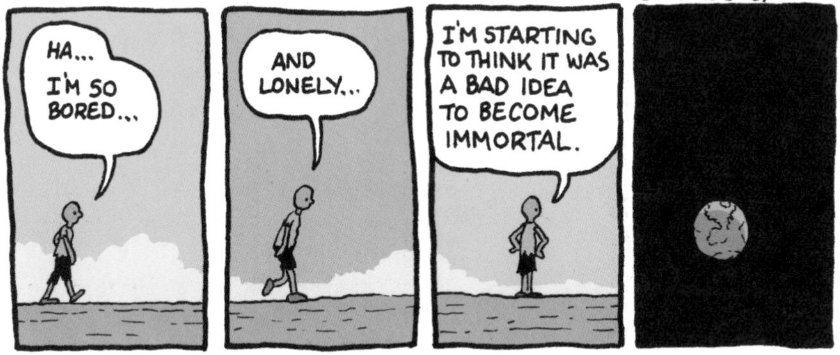
HA...
I'M SO BORED...
AND LONELY...
I'M STARTING TO THINK IT WAS A BAD IDEA TO BECOME IMMORTAL.

MON AUG 19, 2013

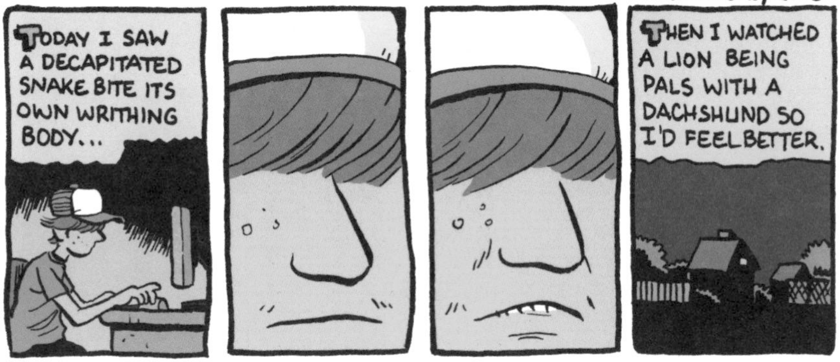
TODAY I SAW A DECAPITATED SNAKE BITE ITS OWN WRITHING BODY...
THEN I WATCHED A LION BEING PALS WITH A DACHSHUND SO I'D FEEL BETTER.

TUE AUG 20, 2013

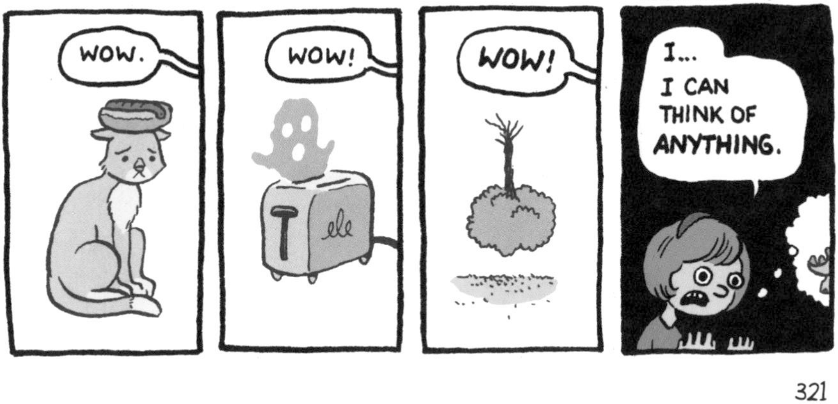
WOW.
WOW!
WOW!
I...
I CAN THINK OF ANYTHING.

WED AUG 21, 2013

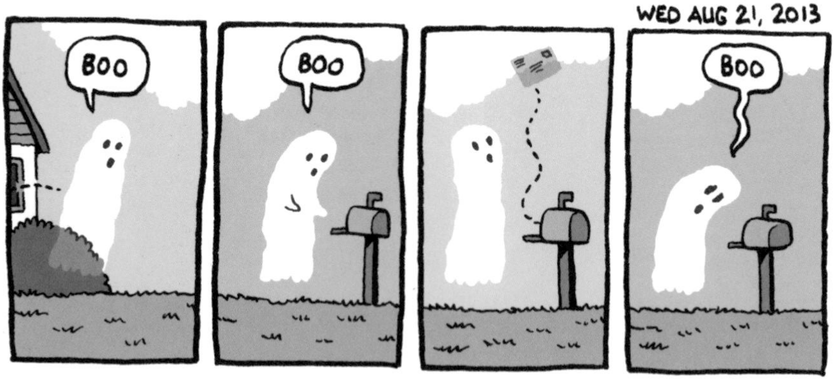
BOO
BOO
BOO

THU AUG, 22, 2013

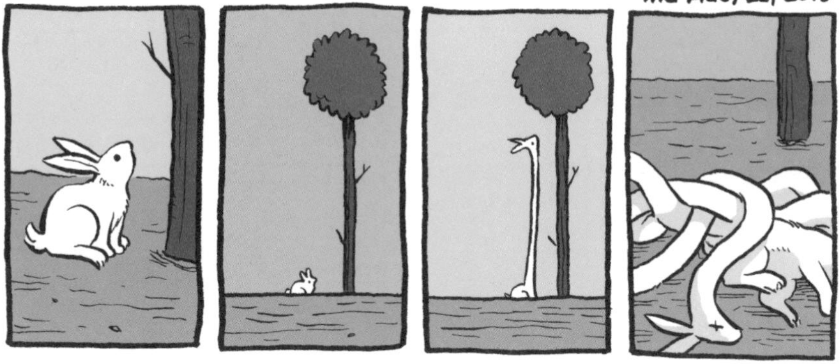

FRI AUG 23, 2013

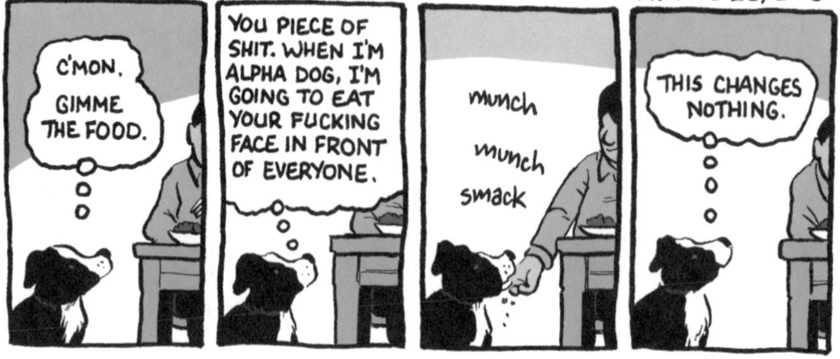
C'MON. GIMME THE FOOD.
YOU PIECE OF SHIT. WHEN I'M ALPHA DOG, I'M GOING TO EAT YOUR FUCKING FACE IN FRONT OF EVERYONE.
munch
munch
smack
THIS CHANGES NOTHING.

SAT AUG 24, 2013

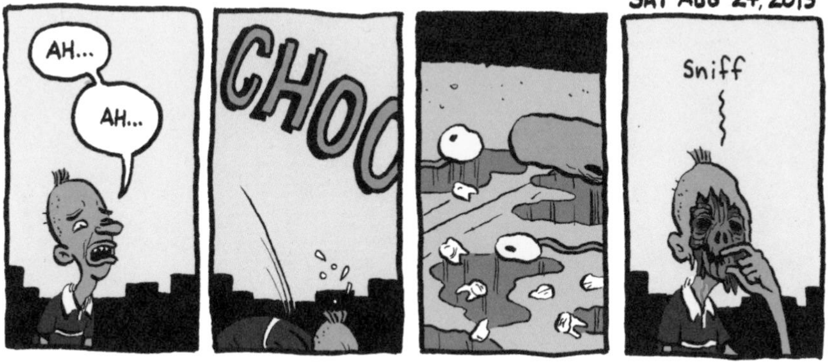
AH...
AH...
CHOO
Sniff

SUN AUG 25, 2013

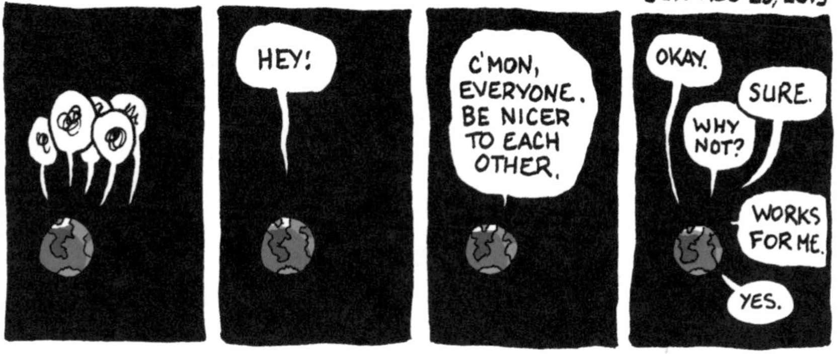
HEY!
C'MON, EVERYONE. BE NICER TO EACH OTHER.
OKAY.
SURE.
WHY NOT?
WORKS FOR ME.
YES.

MON AUG 26, 2013

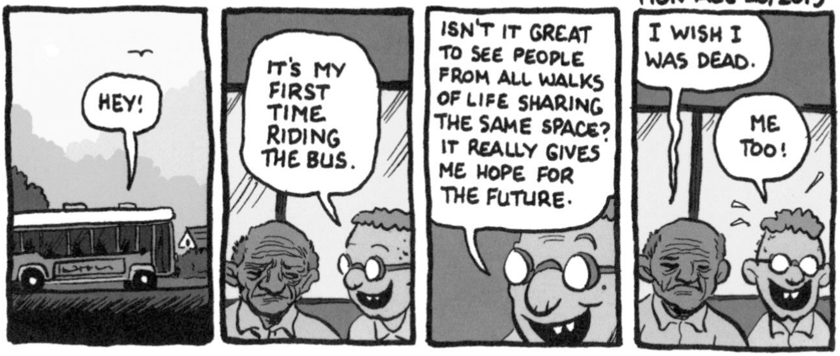
HEY!
IT'S MY FIRST TIME RIDING THE BUS.
ISN'T IT GREAT TO SEE PEOPLE FROM ALL WALKS OF LIFE SHARING THE SAME SPACE? IT REALLY GIVES ME HOPE FOR THE FUTURE.
I WISH I WAS DEAD.
ME TOO!

TUE AUG 27, 2013

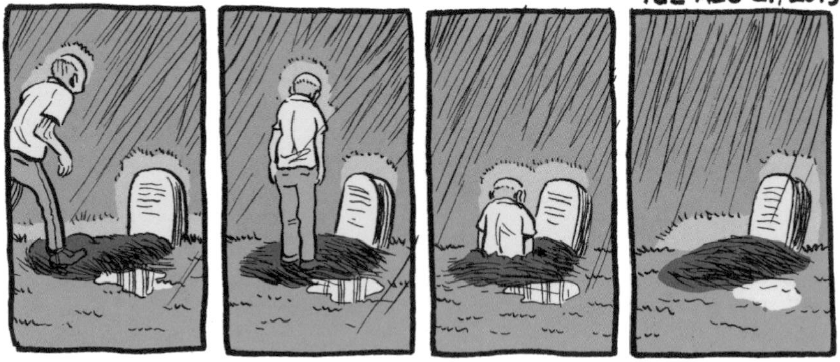

WED AUG 28, 2013

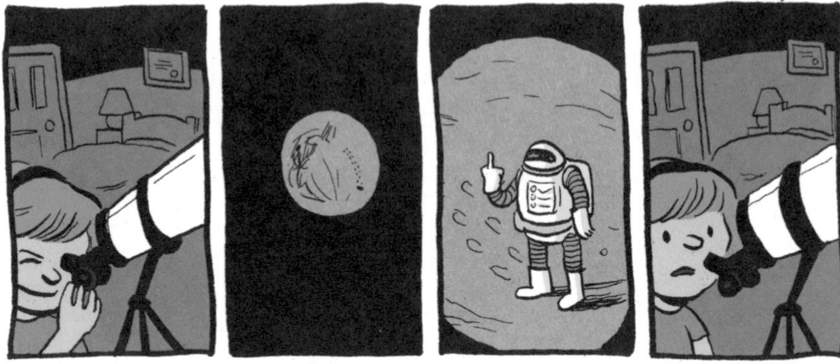

THU AUG 29, 2013

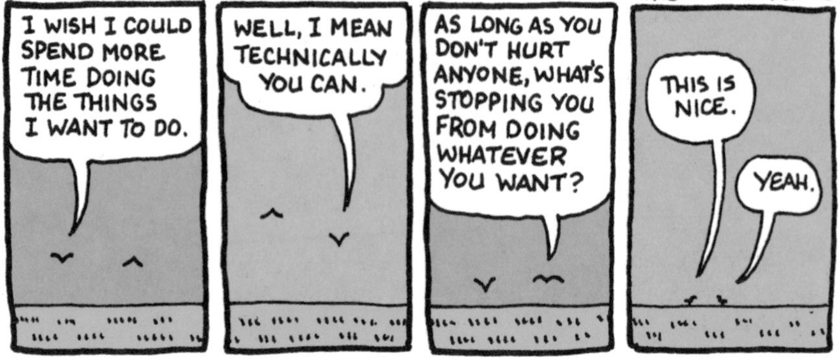
I WISH I COULD SPEND MORE TIME DOING THE THINGS I WANT TO DO.
WELL, I MEAN TECHNICALLY YOU CAN.
AS LONG AS YOU DON'T HURT ANYONE, WHAT'S STOPPING YOU FROM DOING WHATEVER YOU WANT?
THIS IS NICE.
YEAH.

FRI AUG 30, 2013

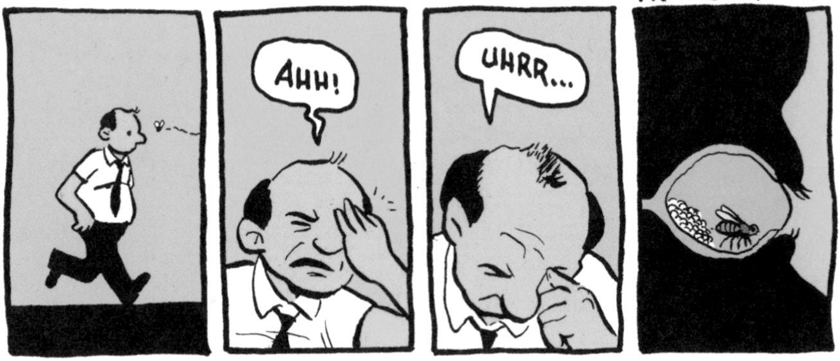
AHH!
UHRR...

SAT AUG 31, 2013

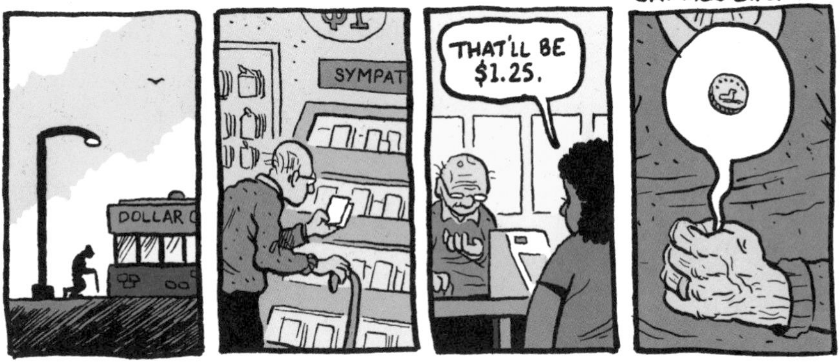
DOLLAR
SYMPAT
THAT'LL BE $1.25.

SUN SEPT 1, 2013

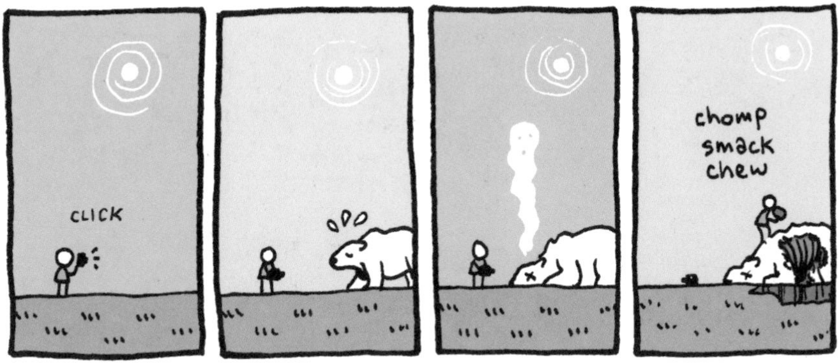
CLICK
chomp
smack
chew

MON SEPT 2, 2013

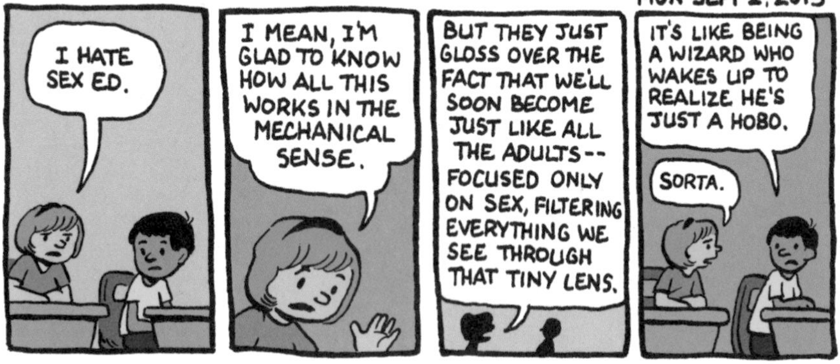
I HATE SEX ED.
I MEAN, I'M GLAD TO KNOW HOW ALL THIS WORKS IN THE MECHANICAL SENSE.
BUT THEY JUST GLOSS OVER THE FACT THAT WE'LL SOON BECOME JUST LIKE ALL THE ADULTS-- FOCUSED ONLY ON SEX, FILTERING EVERYTHING WE SEE THROUGH THAT TINY LENS.
IT'S LIKE BEING A WIZARD WHO WAKES UP TO REALIZE HE'S JUST A HOBO.
SORTA.

TUE SEPT 3, 2013

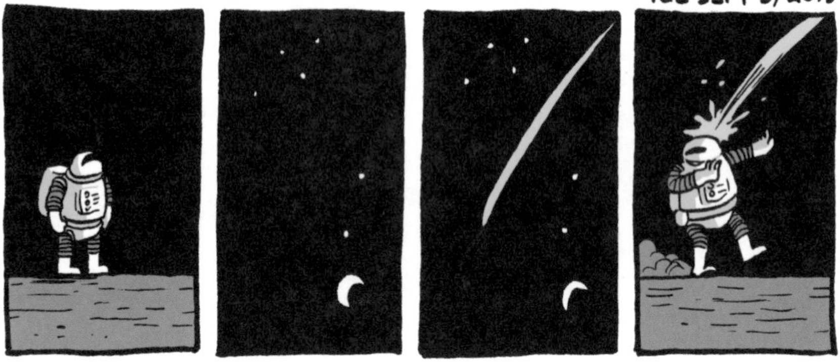

WED SEPT 4, 2013

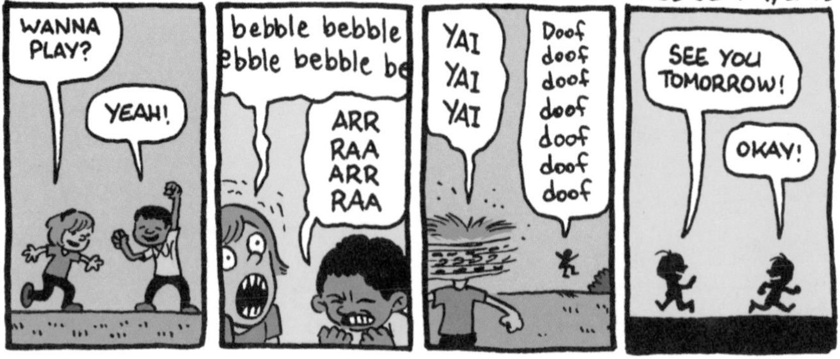
WANNA PLAY?
YEAH!
bebble bebble
ebble bebble be
ARR RAA ARR RAA
YAI YAI YAI
Doof doof doof doof doof doof doof
SEE YOU TOMORROW!
OKAY!

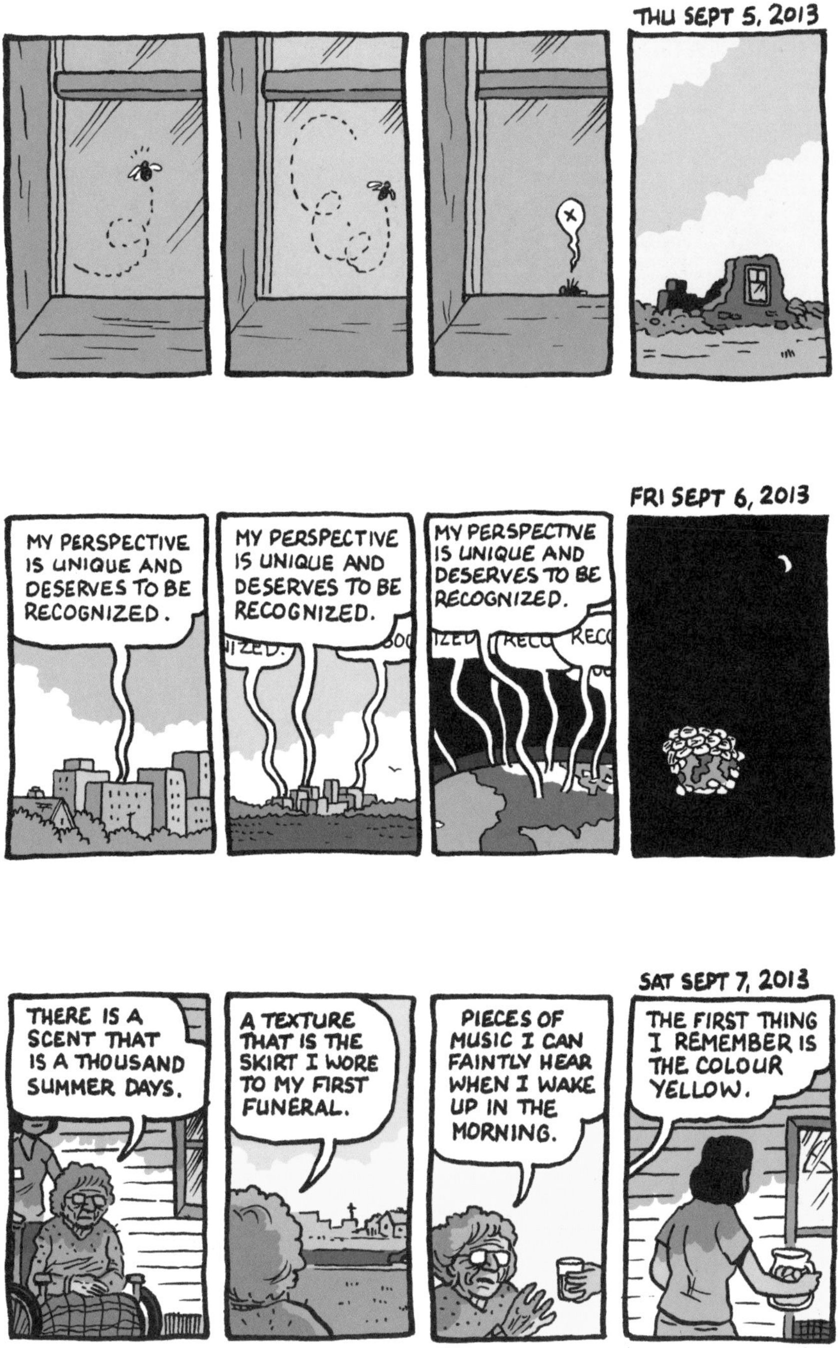
THU SEPT 5, 2013
FRI SEPT 6, 2013
MY PERSPECTIVE IS UNIQUE AND DESERVES TO BE RECOGNIZED.
MY PERSPECTIVE IS UNIQUE AND DESERVES TO BE RECOGNIZED.
MY PERSPECTIVE IS UNIQUE AND DESERVES TO BE RECOGNIZED.
SAT SEPT 7, 2013
THERE IS A SCENT THAT IS A THOUSAND SUMMER DAYS.
A TEXTURE THAT IS THE SKIRT I WORE TO MY FIRST FUNERAL.
PIECES OF MUSIC I CAN FAINTLY HEAR WHEN I WAKE UP IN THE MORNING.
THE FIRST THING I REMEMBER IS THE COLOUR YELLOW.

SUN SEPT 8, 2013

MON SEPT 9, 2013

TUE SEPT 10, 2013

WED SEPT 11, 2013

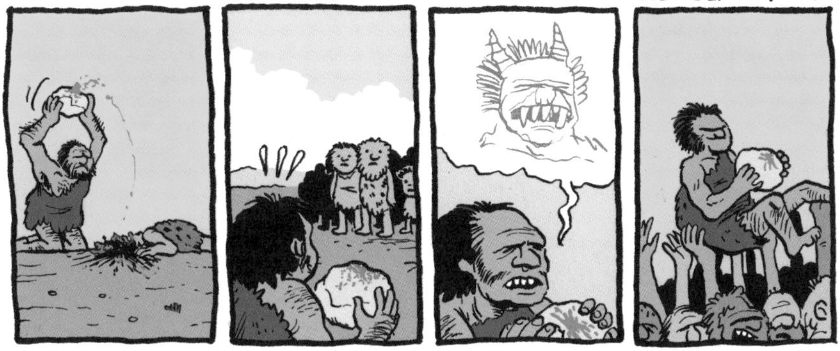

THU SEPT 12, 2013

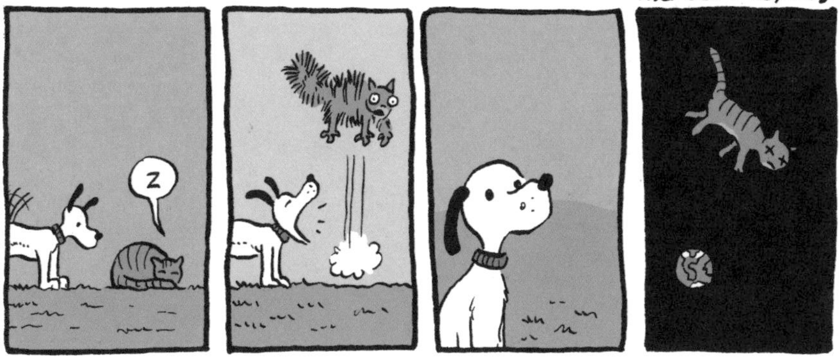
Z

FRI SEPT 13, 2013

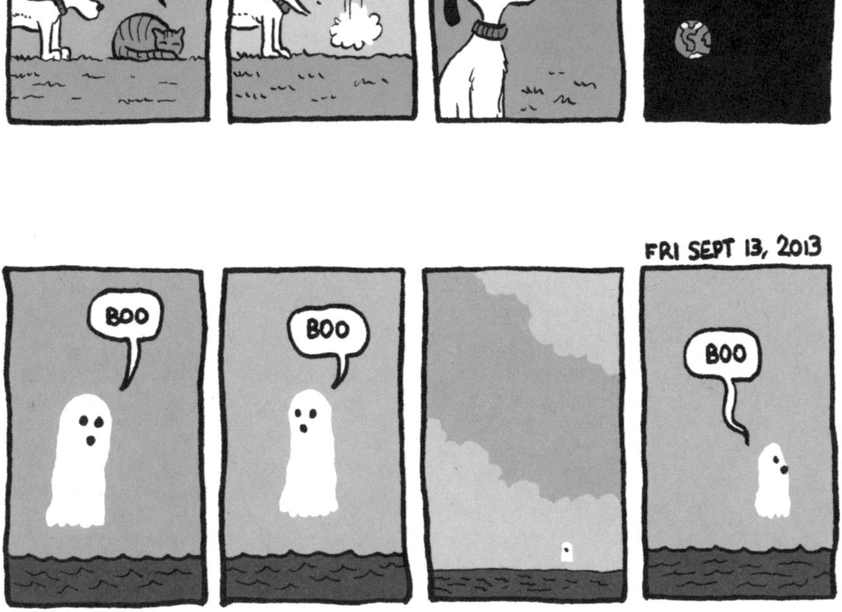
BOO
BOO
BOO

SAT SEPT 14, 2013

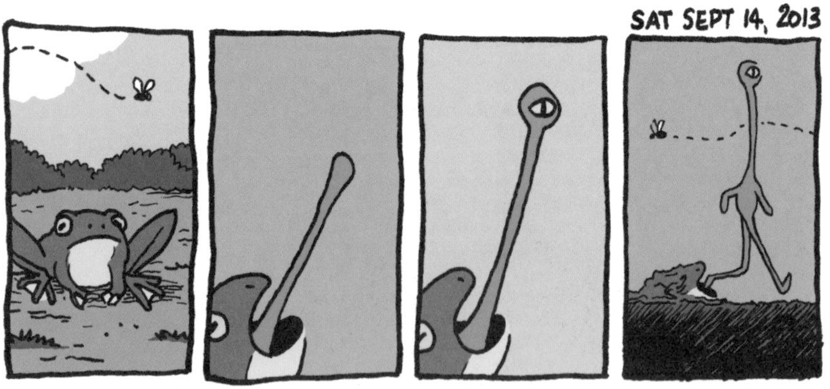

SUN SEPT 15, 2013

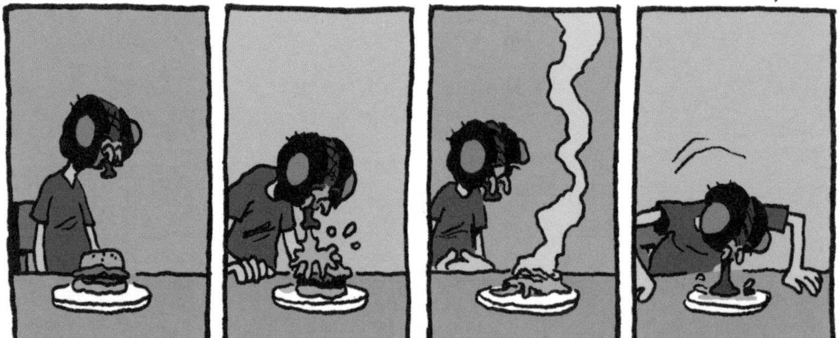

MON SEPT 16, 2013

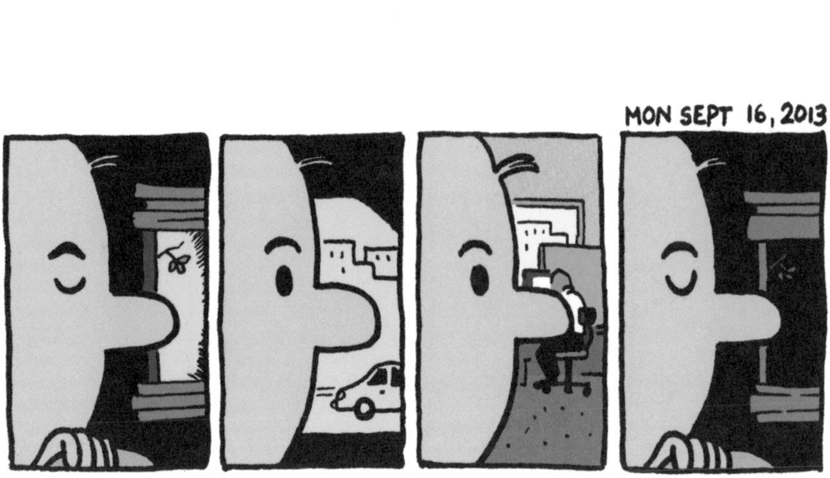

TUE SEPT 17, 2013

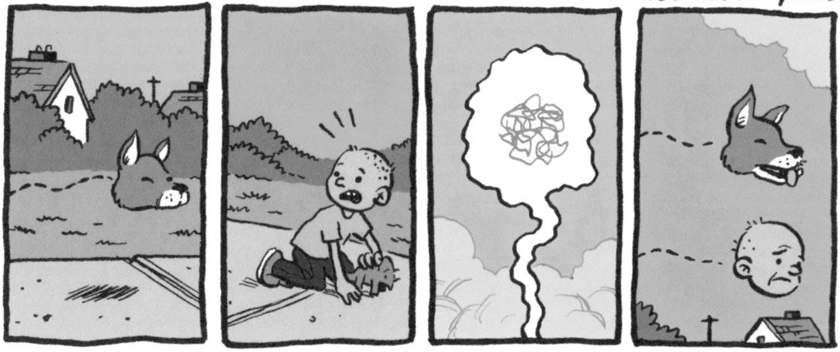

WED SEPT 18, 2013

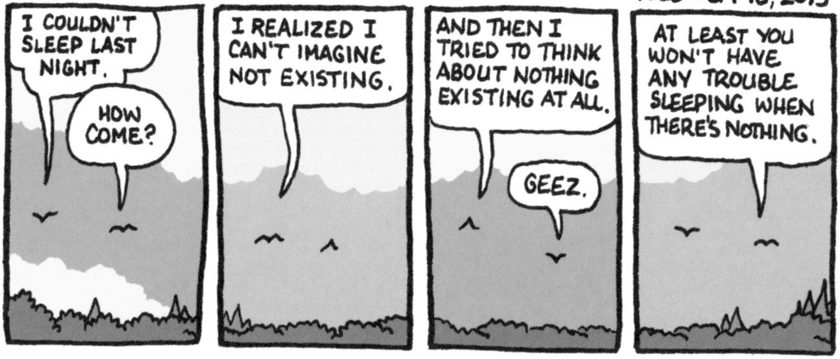

I COULDN'T SLEEP LAST NIGHT.
HOW COME?
I REALIZED I CAN'T IMAGINE NOT EXISTING.
AND THEN I TRIED TO THINK ABOUT NOTHING EXISTING AT ALL.
GEEZ.
AT LEAST YOU WON'T HAVE ANY TROUBLE SLEEPING WHEN THERE'S NOTHING.

THU SEPT 19, 2013

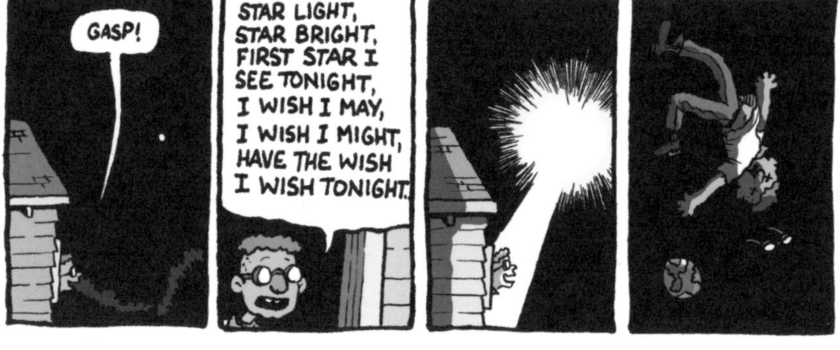

GASP!
STAR LIGHT, STAR BRIGHT, FIRST STAR I SEE TONIGHT, I WISH I MAY, I WISH I MIGHT, HAVE THE WISH I WISH TONIGHT.

FRI SEPT 20, 2013

SAT SEPT 21, 2013

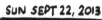

SUN SEPT 22, 2013

MON SEPT 23, 2013

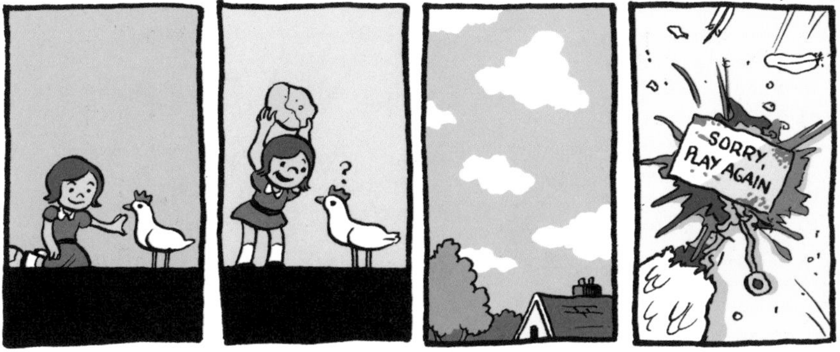
?
SORRY, PLAY AGAIN

TUE SEPT 24, 2013

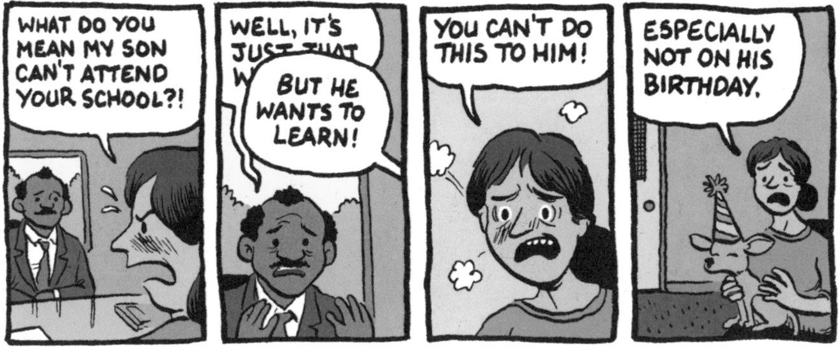
WHAT DO YOU MEAN MY SON CAN'T ATTEND YOUR SCHOOL?!
WELL, IT'S
BUT HE WANTS TO LEARN!
YOU CAN'T DO THIS TO HIM!
ESPECIALLY NOT ON HIS BIRTHDAY.

WED SEPT 25, 2013

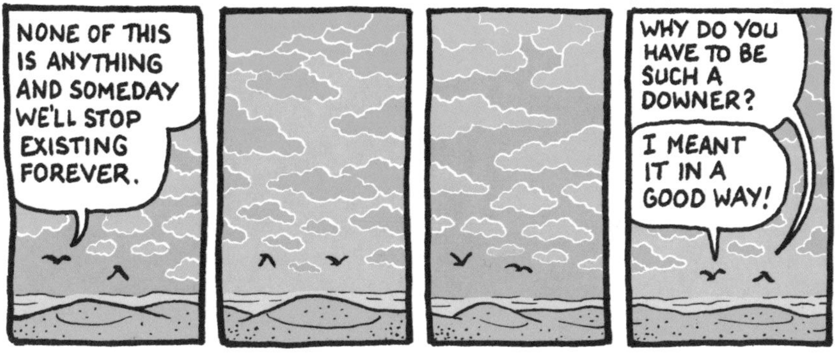
NONE OF THIS IS ANYTHING AND SOMEDAY WE'LL STOP EXISTING FOREVER.
WHY DO YOU HAVE TO BE SUCH A DOWNER?
I MEANT IT IN A GOOD WAY!

THU SEPT 26, 2013

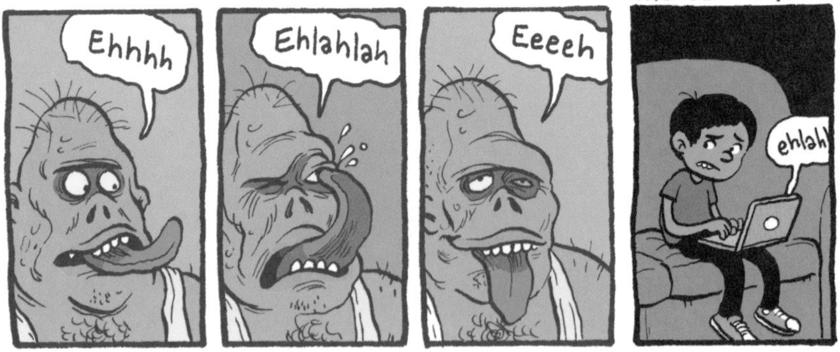
Ehhhh
Ehlahlah
Eeeeh
ehlah

FRI SEPT 27, 2013

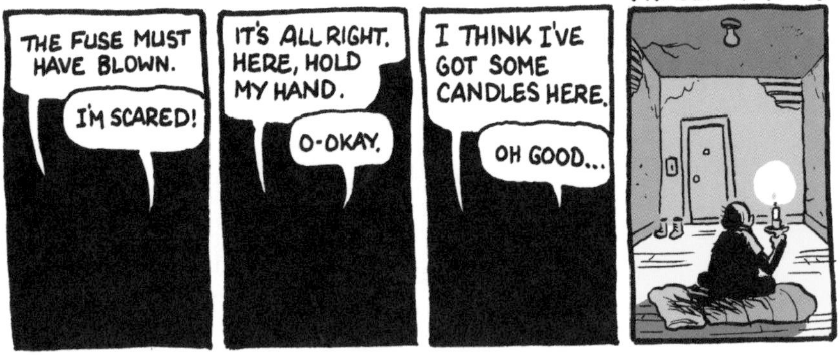
THE FUSE MUST HAVE BLOWN.
I'M SCARED!
IT'S ALL RIGHT. HERE, HOLD MY HAND.
O-OKAY.
I THINK I'VE GOT SOME CANDLES HERE.
OH GOOD...

SAT SEPT 28, 2013

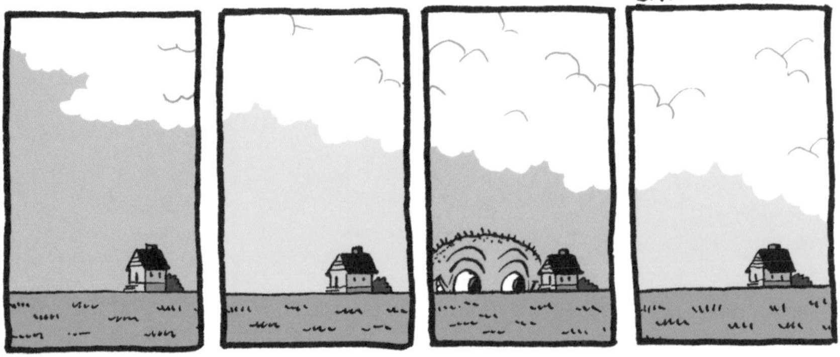

SUN SEPT 29, 2013

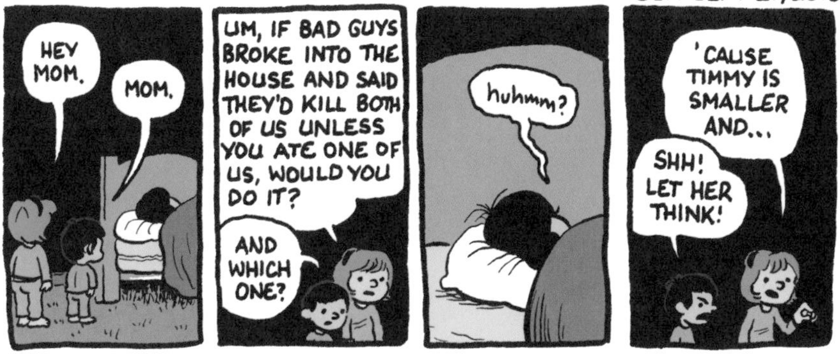
HEY MOM.
MOM.
UM, IF BAD GUYS BROKE INTO THE HOUSE AND SAID THEY'D KILL BOTH OF US UNLESS YOU ATE ONE OF US, WOULD YOU DO IT?
AND WHICH ONE?
huhmm?
'CAUSE TIMMY IS SMALLER AND...
SHH! LET HER THINK!

MON SEPT 30, 2013

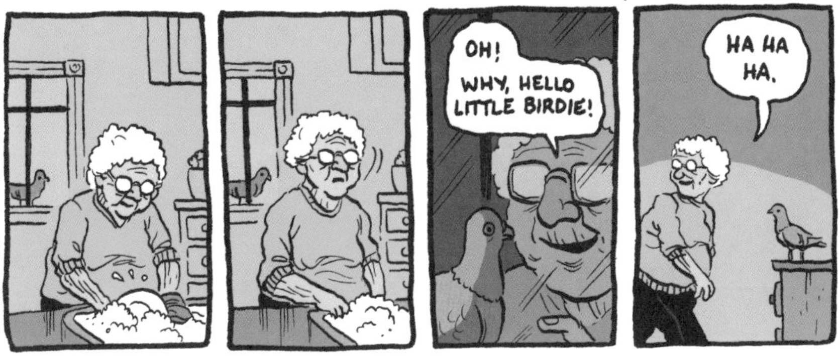
OH!
WHY, HELLO LITTLE BIRDIE!
HA HA HA.

TUE OCT 1, 2013

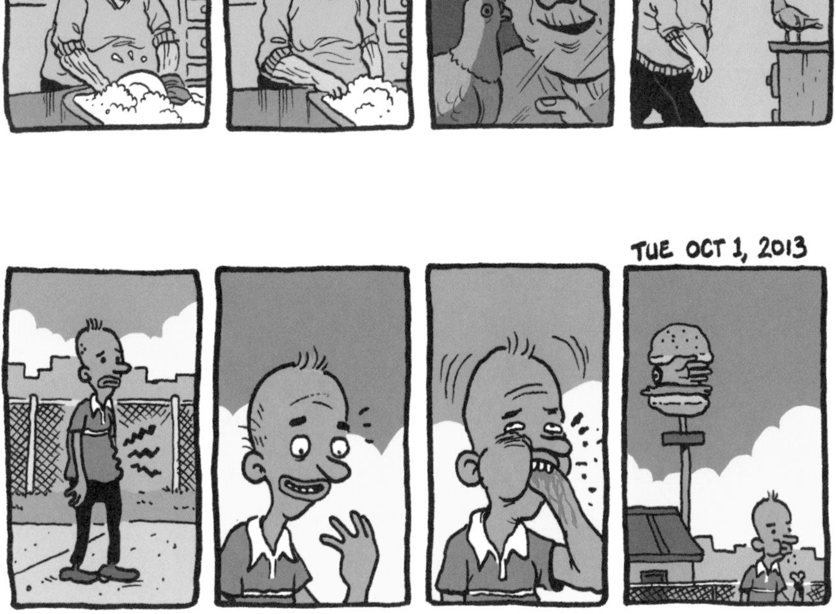

WED OCT 2, 2013

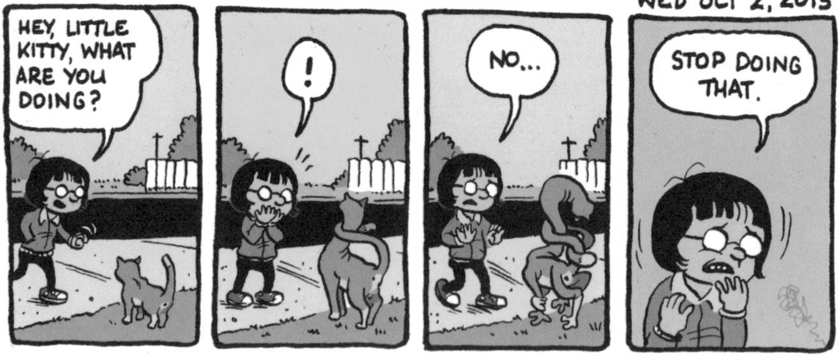
HEY, LITTLE KITTY, WHAT ARE YOU DOING?
!
NO...
STOP DOING THAT.

THU OCT 3, 2013

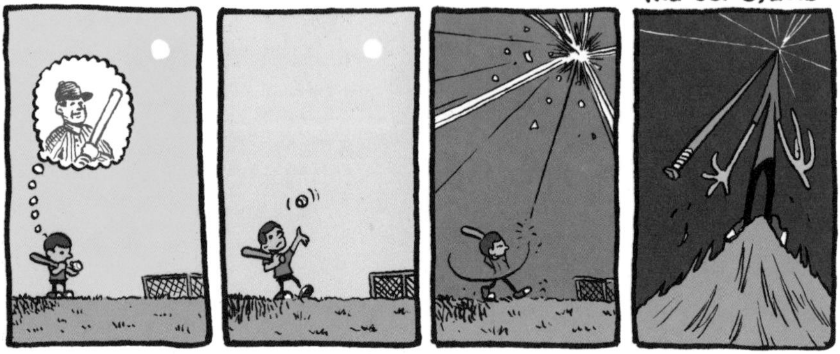

FRI OCT 4, 2013

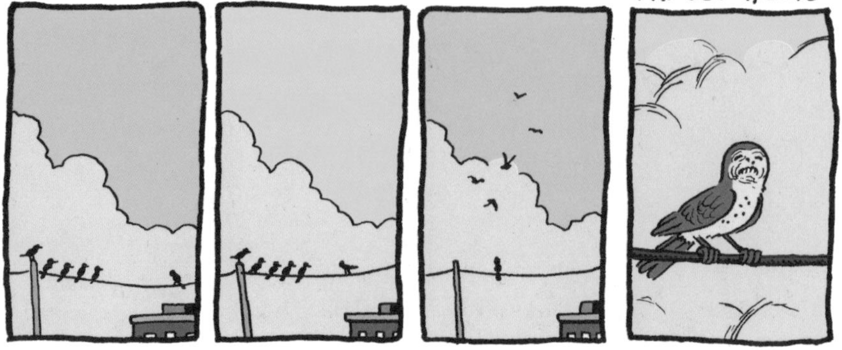

SAT OCT 5, 2013

SUN OCT 6, 2013

slurp...
slurp...
...
Slurp...

MON OCT 7, 2013

JOY! LIFE IS GOOD AND NOTHING BAD EVER HAPPENS!
sniff
♪
♪

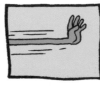

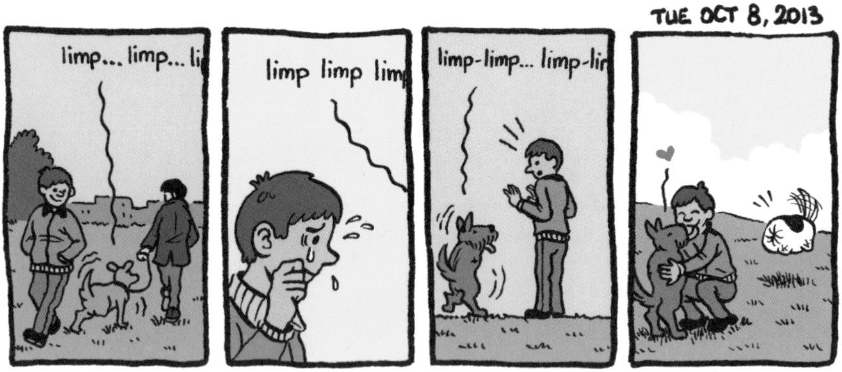
TUE OCT 8, 2013
limp... limp... li
limp limp lim
limp-limp... limp-li

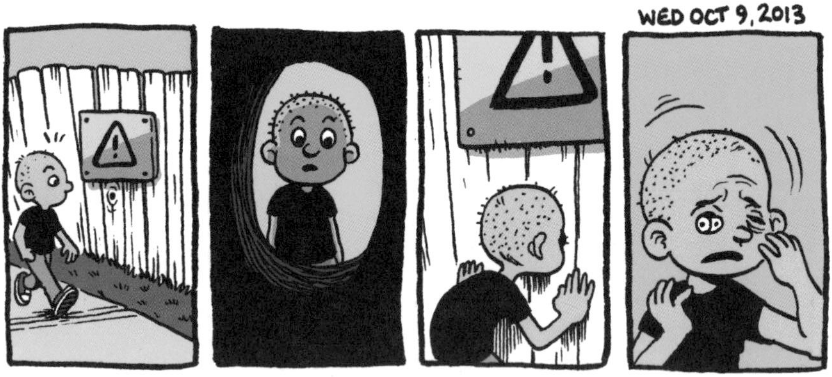
WED OCT 9, 2013

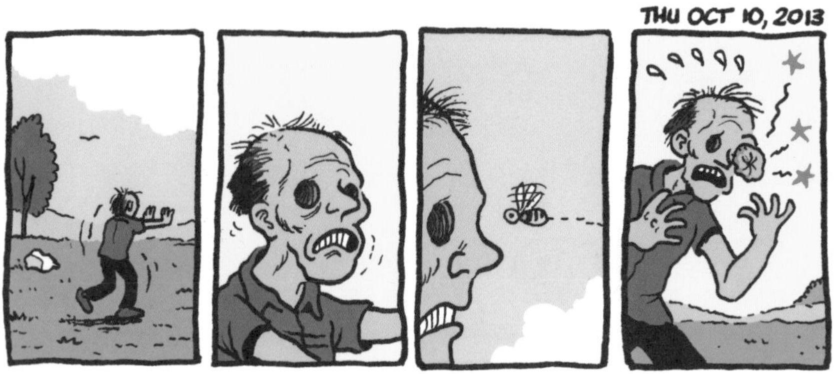
THU OCT 10, 2013

FRI OCT 11, 2013

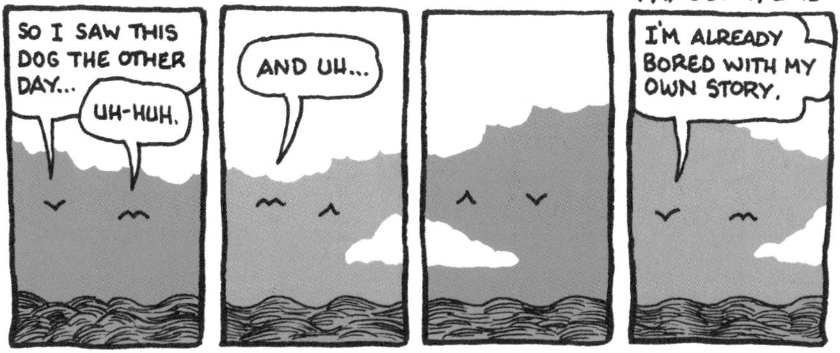
SO I SAW THIS DOG THE OTHER DAY...
UH-HUH.
AND UH...
I'M ALREADY BORED WITH MY OWN STORY.

SAT OCT 12, 2013

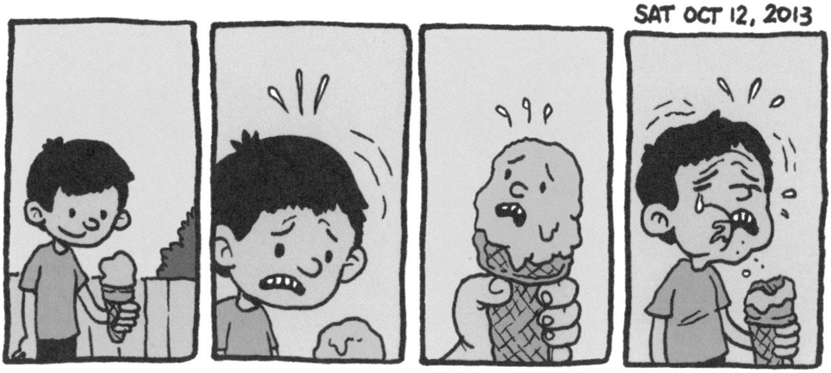

SUN OCT 13, 2013

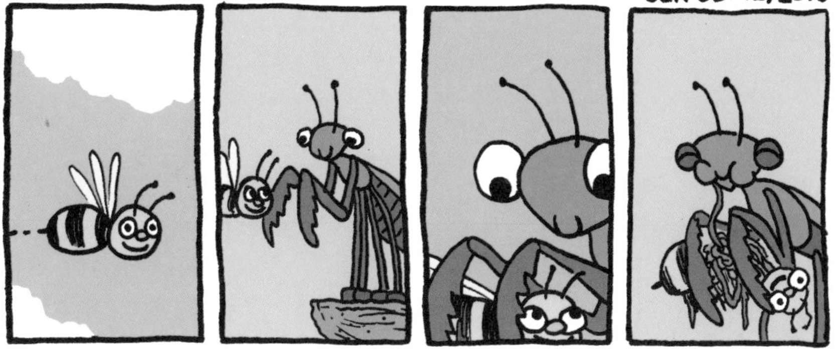

MON OCT 14, 2013

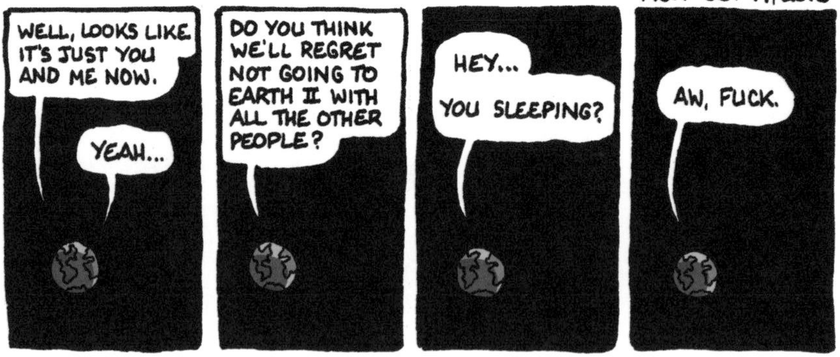
WELL, LOOKS LIKE IT'S JUST YOU AND ME NOW.
YEAH...
DO YOU THINK WE'LL REGRET NOT GOING TO EARTH II WITH ALL THE OTHER PEOPLE?
HEY...
YOU SLEEPING?
AW, FUCK.

TUE OCT 15, 2013

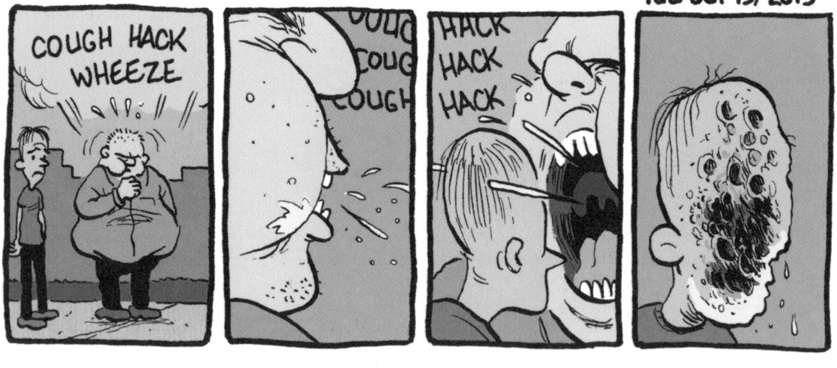
COUGH HACK WHEEZE
COUG
COUGH
HACK
HACK
HACK

WED OCT 16, 2013

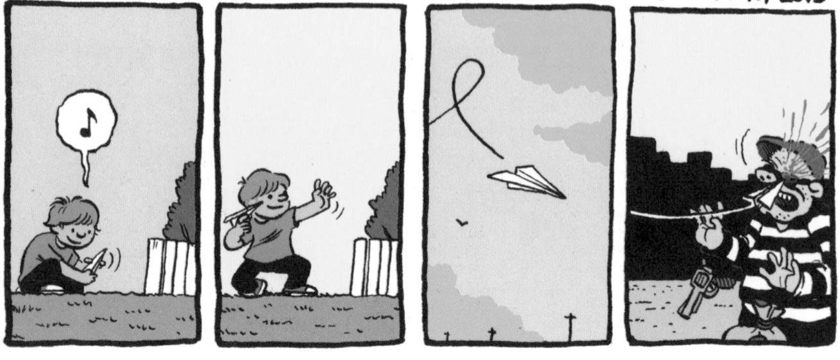

THU OCT 17, 2013

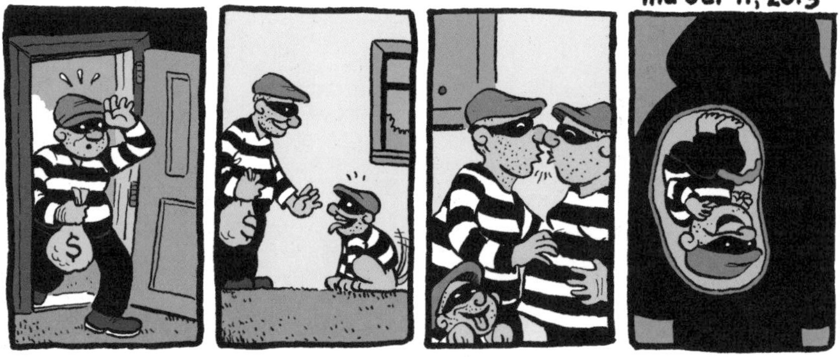

FRI OCT 18, 2013

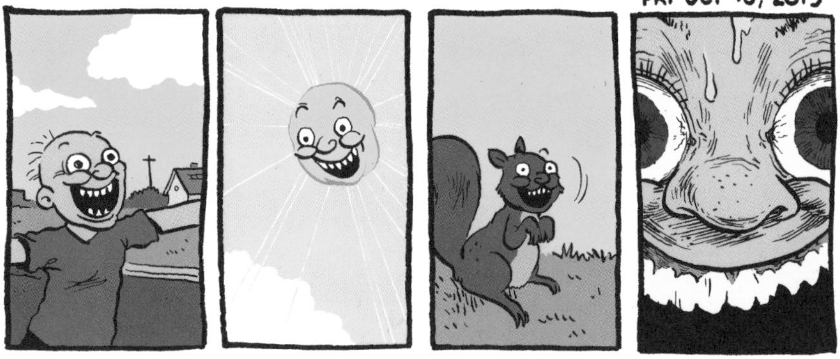

SAT OCT 19, 2013

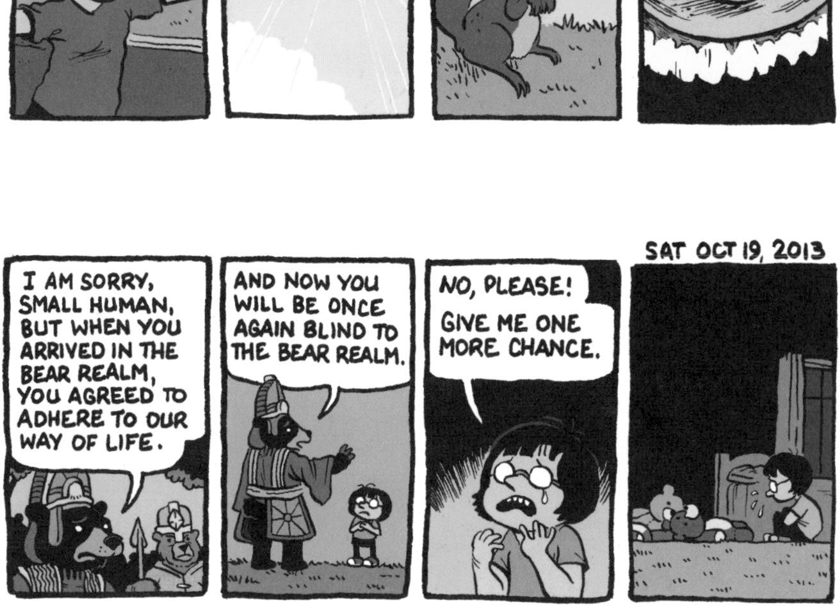
I AM SORRY, SMALL HUMAN, BUT WHEN YOU ARRIVED IN THE BEAR REALM, YOU AGREED TO ADHERE TO OUR WAY OF LIFE.
AND NOW YOU WILL BE ONCE AGAIN BLIND TO THE BEAR REALM.
NO, PLEASE!
GIVE ME ONE MORE CHANCE.

SUN OCT 20, 2013

GRAMMA! TELL ME A GHOST STORY!

OH MY GOODNESS, YOU DON'T NEED TO WORRY ABOUT ANY SILLY GHOST STORIES, DEAR.

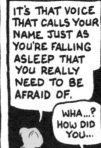

IT'S THAT VOICE THAT CALLS YOUR NAME JUST AS YOU'RE FALLING ASLEEP THAT YOU REALLY NEED TO BE AFRAID OF.

WHA...? HOW DID YOU...

DON'T EVER ANSWER IT. DON'T EVEN THINK IT.

GOOD NIGHT.

MON OCT 21, 2013

THE EYEDROPPER CHIHUAHUA IS NOT ONLY THE SMALLEST DOG BREED...

BUT THANKS TO ADVANCED BREEDING, IT IS ALSO THE SMALLEST VERTEBRATE.

IN FACT, IT HAS FEWER CELLS THAN AN ANT. LET'S TAKE A CLOSER LOOK AT THIS ADORABLE LI'L FELLA...

wheeze

TUE OCT 22, 2013

HEY.

HEY, KID!

NICE FACE.

THANKS, FELLOWS.

WED OCT 23, 2013

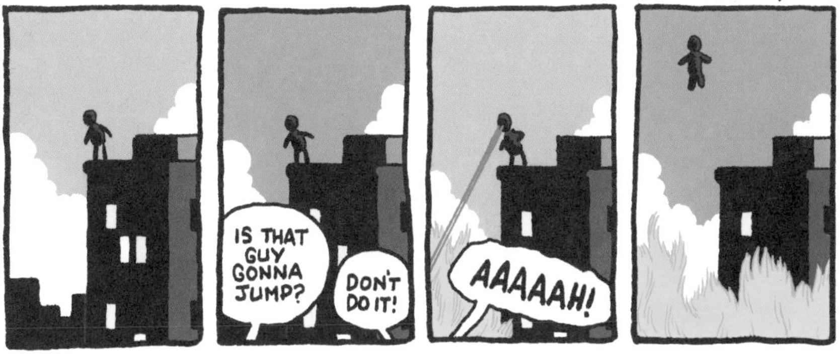
IS THAT GUY GONNA JUMP?
DON'T DO IT!
AAAAAH!

THU OCT 24, 2013

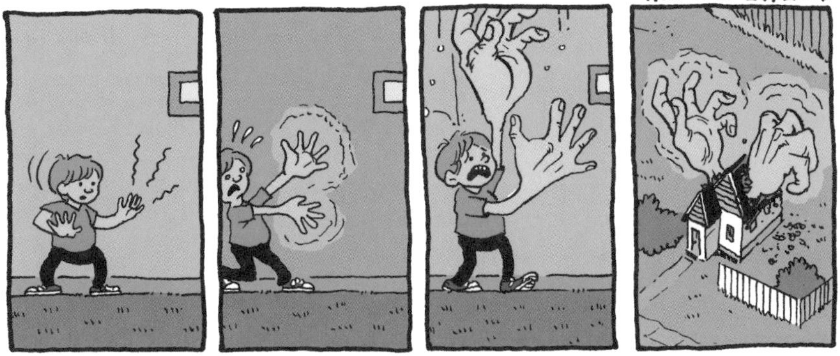

FRI OCT 25, 2013

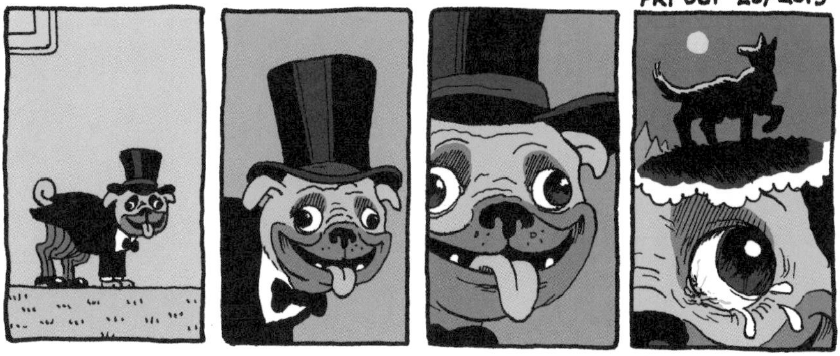

SAT OCT 26, 2013

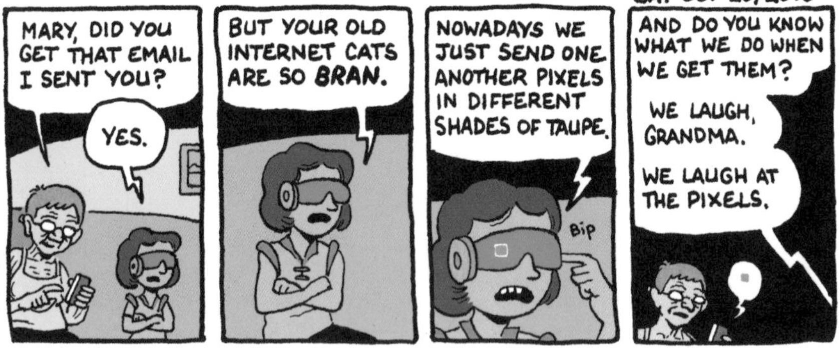
MARY, DID YOU GET THAT EMAIL I SENT YOU?
YES.
BUT YOUR OLD INTERNET CATS ARE SO *BRAN.*
NOWADAYS WE JUST SEND ONE ANOTHER PIXELS IN DIFFERENT SHADES OF TAUPE.
Bip
AND DO YOU KNOW WHAT WE DO WHEN WE GET THEM?
WE LAUGH, GRANDMA.
WE LAUGH AT THE PIXELS.

SUN OCT 27, 2013

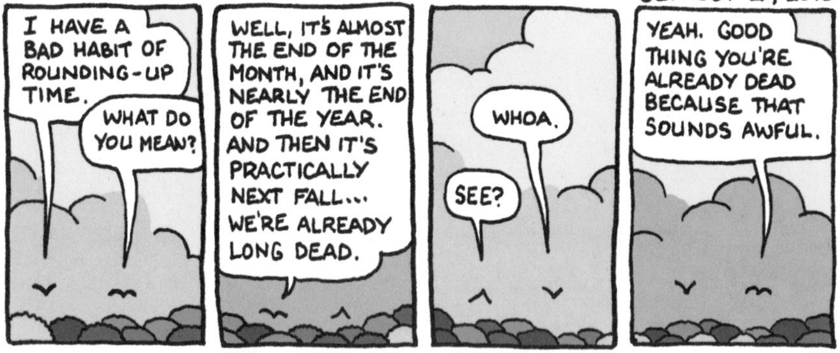
I HAVE A BAD HABIT OF ROUNDING-UP TIME.
WHAT DO YOU MEAN?
WELL, IT'S ALMOST THE END OF THE MONTH, AND IT'S NEARLY THE END OF THE YEAR. AND THEN IT'S PRACTICALLY NEXT FALL... WE'RE ALREADY LONG DEAD.
WHOA.
SEE?
YEAH. GOOD THING YOU'RE ALREADY DEAD BECAUSE THAT SOUNDS AWFUL.

MON OCT 28, 2013

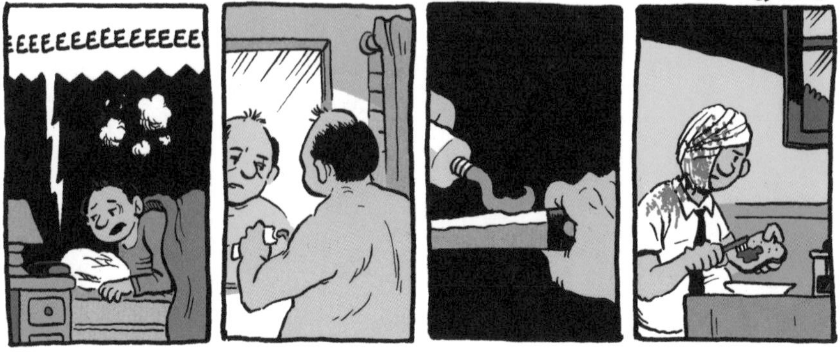
EEEEEEEEEEEEEE

TUE OCT 29, 2013

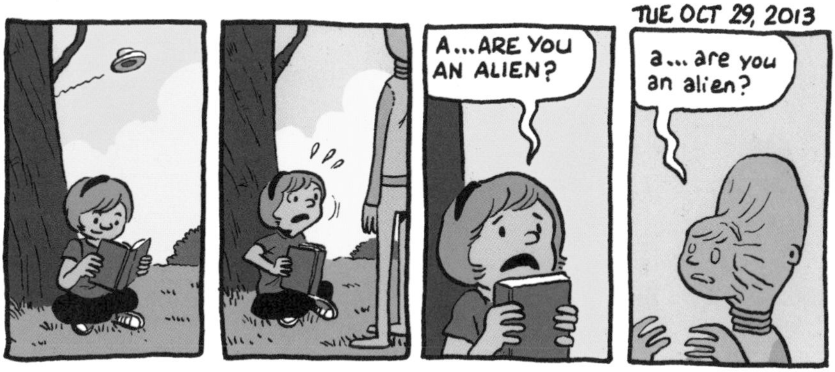
A...ARE YOU AN ALIEN?
a... are you an alien?

WED OCT 30, 2013

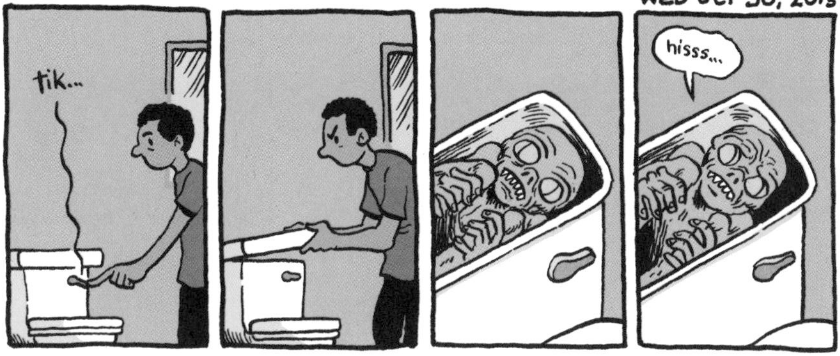
tik...
hisss...

THU OCT 31, 2013

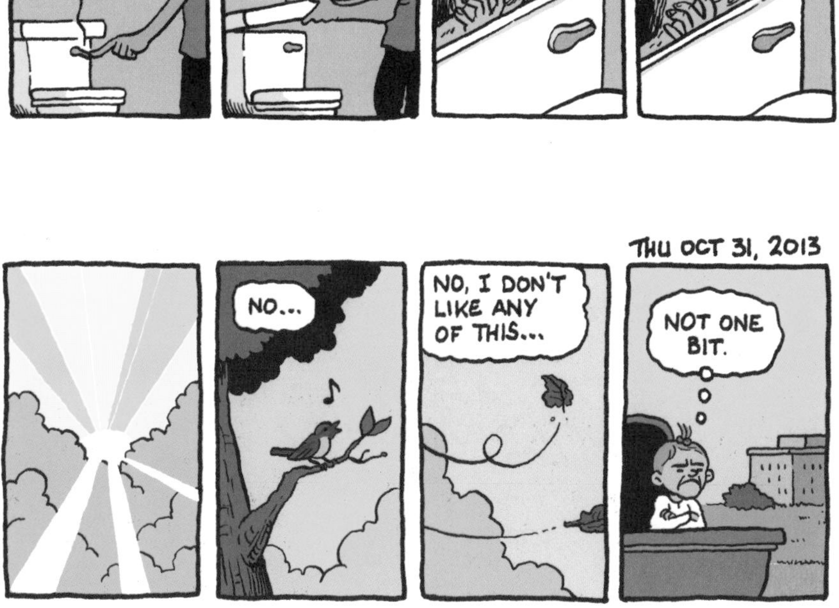
NO...
NO, I DON'T LIKE ANY OF THIS...
NOT ONE BIT.

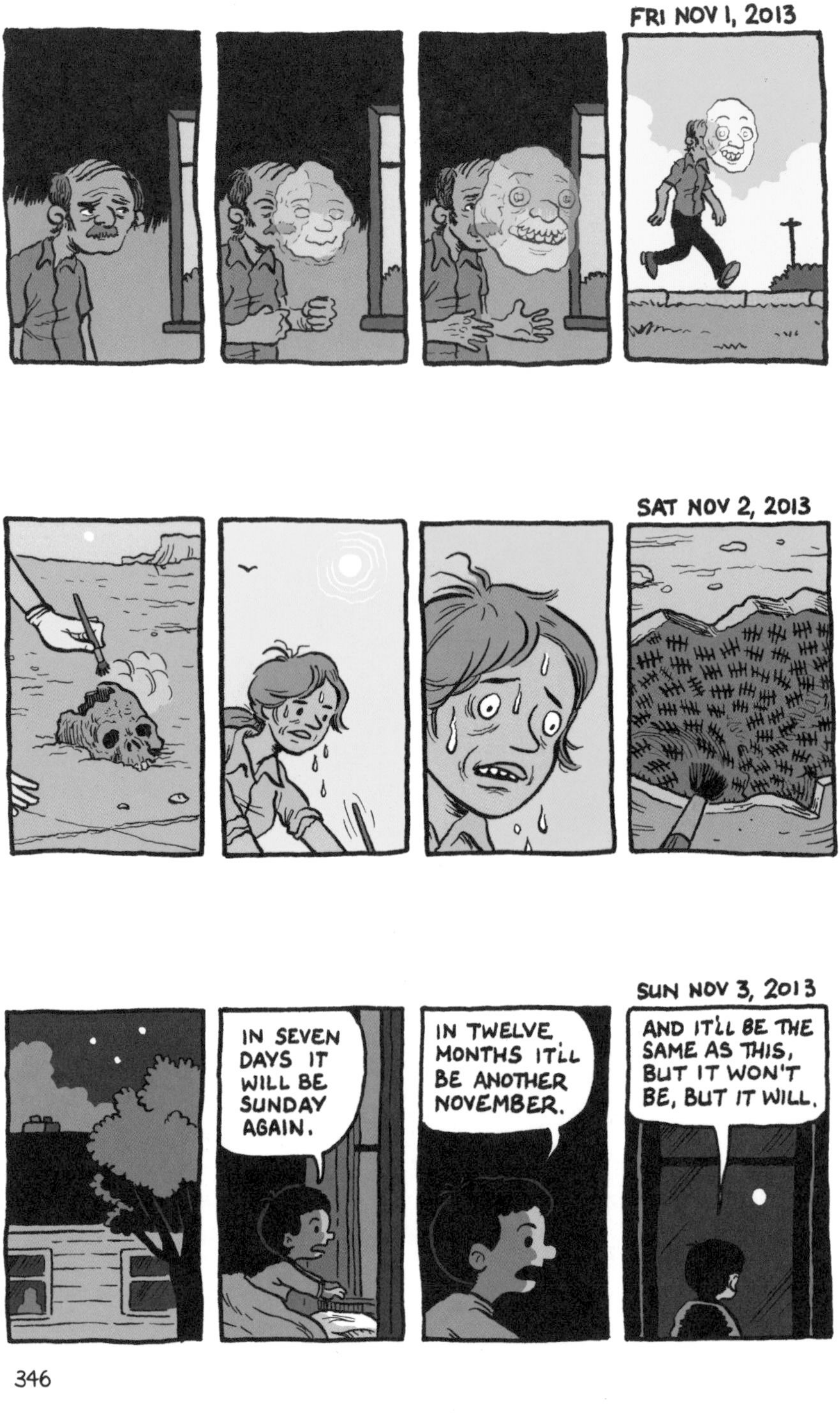
FRI NOV 1, 2013
SAT NOV 2, 2013
SUN NOV 3, 2013
IN SEVEN DAYS IT WILL BE SUNDAY AGAIN.
IN TWELVE MONTHS IT'LL BE ANOTHER NOVEMBER.
AND IT'LL BE THE SAME AS THIS, BUT IT WON'T BE, BUT IT WILL.

MON NOV 4, 2013

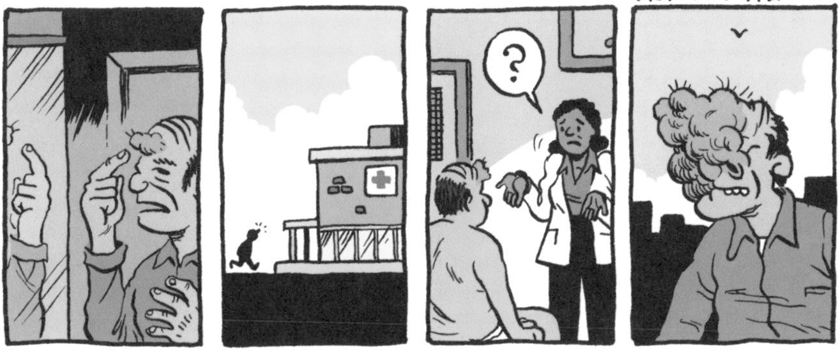
?

TUE NOV 5, 2013

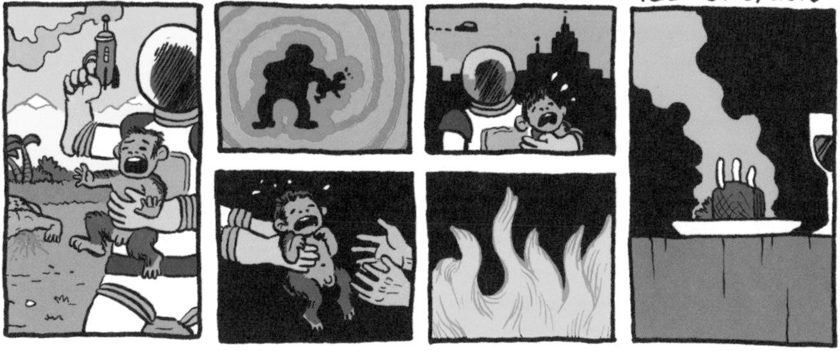

WED NOV 6, 2013

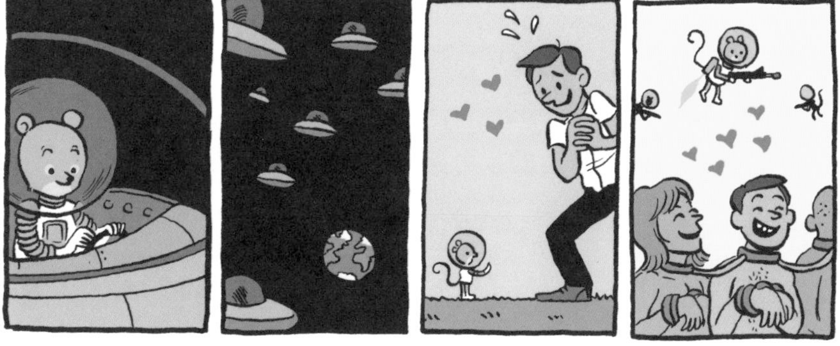

THU NOV 7, 2013

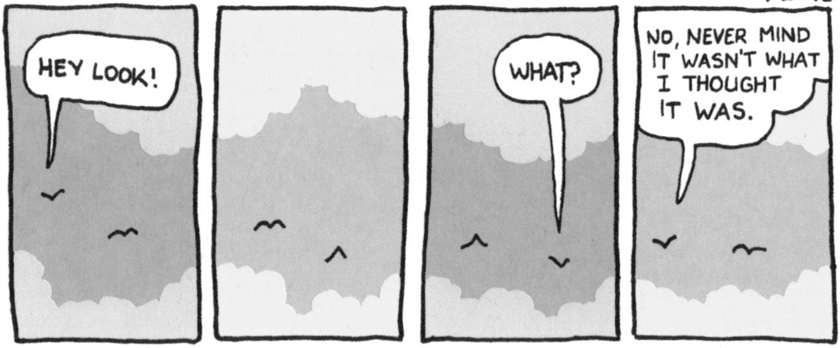
HEY LOOK!
WHAT?
NO, NEVER MIND IT WASN'T WHAT I THOUGHT IT WAS.

FRI NOV 8, 2013

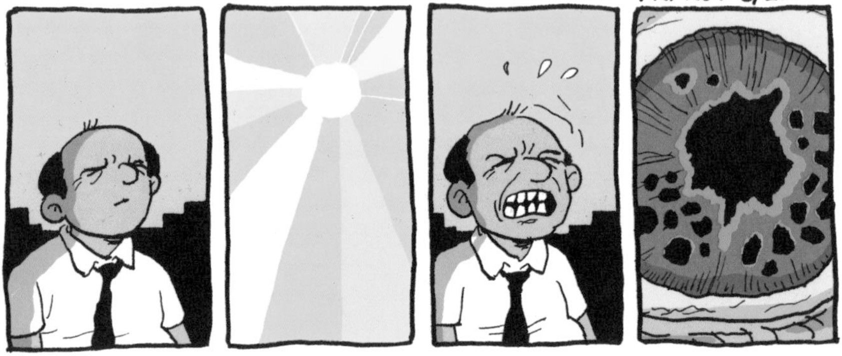

SAT NOV 9, 2013

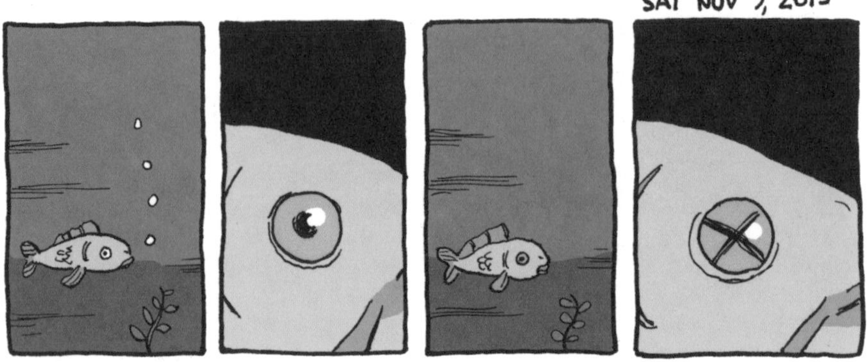

HOW WAS YOUR DAY?

GOOD.

FIRST I WAS BORN, BUT I DON'T REALLY REMEMBER ANY OF THAT. THEN, AS I GREW UP, I OFTEN FELT KINDA AWKWARD ABOUT ALL THE THINGS I DIDN'T UNDERSTAND.

SOME OF THE DECISIONS I MADE DURING THAT TIME STILL AFFECT ME TODAY. OTHERS WERE WITHOUT CONSEQUENCE, THOUGH I STILL THINK ABOUT THEM FROM TIME TO TIME.

OVERALL, IT WAS MOSTLY FINE. I GUESS IT'S A CONSTANT PROCESS OF SEEKING THE BALANCE OF ALL THINGS. THEN TODAY I WOKE UP AND HAD TOAST AND...

WED NOV 13, 2013

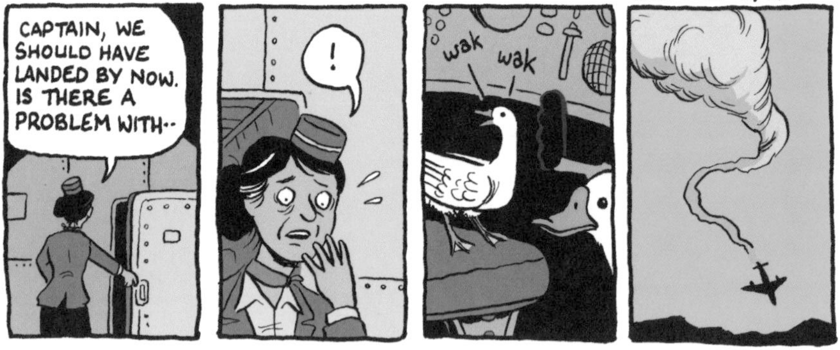
CAPTAIN, WE SHOULD HAVE LANDED BY NOW. IS THERE A PROBLEM WITH··
!
wak
wak

THU NOV 14, 2013

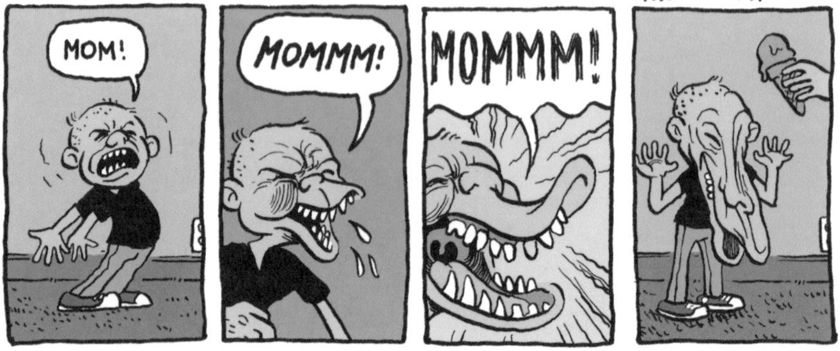
MOM!
MOMMM!
MOMMM!

FRI NOV 15, 2013

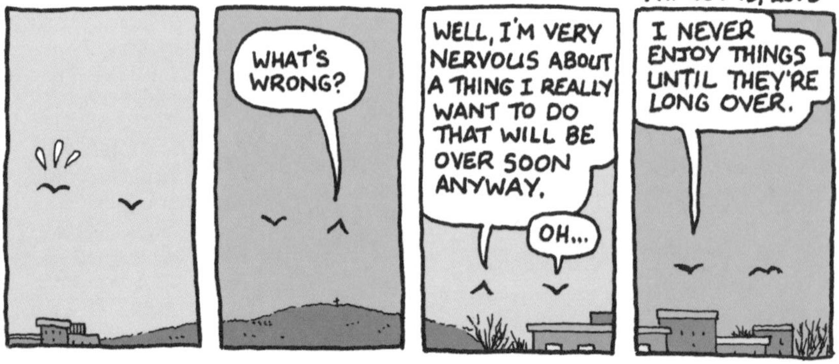
WHAT'S WRONG?
WELL, I'M VERY NERVOUS ABOUT A THING I REALLY WANT TO DO THAT WILL BE OVER SOON ANYWAY.
OH...
I NEVER ENJOY THINGS UNTIL THEY'RE LONG OVER.

SAT NOV 16, 2013

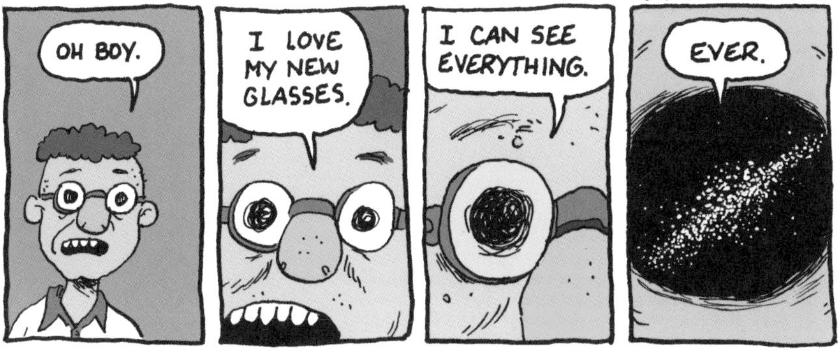
OH BOY.
I LOVE MY NEW GLASSES.
I CAN SEE EVERYTHING.
EVER.

SUN NOV 17, 2013

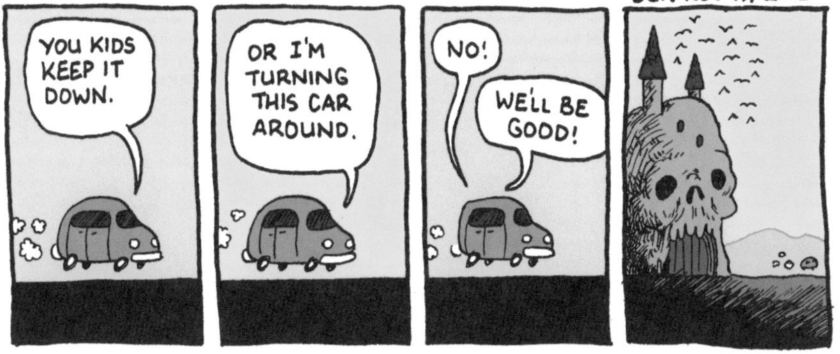
YOU KIDS KEEP IT DOWN.
OR I'M TURNING THIS CAR AROUND.
NO!
WE'LL BE GOOD!

MON NOV 18, 2013

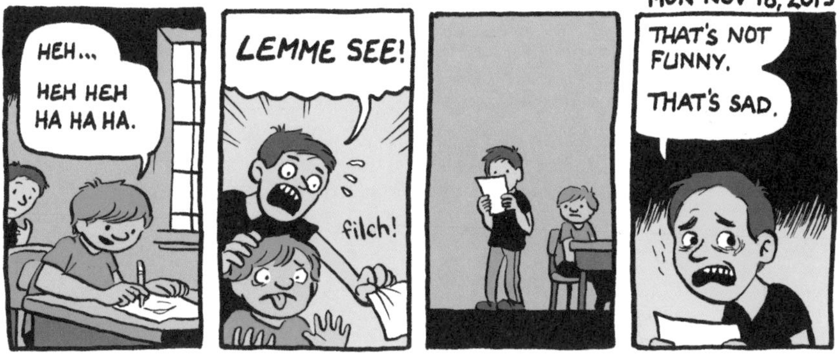
HEH...
HEH HEH HA HA HA.
LEMME SEE!
filch!
THAT'S NOT FUNNY.
THAT'S SAD.

TUE NOV 19, 2013

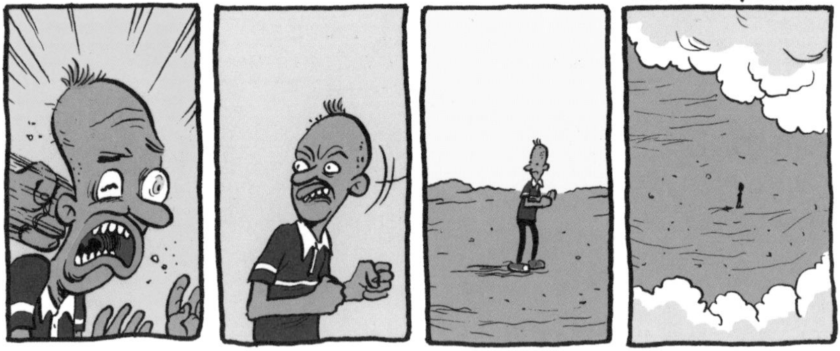

WED NOV 20, 2013

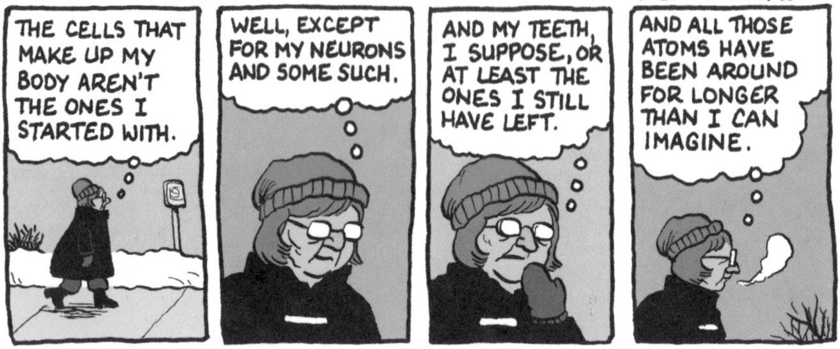
THE CELLS THAT MAKE UP MY BODY AREN'T THE ONES I STARTED WITH.
WELL, EXCEPT FOR MY NEURONS AND SOME SUCH.
AND MY TEETH, I SUPPOSE, OR AT LEAST THE ONES I STILL HAVE LEFT.
AND ALL THOSE ATOMS HAVE BEEN AROUND FOR LONGER THAN I CAN IMAGINE.

THU NOV 21, 2013

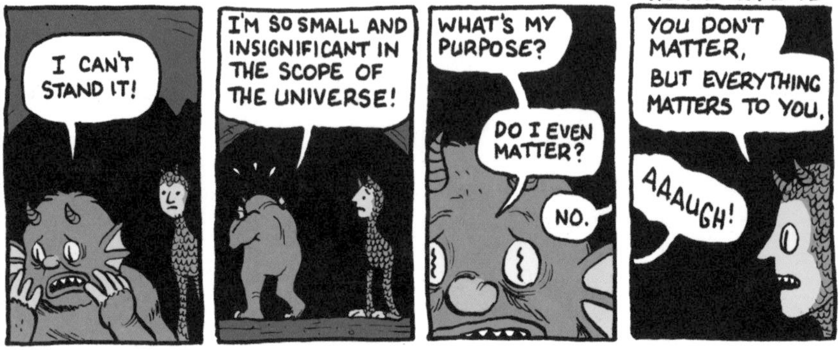
I CAN'T STAND IT!
I'M SO SMALL AND INSIGNIFICANT IN THE SCOPE OF THE UNIVERSE!
WHAT'S MY PURPOSE?
DO I EVEN MATTER?
NO.
YOU DON'T MATTER,
BUT EVERYTHING MATTERS TO YOU.
AAAUGH!

FRI NOV 22, 2013

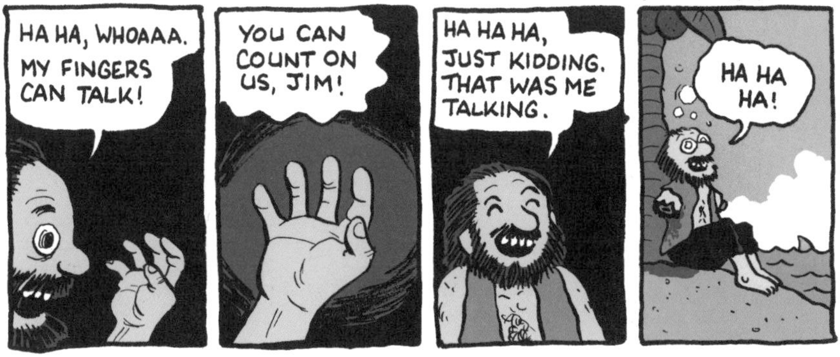
HA HA, WHOAAA. MY FINGERS CAN TALK!
YOU CAN COUNT ON US, JIM!
HA HA HA, JUST KIDDING. THAT WAS ME TALKING.
HA HA HA!

SAT NOV 23, 2013

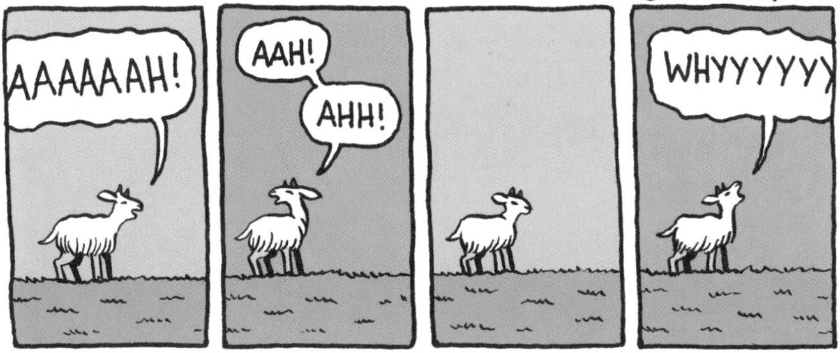
AAAAAAH!
AAH!
AHH!
WHYYYYYY

SUN NOV 24, 2013

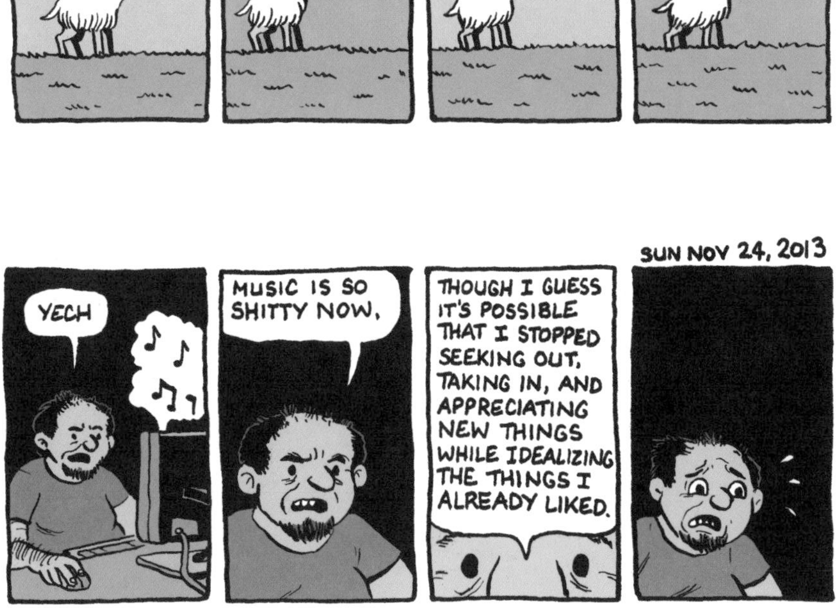
YECH
MUSIC IS SO SHITTY NOW.
THOUGH I GUESS IT'S POSSIBLE THAT I STOPPED SEEKING OUT, TAKING IN, AND APPRECIATING NEW THINGS WHILE IDEALIZING THE THINGS I ALREADY LIKED.

MON NOV 25, 2013

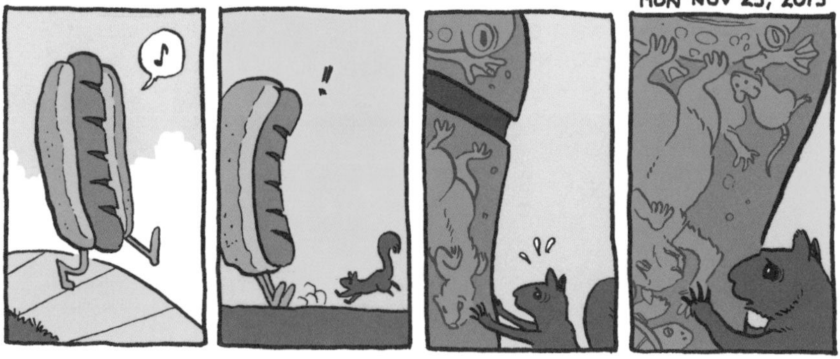

TUE NOV 26, 2013

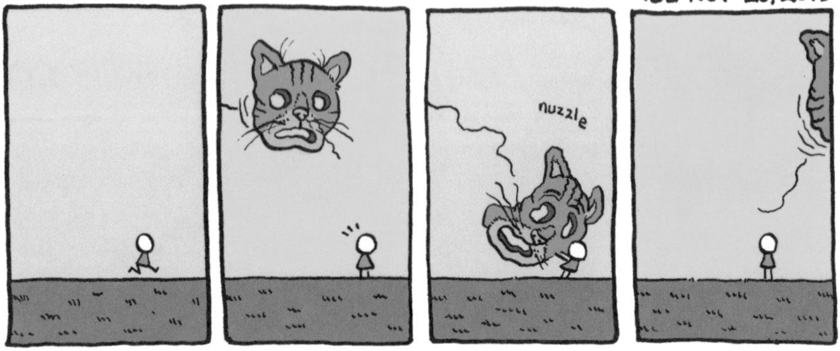
nuzzle

WED NOV 27, 2013

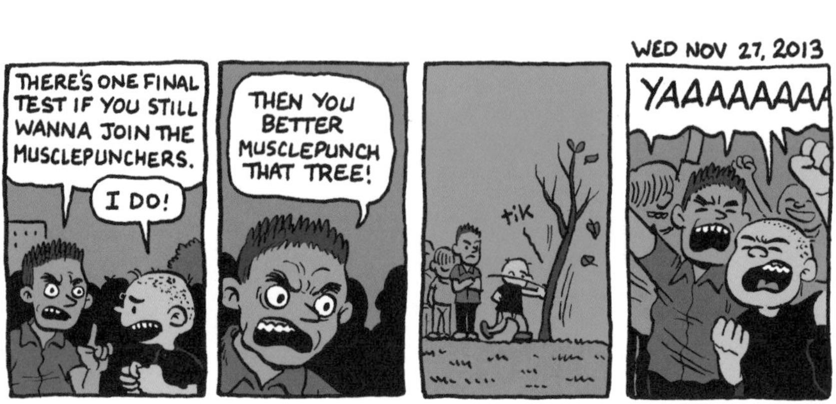
THERE'S ONE FINAL TEST IF YOU STILL WANNA JOIN THE MUSCLEPUNCHERS.
I DO!
THEN YOU BETTER MUSCLEPUNCH THAT TREE!
tik
YAAAAAAA

THU NOV 28, 2013

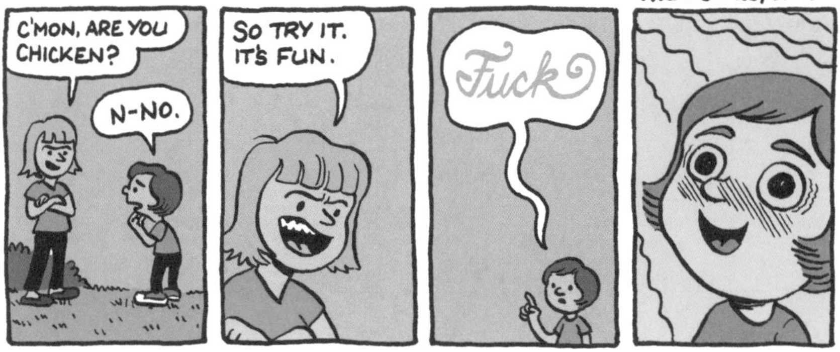
C'MON, ARE YOU CHICKEN?
N-NO.
SO TRY IT. IT'S FUN.
Fuck

FRI NOV 29, 2013

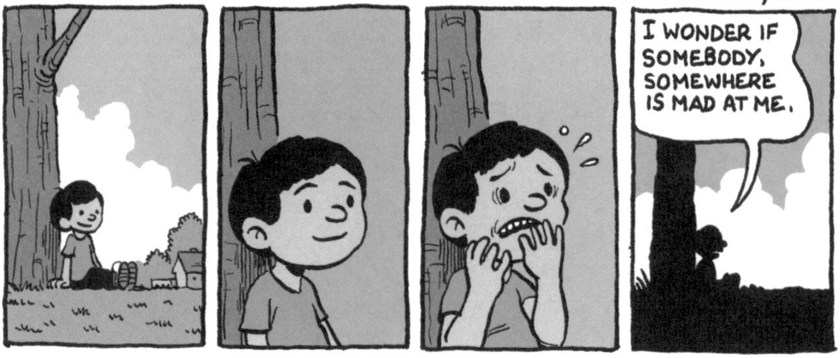
I WONDER IF SOMEBODY, SOMEWHERE IS MAD AT ME.

SAT NOV 30, 2013

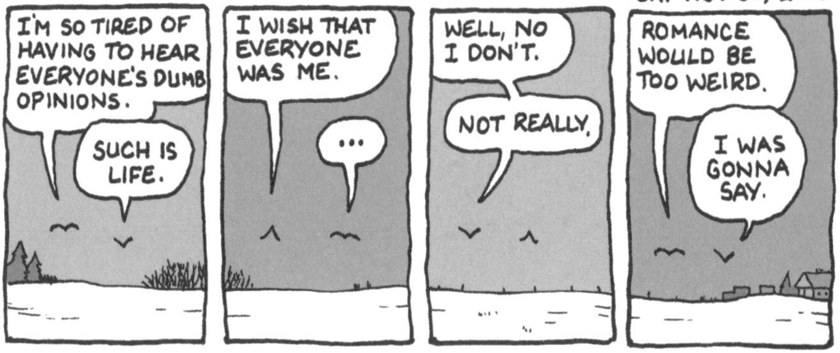
I'M SO TIRED OF HAVING TO HEAR EVERYONE'S DUMB OPINIONS.
SUCH IS LIFE.
I WISH THAT EVERYONE WAS ME.
...
WELL, NO I DON'T.
NOT REALLY.
ROMANCE WOULD BE TOO WEIRD.
I WAS GONNA SAY.

SUN DEC 1, 2013

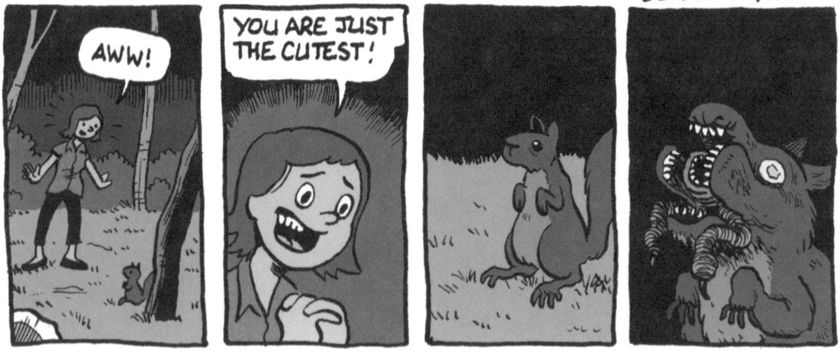
AWW!
YOU ARE JUST THE CUTEST!

MON DEC 2, 2013

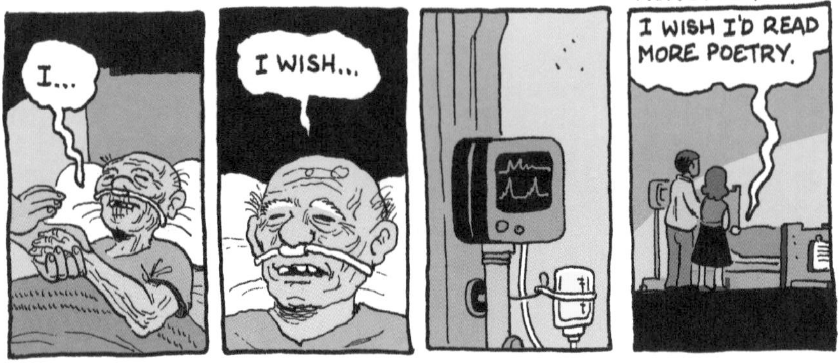
I...
I WISH...
I WISH I'D READ MORE POETRY.

TUE DEC 3, 2013

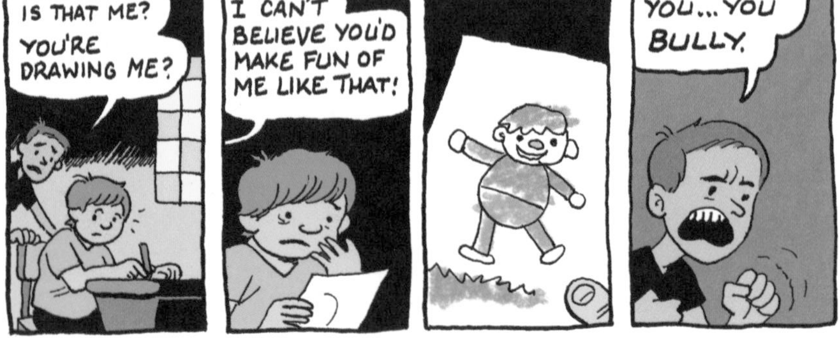
IS THAT ME? YOU'RE DRAWING ME?
I CAN'T BELIEVE YOU'D MAKE FUN OF ME LIKE THAT!
YOU... YOU BULLY.

WED DEC 4, 2013

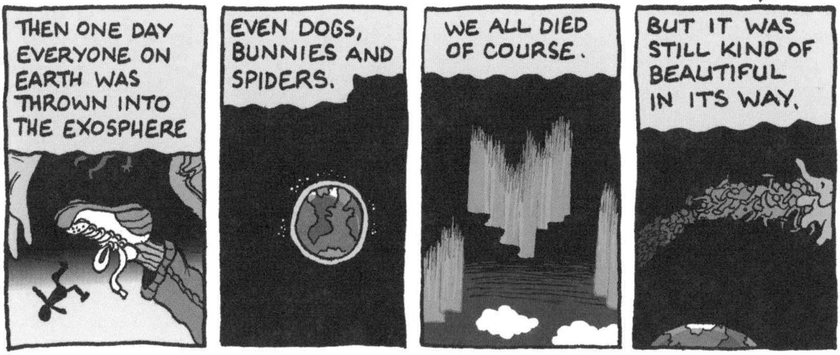
THEN ONE DAY EVERYONE ON EARTH WAS THROWN INTO THE EXOSPHERE
EVEN DOGS, BUNNIES AND SPIDERS.
WE ALL DIED OF COURSE.
BUT IT WAS STILL KIND OF BEAUTIFUL IN ITS WAY.

THU DEC 5, 2013

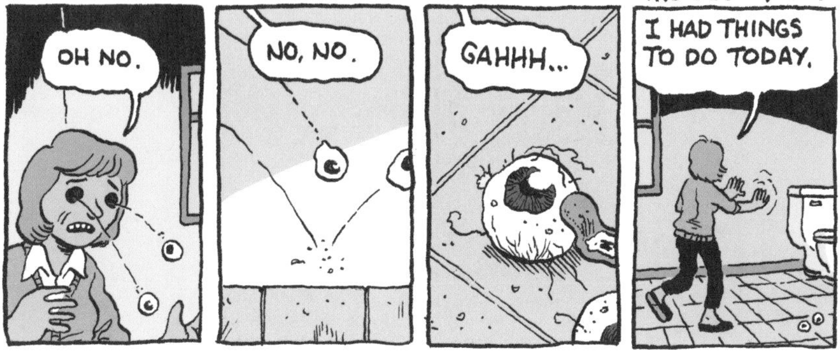
OH NO.
NO, NO.
GAHHH...
I HAD THINGS TO DO TODAY.

FRI DEC 6, 2013

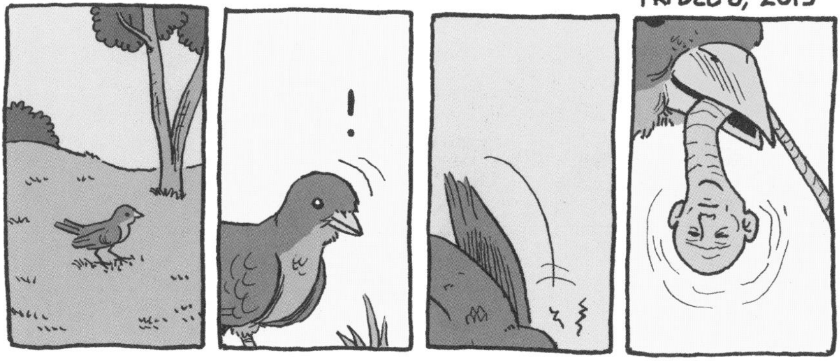
!

SAT DEC 7, 2013

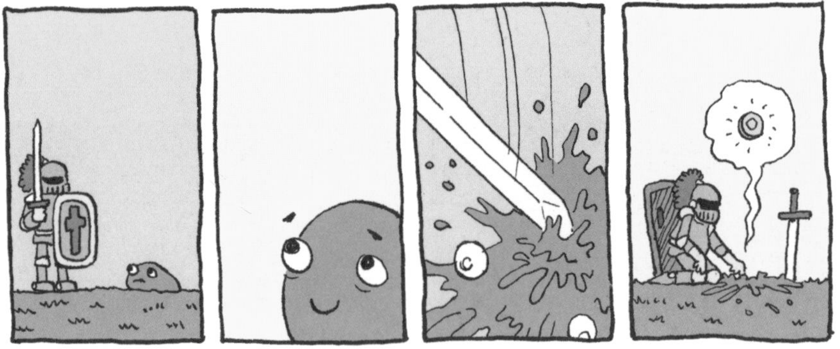

SUN DEC 8, 2013

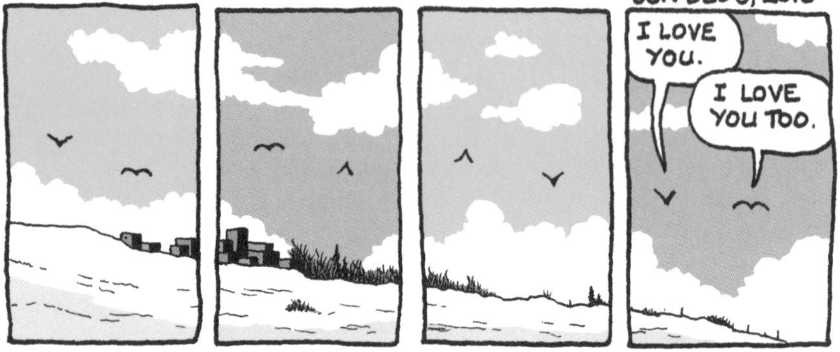
I LOVE YOU.
I LOVE YOU TOO.

MON DEC 9, 2013

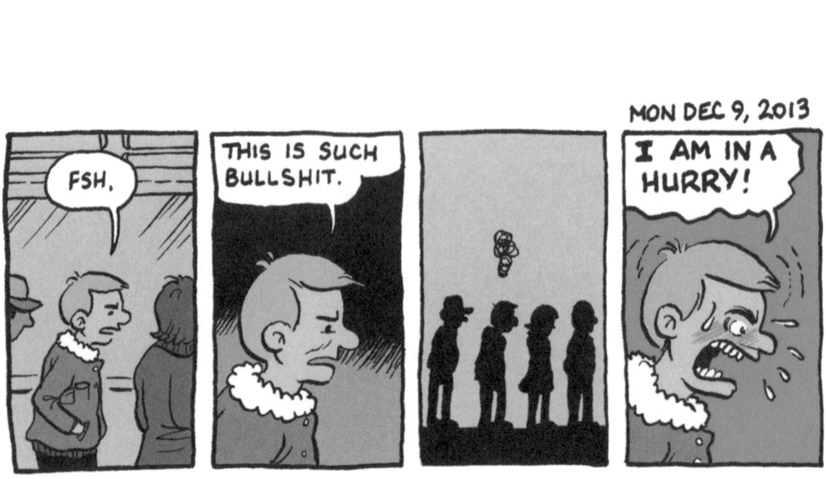
FSH.
THIS IS SUCH BULLSHIT.
I AM IN A HURRY!

TUE DEC 10, 2013

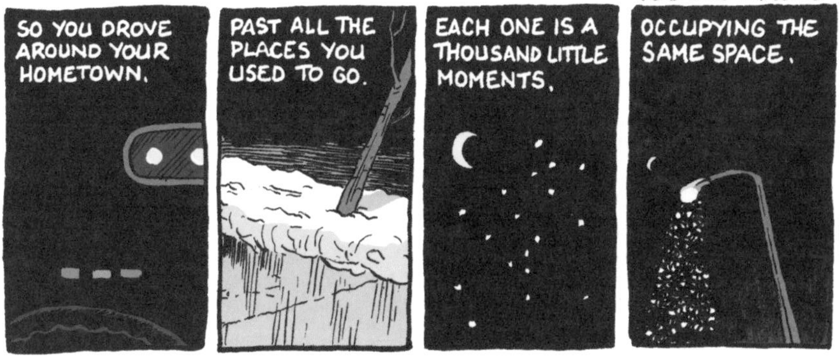
SO YOU DROVE AROUND YOUR HOMETOWN.
PAST ALL THE PLACES YOU USED TO GO.
EACH ONE IS A THOUSAND LITTLE MOMENTS,
OCCUPYING THE SAME SPACE.

WED DEC 11, 2013

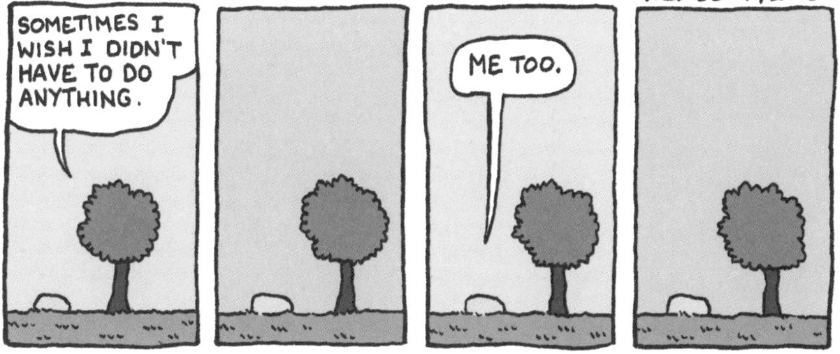
SOMETIMES I WISH I DIDN'T HAVE TO DO ANYTHING.
ME TOO.

THU DEC 12, 2013

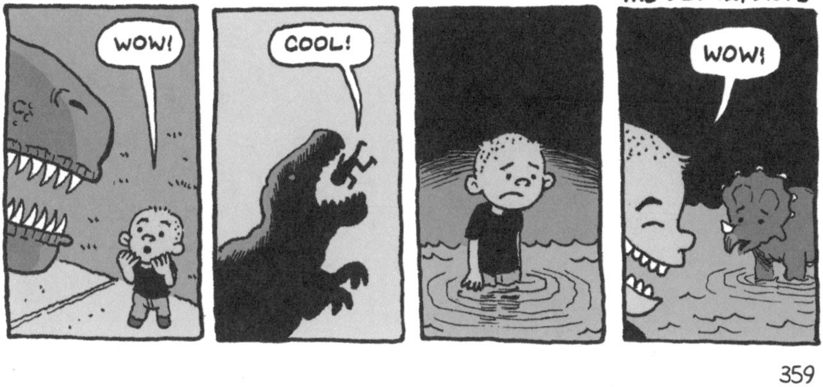
WOW!
COOL!
WOW!

FRI DEC 13, 2013

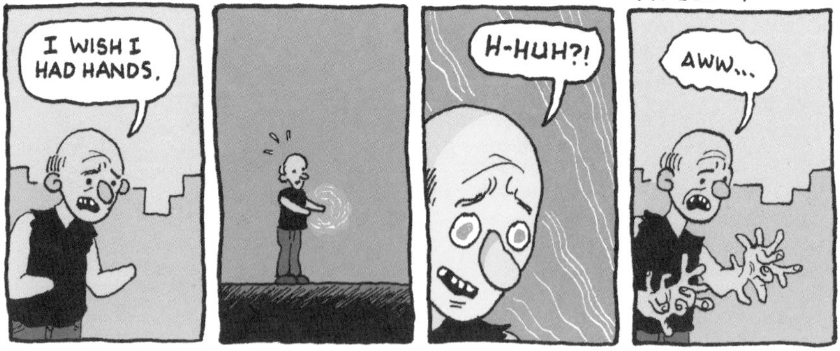
I WISH I HAD HANDS.
H-HUH?!
AWW...

SAT DEC 14, 2013

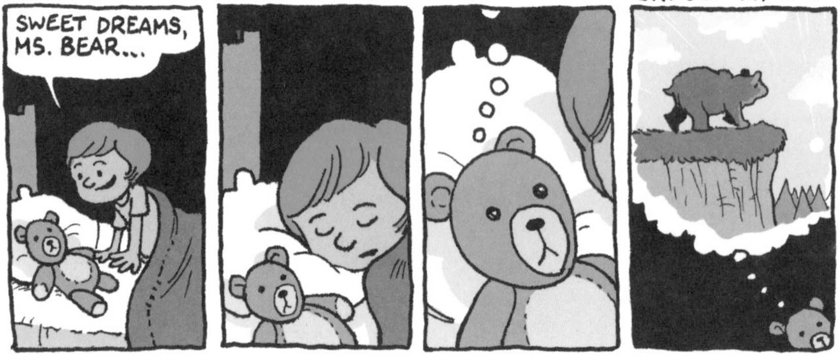
SWEET DREAMS, MS. BEAR...

SUN DEC 15, 2013

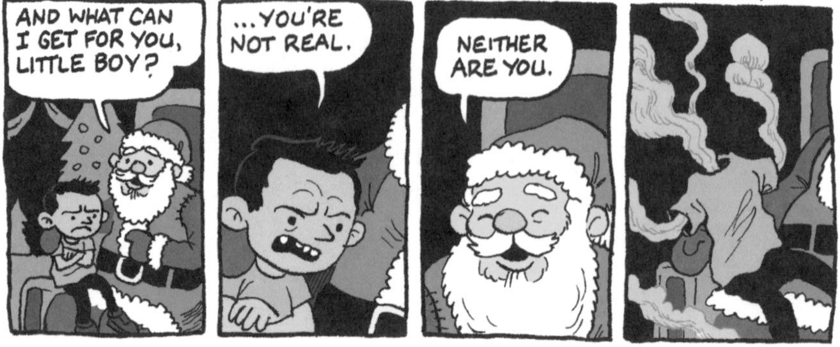
AND WHAT CAN I GET FOR YOU, LITTLE BOY?
...YOU'RE NOT REAL.
NEITHER ARE YOU.

MON DEC 16, 2013

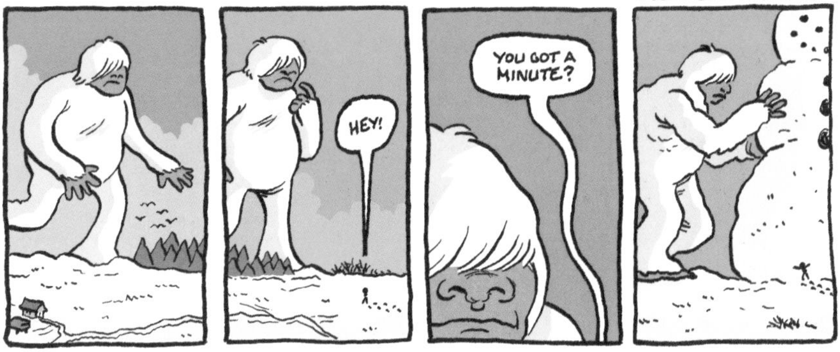
HEY!
YOU GOT A MINUTE?

TUE DEC 17, 2013

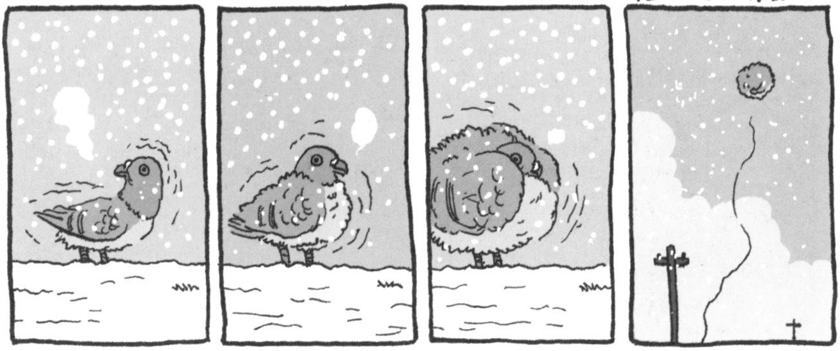

WED DEC 18, 2013

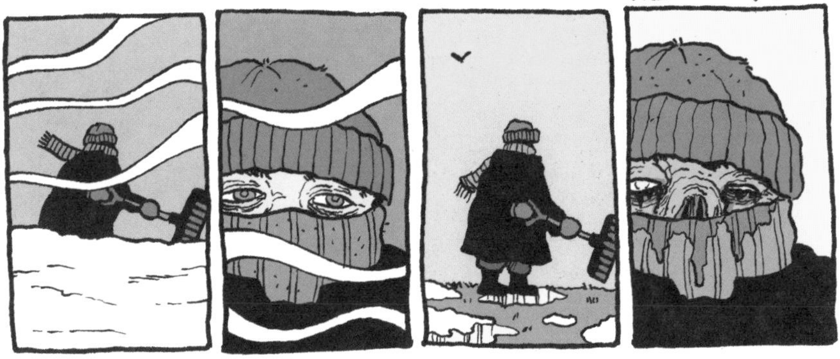

WELL,

SAM WORKED A JOB, WATCHED TV, AND ALWAYS COMPLAINED ABOUT WEATHER AND STRANGERS.

WE'LL REMEMBER SAM UNTIL WE DON'T, AND THEN NO ONE WILL.

ANYONE ELSE?

I HATE THIS TIME OF YEAR.

THAT'S WHAT YOU SAID DURING EVERY OTHER TIME OF YEAR.

362

SUN DEC 22, 2013

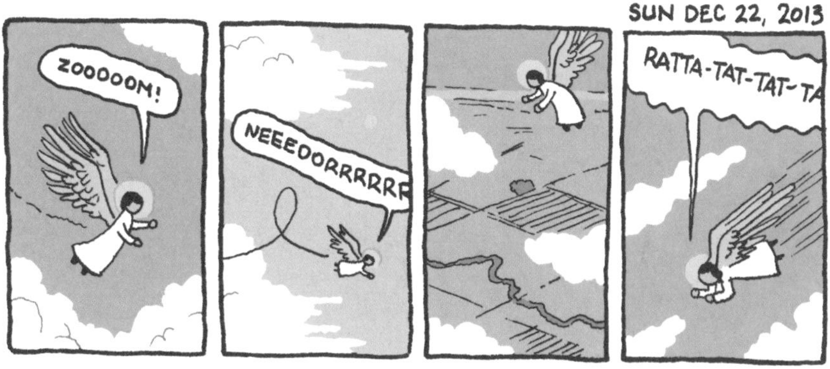
ZOOOOOM!
NEEEOORRRRRR
RATTA-TAT-TAT-TA

MON DEC 23, 2013

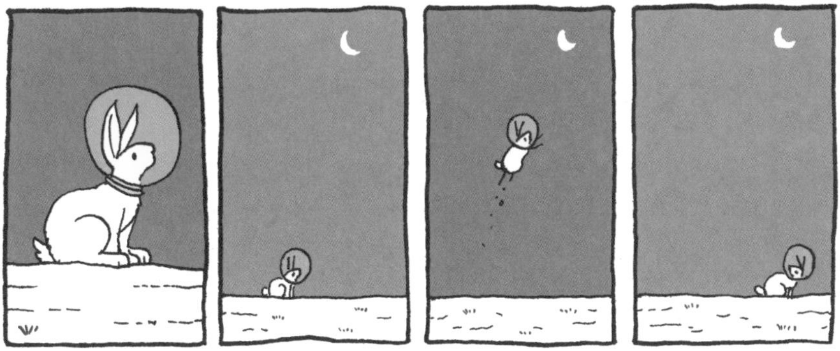

TUE DEC 24, 2013

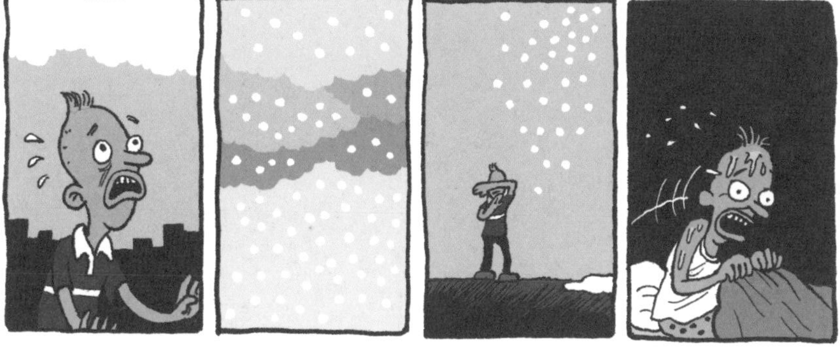

WED DEC 25, 2013

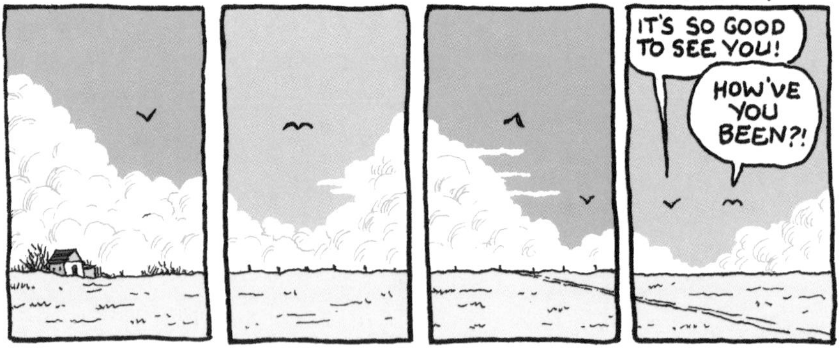
IT'S SO GOOD TO SEE YOU!
HOW'VE YOU BEEN?!

THU DEC 26, 2013

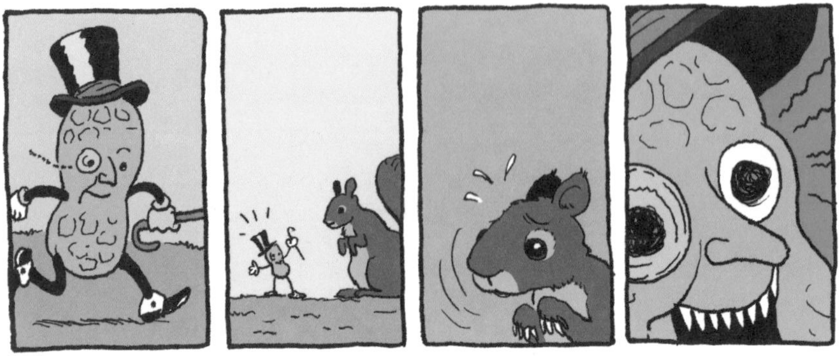

FRI DEC 27, 2013

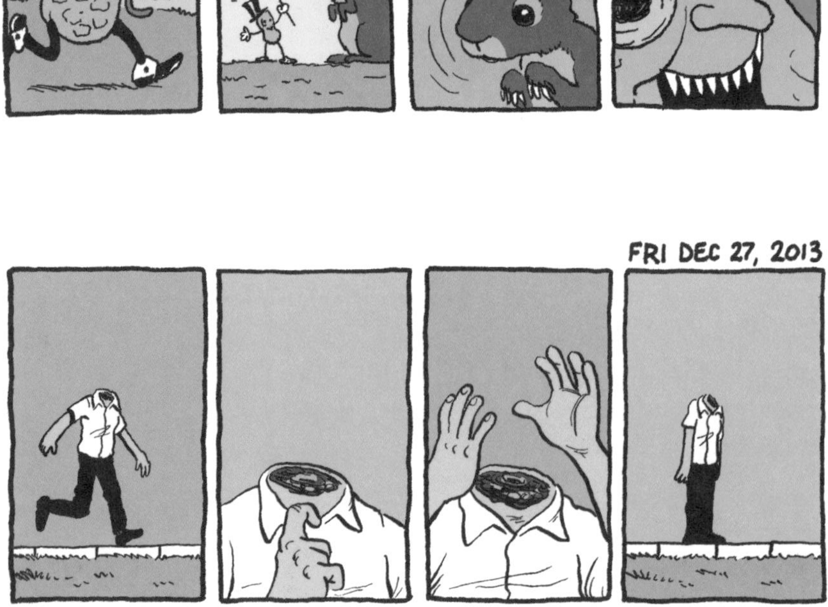

SAT DEC 28, 2013

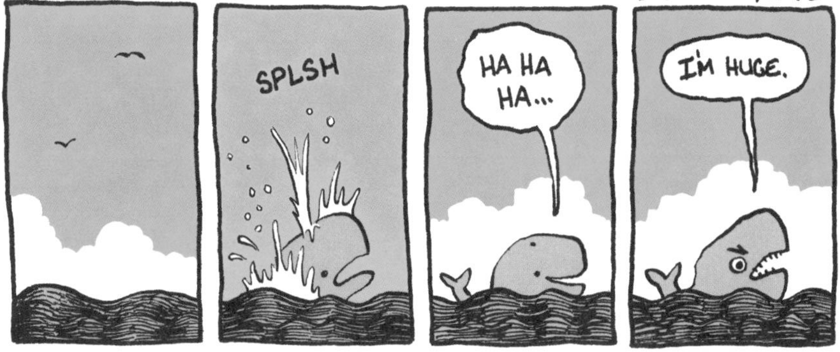
SPLSH
HA HA HA...
I'M HUGE.

SUN DEC 29, 2013

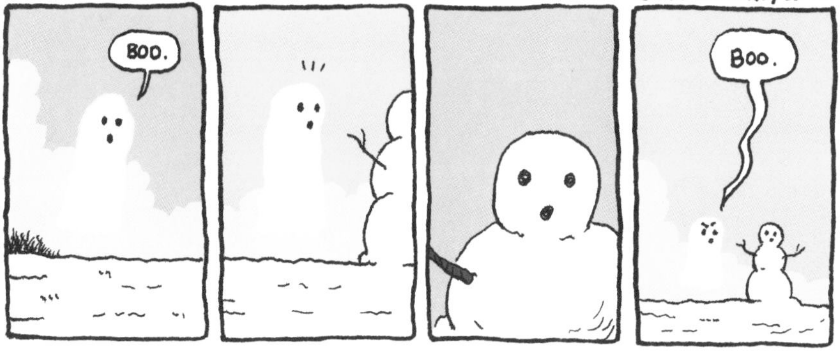
BOO.
BOO.

MON DEC 30, 2013

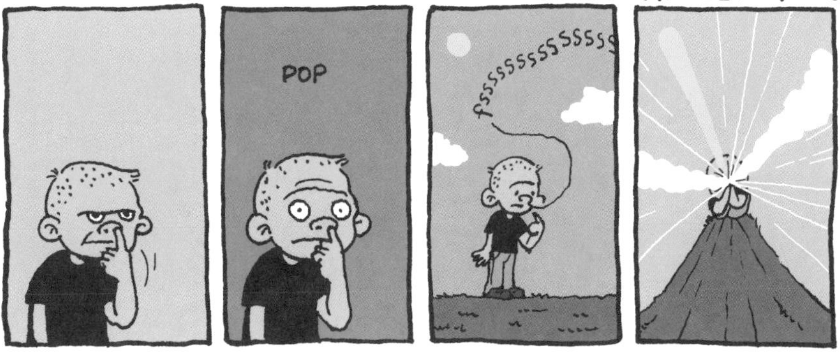
POP
fssssssssssSSSSs

TUE DEC 31, 2013

snap.

366

ACKNOWLEDGMENTS

THESE COMIC STRIPS WERE MADE POSSIBLE THANKS TO EVERYONE WHO PUT UP WITH ME BEING HALF-DISTRACTED THROUGHOUT ALL MINOR AND MAJOR LIFE EVENTS OVER THE LAST FIVE YEARS. THOSE WHO WERE THE MOST PATIENT INCLUDE: LAURA, MY PARENTS, MY SIBLINGS, AND MY IN-LAWS.

THANKS TO MY CARTOONING FRIENDS FOR STUDIO SESSIONS, DRAWING NIGHTS, AND ALL THE HARD WORK THEY PUT INTO THEIR OWN COMICS. AMONG THEM: ANDY WARNER, d.w., BETH HETLAND, PAT BARRETT, JOSH KRAMER, JON CHAD, BILLAGE, SEAN K., JOSEPH LAMBERT, JOSH ROSEN, MARTA CHUDOLINSKA, ADAM AYLARD, JOE OLLMANN, JOHN MARTZ, AARON COSTAIN, ZACH WORTON, AND MANY, MANY MORE.

EXTRA THANKS TO MY BROTHER JONAH, WHO HAS BEEN MY DRAWING BUDDY SINCE WE STARTED SCRIBBLING.

SPECIAL THANKS TO ANNIE KOYAMA FOR ALL SHE DOES, RYAN FLANDERS FOR THE INITIATION, AND OF COURSE, JAMES KOCHALKA.

FINALLY, THANKS TO ANDY BROWN, WITHOUT WHOM *THE DAILIES* WOULD HAVE REMAINED BANISHED TO THE NETHERWORLD OF THE INTERNET. OF ALL THE ANDY BROWNS IN THE WORLD, YOU'RE THE ANDY BROWNIEST.

368

DAKOTA McFADZEAN WAS BORN IN REGINA, SASKATCHEWAN IN 1983.
HE MOSTLY JUST WANTS TO GO ON WALKS AND LOOK AT THINGS.
HIS FIRST BOOK, *OTHER STORIES AND THE HORSE YOU RODE IN ON*,
WAS PUBLISHED BY CONUNDRUM PRESS IN 2013. HE CURRENTLY
LIVES IN TORONTO WITH HIS WIFE.

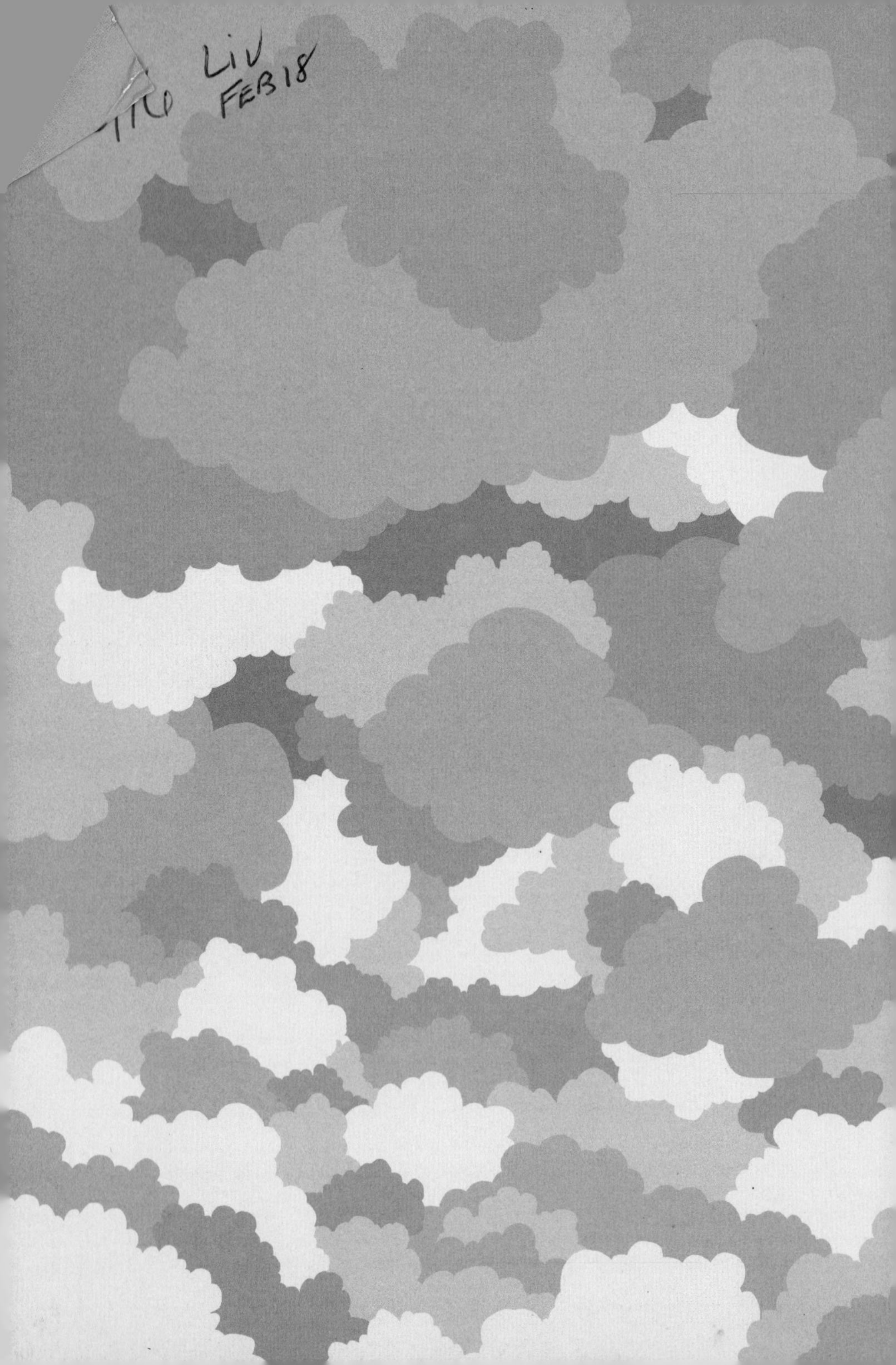